Creating an Old South

Creating an

The University of North Carolina Press • Chapel Hill and London

Old South

Middle Florida's Plantation Frontier before the Civil War

EDWARD E. BAPTIST

© 2002 The University of North Carolina Press
All rights reserved
Manufactured in the United States of America

Designed by Heidi Perov
Set in Bell and Kuenstler Script
by Tseng Information Systems, Inc.

The paper in this book meets the guidelines for permanence
and durability of the Committee on Production Guidelines
for Book Longevity of the Council on Library Resources.

Library of Congress Cataloging-in-Publication Data

Baptist, Edward E.
    Creating an Old South : Middle Florida's plantation
    frontier before the Civil War / Edward E. Baptist.
        p. cm.
    Includes bibliographical references and index.
    ISBN 0-8078-2688-x (cloth: alk. paper)
    ISBN 0-8078-5353-4 (pbk. : alk. paper)
    1. Florida—History—1821–1865.   2. Plantation life—
Florida—History—19th century.   3. Whites—Florida—
Social conditions—19th century.   4. Plantation owners—
Florida—History—19th century.   5. African Americans
—Florida—Social conditions—19th century.   6. Florida
—Race relations.   7. Social classes—Florida—History—
19th century.   8. Frontier and pioneer life—Florida.
9. Land settlement—Social aspects—Florida—History—
19th century.   10. Migration, Internal—United States—
History—19th century.   I. Title.
F315 .B37   2002
974.9'05—dc21   2001053080

Cloth 06 05 04 03 02   5 4 3 2 1
Paper 06 05 04 03 02   5 4 3 2 1

For Stephanie

Contents

Illustrations, Maps, and Tables

ILLUSTRATIONS

MAPS

TABLES

Acknowledgments

The long process of writing a book like this involves one in so many debts of kindness and assistance to other people that one cannot hope to repay them. One is in a sense bankrupt, bound to one's creditors by obligations that cannot be redeemed. At least that is what I hope, for my scheme is this: by remaining in their debt, I plan to remain linked to them. And thus I must first acknowledge my bankruptcy, my unpayable obligations of gratitude, in order to cement that relationship.

Any historian must begin by thanking those who preserve and make available the most basic building blocks of research: the archivists and librarians who have saved me countless times from error, confusion, and most of all, ignorance of some of the fantastic sources I've been lucky enough to examine. David Coles and the staff of the Florida State Archives and Florida State Library alerted this (occasional) migrant to Middle Florida to many sources. David helped me repeatedly after I returned to Philadelphia, supplying xeroxes, citations, and suggestions. At the Jackson County Courthouse in Marianna, Florida, Robert Standland and Dale Herman helped me dig up records that I thought had burned a century and a half ago. For many years, Bill Erwin performed his own archival miracles in the Special Collections Department of the Perkins Library at Duke, matching scholars with sources, using files in his head that no computer could equal. The rest of the staff there, as well as Tim Pyatt, Shayera Tangri, John White, and the rest of the staff of the Southern Historical Collection at the University of North Carolina's Wilson Library also assisted me in countless ways. The staffs of the Georgia Historical Society and the Virginia Historical Society were also unfailingly polite and helpful. Finally, Walter Beyer of the Family History Center in Broomall, Pennsylvania, helped me utilize the genealogical resources of the Church of Jesus Christ of Latter-day Saints. Few scholars are aware that this organization has microfilmed county records from all over the United States, or that the church generously permits nonmembers to use these resources for their own genealogical or historical researches.

At Georgetown University, a group of extraordinary undergraduate teachers and advisers—David Johnson, Alan Karras, John R. McNeill, and Marcus Rediker—set my historical feet on the ground and taught me how to find and write my own way forward. Then, at the University of Pennsylvania, and the Pennsylvania (now McNeil) Center for Early American Studies, a number of mentors, teachers, and friends helped shape me into a professional historian. I'm grateful for the assistance, advice, and examples of Roger Abrahams, Richard Beeman, Kathy Brown, Bob Engs, Nancy Farriss, Jeff Fear, Lynn Hunt, Walter Licht, Roderick McDonald, Charles Rosenberg, Mark Stern, Tom Sugrue, Mike Zuckerman, and for the Department of History in general for its years of financial support while I was a graduate student. Meanwhile, Val Riley and Gladyce Constantine always had quiet words of encouragement and confidence, in addition to making it possible for graduate students to navigate the channels of bureaucracy. I appreciate them very much, as I do Deborah Broadnax — who did the same things, only more loudly.

I also want to acknowledge the assistance of the University of Miami, especially for the two Max Orovitz research grants that allowed me to conduct additional research and complete the writing of this book, and the General Research grant that enabled Richter Library to purchase important microfilms. During my first few years at Miami, tumultuous though they were at times, I developed as a scholar and teacher only with the assistance of numerous colleagues, students, and friends. Some were there every day; some put in precisely the right word at precisely the right time. Without each of them, I'm sure that the last four years would have been much more difficult. In particular, I must thank Edmund Abaka, Ligia Aldana, Robin Bachin, Leslie Bow, Jeff Brosco, Bill Brown, Russ Castronovo, Charles Clency, Fred D'Aguiar, Edwidge Danticat, Lenny Del Granado, Marcia Evanson, Martha Few, Harry and Ruth Forgan, Jennifer Forsythe, Ken Goodman, Paul Hamburg, Kathy Harrison, Whittington Johnson, Jim Lake, Bob Levine, Bob Moore, Sandra Paquet, Rochelle Theo Pienn, Aldo Regalado, Don Spivey, Steve Stein, Kumble R. Subbawamy, Hugh and Pat Thomas, Ruthanne Vogel, and all my students.

In graduate school and elsewhere, a number of friends helped shape both my writing and my life, and I am happy to be able to acknowledge their comradeship, their hospitality, their brother- and sisterhood. They include: Luther Adams, Roseanne Adderley, Stephen Bumgardner and his family, Stephanie Camp, Kon Dierks, Leigh Edwards, Rhonda Frederick, Anne-Elizabeth Giuliani, Kali Gross, Jennifer Gunn, Beth Hillman, Tom Humphrey, Maurice Jackson, Hannah Joyner, Michael Kahan, Bob Kane, Rukesh Korde, Tim Lane, Edward Larkin, Bruce Lenthall, David Meyers, Liam Riordan, Sarah Russell, Randolph Scully, Kristen Stromberg, Phillip Troutman, Karim Tiro, Judy Van Buskirk, Justin Warf, and Rhonda Williams.

The following individuals read and commented on the entire manuscript at various stages, and it is much better, and less unwieldy, as a result of their generous efforts: Charles Bolton, Clark Cahow, Dan Dupre, Hugh Thomas, and an anonymous reader for the University of North Carolina Press. John Hope Franklin and John Lukacs provided timely encouragement. Others pitched in to read and comment on particular chapters, or papers and article manuscripts that became parts of various chapters, including Luther Adams, Stephanie Baptist, John Boles, Stephanie Camp, Jane Turner Censer, James Dorgan, Susan Gray, Steven Hahn, Tom Humphrey, Hannah Joyner, Edward Larkin, John Edwin Mason, Holly Mayer, Alida Metcalf, Marcus Rediker, Daniel Rodgers, William Warren Rogers, Sarah Russell, Chris Schroeder, Randolph Scully, Mitchell Snay, Neva Specht, Karim Tiro, Kirsten Wood, Bertram Wyatt-Brown, several anonymous readers for the *Journal of American History* and the *Journal of Southern History*, and the audiences at a number of conferences.

A special thanks must go to Steven Stowe, who at the behest of the University of North Carolina Press read and commented upon several stages of the manuscript that became this book. His comments were both generous and probing, encouraging and direct. He later identified himself to me, and we were able to continue a dialogue, extremely helpful to me, on the subject of the manuscript. As with the others who have commented upon all or parts of this text, he is not responsible for the errors and infelicities that remain but is surely to be credited for removing many that were once present. I'm also especially appreciative of the editors and staff at the University of North Carolina Press. Mary Caviness and Mark Simpson-Vos have been unfailingly helpful through the whole lengthy process of publication. And most of all, David Perry's support, encouragement, criticism, and willingness to go drink coffee with me at Café Driade have made him an ideal editor.

Harry L. Watson of the University of North Carolina signed on as outside reader for my dissertation and stayed on as mentor and friend. Through access to the resources of the Center for Study of the American South, he also provided me with an academic home in the Triangle during one summer and a year of leave. His thoughtful comments on various stages of my manuscript have made it much better than it could otherwise have been. Although I know he won't agree with all of my conclusions, I hope he'll appreciate the more North Carolina–centric parts of this text. John Thompson and the Department of History at Duke University also ensured that I would have access to the resources of Duke's Perkins Library during a year-long leave in the Triangle area, for which I am most grateful.

I didn't leave Richard Dunn and Drew Faust out when I spoke about those who shaped me at Penn, I only saved them for a few lines later. Richard marked page upon page of my writing with meticulous and thought-provoking comments. He provided a model of scholarship, and a model of how to conduct oneself as a scholar and a teacher. I can also testify that his legendary generosity is no myth. He supplied me with office space and opportunities at the Philadelphia Center for Early American Studies, and when my computer died he lent me his own office and computer. Without his help I would have completed my dissertation at a much later date.

I thanked Drew Gilpin Faust when I finished my dissertation, and I have even more to thank her for now. She helps her students and former students to find their own paths, both as academics and as people with lives and families. And while those who work with Drew do not have to toe a party line, her comments are frank, and she does not do the false favor of hesitating to criticize. Like everything else she says, her critiques are expressed with the collegiality that makes her a role model for aspiring historians. I am grateful to her, specifically for her help, her readings and criticism, and advice in the process of researching and writing the dissertation that began this text, but also more generally for her example. And for this former student, she continues to be an excellent mentor, giving good advice, reading chapters, catching up with the news of former students' lives, and always asking the right questions. Drew is a wonderful scholar and teacher, but an even better person.

Finally I come to family, the most important thing. Those who know me may be aware that my extended family is, in number, more like those of the nineteenth-century South than the families typically claimed by members of the post-twentieth-century academic world. But out of them all, my mother and father have shaped me more than anyone, of course, and I thank them for their love. My wife's parents, Patricia and Robert Nevels, have welcomed me as a son. My daughter, Lillian Faith, came along when my dissertation was completed and I had just begun to work on this book. Now she is old enough to comment—at some length—on the images that accompany the text. And my son, Ezra James, just got here. Children aren't owned—much less made in their individuality—by their parents. They are only borrowed, and I'm thankful for the privilege of owing them my love and care. Last and most, for family and friendship, for patience and strength, for moments of joy and years of love, I thank Stephanie.

Creating an Old South

Introduction

Origins and Outcomes

An origin is a beginning which explains. Worse still, a beginning which is a complete explanation. There lies the ambiguity, and the danger!
—Marc Bloch

Captain George Washington Parkhill lay face up in the growing daylight on the battlefield at Gaines Mill. As the Confederate soldiers moved past his body, forward in Robert E. Lee's furious hammer blows against the Union flank, only the flies remained with him, settling on his gaping mouth and the wetness of his eyes. His cousin, Lieutenant Richard Parkhill, soon came rushing back. He had seen the fatal bullet's impact: "When he fell it almost killed me. I was so much excited I scarcely knew what I was doing. The men over all wanted to lay down and they did so, when I walked down the line & told them to avenge their noble captain's death. [T]hen the balls began to fall like rain, but they all gave a yell and started towards the enemy."[1] Now Richard gathered the other officers and they carried their dead captain from the field. With solemn care, they took him back to Richmond, where his wife, Lizzie, waited among the couple's Virginia kin for news of the day's battle. The unexpected sight of her husband's corpse devastated her, reported a relative: "O! I *never* in my life witnessed a *sadder* scene than that young wife clinging to the lifeless form of her soldier husband." In the days to come, she buried "Washington" and prepared to return to their home in Leon County, Florida.[2]

Parkhill's death paralleled that of his Leon County neighbor Colonel George T. Ward. Earlier in the spring of 1862, as Union general George McClellan pushed Southern troops under Joseph Johnston back from Williamsburg, the Confederate command ordered Ward's Second Florida regiment to make a countercharge. "On reaching the fallen timber," wrote one survivor of what followed, "the advancing lines of the Second Florida were blunted, and opened fire. It was here that the fatal bullet pierced the heart of Ward and terminated the life of that heroic soldier and accomplished gentleman.... [I saw him] disdaining to seek the partial protection offered by the fallen timber."[3] Union fire forced the Confederates to fall back to their previous position, but the Second Florida later sent a party out to recover Ward's body. The names of these men read like a list of the planter families of Leon County. Officers George Call, Theodore Brevard, C. Seton Fleming, Eben Burroughs, and David Maxwell all ventured into the no-man's-land, seeking to protect from desecration and dishonor the body of their peer. And in the midst of their attempt to recover Ward's corpse, Union riflemen shot and wounded Lieutenant Fleming. Now he, too, lay on the field. Another party went back to get Fleming, and yet another soldier fell.

Like knights-errant in the plot of a historical romance, the Parkhills, Ward, and Fleming played the part of the cavalier. In the imagined drama of their class, the bold Southern planter fought with courage, leading his loyal yeoman troops in brave charges, dying with honor. His death was momentous, and the events around it—even the recovery of his corpse— showed the character of the actors involved.[4] The deaths of Ward and Parkhill thus offered surviving elite men numerous opportunities for talking about a planter gallantry that echoes myths, both theirs and ours, of an "Old" South. While Florida might seem less Southern now than some of its neighbors, definitions of regions, like the regions themselves, change over time. Thinking of Florida as part of the South was second nature to those who lived there before the Civil War, particularly those in the plantation region of "Middle Florida," which stretched from the Suwannee River west to Jackson County on the western bank of the Apalachicola River.[5] This plantation belt, which centered on Tallahassee, was a part of the same economic, cultural, and political subregion as the states called the "Old Southwest" by historians. These states also included Mississippi, Alabama, and Louisiana, as well as Tennessee, Arkansas, and eastern Texas. Elite men who moved to Middle Florida after its acquisition by the United States in 1821 sought, as did planters throughout the Old Southwest, to prosper and rule through the acquisition of land, control of dependents, and staple crop production. By 1860, the enslaved numbered over half of Middle Florida's 75,000 inhabitants.

Despite this history of tumultuous movement, our traditional belief that the South is distinct from the rest of the United States leads us to think that the "frontier" did not shape the slaveholding states. "Frontier" is, of course, almost as loaded a term as "South." For whether Americans dream of a place that tests and refines white men, of the advancing edge of "civilization," or of a crucible for democracy, they have often imagined the frontier as the place that distills the nation's deepest tendencies. The frontier shaped the United States, and the essence of the United States is the frontier.[6] The South, as a region settled in large part by the enslaved and those who claimed ownership over them, does not fit easily an image of the United States as a land where settlers won freedom from the wilderness. Indeed, in textbook after textbook, the Southern frontier either does not exist or is a specialized zone of "Indian" traders and outlaws. When planters, slaves, and nonplanter white farmers arrive on the scene, the Old Southwest becomes a reproduction of the coastal plantation kingdom and its social relations. After all, according to the traditional ways of celebrating American history, slavery is an undemocratic, un-American exception. Where it existed, as in the Old Southwest, its presence prevented the yeast of frontier democracy from fermenting. Southwestward migration, then, simply transplanted society unchanged from old plantation regions, and a society with the uniquely American characteristics shaped by the frontier did not develop.[7]

Perhaps, however, the Southern frontier was all too typically American. In any case, much that has intervened has made it difficult to perceive on its own terms. The 1862 dramas that surrounded the deaths of Ward and Parkhill, for instance, stand between us and the settlement of Middle Florida, blocking our view. Both before and after the Civil War, men and women of the planter class erected a wall between the future and the past, making the remembered history of migration to Middle Florida look like Parkhill's last charge. In their accounts, local history became a ranking of the old names transplanted without event from old societies: "Here were Meades, Randolphs, Eppes, Keiths, Carringtons, Bollings, Walkers, Taylors, Calls, besides a score of other good Virginia names."[8] After the Confederacy's fall succeeded those of Ward, Parkhill, and hundreds of thousands more, its defeated survivors redoubled the effort to make the prewar South look changeless, without internal conflict, in a word, "Old." One survivor of Middle Florida's planter class wrote of the time before the war as timeless, in a region where "there was none who were poverty-stricken," in her words, a veritable "Eden."[9]

Pious descendants of Confederate heroes are not, however, the only ones responsible for making the antebellum South look like a changeless realm. Visions of moonlight and magnolias began with Southern mythmaking but lean on the stories told by historians. Yes, with one hand, scholars do unravel the myths woven about the Old South by its defenders. Yet despite their efforts, the image of a changeless South remains alive. For with the other hand, some spin out the thread of another vision, one that inadvertently supports the notion of the South as a static region. In the scholarly version, the South had by some particular point in time achieved an essential set of conditions like slavery-based cultivation and planter hegemony—it had become the Old South. Communities that appeared to break out of this mold, or to follow a different pattern, were in reality either moving inexorably toward their Old South destiny or mere exceptions to the rule. Perhaps if we could identify the crucial characteristics and institutions of the plantation South as a state of being, the essence of the distinctive region, we might be able to understand why racism and slavery have blotted America's supposedly exceptional history, and why the Civil War tore apart the republic.

Popular and scholarly assumptions may well have diverted historians from looking at the plantation frontier. They have written relatively little about nineteenth-century expansions of the plantation system into areas like Middle Florida. Instead, they have focused their efforts on older areas in an attempt to identify the elusive characteristics that made the South so Southern, so different, so "Old." The concentration on relatively stable plantation regions like low-country South Carolina has led some scholars to depict the antebellum South as a region governed by the repetitive dynamics of master-slave interactions.[10] In other cases, historians identify the colonial and revolutionary eras as periods that shaped distinctive Southern social relations into the form that they held until the Civil War. Still others see the years around 1830 as an important period of change, arguing that Northern attacks on Southern slavery prodded the region to a new consciousness of itself as distinct.[11] Even in this last version, outside forces and national political struggles drove change, not the movement south and west of millions of Southerners. That movement appears as little more than a footnote, or at most the working out of an already true theorem: planter-dominated society and culture long established in the older states were transplanted to places like Middle Florida.[12]

The idea that the unique qualities of the antebellum South lay in some essence first distilled along the James in Virginia, or in the rice swamps of coastal South Carolina, parallels the view of history acted out by George Ward and George Parkhill. The contemporary narratives surrounding their deaths drew upon antebellum myths of a confident slaveholding class that ruled a stable realm with the willing support of deferential common whites. The death dramas of Ward and Parkhill harmonize with the very different notes sounded by historians on the origins of Southern society, culture, and character. The related belief that the course of the Civil War proves our theses about the nature of the pre–Civil War South could lead us to assume that the nineteenth-century mythmakers had it right: Middle

Florida was a shoot from the stem of Virginia or Carolina. The specific process of its settlement mattered little in understanding either the experience of the migrants who settled that area, or what the region came to be by the time Ward, Parkhill, and their obedient troops marched off to war.

Although every Middle Floridian had a vision of the future, a vision shaped by their respective pasts, no one knew what was coming. No one called the era in which they were living "antebellum." Too often, histories of the nineteenth-century South have looked like a cascade of inevitability: racism divides the lower classes, hegemony reigns, the rich, the white, and the male remain in charge. The Civil War comes, right on time. Such histories become monologues trooping to a foreordained end. Not coincidentally, many of them also focus heavily upon records generated by the elite. Such a bias can be difficult to avoid. Imbalances of power often prevent the less powerful members of the human family from leaving much in the way of written sources. And the even greater bias of foregone conclusions, from supposed origins to certain outcomes, can lead us to impose historians' own definitions of what acceptable ends to oppression might be, and how people in the past ought to have sought those ends. Once we have made such an imposition, our task and our argument become circular. For instance, some historians argue that the fact that a great many nonplanter whites fought on the side of planters during the Civil War, and that at the same time, the enslaved did not rise up and slay every white person in sight, prove the existence of a prewar Southern society shaped by the willing consent of subordinates to planter hegemony. Here, antebellum history foreshadows the war, which in turn retroactively proves what the South was all along.[13]

Foreshadowing crams stories about the past into narrow equations whose terms march neatly forward to an outcome that we, of course, already know. From outcomes, we leap to conclusions about why things happened, and misunderstand what they meant to the actors involved, and to spectators like ourselves. Middle Florida's history did not move in a straight line from settlement to some inevitable conclusion in tragic battlefield scenes such as the ones in which Ward and Parkhill starred as doomed cavaliers. Nor does a focus on origins help matters. Planter movement did not produce an easy transplantation of hierarchies that may or may not have been solidly established in the Old Dominion, from which so many of the Wards and Parkhills of the area hailed. We cannot measure this history from determinate beginnings, or from apparent results. For upon closer inspection we find a different story in Middle Florida, one that inevitability cannot contain. There, migration and settlement on the plantation frontier dramatically transformed the elements of society and culture inherited from the eighteenth-century Southeast. In fact, migration and settlement and the conflicts that they provoked would help to create the historical perceptions that shaped still-living ideas about what the words "Old" and "South" mean when paired together.

The regimes of slavery that sprang up in the colonial Chesapeake and South Carolina would shape the South's development into the early nineteenth century. But the expansion of the cotton frontier remade the elements of the eighteenth-century region, shaping a new Southern society through its repeated settlements and unsettlements. Masters, mistresses, slaves, and nonslaveowning whites, especially those who moved to the Old Southwest, all lived in a world in flux, and all had their own ideas about what the frontier would be. Many migrants born in the older seaboard states spent major portions of their lives in new regions. The experience of constant change shaped both their lives and the society in which they were embedded. For example, John Branch, a planter and politician from Halifax County, North Carolina, was born in 1782 and grew up amid the political and economic changes of the Revolutionary settlement. He saw the expansion of cotton production in the seaboard states, the end of the African slave trade, the War of 1812, the opening of an empire for slavery to the south and west, and the rise of Jacksonian politics. Branch moved to Middle Florida in the 1830s. He lived there through most of the area's many changes, and died (back in Halifax County) in 1863, in the midst of the Civil War. Branch's experience of constant change and movement was typical. Between 1790 and 1860, millions of white and black settlers moved across the Appalachians into the Mississippi Valley, and down the Atlantic coastal plain south and west. And most important was the fact that migration and settlement sparked constant conflict and change. During the decades after 1821, when American settlement in Jackson and Leon Counties began, local planter rule was tenuous and contested. At times nonplanter white men rejected the leadership of "gentry" like Branch and at others led planters on paths that they had not planned to travel. Women and slaves were often less than content in the households that Branch and his peers ruled.[14]

As settlement of the plantation frontier proceeded, the older coastal regions continued to be considerably important to the region as a whole. But the South that ultimately fought for its independence as a slaveholding white man's republic emerged from crisis and conflict within the newer states and territories. So, too, did its myths. In fact, Ward's and Parkhill's seeming confidence rested on the successful and recent contrivance of the stories that such men told themselves in order to forget the unsettled past of their own fathers. Influenced by both local and national developments, members of Middle Florida's planter class redefined themselves as historically distinct from their counterparts in the North: they were supposedly the chivalrous rulers of a harmonious, hierarchical society.[15] Resisting that definition was a more complex reality: a struggle among the classes and factions that divided whites and, beneath them, the enslaved African Americans who watched and waited. The myth, in compensation, offered planters an imaginary history of stability, a dream genealogy of seamless rule that held that white alliance across classes was a constant, and ignored the harsh effects of planter-directed frontier disruption upon the enslaved.

When we consider the Southern plantation frontier, we lift aside layers of myth to re-emphasize the role of migration and, indeed, change in the history of the nineteenth-century antebellum South. With that as my goal, the following chapters begin by describing the process of migration to one corner of the plantation frontier—Middle Florida. They show how friction between antagonistic groups eventually created a South that to us could look inevitable, or even "Old," if we are not cautious. Within Middle Florida, I have chosen two counties, Jackson and Leon, on which to focus. Depth and richness of sources helps to distinguish them, and the differences between the two also tell us much.[16] They were part of one history, however, one that reveals that the origins of migrants to Middle Florida do not themselves explain what happened on the plantation frontier. There, people changed to deal with a new set of social forces and a new physical environment. And this experience, more than the area's status on the geographical edge of the United States, as a border between white and Native American territories or even as an area being brought into the commercialized Atlantic economy, reveals the way in which the Old Southwest was a frontier. In Middle Florida, planters, nonplanter whites, and enslaved African Americans interacted with each other in new ways because they were on ground unsettled in every political, social, and cultural sense.[17]

Of course, the people who moved from the old states to new territories could never completely escape the living hand of history, any more than those who stayed behind could in turn avoid the frontier's growing presence in their political, economic, and other calculations. Mythological versions of Virginia eventually served as the ideal society of planters who came to Middle Florida. Less wealthy whites, however, often looked on the lack of democracy and explicit deference that they remembered of the old states from which most came as political hell. For them, the ideologies of white male independence enshrined in memories of the American Revolution showed the way to political heaven. Planters, slaves, and nonplanter whites brought their own experiences and ideas with them to Middle Florida. But the contradictions between what each of these groups carried as memories, desires, and interpretations, as the text moves on to show, helped to shape the conflicts that erupted once migrants reached Jackson and Leon

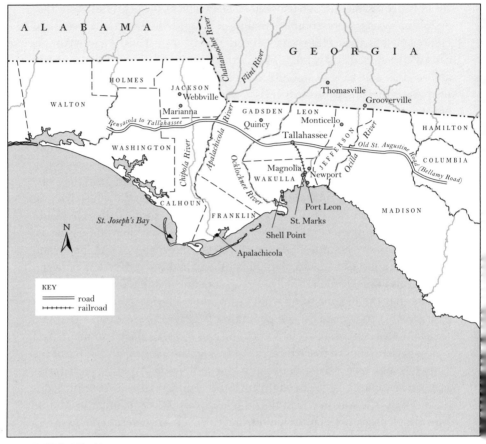

Middle Florida, c. 1843

Counties. In particular, the wealthiest whites may have wanted to reproduce their preeminence in the tidewater counties from which they hailed, yet they found upon arrival in new districts that older verities of political and cultural power became open questions.

Among whites in particular, power was expressed and understood as manhood, and the status of manhood was often derived from the use of political or other kinds of power. Therefore this story of Middle Florida concentrates on the issues of honor and masculinity, which shaped public and private conflict on this stretch of the plantation frontier. While this story does not ignore women, it cannot accord to debates over womanhood the same space it does to arguments over manhood. Of course, the ability to talk about battles between men as struggles over manhood builds upon an extensive historical literature that already exists on Southern women, especially of the planter class. These histories have taught us to recognize the gendered character of many social and cultural relationships.[18] Indeed, on Middle Florida's plantation frontier, arguments about political power were often disagreements about who could claim the authority over self and others that went along with manhood in a society where only men ruled, and only those who ruled were considered fully men. The converse was also true: conflicts over manhood—what it was, who had it, who did not—were also conflicts about political power. For instance, white men who were not planters first resented, then challenged, the arrogant posturing of planter men, sparking conflicts that occupied much of the public life of Jackson and Leon Counties, until an uncertain resolution brought some measure of peace in the 1840s. While nonplanter white men remembered the democratization of masculinity, memories of political and economic disaster and cultural humiliation haunted planters' frontier past during the 1850s. These ghosts motivated the compensatory idea that the South was "Old," a society stabilized by lower-class deference and ruled by the benevolent descendants of cavaliers. Middle Florida's Old South was an idea of recent vintage when Parkhill and others carried its script into battle.

Meanwhile, a majority of those who came to the plantation frontier did not choose to move. While many planter women, for instance, supported the decision to move, others opposed removal to Florida as a threat to health and the ties of kinship. In either case, the pains and disruptions they endured, though real, paled in comparison to the massive tragedy of unfree migration. Enslaved African Americans had little choice in their forced removal to the plantation frontier, which exposed them to repeated disruptions and dangers. Theirs was a tale of migration, but not of eventual settlement, for there was no stability for them while slavery lasted. Still, enslaved African Americans did everything that they could to rebuild family and community, while never forgetting the losses of their westward passage. They, too, experienced and constructed a frontier history, one far different from the pasts in which whites believed.

People lived and acted within the contexts of the material realities that constrained and shaped life on the plantation frontier, and in the midst of political debates that stretched far beyond the borders of one group of Florida counties. In politics, settlers spoke about and acted upon some of their deepest beliefs. In their economic acts, they did the same, even if the grammars and vocabularies of the two practices often seemed to contradict each other. Social and political life can show us that people who came to Jackson and Leon Counties brought differing ideas about race, family, government, and manhood. And we can see that the political and economic struggles that ensued from the clashes between such differences reshaped both the material world and the social relations of power in Middle Florida. Thus they form a central strand of this book's braided argument. Yet such conflicts were not the only paths along which the threads of Middle Florida's story spun out during these years.

In order to tell a story of the settlement of Jackson and Leon Counties that is not a monologue foreshadowing inevitable conclusions, one must also listen to the ways in which people told themselves and each other who they were; how they got to be that way; where they wanted to go next. And to hear these stories, the historian must also use varied sources, and various tools to interpret them. The past comes back to us, not only in statistics, letters, and straightforward news but also in the stories buried in folktales, humor, and other unexpected places. Using whatever methods I can, I excavate and interpret these sources, and put them into relief against the lives of all Middle Floridians.[19] They tell us, in turn, that planters did not always have the upper hand, even though the powerful often constrained other people, and almost all whites exploited the labor of African Americans.[20]

The antebellum history of Jackson and Leon Counties shows us that the Old South did not grow from the replication of an older South. Instead, migrants, during years of alternating crisis and prosperity, created in the Southwest new social and cultural arrangements that we now interpret as characteristic of an entire region.[21] The process was contingent, unplanned, and riddled by conflict, especially among white men. Different classes, and different factions within the migrant elite, all fought each other, and all fought over the idea of manhood in general. The history of migration and settlement shaped an uncertain course, driven by the decisions and acts of thousands of people. By 1860, a Middle Florida emerged, one that some claimed was both Southern and Old, but also one that no one could have predicted in 1830, or 1840. What took place in communities on the plantation frontier is far more than an interesting sidelight to Southern history. In these processes, planters, common whites, and enslaved African Americans remade their world through compromise and paradox, incidentally and accidentally making the South that went to war in 1861. Their series of new and newer Souths even gave birth to the idea of an "Old" South.

So let us go back, beginning no longer with the Civil War—which will stand instead as a product, rather than a proof, of what came before it —nor with the supposed origin of quintessentially Southern culture or social arrangements. Instead, let us start at the point in time and space when the area called Middle Florida became part of the United States, and then we will travel forward, roughly in this order: land, migrants, migration, and conflict. First comes the land: while the unfolding history of the South's plantation frontier was a play in which the actors did not know their lines, for there was no script, there was at least a geographical stage. On that space the first actors sought to mark out their own places. As early as the 1810s, American whites had looked south to Florida, then claimed by Spain, as a place where they hoped one day to establish plantations and appropriate wealth from the labor of enslaved people. But in Middle Florida, as everywhere else on the plantation frontier, someone else was already there. In fact, by the early eighteenth century, various bands of Muskogee-speaking Amerindians from the Creek Confederacy had supplanted in Middle Florida the Apalachee peoples, who were wiped out by Spanish colonization and English massacre.[22]

Most prominent of these Florida residents were the various "Seminoles," a term that may have meant "wild men" in Muskogee. The Tallahassa band lived around the vanished Apalachees' "old fields" that would become the site of Tallahassee, and the Mikasuki band became the namesake of the large lake just to the east. The Apalachicolas, who were also Creeks but not, strictly speaking, Seminoles, gave their name to the river formed from the confluence of the Flint and Chattahoochee. The various bands thrived on fertile land that supported both hunting and farming. In the northern two-thirds of the region, clay and hammock lands supported thick hardwood growth, while pine and saw palmetto covered the sandier soil that stretched in a belt twenty-five miles wide north from the Gulf of Mexico. The soil was particularly rich in what would become Leon County, around a series of lakes — soon called Miccosukee, Lafayette, Jackson, and Iamonia — and in the Chipola, Chattahoochee, and Apalachicola River floodplains in Jackson. Southward lay the harbors of the shallow St. Marks River, where Florida's longtime colonial ruler Spain had maintained the fort of San Marcos since the seventeenth century, and to the west, Apalachicola Bay.[23]

The Seminoles learned, however, that white empires would not leave them to enjoy Middle Florida. Great Britain controlled once-Spanish East and West Florida after the 1763 settlement of the Seven Years' War, and even after the 1783 Treaty of Paris returned Florida to Spain, British traders continued to operate out of the stone fort on the St. Marks River. Americans in Georgia and Alabama accused them of luring their bondpeople to flee south to the Seminoles. Although the Seminoles had "slaves," many were runaways and descendants of runaways who had fled Georgia and South Carolina for the Florida Indians and lived in quasi-independent enclaves. Andrew Jackson and other American leaders found that both the War of 1812 and the presence of these semi-independent black communities made good excuses for chastising the Seminoles, the Spanish, and English traders. First, raiding parties from Tennessee and Georgia broke Indian power east of the Suwannee. Then, in 1814, Jackson, who had just defeated the Creeks at Horseshoe Bend in Alabama, crossed the border into West Florida and seized Pensacola. Even after the Americans withdrew from Spanish territory in 1815, a fortified enclave of escaped slaves and black Seminoles on the Apalachicola became the focus of further conflict. Georgia and Alabama slaveowners claimed that this "Negro Fort" posed a threat to the stability of their mastery. The gunboats of an 1816 expedition bombarded the maroons, who had raised a red flag indicating "no surrender," until the fort's magazine exploded, killing dozens if not hundreds. The remnants limped into the woods and swamps. Many sought refuge in Seminole villages farther east and south.[24]

The destruction of the Negro Fort did not end border conflicts. In March 1818, Andrew Jackson took advantage of loosely worded orders from Washington, turning skirmishes with the Seminoles into a full-scale invasion designed to make the southern border of the United States finally safe for slavery.[25] After crossing the border at the east bank of the Apalachicola, Jackson marched east to the Tallahassa villages. There he rooted out the few remaining warriors, women, and children, burned the towns, and destroyed the livestock. The general then seized the fort at St. Marks, where he occupied himself in hanging Seminole chiefs and British Indian traders. In the midst of the controversy that followed, American expansionists pushed for official recognition of Jackson's supposedly unauthorized invasion. A treaty signed in 1819, and ratified by both sides by 1821, sold Florida to the United States, making Washington responsible for settling both claims by Americans against the Spanish government and private land claims.[26]

President James Monroe appointed Andrew Jackson the first governor of the territory, and Florida's new chief executive traveled to the old Spanish capital of Pensacola to witness the ceremonial changing of the flags on July 17, 1821. Jackson would find his authority more constrained than it had been at the head of his conquering armies. The territory was a form of government somewhere between a subject colony and an equal state. Congress and the Executive Department jointly supervised territories, appointing many of the officials but granting the people increasing rights to self-determination until, once they had reached a population of 50,000 white inhabitants, they could apply for statehood. Congress appointed the Legislative Council, the representative assembly of the territory, for yearly terms until 1825, when it became an elected body. Jackson could not sort out the squabbling of the council in his short but stormy tenure in Pensacola, which ended in 1822. He resigned with relief, and Monroe appointed William P. DuVal, a Virginia-born Kentuckian, as Jackson's replacement.[27]

Courts and claims commissions would take decades to sort the legiti-

Apalachicola River (from Francis Comte de Castelnau, Vues et Souvenirs de l'Amérique du Nord*)*

mate from the fraudulent among Spain's land grants, both large and small. In the meantime, the federal government owned all of the rest of Florida, but the need to survey and sell the land grew more intense as American whites poured over the border. The events of the First Seminole War had brought Middle Florida directly into the consciousness of Southern migrants. News spread of the fertile lands along the Apalachicola River system and around Lake Miccosukee. Several hundred North Carolinians who had earlier settled in Georgia and Alabama soon trickled down the river valleys. In 1822, their numbers had grown large enough that the territorial government requested that Congress officially establish Jackson County, on the west bank of the Apalachicola and Chattahoochee Rivers. While Jackson remained a part of a separate federal judicial district, geography and economics would link it to the rest of the Middle Florida district that soon began to develop to the east.[28]

By 1823, it became obvious that neither Pensacola nor St. Augustine was acceptable as the center of territorial government. Commissioners traveled to what soon became Leon County and selected the present-day site of Tallahassee as the location for the new capital of Florida. The Tallahassee "Old Fields" were geographically convenient, since they were located midway between St. Augustine and Pensacola. Middle Florida also contained hundreds of thousands of acres of rich land suitable for plantations.[29] And although neither the Spanish nor the English had established plantation agriculture in Middle Florida itself, institutions of slavery were already firmly established in the territory as a whole. As in coastal Georgia just to the north, racial slavery was the backbone of commercial agriculture in the narrow strips of plantation near St. Augustine and the lower St. John's River. Several American planters, such as South Carolinians Abram Bellamy and his father, John, who would eventually settle in Middle Florida, had already moved to the territory's eastern coast. Benjamin Chaires, originally from North Carolina, stocked his plantation near St. Augustine with slaves smuggled in from the Caribbean and Africa. He soon relocated to Middle Florida, where he became the territory's wealthiest planter.[30]

After the commissioners identified the site of the territorial capital, the process of surveying and selling the public land could move forward. Surveyors mapped the public domain of Middle Florida onto a rectangular grid invented by Thomas Jefferson for the Northwest Territory. From Tallahassee, surveyors and their assistants, contracted by the mile, ran a "base line" east and west and a "meridian" north and south. Then they marked off and numbered townships along these lines: six miles square, divided into thirty-six sections measuring a mile on each side.[31] Yet even as the future site of Tallahassee became the central point on the grid of public lands for sale, Tallahassa Seminoles who followed the venerable and feisty Neamathla remained a threat to Middle Florida's plantation future. An 1822 estimate had counted some 2,000 Indians west of the Suwannee. In September 1823, a group of federal commissioners met at Moultrie Creek and presented the chiefs with an ultimatum: sign a treaty confining the Seminoles to the central part of the peninsula or be deported by the unleashed force of unrestrained white settlers. Despite objections, all of the chiefs present signed a document that commissioner James Gadsden privately described to Secretary of War John C. Calhoun as being "in large measure a treaty of imposition." The treaty of Moultrie Creek cleared the last obstacles to settlement. Except for the friendly chiefs along the Apalachicola, now confined to eight square miles, and the inhabitants of Neamathla's village near Tallahassee, the Seminoles and their black allies had to move south to much less fertile land. Within a year, Governor DuVal and increasing pressure from white settlers forced Neamathla to leave his reservation.[32]

Meanwhile, the territorial and federal governments threw up the mechanisms for creating civil government and a territorial capital in Leon County. In March 1824, Governor DuVal proclaimed that the Legislative Council would meet that fall at Tallahassee. The council established Leon County that same month. In April, settlers began to arrive at the hill that would become the site of the capitol building. Several erected a log structure that would house the first few sessions of the legislature. Benjamin Tennille surveyed a town plat for Tallahassee, dividing a 160-acre plot into 160 town lots. On the first Monday in April, the capital's land commission cried off the property at public auction. The sale of Tallahassee lots brought in over $45,000. Soon an array of buildings rose up. Most were ramshackle log cabins or rough-hewn frame houses made of "puncheon boards" and split logs. Early travelers noted that "Tallahassee has all the appearance of a town hastily built, very little taste displayed in the construction of the houses, & they are not substantial."[33] Still, while its architecture might not have met cosmopolitan standards, Tallahassee and the region around saw in the next few months a flood of migrants from throughout the Anglo-Atlantic world, especially from older areas of the South. They brought with them not only resources but also plans and ideas. None would work out as expected, but now the stage was set, and the uncertain acts of migration and settlement began their haphazard course.

One

The Peculiar Benefits of Florida

In 1827, Virginian John Parkhill bid farewell to his wife and his two-year-old son George and journeyed south to look for land. In his diary, Parkhill wrote, "I left Richmond in Virginia the evening of 15 April 1827 in company with William Copland [his brother-in-law] with the view of visiting in Florida, examin[ing] the land & purchase if found of superior quality & the situation healthy."[1] Riding stagecoaches south, the two men reached Augusta, Georgia, where Parkhill and Copland had to purchase horses for the rest of the trip, since no stage ran to the Tallahassee region. As they crossed Georgia, the whole Upper South seemed to be on the move. In Augusta, they had "put up at the Eagle Tavern kept by a Mr. Kennedy from Hanover, Virginia." Later they encountered a Dr. Jones, a planter from Halifax County, North Carolina, on his way to his new lands in Jackson County. Parkhill found a sort of comfort in the familiar origins of other elite settlers, but he also noted that now he saw them in a new physical environment. Through southern Georgia, he continually noted the kinds of soil and the types of trees, but found little of promise in the land itself until they reached Middle Florida. There, the soil looked fertile, and the weather was also quite promising—mild, but not yet too warm for Parkhill. In northern Leon County, they met a recent migrant "born in Southampton County, Virginia." Good soil, good weather, and the presence of other migrants from Virginia and North Carolina all confirmed the positive reports Parkhill had heard of Middle Florida. After looking around for a few days, Parkhill bought 480 acres and headed back to Virginia to collect his family, including brother Samuel Parkhill, and his slaves. Samuel purchased land near John's plantation, Tuscawilla, on "Black Creek" ten miles east of Tallahassee. William Copland also returned with slaves, and settled near the Parkhill brothers.[2]

At about the same time a much less wealthy and much older man named Isaac Hay was making his own long journey to Leon County. With the help of son Reubin, who had come up from his own small farm in Leon to Washington County, Georgia, Hay gathered his meager belongings and loaded them on a rickety cart pulled by a broken-down horse. Perhaps Isaac took one last look at the pine-covered, barren tract that he was abandoning. While passing through the same "piney range," Parkhill had written that "in consequence of it being poor, there are but few settlers, and those generally poor with no negroes." Those of Hay's neighbors who had tried to work better soil had already left, unable to purchase the land where they squatted before speculators snapped it up at government land auctions. Hay's own journey south had begun twoscore years earlier in North Carolina, and he was still "poor with no negroes" and had little or no land to call his own. The much younger Parkhill brought slaves, money, and prestigious possessions when his wagons creaked over the Florida border into Leon County. The aged Hay's cart still held only the spare tools of a poor white man: a homemade grindstone and a set of coopering implements, all valued at $7.50.[3]

Men and women like John Parkhill brought to Middle Florida resources and agendas different from those more like Hay. The distance between these groups, a contrast in wealth, power, and even basic rights to citizenship that had emerged from the crucible of the colonial South, became more contested during the Revolution and the new republic. Although the exact dividing line between planter and nonplanter whites is always difficult to draw, clearly the distance between the circumstances of Parkhill and Hay made all the difference in the world. Men who owned ten or fewer slaves—particularly those who, like Hay, owned none—had to work with their hands. But men who owned more than ten slaves, especially those who, like Parkhill, owned many more, did not have to spend day after day toiling under the hot sun. They had the time to dream bigger dreams, especially about the plantation frontier's "peculiar benefits." They also had the power—or so, with good reason, they believed—to shape the reality of migration south and west along the rough lines of their visions.

Migration to Florida, like movement to other states and territories of the plantation frontier, held out to Parkhill and his peers the possibilities of fertile land, staple crops, and profits to be made, especially when compared to those offered by their old states. Wealthy men in the Chesapeake and the Carolinas coveted the soil and the warm weather of Florida, which seemingly provided a perfect climate for export crops like cotton and sugar. At the same time, most educated white men feared the frontier's dark side, at least a little. There, reports had it, disease spread like a metaphor for the social and cultural environment, and society regressed to a barbaric stage: planters' control over slaves slipped; lesser whites turned saucy. Even their own civilized self-restraint risked peril in regions that produced not natural aristocrats but "hot-blooded fellows," scrambling for control over resources. Such climates made "rascals . . . like maggots they seem to flourish most in putrid masses—and the farther south one gets the more plenty they are."[4] Yet powerful desires drew planter and merchant men to brave their fears and turn their faces south and west.

"THE MOST VALUABLE SOUTHERN COUNTRY"

The settlers who left the most information about their movement to Middle Florida were wealthy ones like John Parkhill. But that fact has not made it easy to understand or agree on who or what they and other Southern planters were. Many historians have depicted this class as a pseudo-aristocratic group shaped by the fact of slaveownership. Supposedly, anticapitalistic dynamics of master-slave interactions made the system of plantation slavery into a premodern method of labor control. That, in turn, allegedly produced white men and women defiantly opposed to modern economics and culture. Southern planters were, however, a part of the capitalist world-system. They directed, in fact, what was at times its most profitable and important producing sector. If plantations were not themselves strictly capitalist enterprises, they were certainly enterprises shaped by Atlantic capitalism.[5] And slavery in the United States—whether as a social relationship between individuals or as an economic institution that relied upon worldwide markets for its products—was in the midst of rapid change during the first half of the nineteenth century. As Yankee society changed under the pressures of commercial and technical intensification, wealthy men in the Chesapeake and Carolinas moved south and west in the 1820s and 1830s, expanding, intensifying, and transforming Southern agriculture, and reshaping the Southern ruling class.[6]

When they discussed the possibility of moving to Middle Florida, planters emphasized migration's dual benefits for commerce and family. To Southeastern planters, the frontier of the Southwest offered a cluster of qualities—land, climate, and openness to slavery—valuable because planters could convert them into cash crops. "In time," wrote one early migrant to Middle Florida, "[this will] become an important Southern slaveholding state—producing as its staples, cotton, sugar, rice, and fruit." Yet despite the modernizing effects of long-distance trade, and the potentially individualizing effects of movement to far-off places, planters did not seize the frontier's commercial opportunities as isolated, profit-maximizing individuals. Even as they focused on the importance of creating wealth through production of staples for the world market, Southern slaveowners like John Parkhill relied heavily upon bonds of kinship.[7]

Among planters from the seaboard states, who would supply the majority of Middle Florida's elite, family ties shaped personal identity.[8] And instead of dissolving kinship, migration to the plantation frontier accentuated and reinforced the ties of family and extended family. Many planters moved to Middle Florida for the specific purpose of helping to maintain or acquire honor, wealth, and political sinecures for family members. While the experience of mastery over large numbers of enslaved African Americans shaped white men and women in deep and subtle ways, the explicit defense of slavery, and of themselves as a slaveholding class, was not yet foremost in planters' conscious minds. In the 1820s and 1830s, elite men and women moving to Florida spoke about their concern for supporting their families, rather than about the need to expand the system of slavery in order to save it from abolitionist pressure. They turned toward Middle Florida because it, like other frontiers of the Old Southwest, seemed to promise the wealth and power of planter families' dreams.[9]

The peninsula's geographic position on the flank of the plantation South fascinated Southern writers, like one who stated in 1830, "Florida has always been a subject of lively interest in the United States, both before and since it came into our possession."[10] Prospective emigrants in Maryland, Virginia, North and South Carolina, and Georgia learned of the area through a variety of channels: from private letters, oral reports, local newspapers, national journals, and books. Accounts of Florida began to appear in national publications like the Washington newspaper *Niles' Register* as early as 1817. By 1823, at least four authors had contributed their descriptions of the new American territory to the growing trans-Atlantic book market. Early accounts mentioned only the East and West Florida regions, but soon prospective settlers began to hear of the fertile region in between the two. In the early 1820s, surveyor John Lee Williams produced a series of newspaper articles that described the area of fertile soil that stretched from the Apalachicola Valley to the Suwannee. He ventured his opinion that the small trading post at St. Marks "will even be the principal port of this section of land."[11]

Writers, travelers, and readers imagined a geography for Middle Florida, mapping it as the best of possible worlds for planters who wanted to "remove" from the older Southern states. Unlike earlier settlers in the West Florida parishes of Louisiana, or the slaveowners even then moving to Texas, they would not have to lead local revolutions to force colonial powers to surrender the territory to American planters. In contrast to Missouri, there would be no congressional challenge to the legality of slavery in

Florida, where Spanish, English, American, and Native American settlers had long claimed mastery over enslaved people. And unlike many parts of Missouri or Arkansas, lengthy growing seasons and excellent soil characterized Middle Florida: "These trees [around Tallahassee] are a proof of the vigour of the soil. . . . It possesses an inexhaustible fertility." Alluvial areas along the rivers promised to be as fertile as the Mississippi Delta. Just like migrants to Mississippi or Alabama, Middle Florida settlers could grow cotton. In fact, the earliest pioneers were supposedly already raising prodigious quantities on the new soil, under the sun of the long growing season. A Leon County correspondent reported in 1826 that "Cotton was as high as my head on horseback."[12]

Florida was all that Mississippi, Alabama, or other Southwestern states could be for the restless planter, and perhaps even more. The subtropical climate imagined for Middle Florida permitted dreams of two additional crops that only increased the area's already potent allure. Writers noted the sandy patches that dotted the soil of the inland districts of the counties around Tallahassee but also argued that this seeming drawback was one of Middle Florida's more attractive qualities. Sand and heat created an ideal environment for the long-staple, or sea-island, cotton plant. This form of cotton commanded prices several times that of the ordinary short-staple varieties. Textile manufacturers used its long, silky fibers for "superfine" cloths, but before the settlement of Florida, this variety thrived only along the coasts of South Carolina and Georgia. After 1821, pioneer planters reported early yields of five to seven hundred pounds per acre of sea-island cotton. Thus they held out to ambitious planters the allure of a crop hitherto reserved for low-country aristocrats.[13]

Even more significantly, Middle Florida's climate appeared to permit the cultivation of sugar cane. Sugar was, in the words of one Middle Florida settler, a "higher game," played for deeper stakes than cotton. Planters in Virginia or the Carolinas knew tobacco and cotton and the rewards, and failures, those crops could offer, but sugar promised something far greater. Migrants' fascination with the sweet staple underscored their interest in becoming a part of a world of trade, commerce, and power that transcended regional and even national boundaries. Would-be settlers eagerly consumed claims made by the *Tallahassee Floridian* that cane planted in Leon County hammocks or Jackson County's floodplains would produce "equal if not superior to the best Mississippi [River] bottoms" in Louisiana. The article, which was copied in the national press, reported that "We have now in our office ten stalks of sugar cane, raised on the plantation of Dr. Weedon, the produce of a single joint, weighing *fifty and a half pounds.*"[14]

Stories about Florida sugar aroused potential migrants' economic calculations to fantasies of the Caribbean model of planter power, wealth, and ease. Jamaica planters were still among the richest men in the British Empire, and in the previous century they had symbolized colonial power. Thus, like Virginian Francis Eppes, many men moving to Middle Florida planned to "begin life anew as a sugar planter." Leon County's Thomas Brown sunk $20,000 in his sugar works, while Jackson County settlers also invested heavily in the dream of sweetness and power. In the fall of 1829, Latimus and Marcus Armistead, Virginians who operated a merchant house at Aspalaga on the lower Chattahoochee River, sold sugar boilers to planters Richard Holmes, Peter W. Gautier Sr., T. Watson, and Sextus Camp.[15]

The imitation of the West Indies soon became a local vogue. The presence of a few imported Caribbean planters and white artisans associated with the sugar-making business further encouraged dreams of converting cane into superprofits. Brown recruited a Cuban sugar-making expert to run his mill, while the mere mention of Jamaica was a shorthand assurance of sugar expertise. Jamaican expatriate Farquhar McRae attained a sort of local agricultural celebrity. His articles extolled the possibilities of Middle Florida sugar planting, recommended high-quality syrup-refining equipment, and simulated on paper the hypothetical plantations "B" and "D." "B" grew only cotton, while "D" made both cotton and sugar, recording a higher return on his investment. Others hopefully asserted that Middle Florida sugar grew more like that of Jamaica than did Louisiana cane. Even after frosts in the late 1820s destroyed several cane crops, writers assured prospective migrants that Florida's climate would permit the production of sugar.[16]

Sugar was merely the most glamorous of the many enticements offered by Jackson and Leon Counties. As Governor William P. DuVal wrote in 1824, the costs of the acquisition of Florida seemed like nothing compared to the benefits: "The interior is, in my opinion, the most valuable Southern country I have ever seen. . . . This region produces Sugar Cane and Sea Island cotton in greater perfection than any other part of the Southern Country." Moving to the bottom line, he concluded: "I have no doubt that this tract of Country [the Middle Florida counties] alone will sell for more than the Florida debt."[17] Florida, boosters claimed, would be a sort of superplantation that combined the advantages of both the United States and the West Indies. Eventually, planters had to give up the dream of recreating the sugar islands, and sea-island cotton did not became a major local crop until the 1850s. But in the 1820s, no one doubted that plantation production of staple crops would dominate Middle Florida. Florida offered the classic bases for planter wealth: available plantation land and prestigious government offices that provided sinecures to family members while also allowing elite control over economic development. As one local resident suggested in an 1832 toast, it only needed proper attention from the federal government in order to become a state as rich as others in the South: "The Territory of Florida—Uncle Sam's only Southern plantation, it needs ditching and fencing—Let him look to it, if he wants a good crop."[18]

Despite Florida's multiple and complex attractions, planters might not have taken on the task of having the territory ditched and fenced had they been satisfied with the futures they faced in the old states. In 1836, a relative of the numerous planters who moved to Middle Florida from Halifax County in the eastern North Carolina cotton belt recorded his impressions of a visit to a local market town: "Our Stantonburg friends seem in earnest about moving to Mobile. They are selling off very fast and have rendered their stock of dry goods very low. . . . Poor old Tarborough seems to be retreating every day; our feelings and interest say we must leave it very soon." "Feelings" of fear about declining family fortunes intertwined with calculated economic "interest" in the minds of elite men and women in the older Southeastern states. Both urged planters to leave, lest they miss their chance and be stuck in places that were "retreating every day."[19]

Feelings could be powerful spurs to migration, especially given recent threats to elite power. The volatile business cycles that shook the Anglo-Atlantic world after 1818 imparted the urgencies of self-doubt and threatened family honor to many planters' discussions of migration. By the 1820s, Richmond merchant-planters Robert and John Gamble had experienced tremendous ups and downs in the commercial economy. Ruined once by the embargo of 1807–9, they recovered by investing in the James River canal. Then the panic of 1819, and various hiccups in the business cycle of the 1820s, prostrated the Gamble brothers' fortunes once more. "Their property was once large," said an English friend, "but after too sanguine a speculation, they were wound up in the panic of 1827." Meanwhile, in 1828, North Carolinian Richard Parish wrote to his son William, complaining of his own economic woes. He then mentioned their kinsman Nathan Byrd, a merchant and planter: Byrd was "still in great embarrassment and the prospect ahead is most gloomy." Economic failure could threaten the status of planter men and their families in multiple ways. The term used for overwhelming debt was often, after all, "embarrassment," implying paralyzing, dishonorable exposure. The appearance of economic independence and success—of both self and family—was essential to planter confidence.[20]

Fearful of the embarrassment, planters in the Chesapeake and Carolinas blamed recent decline on the supposedly worn-out soil of their region.

This was a time-honored mode of communal self-criticism, particularly in Virginia. There, Mary Randolph, the wife of Francis Eppes, wrote to her cousin in 1827, a year before Eppes would move to Leon County: "These gullied worn out fields, and this unfinished leaking hull of a house, have become more than ever distasteful to both Francis and myself, and we needed little before to render them altogether odious." Her keen sense of family interest recoiled when she looked out at Virginia's fields: "Tobacco is the only thing which can be made here, and after vast labour and expence, in raising and manufacturing the vile weed, and acquiring both skill and judgment in the business, to find still that no profit must be expected, is disheartening indeed."[21] Breast-beating about worn-out soil and "vile weeds" painted Virginia planters in the gray hues of a declining ruling class while also suggesting that the fault lay in the soil rather than those who supervised its tilling. Increasingly, residents and travelers alike saw the Old Dominion as an "old field" of the South: a state grown too sterile to produce staple crops; good only for raising black slaves and white pioneers to clear and settle Uncle Sam's newer plantations.[22]

Fears about soil exhaustion served as metaphors for concerns about declining family power, but after the panic of 1819 the material basis of planter power—their "interest"—faced clear threats in the form of climatic change and economic stagnation. Soon after the 1793 invention of the cotton gin, farmers learned that cotton would grow in commercial quantities as far north as the southeastern counties of Virginia and the Roanoke Valley of northeastern North Carolina. But in the 1820s, a global decline in temperatures moved the northern limit of cotton cultivation farther south, rendering useless large areas of cultivation. This shift in climate helped drive planters south and west. In addition, a lack of ports stymied commercial growth throughout North Carolina, particularly in the planter-dominated coastal plain. Meanwhile, intensive cotton cultivation since the 1790s had allegedly worn out and gullied fields throughout neighboring South Carolina, and even eastern Georgia.[23]

By the end of the 1820s, the acquisition of Florida, the Creek lands in Alabama and Mississippi, Arkansas, and the Red River lands of Louisiana created an additional pressure on distressed Southeastern planters. Some called it a "fever," while one Florida migrant described it as the "spirit of emigration." A North Carolina woman reported that "Aunt Betsey has broken out with the Florida humours again and is rather disposed to think it the catch." The writer's cousins also wanted to move: "Susan and William are both broken out." To some observers, the scramble to leave the old states seemed irrational, driven by a disembodied spirit that rushed among neighbors like miasmas, the swamp mists blamed for malaria and other fevers.

News of departures seemed to seep through neighborhoods, followed by a common symptom: the desire to ensure that one and one's family would not miss the chance at wealth and power in a new land. Letters from friends and relatives who had already moved reiterated and exaggerated the wealth and success available in Middle Florida. After receiving a letter from his uncle Thomas Randall, Thomas Hagner could think of nothing but "Southern advantages" of lawyering around Tallahassee: "I am indeed so charmed with the prospect he holds out, that the good fortune he depicts as the fruits of the proper application of the circumstances which would surround me there, already almost stares me in the face."[24]

The extended family networks common in older plantation areas shaped decisions to migrate. But in the process of exploiting the plantation frontier's potential wealth, wealthy white men came to rely more heavily than ever on the power that came from kinship ties. Few planter men could afford to move by themselves, or to isolate themselves from the influence and assistance of brothers, fathers, adult sons, cousins, and in-laws. Virginian William Nuttall and his father and brothers carefully planned their move to Leon County, and William and his brother James came down to establish a plantation in 1827. When John Branch, Andrew Jackson's first secretary of the navy, appointed his cousin Eli Whitaker as inspector of the navy's live oak forests in 1829, Whitaker's ensuing journey to Florida to look for promising stands of timber for naval vessels was little more than a cover. In reality, he was prospecting for cotton land that Branch and his other Bradford, Whitaker, and Cotten relatives from Halifax County in North Carolina hoped to buy.[25]

Elite white migrants carefully maintained family ties that extended across states, households, and generations. Attention to family began with patriarchs like John Gamble, who stood at the centers of extensive networks of kin. Gamble's numerous relations of the Gamble, Wirt, Goldsborough, and Cabell families, many of whom moved with him to Florida, referred to him simply as "Uncle John," regardless of their specific genealogical relationship to him. Here, too, both feelings and interest combined. The words of such elders, who frequently dispensed political and economic favors to family members, carried considerable emotional and practical weight. Anna Wills assumed that when her father, Cary Whitaker, decided to move to Jackson County, he would open the floodgates: "I am as interested as anybody[,] for if you move you expect to carry all my Brothers and Sisters with you." These older men felt responsible for maintaining the standing of the clans that surrounded them. Cary Whitaker explained why he wanted to set up a Jackson County plantation that he hoped to hand over to his sons: "We make immense sacrafices [sic] for gold. It was the love of money caused me to leave home children and friends, in order to attain it, the main object was to leave something to give my children."[26]

Younger men, in turn, relied upon the advice and assistance offered by their powerful older relatives. Thomas Hagner asked his uncle Thomas Randall, judge of the Middle Florida circuit, for guidance: "I have more than once turned to Florida as the scene of my future trials and labors, and have consulted uncle Thomas on the subject." Once settled in Tallahassee as a successful lawyer, Hagner in turn offered to help establish his brother in Middle Florida: "It may be in my power to do much for him here, and I would like him not to conclude any arrangement until he advises me." Migrant planters certainly calculated the individual benefits of escaping declining plantation economies and settling in booming cotton regions. But complex considerations for both nuclear and extended kin networks also made movement attractive, as one observer of Middle Florida's planters noted in 1830: "The difficult problem of uniting good society with profit, in the old States, they could not solve. They have come out, therefore, to live simply, if not severely at first, to take advantage of cheap and rich lands, and of profitable staples, and thus to rear estates for themselves and children."[27]

Despite the pressures of feeling and interest, planter men and their families sometimes doubted the wisdom of migration to a "severe" frontier. Some elite women who would stay behind feared the loss of their relatives. Mary Ann Gregory cautioned William H. Wills against leaving their North Carolina neighborhood to follow his father-in-law, Cary Whitaker, to Middle Florida. She warned that there was much to lose in "breaking the chain of early acquaintants." The ties of kinship in the older states were close and strong, and some feared that such relationships could not be transplanted to the frontier. Cary Whitaker's daughter Anna Whitaker Wills herself strongly urged her father not to settle in Jackson County: "I do not like that Florida plan at all, I can tell you. I have thought all along mine was the best way." She offered instead a prescription used by many to finance their continued residence in the older plantation states: "Stay home, sell Negroes, pay up. The balance is *yours* if you have only ten left. . . . Do so [i.e., do as] I say. You may think I have no right to dictate to my *father.* But if that Father goes away and leaves me, I will have none to dictate to and I want him to stay here where I can see him one in six months if no oftener."[28]

Other women feared disease and Indian attacks. Anna C. Gradner, a daughter of Richard Parish (who moved to Leon County in the late 1820s), worried that Seminoles would harm her relatives: "I should not like to be so near the Indians myself. I think you had all better leave Florida and come back again to No. Carolina it is by far the sweetest place." Anna

Wills feared for her father's health in the warmer Florida climate: "I say again I do *not* like the plan you are too old to brave the southern climate." And Martha Bradford's kinswoman wrote: "Unless it [Tallahassee] proves healthier than it has done lately, I shall not be anxious to move.... I would prefer a healthy country to a rich and sickly one, for what is prefferable [*sic*] to health?" [29]

Women generally assumed that they played at least a secondary role in the decision-making process. Indeed, evidence from Middle Florida suggests that they assumed a more obvious role in discussions about migration than in any of the other political or economic decisions made by planters until the Civil War. Their reactions to the idea of removal usually rested upon the perceived effect of migration upon their relationships to kin and family. Those who thought that they would be able to maintain close ties to family were more likely to support migration, while those women who would be left behind in the old states, or isolated on the frontier, tended to disparage the idea. The women of the Eppes and Randolph families urged the family to move somewhere, and, as Francis Eppes reported, "the Girls prefer Florida." They urged Florida rather than Louisiana upon him with great force. In fact, his sister-in-law Harriet Randolph was in her vehemence "not the least masculine of the set." Florida it would be, then, and meanwhile, Mary Eppes urged her female correspondents to join her in the area of the plantation frontier where she would settle. She gave her cousin Jane Randolph (whose own husband had mentioned emigration) a glowing account of husband Francis Eppes's land-prospecting trip to Middle Florida with Thomas Brown. Mary emphasized that the region was surely "perfectly healthy—Louisiana, whether in the neighborhood of your brother's settlement, or in the Attacapas, [Francis] seems rather averse to from hearing that fevers begin already to prevail." [30]

Certainly plantation mistresses were not immune to "the Florida humours," the "fever" for emigration, or the desire for family power and wealth. Catherine Wirt looked out her Richmond window at the rain and saw in her mind's eye the waterlogged cotton growing on the family's new Middle Florida plantation, "Wirtland," to which she and her mother were preparing to move. "Oh these rains and our poor crops," she wrote, thinking of their need to make enough money to pay off crushing debts. She was concerned about both ties of affection and the need for the family to reverse its economic fortunes when she begged for more frequent letters from Middle Florida. "Remember," she wrote, "how our earthly hopes and affections are gathered up in your dear troupe." Mary Eppes, after arguing for emigration, reported success: "Mama is quite willing to remove, I believe, and the girls [her sisters Harriet and Lucy] wish it exceedingly, and even Papa, who opposed it at first (who would have expected opposition from him, on such a scheme), seems to be coming round." Supporting husband Francis's desire to move, she urged on her initially reluctant father. Both of these men would gain wealth and government office from resettlement in Leon County. Mary would also benefit, though perhaps in more limited ways, from family success.[31]

Planter men sometimes took into consideration the hopes and fears of female kinfolk. They did have similar worries. Many noted their fear that disease haunted the hotter environment of plantation regions farther south. R. H. Bradford, John Branch's elderly uncle, cautioned his nephew: "I confess I am afraid of these climates so near the tropics—the fevers are always formidable." If Florida, like the West Indies, permitted sugar production, perhaps it also was a "white man's grave," replete with endemic "agues" (malaria) and yellow fever. Perhaps, Bradford warned, this "land of promise" also "promises graves to the adventurers who go to try it!" First-hand reports told potential settlers that malaria and yellow fever could strike throughout the Old Southwest, but disease also served both men and women as a metaphor for broader concerns about the frontier environment. Paired with the fear of illness in planter discussions was often the fear that on Middle Florida's plantation frontier, migrants might degenerate into savagery. Although optimistic that civilization would prevail, "X, Y, and Z" hinted at this issue in 1834: "He who has never tried a new country, cannot anticipate the privations, labour, and disappointments he must encounter in subduing the forests, in rearing a civilized home in the midst of a savage wilderness."[32]

The fear of regression to barbarity made sense in the context of contemporary views about history. By the beginning of the nineteenth century, many educated Anglo-Americans believed that human societies passed through particular stages of complexity and civilization. "The *infant* state of settlements," wrote one migrant to Middle Florida, "is, like the infant state of the world, a *savage* or barbarous state." The "states," as this writer had it, ascended in ranks from savagery, to agriculture, to commerce. The exigencies of life on a new frontier could drive men accustomed to living by farming to regress into savage hunters or barbaric herders. Settlers in other areas had already shown a disturbing propensity to exhibit behaviors violent even by the standards of the South, where slavery and the persistence of dueling institutionalized violence. Just as "miasmas" supposedly caused fevers, the unsettled frontier environment caused regression to an earlier stage of historical development.[33]

The apparent loosening of customary modes of social and personal control frightened planters. Middle Florida's first migrant planters complained of the proximity of the Seminoles and the restiveness of slaves until Governor DuVal forced Neamathla out of Leon County. But rashes of advertisements for runaway slaves continued to break out in local newspapers. Even planters' psyches suddenly seemed uncontrollable. Early news of shootouts between Tallahassee political factions prompted one South Carolina observer to complain: "The country may be very fine and its productions such as to offer considerable inducements to emigrants, but the above account does not say very much in favor of the refinement of those who are already there." The writer called Florida "The Rogue's Paradise" and hinted that the climate and the unsettled nature of the plantation frontier might be responsible for such unrefined and uncivilized behavior: "These hot-blooded fellows, perhaps, will kill each other off after a while, and make room for a more peaceable population."[34]

Despite fears of degeneration from within and rebellion by the lower orders, many planters decided in the 1820s and 1830s to leave the older states and move to Middle Florida. These migrants remained confident that they would be able to reconstruct Southeastern models of deference by nonplanter whites and submission by slaves in a new country. Faced with the vision of savagery, Joseph M. White, territorial delegate to Congress, insisted upon imagining instead a Middle Florida that supported planter "interest"—for him, "a happier prospect." He pointed with hope to "the condition of Florida West of the Suwannee [Middle Florida]—filling with emigrants from every portion of the union—Forests falling before the ax of industry and fields of cotton blossoming where they stood—I will shew you a city in the place of a wigwam—and a press inculcating the mild principles of republicanism, where the war whoop was lately heard."[35]

Only time would tell how well the dream of making Middle Florida into an industrious quarter of the civilized world, in which the men of planter families could have both wealth and good society, would work out. But making the decision to migrate to Middle Florida as members of extended families, planters sought to escape what they saw as the depressed possibilities for commercial agriculture in the Chesapeake states and the Carolinas. Middle Florida offered them exciting kinds of power, represented by the myth of the sugar planter, and the reality of a new territory in which wealth and office would be up for grabs among family-based factions. Although some women objected to the disruptions and dangers of migration, the frontier's benefits for families intrigued others. And so elite migrants decided to become "Florida gentlemen," as one woman called Leon County settlers, and prepared to move south and west.[36]

Between 1821 and 1840, dozens of wealthy white men from planter backgrounds migrated to Jackson and Leon Counties. Following the same patterns as John Parkhill and his brother-in-law, they traveled south, prospected for land, and then returned to the old states. Planters next assembled family and slaves and headed south in overland caravans. By 1827, planter settlement was in full swing in both counties and did not stop for another decade. Thomas Brown came to Leon County in January 1827 and found that "there were but a few plantations then open and in cultivation." When he returned a year later, the face of the country was changing. New plantations and farms spread through the forest. Benjamin Chaires had begun clearing his plantation "Verdura," due east of Tallahassee, and his numerous sons had settled nearby. Around Lake Miccosukee, men like Robert W. Alston and his sons Willis and Augustus (from Halifax County, North Carolina, by way of Hancock County, Georgia) settled on the rich soil around the water. Meanwhile, in Jackson County, North Carolina planters from the Roanoke River valley filled up the best lands along the Chipola. Others settled on the rich but thickly forested bottomlands along the Chattahoochee and Apalachicola Rivers.[37]

Planters usually migrated with extended families and settled near their relatives, allowing the speedy development of visiting patterns that resembled those of the older states. The Parkhill brothers and William Copland all established their households on Black Creek. The Randolph and Eppes families also settled in the same neighborhood. Just over the Leon County border to the east, in Jefferson County, the Gamble brothers set up their plantations, Waukeenah and Welaunee. Their Richmond relative Abraham Cabell settled only a few miles away. Thomas Randall, married to the Gambles' niece Laura Wirt, bought land and built his house in the same area in 1827. Her father, former attorney general of the United States and noted author William Wirt, bought several hundred acres nearby with the intention of also creating a plantation. He died before he could move to Florida, but his widow, Elizabeth Gamble Wirt, and several of his children did live there during the 1830s.[38]

When the Branch, Bradford, and Whitaker families, an intricately related network of North Carolinians from Halifax County, moved to Middle Florida in the early 1830s, they settled around each other north of Tallahassee. Four Bradford brothers, John Branch, several of his adult sons, sons-in-law, nephews, and three adult Whitaker men bought land, most of it in the two townships north of Tallahassee (in the first range east of the meridian). There, friends and relatives maintained and intensified kinship relations

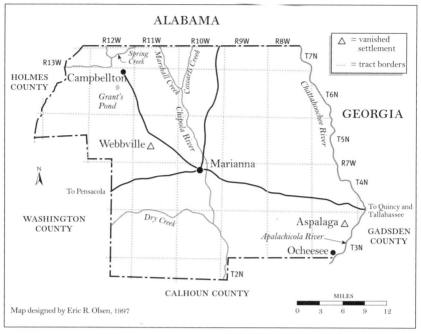

Jackson County, c. 1843

transplanted from the old states. By 1840, at least sixty-eight members of the Branch-Bradford-Whitaker clan lived in their Leon County neighborhood. Jackson County planters also maintained transplanted family ties. In 1836, high land prices in Leon forced Cary Whitaker to purchase in Jackson. But even there he could settle near cousins of the Baker, Roulhac, and other Roanoke Valley families: "I sometimes go and stay the night at Dr. Jno. B. Baker's. . . . I also met with your uncle Simmons. The new comers here from N.C., well independent of others, form a good society." Middle Florida's Achille Murat noted: "A planter never comes alone; he persuades some relatives and friends to emigrate with him, or at least to come and see the country; the greater part of these visitors settle there. In the midst of this infant plantation, he lives happy and tranquil at home."[39]

Among such groups of planters in motion, exchanges of assistance flowed constantly between male relatives and crossed generational lines in both directions. Wealthy settlers relied heavily upon the help of family to realize dreams of cotton fields and sugar houses. North Carolina planter Richard Parish paid off debts incurred by merchant/planter Nathan Byrd in the creation of Byrd's Leon County plantation. Byrd's son Flavius was already married to Parish's daughter, and Parish himself soon moved to Leon

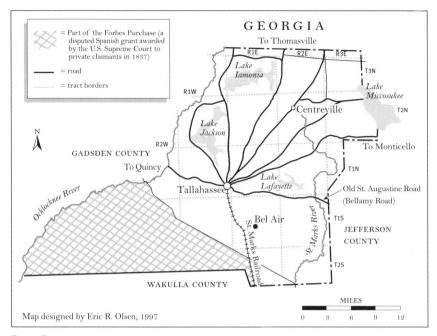

Leon County, c. 1840s

County. While elders helped many younger men, William R. Taylor gave his father "the sum of Eight Hundred Dollars,""the amount," John Taylor wrote in his will, "which he advanced to his mother and myself to enable us to move to Florida." In addition to the large numbers of family members who actually moved together, kinship networks and business associates who remained in the old states but wanted to invest in the returns of the cotton frontier financed many planters' resettlement. William Nuttall's brothers and father conceived his plantations Chemonie and El Destino as a cooperative venture between the four Nuttall men. While William and James, as noted earlier, went to Florida, the other two stayed in Virginia and supplied them with cash and slaves.[40]

Although cash and capital were often in short supply on the frontier—Francis Eppes sold a family clock from grandfather Thomas Jefferson's Monticello to raise money for his move—many could turn to relatives for both. When John Parkhill needed to pay off a debt of $530 in 1830, he turned to his Richmond-based father-in-law Charles Copland. Copland paid Parkhill's debt in return for a mortgage on a slave named Peter, a couple of mules, and some farm equipment. Although a mortgage may seem less than open-handed generosity, if Parkhill was unable to pay when the note became due, Copland would surely have extended it for him. This was the advantage of dealing with one's kinfolk. Cary Whitaker, who faced numerous difficulties in his attempts to set up his Jackson County plantation (including the mishap of a barge that overturned, sinking his crop of cotton in Apalachicola Bay), borrowed money from his nephew Richard Whitaker. Some six years after moving to Jackson County, Whitaker still had not yet redeemed his note. Although he admitted that "there is a debt I am anxious to pay," he knew that he could put off repaying his nephew still further without fearing a legal recourse.[41]

Acquaintances and business associates from the old states may have been less generous than relatives, but they, too, provided an important source of capital to migrant planters. In the personalistic, chaotic commercial world of the early-nineteenth-century plantation export economy, merely to have access to large-scale credit was a tremendous advantage possessed only by the most successful planters in Leon and Jackson Counties. Before the 1830s, Middle Florida could not claim any lending institutions that could supply the significant amounts needed to buy land or slaves. Instead, well-connected men obtained loans from business acquaintances before migrating south to frontiers parched for credit. Leon County planter and speculator William P. Craig (originally of Maryland) borrowed $13,000 from George Lorimer, a Virginia merchant, in the early 1830s. Craig spent much of the money on increasing the size of his slave force. Soon after, James H. Lorimer, a relative of George Lorimer, moved to Tallahassee. When Craig wanted to put off repaying his original debt, he went to James, who took over the debt to his kinsman in return for a mortgage on Craig's slaves. Thomas Brown obtained loans from business acquaintances in the course of his relocation to Leon County. Brown borrowed money from John Dickenson, which he invested in sugar-making apparatus and a sugar-refining house. Brown mortgaged Dickerson many of his slaves but also mortgaged many of the same ones to Philip Alexander of Virginia and to Horatio P. Vass, a Baltimore merchant related to the Gamble brothers. Brown used these loans to pay off $27,000 of various debts owed to merchants throughout northern Virginia. His sugar-making endeavors failed miserably, but not because any lack of credit kept him out of the "higher game."[42]

After deciding where to settle, and how to raise money, elite migrants wanted to begin establishing their plantations as quickly as possible. Those who arrived in Middle Florida with their slaves before land actually went on sale began clearing the woods before they held legal title. Most planters arrived after government land auctions began (1825 in Leon County, 1827 in Jackson County) and so bought their acres before beginning the process of clearing. And this undertaking was laborious: some settlers re-

Plantation on Lake Jackson (from Francis Comte de Castelnau, Vues et Souvenirs de l'Amérique du Nord*)*

duced the difficulty by girdling the trees; but many had every tree cut down and the biggest roots grubbed up from land intended for cotton cultivation with the plow. Slaves turned next to erecting cabins and enclosing fields.[43] Meanwhile, planters hired white artisans to make many of their cotton gins, cotton presses, and sugar works. Men like Isaac Hay's son also hired themselves out by the day or week to split rails, and dug the wells for most plantations, since slaves were too valuable to risk on such dangerous jobs. White hunters and Indians supplied plantations and stores with necessities and commodities from the forest. Thomas Brown's daughter remembered a Seminole, called Tiger Tail by whites, who sold venison and game to William DuVal.[44]

Most work, however, fell to the hands of enslaved African Americans. "How [else]," asked Achille Murat from his well-stocked Jefferson County plantation Lipona, "are great capitals to be employed in agriculture, in a new country, without slaves?" And great capitals had to produce profits: after clearing and fencing the land, migrant planters hurried to bring crops to market. When Francis Eppes returned to Florida with his Virginia family in 1829, the slaves he had left behind had already planted a large field of cotton. Those migrants with relatives could rely on kinfolk to super-

Port of Magnolia (from Francis Comte de Castelnau, Vues et Souvenirs de l'Amérique du Nord)

vise the clearing and preparation of land. When Eli Whitaker moved down from Halifax County, North Carolina, in late spring of 1835, his son Richard had already superintended planting operations on both of their plantations: "I have about 60 acres planted in cotton." Eli, seeing this fine beginning, rented more land and added to his cotton in cultivation by the middle of May. The sharing of labor and supervision encouraged Francis Eppes first to send his laborers to build cabins for his Randolph relatives, and then to borrow their slaves for field labor.[45]

As plantations emerged from the woods, cotton production soared. Jackson County planters had brought bales of the staple to sale before Tallahassee was founded. In 1826, the *Pensacola Gazette* reported, "During the past week a considerable quantity of cotton came into the market and among that particularly entitled to notice were two lots raised upon the Chipola and in the Holmes Valley." From a trickle in 1824, by 1828, Apalachicola shipped 55,000 bales of cotton from the Chattahoochee/Apalachicola River valley, an area that included both west Georgia and Jackson County. In 1828, a local editor reported that Jackson County planters, dissatisfied with the limitations of the harbor at Apalachicola, proposed to build a canal to link the Chipola River to St. Andrew's Bay. Leon County schemers founded the towns of Magnolia and Port Leon on the St. Marks River to ship the produce of Leon and Jefferson Counties. Others planned canals, or tried to obtain government contracts to clear rivers, all seeking to link cotton and sugar producers with their markets.[46]

By 1830, most of these planter dreams appeared to be bearing early fruit. A class of powerful families who relied on slave labor to produce export crops was emerging in Jackson and Leon Counties (see Table A.2). Twenty-three households in the former county and forty-one in the latter reported owning more than twenty slaves. By 1840, these numbers had increased still further. In Leon, ninety-four white households reported enough slaves to put them in the planter category. Jackson's 1840 U.S. Census was taken incorrectly and does not report individual slaveholdings. But the majority of an 1838 territorial census survives and lists thirty planters in the county: almost 8 percent of the white households, up from 6 percent eight years earlier.

In the early 1830s, economic differentiation among whites in Middle Florida grew out of the resources—enslaved laborers, access to credit, knowledge of the commercial world, and political connections—that the most successful brought with them. The planter men and women who moved to Jackson and Leon Counties sought much for themselves and their families. Thus one observer claimed, "The manners, the intelligence, and the knowledge of the old States are to be found in this new territory. Many who have felt the influence of the best society in Europe and America, are to be found among its planters. . . . Wealth, however, is not their sole object; the comforts and humanities, if not the elegancies of civil life, they endeavour to catch by the way in their pursuit of ulterior objects. These views have brought together, particularly in the Tallahassee district, an improved and improving class."[47] The accumulation of wealth and political power would allow planters, early in the life of territorial Florida, to create a society and a political economy designed around their own interests and desires. Within a mere five years, Middle Florida already began to look something like the superplantation envisioned in the early 1820s by William DuVal and others. Cotton and sugar grew to maturity in fields free from Seminoles, and enslaved African Americans harvested them. Bales, bags, and barrels rolled forth from new ports into the hulls of ships bound for Liverpool and New York. Meanwhile, the existence of transplanted ties of family assured the nervous that they were civilized rather than savage. Still, economic power was not the only component of feelings and interest; nor the only object sought by those who called themselves "men of capital and respectability" on the move.[48] Seeking other kinds of distinction, planter men strutted before other white men on the stage of politics, like masters before slaves. And even while this "improved and improving class" sought to tame the forests, themselves, and anyone else in the territory, less wealthy whites like Isaac Hay were also filtering south into Jackson and Leon. They came with a different vision for the frontier, one that would ultimately bring them into conflict with planters.

Countrymen

In 1832, a few years after moving south from Georgia, Isaac Hay asked a Leon County lawyer to help commit to paper his petition for a pension as a Revolutionary War veteran. The intent of the application undoubtedly led Hay to emphasize his patriotism and service in order to boost his chances of receiving a pension. Yet even the rhetorical plea for support from a country to which he had sacrificed his youth subtly underlined the differences between men like Isaac Hay and those like John Parkhill. When Hay told the story of his long odyssey south to Middle Florida, he did not emphasize considerations of feeling and interest, or the recent ups and downs of the Atlantic economy. And although one might assume that every white man in the antebellum South dreamed of becoming a planter, he did not speak of wanting to leave a plantation to his children.[1] Instead, he began with the United States' fight for political freedom, a story that set in relief his own long search for economic and political independence. In 1777, Hay recalled, he enlisted in the Continental line. No mere sunshine soldier, he survived Valley Forge, fought two more years before being captured at the fall of Charleston in 1780, and then endured a year in British hands. After the war, unable to claim bounty lands promised by the state of North Carolina, he sold his rights to them. Perhaps he needed to pay debts, or perhaps he wanted to purchase coopering tools and materials. Despite his artisanal skill, the illiterate Hay never made enough money to become a landowner in Greene County. Thus he never attained the right to vote in North Carolina, where the ballot was restricted to propertied white men. The homage that his yeoman neighbors might have paid him as a Revolutionary veteran therefore never translated into respect when the gentry and yeomanry of Greene gathered on courthouse days.[2]

Perhaps when Hay left eastern North Carolina, he hoped to achieve what he felt his hard service in the Continental line had earned him and his descendants: independence, freedom from aristocratic rule, and manhood.

Hay and his peers believed that the Revolution should have guaranteed their cultural and political status as free white men. So, for instance, did a neighbor who eulogized Ansel Ferrell, another Leon County yeoman from North Carolina who had stood up to fight even as Cornwallis and Tarleton marched over the length of the South: "He lived through the gloomiest days of the Republic, and poured out his blood that his posterity might be free." Hay did not want to be seen as seeking dependence on government largesse, either. He emphasized that until recently "he was able to labour and maintain himself, and was unwilling to receive anything from the government until necessity actually require it." Some time around 1800, when he was approaching fifty, Hay bought 200 acres of poor land in Washington County, Georgia. In 1818, he sold that tract for $150, well below the price he had paid for it, and used the money to buy a nearby eighty-acre tract. This land he worked "as long as it was worth cultivating or I was able to cultivate it, and finding that I could neither sell nor lease it to add to my maintenance, I gave it to my son Reubin Hay." Planters hoped to leave working plantations, and slave quarters full of young workers, to their sons, but all Hay could pass on was a patch of Georgia sand that his son later abandoned as worthless. He and his posterity had not yet found economic independence, or the real freedom that depended on that prerequisite. So Hay and all his sons took roads southwest, still searching.[3]

SOURCES OF MIGRATION

Like Isaac Hay, most non-elite white migrants to early Jackson or Leon County came from the coastal plain that stretched from the Chesapeake south through the Carolinas into Georgia. During the years of the early republic, the experience of continued economic and political inequalities in these planter-dominated counties limited yeoman aspirations and shaped common white migration and settlement to the Old Southwest. Such nonplanter white men often feared that their "betters" wanted to impose deference and dependence upon the white lower classes, and so they moved south and west.[4] Planters on the frontier called such men, among other things, "countrymen." The word smacks of contempt, but it also suggests the uncertain, changing status of such men in ways not readily revealed by terms like "common white," "poor white," or "yeoman farmer." Such terms, in historians' hands, pin down status by specific economic measures of land- or slaveownership. These measures matter and should not be discarded, but on an unsettled frontier, outcomes and yardsticks were perhaps less important than uncertainties. Planters, for instance, suggested by the term "countryman" that these men came from the unknown depths of the new country. Clearly such people were not planters. Their surnames, families, and resources were not those of the migrant elite. But whether or not a countryman was today—or would be tomorrow—a propertyless drifter, or a thrifty, land- and slaveowning farmer, the patriarchal head of his own household remained uncertain. Even migrant countrymen themselves did not know their status, for a firmer definition of it lay only in the future. Would they establish independence as yeoman farmers, or would they face another uprooting, becoming once more poor white men moving to another frontier? Finally, they were also countrymen, with an accent on the final syllable, because in their quest they sought to claim and assert manhood. Both they and their planter counterparts focused upon their status as men —or, perhaps, as males who failed to reach that status. "Countrywomen" were also with them and would play crucial roles in making males into men on the plantation frontier. And yet both planter and nonplanter men had a great deal of difficulty in even acknowledging the work and presence of such women. For both, countrymen were a class of males seeking to be men, and all others in their households were invisible.[5]

Between 1820 and 1830, thousands of these nonplanter white migrants arrived in Jackson and Leon Counties. Just for the purposes of tracing some of them, one might count all men owning ten or fewer slaves as country-men, so long as we remember that this measure is not absolute. Members of the new frontier elite recognized migrants who were somewhere above this partly arbitrary measure as potential peers. Below it, white men and their families clustered, in planters' perceptions, in a barely differentiated mass. Abraham Cabell, for example, was not certain in 1828 whether his new neighbors were "plain unpretending farmers" or drifters "from Georgia with little to recommend them." He distinguished among them but also separated all of these countrymen from himself and his kin. The country-men distinguished themselves from him as well, and they did so in part because of the inclination of those like Cabell to class them all as different from and below him.[6]

The 1830 U.S. Census of Population counted 339 Jackson County house-holds owning ten or fewer slaves, totaling 1,716 white inhabitants. In Leon County, the census-taker found 480, containing 2,681 whites. They were by far the majority of white inhabitants in these new settlements: 84 percent in Jackson County; and 80 percent in Leon. Because migrants' experiences helped to shape their aspirations, the geographic origins of the countrymen who moved to Middle Florida educate our guesses about what they hoped to obtain on the plantation frontier. A combination of census, court, church, and genealogical sources allow us to trace the migration patterns of 174 of

TABLE 2.1. *Origins (c. 1820) of Countrymen in Jackson and Leon Counties in 1830*

Origin	Jackson Number	Jackson Percentage	Leon Number	Leon Percentage	Total	Percentage of Total
Ala.	7	11.9	2	1.7	9	5.1
Ga.	21	35.6	28	24.4	49	28.2
Md.	3	5.1	4	3.5	7	4.0
N.C.	14	23.7	33	28.7	47	27.0
S.C.	6	10.2	17	14.8	23	13.2
Va.	6	10.2	17	14.8	23	13.2
Other South	2	3.4	8	7.0	10	5.7
North/foreign	0	0.0	6	5.2	6	3.5
Total	59	100.0	115	100.0	174	100.0

Sources: Jackson and Leon Counties Households Database; 1830 U.S. Census returns for
Jackson and Leon Counties
Note: Countrymen are white household heads owning 10 or fewer slaves.

the 819 white Jackson and Leon County household heads who owned ten or fewer slaves in 1830.[7] Table 2.1 reveals that the largest number of these migrants came, most recently, from Georgia. In the first two decades of the nineteenth century, a series of Indian treaties and outright dispossessions opened up much of southern and central Georgia for settlement. But North Carolina was a close second, and many of the Georgia settlers had come originally from the Carolinas. Maryland and Virginia were less significant sources of common white migrants to Middle Florida, in contrast to these states' prominent roles in supplying slaves and well-connected planters to the cotton frontier.[8]

North Carolinians like Isaac Hay and Ansel Ferrell had abandoned a state whose growth had slowed to a crawl. As early as the 1780s, thousands of Carolinians left the "Old North State" every year. Those from the piedmont and mountain counties often headed west to Tennessee, and later, Mississippi, Arkansas, and Texas.[9] Those from the coastal plain's pine-covered necks of poor land between rivers, swamps, and endless sandy stretches back of the plantations, headed more south than west. Whether they traveled directly or, like Hay, moved several times over the course of a generation, most of those who ended up in Florida came from the eastern regions of North Carolina, as Table 2.2 shows.[10]

Economic factors helped drive countrymen south and west. Land in coastal counties had been scarce for years, and the soil in the piney woods districts behind the coast was thin and infertile. To make matters worse, during the first decades of the nineteenth century, the rise of cotton as a cash crop in the North Carolina coastal plain drove up the price of land

TABLE 2.2. *Regional Origins of Jackson and Leon County Countrymen from North Carolina, 1820–1830*

Regions	Jackson	Leon	Total	Percentage
Albemarle Sound	3	2	5	12
Roanoke Valley	1	2	3	7
Central Coastal Plain	5	17	22	52
Rice	2	3	5	12
Piedmont	0	4	4	10
Mountain	2	1	3	7
Totals	13	29	42	100

Source: Jackson and Leon Counties Households Database
Note: 42 of 47 common white emigrants from North Carolina could be identified by county of origin. The other five were excluded from this table. Albemarle Sound counties represented here include Camden, Pasquotank, and Washington; Roanoke Valley: Edgecombe, Halifax; Central Coastal Plain: Beaufort, Bladen, Columbus, Craven, Greene, Lenoir, Onslow, Robeson; Rice: Brunswick, New Hanover; Piedmont: Cumberland, Granville (both border the coastal plain), Rowan; Mountain: include Rutherford and Surry.

beyond the means of countrymen. The growth of the new cotton gentry of the Roanoke River counties of Halifax, Edgecombe, Warren, and Northampton led to increased concentrations of slaveholdings, lower wages for poor white laborers, and new levels of social differentiation. Ansel Ferrell, born about 1762 in Halifax County, found that the growth of the cotton economy limited his ability to achieve economic independence. Ferrell, who had fought the British at Guilford Court House, spent many of the years after the war in Nash County, the heart of the planter-dominated Roanoke Valley. He could only obtain land by seeking out and patenting gores, the muddy and unclaimed acres sandwiched between larger tracts along the county's swamps. Without vast amounts of slave labor to drain and fill the rich man's leavings, Ferrell's swampland probably produced little more than subsistence. Although possession of the swampland gave Ferrell, who never owned more than one slave, the fifty acres he needed to claim the right to vote, his marginal economic status was hardly the experience of mastery over an independent household that most white men craved.[11]

In fact, many yeomen and poor whites experienced the coastal plain's inequalities as a state of dependence that called into doubt their own manhood. White men defined themselves and each other by their difference from dependent women, slaves, and children. They attempted to prove their status by ostentatiously rejecting all that smacked of membership in such unmanly groups. In contrast to dependence, "independence," whether political or economic, wrote one migrant to Middle Florida, "infuses pride and manliness of feeling—confidence and buoyancy of action—strength and power of thought." In the early republican South, that meant control over a household and its dependents, and recognition by the community of men as someone with honor. Recognition for one's manly honor, that quality ascribed to a masculinity that rejected any insult or condition smacking of effeminate submission, played out in a variety of day-to-day encounters, which are described in more detail in Chapter 4. But the lack of land and economic independence in and of itself called into question the status of those males who could not direct their own labor, and that of wives, children, or slaves. To be in the position of taking orders, as tenant or employee, from another person suggested slavery, blackness, and femininity. Laboring for wages, paying rent for the use of land, or making cash crops in order to buy the food that one's family would eat through the winter could also put a man on dangerous economic and psychological ground. Other white men came to control one's fate. The prices paid for one's crops fell, creditors and landlords demanded repayment, and employers issued humiliating orders.[12]

Yet countrymen may have squirmed most of all under the political and cultural constraints imposed by a planter class that still assumed other white men would defer to its traditional power. Voting restrictions imputed to unfranchised poor white men a servile inability to make independent decisions. And like that of Virginia, North Carolina's system of government imposed strict property requirements for voting and officeholding while overrepresenting the planters of the eastern counties. The system thus managed to disfranchise common whites from both the eastern and western counties, as did the processes of local governance and justice. In North Carolina, as in Virginia, the state legislature appointed county court judges for life. These men, inevitably well-known planters and merchants, oversaw all functions of local government and were at times able to order about the bodies of future countrymen like so many slaves or women. In 1782, for example, the worthy judges of Cumberland County in North Carolina ordered the sheriff to summon recently returned Revolutionary soldier Rhesa Oliver and his father "to answer such things as are alleged against them." The pair fled the county. Oliver resurfaced a half-century later on the Florida frontier.[13]

Political inequality irritated Revolutionary veterans and their sons, or so one must conclude from what they preferred when they had a choice. For instance, in the early nineteenth century, Nathaniel Macon, a planter-politician from the Roanoke Valley, used a rhetoric that praised yeoman ideals of simplicity, republicanism, and white patriarchy. He followed preaching with personal practice, at least in his exaggerated (and selective) rejection of distinctions among white men. The latter included his well-known choice to live in a humble cabin, although he owned a vast plantation in Warren County. Macon was apparently widely popular among country-men.[14] Yet he was an exception: despite the legacy of the Revolution and the Jeffersonian struggle against federalism, most members of the Southern planter elite were unwilling before the 1830s to abandon older expectations of yeoman political, cultural, and social deference to their rule. Rich men wanted to be called "squire." Many planters drew a sharp line between men like themselves and uneducated countrymen. Planters' wives snubbed the spouses of common white men. Even planters' slaves affected to despise "po' buckra." Thus, as cotton wealth transformed the economic structure of the Southeast, Nathaniel Macon feared what the rise in economic and political inequality among white men might do to the virtue, or manhood, to use the direct translation of the word's Latin roots, of the republic. His yeoman constituents feared what it meant to them as men.[15]

The desire for economic and political independence, and the lack of such necessities in the old counties of the coastal plains, propelled common white men out of the coastal swamps and the pine flats. They hoped, in new states and territories, to establish themselves as independent landowners, and to demand that planters treat them as equals and as men. Theirs would be a lengthy journey. Some headed first to closer destinations, but circum-stances forced them ever southward. Members of the Cone family, for ex-ample, lived in Martin, Tyrrell, and Beaufort Counties in North Caro-lina during much of the eighteenth century. William Cone, from Beaufort County, married Keziah Barber during the 1760s. They moved to Anson County, on the frontier of white settlement. After returning to Beaufort around 1780, perhaps because of the disturbances of Tory-Patriot conflict in the backcountry, they relocated to Chesterfield County, across the South Carolina border. There, in a planter-dominated parish close to the Tide-water rice swamps, Keziah gave birth to their last daughter, Nancy. By 1800, they had moved on again, to Bulloch County, Georgia, where Nancy married another expatriate Carolinian named John Hagan in 1801. After the birth of one daughter, the young couple moved with other Cones and Hagans to the coastal Georgia County of Camden. There, Nancy bore at least six more children before her husband died.[16]

The experience of this movement taught common whites that establish-ing economic independence was also difficult on the Southern frontier. Like Isaac Hay, many were unable to purchase or hold on to the tracts that they had settled and improved. Speculators bought up the best Georgia and Alabama tracts, and the remaining poor land did not permit farmers to raise much besides livestock. By the time migrants improved their lands enough to make the money to pay for their acres in cash, and made the long trek to far-off land offices, they often found that rich speculators had already purchased the ground from under them. Thus the image of the speculator became another face in the gallery of those who supposedly thwarted dreams of yeoman independence. Opposition to "speculation" would become a typical political stance of common white migrants.[17]

By the early 1820s, migrants in Georgia, Alabama, and elsewhere began to prepare to move on once again. During April 1825, in Camden County, Georgia, Nancy Cone Hagan took her leave of the small Baptist church where she worshiped. Her husband, John, was dead now, and her two eldest daughters, Mary and Eleanor, had married men who planned to stay in Georgia. With relatives Lewis Cone and Martha Cone and neighbor Benjamin Hagan (a native Kentuckian who had moved to Georgia, and no relation to her husband), who was already expressing a serious interest in her daughter Elizabeth, Nancy planned to move to the rich new lands of Leon County. The soil there was reputedly much better than Camden sand, and she had to make some sort of provision for her five other children. Like many migrants of the yeoman class, she left with other members of her nuclear and extended families, although the severing of other ties of kinship, friendship, and religious fellowship still troubled her deeply. But given her need to raise her remaining children and provide land for at least her two sons, Nancy Cone Hagan felt pressed to leave. She asked, in the form of a poem that she read before the church, for the blessing of her peers:

All you that feel fellowship come give me your hand,
Dismiss me by letter from this little band.
I hope to find brethren wherever I go.
I wish to serve Jesus as well as I know

. . . .

On the tenth day of April I shall bid you farewell
And my old habitation wherein I did dwell.
Perhaps my dear brethren no more for to see,
But away among strangers for lifetime to be.

. . . .

Do you, my dear brethren and sisters, agree
To live in the spirit of pure unity?
Remember what Joseph to his brethren did say.
Be careful and do not fall out by the way.
And when our labor and life it is done,

Our Saviour in glory will bring us straight home.
We will sit down together on Canaan's bright shore
Where weeping and parting and sorrow no more.[18]

In the pocosins and piney woods of the coastal plain of North Carolina, the rural neighborhoods of the piedmont districts of several states, in South Carolina's low country, and on Georgia's desolate frontier, people like Nancy Hagan said goodbye to neighbors and kinfolk. They loaded up oxcarts, herded livestock and children, and dragged unwilling slaves from spouses owned by other white masters and mistresses. Large family groups made the journey together. Chesley, Francis, Benjamin, and Needham Boatwright and their families, for instance, left Colleton County in the South Carolina low country, and by 1820 were living on the Georgia frontier. Sometime between 1824 and 1830, they all moved again, this time to Leon County. The families had some twenty members, and Benjamin owned one enslaved African American, a teenage girl. With their wagons and cattle, they must have formed a large party. A writer on the same road south through the piney woods of Georgia described a similar group: "The effect was quite picturesque—the people being grouped round the fires, while their animals were dimly seen feeding in the vicinity." [19]

Families like the Boatwrights usually reached Middle Florida before the largest waves of planter migration. Some had entered Jackson County even before Florida became a U.S. territory. At least thirty-one households settled along Spring Creek, a tributary of the Chipola in northwest Jackson, by the end of 1821, and others were trickling into the rest of the county. Many followed the "Coffee Road," which ran west through south Georgia, and then rafted their wagons, stock, and families down the Flint or Chattahoochee River. By 1824, settlers were pouring into what soon became Leon County. Some blazed trails south from the Coffee Road, while others came via the still incomplete "Bellamy Road" that was supposed to run between Jacksonville and Pensacola. The first settler on the site of Tallahassee was John McIver, who arrived with a wagon and his family in April 1824 at the hill that became the center of town.[20]

Upon reaching Leon or Jackson County, countrymen who saw in Middle Florida's soil the promise of becoming landowning yeomen picked likely spots and stopped their journeys. Achille Murat, an early migrant planter, recalled meeting settlers' parties in the woods: "a cart loaded with household furniture and children, and one or more men escorting about thirty cows and hogs." The men were always looking for unoccupied potential farm sites: "[Often] the head of the family has asked me some details relative to the country, and requested me to direct him to the creek, or the nearest spring." Although planters often depicted squatters as lazy, Murat had to acknowledge their energy in establishing new farmsteads: "A week after, I have been astonished to see a good hut there, a field of cattle, and some poultry, the wife spinning cotton, the husband destroying the trees by making a circular incision in them, called a girdle."[21]

Lesser command of labor power and capital constrained the countryman's choice of farm sites. Thick hardwood trees in the alluvial soils along the Chipola, Apalachicola, and Ocklocknee Rivers and Leon County's lakes promised fertility. But clearing the hardwoods took man-years of labor, so nonplanter whites left the river bottoms to men who owned dozens of slaves. Settlers with less labor power available to them could deaden the trees by girdling them, as Murat reported, but several seasons had to pass before they could finish clearing a field using this technique. Considerable work remained in rolling, chopping, and burning fallen trunks and underbrush. After deadening some trees, most settlers began clearing and fencing a field of at least several acres for the corn and other crops that they would need during the first year. Meanwhile, migrants burned the brush that grew under pine trees to clear the way for grass on which game and open-ranging cattle and hogs could forage. The broad, shallow lakes also shrank during the summer, leaving a bed of plants. Finally, would-be yeomen built houses of logs on the simple single- or double-pen designs familiar to all Southerners by the 1820s. Murat noted that their dogged labor reshaped the landscape: "Under their hands the country soon assumes a new aspect: every seven or eight miles rise up huts, formed from the trunks of trees."[22]

Occupying and clearing land was not the same thing as owning it. As surveyors marked out townships and sections on Land Office plats, the land auctions approached quickly. Tracts near Tallahassee would go on sale in early 1825, while some Jackson County sections went on the market at the end of the next year. Unable to bid high against men armed with large amounts of ready cash, countrymen had either to settle for the least desirable land or to hope to take advantage of a "preemption." The latter legal device, a much-debated loophole in the federal land laws, allowed settlers who arrived in a territory before a given date to preempt or remove from the auction process a small amount of land on which they resided and which they had cultivated. The preemptor had to register his claim and secure approval before the land went up for auction. If he did so, he had to pay no more than the government minimum price—in the 1820s, $1.25 per acre. He also had to make a minimum purchase of at least an "eighth" of a 640-acre section. An 1826 law passed by Congress allowed all pre-1825 migrants to Florida to preempt up to a 160-acre "quarter" from auction, which did little, of course, for those in Leon County whose land had been sold out from under them in 1825. An 1830 law would extend preemptions to additional settlers.[23]

Opponents of preemptions claimed that they undermined the federal government's own claim to the land by rewarding instead of condemning squatters. Such abstract contradictions paled next to the more vital ones of the actual process of yeoman settlement. Taking advantage of preemptions demanded not only hard work from entire households but also cash. Obtaining either labor or money involved the migrant countryman in a series of contradictory relationships. In Middle Florida, economic independence may have made a migrant countryman into a settled white man, but he could never obtain it through his individual efforts. At every step of the way, from the first stages of land-clearing through the production of crops for food or cash, men called upon the labor of dependents and of extended family. Only dependence on the work of wives, children, slaves, and relatives could make him independent. The necessity of relying at least briefly on the production of cotton, the price of which depended on the vagaries of far-off markets, was similarly paradoxical. Market crops like cotton often forced one to go into debt in order to begin production. Yet only cotton, wage labor, and other forms of market participation could produce the cash that would buy land. Land, in turn, ultimately protected farmers from the market's vagaries and gave them status as independent men in a hierarchical society full of dependent people.

Squatters who began to clear tracts coveted by speculators knew that they had to accumulate cash if they were going to be able to preempt the land in which they were investing large amounts of labor. Most migrant planters obtained credit from family members or other elite individuals, but few (if any) of common whites' relatives were wealthy, or part of the commercial world. If they had possessed money, they would have been much less likely to leave their old homes in the first place. A handful, like Nancy Hagan, were able to sell old land to help finance their resettlement. She bought eighty Leon County acres from her neighbor Paul McCormick in 1826, soon after moving from Georgia. In 1833, she financed the purchase of some unoccupied government land by selling her nineteen-year-old slave Henry to McCormick for $600.[24]

Family labor extracted and directed through the relations of hierarchy between man and woman, white and black, and adult and child was essential to the process of turning woods into fields, and squatters into independent yeomen. The Singletary brothers, Brayton, Benjamin, and Nathaniel, from Bladen County, North Carolina, and their father, Revolutionary War veteran Joseph Singletary, marshaled hard work from a variety of sources in order to clear even the few acres that they would purchase. Only Benjamin owned any slaves: a male and a female, who may have been under sixteen at the time and thus of lesser usefulness in the fields. The men themselves shared the work. Joseph, born in 1762, probably did less strenuous labor than he had done as a younger man. In 1830, the three sons all listed additional adult males, possibly Joseph's grandsons, among their households. In all, seven men and several boys were available for felling and girdling trees, rolling logs, and grubbing roots.[25]

Women's labor was as essential as that of adult men. Consigned by custom and law to the direction of the male head of household, women performed almost every kind of task on small farms. Six white adult women lived in the four Singletary households, along with thirteen boys and four girls. No Middle Florida accounts mention white women doing the labor of clearing land. Yet the Singletary women, the young female slave, and the girls certainly did most other kinds of field labor. In Jackson and Leon Counties, white women worked the fields: Ellen Call Long, a planter's daughter, claimed that "the 'cotton patch' or 'potato hills' leave no time for ornamental gardening" for the common white woman. Men, women, and children together tended crops and livestock, although women probably did not plow. In addition, women performed all sorts of other tasks crucial to the survival of the household: gathering firewood and caring for children and livestock. Women also produced many goods at home, as Murat's account of the squatter woman spinning cotton indicates, and raised poultry and vegetable gardens. Children no doubt pitched in where they could when young, and after reaching the age of ten or twelve, spent increasing amounts of time in the fields with fathers, uncles, older siblings, and, of course, mothers.[26]

Although the bulk of the Singletarys' labor came from white family members, countrymen who owned enslaved African Americans could add their contributions to those of other dependents. In 1829, the judicial authorities of Leon County hanged an enslaved black woman named Jane on what became known as "Gallows Hill" to the west of the capitol, on the present site of Florida State University. She had allegedly killed her infant. Her owner, Paul McCormick, must have been disappointed with the whole series of events, for Jane had been his only slave, and the birth of the child had briefly doubled his personal property holdings. In Jackson County, while planters disproportionately held enslaved men, females were by far the majority among those owning ten or fewer bondpeople. The same pattern held true in Leon County, where in 1840, yeomen like McCormick, who claimed five or fewer slaves, together owned 584 slaves, 331 of whom (57 percent) were females. Countrymen expected women like Jane to augment wealth through reproduction. Thus Leon County's Thomas Coleman advised his son John to trade their single slave, the "negro man Abram," for a young woman "less advanced in years" as soon as a good opportunity arose. Yeoman farmers, too, extracted plenty of production from African American women. In addition to hoeing, plowing, and harvesting the crops, enslaved women helped with household tasks.[27]

Although common white slaveowners worked alongside their bondpeople in the fields, and often slept and ate under the same roofs with them, they were no less racist and exploitative than their planter neighbors. Surely yeomen pushed slaves harder at labor than wives, children, or themselves. Jackson County countryman Moody Burt provides an illustrative, if extreme, example of exploitation. In 1829, he hired his six slaves to the Armistead brothers, local merchants who employed them at their sawmill. Enslaved workers rented for high sums on the labor-short frontier, and Burt apparently decided that he could live a life of relative ease on the proceeds of his hands. While they worked in the sawmill, he purchased copious quantities of whiskey, and even "two oz. spanish flye," most likely in an attempt to seduce some unfortunate woman. Clearly the hard labor of slaves enabled Burt's squalid version of masculine independence.[28]

Even when they owned slaves, countrymen had to get their hands dirty every day in order to acquire land. While planters relied on credit from relatives, common white men lent their own labor to sons, fathers, brothers, and other kin. Activities like log-rolling, gathering cattle from the woods, or corn shucking demanded large quantities of manpower. Even with the contributions of one or two slaves, one household alone could not accomplish such tasks. Contemporary accounts suggest that white men linked by ties of kinship gathered to make major labor projects into social occasions. Collective labor reinforced the bonds of extended family that had kept migrants like the Singletarys together on the long journey south. Still, by 1829, only Brayton and Benjamin Singletary appeared as landowners in the Leon County tax rolls. Even though their large extended family gave them access to more labor than many of their peers, the difficulties of obtaining cash constrained the Singletarys' ability to acquire freeholds.[29]

Early settlers may have feared that market production linked them in dependent relationships to creditors and distant markets, but they could not wish away necessity. Families worked together to clear land and grow crops, but in order to purchase their eighths, countrymen needed to obtain cash. As on other American frontiers, livestock formed the first market commodity. Achille Murat wrote that the "population of Squatters is very numerous. . . . [I]t attracts the speculator in cattle." Countrymen allowed stock to run loose through the woods and gathered herds up each year or so to brand, pen, fatten, and sell them. Herders drove their stock north and east toward Georgia plantations, or south to Apalachicola and St. Marks, to be shipped to Cuba or New Orleans. Others sold cattle, hogs, and sheep to local plantation owners short on provisions and in need of food for family and slaves. During the first years of settlement, some even mortgaged animals to obtain land. No wonder Murat claimed of nonplanter whites, "According to their morality, cow-stealing is the greatest crime." [30]

Resourcefulness characterized migrants' efforts to earn cash in the first decade of white settlement in Middle Florida. In 1826, for example, Drury Vickers successfully petitioned the Legislative Council for the exclusive right to run a toll ferry on a section of the Ocklocknee River. Ferries offered opportunities to make money without the heavy investments of scarce capital needed to build mills. In 1835, John Sewall refused to vacate land claimed by Georgia land magnate Farish Carter at the "Old Ferry" on the Chipola. Carter's agent, Jackson County planter Richard Long, wrote that Sewall "said he should defend his wright [sic] against you or anybody else." Others hunted deer and trapped otters, trading skins and pelts for cash or credit at stores like that of the Armistead brothers at Aspalaga in Jackson County. Some made grindstones for mills, shaping them with hand tools at their cabins deep in the woods. Hauling them to trading posts, they exchanged them for money or essential supplies. Wage labor for planters also supplied cash. Artisanal work, labor in the fields, well-digging, and overseeing slaves all earned money. While both parties needed it, wage labor could be an uncomfortable relationship for yeomen and planters alike. For the employee, this was too close to the master-slave relationship; for employer, too far away from familiar modes of authority. [31]

The most common way to earn cash was by growing and selling cash crops. In the imaginations of elite migrants, cotton, along with sugar—whose capital requirements were well beyond the means of even most planters—was their connection to the wider world and all it had to offer. In contrast, would-be yeomen hoped that cotton would allow them to defend themselves from that world. In the ideal, cotton led to cash, which led to land, which led to economic and other forms of independence. Thus countrymen hoped to escape the necessity, if not always the opportunity, of market production. Yet the attempt to produce a cotton crop was a gamble for a household that possessed limited labor resources. Each day of work in the cotton patch was one less day spent on producing food crops. Even creating cotton fields cost and risked more than clearing land for corn, the source of bread. Planters preferred to have their slaves clear large fields of trees, stumps, and roots so that they could use plows, while yeoman migrants initially cropped small amounts of cotton with hoes in clearings between the trunks and roots of deadened trees. To produce significant quantities for the market, countrymen had to use plows. Plowing freed up valuable family labor for the task of hoeing for corn but required large initial investments of labor in grubbing up roots to prepare the soil for cultivation.[32]

Even after countrymen had cleared land, labor shortages forced crucial decisions about resource allocation. Cotton's labor bottleneck at the harvest stage—a single worker could pick much less cotton than he or she could cultivate—meant that even specialized planters assumed that they could produce no more than four or five bales of cotton per full hand. Countryman settlers had many other labor requirements and much smaller supplies of labor than their wealthy neighbors. Still, a few bales of cotton each year could go a long way toward making a countryman into a landowning farmer. South Carolinian Jacob Horger, for instance, arrived in Leon County in 1828 or 1829. He had four slaves, a wife, and at least two teenage sons. Horger managed to purchase some land auctioned for unpaid debts. But in so doing, he entered into debt himself, signing a note to borrow the money from a local merchant. In 1830, Horger and his household made five bales of cotton that he sold to Miles Blake's store, along with several dozen eggs. The poultry were probably an additional responsibility of Horger's wife. In return for the cotton, Blake paid Horger's note with cash, converting cotton into land.[33]

Countrymen made cotton to serve the ends of independence, to make themselves equal to other white men in a society full of dependents. The strategies employed by Benjamin Hagan, Nancy Cone Hagan's son-in-law, suggest that countrymen used the market as a tool to that end but that they did not waste much time on the improbable dream of becoming a planter. In 1827, Benjamin (no relation to Nancy's deceased husband) married Nancy's teenage daughter Elizabeth. He also purchased a quarter section (160 acres) of land that he had probably first settled in 1825. His mother-in-law purchased the quarter section to the north. These tracts were about ten miles east of Tallahassee, on pine land of average quality. By 1830, Elizabeth had given birth to two daughters and Benjamin had acquired a young woman named Kost who could help out in the fields and the house. He also borrowed labor from his mother-in-law's four slaves and his brothers-in-law Fletcher and Jesse, who were still teenagers. Benjamin was probably the only full-time field worker, although his wife must have worked in the fields as well. By 1830, Benjamin had cleared two fields from the woods that covered his quarter section—one of thirty-three acres in the northern half of his quarter and another of undetermined size to the south. He probably raised little besides corn, which was not only the source of bread but also an alternative cash crop for yeoman settlers.[34]

By this point, Hagan owed several hundred dollars to local planter and speculator Hector Braden, who may have sold him the enslaved woman Kost. After making enough money to buy his quarter section from the government, perhaps through the sale of corn to neighbors like Samuel Parkhill, Benjamin Hagan found a way to solve his continuing labor shortage and make some needed cash to pay off debts. In 1831, Benjamin rented much of his land to John L. Taylor. While Taylor cultivated the open thirty-three-acre field, Hagan and his family continued to clear and work the southern half. Benjamin required Taylor to plant mostly cotton, although he was permitted to run a few rows of corn across the field, as long as they were far enough apart to prevent the corn from wearing out the soil. By requiring him to grow cotton, Hagan ensured that Taylor would most likely have the eighty dollars to pay him at the end of the year. He also offered to let Taylor use the northernmost forty-four acres of the quarter section for free, for three years, if Taylor could clear them during 1831. If he did so, in 1832–33, Taylor could plant any crop he pleased on the new field. Hagan also neatly sidestepped another problem presented by cotton production—the need for a cotton gin. Most yeomen did not own one, and common whites who used a planter neighbor's gin might feel involved in uncomfortable relations of clientage. Hagan escaped this situation of dependence by requiring Taylor to place himself in a deferential position to a nearby planter. Hagan still got his eighty dollars, and on the new field in the southern half of the quarter, he, his family, and his slave would grow their subsistence crops.[35]

Though illiterate, Benjamin Hagan was not ignorant. While his tactics would not have worked for everyone, most countrymen strove for the status that Benjamin eventually attained. He had worked very hard, extracting the maximum possible amount of labor from his family and slave for five years, all in order to obtain a clear title to land. Now he would not have to ask another white man to let him use his cotton gin or whether he would like to buy some corn for his slaves. In one figurative motion, Hagan revealed that he recognized, and that he had a plan to escape, the dilemma of dependence. He illustrated his goals, and those of his peers. Countrymen did what they had to do to achieve independence and manhood. The necessity of economic independence, which was as much an imperative of manhood as of economic calculation, was more important to them than fear of, or desire for, participation in the market. But they never accomplished independence by themselves.

Through the physical production of crops and reproduction of households, and in the masculine authority developed in the extraction of labor, mastery over dependents made a new freedom for countrymen. Through the 1820s, those households grew in Middle Florida, and grew together. Slowly they carved the woods up into discernible neighborhoods, each referred to as a "diggins."[36] This was an apt term from our perspective because it calls up a picture of what such a settlement must have looked like. Each was a few openings of raw dirt in the woods: three, four, or more log cabins close to each other where eighths of sections ran together on surveyors' plats. In the fields, one might see men and women, often both black and white, digging and hoeing together. Some days each field had its own workers, but on others, all the families of the various farms—for all the whites were siblings or cousins or in-laws—were gathered in one, harvesting a crop or straining to roll logs off the bare clay. Other days family members might shuck corn by the cabin, or grind cane for molasses. In a cold snap, the men slaughtered hogs together while women sat near a stick-and-mud fireplace, laboriously picking seeds from the cotton piled in their laps. Such neighborhoods, like the Spring Creek/Grant's Pond settlement in Jackson County, or the Centreville/Pisgah Church community of Leon County, took shape slowly. At first, the main ties between households were ones of extended family, predating the move to Middle Florida. But as freeholds met through the woods, each "diggins" grew more close-knit and distinctive, gradually carving its place on the social maps of Jackson and Leon Counties.

Maneuvering through the snares of dependence, some countrymen acquired cash, took advantage of preemption laws, and obtained land. During the first series of land auctions, townships around Tallahassee moved quickly into the hands of speculators. But some countrymen managed to purchase decent land, and by 1829, at least 19 percent of Leon County countrymen owned land, although only 13 percent of their Jackson County counterparts did so. (See Tables A.3–A.5.) Landowning remained fairly static through the 1830s in Leon County, for which the 1839 property tax list survives (as it apparently does not for Jackson). Some Leon County countrymen increased their slaveholdings and moved into higher categories, while others in the lower slaveowning categories were town-dwelling artisans. Many remained landless farmers, squatting or renting because they could not find affordable, decent land in a county dominated by migrant planters.[37]

Migrant countrymen cemented their status as landowners at the Tallahassee Land Office. Even at this point the gate was narrow: would-be yeomen had to be ready with cash in hand by the time the township on which they had settled went up for sale. If they were even a dollar short, they risked losing tracts that they and their families had in some cases already cultivated for a decade. On the first day of 1827, John Williams arrived at the Land Office. Land in the Spring Creek neighborhood of northwestern Jackson County was on sale for the first time, and Williams and other Spring Creek settlers were ready. He bought eighty acres on the Alabama line, which his family had already farmed for several years. His neighbor Duncan Anderson bought seventeen acres, and son or nephew William Williams had purchased eighty on December 30. They may have encountered or traveled with neighbors Powell Smith and George Caldwell, who also entered land on the books at the same time. On the first of January, Nancy Phillips, the neighbor of Anderson and Williams, "perfected" or received the official title to a claim originally made by her deceased husband, Abraham. Other settlers purchased land in a neighborhood some three or four miles to the south near present-day Grant's Pond. But still more were not ready, and speculators purchased the most desirable tracts. Land magnate Farish Carter bought three quarter sections along Spring Creek, and his business partners Charles Williamson and James Webb bought four more. The Kentucky Deaf and Dumb Asylum, granted a township by the federal government, also hoped to make money by speculation. They took up vast quantities of real estate in Jackson County, including almost a third of the Spring Creek area.[38]

Of course, speculators did not mind to whom they sold their land. Countrymen could deal with the men with "long pockets" if they came prepared to pay the price. Jackson County's Thomas Goff gave the adequate security demanded by Carter and his agents, who then allowed Goff to pay over two years. In 1830, John Smith negotiated with Farish Carter's nephew and agent J. H. Walker for a quarter section next to the land bought by his brother Powell Smith. Carter had paid $300 for the 160 acres but was now asking $600. Smith, who owned six slaves, may have been able to raise the money. Others could not and were left landless. Neither preemption nor private purchase was an option for such settlers, and so Walker reported to Carter in 1831: "I am fearful that your Spring Creek lands will not prove as profitable as some of the others. There are more people of limited circumstances there, than in the other part of the county." By "profitable" lands, Walker probably meant the districts along the Chipola River, where planters had started to settle.[39]

Late-arriving countrymen were rarely able to purchase land immediately, but renting was a journey unlikely to lead them to landowning status.

Speculators, distant from their lands and suspicious of nonplanter settlers, were reluctant landlords: "[F]ew people there, who wish to rent, are as responsible as could be wished. Renting out land here is a bad business, and the rent difficult to collect." Undoubtedly irritated at the power of speculators to take up so much of the landscape, countrymen often behaved in ways that landlords thought irresponsible or disrespectful: "There are but few persons of character that rent at all, & those who will use the land so as not to ruin it. . . . Where small places have been rented out it has been to trifling fellows." If family ties did not keep common white tenants in their frontier neighborhoods, these "trifling fellows" could pick up and leave long before landowners or their local agents could take any action. Landowner Jesse T. Bernard nearly came to blows with "Old Captain Sharpe who has been cropping with me. I sent over there this morning for some corn, and he refused to let me have any. I then went over there myself and spoke to him, and he flew into a violent passion." In other cases, as Thomas Baltzell complained, "Men have deferred paying so that the trouble of collecting is almost equal to the value of debt."[40]

Despite the problems of renting and the growth of speculators' holdings, many squatters managed to survive for a time within the interstices of yeoman neighborhoods on the still sparsely settled frontier. Landless whites procured subsistence, or perhaps even a little cash, from one clearing for a cabin and another farmed for a patch of corn or cotton, and the resources of the woods and streams for food and for pasture. They squatted precariously on unoccupied land owned by absentee speculators or the federal government. In April 1831, J. H. Walker rode the fifteen-odd miles from his plantation on the Chipola up to his uncle Farish's lands to report that "I have been up to your Spring Creek lands and find all of the sections you mention have setters." Next to Owen and John Williams, for instance, lived squatters William Pulliam and Zachariah Coward. Pulliam owned one slave, but he and his six family members had probably arrived too late to obtain a preemption. Coward was a slaveless man who migrated from the Barnwell district of South Carolina with his wife and no other family.[41] Squatters seeking to survive on the plantation frontier also settled around nearby Grant's Pond. Eleazor Early, a single white man between fifty and sixty, lived close to the pond itself. The destitute Early could not obtain land and had disappeared from the county by 1840. A mile away was another squatter, Eley Bedgood. Bedgood had come from Washington County, Georgia, and before that had probably grown up along Albemarle Sound in North Carolina. He was in the neighborhood still in 1838, but by 1840 he had vanished.[42]

One of the reasons squatters could survive for a time on the sandy acres that planters were not eager to clear was that Middle Florida courts had too much criminal- and debt-related business on their hands to waste time with actions for ejectment from either private or public land. And many squatters might have simply disregarded such actions, given what one official called "the habits[,] manners and moral character of the intruders on the government lands." Stubborn squatters on Spring Creek and around Grant Pond appeared lazy and shiftless to wealthy commentators, like the Jackson County doctor who referred to such a man as "a poor & worthless piney woodsman." As planters extended their holdings, and landowning yeoman families looked to provide freeholds for sons reaching maturity, the least wealthy settlers remained landless. They, or after 1840, their sons and daughters, often left Jackson and pushed farther west, or south into the main peninsula of Florida.[43]

Meanwhile, those who stayed behind, built. Like the Spring Creek area, each "diggins" ultimately rested on the families of white farmers who obtained land. A close look at Leon County's Centreville neighborhood reveals that kinship ties enabled countrymen not only to become yeomen but also to establish coherent communities. By 1830, a new group of emigrants had begun to settle the second township north and east of the Tallahassee meridian. This chunk of piney hills and yellow loam soil had gone up for sale in 1827, but most planters and speculators bypassed it in favor of the rich lands around Lake Miccosukee. Large portions of the township remained unsold for a couple of years, until the arrival of families led by men with German-sounding names like Conrad Houck, Jacob Horger, Adam Gramling, Jacob Stroman, and Jacob Felkel. All had deep roots in the German neighborhoods of the Orangeburg district of the South Carolina Middle Country, where many had been members of St. Matthew's, a Lutheran church.[44]

The Centreville settlers had migrated from one plantation district to another, but they were hardly planters. In 1830, Houck owned two slaves, and Horger, four, and the only reason either of these men, the first two of the group to arrive, owned any land was Horger's previously mentioned purchase at a marshal's sale of bankrupt property. The Orangeburg migrants had large families and close ties of common origin, made closer in Leon County by a penchant for intermarriages among their families. Of Jacob Felkel's children, Elizabeth married a Stroman, David wed Mary Houck, and Susanna married Daniel Houck. Casper Houck's son John married Frances, another Felkel daughter, and Elizabeth Houck wed a Gramling. The families bought land close to each other and joined the tiny Pisgah Methodist Church, at that time meeting in a "brush arbor" near the Centreville crossroads. Some had already converted to Methodism in South Carolina, and, for others, it served as the best available substitute for their Lutheran upbringing. The Orangeburg families, especially the women, soon became the numerical backbone of the church.[45]

Some of the men who transplanted their households to what soon became known as the "Dutch Settlement" may have brought more resources than the settlers along Jackson County's Spring Creek possessed. The original householders established their farms, and sons and brothers like Melchior and Casper Houck, who had accompanied their brother Conrad, then seeded off new households.[46] After Orangeburg migrants began to buy land in the early 1830s, some even bought slaves on credit when cotton prices soared during the middle of the same decade. No doubt Adam Gramling, for example, thought that his purchase, on credit from planter James Gadsden, of the enslaved family of Ned, his wife, Patience, and their children, Edward, Sarah, and Alfred, would soon pay for itself. The most successful of the Orangeburg migrants eventually rose above working in the fields as they grew old, slowly increasing in wealth. But most of the Houcks, Felkels, and Gramlings remained yeomen, owning few or no slaves and working small plots of land.[47]

Still, the men of the Dutch Settlement were frontier success stories. They achieved independence through their abilities to command labor from relatively large numbers of mostly white, but also black, household dependents. They could also borrow labor and other forms of assistance in their "diggins" from peers bound to them by multiple ties of kinship and affinity. Many other Leon countrymen had fewer resources of labor and family, helping to produce a countywide degree of mobility similar to that of Jackson. Those who stayed turned, in the long run, toward safety-first farming. Once limited market participation and the labor of dependents had produced economic independence, many yeomen, like Leon County's Kidder Vann, withdrew labor from the risks of cotton growing and concentrated on ensuring subsistence. Vann bought from the government forty acres to the west of Lake Jackson on the Leon/Gadsden County line. When he died in 1837, he left a meager inventory of possessions worth $303.25, or about one-fourth of what one adult male slave would have cost in that year. Vann owned no cotton, but he did possess a grindstone and barrels for corn. He also had eleven head of cattle, twelve hogs, butchering knives for the hogs, a gun, two hoes, an ox plow, a mare, and a Yankee clock valued at $55.[48]

While Vann was obviously not completely averse to participating in a market that could bring him consumer goods like the clock, once he had paid for his land he may have feared committing his shallow resources to the risky pursuit of cotton dollars. If he devoted his limited acres, and more important, his limited labor resources, to growing cotton, he might not have enough food for his family. Not all yeomen followed Vann's strategy to the letter. But for several of the Pisgah yeomen, even limited gambles on the market like Adam Gramling's slave purchase failed when the cotton boom turned into bust after 1839 in Florida. Most barely preserved their landholdings. Ensconced on their own land in a neighborhood of relatives and peers, and chastened by the failure of market gambles, they returned, like Vann, to the strategy of subsistence farming.[49] And so in "diggins" like Centreville, a relatively stable group of yeomen may have hoped they had achieved a true independence, the foundation of manhood. One of their own number joyfully outlined that which both made possible and marked the subsistence of a countryman who no longer depended on any planter:

Corn in the barn loft,
Poultry in the yard
Bacon in the meat house
And a barrel full of Lard
Coffee in the little bag
And "Sugar in the Gourd."
Hurra! Hurra! Hurra!![50]

Yet, although corn in the barn loft would get one through until the next crop came in, there was more to independence, honor, and masculinity than economic self-sufficiency. Other issues, both material and symbolic, were sparking conflict over questions of manhood, honor, and independence in early Middle Florida. Divisions between family-based groups of planters were also creating disagreements that would involve all Middle Floridians in their coils. Conflicts and fears became evident as early as the first series of land sales, between 1825 and 1827, which inspired charges of corruption and clashes among elite migrants. Perhaps not all was well—perhaps planters would not find the power they sought, or perhaps yeomen would not find the independence they craved. Perhaps such aspirations were mutually exclusive.

Countryman resentments, and planters' own fears of a loss of social control on the frontier, were also the dark subtexts in the October 6, 1826, issue of the *Pensacola Gazette*. Readers opened the four-page paper to find breathless news from Jackson: "The body of a man partly buried in the mud was accidentally discovered, in the Chipola swamp, near Webbville on Sunday evening the 24 Sept." At first, no one could identify the corpse. After the five stab wounds that had killed him, the efforts of dogs and buzzards, and a week or more in the swamp mud, his face was unrecognizable. Near the spot where he lay, searchers found the signs of a struggle in the brush, two sets of footprints leading into the swamp, and only one coming out again.[51]

As more facts emerged, Jackson's wealthier settlers felt increasing unease. The body was clad in plaid homespun, the garment of the country-man, but the victim, they learned, had uncallused hands: "He did not appear to have been a labouring man." Within a week, general consensus identi-fied him as Leroy Morris, "a stranger who had been in the country [i.e., in Middle Florida] but a few weeks, and who, it was supposed, had brought money with him for the purpose of purchasing land." Like many wealthy migrants, Morris, a planter from Alabama, had scouted out fertile land with money ready in his purse. Unfortunately for Morris, although several brutal murders had already occurred in Jackson County by 1826, law enforcement was virtually nonexistent. In the empty spaces of the woods, planter-run militias and patrols could not enforce the law. In contrast to the situation in long-settled areas, on the frontier, neither custom not familiarity could hold subordinates in their places.[52]

More pieces of the puzzle seemed to fall into place when suspicion came to rest on a young and apparently rootless countryman named Anderson Todd, who had associated with Morris for a few days. Allegedly, after learn-ing that Morris was carrying hard cash, Todd had invited the planter to look at some hammock land in the Chipola swamps. Perhaps most planter men had been in similar situations when they first migrated. The search for land forced them to depend, however briefly, upon the expertise of strangers. After luring his unwitting victim into the woods, many believed, Todd had butchered Morris, stolen his purse and horse, and ridden off for Alabama. The gentry of Jackson County quickly came up with a reward of $170, a substantial sum that indicated the level of their concern (although Todd was apparently never caught).[53]

Morris's murder fed elite fears about the potential instability of planter order on the frontier. In the woods and swamps, social distinctions might regress to those of divergent degrees of cunning, or of skill with a dirk. No doubt few yeomen would have approved of Todd's actions. A model prob-ably more to their tastes was that offered by Benjamin Hagan. But Hagan's accomplishment of mastery and economic independence was an ideal not readily duplicated, much less recognized as a sign of equality by the migrant elite arriving day by day in Middle Florida. They and their slaves were forcing countrymen off land farmed for several years, and they were also asserting political and social authority over the frontier. Migrant country-men like Benjamin Hagan, the Singletary brothers, and Kidder Vann might have felt that they, too, had a bit of Anderson Todd in their hearts as they watched speculators squeeze the levers of land acquisition. Meanwhile, elite factional battles over political power insulted nonplanter whites' political manhood—or so countrymen thought. The forms of violence used in poli-tics were often more symbolic than the kind apparently carried out by

Todd, but perhaps were even more threatening. Before examining them further, however, we must turn to a third group that migrated, and not by choice, to Middle Florida. Behind every white dream of frontier power and independence, even those of countrymen, stood another form of violence: slavery.

Forced Migration

Hulda Morgan, child of enslaved African American parents, was born in the year 1800 on Robert W. Alston's plantation in Halifax County, North Carolina. Alston owned Hulda's mother, Lucy, but her father, Spencer Morgan, lived on one of the many other neighboring plantations along Fishing Creek, which ran through one of the richest districts in the state. Just two years later, Alston moved to Hancock County, Georgia, separating Lucy and Hulda from Spencer Morgan. Hulda grew up in Georgia, but in the late 1820s financial pressures and the violent behavior of Alston's sons forced another planter migration, this time to Leon County. But Hulda was left behind in Hancock County on a plantation still owned by Alston. For almost ten years, this second move separated her from most of the other members of the Alston slave community. In 1835, Robert Alston and his sons moved the rest of the laborers they owned, and many more that they had purchased on credit, to their farms along Lake Miccosukee in Leon County. Although Hulda, by then thirty-five, may well have left in Hancock County an "abroad" husband owned by another master, in Leon she met and married Cudjo Alexander. Thus she took part in the creation of a new black community on the cotton frontier. Yet, within a couple of years the Alstons' erratic though hardly atypical behavior destroyed it. The Alston sons Willis and Augustus each met a bloody demise in a series of politically inspired feuds, and the debts the two had compiled during life necessitated the sale of most of their estates. Willis had already dealt away many of his slaves to raise money for new planting ventures in Texas. Robert Alston was also deeply involved in the cotton frontier's shaky financial schemes and had to bargain away many of his bondpeople. While Hulda was lucky enough not to lose Cudjo and at least three of her children, she saw neighbors and kin carried away to the auction block. Her experience of separation and loss was typical. By the time slavery in Florida ended in 1865, most freedpeople old enough to remember another state could tell similar stories.[1]

Hulda Alexander experienced the third term in a long series of forced migrations survived by Africans and African Americans as peoples. The first began with enslavement in Africa and the journey to the Atlantic coast. The second term was the Middle Passage across the ocean. The first two each involved violence, dispossession, and death.[2] The third was not so violent or deadly, although it could certainly be both of those things at times. The brutality of movement within the Western Hemisphere to new plantation regions lay, more than anything, in the fact that it broke up the communities created by survivors of the Atlantic slave trade and their descendants born in the Americas. Throughout the centuries of New World slavery, such forced migrations moved enslaved Africans around the Caribbean and Brazil, but nowhere did the population movements associated with the internal expansion of the plantation system involve such a high percentage of slaves as in the nineteenth-century U.S. South.[3] There they affected in one way or another every enslaved African American. Even those not moved by owners lost family and friends to the relentless quest for new lands and new crops.[4]

Between the early generations' adjustments to the aftereffects of the Middle Passage, and emancipation, the experience of forced migration to the south and west was the most important development in North American slavery.[5] In the course of this movement, from the 1780s until 1865, slaveowners and dealers transported over a million people to the plantation frontier. Those sold to slave traders by owners in the old seaboard states usually never saw friends or family again. Those moved by their owners also faced considerable family disruption and separation, and all blacks encountered a frontier environment rife with danger. The traumas and disruptions of forced migration shaped the lives of the enslaved in early Jackson and Leon Counties, and the memories of separation would mark the lives of African American migrants who survived on the Florida plantation frontier.

ORIGINS OF A FORCED MIGRATION

A remarkably detailed set of documents enables us to map the forced migration of the thousands of slaves brought to Jackson and Leon Counties. In the years between 1866 and 1872, over 1,000 former slaves applied for accounts with the Tallahassee branch of the Freedman's Savings and Trust Bank. Many of the applications were incomplete, but others recorded considerable information, including age, birthplace, and names of parents, spouses, siblings, and children. In some cases, names of mas-

TABLE 3.1. *Birthplaces of Enslaved Migrants Recorded in Freedman's Bank Records*

State of Birth	Number of Ex-Slaves	Percentage
Alabama	11	2.7
District of Columbia	4	1.0
Georgia	62	15.1
Kentucky	6	1.5
Louisiana	3	0.7
Maryland	34	8.3
Missouri	1	0.2
North Carolina	124	30.2
South Carolina	48	11.7
Tennessee	7	1.7
Virginia	111	27.0
	411	100.0

Source: Register of Signatures of Depositors in Branches of the Freedmen's Savings and Trust Company, 1865–1874, Tallahassee, Fla., Aug. 25, 1866–June 15, 1874, National Archives Microfilm Series (NAMS) M816, Roll 5

ters, the year of removal to Florida, and even lists of relatives lost in their westward passage bring individual ex-slaves, such as Maryland-born John Green, to life.

In 1839, William P. Craig sought to enlarge his labor force. Obtaining a loan from the Union Bank of Tallahassee, Craig traveled back to Maryland to purchase slaves in small lots. John Green, then about sixteen and at the peak of his sale value, was one of those whom Craig bought, as was his sister Mary. This sale severed them from the rest of their family. In the late 1860s, Green reported that he no longer knew if his parents, Allen Green and Amelia, were still in Maryland, or even whether they were alive or dead. Nor had he heard from Priscilla, Sarah, Robert, and Allen, brothers and sisters also left behind. John Green's passage from an older area of the South to the frontier illustrates both a common pattern of slave removal, and its common outcome in family separations.[6] In all, some 411 black migrants to Leon County left enough information to enable us to begin to reconstruct their movement to the cotton frontier. We can begin by identifying the sources of migration through the birthplaces recorded by ex-slaves (see Table 3.1).[7]

Nearly two-thirds of these forced migrants came from the so-called Upper South—the Chesapeake states of Virginia and Maryland, and North Carolina. While nineteenth-century abolitionists decried the Chesapeake states as gigantic breeding farms that raised slaves for sale to the cotton

TABLE 3.2. *Regional Origins of Enslaved Migrants from Virginia Recorded in Freedman's Bank Records*

Regions	Number	Percentage
Tidewater	19	30.0
Southside	10	15.9
Northern Neck/Northern Virginia	10	15.9
Piedmont	21	33.3
Valley/Mountain	3	4.8
Totals	63	100.0

Source: See Table 3.1.

Note: Tidewater counties represented include: Chesapeake, Elizabeth City, Essex, Lancaster, Middlesex, Norfolk, New Kent, Isle of Wight; Southside: Amelia, Bedford, Brunswick, Charlotte, Dinwiddie, Prince Edward; Northern Neck/Northern Virginia: Fairfax, Fauquier, Loudoun, Stafford, Spotsylvania; Piedmont: Albemarle, Goochland, Henrico (including all Richmond city), Madison; Valley/Mountain: Botetourt, Cumberland, Washington.

states, North Carolina was also an important source of unfree migrants. The Freedman's Bank records allow us to map even the specific counties of origin of many enslaved migrants (see Tables 3.2 and 3.3). Thus we can see that like so many of the countryman migrants to Jackson and Leon Counties, most of the slaves came from old plantation districts within Virginia and North Carolina. These areas served as seedbed regions for movement west and south. Planters, slaves, and countrymen departed in droves from Virginia's Tidewater and Southside, which had once specialized in tobacco. Another such area was the Roanoke Valley of North Carolina's coastal plain, which produced over half of the enslaved migrants from that state. Some had been owned by planters from that region who sold their slaves into the domestic slave trade, while others were marched southward by migrant elite men like John Branch who were seeking to carve out new plantations in a more reliable climate.

The Freedman's Bank records also reveal the way that the movement of enslaved African Americans to Middle Florida changed over time. Table A.6 outlines the flow of slave migration from 1821 to 1860. The 152 migrants who provided both dates of arrival and state represent only a small portion of the thousands brought to Leon County, but they form a substantial sample of the wider movement. Combined with other data, this information paints a sequential snapshot of Middle Florida's place in the ebbs and flows of the wider westward passage. For instance, most slaves brought to Middle Florida during the 1820s (almost one-quarter of the overall total) probably came with their owners. One reason may have been legal barriers to import for sale: the laws of the territory of Florida ostensibly prohib-

TABLE 3.3. *Regional Origins of Enslaved Migrants from North Carolina Recorded in Freedman's Bank Records*

Regions	Number	Percentage
Albemarle Sound	4	5.4
Roanoke Valley	42	56.8
Central Coastal Plain	16	21.6
Rice Counties	2	2.7
Piedmont	10	13.4
Mountain	0	0.0
Totals	74	100.0

Source: See Table 3.1.

Note: Albemarle Sound counties represented include Perquimans, Washington, and Hertford; Central Coastal Plain: Craven, Johnston, Lenoir, Onslow, Sampson; and Piedmont: Cumberland, Granville, Mecklenburg, Orange, Rowan, Wake. The only rice county represented is New Hanover.

ited international imports and limited the domestic slave trade. In 1823, the second session of the Florida Legislative Council levied a $300 fine on each slave brought into the territory for purpose of sale. The government of the territory, and Florida whites in general, particularly feared that slaves convicted of crimes, or accused of participating in conspiracies, would be sold south.[8] These laws were easy enough to evade, and no record of anyone paying such a fine survives. In 1829, the *Tallahassee Floridian and Advocate* proclaimed the sale of forty-four slaves at auction but denied that they were part of the slave trade: "These Negroes were particularly selected by a gentleman of Virginia for the purpose of settling a plantation in this Territory, but his health being bad he has declined making a settlement." The advertisement gave readers plenty of time to prepare for the anticipated sale: "The above Negroes are expected at Aspalaga in 10 days."[9] While the "gentleman of Virginia" may have first wished to settle in Florida, and then changed his mind, that premise seems unlikely. Had their ostensible master wanted to return them to Virginia, he could have done so. Most likely, the captive blacks formed a coffle driven by a slave trader who had hit upon a new way of evading the law.

A more important factor in minimizing the slave trade during the first decade of American settlement in Middle Florida was the relative dearth of capital. While a few planters like Leon's Benjamin Chaires could buy dozens of enslaved people, others had to use the financial resources of their extended families just to secure fertile land. During the 1820s, the major flows of the slave trade to the Southwest went toward the Louisiana sugar districts and the plantation regions of Alabama and Mississippi.

Then, in the 1830s, local planters created a financial institution called the Union Bank, which supplied an influx of capital and financed an increase in the domestic slave trade to Middle Florida. In the next decade, economic problems depressed forced migration. By the 1850s, when an upsurge in cotton prices provoked more planters to move to Middle Florida, relatively few slaves came to Leon and Jackson from the Chesapeake, one of the main source regions for the domestic trade. Newer plantation frontiers, like Texas, or Louisiana's Red River valley, probably attracted the bulk of that supply during the last decades of American slavery.[10]

Slaveowners' removals probably dominated the first wave of slave migration to Middle Florida. Critics of slavery focused exclusively on the notorious interstate trade, implying by omission that those sold must have suffered considerably more than those carried south and west by owners. The experience of Middle Florida's forced migrants suggests, however, that making such distinctions is less important than understanding the disruptions that affected all the African Americans caught up in this southwestward passage.[11] In fact, for enslaved people, all journeys south to Florida began with painful separations. To understand why, we should return to the tables above, which show that most of the participants in this forced migration came from plantation districts near the Atlantic coast. In these densely settled regions, kinship networks that first began to develop as early as the beginning of the eighteenth century stretched from one plantation to another. "Abroad" marriages, formed when a man married a woman owned by another master or mistress, were extremely common. Fathers visited wives and children on the weekends and on holidays. Multiple, repeated divisions of estates by death and marriage created slave communities split among several masters or several plantations. Thus a child might grow up with his or her mother on one plantation, with a father owned by another white family a few miles away, and with grandparents, uncles, aunts, and cousins, or even siblings on neighboring properties owned by the planter's siblings and relatives.[12]

Kinship networks helped to provide a sense of community and common values for the enslaved. At the same time, they were fragile webs easily torn by the whims of white people. Even when whites moved all the slaves from one plantation to Florida, or when related slaveowners moved together, they necessarily divided husbands and wives, parents and children, and all manner of extended kin from each other. In 1835, for example, John Walker, then in his mid-twenties, was taken by his owner to Florida. Walker's first wife, Emma, and a son, John, remained in Culpeper County, Virginia. A year later he heard that his wife had died. Sales and removals had earlier divided Walker from his siblings, Jackson, Francis, and Amy and Betsy Lewis, who ended up somewhere in Tennessee. Also typical was the experience of William Keno, who left Frederick County, Virginia, as a child with his owner John Dickerson in the same year that Walker was taken from Culpeper. Keno's mother, Becky (also taken by Dickerson), had an abroad husband, Peter, whom William and his siblings never saw again. They may have felt the same loneliness that William Sparks, taken south with his mother by William Kirksey in 1841, impressed upon a Freedman's Bank official in recalling his "father Daniel left alone in Virginia."[13]

Planters were not the only whites who destroyed black families. Women and children owned by yeomen faced almost inevitable separations from spouses and other family members when their masters decided to move to Middle Florida. When North Carolina yeoman John C. Moore decided to move to Leon County in the 1830s, he separated his slave Ellen Paine from a spouse, parents, siblings, and extended family. According to Paine, she "ha[d] no brothers or sisters here" and did not know if her mother was alive or dead.[14] Every removal of slaves by owners rent asunder webs of kinship that draped across old plantation districts. Peter Carter, born around 1802 in Halifax County, North Carolina, had already suffered the loss of his mother, probably through early death. Then he lost his sister Cibby when his owner sent him to Leon County in 1839. Along with him went his wife, Mary, and his daughter, Milley, but his son, also named Peter, remained behind. The younger Peter Carter may have already been sold to another Halifax planter, since otherwise a young male hand would have been a prime candidate for the frontier. In addition, the elder Carter's own father, his stepmother, two siblings, and fifteen step- and half-siblings remained behind in North Carolina. Most of them belonged to yet another master or masters. Thirty years later, Peter Carter had not forgotten them, and they probably had not forgotten him either.[15]

JOURNEY AND ARRIVAL

For many enslaved migrants, the forced journey south drove home a deepened understanding of one central fact: that to be enslaved meant that someone else could dissolve one's very life. And understanding provoked varying responses. The emotions of separation often led to open opposition on the day of departure. The enslaved used various strategies to try to prevent separation. Slaveowners countered by using force or treachery to deliver slaves to new buyers, or to split them from families. One woman tried everything possible to keep her daughter with her in Virginia. When the girl's Florida-bound owner refused her pleas, she symbolically refused consent in ways that seemed irrational to whites but expressed her rage and loss: "You remember what a fuss Old Milly made about Betty. The old scamp kept all of her clothes and bedding and all and refused to give them up, so all the servants say, & the girl when she got here, had nothing but the shirt on her back." [16]

Just as planters breezed over the scars inflicted by the separation of African Americans like "Old Milly" and "Betty," they seemed not to notice or remember the difficulties of the ensuing journeys south. Thomas Brown certainly seemed to think that the people he marched down to Leon enjoyed the trip as much as he did. In 1826, Brown brought some sixty of his slaves down to Leon County from northern Virginia. After locating some land on the southern fringe of Lake Jackson, he hired out those slaves and returned north. In November 1827, Brown "started for Florida with his cavalcade—one hundred and forty odd negroes." In Brown's memory, the "cavalcade" may have seemed a romantic idyll. Brown noted off-handedly that white men rode on horseback and white women rode in coaches, while most slave children and all adult blacks walked. At night the blacks slept in "open tents—one long strip of cloth," while the white family slept in tents with walls and doors. Migrants who walked fifteen or twenty miles a day, the pace set by Brown on his two-month journey to Tallahassee, were likely exhausted by the time evening came. Yet each night in camp, Brown insisted that when the "old fiddler—Uncle Jenkins . . . drew his bow, it was a signal for the negroes to dance" and entertain the whites. [17]

In another case, when the Randolph and Eppes families moved south to Leon in 1829, the party traveled an average of at least twenty-five miles a day in the hot weather of June. Most of Eppes's twenty-odd adult slaves walked. Slave children rode in wagons, where, cramped and cranky, they fought like any other traveling youngsters: "There is a continual *yell* issuing from the backs of the waggons." While the black women prepared the evenings' meals, the white women rested in nearby inns or "[took] a regular loll before dinner" in the shade of a nearby tree. And if Harriet Randolph reported that the whites were "all much thinner than [when] we left home," what of the unfree travelers who walked while the master class rode? The slaves' clothes, at least, had worn thin and ragged: "We have taken off it [a wagon cover] a shirt for Jordan who was literally naked. . . . [Agnes and Nanny] wore out each a suit completely on the journey, & have been so indecent lately, and indeed in such absolute want, that I did not think it right to carry my economy any farther." [18] Other slaves died from disease or accident along the way. Planter Eli Whitaker reported to his brother the painful death of an enslaved woman on the road south from Halifax County in North Carolina's Roanoke Valley. She fell into an open campfire, an event described laconically as "the regrettable circumstance of Mr. Nash's girl Lucinda getting burnt, suffering, and dying."[19]

Planters' removals from the old states disrupted African Americans' ties of kinship and community there, but slaveowners also undermined the possibilities of rebuilding kinship and community among those that they moved. After reaching the territory, some white migrants sold slaves to raise funds for purchasing land and equipment. In addition, many selectively structured the slave forces that they moved to the Old Southwest, bringing young workers and leaving older slaves in the old states. North Carolinian John Branch left some slaves to maintain his Whitfield Place plantation in Halifax County long after he had established Live Oak and Waverley just to the north of Tallahassee. His cousins Absalom and Cary Whitaker did the same. Older enslaved people remained in the Carolinas and Chesapeake to maintain these plantations and provide summer homes for wealthy whites trying to escape Florida heat.[20]

Clearing frontier land for cultivation was brutally physical and exhausting work, best suited, whites believed, for young African American men and, to a lesser extent, young women. In order to grow cotton or sugar, slaves first had to clear acres of thick hammock growth, cut down massive live oaks, grub stumps out of the red clay found on the best lands, and burn and roll logs from the fields. So, like frontier slaveowners in other parts of the Old Southwest, white settlers in Middle Florida separated families and bought judiciously in order to maximize the available amount of labor. In the process they created slave forces unbalanced by sex or age, destroying existing family structures and limiting the possibilities of their reconstruction. In 1826, for instance, of the fourteen slaves owned jointly by the brothers Hugh and William Campbell, only three were female. Four years later, Leon's Samuel Parkhill, "a pushing man," owned twenty-one enslaved African Americans. Seventeen of them were male and under the age of thirty-six, and four were female. His brother John owned fourteen male and six female slaves, and John's brother-in-law William Copland claimed six males and two females. None of the African Americans owned by Copland were over twenty-four. Jackson County's migrant planters were no different. Tailored removal from old plantations and purchases meant that Peter W. Gautier Sr. owned thirty-four men, twenty-seven of whom were under twenty-four. Of his thirty-seven women, twenty-three were similarly young. Gautier's son Peter Jr. owned nine males—eight younger than twenty-four. Only one of his seven females was older. Robert Ricks, a native of Southampton County, Virginia, owned forty-one slaves, and all twenty of the females were less than twenty-four years old.[21]

The wealthiest planters often owned labor forces skewed obviously by age (and to a lesser degree by sex). According to the 1830 U.S. Census, Leon County's Benjamin Chaires, reputedly the wealthiest man in the territory, owned 213 slaves, 127 male and 86 female. Seventy-two of the males were between ten and thirty-six years old. Only one was over fifty-five. None of the females was over fifty-five, and only seven were over thirty-six. Through selective migration and purchase Chaires had created a labor force strong—and young—enough to clear the fields of his plantation, Verdura. Among his slaves of working age, two-thirds were male. Out of all his slaves, only sixty-five, the children ten and under and the one man over fifty-five, were likely to have escaped intense daily field labor. The entire slave community contained only one real elder. Young parents on Verdura, already responsible for a full day's labor, could not expect the childcare and informal education that older men and women provided in more settled slave quarters.[22]

Although not as skewed as the extreme example offered by Benjamin Chaires's plantation, Jackson and Leon Counties' overall slave population structures revealed planters' truncation of slave communities. In both counties disproportionate numbers of both bondmen and -women were in the age group between ten and thirty-six. These were the most valuable slaves, including those who were at the peak of productive and reproductive capacity, or those who were just moving into that group. In Leon County, 55 percent were between the ages of ten and thirty-six, and in Jackson County, 58 percent fell into this category. The source states, and old plantation districts in particular, provide a strong contrast. In two counties that sent many bondpeople to Middle Florida—Essex County in the Virginia Tidewater and Halifax in North Carolina—only 45 and 46 percent, respectively, were between ten and thirty-six. Meanwhile, the population of the source states and source counties contained many more middle-aged and elderly slaves than did Middle Florida.[23]

Owners even took mothers from their children if it served their purposes. Local historians have depicted North Carolina–born aristocrat Hardy Croom as a kind paternalist, possibly because of his absent-minded fascination with botany. Croom's Middle Florida planter peers mourned the tragic 1839 wreck of the steamship *Home* off the Outer Banks, in which he and most of his family drowned. William Kenyon, born around 1818 on the Croom plantation in eastern North Carolina, might have seen Croom, who had separated the infant Kenyon from his father, in a different light. Around 1828, Croom moved Kenyon and his half-brother Martin Clark to Gadsden County (just west of Leon) and left Kenyon's mother, Cherry, behind on his North Carolina plantation. She may have been in her late thirties by then, declining in fertility and laboring power, while Kenyon and Martin

Plantation on Lake Lafayette (from Francis Comte de Castelnau, Vues et Souvenirs de l'Amérique du Nord*)*

were almost teenagers. Croom put the boys to work clearing new ground for cotton. As they grubbed up live oak stumps, amidst the smoldering logs piled in the fields, the two boys must have realized that they would probably never see their mother again. Shortly after the Civil War, William Kenyon reported that he "does not know if she is living."[24]

Florida's migrant masters left little information explaining how they decided which slaves to take and which to leave, or even noting that they had made decisions that separated families. The objects of planters' manipulations remembered things more vividly. Selective removals of the young created Florida slave quarters without elders, and often with unbalanced sex ratios. The slave communities of the Chesapeake and Carolinas had lost vital productive and reproductive elements. Slaveowners' division of one established plantation population into two skewed, geographically sundered groups inflicted emotional scars that ex-slaves continued to find painful three decades and more later. As we have seen, Leon planter Thomas Brown attached little import to his decision to leave some slaves in Virginia. But one of the "old negroes" left behind was Jack Paine, now lost to his wife, Della, and children, Charley, Willis, Harriet, Julia, Ann, and Abram, all of whom went with Brown to Leon County. Years later, Charley Paine remembered, even if Brown did not, that a migrant slaveowner had wrenched apart his family to create a plantation in Middle Florida.[25]

SLAVE TRADES AND SLAVE POPULATION

After tearing apart abroad marriages, disrupting kin networks by tailoring workforces taken to the frontier, and marching enslaved African Americans south to Middle Florida, Leon and Jackson County's migrant planters were not yet done with adjustments to their property. Two kinds of slave trades completed the array of unfree migrations to Middle Florida. The first was different from the interstate slave trade that we tend to imagine—the commercial operation in which professional slave traders purchased large numbers of people in the selling states to ship or march them south and west. During the first decade of settlement in Middle Florida this kind of trading involved a relatively small volume of slaves. Frontier chronicler Achille Murat, who owned slaves in Leon and Jefferson Counties, reported another, temporarily more important kind of trade as a typical part of plantation creation. "The planter having returned home, sold his lands and house, and added to the number of his negroes," engaging in what we might call a "planter-borne trade," purchasing slaves specifically for the purpose of stocking his raw plantations in the Old Southwest. Murat himself planned such trips to the Upper South in order to staff his own plantation, Lipona. In 1834, he wrote that he would "probably go to Maryland and Virginia in quest of negroes" and asked political ally and neighbor John G. Gamble to use his banking connections to find information on slave prices in the Chesapeake region. He wrote to Thomas Botts of Fredricksburg, detailing his plans: "I will probably invest during the month of December next from $10 to $12,000 in negroes and I intend to go myself to the north for the purpose. I will try first in the Baltimore market, but it has been suggested to me, that by enquiring of professional friends in Virginia, I would perhaps, hear of some person either willing or compelled to part with their gang, which would enable me at once to complete my purchase."[26]

The planter-borne trade as a whole was every bit as flexible as Murat. Florida slaveowners trolled the old plantation regions, willing to purchase individuals, family units, or even small slave gangs. They visited slave markets, slave traders, estate sales, and any master or mistress willing to sell. Sometimes slaveowners themselves brought new purchases down to the territory. Samuel Parkhill bought Edmund and his wife Rebecca from a trader in Hamburg, South Carolina (who had originally purchased them in Petersburg, Virginia), and transported the couple to his plantation on Lake Iamonia in Leon. Meanwhile, Samuel's brother John Parkhill wrote the Reverend William Atkinson of Virginia, inquiring about the upcoming auction of the parson's uncle's estate. Parkhill, who planned to send an agent to the sale, wondered if the slaves would be sold together or as individuals, if any were mechanics, and "are they of a good moral character? Will they be sold on time or for cash?" Planters hoped to strike their own deals with Upper South slaveowners that would eliminate the higher prices imposed by middlemen.[27]

The differences between the experiences of slaves brought to Middle Florida by their Upper South owners and those brought by various slave trades, may have been less important than their common characteristics of disruption, hardship, and separation. The addition of the planter-borne trade further blurs lines between the slave trade and planters' migrations.[28] Once they arrived in Middle Florida, unfree migrants were thrown together in the same patchwork communities. Most forced migrants landed in slave quarters that housed more than twenty slaves. By 1830, in fact, 48 percent of the slaves in Jackson and Leon Counties lived on just sixty-four plantations.

During the 1830s, local slave populations expanded and changed. The domestic slave trade, initially a minor source of Middle Florida's enslaved laborers, became the major source of field hands for elite white men. The chartering of the Union Bank in 1833 unleashed a flood of credit. Attracted by the smell of standing money, interstate slave traders brought thousands of enslaved migrants to the region during the next few years. John Gamble and his brother Robert, who had come to the territory with a few dozen slaves between them, acquired 193 and 128 enslaved African Americans, respectively. Samuel Parkhill increased his holdings to 198, and John Parkhill and George Ward accumulated 61 each. By the latter part of the decade, Tallahassee became a fairly important terminus of the domestic slave trade from the Upper South to the Old Southwest. Some of the captive migrants came overland from Virginia, Maryland, and the Carolinas, while coastal trading schooners transported others from the slave markets of New Orleans to St. Marks or Apalachicola.[29]

The slaves who came to Middle Florida in the Union Bank–funded burst of the slave trade walked the hardest of all paths to this plantation frontier. Few slaves on the block held any power over their destination, and most had already been separated from their relatives before ever reaching frontier auction blocks. One exception was a man whose 1844 attempt to prevent the destruction of his marriage was recorded by a traveler: "One old fellow said he did not care who bought him if they did not take him from his wife but 'if they do, see if I work'—and his compressed lip told that he was determined." Yet even this scene, which may have ended in the purchase of both husband and wife by the same person, suggests the misery that the full-blown trade typically caused. Charlotte Moore, born in Maryland, was sold away from her parents and moved to Middle Florida as an orphan in a slave trader's drove. Even after several decades had passed, she had "no other relations in this place," aside from her husband and children. Florida planters who purchased slaves at traders' auctions bought lonely individuals, like Stephen Robison, taken from all of his family in North Carolina by slave dealers in 1835.[30]

Slaves like Robison and Moore probably experienced the most difficult adjustments of all to Middle Florida's slave quarters. Yet, at the same time, the rapid importation of enslaved migrants in the 1830s created a population large enough to form the basis for new communities. All enslaved blacks faced together the same challenges of distorted population structures, the loss of family members, and the unfamiliar frontier environment. The bank's loans to planters and the rise of the slave trade meant that plantation slaveholdings grew rapidly in size. Among other things, this growth opened more possibilities for marriage between slaves divorced from former partners by forced migration (see Table A.8). Fifty-seven percent of Jackson County slaves and 70 percent of those in Leon lived in groups of more than twenty. Yet although the high proportion of enslaved migrants on large plantations seemed to offer a basis for reconstructed community life, especially in Leon County, the nature of the cotton frontier would inflict repeated blows on the people who always bore the burdens of ups and downs in the plantation economy. In the meantime, they were already facing other obstacles to survival, such as the natural environment invaded and transformed by the expanding plantation realm.

DISEASE AND CLIMATE

Forced migrants to Middle Florida encountered a host of new dangers, including living and working conditions very different from those they had left behind. The frontier environment into which masters' removals thrust bondpeople was a hazardous place. Yellow fever and malaria ravaged both white and black inhabitants of Middle Florida. The first disease affected mostly town dwellers, and appeared infrequently, always in the form of an epidemic. A fragile species of mosquito was the vector that carried the "yellow jack." Some years, during the late summer or early fall, ships from the Caribbean brought yellow fever to Middle Florida and it ravaged the area, as it did most spectacularly in 1841. Yellow fever was acute and often fatal, but, on the other hand, its survivors were immune to future attacks of the virus. The endemic disease malaria was not always fatal but chronically sapped the strength of survivors. People who got malaria either died within a few weeks, or suffered from the disease throughout often shortened lives. In January 1844, planter L. B. Whitaker reported, "[Enoch] has a return of the chills, though he has gone to work." Enoch undoubtedly faced a lifelong battle against painful fevers. Malaria lurked near almost every plantation, carried by several species of hardy mosquito, although nineteenth-century science attributed its chills and "agues" to some sort of deleterious influence from the miasmas that rose from swamps and low-lying areas. Planters who could afford to do so spent Middle Florida's late summer "sickly season" in their home states or in northern resorts, leaving overseers and slaves to face the fevers.[31]

In 1836, Eli Whitaker reported something unfamiliar from his new settlement in Leon County: "One of our field hands, our youngest son, & myself have been sick since Augt. come in with something like the ague or chill & fever." Although many of the African Americans brought to Middle Florida inherited from their African ancestors certain amounts of resistance to tropical fevers, even in African regions of endemic malaria, much of the population did not possess such defenses. Thus, many black migrants suffered from malaria as well. In addition, the forms of malaria that affected both blacks and whites on the Florida frontier were different from those they had encountered in the established plantation districts of Maryland, Virginia, and North Carolina. These regions were less strenuous disease environments than either West Africa or the rice swamps of coastal South Carolina and Georgia, leaving most slaves transported to Middle Florida ill-prepared for what many would encounter. While the malaria type in the Chesapeake and North Carolina was the typically less dangerous *vivax*, migrants to Middle Florida battled high frequencies of the more deadly and often unfamiliar *falciparum*.[32]

Planters' decisions that shaped the pattern of settlement in Middle Florida further increased the risk of illness for slaves. In Leon County, placid lakes and shallow ponds dotted the landscape. As the lakes receded in the summer, they left excellent pasturage but also puddles that formed ideal breeding zones for mosquitoes. Although early-nineteenth-century medicine understood that there was a connection between proximity to standing water and summer and fall fevers, dozens of planters settled next to Lakes Jackson, Iamonia, and Miccosukee. And the most fertile soil lay near water. John Parkhill noted in 1827 that he feared that Leon's many lakes would cause unhealthiness, yet he located his slaves close to several bodies of water on his Tuscawilla plantation. They suffered accordingly. Likewise, Henry Partridge's father removed from South Carolina to Lake Miccosukee in the 1830s, only to lose most of his slaves to "a fearful mortality on the newly cleared farm." [33]

Most Jackson County slaves faced a particularly intense disease environment, since so many of the largest plantations there sprang up along the Chipola River or along the "bottoms" of the Chattahoochee. Like their counterparts elsewhere in the Southwest, Jackson planters found the bottoms "very rich, but . . . liable to inundation," yet they set African Americans to labor in an area that "has the reputation of being the sickliest place in the County." Every year the rains of the early summer and the life cycle of the mosquito brought danger to unfree migrants in the rich lands favored by planters. In June 1851, W. W. Boykin, overseer of George Gray's Jackson County plantation, noted: "In regard to the general health of the negroes it has been quite good. Some cases of the fever." In August, Gray was safely ensconced in North Carolina but the insect had made its Florida rounds in earnest, as Boykin reported: "[T]he negroes is quite sickly they are down constantly with the fever." Meanwhile, slaves continued to work late into summer evenings in fields by lakes, or in river bottoms. [34]

In their quest for cotton profits and family power, planters were willing to gamble the health of migrant slaves. In fact, the transformation of the frontier environment, which white settlers directed, made diseases more prevalent. Early letters claimed that the area was healthy, and one slave-owner writing in the late 1840s suggested that the bad years had come only after 1832. He may not have been entirely wrong. Settlers' creation of a new ecology in Middle Florida changed what had been a relatively healthy place into a deathtrap. In the cleared forests and plowed fields after early summer's hard rains, water stood in the soaked soil between furrows and in holes dug in roads by wagon wheels. Rain barrels and cisterns filled. Saw- and gristmills, like the one Thomas M. Bradford erected south of Tallahassee in the 1820s, created more standing water. The flood of new food for mosquitoes was even more important than the medium of water. By the 1830s, 15,000 people had poured into two counties where once only a handful had lived. The supply of new blood surely caused an explosion in the mosquito population. [35]

The heat of the long Florida summer also threatened the health of enslaved laborers unused to the new climate and overworked in the rush to finish hoeing cotton or corn. Pulling fodder, which often took place in August, "is always a hot time[,] that work," as one Florida master admitted. His solution was to "give them a hot tub of molasses & water with a little vinegar in it to drink, what is commonly called 'switchel.'" Overwork in the heat brought slaves' resistances to disease even lower, and was simply physically difficult to endure. One hot July, Ann, a slave at El Destino plantation in Leon, "fainted twice in the same day." The sun was so blistering that a "mare fell down dead." A month later, "Coatney, Phillis, Venus, Eliser all fainted in the heat it being the hottest day we have had here." The new work regimen also prevented many enslaved people from growing their own food to supplement the meager rations supplied by planters, and separation from kin and friends produced psychological depression. Together with these factors, overwork in the heat left enslaved African Americans vulnerable to the dangers of the frontier environment.[36]

On El Destino and Chemonie plantations in eastern Leon County, enslaved migrants brought to the territory by William Nuttall never made much headway against the frontier's health hazards. Chemonie, started in 1840 or so to employ some of the many laborers owned by William's widow, Mary Savage Nuttall, and her second husband, George Noble Jones, was particularly unhealthy. The plantation's overseers left records of births and deaths during the years 1841, 1847–49 (the 1849 record stops in mid-April), 1852, and 1855–56. Over this span of almost six and one-half years, twenty-four children were born in the Chemonie quarters and at least nineteen of the slaves there, including eight infants, succumbed to various ailments. This was hardly the annual increase of ten percent that Jones claimed in a letter defending his plantations. Jones sometimes blamed his overseers for the lack of growth, while a twentieth-century historian who read the plantation's journal blamed the slaves' frequent sickness on the "lack of economic incentive as the hands frequently magnified their petty ailments to get leisure."[37] The many deaths and the slow growth of the Chemonie slave population suggest instead the difficulties of the frontier environment in Middle Florida.

THE EFFECTS OF SEPARATION

In contrast to the migrations of planters and common whites, which relied upon and reinforced kinship, forced removal to the plantation frontier attacked and dissolved the family bonds of enslaved African Americans. Enslaved migrants responded to this disruption in a number of ways, and their frontier story is in large part one of their attempts to deal with forced migration's assault on family and self. In the long run, they would reconstitute and replace some of bonds broken by the decisions of white owners. But in the short term, the dislocations and dangers of enslaved life prevented any opportunity to rebuild. Again and again, their efforts at building lives and families met with frustration, and they had to admit tactical defeat. Whether they were taken by slave traders or by masters on the move, unfree migrants had to confront the reality of loss by the end of the first day's journey south. One Maryland slave, sold to a trader who carried him to Georgia's cotton frontier, recalled bitter despair that nearly overwhelmed him: "It appeared to me that the cup of misery was full—that there was no hope of release from my present chains, unless it might be to exchange them for the long lash of the overseers of the cotton plantations." What could he do? Like many, his spirit staggered as he thought of the apparent impossibility of reunion with his family, which increased with every mile the line of bondpeople marched south: "I seriously meditated upon self-destruction, and had I been at liberty to get a rope, I believe I should have hanged myself. . . . I had now no hope of ever seeing again my wife and children, or revisiting the scenes of my youth."[38]

We know very little about slave suicides because masters did their best to cover up the occurrence of this last act of resistance. Even among the vast majority of unfree migrants who did not take their own lives in despair, certain African Americans torn from the ties of home and brought to Middle Florida clearly never recovered. William Stephens was born in Lenoir County, North Carolina, about 1804. By the 1830s, he had a wife and nine children, who belonged to another master. But then his owner carried Stephens to Florida. The same white planter also sold William's brothers Robin, Willis, Levi, and Staley to different states, while sister Harriet died in North Carolina. Shortly after the removal to Florida, Stephens' father died. Although not yet parted from his mother, William Stephens had lost the rest of his immediate family in the course of one planter's migration. Perhaps he mourned his wife, Sally, the most, for he did not remarry and had no more children.[39]

Enslaved migrants might well have rejected the notion of rebuilding families. Some, like Africans caught up in the Middle Passage, probably wondered whether it was worthwhile to bring a child into a world where whites could sell the baby away from them. The enslaved woman Jane (mentioned in Chapter 2), convicted of infanticide, was supposedly the first person hanged in Tallahassee. Some remained isolated from family relationships for as long as slavery lasted. Fanny Henderson, who was born around 1805 in South Carolina and carried as an adult to Florida, spoke to a Freedmen's Bank officer in the late 1860s who reported that she "says she has no relations at all." Others lost basic aspects of their identity. Melvina Whitehead, brought from Georgia, had no idea how old she was. She had no family to remind her of when she was born.[40]

Yet most enslaved migrants sought ways out of despair and dislocation. The frequency of attempts to escape—the most direct way out—led traders to shackle slaves together. African Americans separated by owners from spouses in abroad marriages often tried to run from slaveowners' caravans before they got too far south. Martha Ann Hill, taken from Nashville, Tennessee, at the age of nineteen, was, as she put it, "lost on the way" to Leon County in 1832—in other words, she attempted to escape to her husband, William, who remained behind in Tennessee.[41] Once in Middle Florida, many black migrants tried to go back to their families in the older states. In 1841, a twenty-four-year-old man named Henry escaped from Samuel Richardson's Middle Florida plantation. Richardson feared that Henry had forged a pass and was certain that the he would make a daring attempt to return home: "He has relations in Richmond, Va., from whence he was purchased two years since, and to which place he will no doubt attempt to make his way." Like others dragged south, Henry may have counted the rivers and memorized the names of towns along the way. Slaveowners believed that fugitives aimed for their old neighborhoods and families, not for the still more remote and less well known free states. In 1828, Joshua Croom announced in the *Tallahassee Floridian and Advocate* that Hector, twenty-two, and Simon, sixteen, had run from his Jefferson County plantation. For the previous ten years he had kept them at his plantation in Alabama "on the Muscle Shoals on the Tennessee River . . . where I expect they are making."[42]

Several reasons made women less likely to run for the old plantation regions than men (see Table 7.1). Women separated from their abroad husbands and taken to Florida often brought children with them. Children hindered escape, yet to leave them behind would have created another painful separation. Judge Thomas Randall's slave Rebecca may not have had children when she attempted to flee back to South Carolina in 1835. Others refused to let the long odds against escape with children intimidate them. Entire families sometimes tried to run away. For example, in 1839, George and Lettus carried five children with them as they escaped a Middle Florida plantation. But the Carolinas and Virginia were a long way from Middle Florida, as enslaved men and women knew. What would they do when they returned? Could they live in the woods, on the outskirts of their old plantation, for the rest of their lives? Some preferred taking even this risky gamble, but for others, the odds were too long. In the end, most forced migrants to Middle Florida tried to find some way to survive their new conditions.[43]

In a world where many sureties had disappeared, brief moments of connection to the people and places where they had formed their identities helped some enslaved migrants to Middle Florida maintain the will to survive. Planters occasionally passed news about slaves in letters to other members of the white family, who then told related slaves. In 1837, plantation mistress Lydia Parish wrote to Caroline Turnbull, asking her to "[t]ell Dick Sally is in good health and sends her love to him." The Parish family was trying to reconcile a man to separation from his wife. However even that level of expressed concern was rare before the 1850s. Very few Middle Florida planters mentioned slaves by name in letters, except to describe their insubordination and consequent punishment, or perhaps to plan their sale.[44] Most slaves had to rely on fugitive bits of information that traveled to and from the plantation frontier by word of mouth. Since so many Middle Florida slaves hailed from the same areas of the old states, some African Americans heard news of relatives through later emigrants from their own native regions. Isaac Wood, born in North Carolina's Onslow County around 1815, was taken from his home in 1827 to Gadsden and then Leon County in Middle Florida. He learned that his father, Luke Purlock, had died in South Carolina in about 1856. But most of the bondpeople caught up in the southwestern migration never learned anything of those they left behind. Wood, for example, never discovered what happened to his siblings Luke, Louis, David, and Kitty after the estate they lived on was broken up and sold in 1845.[45]

For a lucky few, long years of absence, relieved by occasional rumors and word-of-mouth messages passed by later migrants, came to an end in joyous reunions after emancipation. Willy Williams, a woman brought with her brother to Tallahassee from Maryland's Eastern Shore, survived many years as the cook for the Hayward family. After the Civil War, Williams's mother, Rachel Fitzgiles, traveled from Maryland to Leon County to visit her daughter, son, and grandchildren. Duimie Harrison, born in Florida in the early 1830s to parents owned by the Hawkins family (migrants from Halifax County, North Carolina) eventually moved to Halifax with her mother and father after freedom came. This brought about a reunion for her parents and close relatives whom Duimie had always heard about but had never known.[46]

For most slaves, however, reunions never happened. Cast into Florida, they had to make their lives there. Words from the old home were bittersweet reminders of family and of ties of remembrance and affection that masters could disrupt in the flesh but could not obliterate in the mind and heart. Messages gave strength, but the long years' journey of the exiled was still arduous. A letter from a Virginia slave named Lenn to his appropriately named sister Memory in Tallahassee reveals a combination of resignation and fortitude. Written in 1858, the letter shows that Lenn and Memory, separated in the late 1820s, knew that they were growing old and would probably never meet again. The absence of each was still an open wound in the other's life. Lenn gave news of individuals from their extended family— sixteen African Americans, scattered across the Southside Virginia county that was presumably Memory's original home as well—and then closed his letter, not giving up all hope of seeing her again but having to trust in a more moral world beyond white control: "The first appearance of my illness was in June [?] 1855. I have never been well since. . . . And now, I must draw to a close by requesting you to remember me in your prayers. I ardently long to meet you in heaven, may it be our happy lot. Write me soon and I will answer your letters. Affectionately, your brother."[47]

THE VERNACULAR HISTORY OF THE
SOUTHWESTWARD PASSAGE

Despite a few scattered letters like the one that Lenn somehow sent to Memory, important obstacles stand in the way of our ever knowing what forced migrants said to each other about their conditions and their experiences. The relative scarcity of sources might seem an insuperable barrier to understanding the depth of the tragedy of forced migration to Middle Florida. Indeed, a generation ago, about all that social historians found was that the enslaved rebuilt the basic structures of family life. From this finding they infer that the culture of the enslaved was in essence the same in both Southeast and Southwest, both before and after forced migration. After all, many emigrants built and rebuilt families on the plantation frontier, just as they or their ancestors had done in the old states. What, then, was the difference between those moved and earlier generations?[48]

The existence of a social fact like the family cannot explain what new and old families actually meant to the people who remembered severed relationships, and built new ones. Consider the example of Joe Kilpatrick, separated by force from his North Carolina wife and daughters, Lettice and Nellie. After being brought to a Leon County plantation, he took a five-year-old boy named George Jones, orphaned by the slave trade, into his cabin. Kilpatrick raised Jones as his foster child, and, as an adult years later, Jones named his own daughters Lettice and Nellie. He had never met them in the flesh, but he remembered them as real sisters.[49] This example shows that enslaved African Americans memorialized lost relatives in the names of the young and testifies to the enduring strength of the memory of family. At the same time, however, it suggests the continued suffering of men and women in Joe Kilpatrick' situation. As he told George the stories that made Lettice and Nellie real sisters to the boy, Kilpatrick also reminded himself that he had been torn from his family.

Yet he told the stories. One wonders what larger point he was trying to convey to the boy by doing so. What did he want Jones to learn about forced migration, and about slavery? And what did such exchanges, repeated over and over between enslaved people on Middle Florida's plantation frontier, mean for African American ideology and culture? Although whites in the antebellum South went to a great deal of trouble to prevent enslaved blacks from recording their experiences on paper, two types of sources from former slaves offer possibilities for answering such questions. Narratives written in the nineteenth century by escaped slaves and published by Northern abolitionist presses are the first type of source, and they are one of the most unalloyed deposits of black voices. While often transcribed or edited by Northern or British whites, this variety of slave testimony often contains fewer biases than the second type, the interviews of surviving ex-slaves conducted in the 1930s by employees of the federal government's Works Progress Administration (wPA). White abolitionist editors may have tainted some of the nineteenth-century narratives, but the wPA interviews of elderly former slaves often suffered from worse distortions. Southern whites conducted the majority of these interviews. In many cases, the child or grandchild of the interviewee's former owner interrogated a deferential or understandably suspicious ex-slave. Florida and Virginia, however, were exceptions. In these two states, different hiring practices prevailed in the wPA offices, and African American folklorists, historians, and writers working for the wPA conducted many of the interviews with ex-slaves. Thus an interesting set of comparisons can be made between the Florida interviews and published nineteenth-century narratives.[50]

The antebellum narratives represent the birth of an African American literary tradition. They contain many of the themes that continued in the literature of postemancipation and twentieth-century writers—the psychological war with slavery's legacy, the prospects and perils of black manhood, and the role of movement and migration in shaping African American cultural and family life. Anticipating the literature sparked by the next century's Great Migration, many ex-slave narratives encompass two movements, the first of which was the passage south familiar to most African Americans in Leon and Jackson Counties. Fugitives like Charles Ball, author of *Fifty Years in Chains*, Solomon Northup, author of *Twelve Years a Slave*, and William Wells Brown were able to escape slavery, adding a second, or northward, motion to the narrative.[51] In their texts, such narrators pictured the prior, forced migration south as a revelation about the ultimate realities of slavery. For instance, the enslaved woman Lydia, whom Charles

Ball befriended on a cotton plantation, became the focus of repeated scenes in his narrative. She comes to stand as a model of the damage that forced migration could do. Initially, Lydia was the maid of a wealthy young Maryland woman, and fairly well treated, but then her owner sold her to traders who took her to the cotton frontier. There, on a plantation belonging to South Carolina aristocrat Wade Hampton I, she discovered that her old life as a house servant in the Chesapeake had left her ill-prepared for the cruel realities of frontier cotton plantations: "I have several times been whipped unmercifully," she told Ball, "because I was not strong enough to do as much work with the hoe, as the other women, who . . . have been accustomed from their infancy to work in the field." [52]

Not all narrators—or the enslaved men and women whom they encountered in forced moves south—were house slaves, and few had led a pampered existence in the older states. Yet the movement to the cotton frontier still came as a revelation of the extent of cruelty possible in slavery. Forced migration disrupted old arrangements and accommodations, making barely tolerable situations intolerable for some, and the already-intolerable ones, deadly. Southwestward passages sparked clear condemnations of the white society that made black folks into unwilling migrants. Symbolic acts of white betrayal often led ex-slave narrators to depict the violence of such incidents as a symbol of a wider crime. Whites had seized both Charles Ball and Solomon Northup (who had been a free man) through subterfuge and delivered them up to slave traders. Northup's brutal beating in the slave pens of Washington may have taken place, in a geographic sense, in the Chesapeake. Yet he already had been dragged onto the map of still more brutal social relations that characterized the forced migration of African Americans to the plantation frontier. Such an encounter with the extraordinary physical torture associated with the Southwestern states, and with forced migration, often inspired a deeper knowledge still about the essential depravity of slavery and white slaveowners. [53]

The central role played by the move south in nineteenth-century ex-slave narratives is no accident, no mere device of individual authors' creativity, or white editors' Victorian conventions. As the records of the Freedman's Savings and Trust Company, Tallahassee Branch, suggest—and almost all sources from antebellum Middle Florida that mention slaves concur—forced migration to the cotton frontier was a crucial event in the lives of millions of slaves. Published narratives dovetailed with the local experience of forced migration to Middle Florida, suggesting that the stories written by literary fugitives like Charles Ball developed out of tales that forced migrants told each other and their children. Late at night around the fire, on the front porches of cabins, or at brush arbors in the woods, enslaved African Americans unrolled their narrative of the southwestward passage. In exchanges like the ones between Lydia and Charles Ball they constructed a vernacular historiography that depicted forced migration as the revelation of slavery's deepest cruelties, and as the most dramatic event in their lives.

The fugitive ex-slave's narrative contained many pieces of vernacular history-telling.[54] Quoted or direct speech like Lydia's was not the only example. In fact, authors or editors often cleaned up dialogue. What was still more important survived: the ways in which survivors told stories, their common structures and concerns that hint at the ideals of an entire culture.[55] Ball's own tale, and all other narratives of the forced migration south build on the skeleton of a vernacular form of African American slaves' narratives. In this form, slaves told others their stories: for example, where they were born, who their parents were, and how they came to be in Middle Florida. If a father or mother was telling this story to a child, he or she set forth a demonstration—and a critique—of slavery's true nature.

Oddly enough, autobiographical histories very much like those Ball encased within the structure of his nineteenth-century fugitive's biography also appeared in the very different Florida WPA interviews. Within the reported dialogue between interviewer and interviewee, another, much older, thread of exchange of meaning runs close enough to the surface for the historian to pluck at its outline. When discussing their parents, these ex-slaves often began by describing their origins in the plantation regions of the older slave states. Many traced one or both sides of their genealogy backward to the beginnings of the masters' migrations southward to Florida. Patience Campbell, who had been born a slave in Jackson County, reported that her father's family came from South Carolina. Margaret Nickerson, enslaved in Leon County, knew the name of her maternal grandmother, Phoebe Austin, who remained in Virginia while Margaret's mother and uncles were brought to Florida. Before emancipation, African American parents described their separated families and distant places of birth to their children. The migration south and its attendant separations were important both to the parents' understanding of their own lives and identities, and the children's construction of their origins. The WPA interviews contained similar descriptions of migration. In each, migration revealed the truth about slavery. Slaves in the Southeast, of course, knew that the institution was terrible. But before masters and traders hauled them southwest, storytellers asserted, they had not known how bad it could be.[56]

Forced migration had a particular relationship to human freedom and human crime in the WPA narratives. Strangely, given the extremely low number of free people of color in antebellum Middle Florida, a reader of the interviews encounters frequent explicit and implicit claims that parents or grandparents were free and were "stole" and brought to the Deep South to be slaves. This phenomenon takes one of two forms: explicit claims of free ancestry; or unexplained descriptions of the cause of migration as being "stole." Although we are beginning to realize that the kidnapping of free blacks was more common than once thought, some of the explicit claims of free ancestry might still sound implausible. Ambrose Douglass claimed that his parents were free people in Detroit who returned South to visit relatives still in slavery and were reenslaved themselves, with their children. Samuel Smalls claimed that his father, Cato Smith, born in Connecticut to domestic servants freed while he was a child, came south as a free man, working as a carpenter. Smith supposedly voluntarily indented himself for seven years to the Florida owners of the woman he loved. Eventually the seven years became indefinite. Many of these stories may be true in the strictest sense. More important, these legends of reenslavement served as myths of origin, told by parents to children to explain their own bondage as a kind of trickery and theft perpetuated against people who should be free. In them, forced migration came to symbolize the wider theft of freedom that was enslavement.[57]

Other descriptions of forced migration concur with the legends of kidnapping of free blacks, depicting the process of forced migration as an act of theft. Margaret Nickerson said of her family, "My mother and uncle Robert and Joe were stol' from Virginia and fetched here." Although in the WPA interviews, the term "nigger stealers" sometimes referred to lower-class white outlaws, slave parents also used it to describe all slave traders. Interestingly, in his more literary memoir, formerly enslaved author William Wells Brown, another victim of forced migration, also defined the peculiar claim to property in other people as theft: "I was born in Lexington, Ky. The man who stole me as soon as I was born, recorded the births of all of the infants which he claimed to be born his property."[58] Like the interviewees, Charles Ball, Solomon Northup, and other narrators all describe moves south that begin in kidnappings, depicting forced migration as a robbery of the person. This way of telling the story of forced migration rejects as criminal the essence of masters' claims that slaves were chattel, that they had the right to sell and move people.[59]

In their personal histories of this passage to the South and West, survivors asserted that slavery was theft, not just of labor, but of people stolen from the webs of community and family that had raised them. They rejected the sort of paternalist rhetoric eventually elaborated by some Southern whites: defenders of slavery would argue during the 1850s that ownership entailed a kinder relationship between rich man and worker than did the North's "free labor." But the hints included by ex-slaves in their autobiographies suggest that in the midst of surviving and trying to make sense of forced migration, enslaved African Americans were already describing the deepest injustice of slavery as lying precisely in the relation of ownership that allowed one human being to buy and sell or move and separate others, to treat them as *movable*, chattel property. Slaves did not argue that physical cruelty, sexual abuse, forced labor, or any of the other cruelties inflicted by Southern whites were any less morally wrong. They simply ranked them as the evils of their condition, deciding that the constant threats and experiences of sale, migration, and separation were at the foundation of slavery's cruelties. As Margaret Nickerson pointed out, this injury hovered as an ever-present threat over Leon and Jackson Counties: "I never saw a nigger sold, but dey carried dem frum our house and I never seen 'em no mo'. . . . I ain't never seed no slaves sold by Marster Carr, he wuz allus tellin' me he wuz gonna sell me but he never did—he sold my pa's fust wife though."[60]

The recurrence of the metaphor of stealing within the narrative thread of migration in both ex-slave narratives from the nineteenth century and WPA interviews collected in Florida during the 1930s, makes one suspect that vernacular forms were the basis for more "literary" narratives of removal to the cotton frontier. After all, published antebellum works were unlikely to have influenced the often illiterate ex-slaves interviewed by WPA workers in Florida. Although chronologically the WPA interviews come much later, we might consider interviewees' discussions of slave "stealing" the genealogical siblings of similar narrative forms found in nineteenth-century published accounts. The common ancestor of all was the narrative told by parents to children, or by Lydias to anyone who would listen. And prior even to those were the histories recounted by many enslaved Africans about the theft of their persons. When asked how old he was, one enslaved Florida man, born in Africa, replied: "Me no know, massa, Buckra man steal niggar year year ago." A more lengthy narrative from Shack Thomas's African-born father also draws direct parallels in regard to theft between the two slave trades.[61]

Oral autobiographical accounts presented in the slave quarters told young slaves where their parents came from and how they got to Middle Florida. They expressed the loneliness and pain of separation and rejected the legitimacy of the masters' rule. Fugitives who later told their lives to white interlocutors could not always control the precise language in which their tales would be told in print. But in deeper ways, dialogue with other slaves had already shaped the fugitive's story along the lines of autobiographical accounts presented in the quarters. The thread glimpsed in that pattern resurfaced a lifetime later in WPA interviews. There again shone in the weave of the recounted past the searing instruction of migration, and the vehement rejection of enslavement as theft. Around such a narrative African Americans torn from different places, bereft of many or all family members, could describe their common predicament. Like the various groups of whites that came to the Middle Florida frontier, enslaved African Americans created ways to understand and explain their experiences. Their story, like their experience, was vastly different. Countrymen and planters seemingly reconstructed their families in the process of migration and settlement, making them more independent and powerful. That process depended on the destruction of black families, a bitter irony of which forced migrants were well aware. Unlike planters, who initially imagined migration as a process of creating a civilized society in the wilderness, or countrymen, who saw removal as a chance to make the Revolutionary idea of white male equality into reality, the enslaved never saw the frontier as a site of freedom.

Forced migration in the antebellum South shaped the life of every African American, whether taken or left behind. For those taken to Middle Florida, like Joe Kilpatrick or Hulda Alexander, the pain of forced migration never receded completely from view. The number of ex-slaves who mentioned lost relatives—75 percent of the 216 interviewed at length by Freedman's Bank employees—underscores the fact that most African Americans in Jackson and Leon Counties never again saw the people whom they lost in the course of their removal. Their vernacular history of the frontier had to begin with their experiences of loss, and then they had to choose a path along which to move forward. One day they passed the lessons they learned on to a younger generation. Almost always, they spoke in the same narrative vein: forced migration was a process of white people stealing blacks from families and homes. It revealed the true relationships of the institution and underscored the fact that African Americans could never trust slaveowners. They had to understand the central role forced migration played in slavery and in their own lives as enslaved people, in fact, in order to survive their movement. The process of understanding the history of their own forced migration, even as it was going on, was in fact the basis of their new life and new community in Middle Florida. Can we not see them now, sitting in front of the fireplace in a ramshackle cabin, or in a moment snatched from hoeing cotton, witnessing in a "hush arbor," or resting on a front porch in the cool of an evening, saying, like Lydia, "I have been here almost two years, and came from. . . ."[62]

Hot-Blooded Fellows and the Flush Times of Middle Florida

One evening in January 1825, Joseph White, a candidate in the upcoming spring election for the post of territorial delegate then held by Andrew Jackson's protégé Richard Call, was walking down a Pensacola street. Suddenly, Call's ally (and the mayor of Pensacola) Peter Alba Jr., "a man of gigantic size and athletic strength, armed with a large bludgeon and a *stiletto*," rushed from the shadows and began to pummel White. While friends served as lookouts, Alba thrashed White with his club. He then attempted to sever the Kentucky-born politician's ears. But White managed to extricate himself from Alba, all appendages intact, with the help of a friend. He then beat a judiciously rapid retreat.[1]

Alba's attack was merely the latest installment in a long series of exchanges between Call and White, who had been at loggerheads since their arrival in the new territory. In 1822, at the first session of the Legislative Council, White, who had just moved from Kentucky to Florida, defeated a bill sponsored by Call. Call's proposal would have made it easier for speculators to obtain title to unconfirmed Spanish grants. The disagreement set the tone for a form of politics "divided into factions and cabals," as one observer put it, which became still more fractured as planter migrants poured into Middle Florida. Here, where the greatest riches of the territory waited, issues of land speculation and ownership had already provoked new conflicts between migrant planter-politicians. White, who served on a commission to decide the validity of land grants made by the Spanish government before 1818, had in 1824 denied Call's probably fraudulent claim to a massive grant in the "Chipola Country" of Jackson County.[2]

Call's tenure as the territory's nonvoting delegate to Congress (1823–25) had not prevented him from sparring at long range with White and other Florida critics. In fact, Alba's January 1825 assault was the first blow in Call's campaign for reelection. Next, a few days later, knife-wielding bravos—"hooting, halloaing, and hurraing through the streets"—apparently allied with Call, Alba, and their clique of speculators, broke up a meeting of White's supporters. But then, in February 1825, Call learned that President James Monroe would soon appoint him to a lucrative Land Office position in Tallahassee. The delegate dropped from the race and set his friend James Gadsden to the task of running in his stead against Joseph White.[3]

Even as Call's surrogate waged electoral war on White, the outgoing delegate argued that his erstwhile opponent was dishonored, submissive, and unmanly. Alba's whipping, for instance, had allegedly reduced White's body to that of a chastised subordinate. No one who could not or would not defend the integrity of his body from violation was fit to lead white freemen. "I would ask the gentleman," wrote one Floridian in response to an earlier, similar affair, "does he [White] suppose the militia of the territory would have any confidence in his fighting for the rights and honor of his country should he not retain a latent spark of honor to support his *own* reputation?" White remained in the race, despite the unanswered verbal and physical insults offered by Call's allies. Then, in March, Call, known as "a devotée of the pistol," published a letter in which he denounced White and his friends as "base and unprincipled." White tried to avoid the duel that Call so obviously sought but felt that the code of honor forced him to publish a letter in which he offered to give his enemy "satisfaction." Shortly thereafter, White won the election, defeating Call's cat's-paw Gadsden (as he would defeat him four more times by 1835). Never known for his physical courage, the newly elected delegate left Florida almost immediately, supposedly to take up his post in Washington.[4]

White had won the electoral battle despite coming in second in the pageant of hyper-aggressive planter masculinity. Voters' commitments to such ideals were more complex than was Call's absolute idolatry of honor. But Call continued the feud, finding a ready audience among his peers, even if he did not sway the votes of countrymen from White's column. The issue simmered while White stayed in Washington for the next year and a half. Call and his friends made much of the absence, claiming that White was afraid to return. And if he did return, they would not deign to confront such a coward on the field of honor. They boasted that they planned instead to repeat and perfect Alba's symbolism-charged assault: "We have heard repeatedly," complained one White supporter, "that his ears were to be cut off—that he was to be caned—that the hickory was cut." Call's allies planned to inflict the corporal marks of the humiliated slave or the poor white criminal on White, simply for opposing their leader.[5]

In the meantime, Call found few outlets for his urge to chastise his opponent, although he did seize an opportunity to horsewhip, in public, the editor of a pro-White newspaper. When White did return to Florida in late 1826, the delegate tried to put off the seemingly inevitable conclusion of the feud. Finally, after much delay on his part, the "seconds" appointed by the two politicians supposedly worked out an "honorable and amicable termination" of the disagreements and insults. Yet this was not enough for Call, whose supporters immediately put it about that White, in order to avoid a duel, had consented to an unmanly admission that he had submitted to another man's insult. Still, the most dangerous part of the feud was over, although the two factions headed by White and Call continued their verbal and sometimes physical combat through the next decade. Their partisans would return to the same ground, with Call's friends asserting that White was less than eager to fight, and White's men rebutting the charges and launching more insults at Call.[6]

The feud between Call and White shows some of the constituent elements of politics in the early years of Middle Florida. Elite factions composed of "hot-blooded fellows" fought over the rewards of land speculation and office. Ties of personality and kinship brought them capital and political appointments. To obtain less tangible yet no less coveted kinds of symbolic power, they asserted an aggressive style of planter masculinity that excluded most white men from the circle of honor. In fact, the dramas performed by Middle Florida's planter-politicians revealed their ideas of differences between themselves and other white male settlers. Women and especially slaves were, of course, dependent and unmanly, objects of command, protection, and exploitation. But even other white men were unequal in the eyes of those like Call.[7]

The most basic beliefs held by many planter men, as well as the dynamics of the frontier's mad scramble for resources, meant that Call and his peers simply did not value the idea of equality among white men. They always had to have the last word, to trump everyone else's card, to finish one up in every symbolic exchange. They carried out a never-ending battle to show that they dominated all people around them as they dominated their legions of slaves. If they demonstrated anything less, they appeared a bit too close to unmanly submission. There was no middle ground. Only among family and kin, and not even always then, could planter men rest from the effort to show the public face of one who dominated his surroundings. These beliefs were both unstable and destabilizing. Elite men—and would-be elite men who had come to the frontier to assert and achieve a new status—had to compete with each other over the distribution of the rewards of office, land, credit, and honor. In the course of those struggles, opponents' very opposition sent planters sniffing for insults. Although the dynamics of this contentious masculinity appeared most clearly in the planter duel, they extended into virtually all relations between white men. Planters' vaunting implicit and explicit claims to dominance, and the grasping character of the politics such claims produced, built up an account of resentment. As that mounted, and until it came due, local and territorial politics remained contests waged by factions. The weapons were those of planter manhood, and the tangible rewards were the raw materials of plantation creation—land, credit, and the political positions that commanded the distribution of such resources.

"ENTERPRIZING BOLD MEN"

In the symbolism-charged drama that was early territorial politics, land speculation was an ever-present issue. As word spread about Middle Florida's suitability for plantation agriculture, ambitious politicians and speculators began to jockey for the right to profit from public land, the early frontier's most valuable resource. Although nobody admitted in public to being a speculator, many white men sought to get rich by purchasing land low and selling it high. As William P. DuVal, for many years governor of the territory, stated bluntly in 1826, "The citizens of Florida are enterprizing bold men and . . . do not bring but come to acquire fortune." To command this process, ambitious men like Richard Call or Joseph White needed control over public office, a new territory's second-most-valuable resource. They had seen the process before in Kentucky, Alabama, and elsewhere: land speculation and political office marched hand in hand to create wealth and power on the frontier.[8]

Yet no one could begin to buy plantation land low and sell it high until surveyors mapped the public domain of Jackson and Leon Counties. As late as 1824, complained the members of the Legislative Council, "The planter cannot emigrate to Florida, because he cannot purchase lands with a clear legal title." They feared that the possibilities of "sugar and cotton and the more valuable tropical staples . . . lay dormant."[9] All Middle Florida settlers were still by definition squatters on unsurveyed government land. Finally, early the next year, President James Monroe ordered the Tallahassee Land Office open for business. He appointed Richard Call as receiver of public monies, and George W. Ward as registrar of public lands. Call and Ward were protégés of Andrew Jackson, who had used his prestige to ensure their advantageous positions. For the next decade the two men would use the Land Office to divert land and profits to a clique of allies and relatives known collectively as the "Nucleus." And their specific duties would enable extensive intervention in land distribution. Ward recorded the purchaser of each tract and, with Call, supervised the auction process. Call's duties included accepting payment for government tracts bought by private individuals, issuing deeds for purchased land, and awarding preemptions.[10]

The implementation of preemptions proved a particular source of controversy. Whereas some individuals who took advantage of this law were prospective planters, most were small farmers short on cash and dependent on family labor.[11] The latter group of settlers dreaded having to compete with speculators in government auctions. Speculators, charged Joseph White, "flock to the country like vultures at 'death's prophetic knell,' traverse all the roads made by honest settlers; survey the whole district; take notes of every well-improved place; [and] ascertain whether there is a spot endeared to a planter, on account of it containing the bones of a wife, child, or friend." Using this information, "when the sale begins, the planters are informed privately" by the speculators "that, unless they pay so much to this 'holy alliance,' their farms and houses will be taken from them" by wealthier bidders at the auction.[12]

Because preemptions would presumably enable "honest" settlers to protect "well-improved places" from flocking speculators, Call and Ward sought to limit the use and scope of these claims. Sometimes they did so to punish enemies, as when they blocked the claims filed by Peter Gautier Jr., his father, and several other Jackson County supporters of Joseph White. As speculators in their own right, Call and Ward also sought to expand the amount of land open to the auction process. Despite repeated warnings from Washington—even from President John Quincy Adams, ordinarily no supporter of such laws—Call and Ward brazenly obstructed preemptions by every means possible, questioning the terms of both acts and claims in minute and pedantic detail. In December 1826, the receiver and registrar illegally closed their office to claims, just two weeks before the second round of land auctions. Call unilaterally turned down the preemptions of many poor settlers, such as Leon County's Jesse Kent and Mary Fletcher: "We can assign no reason why . . . further than that rumors unfavorable to their [claims'] validity, have reached the Office."[13]

As opponents pointed out, appointed public office allowed Call and the Nucleus to shape to their own local benefit land policies created in Washington. "The abuses and temptations to fraud must occur to every thinking mind," wrote one critic, who added, emphatically, "The combination of receiver with speculators is an infamous thing." The available evidence hints at plenty of sharp practice by Call, Ward, and the cronies they installed in lesser positions. More lucrative than outright theft of government monies—an accusation leveled by some opponents—were the opportunities for insider speculation. The same critic added, "He [Call] possesses no want of fidelity to his own pocket. For my own part I consider his agency in land speculations . . . little short of criminal."[14] Call controlled the auction and preemption processes in addition to obtaining all the benefits of inside information. His power as receiver of public monies also meant that some individuals undoubtedly sold him land at low prices in order to curry favor, and he bought and sold land without pause. In 1825 and 1826, he purchased some of the first land sold in Leon County. After paying a minimal price for 160 acres located within two miles of Tallahassee, Call turned around and sold the same tract two years later to North Carolina migrant John Shepard for $15 an acre, yielding a profit of 1,200 percent. In 1827, he bought several tracts along Lake Jackson for $3,200, paying less than the government minimum for at least one one-thousand-acre chunk. Eventually he sold these, too, receiving several times the original price. Profits like these helped Call to finance mounting purchases of land and slaves. In 1821, he came to the territory possessing little beyond the patronage of Andrew Jackson. By 1840, tax and census records listed him as the owner of 66 slaves, 6,000 thousand prime acres in Leon (and much more elsewhere in Florida), and $20,000 in Tallahassee lots.[15]

Call's Nucleus friends grew wealthy as well, buying and selling furiously from the time of the first auctions of Leon County land onward. Men like David Thomas, Robert W. Williams, R. C. Allen, and Call's cousin G. K. Walker began by administering the survey of government lands. By 1830, they were among the richest white men in Middle Florida. Most were Jackson cronies from Tennessee, a fact that led another critic to ask, "Was not the Georgeans [sic] proscribed by party feeling from participating in the surveys of the public lands of Florida, which was given . . . to those from Tennessee. . . . Have not companies and speculative operations grown from this influence, oppressive to the people?" The "Tennessee surveyors" drew no lines between their access to the Land Office and their activities as land speculators. In fact, they called attention to the connection. In 1826, when R. C. Allen opened a land agency in Tallahassee, his advertisement suggested that migrant planters should work with the Nucleus if they wanted to purchase a plantation site: "Gentlemen who visit this country with a view to permanent settlement, labor under many disadvantages in the purchase and location of lands, which it is believed might be obviated by this office." He listed the receiver of public monies and the governor of the territory among his references.[16]

The use of the Land Office for private gain by the Nucleus contradicted in political action the principles that supposedly dominated political rhetoric through much of the early republican United States. Local criticism of Call and his cronies as "oppressive to the people" attempted to call up popular fears about the use of public office for private gain. In his attempt to claim the title of tribune of the people, Joseph White emphasized that his desire to protect the economic independence of sturdy white republicans motivated his defense of preemption rights: "We want on the borders of the Union, a hardy bold and patriotick [sic] white population to protect the frontier, and I have constantly advocated a policy that will put poor men on the soil." White's allies supported the delegate's self-portrait, lauding his "inestimable talents[, which] have ever been exerted in the hall of Congress against the iron grasp of the heartless speculator." He and other Nucleus opponents claimed to support a Jeffersonian vision of national expansion based on yeoman settlement, one that also rejected the use of public office for private gain.[17]

While the members of the Nucleus had certainly not learned the political importance of judiciously praising such ideals—indeed, that helps explain their remarkable lack of success in open elections—they were merely more frankly open than their peers. Despite his effusive use of the language of virtue, White gave no indication that he would have been any less grasping in the Land Office than Call. When opponents criticized the delegate for serving as the legal counsel for the heirs of Spanish claimants for Florida land, White's friends mounted a defense that sounded much like that used to justify the speculations of Call and the Nucleus: "There may be some few . . . who under the influence of *sinister* and *party* motives would *at this crisis*, ask this worthy public servant to relinquish all claims to professional exertions, on which he is mainly dependent." Most planter migrants readily put aside the qualms and quibbles of virtuous rectitude in order to grasp as many "claims" to land and office as possible for themselves, their extended families, and the political factions to which they belonged. After all, if migrant planters were denied the opportunity to construct powerful frontier empires through land speculation and political office, they were being treated like mere countrymen, or even slaves. "What places of employment are left to the Virginians, the Carolinians, and the Georgians?" wailed "Moon Light," a critic of the Nucleus. "Ans[wer]: felling the trees, draining the low grounds, tilling the soil."[18]

Despite "Moon Light's" fears, the Nucleus was hardly the only faction to profit from land speculation, and its opponents were hardly reduced to enslavement. Joseph White and his allies engineered many successful ventures. White was closely connected to Georgia's Farish Carter, who, along with associates Seaton Grantland and Charles Williamson, made massive land purchases in both Leon and Jackson Counties. Williamson alone bought almost 10,000 acres in Jackson during a two-week-long auction in May 1827.[19] Carter managed his Jackson County lands first through his nephew J. H. Walker, and later through Jackson County planter and Joseph White ally Richard H. Long. Carter and his friends manipulated preemption laws and fixed auctions throughout the Southwest. One ally wrote Carter from a Mississippi land sale, "The Georgians have understood each other, & got along well, and will continue to do so. Franklin will get his land as low as could be desired." These speculators counted on the assistance of White and several other tame Congressmen.[20]

Joseph White's land business prospered as well, perhaps because of a constant flow of capital from his ally Carter. By the 1830s, White owned Casabianca, a Jefferson County plantation just east of Tallahassee, 250 slaves, and enough cash to travel frequently to Europe. Although Call and White represented the extreme viewpoints of territorial leaders on the question of preemption rights, both were planters and speculators in frontier land, obviously bent on benefiting family and self. The Nucleus and White's faction were not the only groups of men trying to seize the potential wealth of the Florida plantation frontier, either. Jackson County men like James Webb and Call's opponents Peter Gautier Jr. and Peter Gautier Sr. speculated heavily. Hector Braden and John Bellamy began to buy large chunks of land—later resold in smaller parcels—as soon as the first townships around Tallahassee went on sale.[21]

In Leon County in particular, "intrigues and knavery the most unblushing display[ed] themselves in all their lustre," as outside interests and wealthy settlers alike invested heavily in plantation frontier land. Virginian Richard Hackley tried to make good a suspicious claim of Spanish origin, the Alagon grant, while even the aged Marquis de Lafayette sought his pound of flesh. In recompense for service in the American Revolution fifty years earlier, Congress granted the French patriot all of township one, range one, north and east—a square six miles by six, located next to Tallahassee. Through agents Daniel Burch and Robert W. Williams, speculators in their own right, the republican nobleman sold the land piecemeal to finance his old age and his children's prosperity.[22]

Whether they relocated to the Old Southwest or not, individuals and families in the South—and in fact throughout the wider Anglo-Atlantic world—speculated on the creation of new plantation economies. The alliance between Farish Carter and Joseph White was one example of the phenomenon. Ties stretching far beyond Florida also permit us to acquit Richard Call of at least one of the crimes of which his opponents accused him—that of rank theft from the receipts of the Land Office. Using the advantages afforded by his command of the land auction process, one can see how Call bought and resold land at high rates of profit through the 1820s. But during that decade, Land Office and Leon County deed records suggest that he bought even more than he sold, while also plowing large sums into the purchase of slaves.[23]

How could a young man who had come to the territory with nothing spend tens of thousands of dollars on land purchases? One of the factors that ensured that no one would ever confuse a hot-blooded fellow like Call with a countryman was his ability to take advantage of connections to elite men and women in other parts of the Anglo-Atlantic world. Andrew Jackson's patronage provided contacts that supplied the capital needed for Call's purchases and ventures. Call bought and sold land for Philadelphian Thomas Dunlap and his family, who in turn helped him come up with money, like the $22,000 that he paid to Seaton Grantland for 5,420 prime acres in 1831. Connections, not pilfered cash, accounted for Call's wealth. The same held true for other Middle Florida speculator-planters. When Virginia migrant William Nuttall promised in 1833, along with Maryland natives Hector Braden and John P. Craig, to pay over $46,000 for one-half of Lafayette's township, they borrowed the money from John Dickenson of Caroline County, Virginia. Braden may have met Dickenson in the circles inhabited by other individuals who had lent him money, such as Philadelphian Joseph Miller and Alexandria's Joseph Janney.[24]

A web of long-distance finance helped to support the process of planter migration and settlement, binding men in the new states to relatives and associates in the old. Kinship groups of planters who came to Jackson and Leon Counties initially looked north and east for old allies, rather than around them for new ones. The process of land speculation meant that power often flowed from appointed political offices, which also could depend on contacts outside of the territory. Within the territory, two factors combined: the intense competition for juicy tracts of land; and the fight to maintain one's hold on the types of public office that brought opportunities and prestige. The volatile mixture of these factors helped to encourage "enterprizing bold men" who came to Florida to "obtain fortune" to fight each other in the manner of "hot-blooded fellows."

FACTIONAL POLITICS

The competition between planter-politicians for power and wealth was hardly what countrymen had hoped to see dominating the frontier. But in the 1820s and 1830s, the very nature of territorial Florida's politics limited the ability of nonplanter white men to force leaders to respond to the wishes of voters. For example, in 1825, three years after the establishment of Jackson County, the county court there selected a committee to choose a permanent site for the courthouse. After the committee picked a spot on the Chipola River, two of the three judges on the county court voted—over the vigorous dissent of the third, William Pope—to throw out their report and start over. "It appears," wrote a local man to territorial governor William P. DuVal, "that the citizens of Jackson County ever have been and are more contentious and refractory than any other county in your jurisdiction." The committee then turned to a crossroads called Webbville, where a few stores and houses had already sprung up. Webbville took its name from James Webb, who owned much of the proposed town site. But as soon as surveyors had sectioned the new site into lots, the territory's Legislative Council stepped in. It ordered the selection of a new commission, which once again picked the Chipola River site. Again the county court refused to act on the council's recommendation, and the Webbville settlement continued to grow, serving as the de facto county seat for Jackson's 2,500 inhabitants.[25]

Webb, an ally of territorial delegate to Congress Joseph White, stood to profit if his land became the site for the courthouse and the town that would probably develop around it. So did his friends Peter Gautier Jr. and Sr., and county court judges Jacob Robinson and Thomas Russ. They all owned land in or near Webbville. On the other hand, the Legislative Council's influence was not wholly innocent, either. Robert Beveridge, a wealthy Scotsman who lived in Maryland, had already staked out a claim to the proposed Chipola River site. Beveridge was an associate of Richard Call and his Nucleus allies on the Legislative Council. Following the 1827–28 land sales that confirmed Beveridge's title to the town site he was calling "Marianna" after his wife, he sold them a number of town lots.[26]

The county court refused to act, but the Legislative Council proceeded with plans to make Marianna the county seat. Joseph White forestalled their project by taking the matter to a higher level. Wielding a petition signed by a majority of Jackson's voters, he persuaded a committee of the House of Representatives to overrule Florida's Legislative Council and order a countywide referendum on the courthouse site.[27] But while Congress was in recess during the summer of 1828, Beveridge and company offered the county a bribe, promising to build a courthouse from private funds at Marianna. To ensure their victory, Nucleus politicians sold low-priced land near Marianna to Lackland Stone, a Jackson County representative on the Legislative Council. Stone, who had previously backed Webbville, switched his support to Marianna.[28]

Furious petitions from the county fulminated against Stone's apparent corruption, and a letter to the *Tallahassee Florida Advocate* angrily asked Stone, "What will become of your honor? Who hereafter will regard your word?" Sarcastically, the author went on to state, "You say truly that the county is much in need of assistance, and that she is at this time largely in debt. I presume that you think that Mr. Beveridge is in the same situation, and that he must be benefited a little as well as the county?" Stone and other council members evaded the House Committee's ruling, and massive popular opposition, by simply imposing hefty fines on anyone who carried on superior or county court business at a site other than Marianna. Beveridge's town became the de facto county seat, although the promised private funds never materialized and local taxpayers eventually had to build a courthouse themselves. Webbville itself dwindled into a ghost town, a quaint rumor in county history.[29]

The contest over the location of Jackson County's seat illustrates several important aspects of the political process in early Middle Florida. From 1821 to the mid-1830s, political struggles focused on land speculation and the closely related rewards of office. The combatants in the electoral, epistolary, and sanguinary battles that dominated public discussion typically represented the factions of elite men who squabbled over such benefits. The territory's distance from national politics certainly played a part in this phenomenon, divorcing local contests from the broad ideological issues that were beginning to call national parties into being. Many offices were awarded by appointment, usually on the basis of personal ties to powerful men in Washington. Party-based ties between men dependent on public support for a commonly shared ideological platform did not play a role in determining officeholding during these early days. Factions that centered around personal friendships and patronage were the result, and factional conflicts were more important to Florida politicians than were their own constituents. Some Florida politicians appeared uninterested, in fact, in appealing to countryman voters. Others became so embroiled in the personal and factional conflicts of frontier Middle Florida that they paid no attention to the wishes of their constituents. The conduct and language of territorial politics added a new layer to the effective disfranchisement begun by land speculation and capped by the aggressive acts of planter masculinity.

Again and again on the plantation frontier determined local planter-politicians attempted to seize benefits for themselves, their families, and their friends. Nearby Alabama, settled a decade or two before Florida, had been through a similar phase, although by the 1820s politicians there had to be more willing than their Jackson and Leon counterparts to cater to the political beliefs of the broad mass of the white male population. On most of the South's frontier, as in the territory of Florida, the restrictions that limited voting to the propertied in many of the old states had disappeared, making a popular appeal essential if one wanted to win elections. And, even though voters in the Florida territory had little to vote for in the 1820s, countrymen believed that a proper republican government, such as that for which their forebears had fought, would promote white male equality. They feared that the powerful loved to use their position to increase their power at the expense of everyone else, subjecting free men to the moral, political, and financial equivalent of slavery. The stakes of vigilance against such decay were high. Countrymen could feel the fear of the republic's potential failure like a punch in the gut. They saw shameful dependence around them every day—after all, almost one-half of the population of early Middle Florida was enslaved. Rarely, it seems, did countrymen reach out in sympathy. Instead, they reacted in horror and rejection, perhaps anxious because they knew that many white men had been and were still dependent, still subject to orders from elite employers, landlords, and judges, even if they could now cast often meaningless votes.[30]

Above all, countrymen insisted that politics begin with the definition of all white men as independent, equal, and manly political actors. Yet only when taught by the hard lessons of popular revolt and public humiliation would most planter migrants learn to put white male equality at least in their rhetoric. From the inception of the Florida territory, politicians divided on lines marked out not by different ways of appealing to voters' ideological beliefs but by exclusive alliances of kinship and friendship. For fifteen-odd years, they were able to get away with it. After the factionalism of Pensacola in 1821–24, Tallahassee saw still more intense struggles between ever-shifting, complex formations of migrant elite men. The Nucleus, of course, fortified the high ground of the Land Office, while Joseph White and his speculator cronies contested their dominance into the 1830s. The Nucleus imported new relatives, setting them up in positions of local power: "Whenever a new office is created or set adrift by death," wrote a critic, "some of their number have a cousin cut and dryed, to lay hold of the post."[31]

For young elite men who hoped to get ahead, factionalism helped to secure one's feelings and interest in a new country. No wonder that men would fight verbally and physically, and even risk death for faction and family. Joseph White's brother Everett, a Legislative Council member, died in an 1836 duel with Jefferson County politician Abram Bellamy. Nephew Oscar White, meanwhile, fought a celebrated battle with Richard Call's protégé Leigh Read in 1833. When the two combatants had fired their pistols in vain, they wrestled in the dust and stabbed at each other with knives. Call's cousin George Walker, Read's second, "stood over the two, with cocked pistol, threatening to shoot any man who interfered."[32]

The Nucleus and White's relatives were far from being the only factions that struggled for economic and political dominance during Middle Florida's first years. In and around Tallahassee, Maryland emigrant William Wyatt, William Nuttall, and Governor William DuVal and his extended family of Kentuckians traded verbal and physical blows, forming and re-forming alliances in a continual process of factional mitosis. Looking back from 1839, the pseudonymous "Office-Hunters" described the previous fifteen years thusly: "We have all been here like a litter of hungry sucking pigs, squealing and rooting each other from the teats." DuVal, charged observers, was "all things by turns and nothing for long." He constantly shifted political alignment. In the early 1820s, he supported Joseph White and opposed some plans of the Nucleus. After charting his own course for a few years, DuVal came down on Call's side. Even Call changed his alliances as necessary. In 1833, he pushed aside the perpetually defeated James Gadsden to run for territorial delegate with DuVal's backing. Opponents charged that settlement had lessened the power and the benefits that Call could squeeze from the Land Office: "It was not convenient for him to offer until the land office 'tit' was sucked dry: but now, it seems, it no longer gives milk, and he must take to rooting."[33]

The politicians of territorial Middle Florida could afford to ignore the will of their constituents for two reasons. First, a considerable number of government officials were appointed in Washington, including the governor, Land Office officials, and most law enforcement officials, like judges and marshals. Once in place, they had only to stay in the favor of the federal administration in order to remain in office. William DuVal, for instance, who formed alliances with both John Quincy Adams and Andrew Jackson, held his post from 1822 to 1834. He, in turn, had the power to name many other officials, which, Joseph White charged, included "a regiment of Colonels. . . . Six of them have died Sots and several others to all appearances are destined for the same end." But even in the case of the positions settled by popular ballots, planter factions dominated the field. Economic and social prominence plainly commanded name recognition essential to election in a territory lacking organized political parties. In some other areas of the country, new forms of party organization were improving the ability of ordinary voters to impose ideological conformity on candidates (and vice versa, of course). In such places, political candidates took sides on ideologically charged issues like internal improvements, the "monster Bank," and nullification. Yet Florida planter-politicians were able to ignore such topics — at least for a few years.[34]

Middle Florida's politicians did not have to listen to ordinary white men, and often did not even hear them. In the rare case in which popular votes mattered in territorial Middle Florida—that of the biannual election for congressional delegate—countryman voters obviously preferred White to Call and his cronies, thus making the best of a bad bargain. Yet even that test of popular sentiment was not safe from the manipulations of factional struggle. In 1831, Governor William DuVal threw out the result of Joseph White's narrow reelection over James Gadsden. DuVal invalidated the returns from enough pro-White precincts to force a "tie" and called for another election. White's partisans exploded in outrage—"If the majority had been for Gadsden," hissed one, "can any man believe we should hear of another election?" At a Leon County barbecue hosting White, another man taunted DuVal, who bragged of his close friendship with Andrew Jackson, with his support of the South Carolinian Gadsden: "Gov. DuVal—he has given us the first fruits of nullification by setting aside an election of the people."[35]

The delegate himself declared that he would not campaign in the farce of a second canvass. The newspapers battered DuVal, using republican principles to charge him with corruption. One mischievous satirist published a narrative entitled "ANOTHER DREADFUL STEAMBOAT DISASTER"—an account of the crash between the "Joe White" and the "Billy DuVal." The latter, "though originally a good Boat, is now old, and some of her main timbers considered unsound—she has generally been patronised by the monopolising aristocrats and land speculators of Tallahassee." In real life, as in the story, the steamboat "Billy DuVal" suffered severe damage in the collision with "Joe White." DuVal's "trip up Poll Book River to TIE Landing" ended in embarrassing failure: newspapers abused him, and White won the second election without campaigning or acknowledging its validity. DuVal's brazen attempt, though defeated, to overturn the results of a popular election suggested to many that Florida's territorial politicians sought to disfranchise the yeoman voter in their quest for factional power.[36]

The anger of countrymen was fruitless during this period, however. They lacked both power and committed allies. Even the newspapers' critique of Middle Florida's politics rarely emanated from yeoman sources during the first decade or so of settlement. Many of the complaints about the tenor of Florida politics came from elite men like Joseph White: one newspaper sarcastically commented on "the oft-told tale of his supreme disgust with Florida politics." Federal judge Thomas Randall complained of the "violence and intolerance of party spirit" that prevented Middle Florida from living up to the early promise offered by the "intelligent, well educated men" who had moved there. White was, of course, a prime mover in factional controversy, while Randall's complaint suggests an essential social conservatism. They were hardly the voices of the yeoman settler. Other denunciations of politics as practiced issued from the pens of newspaper editors, often transplanted Yankees accustomed to a conservative, quasi-federalist version of politics by the better sort. In 1829, the editor of the *Tallahassee Floridian and Advocate* announced that "the political slang of expectant partizans will not be retailed in this journal, as it generally originates in private animosities, and always has reference to subjects which, from our present situation, are matters of no interest." Such old-fashioned denunciations assumed that anything short of elite-approved consensus was a bad outcome for politics.[37]

Countrymen did express their disgust with Middle Florida's politics, and they directed their opposition at the implications of both the policies and style of planter-driven politics. But their voices from before the end of the 1830s emerge only rarely from surviving documents. Indeed, their relative absence suggests the inability of ordinary white men to make their voices heard in the din of the factionalized politics of early Middle Florida. The very structure of territorial politics disfranchised most white men. And the style of politics, especially the aggressive assertion of an exclusive masculinity in planters' interactions with each other and with countrymen, denied the independent manhood of even property-owning migrant yeomen. That style also revealed much about elite men and the ways in which they viewed their world.

WHERE I RULE, I RULE IMPERIOUSLY

In Middle Florida, as elsewhere in the antebellum South, ideals of manly honor structured the interactions and identities of white men, shaping Southern politics, culture, and society. Desire for mastery and antipathy toward submission dominated the individual consciousness and collective unconscious of white men who moved to Florida. Virtually all white men agreed on the need to reject and resist—by violence, if necessary—the attempts of others to force them into a position of subordination. This was the essence of honorable behavior, and it distinguished free men from slaves and women. Some elite men even argued that this ideal of the honorable man, ever willing to risk his life in the forum of the duel in order to preserve his reputation, could smooth interactions between white men. If all white men were ready to defend their honor with violence, wise individuals would treat each other with the precise manners necessary to avoid offense.[38]

Perhaps the vision of manhood enshrined in the duel might have reduced violence if everyone in Middle Florida expected all men, or even all white men, to act on, and to receive, the same rewards of "manhood." Whether one looks at a single place in time, or compares several across history, ideas about masculinity in various classes and cultures are certainly alike in a most basic sense—they are usually very different from ideas about femininity. Men have to prove and achieve their masculine status through a series of tests and behaviors, such as violence, productivity, sexuality, or leadership, which set them apart from women. In most societies, achieving the status of "manhood" has not only imposed different requirements on its would-be possessors but has also brought them rewards greater than those allocated to women, children, and grown males considered less than men.[39]

But the meanings of manhood are neither changeless over time nor uniform among different classes within a single society. In the antebellum South, almost all white men could agree on some basic precepts of what being a man actually meant.[40] White migrants to Middle Florida certainly considered enslaved males, for instance, to be unmanly. But on other matters, such as the status of countrymen, there was more debate. Planters' common belief that countrymen were less independent, less manly, and less entitled to the rewards and respect due to men revealed clear differences between white masculinity and white equality. In fact, planters did not really believe that white men of different classes were equal. And, not only were planter ideas about manhood at odds with those of countrymen, but Middle Florida's early history shows us that the ways in which planters attempted to live out those ideas inevitably caused unceasing friction between white men of all classes.

The icon of elite frontier masculinity was the "hot-blooded fellow" who not only submitted to no one but also attempted to compel obeisance from all others in his world. Planters learned this role on the stage of the plantation. A French traveler who visited Middle Florida in 1837–38 noted that because the typical planter was "accustomed to exercise absolute obedience over his slaves, he cannot endure any opposition to his wishes." Perhaps the best example was Richard Call, who refused to act in any way that possibly could be construed as submission. No one could criticize his public conduct as land official or, later, territorial governor without facing his wrath—for to respond with anything short of a challenge to such critique was, in Call's mind, unmanly surrender. Even the voters of Florida could not expect to hear him say anything that possibly could sound as if he were catering to the wishes of a majority. "I am not calculated for a successful politician," he bragged, "so far as success must depend upon a time-serving humiliating policy which would degrade the reputation of a gentleman. . . . I will not lie, fawn, flatter, and deceive—be it so: I care not; I am able to take care of myself."[41]

To "fawn," to speak in the uncouth political vocabulary of the countryman public would constitute degrading submission of Call's proud self, and Call would not give way to anyone. Call also insisted that no man could oppose him without setting up a confrontation from which he would emerge victorious and the other humiliated. His long feud with Joseph White, for example, showed Call's intractable desire to reject all contradiction and criticism as an attempt to deny him the mastery in public that he acted out on the plantation. He stridently insisted that "there lives not a man that dare breathe an insinuation against the reputation . . . of Gen. Call." Of course, saying that no man dared speak was the same as arguing that all who did not speak remained silent out of fear, and thus were unmanly slaves to cowardice. Thus Call interpreted all opposition as an attempt to strip him of his manhood, to which he must react with violence, and asserted that all who did not oppose him were less than men.[42]

Call's manner angered more than his political opponents. The proud Tennessean and his peers sowed insults like dragon's teeth upon the yeomen soil of Middle Florida. Call not only opposed the use of preemptions, which directly threatened yeoman independence. The menacing language that Call directed at his opponents also showed his belief that steep hierarchies of manliness and honor separated independent planters from dependent common whites. "Where I rule, I rule imperiously," said Call of his own political philosophy. Yeomen wanted nothing of imperious rule—unless, perhaps, they were speaking of ruling the other inhabitants of their own households. A phrase, borrowed from Thomas Jefferson, was used by a local newspaper to appeal for countryman votes while evoking their aversion to such assertions of power over independent white men: "Some men are not born beasts, and others *booted and spurred to ride them.*"[43]

In their precarious state between dominating rule and a dependence that could not fail to evoke slavery, countrymen wanted to hear nothing that suggested any white man should be ridden booted and spurred. The horse, a beast of burden, was a fearful political symbol of masculine anxiety; one that could suggest a physically powerful yet dependent animal subordinated by a truly powerful man. Indeed, countrymen tried to turn the horse image on its head both in political ideology and in daily interactions. The French visitor Castelnau reported seeing one young man spoiling for a fight as he rode into a Middle Florida town: the rider cantered his horse around the courthouse square and "after having imitated a cock [an animal that fights to the death rather than submit, and rides rather than being

ridden] . . . cr[ied] out from horseback: 'I am a horse but I defy anyone
to ride me.'" But if Call realized how countrymen would react to the rank-
ings that his language suggested, he did not care. His own use of horse-
related language specifically rejected equality among white men and depicted his own process of attaining power as the humiliation of other white
men. Call proposed to reduce one opponent to his beast of burden, asserting that he would "ride [him] . . . 'with a stiffer bit and ranker rowel, than
he had been rode with [before].'" Perhaps white men on the frontier did
not interpret Call's metaphor as a sexual threat, but certainly to be "ridden" promised to make one submissive and dependent, like a woman or a
slave. Many had heard that Call once attempted to rape Peggy O'Neale
Timberlake, later wife of Governor William DuVal's successor, John Eaton.
Using a fireplace shovel, Peggy fought off Call's attempt to ride her. Call
still later proclaimed her as lacking in virtue. Call's words and attempted
actions equated the ridden (or even those whom he threatened with riding)
with the unvirtuous, male political opponents with feminized or female objects of domineering sexuality.[44]

Land policies and political language smacked of a desire to put boots
and spurs on the feet of the Nucleus and saddles on the backs of other
white men. Thus yeomen would have been foolish not to fear that·the class
divisions and hierarchies of white manhood of the tidewater South were
alive and well in the minds of planter-politicians on the plantation frontier.
If anything, such attitudes seemed even more explicit in Middle Florida.
The political combat of the frontier was open and vicious, and planter-
politicians' furious responses to criticism and challenge revealed assumptions about inequality among white men that older and more stable political
structures might have kept muffled. Call and his ilk habitually attempted
to mark opponents with precisely the same insignia of being ridden that
planter-dominated courts inflicted upon poor white (but not planter) criminals: horsewhippings, brandings, severed ears. Other aggressive planters
behaved much like Call and his allies did in their conflict with Joseph White,
attempting to whip those whom they wanted to portray as not even worthy
of the challenge of a duel. Such assaults marked their victims as almost beneath the notice of elite men, supposedly excluded from the ranks of those
whose manliness meant that one at least had to duel them. Those who
carried out such actions saw them as politically significant, assuming that
other Middle Floridians would see the whipped as unmanned, and the one
who whipped as honorable. By using this kind of tactic planter-politicians
also implied that they had the right to humiliate those of lesser status who
dared "breathe an insinuation."[45]

In his obsession with the defeat and humiliation of all opponents, Call

Tallahassee street scene (from Francis Comte de Castelnau, Vues et Souvenirs de l'Amérique du Nord*)*

was merely the most extreme exemplar of a style of masculine behavior that possessed many planters and politicians on the Florida frontier. Even the duel, a standard by which elite men measured their manhood and that of others, rested on an assumption of inequality that excluded not just blacks and women but almost all white men as well.[46] In fact, the duel was in one sense everything to planter men, an ideal receptacle spilling over with those values of planter manhood that set them against each other and against countrymen. The duel's protean footprint was everywhere: whenever tension rose between planters, whenever they discussed anything that raised the question of which white men should have political and economic power in Middle Florida, planters' words and actions reeked of its insults, of its implied gunpowder. Some planters who considered themselves honorable did oppose dueling, often on religious grounds. But these men were about as logically consistent as the corporate executive who thinks that monopoly is morally wrong. They were individuals uncomfortable with the obvious implications of their own beliefs.

The duel and the words and actions that preceded it symbolized planter manhood and illustrated the deep and powerful thirst for dominance that made territorial Middle Florida so unstable. To understand this, we must

remember two crucial elements that made the duel so useful, as act, metaphor, and reservoir of language and imagery, to planters bent on "proving"
that they were masters over their worlds. First, it was exclusive, not inclu-
sive. Planters used the duel and its ceremonial apparatus as tools to draw
sharp lines between themselves and the dishonorable, dependent, and unmanly in society. Second, it was both unstable and destabilizing. Rather
than channeling conflicts into formalized violence, the duel increased the
frequency of street fights and shootings by turning planter men into hot-
blooded fellows bent on proving their mastery to and upon all who crossed
their paths. Instead of establishing the honor of all involved, the duel as
practiced enabled elite men to impugn the manhood of everyone who dared
to oppose them. Consequently, instead of solving disputes, the duel created
additional ones.

Few white men, planters claimed to believe, could actually participate
in the duel's deadly formality. Public opinion, the refusal of planters to respond to challenges from "lesser men" with anything other than horsewhippings and canings, and selective prosecution all excluded countrymen from the planter duel. Legislative Council member Benjamin Putnam,
arguing against a stronger antidueling law, "took a nice distinction between 'gentlemen' and the common vulgar crimes act for 'loafers and blackguards.'" Putnam assumed that only the aggression committed by dishonorable men was a social problem; upper-class men had a clear right
to reply to insult with deadly violence. The territorial courts of Middle
Florida agreed with Putnam. In contrast to the frequent prosecution of
countrymen for "riot," "affray," and "mayhem," judges did not enforce the
antidueling laws on the books. Planters on the Legislative Council even
mustered enough votes in 1831 to repeal the merely symbolic existing stat-
ute.[47] Their use of the code of honor to ensure social and other forms of
stratification was not unusual. The rise of the duel in the Western world
from the eighteenth century onwards was in part an effort by men who had
made their money from new forms of commerce and production to cement
their status as "gentlemen" through codes and rules and choreographed
violence.[48] But what was more important than the code was the way planter
honor worked in practice, as opposed to advice books' descriptions of idealized duels in which all participants followed the letter of the "rules." In
Middle Florida elite migrants believed that they had to inflict preemptive,
dishonoring strikes on all those who opposed them. They had to rule, and
rule imperiously.

The prescribed mechanisms of the duel's preliminaries allegedly confined incidents of even the most orderly violence to the spatial outskirts of
society, and conferred respect on all who followed its rules. Nothing could

have been further from the truth in Middle Florida. The duel as practiced encouraged men to break its formal rules and show their aggressive potential for violence in order to avoid being taken as submissive. While the seconds exchanged notes, chose the ground, time, and weapons for the formal encounter, combative planters sought to jump the gun. They used the time between initial provocation and the actual ceremony to plot and launch assaults that would humiliate their antagonists. With such actions, like Peter Alba's attempt to "chastise" Joseph White, assailants hoped to seize the high ground of honor and deny membership in the community of men to political rivals. When Leon County politician William Wyatt punched Nucleus stalwart Isham Searcy in a session of the Legislative Council, he made certain that the newspaper-reading public knew about the way in which he had taken "full satisfaction" for an alleged insult by Searcy. The "posting" of an individual for allegedly being too cowardly to fight, which meant much the same as horsewhipping him, also played a role in public perception—or so thought the partisan press, who reported such occasions with glee. And all these attacks, observers recognized, were a significant part of political combat and campaigning. "Citizens" already knew the answer to the sarcastic question that he posed about the repeated attempts by Nucleus allies to threaten and assault Joseph White: "What can be the reason that for years past, especially about the time of an election, the public mood has been inflamed by repeated menaces of attack on this individual?" The reason was that the Nucleus sought to shame and feminize their opponent.[49]

Preemptive and violent attempts to deny, by figurative emasculation, the worthiness of a rival's right to challenge an individual in any way could take deadly forms. One evening during the Second Seminole War, a dispute arose among the planter officers of a Leon County militia unit camped in the wilds of East Florida. Lieutenant William Ward, son of Nucleus leader George W. Ward, brought a petition from his enlisted men to the campfire of his superior Col. George Parish. Angry words passed between Ward and Parish, raising the possibility of a formal challenge. Col. Augustus Alston, sitting with his friend and Lake Miccosukee neighbor Parish, showed that he considered Ward and his common soldiers impertinent by roaring out, "Shoot the damned dog!" Parish promptly raised his loaded pistol and murdered Ward. In a Jackson County counterpart to this incident, a lawyer named B. F. Wood and a farmer named Jordan, who had argued with each other the day before, encountered each other on a country road. When Jordan, who was unarmed, would not move aside, Wood simply blew a hole in Jordan's abdomen with his shotgun. Such encounters did not proceed along the script of the formal code of honor. Instead, they happened because planters were willing to use violence to defeat any individuals who stood in their way, and since their opponents might be just as willing, it was better to bring their own willingness to bear as soon as possible.[50]

Occasionally the period of preparation did not explode into dishonoring violence, but even in those cases—rare as they were in Middle Florida—the very ceremony of the duel still contained dangerous and destabilizing implications. Supposedly, if both sides punctiliously followed the rules, each man, whether dead or alive, came home from the dueling ground covered in the laurels of honor. Because no one was dishonored, neither combatant (nor their surviving families) would seek vengeance after the encounter. The feud could stop, rather than consuming generations of participants on each side in its bloody exchanges. Yet on Middle Florida's plantation frontier, the ceremony's ambiguities attenuated its ability to contain the hot blood of violent fellows, and provoked long chains of vengeance.[51]

What, after all, were angry planter men trying to prove in the ceremony of the duel? Were they trying so hard, as some men argued in the pre–Civil War South, and some have argued since, to display an honorable self-control that they would encounter even death before displaying cowardice? If that was the case, then the duel could shed honor on all involved, no matter who won or lost, so long as they followed the ceremony's exacting rules.[52] Yet many planter men acted as if they believed that almost nothing could compensate for the dishonor poured upon those who suffered physical or metaphorical domination, even if only for the instant it took to receive the slap of a word or a blow from an assailant's fist. The latter was particularly troubling, perhaps because the people most often physically abused in this society were the enslaved. Being placed, for however short a time, in the same situation as an African American caused great anxiety. In one incident, a bully punched the cousin of Florida planter John Taylor repeatedly, until Taylor's kinsman grabbed a shotgun and killed his assailant. But another cousin worried that by being beaten, his relative had been stained so badly that even the death of his attacker could hardly wipe out the insult: "I am very sorry that John had to commit the deed and still more hurt to hear that he did not act bravely in this matter. He suffered himself to be dragged through the streets of Livingston before he would *fire.*" The ideal of planter manhood was impossible to achieve: the perfect man of honor who could not be criticized, mocked, touched, punched, or shoved. The only way to erase a mark of submissiveness was to kill one's opponent. Even then the relentless need to dominate made planter men unsure if they had scrubbed white the stain on their mastery of the world.[53]

When duels proceeded to consummation, participants and/or bereaved relatives often believed that the result thus produced was one of domination that needed to be wiped out, rather than the affirmation of the equal honor of the two combatants. Two men faced each other down, and given the beliefs of most men about what it meant to be a man and a master, both could not come out of a contest with their honor intact. One man lay dead, silenced and defeated, while the other still stood. Indeed, instead of a site of equality among honorable men, the duel was just a highly refined and masked form of vengeance, one more struggle in the endless quest to have the ruling word. No wonder that in Middle Florida, insulted relatives of the deceased typically took up the exchange, continuing the feud. George T. Ward, brother of the William Ward mentioned above, hoped to speak a supreme insult when he sought out his brother's killers. Although George Parish somehow eluded him, Ward found Augustus Alston at Fisher's Hotel in Tallahassee. The bereaved brother slashed Alston's face with a riding crop, Alston challenged Ward, and Ward, who still had more to say, accepted. In the first exchange of fire at the dueling ground in southwest Leon County, Alston badly wounded Ward. The formal rules of the encounter would have permitted both to retire, their honor proven. But Ward still wanted to blot out the words that Alston had spoken. He fired four separate pistols with a wounded arm, literally crawling toward his opponent on hands and knees to shoot once more before collapsing from the loss of blood.[54]

Slavery shaped planter selves, and two men who sought to rule and rule imperiously could not oppose each other peacefully. Both men could not show themselves as equally honorable. One man or one family had to win, and everyone else had to lose in the world of planter honor. As planter families and factions jockeyed for dominating power on the Middle Florida frontier, they used insults and actions associated with duels as the language of their political contest. Thus they revealed a sense of masculinity that at some level needed to make everyone else—at least everyone not allied to oneself—a slave so that the self might be absolutely free. The duel distilled, fortified, and made obvious this attitude. But it was only the most extreme form of the strain that infected planters' relationships to all others on the plantation frontier. As a consequence, hot-blooded fellows produced precisely the disorderly politics, society, and selves that many planter migrants had feared. Meanwhile, countryman observers could see that the imagery and language of cross-class and cross-race humiliation used by squabbling planter-politicians' revealed that hierarchies of manliness and honor supposedly divided white men. They could all guess that countrymen ranked, of course, at the bottom of that pyramid. Even when planters were the objects of dishonoring attacks, such tactics resonated with a belief that one should drive opponents down to an emasculated level allegedly inhabited by countryman "loafers and blackguards." So the account in which nonplanter whites chalked up planter-politicians' manifold insults to white male democracy grew and grew. And then, Florida gentlemen outdid themselves, erecting as government policy the clearest evidence yet that they believed that only some white men could claim the benefits of manly independence.

A HANDSOME ESTATE WITHOUT
ADVANCING A SHILLING

During the 1830s, Middle Florida's kaleidoscopic politics shifted once again. The catalyst for this change was the energy supplied by a cluster of migrants from Virginia, whose scheme for redirecting international supplies of credit captured the minds of fellow planters. What came to be called the Union Bank of Florida actually copied its organization from a species of financial institution that sprang up across the Southwestern plantation frontier during the early 1830s. Like these other institutions, the Union Bank of Florida was an attempt by migrant planters to control their own economic destinies. Relying upon the desire of European and Northern investors to make huge profits by lending capital to frontier cotton plantations, planters created their own financial institutions. Then frontier masters with the proper credentials would be able to purchase slaves and land at their own discretion. Flexing the muscle supplied by their control over the world's most important raw material, planters hoped to use the financial independence supplied by the banks to respond to the cotton market's ups and downs, and to support their families' "interest."

As the 1820s became the 1830s, the rewards of control over public land sales declined. Much of the best land had already reached the auction block, although some remained unsold on Land Office plat books because of the lack of ready cash in the local economy. As this cause for factional combat among Middle Florida's planter-politicians declined, Nucleus ties to Washington also weakened after the "Petticoat Affair," the crisis over Peggy O'Neale Timberlake Eaton's propriety or lack thereof. Richard Call's stranglehold over federal patronage loosened, and one newspaperman noted that "the Nucleus is no longer the hive from which swarms of officers go forth to suck honey from the Treasury blossoms." By 1833, Call saw the need to seek direct political power, leading him to run against Joseph White for territorial delegate to Congress. And while Call tried to maintain power, William DuVal lost favor in Washington, especially in the wake of his unsuccessful trip up "Poll Book River." [55]

As the flow of power and wealth from the Tallahassee Land Office ran dry, Middle Florida planters began to chafe under other constraints to economic growth. Even as cotton prices looked as if they might begin a long-hoped-for rise in the early 1830s, settlers could not take full advantage of that development. The chronic lack of currency, a problem that plagued many frontier communities, meant that most settlers lacked the cash necessary to purchase enough slaves to bring their acres under full cultivation. While almost every financial institution issued some kind of paper money, much of it was worthless outside of its state or community of origin. The most reliable money—that most likely to trade at or near "par," or face value—tended to gravitate toward New York and other centers of commerce. But as governor, William DuVal had vetoed a series of proposed banks that might have expanded the local money supply, and plans to establish a local branch of Nicholas Biddle's Second National Bank had also come to naught. In the 1820s, DuVal had courted yeoman support, "acting with a single eye, to the public good," as he claimed, by opposing the early bank proposals. His zealously anti-bank lieutenant, Territorial Secretary James Westcott, who acted as governor during DuVal's lengthy Kentucky vacations, vetoed two others in 1832.[56]

During the next year, however, DuVal signaled that he was ready to cooperate with other factional leaders in forming a local bank. "The time has arrived," he stated, "when the great planting interests of Florida call out for such an institution." John Gamble and his Virginia friends responded with a proposal that promised to be the solution to planters' problems. Gamble was no stranger to the schemes for money-making, internal improvement, and economic expansion that were so common in the United States during the first half of the nineteenth century. As a Richmond merchant, he and his brother Robert had obtained a contract to construct one section of the James River and Kanawha Canal. The Gambles also traveled to Europe, where John made numerous financial contacts. After spending their first few years in Middle Florida rebuilding from losses suffered in the 1820s, the Gambles and their allies felt confident enough to mobilize their considerable resources behind a bank project. Marriages and joint economic ventures had brought the Randolphs, Parkhills, Browns, Nuttalls, and other families of Virginia migrants into John Gamble's orbit, and he had built alliances with both Richard Call and William DuVal as well.[57]

With support from DuVal and the Nucleus, the charter for the Union Bank of Florida was proposed in February 1833. The Legislative Council approved it by a vote of ten to eight. Gamble was to be president, and fellow Virginians John Parkhill and Thomas Brown were cashier and head teller, respectively. The only Middle Florida representatives who opposed the proposal were Abram Bellamy, a Jefferson County politician who modeled himself after North Carolina's Nathaniel Macon, and Thomas Bradford, a Leon County sawmill owner. Both were favored candidates of local countrymen. Soon after his vote, however, Bradford suddenly faced a series of indictments for alleged sexual offenses. He soon departed the county for Alabama. Having passed the bank charter and disposed of local opposition, Middle Florida's planters rejoiced to see Governor DuVal proclaim the Union Bank the "true planters' bank" and sign it into law. "We congratulate the planters on the establishment of this institution," wrote the editor of the *Tallahassee Floridian*, "as calculated to promote the interests and develop the resources of this country."[58]

The Union Bank's charter called for an initial capitalization of one million dollars, with the option of later expanding to three million. Local landholders subscribed for the stock of the bank, for which they paid by granting mortgages on their land and slaves. The actual cash that made the wheels of territorial finance turn was to come from the sale of thousand-dollar bonds, redeemable in the 1860s, at 6 percent interest. The territory of Florida issued these bonds and backed them with its own pledge to repay them should the bank and its stockholders default. The bank then planned to lend the money from those sales back to shareholders, giving them in hard cash up to two-thirds the on-paper value of their mortgaged property.[59] This was only one of dozens of speculative schemes mushrooming into existence across the United States during the boom of the early 1830s. By 1837, Southern planter bankers like John Gamble had convinced Northern and European investors to funnel almost fifty million dollars in capital to upstart banks in return for state-backed bonds issued to banks by state and territorial legislatures.[60]

A few politicians, such as Abram Bellamy and James Westcott, questioned the legal right of eighteen Legislative Council members to burden the people of Florida with "faith bond" debts that would last for thirty years. Others wondered whether Florida's obligations as a territory would transfer to Florida the state, once that hoped-for status could be achieved. In response, Gamble and other Union Bank backers lined up a quartet of esteemed Northern legal experts, including Daniel Webster, who declared that a state was responsible for fulfilling legal obligations incurred while in territorial status. Armed with this benediction, Gamble opened the bank's books in early 1834 and began taking subscriptions for stock. But not all of those who subscribed, especially countrymen and less wealthy—or politically powerful—planters received stock. In addition, members of the bank clique served as assessors, raising complaints that they were not evaluating all property equally but instead favored their friends and relatives. The as-

Union Bank of Florida one-dollar note (Special Collections, Perkins Library, Duke University)

sessed value of one's mortgaged property determined the amount of stock one could acquire, and the amount of money one could borrow. And not all were happy that the bank—required by law to make itself accessible to all Florida citizens—only opened branches in Tallahassee, Pensacola, and Marianna.[61]

In the middle of 1834, Gamble headed north to New York and Philadelphia with a thousand bank bonds in his portfolio. He was prepared, if necessary, to draw on his contacts at Baring Brothers and other London houses, but by September, he had apparently sold all of them to U.S. investment bankers, whom his sister Catherine Wirt called his "New York confederates.". Gamble arrived home with one million dollars in cash to lend and found himself "hailed with the most lively testimonials by our citizens." An expectant Middle Florida believed that "[t]his sudden influx of capital cannot fail, if prudently expended, to advance the prosperity of this country and develop its resources." The bank began to lend money immediately, and within six months the local plantation economy was expanding rapidly, leading to a state of excitement. "The way we are going on here," wrote one local planter, "would make your hair stand on end. I mean in the matter of Banking. . . . A small territory, without a dollar, borrows millions founded on its land and negroes."[62]

The touch of money quickened economic life across Middle Florida. Slaves marched in, chained in traders' coffles. Cotton rolled south in heavy wagons toward the ports on the St. Marks River, or on barges down the Chipola to the Apalachicola in Jackson County. Local planters credited the Union Bank's efforts for the district's heady prosperity. Looking into the future, they saw even more of the same rapid development, including projects of commercial modernization that would assist the construction of ever greater planting empires: "The man who once with his hundred hands felt '*the pinch of the shoe*' for the want of 'a *bit* of ready cash' can now speculate in the stocks of lands, Rail Road, navigation companies—can now build up or destroy towns. Truly! Florida is yet the country."[63] Hopes for economic power seemed well on their way to fulfillment in the heady days that followed the sale of the bonds. Gamble's initially doubtful brother-in-law Thomas Randall wrote, "I have become a convert to this scheme . . . it is infallible here I assure you." Currency was plentiful. Local men launched ambitious projects, founding new towns like Port St. Joseph (intended as a competitor for Apalachicola) and Magnolia and Port Leon on the St. Marks River. In between "build[ing] up and destroy[ing] towns," Leon County planters helped create a railroad between Tallahassee and Port Leon, speeding the flow of their product to ships bound for Liverpool's cotton markets. The Legislative Council chartered another institution based on faith bonds, the Southern Life and Trust Insurance Company. This corporation never sold many of its bonds, which nonetheless did not prevent it from lending paper money. And in 1837, Richard Call—now the appointed governor of the territory—prepared to issue another two million dollars of faith bonds, to make up the rest of the Union Bank's total authorized capitalization.[64]

Yet the Union Bank had not united all of Middle Florida's contentious and powerful planter families. Some remained untouched by the scheme's benefits, even as the wealth of Gamble and his increasingly powerful faction inflated rapidly. In the finest traditions of frontier politics, these men used their control over the bank to distribute wealth to their families and friends. John Parkhill, cashier of the bank, wrote to kinsman Francis Eppes, recording the advantages that a Mr. Bolling, a relative or friend from Virginia, might obtain if he moved to Middle Florida: by mortgaging slaves, he could get stock "which would enable him to borrow $22,000. . . . [T]herefore he could secure a handsome estate without advancing a shilling except the interest." By leveraging his slaves, Bolling could obtain a huge sum of cash that would allow him to buy a plantation and additional laborers. But could everyone expect the same treatment? Perhaps not, since Parkhill continued, "I would rather Mr. Bolling should get it than anyone else."[65]

Two additional tactics enabled a favored few to expand their wealth beyond measure. First, someone such as Bolling, closely allied to the bank's ruling clique, could expect a highly favorable valuation of his mortgaged property, increasing the number of shares of stock he could "buy" and the amount of money he could borrow. Second, a reapportionment of stock in 1838 let few new subscribers in on the money collected by Gamble's sec-

*City of Apalachicola (1837), by N. Calyo, probably from a sketch by H. A. Norris
(Archives and Special Collections, Richter Library, University of Miami)*

ond sale of bonds. Instead, eighty-eight original stockholders received 90 percent of the new shares, supposedly to recognize the increased value of the property they had acquired from the first round of loans. Thus they could borrow still more money from the bank, pyramiding their wealth upon overlapping mortgages. A later investigation would find "its operations confined to a small circle. It was intended to be a public institution; we find it more nearly a private one. One-fifteenth of its shares are held by one man, one-sixth by three men, one-third by eleven." Those eleven were, in order of the size of shareholding, John Gamble, Samuel Parkhill, Robert Gamble, Hector W. Braden (the Maryland-born associate of Virginian William Nuttall), Elizabeth Wirt, Achille Murat, married to a Willis of Maryland, William P. Craig (a Chesapeake migrant and Nuttall's partner), and John Parkhill. After these eight—all tied to the Virginians in some way—came South Carolina's Benjamin Whitner, and then more Virginians: William Nuttall, and Francis Eppes.[66]

The Union Bank epitomized Middle Florida's factionalized, family-based political system. A clique of planters seized control of the reins of power and used their position to distribute the rewards of office and credit, rightfully possessed by all white men, to their kinsmen and allies. Gamble, not so confrontational toward other men of his class as was Call, included more of his peers in his distribution of rewards than had Call during the heyday of Nucleus control over the Land Office. But Gamble's actions rested upon the same basic set of beliefs. To many planter migrants, only wealthy, independent white men qualified as masters. Only they should control government, and among them, only members of their own faction were to reap the rewards of power. There was nothing wrong with using government as the engine to collect from the many and distribute to the few. The Union Bank was not so far in spirit from the duel—each admitted only a few to its circle of honor, each permitted only a few white men to obtain the honors and benefits of manly independence, and each was, ultimately, unstable.

Although supporters of the Union Bank of Florida had pitched their pet project as a source of credit to all farmers, to countrymen it soon became obvious that this institution did not support the independence of every white man equally. The bank, many came to fear, would enslave common white men, subjecting them to years of debt, without any of the benefits of credit. The Union Bank and its ruling clique would be "their masters," presumably making white men into slaves. Without a response to this insulting program of action, the bank's clique would believe that the "community [was willing to] yield themselves, voluntarily, to shameful vassalage."[67] While some observers still reported that "the countenance of everyone seems lit up with joy," others began to hear grumbling. And in

1837, the Bank of England shut off commercial credit to the cotton trade, panicking America's overheated economy. In response, the Union Bank suspended specie payments and sent John Gamble to Europe, where he sold the remaining two million dollars of faith bonds.

Early Middle Florida politics had become a stage on which planter men strutted in masculine roles that excluded nonplanter whites and provoked constant factional conflict even among planters themselves. Out of the unformed material of the frontier, planters sought to carve personal and familial empires just as they forced slaves to carve cotton plantations out of the woods and swamps. Attempting to master politics, planters used all the resources at their command: capital from outside to aid in their land speculation; allies in male kin to fill out the ranks of factions; and tactics from the duel's assertive styles of masculinity. Those who lost in these exchanges of insults, horsewhippings, and gunfire were less than men. Like slaves, women, or even countrymen, they could not master their world. The flush times of Middle Florida served best "hot-blooded fellows" like Richard Call. Yet even as John Gamble sailed to Europe in 1838, ready to bilk investors of two million dollars more, the debate was not over. Despite the important role that would be played by planters who felt excluded from the El Dorado of the Union Bank, in the long run, opposition to the Union Bank would rely upon the anger of countrymen denied the rewards of frontier politics and government: money and manhood. As one Floridian asserted, to be worthy of the name, a free man had to resist subordination to the command or the interest of any other man: "It behooves everyone who has a regard for his rights, to set his face against every attempt to carry things by threats, or by a vain presumptuous, and arrogant disposition toward those who will not bow the knee and shout hosannah."[68] For these men, who did indeed hold their "rights" in high regard, the Union Bank was apparently institutionalizing a "ragocracy": a class of men whose aristocratic pretensions rested only on flimsy paper money, and on equally shoddy claims to an exclusive and vaunting white manhood. A reckoning was coming, one that grew, like the political climate of Middle Florida, from white male ideas of manhood and honor. But these ideas would not be those held by migrant planters. Instead, countrymen would make their own response.

Jack in the New Ground

One time away back there was a boy named Jack. He and his
folks lived off in the mountains somewhere and they were awful
poor, just didn't have a thing. . . . Well, Jack decided one time he'd
pull out from there and try his luck in some other section of the
country. . . . He went on, went on, and pretty soon he came to a big
fine stone house up on the road. . . . A man came to the door, says,
"Hello, stranger. . . . Why, Jack, I'm the King. . . . Can ye clear
newground?" "Why, that's all I ever done back home."
—from Richard Chase, *Jack Tales*

Like the mythical trickster Jack, countrymen came to Florida
ready to clear new ground. And like Jack, they encountered many difficulties in their quest to escape poverty and reach manhood. For them, the new
ground of Florida was all one "diggins," in whose raw fields they sought to
clear room for their own manhood. Encounters with others like them, with
planter men, with "country" women, and with enslaved blacks took place
all over that new ground: in planter-dominated courthouses, in the more
egalitarian male spaces of tavern and crossroad, in the churches built on
the tireless efforts of women, and in rural neighborhoods. In some of these
places, planter men strutted, and used violence, contempt, and exclusion
to keep down insolent types. Countrymen turned against them trickery,
defiance, and other tactics, asserting their own manhood. Meanwhile, the
women of the latter class, seeking slightly different goals, used admonition
and prayer to reform men. Jack's status and character, it seems, mattered
to many in Middle Florida.

Jack is an appropriate figure for the countrymen of frontier Middle
Florida. Although many of the particular versions of "Jack Tales" that we
have were written down by folklorists who interviewed informants scattered across the early-twentieth-century South, we know that both Jack

and other tricksters were present, in both speech and spirit, on the Florida frontier. The fact that most such characters were male is no accident. In frontier Middle Florida as elsewhere, trickster tales served as instruction, advice, and means for navigating the difficult journey to manhood. Characters like Jack often appear at the borders of societies. They crop up in periods where much is uncertain: the new grounds of histories and cultures. For every countryman in the antebellum South, manhood was a new ground, a status that self-appointed superiors were unwilling to grant. Jack's tricky tactics and bold defiance would serve him well in this quest for manhood. Countrymen on the Florida frontier learned much philosophy from "dandy Jack" and his "moncky capers," as one planter referred disparagingly to the character and his stories. So if the duel was the touchstone of planter manhood, the trickster's laugh was the "one time way back" of yeoman masculinity. The trickster stories of history change, and with the passage of time, new grounds grow over with crops and eventually become old fields. The usefulness of yeoman masculinity as a counterweight to elite power would in time disappear. But before that could happen, Jack in the new ground had to remake the relationship between planter and yeoman men.[1]

In the 1830s, some Middle Florida countrymen had acquired land through potentially risky excursions into the market. They wielded mastery over dependents and slaves. Now they turned to trying to insulate themselves from the vagaries of the market, where "[t]he man who has a competency today, may be plunged into the depths of poverty tomorrow," and to the task of passing on hard-won economic independence to their sons.[2] Despite the success of some at these endeavors, the planter-countryman relationship did not change. Away from the fields and woods, the sites of mastery over black and white dependents, countrymen encountered Jackson and Leon County planter men at other sites where who was dependent and independent remained uncertain: taverns, horse races, and militia musters; Tallahassee's public market (known as "Rascals' Square"), where small farmers sold their crops; and in courtrooms and at polling places. At these and other places in Middle Florida, planters tried to enforce their own definition of masculinity. Under this code, those who did not and could not rule their worlds like plantations were hardly planters' equals.

The question of whether countryman and planter were allies or enemies is an important one for history. If we look only at the apparent cooperation of poor and rich in the Civil War — at least at the beginning of the war — the relationship between planters and common whites may appear to be one of collaboration between unequals, or hegemony. Perhaps the two groups confronted each other on certain issues, but on questions of race and gender —

Four views of Middle Florida (from Francis Comte de Castelnau, Vues et Souvenirs de l'Amérique du Nord*). Clockwise from top left:* Indian village on Apalachicola River; Apalachicola River; railroad at Tallahassee; arsenal at Mount Vernon.

their beliefs about the status of blacks as slaves, and women as domestic dependents—they forged an alliance that went beyond seeming antagonism. In some cases, historians even seem to imply that planters manipulated and tricked yeomen into supporting a Civil War fought mostly for the defense of chattel slavery. The South's peculiar institution supposedly brought "real" (i.e., material) benefits and power only to the ruling class. Thus the ruling class had to—and was able to—trick yeomen blinded by racism and other ideologies into going along with the planters' program. In this fable of puppeteer planters, consent to elite power was the repeated pattern of white class relations in the antebellum South.[3]

Planters and yeomen did agree on certain key questions. African Americans, most nonslaveholding Southern whites believed, belonged in slavery. Further, most white men saw masculinity and femininity as antithetical and believed that to lose the first led one to a state little better than the second. But these two groups of white men also disagreed on issues so basic that conflict was inevitable. Countrymen and planters certainly had different ideas about what made a man, and what that meant in the practical terms of relations between the poor and the wealthy. Most planters seem to have assumed that a modified deference would remain in place on the frontier, and that countrymen would remain in a state that all white men thought of as inferior in manliness. Countrymen, however, believed that all white men were equal, in part because all ruled dependent women and blacks. In contrast to planters who placed faith in the exclusivist violence exemplified by the duel, countrymen believed that violence established a masculinity that could theoretically include all white men as equals. Using the extravagant physicality of their rough-and-tumble fighting and the aggressive trickery of their stories and rituals, yeomen made their own case for manhood on their own terms.

We might read the sturdy independence of Jack, or the rough-and-tumble violence of those who tried to follow his example, as romanticized individualism. The exceptional "Jack," as in the story above, might have broken free of old constraints to define himself exuberantly, while most of his peers remained trapped between deference and independence. But such was not the case, and countrymen rose as a group rather than as isolated individuals. Nor were male peers the only members of community and family from whom countrymen needed help in their quest for manhood on the new ground of Florida. Reliance on the efforts of dependents made yeoman economically independent, and women in particular also enabled other changes that lifted all countrymen from political dependence to what they would consider political manhood. Women bound to countrymen by marriage, blood, and church communion consciously sought to reconstruct

yeoman masculinity in a more evangelical model. The ability of such re-
forms to ameliorate the lives of white dependents was limited. Yet widows
and matrons, in the process of trying to make life more livable by modi-
fying the behavior of men, built church communities into the centers of
wide neighborhoods. The rise of a new local politics grew upon the political strength of those neighborhoods. Political change would confirm, in a
new ground, countrymen as simply white men.

JACK GETS STROPPED

Just as there was more than one sort of white man, there was more
than one set of meanings for manly violence in early Middle Florida. But
at first glance, the sheer ubiquity of violence might have seemed more significant than its meanings. In the 1820s and 1830s, aggressive masculinity
pervaded the places where male Middle Floridians gathered. The muddy
streets of Tallahassee, Marianna, or Apalachicola on market and court days
were single-sex environments, often made both exciting and dangerous
by liberal applications of alcohol. People of all ages and conditions came
together at polling places at election time, barbecues, crossroads doggeries,
and communitywide retreats like Shell Point on the gulf coast of Leon (later
Wakulla) County or the Big Spring in Jackson. Meeting places gave men
the opportunity to acknowledge other men as equal members in the circle
of honor or to insult them, leading to conflict. "As for bloody noses," claimed
the Comte de Castelnau, a Frenchman who visited the region in 1838, describing a Middle Florida town, "they were so ordinary that one might as
well have considered them universal." Both long feuds and casual words
could lead to tragedies like the chance encounter at a Fourth of July barbecue near Marianna that led Jesse Montfort to kill Isaac Swain in 1831; or
the series of drunken arguments that led John Waters to shoot seventy-
five-year-old David Jones in June 1835. White men from all levels of society
seemed to be equipped with hair-trigger tempers. One might easily take reports like those of Castelnau as evidence that all white men believed in the
planter version of manhood. He saw one crossroads town as nothing but a
saturnalia of brutality: "The entire village seemed to be fighting; here two
drunken men were dragging themselves along to attack each other; there
farmers were amusing themselves by lashing unfortunate slaves, laughing
to split their sides at their contortions and cries; farther on young men were
blaming themselves for the murder of a relative, and murderous weapons
gleamed immediately in their hands."[4]

To Castelnau, every encounter between white men appeared to be a contest for domination. From such a perspective, the violence of the "plain people" appeared as a vulgarized dialect of planter duels' scripted actions and speech.[5] A closer look at both individual violence and the violence of the legal system in early Middle Florida, however, reveals clear distinctions. Countrymen did not speak the same language, nor did they seek from it the same kinds of outcomes, as did planters. Nor did society allow countrymen to use violence in defense of their manly honor. Jack again serves as a useful metaphor. In the first part of the story "Big Jack and Little Jack," the former goes to work for "the King." The King states, "I got a rule here with anybody I hire: the first one of us to get mad will get three strops cut out of his back, long enough to make shoestrings." Big Jack agrees to these conditions and works hard: tending sheep, plowing, and so on. Yet the King cheats Big Jack: refusing to provide tools or to feed him. "I never hired ye to eat," he tells Big Jack: "I hired ye to tend sheep." Big Jack responds in anger, "Looks like a man ought to be mad . . . work for somebody all day and starve to death. That ain't no way to do!" Then the King gleefully claims his authority under their earlier bargain. "So the King took hold on him and got him down: got out his knife and cut three strops right out of Big Jack's back." Just like "the King," the court system in Jackson and Leon Counties "stropped" countrymen who resented insult, refusing to allow equal access to the violence that made planter males into men. When countrymen fought out disputes—stating, in effect, that they were men, and therefore they "ought to be mad"—planters inflicted on them punishments more suitable to slaves, denying countrymen the legal right to manly anger.[6]

The legal systems of Middle Florida marked distinctions between one class of white men always allowed to use violence to defend their honor and another without such carte blanche. In 1832, James W. Westcott, scion of elite families from Virginia and New Jersey and political appointee of the Jackson administration, stood before the bar of the circuit court to answer a charge of assault and battery. Westcott was not unique. Between 1825 and 1833, the Leon County grand jury indicted elite men at least eleven different times for various types of assault, battery, and riot (the last being merely a legal term for several people attempting to batter each other). He was one of many who abandoned the strict script of dueling and using fists, canes, and horsewhips attempted to chastise adversaries whom they wanted to dishonor.[7]

Like most men from the ruling class who came before the Leon County court on charges of assault during the 1820s and 1830s, Westcott had little to fear from judge and jury. Despite convicting him of assault, the court fined Westcott a mere twenty-five cents plus a few dollars in costs—a typical slap on the wrist. Even including one anomalous $50 fine imposed on a man who fled bail, the average penalty levied on planters and merchants indicted for such crimes was $6.81. Richard Hayward, a merchant and planter from Maryland, was indicted at least three times for assault and battery and repeatedly faced additional charges of carrying concealed weapons and gambling. Somehow, however, Hayward never paid a fine larger than ten dollars, and that was for a gambling conviction. The judicial system rarely levied any punishment for manslaughter, the category under which homicides committed by elite men were prosecuted, if they were prosecuted at all. The ways in which elite men settled disagreements with others—whether by dueling putative peers or by "horsewhipping" inferiors—were apparently beyond the law's purview.[8]

Matters for yeomen and poor whites brought before the bar stood somewhat differently. While David C. Wilson, a Tallahassee merchant, received a fine of fifty cents plus costs for a riot conviction in April 1833, when the court convicted Jesse Wiggins, the son of a yeoman, for the same crime one year earlier, it charged him one hundred dollars plus costs. Wiggins, of course, had much less ability to pay a large cash penalty than merchants or planters who dealt in the cash economy on a day-to-day basis. Such inequity was typical: planter John S. Taylor, convicted of assault and battery in 1830, paid one dollar, but the landless Joel Yancey, found guilty of beating someone up two years earlier, was fined sixty dollars. In all, the courts assessed the twenty-one countrymen convicted of assaults, batteries, and riot a mean fine of $65.86.[9] Judges and juries convicted the poorest defendants at higher rates than members of any other group, but they also assessed heavy fines against Leon County yeomen. Several of the slaveless whites convicted were actually members of yeoman families. Others like slaveless farmer Edward Ballard, who had lived in Leon County since its founding, were hardly transients. The circuit court convicted him of assault with intent to kill in 1828 and fined him five hundred dollars plus costs, clearly an unpayable punishment for a subsistence farmer. Sentences usually mandated that criminals remain in jail until they paid their fine. Once they were assessed an overkill fine, men like Ballard faced an unpleasant choice. They could languish, humiliated by their bondage, in unhealthy, ramshackle county jails, or they could escape and leave Middle Florida forever. Most found the latter the more palatable option and fled the county for Alabama, Texas, or elsewhere, leaving only an entry on the "dead docket."[10]

Even the letter of the law discriminated against countrymen, specifically proscribing their favored fighting tactics. Their no-holds-barred style, called "rough-and-tumble" by some, encouraged brawlers to attempt to bite off opponents' noses and gouge their eyes. The Florida legal code called such tactics mayhem: the intentional attempt to maim or disfigure another person; and a conviction justified whipping or imprisonment.[11] In contrast, the courts were reluctant to establish precedents for control over either the form or actual incidents of planters' private violence. The men who sought to crop Joseph White's ears in 1825 were certainly not prosecuted for attempted maiming. The men who dominated the legal and political structures of territorial Middle Florida reserved the right to use blows and bullets to defend their own manhood. Planters always occupied a disproportionate number of the seats on grand juries, and merchants and the more prosperous yeomen filled most of the rest. Elite men also controlled the procedures of the courts. In the first two decades of settlement, judges, attorneys, and marshals did not hesitate to intervene to block petit (trial) juries' decisions that went against planter interests. When jury members, many of whom were yeomen, sentenced the Leon County slave Ben to death for murder in 1828, district attorney and judge cooperated to dismiss the case. Planters did not want to see valuable property swinging from a scaffold on Gallows Hill. Judges, not juries, often assigned fines for assault convictions.[12]

Inequities also existed in the courts' treatment of property crimes. Even rich men accused of dishonorable crimes received lenient treatment: George Chew, the ne'er-do-well, kleptomaniac son of a Virginia planter, never received punishment for his repeated larcenies. Chew received protection from other elite men so long as his sticky-fingered propensities did not become shameful public knowledge, but poor whites who committed crimes against property were expelled from the body politic. Poor whites accused of theft found themselves trussed up in public for whippings, or locked in the pillory where any person could hurl rotten vegetables (or worse) at them. Contemporaries stated that such punishments "amount[ed] to disfranchisement of the offender": white men whipped in public like slaves could no longer count on respect from any other citizen, and were stricken with impunity from voting lists and muster rolls.[13]

"Then boast and bear the crack / With the sheriff at your back / Huzza for dandy Jack," wrote one free black Southerner, well aware of the implications of what whipping "said" to others about the whipped. And thus, like Big Jack, troublemakers, transients, and resident poor whites, slavelike, lost strops from their backs to sheriffs who carried out sentences for early Leon County courts. Bob Penn was given thirty-nine lashes for burglary in 1831. John Pearce, accused and convicted of slave stealing in the same year, was perhaps lucky to escape with only thirty-nine stripes for slave stealing. Pearce and Penn bore the scars—visual signs of their dishonoring—of their ejection from the status of citizen. And although countrymen probably despised thieves enough to support harsh sentences in some individual cases, their most popular representatives criticized the large number of offenses punishable by whipping in Florida. Despite the contempt the typical yeoman may have felt for those who had been lashed and humiliated before others, he also feared the proclivity of the planter-dominated courts to devastate the lives of poor men.[14]

Courts' attempts to deny countrymen equal access to violence displayed planters' beliefs about common whites' manhood for all to see, and also replicated in day-to-day actions the ideology of domination found in the language of territorial politics.[15] Yet during the early years of U.S. settlement in Middle Florida, nonplanter white men found no easy opportunity to rectify these galling inequalities. Small wonder, then, that countrymen apparently feared both sternly real and floridly imagined threats to their status as "Freemen of Florida," to use a phrase then current. Planter-generals, many suspected, wanted to institute a property qualification for voting. If the courts would punish a countryman for the same act of violence that won a rich man admiration, no wonder that common white men were ready to believe that the acts of political clans were *"nothing less than a question of liberty* or *slavery!"* Their greed for power, and supposed desire for deference among white men, threatened the multiple kinds of independence "purchased by the blood of our fathers."[16]

For evidence that such fears had substance—that planters somehow denied them the rights of freemen, whether in the streets or in politics— countrymen looked no further than the Union Bank of Florida. Fastened by planters like an albatross to the territory's neck, the bank owed little to common whites, and gave them less. In 1838, Leon County yeoman R. B. Kerr complained that the Union Bank was "nothing but a system of reciprocal credit" among the stockholders, a gigantic insult that defrauded and oppressed yeomen. It took their money by inflating currency, left them the prospect of future taxes to pay off the bonds, and gave them nothing in return.[17] So long as territorial political culture remained unchanged, however, countrymen could do little but complain privately. But in the meantime, with fists and words, they defiantly continued to claim the right to violence, fighting for honor and manhood in Middle Florida's new grounds.

DOMICILIATED WITH THE PEOPLE

One Sunday morning, Charles Hentz, a young Jackson County physician, dressed up in his best clothes and rode with his friend, an ambitious clerk named Hazard, toward the nearby village of Olive Grove. As they passed "Crawford's doggery," a notorious drinking establishment, a number of countrymen staggered out the front door. "Although it was Sabbath morning," remembered Hentz, they "hailed us boisterously, and told us to get down and come in and get something to drink, and 'dirty our fine clothes.'" The two men refused the offer, and one can hear both wonder and disdain in Hentz's voice as he "rode on to the Ferry, commenting on such a Sabbath morning spectacle." When the two men returned a few hours later, they "rode by just as there had been a grand 'knock down, and drag out' fracas among the miserable wretches." He saw something wild indeed: "Alex Keel was standing in the piazza, with his long hair and beard in a tangled and disheveled mess, slinging his arms and shouting and swearing like a raving maniac; old man Rozier was lying insensible on the floor, where someone had knocked him down—Bill Robison, who had just stabbed an old fellow named Jonah Burns, was jumping on a horse, bare headed, with his coat (an old broadcloth one) torn open from the collar down, and flying out in long black streamers behind."[18] The lunatic brawl, lubricated by whiskey and no doubt sparked by insulting words, shocked the educated Hentz. For a while, his friend also felt intimidated by the wild physicality of these men: "Hazard thought he had come to a wild country." Yet the clerk learned one language of common white culture soon enough: "He soon, through the influence of whiskey, fell to the same level; he got to drinking, was discharged from the store, and threw himself away—domiciliated with the people."[19]

If planters' duels are the royal road to comprehending elite masculinity, physical violence and verbal challenges like those that Hentz encountered that Sabbath morning open a path into the world of Middle Florida's countrymen. For planter men, honor was manhood, and manhood, combining as it did different ideas about race, class, and gender, was identity. So it also was, in one sense, with countrymen. But given their different experiences, goals, and resources, we should not be surprised to learn that nonplanter white men understood manhood differently than did the elite of Middle Florida. Two kinds of encounters or tactics, in particular, show a yeoman masculinity distinct from planter honor. The first kind is the rough-and-tumble fight, like the one that Hentz witnessed at Crawford's doggery, which sometimes offended and sometimes intimidated elite observers. The second is the verbal tricksterism displayed by countrymen among themselves and in their encounters with planters or outsiders: challenges, jokes, and stories that tripped up the arrogant or unwary. These types of expression had dual goals: to prove one's manhood among a circle of white male peers; and to embarrass and humiliate elite men who insisted that they were superior in masculinity.[20]

To be a man, one had to fight. This was a simple fact that poor boys learned from the time they could walk. Family members taught them how to defend their honor in rough-and-tumble brawls, as one traveler to frontier Florida observed: "During the recess of court one of the grand jury men came below and found his hopeful son of some 8 or 9 years of age fighting with another boy. The father looked coolly on until it was ended and then said, 'Now you little devil, if you catch him down again bite him, chaw his lip or you'll never be a man.'"[21] Just as they worked their way out of dependence into economic manhood, countrymen learned and often defended their gendered honor as both individuals and families. Brothers John and James Dickerson attacked Asa Chamberlain four times in the first five days of January 1827. Chamberlain stayed out of their sight until March, when the Dickerson brothers found him in Tallahassee again, and assaulted him with "certain leaden weights and their fists." The brothers knocked Chamberlain down and kicked and beat him so severely that the victim claimed he needed six weeks of bed rest to recover.[22]

Rough-and-tumble fighting was neither more nor less violent than planters' duels. Yet contemporary observers and latter-day scholars described the behavior of men like the Dickersons as unrestrained and even depraved compared to the orderly executions idealized by the code. Combatants tussled and struggled, exchanging punches, gougings, and stabs, assaulting each other in ways that would have produced endless chains of duels between planters devoted to the appearance of invulnerability. Charles Hentz seemed disgusted by what he painted as an undifferentiated, primitive machismo in his characterization of the two Keel brothers, Jackson County rowdies. They were "desperate bad men; particularly Alex, who was a large man, with an immense, tawny beard, and long, tangled, unkempt hair; they were always boisterous, and ready for a fight; it was said they had killed men elsewhere." Still, on the plantation frontier, the countryman's ideals, at war with his own ambiguous place in the world, structured seemingly anarchic rough-and-tumble fighting.[23]

Insubordinate defiance characterized the genesis and the tactics of the typical rough-and-tumble fight. While wide differences gaped between the ideologies of planter and common white violence, both codes emphatically rejected "submission," the sign of unmanliness. Yeomen also defined themselves as different from other groups of people whom they considered unmanly. Women had "bland qualities," compared at least to the "bolder character of men," and African American males, almost all enslaved, were defined in whites' minds by their submission. But at the same time, countrymen were well aware that Middle Florida elite men considered them subordinates: economically dependent; political followers; forbidden to use the domination-obsessed violence of the duel; horses to be ridden.[24]

Submission to the insults of any man was therefore analogous to acknowledging that planters were right: that some white men were less equal and less manly than others. That in turn could suggest that one might not be truly "white," or truly a "man." Rough-and-tumble fights thus dredged up the class politics embedded in white masculinity in the antebellum South. In part because they risked and rejected the condemnation of planter authorities, they revealed countrymen's deep desire to be insubordinate, to be horses that would not be ridden. But fighters' ethic of insubordination ran deeper than a mere contradiction of or simple opposition to elite codes and controls. Instead, the perpetual rejection of submission was a philosophy of life: "Chaw his lip, or you'll never be a man"—fight like a wild man, go too far, or you won't be going far enough. Performances of this creed were almost predictable. At a polling place in Jackson County one election day, a group of yeoman farmers and poor white ne'er-do-wells had already been drinking and acting rowdy. Becoming concerned that they were not acting insubordinate enough, they bullied Charles Hentz into "giv[ing] them some chloroform; they having heard of its wonderful effects in the way of sudden exhilaration." He poured some on their handkerchiefs, and after they smelled the soaked cloths, "a wild scene of confusion took place." The men acted out their manhood, "yelling and screaming, and flying fists created for a while a pandemonium." Hentz meanwhile hid in a locked house but could not escape the brawling countrymen—"one of them came bounding in the window, seeking shelter from one of the Keels, who looked like a raging demon."[25]

Countrymen understood the language of planters' attempts to exert a physically defined superiority over poor and yeoman whites. The aggression of the rough-and-tumbler rebuked elite attempts to denigrate and, through the courts, to force Jack's submission in the new ground. This principle of masculine insubordination shaped much else in countryman culture. Poor white and yeoman mothers and fathers began early in life to teach their children to adopt a posture that rejected deference, specifically striking at planters' cherished symbols of economic and cultural superiority. "The Pine Crackers, the pioneers of civilisation so-called," wrote one man who traveled the "Bellamy Road" across Middle Florida in a fine carriage, "sedulously school their children to suppress the manifestation of any surprise that the equipment of a traveler may excite. I believe nothing horrifies them more than the admiration of external appearance characteristic of a gentleman. 'What are you staring at you little fool? Did you not see anyone before?' So uniform is their attention to this point that I drove daily past their cabins without appearing to attract the notice of the inmates."[26]

While planter honor rested on the appearance of invulnerability and self-control, the egalitarian masculinity of brawlers and hard-working farmers brooked challenge or even defeat but rejected acquiescent subordination. The rough-and-tumble fight showed that the countryman who was bold enough to fight accepted the consequence of bodily contingency. He might win victory, or he might suffer defeat and even maiming—a chawed-off lip or worse. Even if his body was defeated, he had not shrunk from battle. His insubordination proved, to himself and to others, not superiority but equality to any other white man—not what others dared not do, but what he himself would not fear. Yeomen and poor whites did not grow up as the allegedly unchallenged (future) masters of plantations but as both laborer and future master of dependents. Perhaps John and James Dickerson, for example, had seen each other whipped and directed to field labor by their father. They knew and had to accept both mastery and limitation, victory and defeat.[27]

For some veteran brawlers, fighting had marked on their bodies the twin signs of defiance and equality. The countenance of Johnson Cook, an outlaw sought by Leon County authorities during 1839, revealed his refusal to act the subordinate part: "Johnson Cook is between 26 and thirty years of age, weighs 140 pounds. . . . His face and hands are badly scarred with dirks and knives, which he got by fighting; has been stabbed through the muscle of the arm twice, with a dirk, also in the hip." To Leon County's elite, Cook's scars revealed his rough uncivilization, that he "thought there was no more harm in killing a man than there was in killing a hog." Scars were marks of shame, and of bodily vulnerability, in their code of honor— signs that revealed previous events of defeat and "embarrassment." To other white men, including perhaps Cook himself, these marks showed in the defeat and maiming of his body a kind of victory over submission, fear, and defeat itself. Cook would fight, regardless of whether he would win or lose, and that was all that really mattered. Though competitive, deadly, and every bit as brutal in its own way as planter behavior, rough-and-tumble fighting in the streets of Tallahassee and the doggeries of the rural crossroads also created a community of equals. The male who answered the challenge to a brawl became a man, even if left battered in the dust.[28]

Rough-and-tumble brawling was only one expression of an ethic that resonated in nearly every aspect of nonplanter white male culture. Countrymen presented themselves to the world as uncontrollable: "tall, sturdy, bold, addicted to drinking, and habituated to interlarding their words with terrible curses. . . . They leap about and howl and make no effort to restrain their passions." These physical acts signified insubordination and expressed a belief in equality among free white men. Competitive activities, even those that did not involve fighting, contained tests that required males to show both defiance and the willingness to submit one's body to potential damage or defeat. The latter demonstrated courage, but also the belief that while a brave white man was as good as one's fellows, he was also no better, no more inviolable. Drinking, for instance, carried such an imperative. To offer a dram was to offer a challenge to see whom could most readily reject sobriety; or consume the most liquor. The drink was also an invitation to submit one's body to uncontrollable forces in company with one's fellows. The man who refused to join in was a coward and a snob. Tavern habitués reacted with anger to rejection: "When I refused," reported one neo-Puritan Northerner, "they would turn around and look as if they had been shot." [29]

Verbal invitations to drink, or to dirty one's fine clothes, thus contained their own depths and tactics, as did another genre of yeoman self-definition and anti-elite challenge. When countrymen came together, they traded stories, jokes, and insults, creating a dialogue of multilayered meanings that asserted equality among white men. The verbal banter, trickery, and story-telling of backwoods characters were more than colorful raw material for writers. These tales recorded, and their tellings often contained, contests of masculinity. Migrant planters, or travelers like the one who noted this Florida encounter, stumbled in the subtle depths of word games: "A nondescript of the cracker species was seated on a log by the side of some of our fellow passengers who were sunning themselves. The old cracker was smoking lustily. Says he to one of them, 'Stranger, I reckon my smoke ain't agreeable nohow.' 'No it is not,' said the other. 'Well *move* then,' was the polite reply."

The encounter with the "old cracker" contained the essence of the tricksterism so important to the countryman's relationship to the world. Here, a leading question sets a trap, and an officious, educated individual predictably stumbles and makes a fool of himself. The traveler believes himself superior to a "nondescript of the cracker species," but he does not realize how well the object of his contempt understands him. What seems like the offer of a subordinate to oblige his better turns into a demonstration of two forceful messages about power on the plantation frontier: one man assumes that he naturally holds authority over another, and the latter defiantly refuses to grant it. The teller of the joke upended his target, leaving him feeling ridiculed and humiliated, as Charles Hentz felt on one occasion when, "bothered by a wise acre, country ignoramus—like an inexperienced fellow, I suffered him far too much." Hentz hoped that more experience would help him to avoid further encounters in which another man asserted masculinity and equality at the expense of his erstwhile "superior" in the exchange. [30]

Hentz was perhaps too ambitious, for he and his kind were in this contest outflanked. Middle Florida stories of trickster characters were complex dialogues armed with long-honed, multiple levels of meaning. On one level, the man who was tricked became less than a man. The earlier-recounted "stropping" of "Big Jack" depicts his reduction to unmanned, slavish humiliation. But as this story continues, after Big Jack leaves the King's farm, he meets "Little Jack" coming down the road and tells him what has happened. The latter goes on and enters into an identical bargain with the King. But this time it is Jack (the splitting of the lead character into "Big" and less tricky and "Little" and more tricky halves makes an obvious point) who defrauds the other man. Little Jack eats the sheep he agrees to watch, kills the mule with which he promises to plow, cuts down trees to pick their apples, and finally tricks sexual favors out of the boss's wife. The King becomes angry, thus losing both the bargain and his control of the situation. Jack, having already destroyed various signs of invulnerability, ties the King down and cuts three strops from his back, marking the planter as unmanned.[31]

Other characters (including some less well served and preserved by folklore collectors) showed the way in which trickery defied defeat, upended hierarchies, and humiliated the arrogant. "Snell," for instance, made his only known printed appearance in the *Tallahassee Star of Florida* on October 6, 1842. In the story told by the *Star*, the mayor of an unnamed town appeared, hanged in effigy, on the courthouse square one morning. The town looked like Tallahassee, and the mayor resembled the capital's humorless mayor, Francis Eppes. "This high misdemeanor," said the *Star*, "had been generally attributed to an individual named *Snell*, whom everybody seemed to know, and no one could identify." The law could not put its hands on Snell: like any good trickster, he was everywhere at once. In an impromptu court hearing, a judge called witnesses forward and tried to find out the truth about "Snell," whose name meant "quick" or "clever." One who volunteered to take the stand was "a pert, brisk looking little fellow, the ready twinkle of whose smiling grey eye as he winked knowingly to his honor, and leered rather dubiously on the clerk, told as much as if he had said, 'never mind, your honor, I can tell you all about it.'" But instead of clearing up the mystery and enabling the judge to restore proper order to the community, the witness led the court down the pathways of a ridiculous, absurd narrative. Launching into a bizarre story, he claimed to have seen Snell in the woods, riding down the railroad tracks on a teapot "with the steam pretty well up." "And I says to myself, says I, if that ain't *Snell*, it's *Roach*! And I says to him, says I, Holloa! Snell! Is that you? And says Snell to me, says he, 'you be d—.' And this, may it please your honor, is all that I know about the business." The witness had transformed himself into Snell, and so could any other countryman storyteller worth his salt. He duped the court to go with him down the tracks. They hoped to get what they wanted. Instead, he insulted them.[32]

Trickster characters and stories brought together imagination and practice. Their narratives displayed wrecked and broken hierarchies, and imported inversion into performance when they were told in the presence of elite listeners. In the Snell story, the witness's pretense of humility preceded an aggressive revelation of defiance, and the storyteller performed the same act as his character. In contrast to slave storytellers, who were far more beleaguered than the poorest whites, yeoman trickster storytellers could afford to be much more open and aggressive than their enslaved counterparts. The turn of the tale upon elite male listeners flipped the opponent's own rules against him, if, as did the King or the Judge, he lost his temper, or displayed a belief in the same sorts of inequalities that structured the duel. An arrogant planter's own beliefs about gender, after all, condemned the "loser" in any exchange—the one tricked, insulted, imposed upon, embarrassed—to unmanly status. A traveler among the "crackers" along the antebellum Georgia-Florida border noted, "Some of these fellows have a good deal of humor and have a happy facility of making doggerel poetry. A gentleman whose name was N. Burritt was the other day teasing one of these fellows for rhymes." Now Burritt was a well-known local figure and a sometime representative to the Legislative Council. "After a while the cracker commented: 'God made a man and called him Nelson Burritt / After he saw his face he was sorry for it,' thus turning a good joke upon the lawyer his tormentor."[33] Tired of Burritt's patronizing air, the "cracker fellow" turned the rhyme against him. In a sense, he became Snell for an instant, revealing his disdain and rejection of the inequality assumed by Burritt's command that an alleged inferior perform and entertain a wealthy lawyer. This countryman sharply signaled his unwillingness to be badgered and otherwise treated as unequal. He surprised the rich man with a bold insult to his face. Yet his insult contained a twist of humor, and invited a riposte, if the lawyer was quick-witted enough to come back with one.

Few planters could become as adept in the circumlocutions and subtle turns of this brand of verbal combat as long practice had made countrymen. To domiciliate with the people, one had to understand that storytelling and joking were tests not only of one's wits, but also of one's commitment to white male equality. The wise elite man—what Charles Hentz hoped to become, though he never quite succeeded—learned to efface any evidence of belief in his own essential superiority, whether he was attempting to humor lower-class voters, or simply sought self-defense. In Augustus B. Longstreet's story "The Shooting Match," set in a region of frontier Georgia

"Pair of 'Crackers'" *(from Edward King,* The Great South *[1875]; Florida State Archives)*

through which many Middle Floridians passed, the elite narrator, "Hall," riding down a country road, falls in with a backcountry farmer walking to a competition in rifle marksmanship. Hall slows his pace, and the two men begin to talk. After one awkward, straightforward verbal sally, in which the farmer metaphorically unhorses the elite man, the latter has to demonstrate

"Florida Crackers Going to Church" (from Harper's Weekly, *March 20, 1875; Florida State Archives)*

familiarity with this kind of banter "with borrowed wit, for I knew my man, and I knew what kind of conversation would please him most." The yeoman responds: "'Pretty digging!' said he. 'I find you're not the fool I took you to be.'" Had Hall attempted to assert his superiority by insisting that they speak as an elite questioner and a subordinate informant, he might have met a response similar to the smoke-sensitive traveler above.[34]

Tall tales and trickster stories allowed yeoman storytellers to challenge the authority—and thus, by planters' own rules, the masculinity—of the pretentious, while allowing other countrymen to share in the joke. Hierarchies crumbled, if only for a second. Such language games paralleled the ethos of rough-and-tumble fighting. In each case, multiple men, and white men of all classes, could win honor, in contrast to the ethos implied by planters' duels. Still, all African Americans, and white women, certainly remained outside the circle of respect. Yeoman masculinity was no ideology of emancipation, and depended in its execution upon violence, and exclusion. Yet at its core were the hints of an implicit philosophy that undermined even the exclusion of supposed dependents. For the stories and riddles of countryman tricksters also suggest an approach to the body and to material life that found an echo in the imperatives of rebellious equality behind physical insubordination. In these tales, all men and women are subject to the same rules. Even the heroes are not invulnerable, and become subject to ridicule. Unlike planter men, countrymen could and had to accept some limits and defeats, some evidence of mortality, vulnerability, and lack of mastery.

In Middle Florida, Snell, Jack, and a taste for the earthy absurdity of life enabled countrymen to fight, to tell, even to joke into being a sense of self very different from the one that planters fed in themselves, in the process of their hopeless search for imperious rule. While violent, the countryman code of masculine honor did not contain the same insatiable and destabilizing need for supremacy that pushed exponents of the bodily invulnerability espoused by planters' dueling to incessant attempts to master other white men.[35] Instead, in the extravagant physicality of rough-and-tumble fighting, and the complex and earthy humor of verbal exchanges, countryman fighters and storytellers, jokesters, tricksters, drinkers, and rowdies invited and challenged fellow white men to come and dirty their fine clothes. Thus Jack and Snell enacted a society that kept women and blacks down while simultaneously setting up all white men as equals. Those who joined in their circle, as Charles Hentz's friend Hazard eventually learned to do, "domiciliated with" the "people."

COUNTRYWOMEN AND COUNTRYMEN:
RECONSTRUCTING MASCULINITY

The wives, daughters, and sisters of common white men were as invisible to travelers in Middle Florida as they were elsewhere in the South. "The people" were not, of course, only male, and country "men" were not the only nonplanter white migrants. The male-focused terminology of the time suggests the crucial importance of understanding masculinity if we are to understand how power worked among this people and this time. Yet women's presence was essential to both yeoman households and lower-class white communities. As men knew, women worked in field and home, and gave birth to children who became laborers in youth and props to one's old age. They did not always recognize that many women would have preferred to reorganize yeoman masculinity. The wives and daughters of countrymen, scorned as they were by the planter classes, sympathized with and supported the ambition of fathers, brothers, and husbands for independence. But not all "the people" benefited from the exercise of manhood in the fighting, drinking, and verbal contests that erupted where white men came together and tried to assert their status.[36]

On the Middle Florida frontier, the production of household independence, or even family subsistence, extracted a bitter tax. Countrywomen spent their literal lives in producing life. A dozen or more pregnancies, childbirths, and nursing, all in the context of inadequate nutrition and medical care, might rack their bodies. The diseases of the fetid Florida environment also ground women down. Malaria and yellow fever did not claim as many lives in the piney woods as in the damper lowlands, but none was exempt. Children, joys to many parents, were also ephemeral, dying from "the prevailing fevers" with tragic frequency. Said one bereaved mother, "My sorrow is easier conceived than told." Nancy Hagan, who had raised seven children to adulthood, knew well how to speak the typical experience of a mother's loss:

> Dear little Cullen left me, too,
> Up to his father's arms he flew. . . .
> His little smiles so charmed my heart
> I found it hard with him to part.[37]

The migration that made independence possible for men also caused for women the pangs of separation from family and friends. The poverty that made migration imperative was all too obvious to countrywomen laboring in the Southeast's barren fields. Yet necessity does not make forced choices painless. Little wonder, then, that life sometimes seemed a long and weary journey to Hagan, who wrote in 1829: "I am a lonely widow now, my time is almost out. / Forty-seven years that's mixed with joy and grief is already turned about." Another Middle Floridian, widowed and destitute, wrote bitterly, "Mine is the frequent lot of women: poverty, loneliness, and a broken heart."[38]

Husbands and male relatives could also create traumas far more terrible than disease and separation. Rough-and-tumble fighting made a male into a man in the eyes of his peers, if not in those of his self-appointed planter superiors. But violence also exerted control over dependents like wives, children, or slaves. Tensions over economic and other pressures pushed men who already believed in violence as a means of household control into vicious, even deadly behavior. Pleas for divorce from abusive and dangerous men like John Rhymes show up repeatedly in territorial Florida's legislative records. After Rhymes married Mary Lastinger in Georgia, he abandoned her and their children in Leon County for a life of banditry and opposition to authority. Even before then, testified a former boarder, Mary "was badly beaten and threatened to be put to death by her husband." William Waugh threatened to cut his wife's throat, punched her, shot at her, and chased her through the town of Magnolia in the dark. The slaves owned by mentally unstable yeoman John Wadkins convinced him that his wife, Mahala, was sleeping with their neighbor Jesse Butler. He shot and killed Butler and narrowly missed Mahala.[39]

Some women fought back against intimate violence. Although in the ideology of manhood the sign of womanhood was submission, countrymen knew that women did not simply submit. Their refusal to be the simple objects of a male monologue of household domination may have occasionally touched off explosive domestic violence. More stable men accepted, with clenched teeth or with laughter, the distance between the ideals of male domination and the daily realities of life. Men needed women to do so much of the crucial labor of farm and family, especially on the frontier, that most wives had more day-to-day power than the ideal of masculine domination allowed. Some may have had even more: a folk song found from Arkansas to Florida tells the familiar story of the wife who not only controlled her own labor but also had direction left over for her husband's as well:

When I was young and foolish
Thought I'd never marry,
Fell in love with a pretty little girl,
And sure enough we married.

CHORUS:
Rostum, dinkum, dairy,
Prettiest little girl ever I saw,
And her name was Dev'lish Mary.

We'd been married about two weeks
Before we ought to been parted;
Everytime I looked cross-eyed
She knocked me in the head with a shovel [CHORUS]

She washed my clothes in the old soap suds;
She filled my back with switches;
She let me know right off the start
She's a-gonna wear the britches [CHORUS][40]

Stories of rebellious women who cast aside their husbands filled Middle Florida courtrooms and newspapers. Wives sometimes committed adultery because spouses were absent or otherwise unable to fulfill their sexual desires. Alfred Evans spent several months in the woods as a deputy surveyor. Returning home, he found that his wife's open infidelity while he was absent had scandalized their Leon County neighbors. In a similar example, Lemuel Turner was lying in bed, prostrated by an illness, when his doctor, Lewellyn Robertson, announced that he had prescribed Turner some medicine. Robertson added that Sarah Turner should come with him to pick up the preparation. Suspicious, Lemuel crawled out of bed and trailed the pair, and "[a]t no great distance . . . discovered your petitioner's wife and the said Robertson in the act of cohabitation." Of course, men who wanted divorces inevitably charged wives with adultery, and never revealed in their petitions if they had done something that led women to desert them for other men.[41]

Tensions within the household, whatever their cause, subjected many women to abuse and deprivation. Some feared even worse, with good reason. The murder of wives was less common than it has been in late- and postindustrial America, but domestic violence still threatened women with physical abuse and death. John Wadkins, who had murdered the man whom he believed to be his wife's lover and had tried to kill his wife as well, was a neighbor of Nancy Hagan. Her daughter was to marry Benjamin Hagan just a few days after the murder occurred. Nancy composed a warning, reminding her soon-to-be son-in-law to avoid the dangerous male behaviors that could destroy households. Lines from her poem summed up what countrywomen wanted from men:

> Son Benjamin, to you I say
> You've taken my Elizabeth away
> She has left her mother and her friends
> And gone with you this day to spend.
> Oh what courage for a child
> Whose temper is exceeding mild
> O live in love and be at peace;
> That is the road that leads to bliss.
> I hope the Lord will you prepare
> Each other's burthens for to bear
> The warning of poor Watkins take;
> His jealous wrath you will forsake.[42]

Despite the conflicts that existed within many households, women like Hagan could not think of themselves as a part of a group with interests opposed to their men. Instead, she believed that husband and wife should bear "burthens" together "in love and peace." The dust of Middle Florida fields tasted as dry in the mouths of Hagan and her sisters as it did to yeomen.

They, too, felt alienated from the upper class, which certainly considered them alien. Just as the countryman was less manly than the planter, there was something, in the eyes of travelers and planters, less feminine about his wife. Commentators portrayed her as "wretched, with a snuff brush in her mouth," or as a "most disgusting hussy." Countrywomen were aware that they worked in the fields while planter women did not. They knew that the taxes paid by their families might some day go to pay off the territorial "faith bonds" of the Union Bank. The faith bonds boosted planters' land resources and slave property, while women from landless families labored beside their husbands, trying to raise enough money to buy merely eighty acres or one slave. Such women would support the efforts of countrymen to change politics in Middle Florida.[43]

Yet even if they did not pose radical challenges to male dominance over households, women wanted to limit and transform some aspects of countrymen's behavior. Middle Florida women believed that husbands and fathers should not behave in "harsh, cruel, and unnatural" ways, including the physical and sexual abuse that often grew out of drunkenness. Rather than marriage itself, or male supremacy in public affairs, countrywomen decried the everyday evils committed by men who could not live up to their tasks as husbands, even as wives produced and reproduced independence for those men. Improvident men entangled their family's possessions by signing notes of hand to merchants and planters. Some sought to buy land, or a slave. Others lost their money in the gaming parlors and drinking places that filled Tallahassee or river towns like Apalachicola. John Runnell, for example, husband of Tallahassee's Lorena Runnell, became more and more "dissipated" until he finally vanished, and his creditors showed up and took everything except "two helpless infants to support." Alcoholism was rampant on the frontier, and for every married man "found rolling drunk in the streets . . . addicted to drinking," there was a wife afraid that the marshal would soon arrive to attach all of their meager goods. This was another side of countryman insubordination.[44]

Like most other people throughout history, women like Nancy Hagan believed some contradictory things. They accepted the outlines of the male-headed family. Divorce petitions to the legislature frequently complained that a husband who had deserted was refusing to "render [his wife and children] that protection which he was in duty bound to render." But women preferred that a husband be his wife's "bosom friend" rather than a distant or brutal ruler. While countrymen and male planters alike may have agreed that, in theory, men were the absolute rulers of households, non-planter women had rather different ideas. According to Nancy Hagan, men were in charge of marriages because they could protect families from the violence of society. While she thus accepted some of the precepts of masculine honor, her justification of male authority rested on his capabilities and responsibilities for protecting and representing the household rather than on his ability to control the household through physical violence. A husband, Hagan wrote, should "hold a gentle reign / and thus in love with her remain." In fact, she remembered her late spouse, John, as a "companion." A man should, in turn, consider his wife his "mate," a partner with a different role.[45]

Women rejected the deep nihilism that lay beneath the trickster's constant "no." In place of the abuse, drunkenness, and desertion that marred many marriages, women, especially churchgoing women like Hagan, increasingly pushed for a different model of male relationships with women. While Nancy Hagan's poems spoke of love, she meant perhaps not a romantic love but a bond between husband and wife that proceeded from a mutual respect for each other as Christians. Equally important was the alliance of man and woman in building a household and raising a family in the treacherous world. Hagan was exceptional, of course, like any other non-elite person of her place and time who has left us much in the way of written records. Yet her views could not have been too unusual, for friends and fellow church members repeatedly looked to her to mark the passages of life with occasional poems. And her wish that men would fulfill their responsibilities, as she and her sisters understood them, could not have been unusual among women of her race and class. When she put words into the mouth of a bereaved husband, he finally expressed what women like Hagan wanted to hear:

My dear Mariah took her leave
And I am left alone to grieve
Ah, she was everything to me
That I desired a wife to be.
Her bosom glowed with sacred love.
Her thoughts did often soar above.[46]

Perhaps the views of women like Hagan did not challenge their culture's deepest ideas about proper gender order. Yet they did criticize the alcoholism, physical abuse, and desertion of family that sprang from ideas about male household mastery. Amelioration, not revolution, was their goal. At the same time, their thoughts often soared above: Trusting that individual conversion would produce the desired changes in husbands, brothers, and fathers, they pursued individual religious solutions to the social problems of masculinity. In order to reconstruct manhood, they built, little by little, family and neighborhood networks in support of the evangelical churches in which conversion was supposed to take place.[47]

CHURCHES AND NEIGHBORHOODS

Beginning in the mid-1820s, common white migrants from the Carolinas and Chesapeake founded at least a dozen evangelical churches in Jackson and Leon Counties. Some historians have argued that, after eighteenth-century beginnings as institutions whose spiritual and organizational egalitarianism threatened the plantation society that surrounded them, nineteenth-century Southern evangelical churches became realms of yeoman patriarchy where wives and daughters were a silenced majority. True, men remained the most common targets of church sanctions throughout the nineteenth century, especially for offenses arising out of the competitive, egalitarian world of male fighting, drinking, and hunting. But at the same time, men in such churches tried to hold women closer and closer to ideals of sexual and familial quietism.[48] In contradiction to this picture, one group of women in Middle Florida retained a voice. Older and widowed women wielded certain forms of authority in their evangelical congregations, well into the 1840s. Some women, like Leon County's Nancy Hagan, even used church networks and religious language in their attempts to modify yeoman masculinity, although they carried out much of this work in places out of sight of the meetinghouse itself. The web of community that they wove eventually worked independent households and kin groupings together into wider neighborhoods, creating unexpected results for Jack in the new ground. In yet another way, women made countrymen into independent yeomen.

As in most evangelical Southern churches, Middle Florida women were the majority of the pious, despite being less numerous than men in the population of frontier Middle Florida. At Pisgah Methodist in Leon, they formed the clear majority of members before 1841 (57 percent) and of members who joined before or apart from their families (58 percent). As they did throughout the antebellum South, women saw to housing and feeding the circuit riders and new preachers of Methodist and Baptist churches. One group of women did even more. Older women, many of whom were widows, linked the congregation together in the days between meetings. While kinship and geographical origin united early members of many churches, matrons expanded congregations, bringing together with their visits households originally from different states and different families.[49]

Leon and Jackson Counties, could, in those early years, be lonely places for countrywomen. Once married, men and women relaxed in sex-segre-gated groups, participating in activities gendered male or female. In early Jackson County, women stayed home while men went hunting with their peers, rounded up livestock, or traveled to Tallahassee to patent land they had cleared. In Leon County, countryman "diggins" clustered closer to-gether than in Jackson, making visiting easier. When kinfolks and friends did gather together, women were almost always working. Quilting, shelling peas, making cloth, caring for the sick, and helping a sister with childbirth were all part of the production and reproduction of the household. Work brought women of some extended families together, although the constant requirements of productive and reproductive labor, added to cultural pro-hibitions against solitary travel, could also reinforce the relative social iso-lation of individual households.[50]

On the other hand, the older women who helped with the work, cared for the sick, and birthed the babies traveled with much more freedom than their younger peers. The matrons and widows of the Pisgah church, for instance, drew the lines of association tighter until they formed a net that caught some member of nearly every yeoman family in the townships around the church at the Centreville crossroads. Zipporah West, a native of Accomack County on Virginia's Eastern Shore, Elizabeth Conner, "Mrs. Umphries," and "Sister Felkel" visited local women and each other, dispensing help and advice. Such was the testimony of Simon Richardson, a Methodist preacher who rode the Middle Florida circuits for decades. He praised the efforts of the "good old sister[s]" at Pisgah, although he still counted only men as full members. A. B. Longstreet, chronicler of the Georgia frontier from which so many of these women came, recalled, "I love the aged matrons of this land. . . . They are ministers of peace, comfort, and consolation." Physician Charles Hentz admitted both their traditional healing expertise and the im-portance of gaining their respect: "[I] wish to conciliate the old ladies." In her community along the northern edge of Leon County, Nancy Hagan did similar work. Combining midwifery with her religious mission, she trav-eled from Lake Miccosukee to south Georgia, and back again, lending both a skilled set of hands and more spiritual gifts.[51]

The paths Hagan traced in northern Leon County and Thomas and Early Counties of Georgia, bringing news, comfort, and perhaps even sis-terly rebuke for sins, formed a web of social relations in each of the churches she attended. Her poetry encouraged common white neighbors to define family in the terms of the evangelical community. When Theophilus Hardie died in 1833, she composed a poem called "The Widow's Complaint" at the request of his bereaved wife. Hagan wove together familiar religious phrases with her own experience into a gift that she hoped would console Mrs. Hardie:

> My dear beloved husband's gone
> Unto his long and wished-for home
> Forced from this tenement of clay,
> Sweet angels bore his soul away.[52]

Hagan sent a letter (in poetic form, of course) to a mother in Virginia whose daughter, the mother of two children, had died in Leon County. As a surrogate family member, she linked the old states to yeoman families on the cotton frontier, and the households and settlements of evangelical communities to each other.[53] Men ran the business meetings and spoke from the pulpits, but matrons were the foot soldiers of the evangelical army, binding together the women and the yeoman households of the cotton frontier with their visiting habits:

> O how delightful is the day
> When friends together meet.
> They sit and chat the day away,
> Not fearing what they speak.
> With soothing words they then can cheer
> And help each other on.
> The Time so sweet, so quickly flies,
> We hardly know it's gone.
> I then alone with solemn steps
> And intense thought go home.
> Down by my fireside I sit,
> Entirely alone.
> I fetch to mind, for to digest,
> The converse of the day.
> All that is good I do set down,
> And throw the rest away.[54]

As countrywomen aged, their roles changed. Older women had passed the age of reproduction, and no longer needed, in the eyes of men, to be sheltered in the household as valuable sexual property. Widows and matrons were also less likely to do field work, freeing them to visit children, friends, and fellow church members. Older yeomen, if they were as successful as Jacob Felkel (the husband of "Sister Felkel"), sometimes accumulated five or more slaves. There was less need for white women's unremitting labor in such households. Widows like Nancy Hagan, who in 1830 had teenage sons, four slaves, and a nearby son-in-law, could at times count on the labor of others so that they were free to pursue other activities. One perceptive observer encountered three older women on the Georgia plantation frontier going as quietly as Hagan about the business of subterranean community-building. Two of them, both widows, had come several days' journey to visit the third, whose husband was off prospecting for land. Neither they, nor the observer, seemed to find anything unusual in the fact that they traveled unescorted, nor in the amount of news, advice, and commentary they exchanged. At the same time, older women who had spent their adult lives taking care of others felt increasingly lonely as members of their households died or set off on their own. Hagan's husband was dead, and her children were marrying. She had to travel around if she wished to see and serve her family and friends, groups that had expanded to encompass entire congregations.[55]

Women in some traditional societies gain with old age a new license to speak. Especially in matters of morality, where men have not always associated the acknowledgment of women's wisdom with the diminution of male household authority, they have sometimes acquired certain kinds of power. In Middle Florida, some women certainly spoke up in churches. A few even spoke out at political gatherings, perhaps echoing in some ways women's occasional roles as exhorters in early-nineteenth-century evangelical congregations. Nancy Hagan, already an unofficial lay minister and visitor, became a witness in controversial church matters. Her poetry, read out loud on Sundays, summoned wider circles of men to right their moral compasses. In "On the Death of Isom Johnson," she criticized the quintessentially male pastimes of horse racing and gambling. After being killed by a fall from his steed during a race, Johnson became the symbol of what could happen to any sinful young man who did not right his ways:

> Your friend is dead, laid in the clay.
> A solemn call for you today.
> Young men, I pray a warning take,
> And all your vain pursuits forsake.[56]

Hagan would not be silenced. She did not read her poems only to mark the passages of deaths and partings. In 1838, she marched to the front of her church and called upon its members to renew their material and spiritual commitments to building the church as a community alternative to that offered by the sinful world:

> My Christian friends, will you now hear
> A word not whispered in the ear

But spoken aloud to all around
Whose feet now tread this hallowed ground
The worldlings they with minds so rash
To circus riders pay their cash.
And we are young and strong as they,
But yet our preacher gets no pay.

Hagan underlined her call for members by laying ten dollars of her own upon the table. After all, the worldly people found plenty of money for frivolous amusements like Mr. Waterman's traveling circus, which had just left Tallahassee. Thus she shamed a congregation into supporting its preacher.[57]

Hagan's independent streak eventually caused her to lead other members of her church in opposition to its 1842 decision to join the doctrinally conservative "Anti-Missionary" movement. This movement arose from several sources, including dogmatic contentiousness over predestination. More importantly, many male Baptists desired to keep at bay the innovations of modern evangelicalism, such as Sunday schools, or the religious instruction of slaves. These new-fangled ideas supposedly threatened their control over their churches and households. Hagan, in contrast, urged Baptists to "preach this gospel to Ethiope's land," urging the instruction of slaves, and of Indians, too. Although she was a slaveholder, and no abolitionist, Hagan opposed some of the men of her church on these issues, which implicated white male control over dependents. Eventually she and six other members (three of them female) of her old congregation, all excommunicated for pro-mission beliefs, helped organize Liberty Baptist Church, just over the Georgia border in Thomas County. The widow became the new church's first secretary.[58]

Nancy Hagan was, of course, exceptional. Many countrywomen were illiterate, and almost none wrote poetry. Yet the experiences that shaped her life were anything but unusual, and her response to those experiences is thus deeply relevant to understanding how nonplanter white women lived on the plantation frontier. Her beliefs about evangelical religion and about the need to reform men, and her role as a community-building matron, were all typical in frontier Middle Florida. In Hagan's poems, one sees illustrations of a hidden rural world in which matrons and widows were not silenced in, or outside, churches. Like their ability to travel without male chaperones, matrons' ability to speak out as moral guardians rested upon their age, their psychological status as pious community mothers, and their graduation from the laboring and sexual processes of making masculinity. Matrons, who also tended to be the closest allies of preachers, did not run

Southern churches, but neither did they act as if women must be utterly submissive.[59]

Many men of Hagan's class understood that like her, like the "good old sisters" of Pisgah, and like the Mrs. Brown who cared for the ill of eastern Jackson County, women were the glue of yeoman community. Through Hagan's last twenty-five years, almost all of which she spent as a widow in Middle Florida, she was a constant presence in the lives of her children, her neighbors, and her fellow church members. She handled the Florida land affairs of her son Jesse, who had moved out to Texas. Jesse wrote to his mother, begging her to join him and offering to send the money for her journey despite his near penury in the new settlement. But she never made this final migration. She died in 1846, at the age of sixty-five. As befit someone who had offered so much to her God, believed her daughter-in-law, "Mother died happy." Local folklore acknowledged her importance, remembering Nancy Hagan as "a very godly woman" and "a great spiritual power in her church."[60]

The foundations of yeoman community that were laid down by the tireless labors of old women extended beyond the church where the message originated, even to the borders of formal politics. At a public barbecue thrown by pro–Union Bank Whigs in 1840, for example, a countrywoman stood up and interrupted the hosts, derailing their agenda. To one newspaper writer, the refusal of this women to sit quietly at a political meeting came as a shock. "The *finale* was the speech of an old woman at Monticello," he wrote, "who seemed to have got a good hold of one idea at least. 'It's of no use,' said she, 'for the Bank men to come here and make speeches and fine promises to the people.'" She gave her patronizing hosts an unvarnished piece of her mind: "We know what it all means, and we know that when a poor man goes to Tallahassee to enter an eighth of land, he has to take one hundred and fifty dollars in Union money to get a hundred to pay for his land. It's of no *use* for them to talk to us until they make their money better."[61]

This direct intervention in electoral politics was unusual, but "old women" and "aged matrons" had never been entirely silent in Middle Florida. Also significant were the effects of the institutions and networks they had created. In 1839, yeoman churches became the centers of resistance to the Union Bank, the locus of political action, and the places where communities gathered together to hear speeches. The central role of the churches was no accident. They were crossroads where increasing numbers of yeomen gathered on Sundays to worship in groups that bridged kin networks. Yeomen in evangelical churches came to know one another as peers beset by the same problems. There, they created a strength that transcended individual families and households, institutions that previously could do little against the power of land speculators, or the economic problems caused by a legislature beholden to upper-class factions. One day yeomen would no longer need the women who made this possible. In fact, women might even become an embarrassment, as was the old woman at Monticello already to the more educated. Although men would quiet them, they have never been silenced. Their achievements had laid a foundation stone upon which countrymen stood to reach for political masculinity. In the communities built around the churches by countrywomen, men found the collective strength to do what Nancy Hagan strove to do, according to her God's word: "Fear not the men of high degree, nor love the world for wealth, / But shun their ways and visions, too, and all their vain longed pelf."[62]

By the end of the 1830s, at least two systems of masculinity existed among white Middle Floridians. While hot-blooded fellows among the planter class squabbled and shot at each other over political power and status, would-be yeomen held and acted out different self- and collective concepts. Yet, while yeomen felt security and status within the confines of their "diggins," political life, which brought together white men from various neighborhoods and classes, failed to respect them. Worst of all, the Union Bank supplied a favored few with capital, while oppressing all other citizens by making them responsible for the loans of failed debtors. Opposition to planter arrogance was constant. Jack the trickster cut capers in the new ground. And we also know from the things that politicians appealing to countrymen said to potential constituents during the 1840s, that the official denial of the perquisites of manly violence (for instance) to yeomen rankled deeply. But before 1839, countrymen had not confronted with direct political action the power held by speculators, duelists, aristocrats, office-seekers, and Union Bank officials over Middle Florida communities. Thus the following incident marked something new.

On an election day in the fall of 1839, planter/merchant Richard Hayward rode out with his friends, Tallahassee supporters of the Union Bank like himself, to the Centreville crossroads, at the heart of the yeoman neighborhood formed around Pisgah Methodist Church. Hayward, a violently aggressive planter and merchant from the Eastern Shore of Maryland, certainly seemed to enjoy beating and whipping others, perhaps more so than was entirely prudent. He had thrashed the Seminole leader Tiger Tail, helping to turn him into one of the most embittered guerrilla leaders of the Second Seminole War. Even as an old man, remembered an ex-slave, Hayward eagerly administered whippings to both his own slaves and those of his son. Masculinity, the use of physical violence to inflict humiliation, and the dominance of others in hierarchies of slavery, class, and gender were inextricably intertwined in Hayward's life.[63]

On this particular day the Union Bank was at last becoming the issue in a Middle Florida election. Hayward took it upon himself to ensure that all went well for the pro-bank side in a neighborhood that was emanating increasingly loud grumbles against bank power. But when he arrived at the militia muster grounds next to the Pisgah church, Hayward encountered a surprise. There, at the polls, expressing his anti-bank opinions in the defiant tones of Snell, was a bold yeoman named "Governor" Barnes, arguing without restraint for his own anti-bank candidate. Hayward announced his intent to thrash Barnes like a slave, but instead the hot-blooded fellow received a dose of a new medicine:

> Barnes was a formidable antagonist, being a heavyweight and muscular throughout. Stripping hurriedly for the fight, the countryman plunged into Hayward with his head, and while the blow of the latter resounded on it, Barnes got "all underhold"; and then the contest resolved itself into a tug and tussle, neither being able to deliver a blow, until Hayward was pressed against and partly over a cotton gin about waist high, when friends ran to separate the combatants. Hayward begged to be let alone, but they were pulled apart.[64]

Hayward was bleeding profusely from his forehead. He may not have wanted at first to admit what his friends had known, but he was beaten and could have been badly hurt if Barnes had been allowed to continue. Barnes was a rough-and-tumble fighter and had probably done hard field labor much of his life. From the outset, Barnes had made the confrontation into his kind of fight. He stripped off his clothes, a common tactic among non-elite Southern brawlers. But instead of the dueling ground, on the state line, in the presence of solemn seconds, or the courthouse, where the planter-dominated machinery of justice punished slaves and common "loafers and blackguards," Barnes and Hayward fought in Centreville before crowds of hooting countrymen. Rather than planter intimidation, the decisive tactics were now majority force and yeoman insubordination. Hayward had indeed blundered onto yeoman turf.

Hayward had been accustomed to having his way with opponents. If they backed down, they were cowards in their own eyes and in his, and if they fought they did not win: either he or the elite-dominated courts inflicted their punishment. He had thus marked them with submission and slavery, thrashing inferiors, unmanning the insolent. Looking back at this incident from the end of the nineteenth century, the memoirist who observed it is at pains to paint Hayward as every bit as physical as his working-class antagonist. He is no overcivilized aesthete but the ideal of the athletic man. Such were the insecurities of elite white men in the late nineteenth century. But the remarkable thing is not that Hayward was not immediately knocked silly by a muscular man undoubtedly trained the hard way in rough-and-tumble fighting; the significant fact is that Barnes sought out the confrontation in defiance of what Hayward might do to him in a planter-dominated court. In Barnes, Hayward met a man who would not be unmanned by intimidation, or by a defeat expressed in elite styles of punishment. Now, in 1839, Barnes was ready to participate in politics as a white man, equal, in his own eyes, to Hayward, and to fight on his own terms. Hard opposition to the deference that yeoman migrants despised in North Carolina, Virginia, and other states and had quelled in themselves crystallized in this encounter. Hayward and his friends would soon have to realize that they could not intimidate all countrymen. On juries, in elections, and in everyday encounters, yeoman anti-elitism and passion for white male equality was about to become more vocal than ever.

Hayward and Barnes, in this account, later made up their differences. The planter accepted the yeoman's equality in masculinity.[65] In parallel fashion, massive yeoman support for a new politics would compel change, as countrymen forced their views into Middle Florida politics. Perhaps we could call the ascent of yeomen to the acknowledged status of white manhood, and their consequent cooperation in trying to perpetuate black slavery, by the name of hegemony. But even if that would be useful, we must remember that hegemony was not eternal but was made in the crucible of historical events. Yeoman and planter alliances began not with a concerted effort planned in the back rooms of planter manipulation but in the angry insistence of countrymen that they be treated as masculine equals. Countrymen were not, of course, planters' equals in wealth, political power, or even in mastery over women and blacks. But they claimed equality on other grounds, forcing planters to acknowledge their honor, and their right to make claims in politics for the recognition of their own white manhood. The agreements that eventually united white Southern men across the barriers of class were unplanned and contingent. Planters, no puppeteers, did not want to move to their new position. They did not manipulate the ideological debates that led to such an outcome, even if they secretly continued to consider themselves innately superior to countrymen. Soon they dared not say it. On the Florida frontier, common white males had become, they believed, men.

Decline and Fall of the Rag Empire

THE CRISIS OF MIDDLE FLORIDA

"Commerce was king" — and Rags, Tag and Bobtail his cabinet council. Rags was treasurer. Banks . . . did a very flourishing business on the promissory notes of individual stockholders ingeniously substituted in lieu of cash. They issued ten for one, the *one* being fictitious. They generously loaned all that the directors could not use themselves.

—from Joseph Baldwin, "How the Times Served the Virginians . . . The Decline and Fall of the Rag Empire."

One day in late March 1841, idlers lounging on the square in front of Tallahassee's capitol building were treated to a most amusing scene, one that carried a wry taste for anyone who remembered planters leading droves of newly purchased slaves through the square toward the plantation districts. Trailed by a crowd of interested spectators, Deputy U.S. Marshal John F. Kachler strode from the county courthouse a few blocks away to the Union Bank building on the square's south side. In his hands, he held a writ of judgment ordering the bank to pay Dr. J. Mitchell $1,195 in specie. When he reached the bank, Kachler prepared to auction off the building itself, but at the last minute, bank president John G. Gamble and his clerks emerged, carrying sacks of money. They counted out gold dollars and silver half-dollars and returned to the building for more. By the time they had finally counted out enough to cover the debt, Gamble and his employees had given the marshal $400 worth of the bank's last nickels and dimes. The Union Bank had been the financial engine of a plantation frontier and the symbol of elite power. The institution's loans had sponsored the importation of thousands of enslaved human beings into the area and put dollars in the pockets and swaggers in the steps of migrant planters. The bank's direc-

Capitol building at Tallahassee (from Francis Comte de Castelnau, Vues et Souvenirs de l'Amérique du Nord*)*

tors had defied not just the national depression that began in 1837 but even the voters of Florida. By 1841, in order to save the bank from the vortex of debt that he and his allies had helped to create, Gamble was scraping small change off the bottom of the vault. No doubt some indebted folks looked at the sad little canvas bags of coins that backed the extravagant bank notes in their pockets and reflected on how few supplies those pieces of paper would purchase during the coming year.[1]

Few could have predicted the twisting course of change during these years. In Jackson and Leon Counties, war with the Seminoles increased federal influence in local politics, terrified planters with the prospect of disloyal slaves and poor whites, and brought a new sense of vulnerability to the areas raided by guerrilla bands. Then, yeoman electoral revolt and the introduction of a party system swept factions from political power in Middle Florida. Neither intimidation nor conscious manipulation could maintain the old way of deferential politics. Economic transformations added to the sense of confusion, as thousands of court suits crowded the dockets of Jackson and Leon Counties, wiping out planter dreams of commercial power and success. The years of crisis produced a sensation of profound vertigo.

NECESSARILY A FRONTIER

In retrospect, even the most generous of historical estimations must admit that Florida's planter-politicians brought the Second Seminole War upon themselves. Even though the 1824 Treaty of Moultrie Creek removed almost all Native Americans from Middle Florida itself, men with the ear of the federal government, like delegate Joseph White, had urged the complete removal of the Seminoles from the territory. Such planters wanted to excise the threat posed to the stability of plantation order by the Seminole presence. By 1835, the federal government concurred. It abrogated the Treaty of Moultrie Creek and pushed older Seminole leaders into consenting to a move to present-day Oklahoma. In response, younger, more warlike Seminoles, led by Osceola, murdered acquiescent chieftains and attacked U.S. Army outposts in southern Florida.[2]

At first, Middle Florida's elite men welcomed the war, considering it a splendid opportunity to win laurels. Planters associated with the Union Bank and Nucleus factions received plum assignments and rose to high ranks. General Richard Call received a battalion of militia to command. Colonels Leigh Read, Samuel Parkhill, and Richard Parish also led troops off to war. But soon a disheartening series of reverses in southern and eastern Florida provoked a long and bitter conflict between Middle Florida's politicians and the U.S. Army. Each accused the other side of incompetence and cowardice. In 1836, Richard Call, now the territory's appointed governor, assumed control of all military operations in Florida at the behest of President Andrew Jackson. The result was soon military and logistical disaster. Jackson was compelled to relieve his old friend of military command.[3]

A succession of regular army commanders could do little better, however, and although Call continued as governor, his constant carping annoyed Jackson's successor, Martin Van Buren. Call and others, arguing that the regular army had done little of value in the war, continually pressed the United States to take into service mounted militia units led by local politicians. Career generals like Winfield Scott and Zachary Taylor, tired of planter officers' incessant seeking after glory, insisted that most of the volunteers be enlisted as infantry. Marching and tramping was not to the tastes of Florida planters, so they refused to join as foot soldiers. The territory's whites also distrusted generals' attempts to establish treaties with the Seminoles. Settlers insisted that the only acceptable conclusion to the war was extermination of the Seminoles or the removal of all surviving Indians to the west: "If [they remain] located in Florida, all our runaway slaves will find refuge and protection with them."[4]

By November 1839, Van Buren decided that he could endure Call no longer, and replaced him as territorial governor with East Florida judge Robert R. Reid. Call's local allies were furious at Van Buren, but they had pressing military problems to face. After 1837, conflict with the Seminoles had slowly degenerated into a vicious guerrilla war. Tallahassee newspapers argued that whites must destroy Indian cornfields and settlements still hidden in the southern Florida swamps: "The war must be carried into Africa."[5] Like the Roman consul Scipio, originator of the strategy, Seminole bands were already trying to relieve pressure on their home territory by slipping over the Suwannee to strike the enemy at home. Guerrillas began to raid Middle Florida with great frequency, burning houses, robbing wagon trains, and killing whites, blacks, and livestock in Jefferson and eastern Leon Counties. Looking for several specific white planters, Tiger Tail's band raided Green Chaires's plantation in eastern Leon County one night in 1838. They burned the big house and killed Chaires's wife and sister. His daughter hid under a blanket in a cotton field, escaping prowling raiders who searched for more enemies. A raid on Bailey's Mills in Jefferson County in late July of the same year killed a Mr. Singletary, his wife, and two children. This location, one planter wrote in terror, was "entirely within the frontier." Other bands traveled along the coastal swamps by canoe, such as a party of Seminoles that came up the Ocklocknee in July 1838 and killed a man named Lasley and his daughter. To make matters worse, fugitive Creek Indians resisting removal from Alabama raided down the Chattahoochee Valley into Jackson County in 1836, 1837, and 1839, killing more than a dozen whites along the river.[6]

Raids like the one that ravaged Green Chaires's plantation struck directly at planters' need to project a manly invulnerability. Or so one might guess from their complaints. Joseph White had whined to an earlier federal administration that "every plantation . . . is necessarily a frontier." "I will not waste your time by pointing out the perils to which a planter so situated is subjected," White added, and then enumerated them anyway: "The inability to procure relief, when he is threatened with the Tomahawk: the certainty of insult." In their imaginations, planters faced physical torture, the rape of women, and the theft of possessions. They could find no "relief" from this "insult" that struck at the illusion of mastery: not in the law; not in the duel; not in the cowing of subordinates, for Seminoles refused to accept what planters believed slaves and other subordinates acknowledged.

The Seminole War's dangers threatened to subject elite whites to what the enslaved faced every day.[7]

Even old allies perceived the planters of Middle Florida as suddenly emasculated, submissive, unable to assert their invulnerability. When Joseph White went to Andrew Jackson to ask for more troops, the president taunted the delegate with his constituents' inability to defend themselves: "Let the damned cowards defend their country. . . . [T]hey ought to have crushed [the Seminoles] at once if they had been men of spirit and character." Jackson then suggested a drastic remedy for those who could not silence their enemies: "[T]he men had better run off or let the Indians shoot them, that the women might get husbands of courage, and breed up men who would defend the country." If the planters of Florida could not prove their manhood by defeating the Seminoles, then they were bound to be deficient in other areas as well. The president, no stranger himself to the vaunting language of elite Southern masculinity, knew very well what he was saying, and he chased White out of the Oval Office to make his point more clear. This Indian war impugned the ability of Florida's elite males to establish their mastery as men. Planters were supposedly able to protect everything that touched their honor: bodies, reputations, households. If their invulnerability disappeared, what made them distinct from those below?[8]

Thus it comes as no surprise that planters repeatedly expressed fears that the war not only would "desolate Middle Florida and drive off all the negroes," in White's words, but would also destabilize all racial hierarchies. During the first months of 1836, many enslaved African Americans confirmed planter anxieties by fleeing plantations along the St. John's River in eastern Florida. Many of these fugitives joined the Seminoles, who already had "slaves" of their own, and settled in allied villages of "Black Seminoles." No similar burst of marronage occurred in Middle Florida, but each rumor of attack in Middle Florida increased planter anxiety.[9] Just as frightening as the possibility of a revolt of subordinates was the belief that some whites had joined the Seminoles and fugitive slaves. For example, a man named Linton claimed in June 1839 that he had somehow sensed an ambush set for him in the woods along the Leon-Jefferson County border. Sneaking around behind the hammock where his assailants hid, Linton claimed later, he had seen eight Indians and one white man waiting for him to come down a trail. In another incident, when Seminoles slaughtered celebrated naturalist Henry Perrine in his South Florida outpost, a white man allegedly participated in the attack. And an 1841 party that killed and robbed four whites on the Magnolia road supposedly contained twelve to fifteen Seminoles, "headed by one white *devil*." An opponent who scalped and skulked like the Indians, burned with the rebellious slave's thirst for revenge, and was led by white race traitors was a fearful prospect for planters to contemplate.[10] As they sometimes do, these nightmares contained elements of prophecy. And as enemies penetrated "entirely within the frontier," other conflicts bubbled up to the surface of white society itself.

BEGINNING TO FEEL LIKE AMERICAN CITIZENS

Middle Florida's political crisis began with angry debates among wealthy and powerful men about the role and status of the Union Bank. Quite simply, the institution made some of them much more wealthy and powerful than others. In the unbalanced reapportionment of 1838, 90 percent of the shares and new loans went to 88 old stockholders, while 152 new subscribers got only 10 percent. These transactions came on the heels of a suspension of specie—gold and silver, rather than bank-issued paper— payments during the international financial panic of 1837. The institution's refusal to redeem its notes in specie irritated hard-money ideologues like Leon County's James Westcott, as well as the region's countrymen, who argued that the unstable values of bank-backed paper notes created another way for the rich to fleece the poor. During the Legislative Council session of January and February in 1838, Westcott and others attempted to rein in Gamble and his faction. But bank supporters defeated their proposal to put the Union Bank under the direct supervision of the council, calling opponents a group of poor men "with nothing to lose," and thus incapable of responsible oversight.[11]

Among the new, and shortchanged, shareholders were John Branch— a former state governor, presidential cabinet member, and U.S. senator from North Carolina—and members of his extended family. Branch, limited to a paltry few thousand in loans by his late arrival at the barbecue of credit, complained that among the directors appointed to oversee the bank's operations were *"the brother of the [its] President and also the brother of the cashier."* He claimed a principled opposition: "I have deprecated . . . ," he wrote to Martin Van Buren, "the insidious encroachments of a Paper aristocracy. The Banks in this Territory owing to injudicious legislation have the most alarming powers conferred upon them." One newspaper writer satirized Branch's recovery of anti-bank principles that he had not publicly espoused in a decade: "I am opposed to loaning, selling, or bartering away the public credit, unless I or my relatives can get something from it." Indeed, Branch's male relatives, including son-in-law Leigh Read, were growing vocal. Read, a former Richard Call protégé, spoke out against ex-

Nucleus and current bank men. Branch, in fact, blamed Call for both the dominance of the bank faction and a growing rivalry between their families: "[T]he Governor . . . seems to be content to *retain*, or *put* in such persons as are most acceptable to the leading influences in the Bank."[12]

The issue of Florida's status in the federal union had also come to a head. While territorial isolation had rewarded men like Richard Call and John Gamble, they believed that statehood would serve them even better. Citizens allegedly felt the inferiority of territorial status as "vassalage," a "galling and humiliating disfranchisement" that impugned their manhood. Middle Florida leaders argued for immediate statehood, although many citizens in the east and west worried about another vassalage, fearing that the region that dominated the territory would have even more overweening control over a state. By 1837, planter-politicians had mustered enough support in the Legislative Council to call a constitutional convention for the winter of 1838 at St. Joseph, on the gulf coast south of Jackson County. After creating a constitution, Florida could petition Congress for recognition as a state in the Union. Those elected as convention delegates would have the power to shape the state for years to come, so campaigning was intense. Leon County split its votes, electing bank men George T. Ward, John Taylor, Thomas Brown, Samuel Parkhill, and William Wyatt, and anti-bankites James Westcott, Leigh Read, and Leslie Thompson. Jackson sent Thomas Baltzell and Alfred Woodward, along with bank supporters Richard Long and Samuel Bellamy.[13]

Soon after opening, the St. Joseph convention degenerated into a battle between pro- and anti-bank groups. After Samuel Parkhill nominated former governor DuVal to preside, fellow Leon County representative Leigh Read nominated Robert Reid (not yet governor, at this point) in opposition. Reid won narrowly in the first of a series of close victories by a coalition cobbled together by East and West Florida representatives, with anti-bank men from Middle Florida. As the combative James Westcott maneuvered to keep the alliance together, DuVal's pro-bank allies sarcastically thanked him for "his universal action and unlimited efforts to conduct the entire business of the body." "Where," they wondered, "was ever such indefatigable activity, such willing sacrifice of watching and labor evinced on the part of a single individual to save his fellow-laborers from the trouble of thinking and acting for themselves?"[14]

Westcott, born in Virginia but raised in New Jersey, had come to Florida in 1830 already well schooled in party politics by Martin Van Buren. Westcott had been Van Buren's New Jersey lieutenant, helping his allies to organize a system of local meetings and committees, linked to state conventions, which produced ideological platforms and candidates pledged to support them. The victorious candidate who deviated in office from his stump-speech promises to ally himself with others of his party in the legislature could expect repudiation in the next election. Party structure bound politicians to voters, and voters to the nationwide issues and ideologies. Now, Westcott replicated Van Buren's achievement—the creation of the national Democratic Party—on the smaller stage of Florida. His Florida political organization cohered around "party principle," not the personal preference that held factions together. The new party system combined old republican ideologies with the supposed readiness to place any white man of correct political principles into any office.[15]

Westcott organized the anti-bank representatives, as his pro-bank opponents implied, but he was not alone. Recently converted bank opponent Thomas Baltzell of Jackson County, a former DuVal associate, proposed a series of anti-bank resolutions. Robert Reid, Leigh Read, and Abram Bellamy also helped to lead the anti-bankites in the convention. By the time it adjourned in January 1839, they had pushed through a distinctly anti-bank constitution. Its rules required a strict specie basis for new banks and submitted existing organizations to annual examination by the legislature. To cap off their success, the victors announced a meeting at a St. Joseph's hotel to organize a Florida Democratic party. The meeting proclaimed adherence to the "principles" of the national Democrats, including "the Jeffersonian Republican faith" and opposition to abolitionism. They promised to repudiate the factionalism of the previous eighteen years, with all its "personal excitements, not originating in principle." And national Democrats' supposed principle of hostility to inequitable state support for the economic endeavors of a single privileged class began to refocus debate onto the substantial issues that would shape the future of white male freedom.[16]

During the first eighteen years of territorial Florida's history, few politicians had either spoken or acted in the terms of yeoman beliefs about the Revolution's republican legacy of white male equality. The general body of Middle Florida voters simply had not had the choice to vote for representatives who believed in the ideals that they held dear. Countrymen had little control over who ran for office—"nominations" occurred at elite planter gatherings preplanned and directed by "managers." Those who did run were wealthy enough to afford the time and expense involved, and prominent enough to have a reputation outside of their own precincts. But now the old way was changing, and after the 1838–39 constitutional convention, many Middle Florida delegates returned home energized for a crusade against the faltering Union Bank.[17]

The geographical epicenter of 1839's political revolution in Middle Florida was the Centreville crossroads, in the heart of the neighborhood initially knit together by the women of Pisgah Methodist Church. Records do not reveal precisely who called "a large and highly respectable meeting of the citizens of the Pine-Lands" held at the Centreville muster ground near Pisgah on June 22, 1839. Many planters from the area attended, including members of the Branch, Bradford, Ponder, Bembry, and Hunter families. The yeomen, however, far outnumbered the "better sort." Undoubtedly accompanied by women as well, countrymen from the Mattox, Sanders, Shehee, Felkel, Houck, Gramling, and other families appeared in great number. All agreed that the Union Bank posed a serious threat to their manly freedom. "Their confidence had been abused," reported one correspondent. In both planter and yeoman ideas about gender, men who were tricked and did not respond had lost honor, and the bank's directors had clearly perpetrated an insulting fraud on the community, promoting "an elevated few not entitled to more consideration than the majority of our community." To rebut the insult to their economic and political manhood, the men of Centreville pledged that if the bank did not resume specie payment by October 1 of that year, they would not accept its bills in exchange for their cotton crops now in the fields. In order to include yeomen whose main cash crop was not cotton but corn or livestock, the men also promised not to accept Union Bank paper "for anything else which we may have to sell." Most important, they announced their refusal to vote for any candidate in the fall's legislative elections who did not pledge to force the Union Bank to resume specie payments. The meeting's participants pushed candidates to take open stands for or against the bank and promised to use their votes to enforce principles in politics.[18]

The list of men who signed the pledge shows the mixed character of the Centreville gathering. Fifteen might be called planters, including Leigh Read, a man who openly sought countryman support by attacking the bank. Eleven more were yeomen from the area, outnumbering in one fell swoop all the countrymen whose names had entered Florida newspapers because of their political activity in the previous twenty years of American settlement in Jackson or Leon County. Four were members of the Pisgah church, and five others claimed connections to the congregation through the membership of wives or other family members. The meeting proved the model for July and August meetings in Tallahassee of a group now calling themselves "Democrats," in which Centreville yeoman John Felkel participated as a member of the "Committee of Correspondence." Meanwhile, in Marianna, Thomas Baltzell told a gathering of Jackson countrymen that the Union Bank submitted the property of all of Florida's citizens to outside control. Following Centreville's lead, voters throughout Middle Florida during the summer and early fall of 1839 pledged to support only anti-bank candidates in the fall, and candidates in turn promised their willingness to be held accountable. Borne on a wave spreading out from Pisgah Methodist Church, the anti-bank Democrats swept to victory in the fall of 1839, winning three of Leon's four seats and both of Jackson's two, thus controlling the territorial house.[19]

Yeomen began to feel their strength as citizens, and as a potential majority of the electorate. Democrats directly associated themselves with countrymen, at least in political discussion. "We had rather have the opinions of a plain *Democratic* farmer on such questions" as the bank's responsibilities to pay off its bonds, wrote one Democrat, than that of expert lawyers like Daniel Webster, whose pronouncements bank defenders trotted out at every turn. Middle Florida Democrats made ready use of class resentments sharpened by bank inequalities. Their opponents were "gentry," but the anti-bank forces were "the people of Florida." On a national level, pro-bankites' allies, the Whigs, "cannot help letting out . . . their aristocratic feelings." Democrats' attacks on the Union Bank included specific references to cultural and economic inequities experienced by yeomen. While bank debtors, "capitalists and speculators," had acquired "negroes, horses, and merchandise," the failure of the stockholders was likely to mean that the "plain *Democratic* farmer" would have to pay hundreds of dollars in extra taxes.[20]

Meanwhile, the increasing connections to national parties meant that national politics began to have consequences in Middle Florida, beyond who would be in or out of appointed posts: "We began to feel like an *American citizen*," said one Tallahassee commentator. The party system itself was an ideological statement against Middle Florida's factional politics, and Democratic politicians took from the national level not just a model of party organization but also an ideological approach that catered to countrymen. The hostility of countrymen to planters' quest for economic, cultural, and political domination made the Democrats' political rhetoric relevant, and in fact supplied much of its vocabulary and imagery.[21] Such rhetoric was hardly unique to Florida. In other plantation frontier states, voters heard constantly about machinations of supposed "royal parties" bent on destroying the rights of freemen. Floridians employed this syntax later than their neighbors, but they called on the same view of political history as a struggle against plotters bent on driving yeomen into feminized submission. In Jackson and Leon Counties, Democrats identified their enemies with the opponents of Jeffersonian republicanism. Jefferson, editors assured their readers, had warned Americans about people like the Union Bank's aristocratic backers: "Are our young men wiser than the sage of Monticello? Can they see nothing to apprehend in the full bloom of that which alarmed him in the bud?" Like "the Federalists of '98," the Union Bank's support-ers threatened the Revolutionary and republican promise of America. They were "aristocratic idlers, who with corporate privileges levy an onerous tax upon the frugal sober minded and industrious to be expended wholly in luxury and vain parade."[22]

Democrats appropriated the word "people," a word that of course had a long history, and substituted it as a word of praise where others might have inserted the more ambiguous "countrymen." One pro-Democratic writer, possibly the *Floridian*'s editor Samuel Sibley, referred to himself as "John (x) Smith," indicating his commonness with alleged illiteracy and a ubiquitous name. "John (x) Smith" claimed friends in Centreville, the ideological pole of yeoman revolt and Democratic strength and the site of the fight between "Governor" Barnes and Richard Hayward. The Pisgah neighborhood in particular became a local symbol for the party, and a signal of countryman intervention in politics. Years later, Centreville remained the territory of countrymen in the mental geography of Leon County; an uncomfortable place for upper-class whites irritated by signs of lower-class insolence. But in 1840, the editor of the *Floridian* announced his conversion to the Democ-racy by stating that he would attend a barbecue at Centreville.[23]

Recognizing its most numerous constituency, the Democratic press adopted Centreville's language and portrayed every action of the pro-bank side as an attempt to force unmanly submission on the common white citi-zens of the territory. Every political battle suddenly echoed the everyday struggles of yeomen for manly respect in a society divided sharply by class, race, and masculinity. Images of haughty attempts to dominate, of effemi-nate or slavish submission, and of manly resistance proliferated. Country-men, of course, believed that to resist subordination was to be a man. The language of the *Floridian* became visceral, consciously evoking the belief that pro-bank politicians sought to force Florida's white men to submit like slaves or women to their rule: "The Banks are their [the people's] mas-ters," and the community had yielded itself to "shameful vassalage." Those who served the pro-bank men must "submit to all this, and kiss the rod." For many individuals, proof that the pro-bank faction desired to dishonor "the people" came with the Union Bank's 1840 refusal to open its books to inspection by the new anti-bank legislative majority. This was "defiance" of the will of the countryman voting majority, "the grossest insult to the com-mon sense of the people of Florida." The pro-bank press was "submissive and subservient" to the "Lords and Barons of the Bank." But rough-and-tumble fighters would not submit: the "Bank power has not yet got its foot so firmly fixed on the necks of the people as that."[24]

Democrats' language called up fears of enslavement and emasculation, and anti-bank politicians (called "Locofocos" by opponents) promised full and complete enfranchisement as an antidote. Democrats were aware that countrymen resented not only political rhetoric and practice that assumed inequality between white men but also the everyday rituals of crime and punishment that inflicted class hierarchy upon them. Claiming with some accuracy that pro-bank men supported the public flogging of whites, and the status quo of separate law for separate classes, Locofocos in the 1840 territorial legislature attempted to equalize punishments for dueling and those for crimes associated with yeomen, including mayhem (gouging) and cattle maiming. They also attempted to restrict the state's power to mark white male thieves as equal to slaves. Anti-bank politicians removed distinctions between the different kinds of violence used by different classes of white men to defend honor.[25]

Suddenly, yeomen in Middle Florida seemed to be exulting in a new feeling of political potency. The ethic of the rough-and-tumble fight began to displace that of the duel and its obverse face, the chastisement of an inferior. "Governor" Barnes whipped Richard Hayward. So planters wishing to court the newly active majority had to acknowledge yeomen as equal, enfranchised, and honorable. At the meetings, barbecues, and dinners that now mobilized local voters, in both Tallahassee and in the communities of the countryside, political deference evaporated before the eyes of an anxious elite. Just as countrymen asserted their right to the violence of honor, so they also now claimed the manly authority to speak in the challenge and response of public toasts at barbecues and dinners. At a January 1840 Democratic dinner in Leon, nonslaveholder Richard Sanders, a signatory of the first Centreville resolutions, toasted "[t]he last Election Day—long to be remembered and dearly cherished as the day of the triumph of true Democratic principles in this county." William Michael slipped into the vernacular to claim his place on Leon County's class-marked map: "Centreville—the *stomping ground* of true Jeffersonian Democracy." Even planter-politicians who had hitched their wagons to the Democrats might have shifted uncomfortably when illiterate farmer Melchior Houck closed with a rough-and-tumble fighter's challenge: "May God have mercy on the stockholders of the Union Bank, for we shall have none."[26]

MEN OF SENSE VERSUS BLOCKHEADS

From 1839 until the middle of the following decade, the simultaneous collapse of the old factional system of territorial politics and the Union Bank, the engine that supplied planters with a stream of wealth even during the dark days of the panic of 1837, overwhelmed and confused elite society. Many elite white men continued to believe themselves above "the idle, silly, *over-talking, over-balking* mob, which styles itself 'sovereign.'" Perhaps such sentiments were best kept from the public during election time. But that was a lesson that took years to learn. Many planters insisted on learning the hard way, from failures rather than successes. When deference broke down in 1839, they turned first to denial, then to violent coercion, and finally to manipulation in the effort to assert their superiority against insolent upstarts.[27]

The seeming arrogance of pro-bank men reflected, like certain kinds of violence, a belief in an essential inequality among white men. Blithely, bank officials claimed both before and after the pivotal 1839 election that the people of the territory had neither reason nor right to dispute their own responsibility for paying off debts incurred by the stockholders. John Gamble breezily told his "Centreville brethren" that there would be no increase to the bank's capital—debts for which he claimed the territory's taxpayers were ultimately responsible—until the stockholders so decided. In other words, the stockholders could even issue themselves more loans at whim. Gamble also asserted that the legislature could not revoke the bank's 1833 charter, or repudiate the bonds: "High priests of party have declared that the future state of Florida will not be bound by contracts entered into while under Territorial government. But I have no fears that such a principle will be assented to by any legislature."[28]

The pro-bank men tried to characterize the "high priests of party" as a group of outcasts and failures who had whipped up a storm of disruptive rhetoric about equality, all for their own gain. The men who led the Democrats were indeed a mixed group, united by anti-bankism and a willingness to appeal to more popular tactics than hitherto used in Middle Florida. Many had not been prominent in Leon County politics before 1839. Even James Westcott, who had held appointments as territorial secretary and district attorney, was widely seen as an outsider. Others, like Tallahassee's James Berthelot, were just small-time merchants in dry goods. The voices of political outsiders, supported by countrymen, sounded threatening to nervous pro-bank planters shocked by recent defeats. More conservative whites believed that many of those who now spoke up at social gatherings or represented their precincts in county conventions should be following the leads of better men. "We are to have a Social Democracy!" shrilled one pro-bank writer. "Men of education, throw open your doors and your hearts to the illiterate, boorish, savage. Men of taste and refinement consort indiscriminately with the vulgar—men of morals with profane; men of sense with the Blockheads."[29]

Elite men who joined in the popular anti-bank movement faced a different kind of criticism. Pro-bank leaders pictured men like Leon County's Leigh Read as simultaneous class traitors and crude upstarts: "novi homines" or "mushroom men." Read had come to the territory from Tennessee in 1833. At first he allied himself with Richard Call, but by 1837 he had broken with the general, whose family later painted Read as a snake nourished in the pro-bank bosom. More threatening than treachery, or his success at building ties to other planters, was Read's ability to mobilize popular support by seeming more manly in terms that united planter and yeoman masculinity. Read was the only general from Middle Florida to experience any success in the Second Seminole War and was clearly able to inspire confidence in his soldiers. His violent life did not display the exclusionary beliefs personified by his own onetime patron Richard Call. Read fought several duels, but he also fought rough-and-tumble battles. He once supposedly said that he had been "tolerably wild through life," which may have attracted the approbation of yeomen who defined masculinity as insubordination. Drawing common white supporters with an air that suggested he was one of them, Read's masculine charisma obviously irritated his opponents no end.[30]

The success of Democratic Party organization and the appeal of anti-bank policies propelled the area toward open conflict after the legislative elections of 1839. President Van Buren had evicted his critic Richard Call from the governor's office at the end of 1839, and the Leon County Democrats had elected Leigh Read, Hugh Archer, and Nathaniel Walker to the territorial House on an anti-bank platform. Daniel McRaeny, a neutral candidate, was the fourth and final representative from Leon, and he soon joined the House Democrats, backing many of their proposals. James Westcott and his East Florida ally David Levy did not rest on the laurels of their overall majority in the territorial legislature. Westcott, now a territorial senator, began to push an ambitious agenda through both houses in January 1840. The heart of the Democrats' program was an attack on the Union Bank and the other territorial financial institutions, which Westcott called "corrupt and corrupting rag-shop[s]." They quickly appointed a committee to look into the bank's affairs. At the same time, President Van Buren, no doubt with Westcott's encouragement, asked a congressional committee to examine the bank charters of states and territories.[31]

Meanwhile, unused to opposition, Gamble and the Union Bank's supporters lashed back. An epistolary war raged in the increasingly pro-Democratic *Tallahassee Floridian*, as "A Stockholder" rejected all criticism from the anti-bank side, which he characterized as "rabid . . . ravings." John Gamble also flatly refused to allow the legislature to have access to the bank's books. Even after Governor Reid staged a coup in January 1840, appointing an entirely new bank board composed of five Democratic directors, Gamble kept the books from anti-bank officials' hands. Given the extravagant lending policies of the bank, and the evidence of incestuous division of the institution's spoils, many suspected that its accounts contained damning evidence of illegal practices. Despite multiple opportunities for Gamble and his allies to dispel rampant rumors of "'defalcations,' 'overdrafts,' 'illicit loans,' 'kites,' 'partiality,' and 'favoritism,'" they had refused to do so.[32]

The arrogance displayed by bank supporters seemingly provided credence to accusations that Gamble and his allies wanted to impose a demeaning rule upon the countrymen of the territory. The editor of the *Floridian* compared the pro-bankites to the hated Federalists' "black cockade of *98*," accusing them of "claiming to have all the decency, honor, morality, and honesty, these qualities are denied to all that dare to differ with them." By March, enough pro-bank rejoinders had floated around Tallahassee for "Hardest Fend Off" to wonder, in mock reply, "If the [Locofocos] are as poor, and as mean, and as contemptible, as the Federalists say they are, I do not see how they so managed it as to lead, by the nose, the wise, and the learned, and smart Bank folks into such a snare." Given the pro-bankites' words and actions, Governor Reid found it easy to assert, piously, that the bank was oppressing the sovereign people by denying information to the committees. Gamble and his friends, said one critic, were "[g]entlemen led to extravagant and Aristocratic ideas whose reduced Means ill comported with their former habits." They were not only arrogant, but wildly improvident: "When once involved in the new, and I may say Super-artificial credit system introduced by the sale abroad of State security [they] mistook the Stream for the fountain and wasted the Waters with unheedful prodigality."[33]

When the banking and judiciary committees of the territorial legislature finally reported, they unleashed damning indictments of what had been, to all appearances, a special-interest scam operated by Gamble and his friends and relatives. The bank was over $600,000 in the red, and held less than $13,000 in liquid assets. It could not identify with certainty the recipients of over one million dollars distributed in loans. Only the continued injection of outside gold into the Middle Florida economy by the sale of bonds had prevented the bank's currency from depreciating below the value of the paper on which it was printed. "Such is the deplorable condition," intoned the bank committee's report, "of the Union Bank by its own figures."[34]

Outmaneuvered on the new field of popular politics, "gentlemen" refused to surrender to men they considered upstarts and turncoats. Men like

John Gamble steadfastly stuck to hierarchical definitions of political relationships among white men. In their vision, the best men held office, led, and incidentally benefited their families in the course of their possession of office. Yet when a planter man like Read spoke, claiming to represent the political views of common white men, how was one to interpret their aggressive critique of the bank as a source of economic power that separated some planters from other white men? Their attacks threatened far more than institutional policy. For Gamble and others, such debates were not "party" or political matters but barely comprehensible hodgepodges of insult. Certainly Read and Westcott and the yeomen they represented were not legitimate political opposition. These Democrats appeared to follow and cater to countryman interests and styles, rather than the other way around. Pro-bank planters tarred men like Read with the brush of representing a subordinate group that had no legitimate interest in the uses of "public" office for "private" benefit. When "novi homines" questioned the ethics displayed in the process of accumulating benefits, critics also questioned the honor of elite men who had grown rich. Such questions were "private" insults, not fit subjects for public "political" debate. An insulting subordinate had to be chastised, humiliated, and silenced, and neither the courts nor the public needed to involve themselves in such affairs.[35]

In response to their defeat in the fall 1839 elections and to the perceived insult posed by the new political atmosphere, pro-bank conservatives immediately turned to their characteristic forms of violence, attempting to unman their opponents. Augustus Alston, a former director of the Union Bank and a close companion of pro-bank candidate William Tradewell, intensified his ally's repeated slurs against opponent Leigh Read by having one of his slaves "post" the fiery Read as a coward. The latter had disavowed any intention to let the political contest become violent, but when Alston, "the bulldog of his party," sent one of his slaves to tack up a public notice proclaiming Read less than a man, he was sure to get the response he wanted. Most expected the noted duelist Alston to kill Read, an aggressive but unskilled opponent. In the face of pro-bank denials that the duel had political implications, Read charged that Alston's attacks on his honor were an attempt to use exclusionary forms of manhood to silence "the people." "The recent signal triumph," he wrote, "of the people of this county, over the head of a most corrupt, malignant and vindictive opposition, has goaded them to desperation." Something certainly seemed to be goading Alston, who supposedly demanded jager rifles at fifteen paces as the weapons, a recipe for the certain death of one or both combatants.[36]

According to some accounts, Alston ordered his servants to prepare a feast for his triumphant return as he rode off in the morning toward the tra-

A CARD.

A few days previous to the late election, a political altercation took place between myself and an opposing candidate, in which, in repelling an attack, I was compelled to inflict personal indignity. The dispute was of an acrimonious character, but when time had been afforded for reflection, the incident became a subject of mortification and regret ; and early on the following morning, I wrote a note to a mutual friend of myself and the individual with whom I had the difficulty, in which I expressed deep regret at the occurrence, and added that if my advances were received in a corresponding spirit, I should meet and speak to him as if nothing had taken place. I hoped that the matter would there have dropped. Understanding however, that after his arrival at and passage through this city, he was much excited, and that he would probably challenge me, I caused it to be communicated to him, that I did not desire and could not fight him ; and it was finally mentioned to him, that for causes and reasons *which he perfectly well understood*, I could not and would not accept his challenge. Notwithstanding this, and the efforts of mutual friends to accommodate the matter, I was waited upon on the Saturday before the election by a person who at that time held the post of Aid-de-camp in my staff, with a note of the character of which I could learn nothing except that it was not a challenge, but which I had good reason to believe was a peremptory demand for an apology. I declined receiving the paper until after the election, and stated that I would then attend to the matter. On the day after that event, I was again called upon by the same person, and my reply was in substance, that I was informed by the proper authorities that this whole affair was in the hands of a most ancient and honorable association, of which we were all members, for investigation, and as a matter of course, until I understood his note. The affair was, by common consent as I understood, to be left in that situation. I took pains however to reiterate that I entertained no sentiment of hostility to him, and that it would be impossible for me to meet him with hostile intentions.

More than a week had elapsed when I was met while passing to the residence of a friend in my carriage, by this same second, and a challenge from his principal, offered me. I declined it. He did not ask me my reasons for doing so, which I had as I imagined, a just right to expect, and if my reasons had been unacceptable or offensive to him, he might have offered himself in the place of his principal. He left me in a great hurry simply remarking that, "our course is a plain one." I followed him to town as soon as with convenience I could do so. I saw him but once. I sent a friend to enquire what was "*the plain course*," he contemplated. Before the inquiry could be made, he had left Town for the purpose as I was subsequently informed, and believe, of going with his friend to Col. Augustus Alston's to obtain advice.

In the mean time the ancient order above alluded to, had appointed a committee to adjust the difficulty between us, and had required our submission of the whole affair to the arbitrament of three gentlemen. I readily assented to the proposition, and expressed a desire that it might terminate satisfactorily to all. All efforts to adjust the difficulty failed. I had about this time received from the second a letter tendering his resignation as Aid-de-camp. I stated among other things in my reply to this note, that the affair of honor, as he and his principal were pleased to regard the difficulty between us, was rather singular in its character—and that it had the appearance somewhat of being a little in the style of empty bravado. This letter together with other papers, connected with the difficulty will be published in due time.

The challenge had been delivered on Wednesday, but it required training until Saturday, to get them up to the sticking point—and on that day those two individuals backed by Col. Augustus Alston, and a few others, performed the gallant achievement of guarding a *negro man* who was employed to post me, on the pillars of the Executive Office—and other public places. I was invited to witness the show, but I could not have arrived by the hour mentioned in the invitation—and having made up my mind to a different line of conduct, I declined the pleasure, which was in store for me, by the annexed note.* On the following Monday while on a visit to a sick friend, I was waited on by a third individual as the friend of the second in the previous affair with a challenge from that second. The *second* in this last case had made an abusive and scurrilous attack in the newspapers upon a public meeting held in my neighborhood during the last summer—I denounced the falsehood and folly of the piece at the time, and no intercourse had taken place between us since. When the paper was brought to me, however, I received it, and remarked, after reading, that I had heard of it, and had been told that my "*old friend*" Col. Augustus Alston, was originally to have delivered it ; that if he had done so, I should have spit in his face—but having no disposition to inflict such indignity upon the bearer, I spit upon the note and threw it down, adding, that he, the second, might take what course he pleased. I declined giving him my reasons under the belief, that as they had the extreme kindness to raise me from my imputed disgrace by challenging after posting me, the individual, who was now acting as second in this affair, would follow up the course, in which event Col. Augustus Alston would be the second—and a messenger was despatched by him upon the instant for that gentleman. From the boastings of his adherents, my friends expected that he would attack me next morning in the mode, it is known, that he prefers to fair and honorable combat. I went to my plantation after ascertaining that he would not come to town, and remained there until Saturday. On Friday night a gen-

"A Card," by Leigh Read, 1839 (Southern Historical Collection, Wilson Library, University of North Carolina)

ditional dueling grounds on the Georgia-Florida line. Despite his bold front and supposed skills, Alston must have been overanxious, for when the moment of truth arrived, he wheeled, slipped, and fired too soon. As the echoes of Alston's gunshot echoed harmlessly through the trees, Read aimed carefully and shot his opponent down. Alston's death came as a shock to the tleman of my neighborhood came to my house to communicate that while on a visit to town that day, Col. Alston had sought a conversation with him and stated in substance, that he, Col. Alston, would remain in town the following day, for the purpose of giving me a fight : and that he wished my neighbor and friend to communicate his wishes, on this subject, to me.

A friend and relative of Col. A. sent a message by the same gentleman, that if I did not choose to meet Col. A., that he would fight me. To the *latter* message *I* replied, "one at a time, if you please, gentlemen." My disposition of the *former*, was an immediate proposition through two friends, only to meet Col. A., in accordance with his wishes. The letter to his friend, asking him not to crowd upon me too fast, if they all wished to be accommodated, had no necessary connection with the affair between Col. A. and myself, except that *I* had a right to believe from the message, that this friend would be his second. When the letter was delivered, however, they thought proper to make it the subject of an hours' consultation, and although they decided "*not* to *recognize* it," they have retained it in possession. But before this letter was received, this friend of Col. Alston called upon a gentleman whom he presumed to be in my confidence, to enquire what course *I* would take on my arrival in town.—He replied that he was not informed. Upon which this friend of Col. A. informed him that he, Col. A. would fight me any way which I might desire. Subsequently my terms were tendered through one of my friends, but they then concluded to refuse them upon the ground that I had been posted ! I again sent my friends to ascertain absolutely whether he would accord to me the meeting which he had so boastfully sought. *In* the mean time I had received a message through an unauthorized source, that if I would go to Commerce street, " I would be met by *gentlemen*." Who those gentlemen were, I was not informed, except that an armed mob had assembled at the place above indicated, composed of nearly every bitter *personal* and *political* enemy I have in the country. Now as my object was to meet but one person, and that person was COL. AUGUSTUS ALSTON, I could not consent to go to the street mentioned, even though I might be met by *gentlemen*— and though they may have acquired a vast deal of " military reputation " in the recently hard fought field, where paper pellets were the small arms, and placards the heavy artillery, still the temptation was not sufficiently great to divert me from my principal object. I could not, however, ascertain how, or in what manner the *gentlemen* were to have been met. If I could have been distinctly informed that the champion would have *led* them, it is not improbable that HE might still have been gratified.

I have one word to say in relation to my friends. Understanding that I would be attacked by a crowd of the Colonel's *gentlemen*, they rallied around me, with a generous devotion of the most gratifying character. When the invitation was received above mentioned, they were eager for the conflict. They were all prepared to do the right sort of work in such an affair, in the right sort of way, but I would not permit it. There was but one issue in which I felt the least degree of interest; and I was unwilling that others should be involved. Besides, I had promised the authorities of the place, that on my part, nothing like a general fight or riot should occur, unless I was attacked.

It requires no argument to prove that this whole movement against me has originated in political disappointment.—The recent signal triumph of the people of this county, over the head of a most corrupt, malignant and vindictive opposition, has goaded them to desperation. They have singled me out as the object of their mean and pitiable assaults. Unwilling to contribute to their irritation, and desirous of getting on quietly, I made almost every concession to them. They have placarded, denounced, and abused me. They have offered me what they call their grossest indignities ; and by one *coup-de-main*, they have deprived me of all my " military reputation," which is a most deplorable affair, as every body knows. All this does not satisfy them. They have shouted, hooted, and *cavorted*, and although that was no doubt extremely gratifying to the *gentlemen*, still they were not satisfied. I have offered to fight their champion on his invitation—that did not please them. I have offered to fight him, giving him the right of terms—that does not please them. In short, they are the hardest people to please I have ever come across. I have not been able to find it in my heart to raise my foot, much less my arm, against any of the smaller animals of the party : but that great BULL DOG, whose loud bayings have so long kept this city in a state of quiet and tranquility, I had no objection to meet HIM. It would have stirred the spirit more to encounter the Lion of the party, (*if lion there be*) than to have met the hares. I *am fully, thoroughly, and perfectly satisfied, that but for Col. Augustus Alston, I would never have been posted.*

LEIGH READ.

SATURDAY MORNING OCT. 26, 1839.

My Dear, Dear Doctor :

I am mighty sorry that I cannot enjoy the pleasure, which in your kind note of this morning you inform me is in waiting for me at the Capitol Square at 10 o'clock. It would be very gratifying to see myself posted as a coward and scoundrel, particularly as it is very evident that this step on your part is not intended to minister to the delicate nostrils of that knightly gentleman, his Excellency, the Governor. F-a-u-g-h ?

" When knaves and fools upon me are satiric,
I take it for a panegyric."

Your Loving Friend,
LEIGH READ.

pro-bank factions, and especially to his family. When the seconds brought Alston's body home in their carriage, James Randolph—Alston's friend and physician, and one of the antagonists who had provoked Read to fight—extracted the bullet from his corpse. The dead man's sisters, distraught and enraged, reportedly mailed the leaden slug to their other brother Willis, a former Leon County resident who now lived in Texas. Though apocryphal, this story has the ring of truth. The whole Alston clan, male and female, was notoriously devoted to the ideals of violent male honor. Refined Virginia gentry also accepted such violence as necessary, since the Alstons' closest allies in the quest for domination included a Randolph and the Gamble family. The Alstons' devotion came, then, not from some sort of mysterious frontier atavism, but from mainstream planter ideas about manhood.[37]

On January 4, 1840, Willis Alston reached the Tallahassee station on the ramshackle train from Port Leon, where his boat from Texas had landed. Along with political allies like Richard Hayward, Augustus Alston had believed that physical force was the perfect tool to enforce hierarchies of class, race, and gender. His brother was, if anything, more committed to such ideals. Undoubtedly Willis would have felt compelled to avenge Augustus's death no matter what the circumstances, but with his sisters' apparent help, he convinced himself that Read had fought unfairly. By the evening of the fourth, Willis was waiting in the shadows outside Tallahassee's City Hotel. Soon Leigh Read approached the door, bound for an organizational meeting with other Democratic politicos. Alston stepped from the shadows to reveal himself. The two stared daggers at each other, and then Read moved inside. Although Alston's allies later claimed that he was somehow acting in self-defense, they never disputed that he next followed Read into the hall and shot twice with pistols, hitting him once. Ever game, and ever armed, the seriously wounded Read staggered after his fleeing assailant with a sword cane and a derringer, but Alston escaped.[38]

Read convalesced through the spring, and Van Buren appointed him the federal marshal, the chief local law enforcement official, for all of Middle Florida. He watched as bank defenders' verbal counterattacks played directly into the Democrats' hands, but by the summer, more physical blows began to fall in the streets of Tallahassee. When the Democrats of Leon's Ocklocknee neighborhood gathered in late July, they, like participants in similar precinct meetings across the South, charged Whig presidential candidate William Henry Harrison with being an ally of Northern abolitionists. Next they added the provocative deduction that Harrison's supporters—including those in Leon County—were therefore allies of abolitionists. Pro-bank men found out about the accusations from an account of the meeting published in the *Floridian*. Many were already in Tallahassee for a meeting meant to organize a local branch of the national Whig Party. Seething with anger, they gathered and headed into the streets, looking for Locofoco upstarts. Several fights broke out, including one in which Jefferson County Democrat Elias Blackburn used a bowie knife to hold off a group of pro-bank men. Offended planter dignity then shifted its focus to the *Floridian* building. Editor Samuel Sibley was an upstart like so many

Democratic politicians, and his brother Charles had been named district attorney by Van Buren, despite not being related to any of the powerful migrant planter families. Now "[g]roups of angry and indignant bankites and whigs were seen at all corners of the streets [around the newspaper office]. . . . [T]he bar-keepers mixed and stirred juleps and cocktails with remarkable animation." As Willis Alston moved among the crowd, loudly boasting that he planned to cut off Leigh Read's ears as if the newly appointed federal marshal of Middle Florida was an ordinary thief, pro-bank men began to talk about pulling down the *Floridian* office. In printing the Democratic resolutions, the paper had offered "an insult to a gentlemen." The editor himself was no gentleman, so instead of challenging Sibley to a duel, angry bankites threatened to lynch him and other Democrats.[39]

At this point, Governor Reid panicked, and called in a regular army unit that ordinarily guarded Tallahassee from Seminole attack. The soldiers, reinforced by pro-Democratic militia, stationed themselves through the streets and around Reid's house. On August 4, they arrested several pro-bank men, "who were," claimed the detainees' friends, merely making "their way peacefully in the public streets." The next day, a group of Whigs calling themselves "a committee on the part of the citizens of Tallahassee," including former governor William P. DuVal, William Wyatt, Thomas Brown, and others, waited on the governor. There had been no potential for riot, claimed Reid's visitors, and any disagreements that had happened in the streets were, as they later claimed, "a few *angry words* between some few of our citizens in some case of *private quarrel.*" Reid soon withdrew the troops, fearing that he might have offended politically neutral citizens. The newly minted Florida Whigs asserted that by calling out the troops in the first place, he had usurped the rights of citizens: "Scarcely a parallel," they complained, "can be found in the arbitrary conduct of the British Governors in the incipient stages of the Revolution." In contrast to Reid, whom they depicted as a coward, the bankites claimed that they had been ready, in manly fashion, "solemnly determined in defense to resist force by force."[40]

While some parts of the Southwest had already seen shifts in the relations between different classes of white men, most of the ruling class of Middle Florida was not ready for political change in 1840. The Tallahassee riots of August showed that when assertion of authority did not quell dissent, many elite men were willing to turn to violence. Pro-bank men claimed that they were merely settling private disagreements, over which there need be no more public debate than there would be about the horse-whipping of an impudent countryman. The charges that they had mismanaged the bank, had allied with Northern abolitionists through their support of Harrison, and had attempted to intimidate political opponents consti-

tuted, to quote John G. Gamble, impudent "effrontery." By opening for public debate one of the sources of inequality among white men — the wealth
flowing from the Union Bank into the pockets of migrant planters — Democrats called into question the very distribution of power in Middle Florida.
This was so unthinkable that the pro-bank politicians denied the obvious. "I
assure you, sir," wrote one pro-bank legislator of the 1840 riots, "the banks
had no more to do with this quarrel, than the ghost of Banquo." But while
rioters had attempted to chastise their opponents, changing circumstances
soon, like little Jack, turned the tables on them.[41]

STRONGER THAN THE TRAITOR'S ARM

During 1840, Union Bank currency plunged in value, debts
mounted, and the cotton crop burned up from drought. The crop failed, and
with it withered bank supporters' dreams of returning Union Bank currency to its face value. Now nothing could bring enough good money back
into the territory to pay off the layers and layers of debt that structured
elite relations with the rest of the commercial economy. Some blamed the
Locofocos for raising the bank issue and undermining confidence. Many
planters came to realize that the bank was doomed. Most turned to trying to save their plantations. Judge Alfred Balch, a stalwart Jacksonian appointed by Van Buren to preside over Middle Florida's superior courts, reported in April that his arrival to begin the spring term "disappointed the
debtor class who counted on a delay of six months from the want of a judge.
The Creditor class are highly pleased. . . . Very large numbers of actions
of debt are depending in the Courts of this District." By the time that he
adjourned Leon's court session on May 9, Balch had judged several hundred debt cases. Jackson County was in similar straits, although the Union
Bank had displayed less favoritism to that county's planters, denying them
an equivalent opportunity to get into inextricable debt. Though few of the
bank's mortgages had come due by 1840, many debtors had already missed
interest payments, or could not pay debts to local merchants. In other cases,
the new directors "curtailed" debtors' loans, pushing them to pay up immediately in order to increase the bank's liquid assets.[42]

As panic spread through Tallahassee and the countryside in the late
spring and summer of 1840, debtors began to clamor for stay laws. Traditionally, these laws, meant as a firebreak for economic panic, protected only
a portion of property necessary for a debtor's "subsistence," i.e., a small
amount of land, tools, and some livestock. Although this issue brought
together planters and property-owning yeomen, planters wanted to ex-

pand stay laws to cover large numbers of slaves, a difference that would lead these two groups of landowners into disagreement. In the meantime, a meeting held at Centreville in May painted in stark terms the probable result of the legislature's failure to enact a stay law: "[T]he[ir] wives and children . . . would be turned, houseless and naked, into the wilderness, and the creditor would not be benefited, for a sale made for specie would not command a sum sufficient to pay the costs of the execution."[43] Meeting attendees claimed to be "left with no further alternative but an appeal to the supremacy of the people" and argued that the supreme people were instructing their representatives to pass a stay law. Other gatherings allegedly went further, and their wild talk of a lynch law for creditors who demanded specie seemed no idle threat. Local newspapers reported that some creditors had actually been hanged in Arkansas. Yet even as pro-bank men clamored for expansive stay laws to protect their own property, they affirmed the principle of the supremacy of contracts in other situations, claiming that the territory of Florida must back the "faith bonds" of the Union Bank once the stockholders inevitably defaulted.[44]

The failure of Democratic representatives to enact stay laws had much to do with the disparate nature of their Middle Florida coalition. Merchants did not want to stop the process of debt collection, since Northern creditors were pressing them hard. Planters like the Branch family, on the other hand, supported stay laws, as did many yeoman voters. In the middle stood ideological leaders like Westcott, torn between opposition to economic favoritism for any group and the desire to protect economic independence for common white men — many of whom were, on however small a scale, debtors. Indecision had its cost. Middle Florida's pro-bank faction, abandoning, for the most part, its public commitment to the faith bonds, and seizing the issue of stay laws, temporarily rebounded from defeat.[45]

Self-styled "Conservatives" borrowed rhetoric and momentum from William Henry Harrison's victorious national campaign and swept the November 1840 elections, winning three of four Leon County seats in the territorial House, and one of two in Jackson. After his March 1841 inauguration, Harrison began to remove Democrats from key federal posts. Richard Call assumed the governorship for the second time, replacing Robert Reid and (according to Call's brother) pleasing "the people of respectability." The president also removed Leigh Read from his position as U.S. marshal for Middle Florida and installed Minor Walker, a darling of the Virginia set. But Harrison's early death in April 1841 blocked Florida Conservatives' attempts to throw every Locofoco out of appointive office.[46]

Democratic defeat did not mean that the question of white male equality was no longer important to Middle Florida's yeomen. Whig margins of victory were slim and relied in Leon County upon the preponderance of votes cast in Tallahassee, where many residents were irritated by Reid's military occupation of the city in August. Outside of the city, Whigs led narrowly at Miccosukee precinct, where planters like the Alston and Parish families cast their ballots in a straight partisan vote. But at countryman strongholds like Centreville, Democrats won handily. The legislative attempt to roll back the results of the Democrats' offensive against the banks also failed. During the 1841 session of the Legislative Council, the Whigs split between pro-bank and anti-bank factions and accomplished little. Some Leon County representatives wanted to rescue the Union Bank, but others recognized that continued support of the faith bonds crippled candidates at the polls. When Democratic leader David Levy won the spring 1841 election for delegate to Congress, he out-polled pro-bank candidate George T. Ward in Leon, the latter man's home county. The Union Bank was dead as a political force.[47]

Yet the pro-bank Whigs had, literally, one more round left in their magazine. Willis Alston and Leigh Read had been playing a cat-and-mouse game since Alston's January 1840 attack at Tallahassee's City Hotel. Over the next year, the families of Alston and Read each charged that the other man was planning murder. Alston's cousin Augustus Archer first testified that Read tried to force him to assassinate his relative but later changed his mind and claimed that Alston had coerced him into making the first statement. According to Archer, wealthy members of the pro-bank faction promised Archer or Alston money and slaves in return for killing off the immensely popular Read. The tension mounted. Charge followed counter-charge through 1840, and in January 1841 someone fired a shot at one of John Branch's sons as he rode toward his father's plantation north of Tallahassee.[48] The attempted bushwhacking of young Branch was ominous, as was President Harrison's April purge of Democratic officials. Read came to town on April 26 to collect relevant papers for his replacement. As he walked down Monroe Street toward the courthouse, Willis Alston jumped out of the doorway of his friend and in-law Michael Ledwith's home. Leveling a shotgun, Alston emptied both barrels into Read. Bystanders carried the wounded man to Joseph Branch's nearby law office, but there was no hope for survival. Read expired there early the next morning.[49]

As soon as John Branch heard of the assassination of his son-in-law, he rode into town. The father-in-law, bereft of his most powerful political ally, watched with outrage from the street as Alston and his friends "reveled" in a tavern across from the gubernatorial office. Once, Branch and Richard Call had been political allies. Now, when Branch barged into the governor's office and insisted that Call order Alston's arrest on a charge of murder, the governor reportedly laughed at Branch and called him "insane." After a few days, Alston was finally arrested, but his lawyers and allies began to lay the groundwork for a plea of self-defense. They claimed that at all stages "Read was the aggressor" and that Alston knew he would have to kill Read in order to survive. Meanwhile, John Gamble charged, "The feud never had more of a party complexion, than that the individuals belonged to different political parties." Those who stated otherwise—who continued, for instance, to insist that the issues that divided Read from the Alstons were legitimate subjects for public debate—invited additional chastisement and violence: "[Branch] has at different times insulted the whole Whig party with the charge of endeavoring to compress the death of his son in law, by instigating his personal enemies to kill him. . . . And I learn has even thought, or said, that *a Bank* was the instigator." But Archer's claim that Union Bank men offered bank bills and slaves to whoever would kill Read might have seemed poetic truth to many observers, for the crisis over elite power and the bank was the immediate cause of party struggle in Middle Florida during the early 1840s.[50]

Read's enemies continued to nourish the ultimate cause of the party struggle, which was the conflict between incompatible visions of proper relations of power between white men. Their words and actions reinforced the perception that they were aristocrats who thought themselves better than other white men, and received—no matter how dishonorable their deeds—consideration others would not get. Willis Alston awaited trial in the Leon County jail for almost two months after his arrest. Judge Richard C. Allen had consistently denied him bail, but when the district attorney left town, Alston's attorneys rounded up two of the last justices appointed by Call in his previous term. One, David Brown, was a former anti-bank candidate from Centreville. By June 5, 1841, when Alston's attorneys called upon the two justices, the commissions of each had expired. Yet after a meeting between the two and Alston's attorneys, Alston was permitted to post bail.[51]

The pugnacious Alston, once free, set about trying to intimidate the new federal marshal, John G. Camp. "Alston . . . pursued me," Camp wrote, "to the Governor's office . . . [and] treated me with great rudeness." Showing his continued willingness to overpower and dominate opponents, Alston told Camp that he had heard "a Col. Camp had been sent on here who car'd not for dirks, Pistols, Rifles, or Bowie Knives." These were Alston's tools of intimidation, but, he said ominously, Camp may "find his match." After this attempt to bully Camp, a mob of Alston's friends came to town and issued death threats to various enemies. A gang of heavily armed men from the Branch family showed up as well. After much milling about, nothing happened. The next day, Alston skipped bail and fled town, bound for Texas. Alston, whom even friends admitted was a "man of Blood," finally reaped in Texas what he had sown in Florida. A few months later, he murdered a friend of Read in Brazoria. An angry crowd broke open the town jail, dragged Alston into the countryside, and shot him thirty times.[52]

Back in Tallahassee, Whig officers continued to protect everyone involved, in fact or by rumor, in Read's murder. After the justices of the peace allowed Alston to post bail, the Democratic press howled. Perhaps as a warning to the Branch family to cease any plans for vengeance, the courts tried John Branch's son and nephew for carrying concealed weapons to the trial of Michael Ledwith. In 1842, Governor Call pardoned Ledwith, who had been convicted of felony and sentenced to hang for assisting in the assassination of Read.[53] Branch, who had good reason to suspect that other pro-bank Whigs had also been complicit in the murder of his son-in-law, publicly accused Call of covering up a conspiracy. After Branch's accusation, the pro-Whig *Tallahassee Star* jumped into action, issuing a series of editorials that grew ever. Using an irrefutable argument, the *Star* claimed that Branch was insane: "To be sure, he says he is sane. What other lunatic ever thought or said otherwise?" But the *Star* had gone too far, as had the pro-bank Whigs. Violence and coercion had dissolved as useful strategies.[54]

Other, wiser, heads in the Whig Party had already begun to seek to manipulate the countrymen who provided the ranks of their opposition, rather than crushing them into submission. Conservatives remedied their style and headed out into the "diggins" in an effort to trick yeomen into supporting a pro-bank agenda that benefited no one but debt-stricken stockholders. Centreville became the symbolic prize of the 1840 election. If the Conservatives could convince the common white voters who lived near Pisgah church that men who had profited from the Union Bank should be the county's representatives, then the old system of politics might remain more or less intact. A barrage of propaganda targeted the crossroads in the "Pine lands." After the first stay law meeting, the pro-Conservative *Tallahassee Star of Florida* claimed a premature victory: "The people of Centreville met, and passed resolutions directly opposing the doctrines of the locofocoes."[55] Then three Tallahassee politicians, Thomas Brown, Alexander DuVal (son of the former governor), and Edward Gibson (all Conservatives) appeared at the July 4th barbecue traditionally held at the Centreville muster grounds. According to the account of the pro-Democratic *Floridian*, "Some political managers from neighboring places came out to take the good people of Centreville by storm, and drink them drunk with their hard cider politics, but they were mistaken for once in their lives. They found the people wide awake—birds not to be caught with *chaff*."[56]

Members of John Branch's extended family, who lived a few miles west of Centreville, then engaged the Conservative trio in an exchange of toasts. Each side struggled for possession of the support of common white men— or the "people," as the newspapers called them. DuVal flattered his "Centreville friends—hospitable, brave, and intelligent," and the Whigs nominated local planter Kenneth Bembry, the wealthiest member of Pisgah church, for the legislature. Branch cousin John Judge angrily said, "The People of Centreville—may they not prove themselves inconsistent and fickle-minded as has been said of them." A more complimentary toast by Fletcher Whitaker, a grand-nephew of John Branch, repaired some of the damage. Yeoman style then took center stage. A man named Covington directed his hostility toward the pro-bank men whom he felt had tried to gull the "people": "The Cider Barrel, the Whig Liberty Cap—The appropriate image of a Federal party; a perfect emblem of all their arguments being made by grinding and pressing." Then countryman John Brickle registered the "people's" feelings by toasting (at that point, still-living) Leigh Read in rebuke of both the Conservatives' praise of Richard Call, and their earlier nomination of ex-Democrat Bembry: "Gen. Leigh Read—His ingratitude more strong than the traitor's arm."[57]

"Spectator," who had witnessed the scene, commented in the *Floridian* that "the people are true to their ancient faith." Plainly, the "people" were true not so much to the Democratic Party, for they had protested when its representatives did not back stay laws, as to their real "ancient faith": the ideal of white male equality. Yeoman voters were not to be easily taken in by mere condescension from Tallahassee politicians. Two weeks later, a Democratic meeting at Centreville that featured substantial yeoman participation vowed not to support any candidate who opposed a full and continued investigation of the territorial banks. The countrymen proved their point with an overwhelmingly Democratic vote in October, including the rejection of "traitor[ous]" neighbor Kenneth Bembry.[58]

Many citizens charged that the pro-bank men had bought Bembry off with the promise of political support and social acceptance, but they apparently offered David Brown more concrete rewards. Brown, a yeoman farmer and small slaveowner from the Centreville neighborhood, had first made his mark as the least wealthy anti-bank candidate to contend for the honor of representing Leon County at the 1838–39 constitutional convention. But shortly after publicly announcing his candidacy, Brown received a mortgage from the Union Bank. While many other slaveowning yeomen from his neighborhood had subscribed for small amounts of bank stock during 1837–38, few received shares during the reapportionment that followed. Neighbor Adam Gramling, for instance, applied for twenty shares, and was allowed to purchase none. By contrast, the bank directors granted Brown twenty, and a mortgage of $2,000 secured on two slaves and 240 acres of land. His credit was miniscule compared to someone like Francis Eppes, who borrowed $51,000 from an institution run by brother-in-law John Parkhill. Yet Brown, already pressed by several small debts, may have needed the mortgage to save his few slaves and the three "eighths" of land that he now owned. In the spring of 1839, pro-bank governor Richard Call named Brown a justice of the peace for the county, which allowed Brown to add "esq." to his name. In return for the loan and the appointment, Brown served the pro-bank men well with his decision to release Willis Alston on bail. His own neighbors rejected him, never electing him to another office.[59]

In the end, the attempt to manipulate Centreville yeomen failed. Like violence in the streets, or the shooting of the popular Read, the apparent purchase of justice actually helped finish off the pro-bank Whigs as a viable political force. Voters rendered their own judgment. In 1841 and 1842, massive electoral defeats for the Whigs signaled the public's rejection of their tactics. As voters and as participants in political meetings, Middle Florida yeomen had, by the end of 1839, already changed the nature of politics. Popular party "principles" reigned. In 1842, the Democratic legislature officially repudiated the faith bonds, announcing that the people of Florida were not bound to pay the bad debts of the Union Bank's stockholders. Though Call remained the appointed governor until 1844, he could not, as he proudly proclaimed, adapt to the "democratic" era. In fact, he never won a popular election after 1823, although he ran for office repeatedly over the next thirty-seven years. With the new dominance of popular politics, this prototype of the dominant planter, who rode enemies "as [they had] never been ridden before," became a peripheral figure. Years later, as Call lay on his death bed, John Branch's granddaughter wrote, "He has lost his mind entirely, the country will not lose much by his death, poor, wicked old man." His friend and ally John Gamble was also finished, both as a political figure and as a financial power broker. Single-minded devotion to the bank had even led him to feud with his former allies, the Parkhills. "Old G.," wrote one of John Parkhill's friends, ". . . he is a *lunatic.*" Both the old factional leaders and the politics that had ruled Middle Florida for two decades were out of style by the early 1840s. But the catalytic influence of the Union Bank continued for even longer than its death throes.[60]

In May 1842, an individual calling himself "John Caldwell" wrote a letter to the Tallahassee *Star of Florida*. He tried to put into context the cataclysmic changes he had seen over the last three years:

> I was glad to hear an acknowledgment of the hand of God. I have doubts whether the page of History furnishes a parallel for the pressure and universal bankruptcy of '42. But history, both sacred and profane, furnishes us with many lessons, from which we may profit in our distress—let us remember that we are in the hands of that God, that smote the rock in the wilderness and brought forth water. . . . In our prosperity we became idolaters [in 1830s Florida] we denied the position assumed, that the Earth and the fullness belong to the Lord; we set up claims for ourselves.[61]

To "John Caldwell," the crisis of Middle Florida's plantation society was nothing less than the drama of an entire people's fall from grace: the sin of human idolatry, and God's wrathful response. The metaphors he used showed the impact his once-confident peers had felt under the storm's punishing blows. By early 1841, although some politicians continued to argue about the fate of the Union Bank and its bonds, the plantation economies of Jackson and Leon Counties tottered toward collapse. Planters believed their region shrank under the cope of a metaphorical storm that would lay waste to every frontier fortune. "It is true," wrote one, "this District is wealthy, but of what avail are houses, plantations and slaves, when debt hangs like a cloud over them, when specie has disappeared, and exchange gone up to a high rate, when the Court dockets are thronged with suits, and if brought under the hammer, property must be sacrificed."[62] This vision was accurate: once the crash came, it wrecked Middle Florida's financial house of cards. Debt had piled upon debt, and now everything came due. Almost no one could pay what he owed, and many planters faced ruin. Middle Florida planters' confidence, already shaken by political transformations, took another pummeling.

The economic crisis of Middle Florida was part of a wider downturn experienced by the trans-Atlantic commercial world. When a credit contraction in England and in American land markets—the panic of 1837—combined with plummeting cotton prices, northeastern merchants began to call in debts. The full force of the contraction did not really hit Middle Florida until some time in 1839, but by 1840, one dollar of Union Bank money only bought between 60 and 70 cents in hard cash or in the notes of more respected banks. Locofoco assaults raised doubts about the commitment of the territory to back the bank's bonds with its own credit. The legislature's investigation of the institution revealed the bank's own helplessness. It held only $13,000 in specie to back a minimum of $500,000 in circulating notes. By 1842, the Union Bank's bills had plummeted still further, to one-third of their face value.[63]

The steep discount of local currency increased planters' and merchants' costs. Tallahassee and Apalachicola merchants who accepted Union Bank dollars at face value would lose up to 70 percent of the value they had paid to purchase goods from New Orleans and New York wholesalers. By 1840, the merchants who sold barrels of beef, cloth, bagging and rope for cotton, and other goods to Jackson and Leon planters were already in debt to their wholesalers. They raised prices, cut off credit, and refused to accept the worthless Union Bank dollars that were all most customers had. Low cotton prices, followed by an 1841 plague of caterpillars that cut Jackson and Leon County growers' production in half, made the picture look bleak indeed. "The facts are before us, and they are sufficiently painful," moaned one commentator, "specie scarce as hen's teeth, the country flooded with shin-plasters, exchange not to be had." Pressed by their own creditors, merchants had to state plainly, like Tallahassee's J. B. Bull, that they could accept nothing but cash: "Being chased by the frost of the regions North, we are compelled to sell exclusively for cash." But now no one possessed cash worth accepting. Merchants began to take customers to court in order to stave off their own impending doom.[64]

Pressure from Middle Florida merchants, however, was far from being the only economic problem that beset local planters. The whole layered structure of local credit was collapsing. Foreign investors' money, channeled into the territory between 1835 and 1839 by the Union Bank, had become the central source of credit for Middle Florida planters. Between 1837 and 1839, while the wider international economy floundered, Middle Florida's indebtedness to the Union Bank reached a dangerous peak. In Leon County, where 104 of the bank's 139 stockholders resided, planters like Samuel Parkhill continued to borrow without restraint. Supplied with tens of thousands of dollars from the bank that his brother helped to direct, he owed, by 1839, over $100,000 to the bank, local merchants, and other planters. In all, the bank held mortgages to over 94,000 acres and 1,333 slaves in Leon County. Thus, one-third of the first-rate enslaved "hands" in Leon County, and more acres than were actually cultivated officially, belonged to the bank. Jackson County's less favored stockholders made up a smaller part of the population and had granted liens on only 126 slaves and 21,752 acres of land. But clearly the drowning bank clutched in its hands important portions of the Middle Florida's plantation economy.[65]

In addition to demanding interest payments, the bank also curtailed many loans, calling in planters' notes in an effort to recover liquidity and right its balance of payments. By the fall of 1841, the bank's situation was hopeless. Although Leon County's superior court had been idle through much of 1841, as the federal government searched for a replacement for Judge Balch, debtors failed to raise funds sufficient to pay off creditors during their accidental reprieve. Low cotton prices and the failed harvest meant that many actually fell further behind. When a new judge, Samuel Douglass, arrived in late 1841, he brushed aside threats intended to deter him from holding court and announced his determination to clear a docket crowded with lawsuits by desperate creditors.[66]

Douglass came close to accomplishing his goal. He covered eighteen hundred cases between early December 1841 and March 11, 1842, before adjourning and moving on to the next county on the circuit. Day after day, lawyers marched their cases before the judge, and day after day Douglass awarded mortgaged property, or the cash value of unpaid notes, to plaintiffs. On December 29, for instance, among many cases, he ordered John Parkhill (now no longer the Union Bank's cashier) to pay the bank over $2,000 and found that William DuVal's son Alexander owed over $22,000. For stockholders who had made multiple mortgages, the bank initiated multiple suits, one for each. Thus the court ordered William Wyatt to pay the bank $6,000 in several separate judgments on February 16, and on the 19th ruled against him for $11,000 more. Not all suits emanated from the bank; the region's merchants and planters also tried desperately to recover cash from debtors. The toll mounted, until it covered 380 closely written pages in the court's minute book.[67]

Economic disaster saturated public spaces that had once seen performances of planter power. After each court session, advertisements announcing the sales of property attached for the payment of debts plastered the front, back, and even inner pages of the weekly newspapers. As so often happened in such economic crises, the ordinary court process actually made things worse. "Fifteen hundred executions," stated the planters and merchants sitting on the Leon County grand jury, "are said to have issued from our Courts within the last three months, and it is a well-known fact that there is not in the country specie enough to pay on these the legal fees of the officers of the Court—What, then, must be the sacrifice of property!" Plaintiffs demanded specie—hard cash, not worthless bank paper—and court fees were also payable only in specie. Usually the defendant could not pay either fees or debt—if he or she had been solvent, then the case would never have gone to judgment. And so the court ordered slaves, land, and livestock "attached" and sold at the courthouse door. Yet, given the paucity of specie in the "country," few sales brought anything near the amount owed, much less the actual value of the property sold. "The plaintiff, in one of these cases," added the grand jury, "received about one-thirtieth of his original claim, one-tenth of the entire amount of the sale, and the other nine-tenths were required to defray the costs of the suit and collection."[68] Leon County debtors could only sue their debtors to recover money, continuing the domino effect. Debt fell on top of debt and no one had any money to impede a general economic collapse. "It is of great importance to us that we make some collections [on debts] to aid us in getting through the winter," wrote Joseph Branch to his brother Lawrence. "I fear we will be much troubled to get by."[69]

Debt plagued Jackson planters as well, particularly the most wealthy ones. Richard Long wrote to Farish Carter, "Certainly my Dear Sir there was never such a time of suffering for the want of money as now exists." Long later tried to get Carter to assume the mortgages that he and his sons owed to the Union Bank. He probably believed that Carter, one of the richest men in the South, would be able to withstand the general economic pressure. Long's personal ties to Carter might then keep the latter from pressing him for payment. Few Jackson County debtors could count on such treatment, and in November 1841, one commentator wrote from Marianna, "The times are hard, money mighty scarce. . . . Our county is somewhat in debt, but we hope ere long to work out." But many were unable to "work out" of debt. One was Peter W. Gautier Jr., politician and editor of the St. Joseph *Times*, who had left politics and returned to his Jackson County plantation to try to save his estate. There, a Marianna correspondent reported, he was "cultivating 'peas and philosophy,' in imitation of the illustrious Jefferson." Like Jefferson a generation earlier, Gautier proved unable to extricate himself from debt.[70]

The peculiar nature of much of the security for Middle Florida debts complicated the resolution of debt cases. Slaves were a highly mobile and easily concealed form of property, and many debtors took advantage of their capabilities. Some planters secretly dealt to purchasers in other states enslaved African Americans who had been attached by local creditors. When Wesley Adams, a debtor of the Union Bank, reported that twelve of his slaves had burned to death in a fire, his creditors immediately suspected that he had sold them off to New Orleans or Texas. Only a close examination of the charred bodies convinced them otherwise. Other planters absconded in the middle of the night with entire slave forces. Lawyer Joseph Branch, who with his brother Lawrence O'Bryan pursued many Middle Florida debtors in the interest of the stockholders of the Southern Life and

Trust Company, wrote in 1844 that "all of the Neal Negroes, except two, have been run off by Neal and his friends and have escaped into Texas."[71]

In such cases, sheriffs and deputy marshals sometimes scrawled the abbreviation "G.T.T." on the papers that they could no longer serve once insolvent debtors had slipped out of the reach of the law and "Gone To Texas." Texas was, of course, an independent white republic in the early part of the decade, and it became the refuge of many escaped debtors or criminals. Cosam E. Bartlett, the sarcastic editor of the *Star*, preferred to call this phenomenon "Tall Walking," referring to a phrase used in contemporary ads for elegant boots that supposedly permitted the wearer to perambulate while surveying his surroundings in a lordly manner. The editor ridiculed the contrast between pretensions to planter honor and what he saw as the dishonorable reality of running away from debts. Bartlett singled out Peter W. Gautier Jr., "the late witty and talented editor of the St. Joseph *Times*, sometimes called the 'beautiful boy,'" who gave up on peas and philosophy and fled to Texas with his father and their slaves to escape a combined debt of $30,000 or more. "He was lately seen walking very tall—toward Texas, taking along with him some seventy negroes belonging to the Union Bank."[72]

Gautier was a Locofoco or anti-bank man, and the Whiggish Bartlett called his escape "a practical illustration of the doctrine of 'repudiation.'" Thus the editor linked what he saw as the shameful political act of denying that the Florida government and people were responsible for paying off the "faith bonds" with the shameful personal act of running from one's debts. Yet he also saw Gautier's escape as part of a broader phenomenon, "only a specimen of 'Tall Walking.'" The irony of planters who had once strutted tall now slinking off in the night suggests that the economic crisis of the early 1840s battered not only pocketbooks but psyches as well, destroying dreams of power in Middle Florida. Whole families of elite whites left in disgrace—like Gautier, for instance, who escaped with his father, Peter Sr., in-law John Milton, a Jackson County planter, and a train of enslaved African Americans due to be sold off for debt. Bartlett concluded his discussion by comparing "G.T.T." debtors to common white criminals: his last "specimen" of "Tall Walking" was convicted murderer Thomas Horan, a poor white man who had allegedly killed Port Leon's James Murphy in a drunken rage. Horan, after being sentenced to hang, broke out of the Leon County jail and fled on horseback; a posse caught him in Jefferson County. "In the end," Bartlett intoned, some "Tall Walkers" had "stepped a little too low, and were consequently not able to reach Texas as soon as they had counted on." By lumping the Gautiers and Milton with Horan, who was executed on February 23, 1842, Bartlett suggested many things, including both his contempt for Locofoco politicians and the fact that the depression was destroying the fortunes of Democratic and pro-bank elite families alike. Most of all he revealed that economic collapse had undermined planters' claims to many kinds of predominance in Middle Florida. And so many slunk off westward: Jesse Willis from Leon to Louisiana; Ambrose Crane and William DuVal from Tallahassee to Texas, and so on. "Alas," said the editor of the *Floridian*, "They may tell you the stockholders' lands and negroes will pay [the Union Bank bonds]." But "we fear some of [the stockholders] may have to be hunted up in Texas when the time comes to sell them." [73]

The depression of the international economy, beginning in 1837, and the ambitions of local planters had thus touched off in 1840 a general economic crisis of the plantation frontier. Credit policies designed to fulfill planter families' relentless desire for capital and power, and to control relationships to the world economy, had helped to engender overexpansion, opposition, and collapse. Now, in 1842, the Leon County grand jury compared the troubled days in which they lived to "ordinary times." The members of the jury clearly believed that "the destruction of all public and private credit" showed that they were in the midst of a crisis of historical proportions. "The extent and degree of distress," they reported, "is almost without a parallel." The very landscape seemed devastated by the fall of a metaphorical colossus: "When the Banks went down they carried others with them. The commerce and trade of the country was crushed in their fall. . . . And now throughout the broad expanse of our country nothing presents itself but embarrassment, desolation, and ruin." "The hand of Providence is on our land," resolved an 1842 meeting led by ex-bank men like John Parkhill, Thomas Brown, and Richard Hayward. Only God's intervention in history could have brought a once-proud class so low, so suddenly. Men looked for, but mostly feared, what "Publicus" called "a new order of things" that loomed stormlike on the horizon. [74]

Oddly, the crisis would disappear, even before the Civil War, from histories of both Middle Florida and the wider South. So was the view that interpreted the early 1840s as a historical disaster of the first order merely hyperbole typical of the era's public speech? Or did it actually capture a local ruling class's understanding of a series of disasters, now forgotten, that for a time seemed ready to shatter the order of a plantation frontier? The white people of Jackson and Leon Counties had many reasons, perhaps, to believe that the hand of Providence was indeed raised against them. The overwhelming impact of the debt and currency crisis mounted with the highest crests of anxiety about political disruptions and Seminole war.

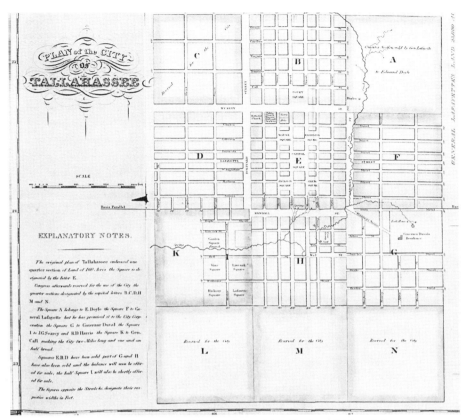

Plan of the City of Tallahassee (Archives and Special Collections, Richter Library, University of Miami)

On top of that came a series of events over which neither once-masterful planters, nor any other human beings, could exert any control.

Drought, plagues of cotton-eating caterpillars, and a devastating 1843 hurricane that wiped out Port Leon were among the area's nearly Mosaic plagues. But the most costly of all was disease. The 1841 outbreak of yellow fever was not the first epidemic to hit Tallahassee. The deadly mosquito-borne virus had appeared several times since 1831. Through the ports of the St. Marks and Apalachicola Rivers, Leon and Jackson Counties were in constant contact with cities where the virus made almost yearly appearances: New Orleans, Mobile, Havana, and Key West. But the 1841 version of the yellow jack was the worst ever in Middle Florida. The epidemic hit early and lasted late, and swept away dozens of Middle Florida's most well-established leaders. The virus (or Providence, as many Middle Floridians argued) proved from the earliest days of July that it was no respecter of persons. Former governor Robert R. Reid was one of the first to die, on July 1. Then victims in Tallahassee and the surrounding area began to drop quickly. Longtime resident Richard Allen died in early August, as the pace of deaths accelerated to eight or nine victims a day. In contrast to previous Middle Florida epidemics, the fever did not remain confined in urban areas. By August, it spread to the plantations. Rain barrels, standing water, and concentrations of victims provided an ideal atmosphere for the virus and its mosquito vector. Countrymen, many of whom lived in low-density settlements and dry areas, were safer than town dwellers, or planters. But slaves, more exposed by their location than anyone, may have suffered dreadfully from the epidemic, despite a partial immunity that some may have inherited from their African ancestors. Their deaths did not make the newspapers, in contrast to those of planters like Eli Whitaker, John Branch's cousin. He and his wife, Mary, sister of the Bradford brothers, perished in September. So did Rebecca Williams, daughter of John Branch and wife of Robert W. Williams. Death hit the Virginia families as well. Samuel Parkhill died at the beginning of September, sending his debt-entangled estate into a spiral of confusion.[75]

Fear spread ahead of the fever. Planters fled Tallahassee for the area around John Parkhill's auxiliary plantation, Bel Air, a settlement in the piney sand hills six miles southeast of Tallahassee. It quickly became known as a safe summer resort for the Tallahassee area's elite, while those not privileged with access to the resort sardonically called it "Scratch Ankle" from the sand fleas that bit planters' legs. But in the meantime, less rational responses held center stage. The merchants and other residents of St. Joseph abandoned the town for good, while in Tallahassee, some tried to deny that the fever was in truth severe. The *Floridian*'s editor, Edward Gibson, complained in August of exaggerated accounts of the rapidity of death by yellow fever. Many said that victims expired in as little as six hours. This, said the editor, was ridiculous, since he believed three days usually passed before the fever became fatal. A few weeks later he, too, perished of the disease—within a few hours after he first showed symptoms. Self-willed ignorance was not uncommon, especially since the "remedies" prescribed by the science of the time could do little more than add to the fever's impact. A visitor reported that "the only way they kept alive was by taking calomel [a mercury-based medicine] by the ounces and now they look more like walking skeletons than like live persons."[76]

By October, the onset of colder weather had finally killed off the disease's mosquito vector, and the fever abated. But the impact had been devastating, both in human and, perhaps, in psychological terms. Though few deaths had occurred in Jackson County, the fever had all but wiped out St. Joseph, one of its main ports. In Tallahassee itself, according to some survivors, 400 out of 1,600 residents died. And in the epidemic's path, death sped the pace of court actions, exacerbating the impact of debt. The executors and administrators of dozens of debt-encumbered estates pressed and were pressed for the final resolution of debts.[77]

Still the region's troubles had not ended. Late in the afternoon of May 25, 1843, a fire began in Tallahassee's Washington Hall, ironically the site of temperance meetings that were supposed to help the town overcome its troubled state. Racing quickly through tightly packed wooden stores and taverns, within three hours the fire burned almost every structure in the business district. From the capitol square north to the wide "200-foot" street where Willis Alston had shot Leigh Read, only the Planters' Hotel stood, alone among block upon block of ashes. No lives were lost, but a committee formed to estimate the damages judged that $650,000 of property had burned. Only two businesses, together worth $18,000, possessed fire insurance.[78]

The Middle Florida elite understood the fire as one more item in a series of disasters; and the overturning of old certainties. Everything that happened to them fit into the paradigm of crisis, and chastisement by an angry God. The recent history of the area, to hear Jackson or Leon elites tell it, was nothing but a succession of reverses and disruptions. In Tallahassee, a committee of local worthies gathered immediately after the fire was put out. They could only ascribe what had happened to incomprehensible forces: "It has pleased an inscrutable Providence to afflict, by an awful calamity, the inhabitants of a city on the frontier of the Union." The once-proud planters addressed an appeal for relief to the rest of the United States: "At five o'clock in the afternoon of Thursday, the 25th of May, the city of Tallahassee, numbered, with a population not exceeding two thousand souls, eighty-nine stores and houses, the theatre of active mercantile and manufacturing industry. In three hours, by a devastating fire, which no exertion could stay, not a solitary store, shop, or theatre of business remained." Middle Florida's elite men felt their once-orderly world spinning out of their hands, leaving them feeling exposed, chastised, and embarrassed. Such words were part of the vocabulary of honor, but they denoted negative states that marked their inhabitants as unmanned. And elite men could not respond to the degradation that such words implied. There was no one to challenge, no one to blame. And at any rate, who among them would have accepted a challenge from men so dishonored as they themselves were?[79]

Despite Middle Floridians' understandable focus on their own particular circumstances, the crisis that overwhelmed Middle Florida's planter class was only one part of a much wider phenomenon. Across the Old Southwest, a decade or more of rapid expansion came to a sudden stop after 1837. Cotton prices plummeted, in part because of overproduction. After the crisis began, frontier planters and merchants paid a double penalty: the recent glut of credit made their money weak, and the ease of obtaining credit had buried most deep in debt. How would they pay with depreciated currency, high debts, and low cotton prices? Most could not, and for ten years after the initial panic, sales for bankruptcy, notices of defaulted debtors, and advertisements for slave auctions covered the pages of Southwestern newspapers. Crisis had more than purely economic causes and effects. The indebtedness and speculation driven by Southwestern banks was a fuse that touched off the potentially explosive resolution of numerous social, political, and cultural contradictions on the plantation frontier. Angry yeomen challenged the political status quo, and social changes followed. Planters' disparate reactions to yeomen who refused to continue to play the subordinate showed their uncertainty and fear. And other changes set in motion by crises of debt altered Southern planters' relationships to the North and to the Atlantic economy as a whole. Perhaps when "John Caldwell" and the other elite commentators of the early 1840s used plague and destruction, storm and biblical metaphor to describe the history through which they were passing they did not exaggerate. In the wake of change, planters, once dazzled by fantasies of frontier power and their own invulnerable manhood, would have to choose new ways to live, both as white men in their local communities and as a slaveowning elite in a wider world. Their society would never be the same again. But no Middle Floridians were as deeply affected by the continued uncertainty of life on the plantation frontier as the enslaved African Americans whose story unfolds in the next chapter.

White Men Are Very Uncertain

SLAVERY AND FRONTIER SOCIETY

The narrative of Daphne Williams does not come to us already labeled as the autobiography of a Middle Floridian. When federal workers interviewed her in the 1930s, the elderly woman lived instead in Texas, where she thought she might be the "mos' ageables' person" in her county. But she was born a slave near Tallahassee, probably in the early 1830s. She claimed to remember seeing the great Leonid meteor shower of 1833, "when the stars fell," and that many who watched thought that the Last Judgment had arrived. In the early 1840s, her owners moved to Texas, taking Daphne with them on a steamboat to Beaumont at the mouth of the Neches River. The rest of their slaves, including her mother and father, had already come out to clear the land and start a crop. The chronology of their migration makes it unlikely that Williams's owners engaged in "Tall Walking," since the field laborers went out to Texas some time before the whites left Florida. Still, they departed in the midst of Middle Florida's crisis, and perhaps because of economic difficulties. Daphne left behind relatives like her uncles Shack and Bob, who were most likely sold on the steps of Tallahassee's courthouse to pay some of the debts that drove her owners west.[1] The whites who claimed her had already sent her mother ahead to set up the new plantation in Texas, so they were separated for several years as well. The experience of arbitrary separation from her child was surely one more reason why Williams's mother "wanted to live till freedom," as Daphne put it. She died after a long struggle, before ever achieving that goal. Daphne would be more fortunate. But her mother's faith that freedom would one day come was certainly astonishing, since her experience had seemingly given her so little reason for such a hope.

Of all responses to the experience of enslavement on the frontier, hope could seem an unlikely one. Anger, discouragement, or despair might seem more likely, for disruption and violence, exploitation and hardship never seemed to lessen. Williams's owners' move had cut off the new ties by which her parents had bound together a life on the plantation frontier. By the 1850s, thousands of such expatriate Middle Floridians were scattered across the Southwestern plantation states, just as Middle Florida itself was filled, and refilled, with the lost and separated from the Southeast. Daphne Williams's story reminds us that the fall of the rag empire in Jackson and Leon Counties marked the lives of enslaved Middle Floridians, and perhaps did so even more visibly than those of the planters who felt emasculated by their sudden self-perception as helpless and defeated. For the enslaved, there was no settlement, only more migration and more frontiers. In Williams's case, the events of frontier crisis sent her to live her life as a Texan, rather than a Middle Floridian. Something so basic as the very geographical space in which she lived out her life reminds us that efforts to rebuild community on the plantation frontier were always subject to the uncertain behaviors of white men and women. Yet black memory and resistance, based in part on a sense of history and what to do about that history, and in part on wanting to see freedom, endured—a persistence that was itself a source of hope.

Even though enslaved African Americans did not participate in the political battles that racked Tallahassee and the surrounding area during these years, the chronology of frontier settlement and crisis was theirs as well. They, too, faced a crisis brought on by the dilemmas of white manhood and the imperatives of frontier dreams. Of course, in their lives, different events were significant, in different ways. Change occurred at a different pace. For instance, African Americans re-created themselves, merging the disparate individuals and families brought by slave trades and slaveowners' migrations into one group, long before squabbling political factions or yeoman and planter whites could do the same among themselves. The courses of action available to the enslaved, and the ways in which they sought to change their circumstances were also very different from those available to migrant whites. Male slaves, for instance, could not afford to couch their resistance in the dilemmas and language of masculinity—at least not in terms that sounded anything like those of either countrymen or gentlemen.

Slaveowners' decisions to initiate forced migration had already transformed both slaves' burdens and the ways in which they looked at the past and the future of enslavement. Then the continued chaos of white society on the plantation frontier—the uncertainty of white men—shaped the conditions in which resistance by the enslaved could—or could not—take place. Paying attention to the chronology of frontier boom and bust thus illuminates the history of change in black society, just as for white. Like the different class-specific versions of white manhood, the dilemmas of black family and community were not constant but had a history in Middle Florida, one on which events like those surrounding the rise and fall of the Union Bank left a mark. And while resistance in Middle Florida could not create a clear victory for the enslaved, we might do well to remember that it rendered uncertain the triumph of those who sought domination over black people.

FAMILY AND FRONTIER HISTORY AT EL DESTINO

In 1835, a man named John Walker was moved from Culpeper County, Virginia, to Leon County. He was forced to leave behind his first wife and two children. Separated from his family, he remarried. Was this because, as slaveowners sometimes claimed when breaking up African Americans' families, people like John Walker simply did not care much about family and thus were not as devastated by such divisions as whites would themselves have been? The evidence suggests that Walker never forgot those whom he had been forced to leave behind. Through messages passed along by later enslaved migrants from the Culpeper area, Walker kept up with his Virginia family, and learned that one of his children had died. But Walker, like countless others, had to choose between despair and rebuilding. His remarriage was not desertion but an attempt to adapt to circumstances beyond his control.[2] Once brought to the Middle Florida frontier, African Americans like John Walker were able to create new families and kinship networks despite disease, separation, and distorted demographic structures. By the late 1830s, unfree migrants were also overcoming whatever cultural distinctions existed between the different groups of slaves brought to Jackson and Leon Counties. Rebuilt families in brand-new quarters could not entirely replace what had been lost, nor erase the painful scars of separation, but most enslaved African Americans doggedly endured the emotional pain of removal. From old and new family ties and marriages, from "fictive" and "real" kin, they pieced together new webs of kinship and community. Such accomplishments were difficult tasks indeed, as the example of African American life on El Destino plantation suggests.

During the 1830s and 1840s, Leon County's El Destino plantation was owned successively by William Nuttall, his widow Mary Nuttall, and then her second husband, George Noble Jones. Nuttall, from Virginia, launched the plantation in 1828, bringing forty slaves from Virginia to clear land at a site on the eastern border of Leon County. His list of the first forty grouped these individuals into seven households (see Table 7.1). Two of them, those headed by Isham and his wife, Mary Isham, and Pleasant and Betty, were two-parent households.[3] Three, including the ones headed by

TABLE 7.1. *Slaves Taken to Leon County by William Nuttall in 1828, by Household*

Isham and Mary	Pleasant and Betsy	Kate	Phillis	Sim	No Apparent Head	Temp
Chesley	Charles	Nutty	Frank	Muriah	Willie	
Demps	Iverson	(Netta)	Reubin	Betsy	Frank	
Stephen	Young	Easter	Haywood	Rachel	Peter	
Emily	Susan	Hannah	Sam		Tom	
L[ittle]	Elisa	Colman			Moses	
Pleasant	Jane				Currie	
Minna						
Melia						
Nancy						
Mary John						

Source: "List of Negroes sent to Florida March 1st 1828," in Kathryn T. Abbey, "Documents Relating to El Destino and Chemonie Plantations, Middle Florida, 1828–1868," pt. 1, *Florida Historical Quarterly* 7 (January 1929): 206–7.

Kate and Phillis, and what appears to be one headed by Sim, had only one parent present—at least once these families were actually brought south. Six men composed another household: each was probably stripped, regardless of existing family ties, from slave auctions or the Nuttall family's holdings. The final migrant, Temp, later the mother of several El Destino slaves, appears to have been a single female living on her own.[4]

We can do no more than guess at the relationships between the various households on the list. Perhaps Pleasant was the brother of Mary Isham, or of Isham, which would explain why the couple named their son Pleasant. Undoubtedly internal relationships of kinship linked at least some of the seven households, but as the case of the six single men suggests, migration had probably already disrupted ties to other households left behind in Virginia. Further disruptions followed movement to Middle Florida. By 1834, El Destino was producing cotton, but rampant disease and Nuttall's constant financial maneuvers had already taken a toll. Twelve of the initial forty forced settlers were already gone. Little Pleasant, Iverson, Frank (Phillis's son), Reuben, Haywood, Muriah, and all six members of the household apparently composed of young single men—Willie, Frank, Peter, Tom, Moses, and Currie—had disappeared from Nuttall's slave inventories. The last six might have gone to the auction block to pay off some of his extensive debts. Alternatively, several or all could have died from malaria, yellow fever, or other diseases.[5]

Photograph of overseer's house, El Destino (Duke University Archives)

Nuttall's slaves responded to repeated disruptions by turning to techniques of survival and support repeated all over Middle Florida. Young
people separated from parents adopted fictive ties of kinship to scarce older
slaves. Foster parents and grandparents insured that orphaned migrants
had food and shelter. And both new and surviving ties sometimes gained in
intensity what they had lost in extension. Siblings who remained together
displayed a visceral desire to help each other. When D. N. Moxley, overseer at El Destino, caught a woman named Venus running away to town,
he hustled her forcibly toward the plantation's jail. She "broke to run, and I
[Moxley] caught her." Her brother Aberdeen reacted instantly: he "caught
up an axe to strike me, and Prince [the black driver] prevented him." Prince
saved Moxley's life, and Aberdeen's as well. But Aberdeen had been willing to kill, and probably to die, to protect his sister. Some siblings, di-
vested of older kin, drew ever closer to each other: Leon County's Henry,
Ned, Lewis, and Willis Johnson, and their sister Delphy Jones made up
a common household long after reaching adulthood. The determination
with which they clung together was one response to separation from other
family members.[6]

The individual and collective desires of planters like William Nuttall—
their "interests" and their "feelings"—kept life in a bubbling turmoil, but
the pot boiled over in the late 1830s. In the next few years, the explosive outcome of white individual and group conflicts finished off many a planter's

dream. Adjustment to the separations brought about by initial movement to the cotton frontier turned out to have been only the first step for enslaved settlers, as new separations began to take place. El Destino was no exception: William Nuttall's 1832 marriage to a Savannah heiress had added many more laborers to El Destino. With her hand in marriage, Mary Savage brought to Nuttall fifty-two enslaved African Americans from the Savages' Silk Hope and Point plantations in the Ogeechee River delta. Some of these slaves, or their parents, had been among the forty-eight thousand Africans brought by slave traders to Georgia in the 1790s and early 1800s. So, while the Nuttall slaves came from a culture produced by two centuries of interaction between Africans, African Americans, and whites in the Chesapeake, those from the Point and Silk Hope plantations mixed immediate African inheritances in their distinctive low-country Gullah language and cultural complex. Nuttall further complicated the process of community formation by mortgaging almost his entire slave force to the Union Bank. He used some of the money to dip into the domestic slave trade, bringing to El Destino many solitary individuals divorced from all ties to family.[7]

Within a decade of El Destino's foundation, then, over one hundred slaves came to the plantation from at least three different sources. Each group brought different cultural inheritances and distinct, though battered, ties of kinship. Then, in 1836, Nuttall suddenly died. Now the sloppiness of the financial ventures he left behind threatened to force the complete liquidation of El Destino's communities. His old business partner and executor Hector Braden sold some slaves and contemplated selling more. The 1840 marriage of Savannah aristocrat George Noble Jones to the young widow Mary Savage Nuttall prevented the complete dispersal of the estate, although Jones sold some of the slaves to pay Nuttall's Union Bank debts. Disease also took a toll, carrying off Virginia migrants Elisa, Emily, Isham, Mary Isham, and Pleasant between 1844 and 1847. By 1847, only fifteen of the original cohort of forty remained on El Destino or Chemonie, a second plantation established with some of Nuttall's slaves.

Yet among these fifteen and their children, many had forged new links of kinship to migrants from the Ogeechee River plantations and elsewhere. Tempy married Georgia native Primus. Easter married Barac, born on the Point plantation near Savannah in 1814. Melia, the daughter of Isham and Mary Isham, married Jimmey. Before her death, Emily married newly purchased Ben Jackson. Stephen married Winney, Sam married Ann, and Jane married Nelson. Others married off the plantation, extending the web of kinship outward. None of the Nuttall slaves married among those who came from Virginia in 1828. Within a generation, enslaved people transported from various regions to the cotton frontier rewove families and communities, albeit in new patterns sharply marked by their experiences.[8]

Marriage mixed various groups of migrants, but as the children of those marriages grew, married, and had their own children, few forgot those lost in the long and destructive processes that had brought them to the frontier and then kept them unsettled. Like other African Americans in Middle Florida, El Destino slaves named children after forebears, especially those left behind or separated from them in the migration to the frontier. Demps, the brother of Chesley (both were sons of Isham and Mary), disappeared from plantation rosters between 1834 and 1844. Then a new Demps appeared, this one the son of Chesley and his new wife, Eve. Iverson, the son of Pleasant and Betsy, was gone by 1834. Twenty years later, Tempy, who could have been his sister or cousin, gave birth to one last child. She called this boy Iverson. And as the ties of marriage tightened between the Savage and Nuttall groups, they began to name children after each other. Robert Habersham, son of Prince Habersham, the driver and one of the most prized slaves brought by Mary Savage from Georgia, called his son Chesley. Melia and Jimmey named a daughter Priscilla, after Prissy, a women included on the marriage agreement that brought Mary Savage's slaves to Florida. Thus, the people living on El Destino began to name themselves as one group, despite their various and particular histories.

The bitter taste of forced migration's brutality and the sweet evidence of survival and rebirth mix as one sees how enslaved people built and rebuilt family and community in Middle Florida. Even where new links of kinship enabled African Americans to follow the El Destino model, the memorializing function of naming marked people with two-sided reminders of loss. Slaves in new communities on Middle Florida's plantation frontier looked both to the future and to the past, and they saw themselves as both weak and strong. Fathers, for instance, named sons after themselves, or their own fathers, carrying names into the future. Jesse Courtney, born in Virginia, left his father, Jesse, and his brother Jim behind. Courtney later named his sons Jesse and Jim. Jackson and Leon Counties' slaves did not forget. Ann Thornton, born in Warren County, North Carolina, saw her sister Trinket sold from Florida to a trader or planter from Mississippi. She named her daughter Trinket, after her vanished sister. Can we believe that people who named children after the lost and stolen did not tell stories like those described in Chapter 3, to youngsters whose very names served as markers of the loss that they had all endured? The younger Trinket would inevitably hear about the older, and what had happened to her. Memorializing fixed the fact of separation in the historical memory of slave communities, and wrote the names of stolen souls as living rebukes to the master class. Such naming was not only a refusal to let slaveowners have the final word in family and community histories but also a ritual that mourned the irretrievably lost.[9]

Despite the ways in which the enslaved survived and even overcame divisions and disruptions like those described in Chapter 4, the uncertainties of white behavior and the grandiosity of planters' aspirations continually caused new problems for African American forced migrants. Even in the 1820s, when the scale of local credit was small, debts compiled in the purchase of land and slaves overcame some frontier planters. In 1829, when Leon County's George Fisher could not pay his notes, the marshal put his property up for sale to the highest bidder, including "a likely Negro Boy, Arch, about eleven years old" and "JACK, CELIA, and her child, SARAH, CHARITY, and BERRY." Thomas Brown, new to sugar planting, delayed the cutting of his cane into November 1829, and a frost ruined his crop. Brown could not pay his multiple mortgages, and scores of his slaves mounted the auction block.[10] Louisa Ross, an ex-slave born in about 1828, remembered that Richmond's Charles Copland gave her mother to his son-in-law John Parkhill, and her father, to son William Copland. When William and John both moved to Leon County in 1827, Louisa's parents migrated to adjoining plantations. Copland, however, soon became bored with the project of clearing land. Looking for ready cash, he sold off his prime hands and rented out his plantation. Soon William "complain[ed] of the misery of idleness, produced as he sa[id] by having incautiously sold his male grown slaves" and wandered off to New Orleans, wondering what to do with his life. But in his attempt to find himself, Copland had taken Louisa's father with him to New Orleans and sold him. Now he was, to her, lost forever.[11]

Planters' desires for frontier power were always risky because they relied upon one of slavery's most consequential elements—human beings could be and were used as collateral, or as sources of ready cash. Schemes built on precisely that fact reached their highest point in the late 1830s, when the Union Bank wrapped all of Middle Florida in an unprecedented tangle of risk. When the bank colossus swayed, tottered, and crashed to the ground between 1839 and 1842, it dragged down masters and slaves in its wreck. As planters bewailed impending bankruptcy, the advertisement for a May 19, 1842, marshal's sale announced in plain type—"31 negroes to be sold on Monday"—that African Americans paid the greatest cost of elite failure. The total disappearance of money from the local economy meant that New Orleans traders were often the only whites who brought the required cash to Tallahassee auctions. The ever-hungry sugar plantations of Louisiana opened their giant collective maw, and kinfolks, spouses, and friends swirled down into the vortex. Traders took Richard Gadsden's siblings Thankful and Thomas to New Orleans. Sancho Thomas, once owned by the Hawkins family, migrants from North Carolina, remembered his brother: "Starling was carried to New Orleans" and no doubt sold in the Crescent City's famous slave market. Not all went to Louisiana: Nancy Williams reported that white men took her brother Owen Williams to Arkansas; and James Givens remembered that his father, James, and his mother, Letty, were sold to Tennessee in 1842. And absconding "G.T.T." whites used enslaved blacks as pawns in the desperate games of failed planters and their creditors. So the planter class caught the black settlers of Middle Florida up in its cycle of reconstruction and re-destruction.[12]

Lists of slaves for El Destino and Chemonie plantations provide a tally of the pervasive instabilities inflicted by the plantation frontier's disorderly white society. An 1847 tally of the Georgia bondpeople brought to Middle Florida by Mary Savage's 1832 marriage to William Nuttall contains fifty-four names. Fifteen were noted as "dead" in 1847—a high rate of death that in a young population signals the impact of epidemic disease. At least eleven had vanished, and were most likely among those sold to pay Nuttall's debt to the failed Union Bank. Most telling of all is the entry for Polly, with its brief notation, "sent by William B. N.[uttall] to New Orleans and sold."[13] Polly's sale, which raised cash for one of Nuttall's many investments, symbolizes the subjection of even the reconstructed stability of black families to the whims, manipulations, and chaos created by white Middle Floridians' frontier dreams. The ventures of planter men and their families risked wealth and honor, seeking more of the same coin. But slaves bore the cost of planters' lost wagers. New African American communities cracked, as auctioneers brought down their hammers to close sales for debt, and would have to be cast once more. The problem for slaves was simply, to quote an enslaved man, that "White men are very uncertain."[14]

THE AMBIGUITIES OF VIOLENT RESISTANCE

The history of a community like El Destino reveals in microcosm one kind of destructive impact, created by frontier boom and bust, on Middle Florida's African American population. In response, the enslaved people of El Destino, or anywhere else in Middle Florida, might well have responded with violence—however futile—to the sequences of white violence that scarred the lives of so many. One might look, in particular, to see if some ideology of masculinity sprang up to drive slave resistance. After all, planters' obsession with dominating masculinity, or yeoman fixation on not being dominated, seemed to undergird almost every conflict among white men. Some African Americans certainly did lash back at the enforcers of arbitrary white power, and began to do so early in the course of settlement. During cotton picking season in October 1827, on Isaac Mitchell's Leon County plantation, one such confrontation erupted between overseer Irvin Kent and an enslaved man named Ben. Ben may or may not have been new to cotton picking, like so many forced migrants from the Chesapeake. But he clearly refused to pick at the breakneck speed urged by Kent, who was eager to help Mitchell make a quick profit from his brand-new frontier venture. At the end of a hard—and evidently contentious—day in the field, Kent certainly told Ben to expect a whipping early the next morning. Ben went back to his hut, sat for a while, and made a choice. Picking up a club, he walked to the front of Kent's cabin, and knocked. When the overseer opened the door, Ben clubbed him to death and returned to his dwelling to await his fate.[15]

Ben sprang from a long line of rebels. From the earliest years of slavery in the New World, bondpeople launched direct attacks on the people and the system that held them captive: revolts, assaults on overseers and masters, open verbal criticism of whites, and running away. In the early years of slavery in the Southeastern United States, the newly enslaved had drawn upon ethnic and religious identities from Africa to organize rebellion. Many believed that they would return to their homeland after death, which emboldened them to confront masters with violence, or to commit suicide. Later, some African Americans turned republican and other ideologies of the American Revolution to the task of asserting their own equal freedom. Religious beliefs adopted and adapted from Christianity also played their part: by the time plantation society had taken root in Middle Florida, Nat Turner and other blacks had reworked messianic expectation as exhortation to apocalyptic rebellion.[16] And then, forced migration to Middle Florida brought separation, new and more difficult kinds of labor, and brutal punishment from barely known whites. Given their recent experiences, we should not be surprised that some struck back, redirecting plantation violence against its perpetrators.

One might choose to see Ben's attack as rebellion against tyranny, as homicide, or perhaps some of each. But he clearly knew that he had also committed something close to suicide. When seized and accused of the crime, Ben had replied that he did not care if he had killed Irvin Kent; nor did he care about the consequences. Arrested, indicted, and tried, he swung from the Tallahassee gallows on May 23, 1828. As Ben and every forced migrant knew, direct resistance to slavery—whether it took the shape of organized group revolts or individual acts—was extremely dangerous. Collective attacks on slavery usually led to failure and violent death for those who led and participated in revolts. In fact, compared to the vast rebellions in black-majority St. Domingue and Jamaica, the less extensive revolts that took place on the North American mainland, where a heavily armed white population outnumbered the enslaved, shrink in significance.[17]

That acts of violence were relatively scarce and that they were often individual and thus restricted in scope might suggest that the enslaved were somehow complicit in their own oppression. Yet such a view would imply that the only kind of resistance that could matter would be that which measured up to a single standard of organized rebellion and revolution, despite situations that varied considerably through the centuries of slavery in North America. Changing conditions could not help but shape new and different forms of opposition. The four hundred thousand Africans transported to the Chesapeake and Carolinas during the seventeenth and eighteenth centuries endured one kind of bondage. Their children and, in some cases, grandchildren and great-grandchildren lived in more stable slave societies and thus experienced something else. And their children, the unfree migrants taken to the Southwestern plantation frontiers of the United States in the nineteenth century, in turn, faced a chaotic and confusing experience of migration, settlement, and then unsettlement.[18]

Such conditions produced people like Ben in addition to creating new risks to accompany every endeavor of direct resistance on the plantation frontier. The white-designed demographics of the domestic slave trade and master-directed movements encouraged violent and direct resistance to masters' authority in Middle Florida, especially before approximately 1840. In the older states, long-established communities relied on parents and elders to train the young in more subtle, less risky forms of opposition to slavery.[19] In Jackson and Leon Counties, masters' truncation of plantation communities produced slave forces weighted heavily toward young, male slaves. In so structuring their labor forces, Middle Florida masters opened up a Pandora's box of trouble. As in virtually every other human society, among enslaved African Americans, older male adolescents and young men produced the majority of physical violence, especially violent individual resistance to established authority.[20] One might possibly view this resistance as a potential crisis spurred on by black manhood. Indeed, young adults, especially men, proved balky, confrontational, and resistant to the dehumanization directed at them on the plantation frontier. Conflicts, like Ben's attack on Irvin Kent, often developed out of the threat of individual punishment. In 1846, an enslaved African American owned by John Branch disarmed a marshal who came to arrest him and boldly flogged the white man with his own whip. Of course, while men were the most likely to enter the court system as defendants, women also fought back. For years, black Middle Floridians, both male and female, remembered with awe the woman who struck back against a whipping in 1849, killing overseer Christopher C. Bryant with her cotton hoe.[21]

Slaveowners, fearful that rebellion was a contagious disease, seem to have kept many incidents of retaliatory black violence out of Middle Florida newspapers and court records. Advertisements for fugitives reveal, however, the large number of slaves who attempted to limit or even reject slavery by running away or turning truant for a time. Some tried to return to their home states, or to find relatives scattered by the slave trade. Others made of running away and truancy a defiant way to reject white control of their labor and their bodies. Susan Bradford Eppes recalled Affie, a black "conjure-woman" who, refusing to live under the control of Edward Bradford, resided in the woods. She returned from time to time to visit the quarters, work her spells, and accept payment in return. The forests and swamps that surrounded most farms and plantations in Middle Florida offered ample opportunities to escape white control. During the season of cotton picking, the numbers of male and female truants exploded. As George Gray's Jackson County overseer reported: "The negroes can't pick to suit some of my neighbors and the Woods is full of runaway Negroes."[22]

In the hammocks and swamps, runaways and plantation slaves could subsist by hunting game and livestock. Therefore masters and overseers considered themselves lucky if they could say, "We have lost no stock this year, except three hogs that were eaten by run away negroes." And both the least settled and the most crowded zones of the plantation frontier provided opportunities for the enslaved to carve out a sort of freedom. In 1833, Charlotte was "supposed to be . . . lerking [sic] about Tallahassee," supporting herself by stealing from local kitchens. R. K. West suspected that Cain, a tall (6'1") man who had fled West's Leon County plantation, would go to Apalachicola and try to lose himself among the day laborers who loaded cotton bales into lighters and ships. River steamboats and sea-going ships were also possibilities. The life of the sailor or steamboat worker was difficult and dangerous, but at least he did not have to labor on a plantation under the supervision of a master or overseer.[23]

The region's newspapers reported runaways in printed advertisements, which provide a panoramic view of that form of resistance. As was the case among African American runaways in other parts of the country, men made up the vast majority—321 of 385, or 83 percent—of Middle Florida slaves who stole themselves. And runaways clearly reacted to, and at times took advantage of, the conflicts and upheavals created by white society (see Table A.9). During the early days, when the population of Jackson and Leon

Counties was still quite small, most runaways reported in Middle Florida were fleeing there from somewhere else. In 1821, Indians under U.S. colonel William Miller captured a group of fifty-eight fugitives from East Florida near the Apalachicola River.[24] In contrast, most of the escapees advertised in the second half of the 1820s were disgruntled migrants who sought to return to their old homes in the Chesapeake or the Carolinas. Then, in the five years after 1835, three times as many runaways were reported than in the years 1831–35. Planters had, of course, used Union Bank loans to import thousands of slaves to the area, and by 1840 controversy over the bank was probably prompting many of these new and enslaved Middle Floridians to flee in order to avoid being sold on the block once again. And during the Second Seminole War, Seminole raiders and white outlaw gangs roamed the woods, providing potential allies for African Americans eager to slip the bonds of slavery. Then, in 1850 and 1851, as local whites debated secession, runaway numbers would explode once again. Perhaps blacks seized upon white unrest as a sign of division and weakness.

Both motive and opportunity for violent resistance to slavery had increased on the plantation frontier. Looking backward, we might be tempted to seek examples of the hyper-masculinized image of violent rebellion and revolution. We might see them as conclusive evidence that the enslaved truly opposed their condition. On the other hand, we might believe that the absence of such examples—what white men of the day would have understood as the only real proof that the enslaved were not submissive to the core—shows complicity by African Americans in their oppression. By the 1830s, an angry and exiled population, composed disproportionately of young and male slaves, lived under the erratic tyranny of Middle Florida's frontier planters. Yet even young enslaved men knew quite well that they did not have the luxury granted to white planter men, who could wrap themselves in the imagery of an invulnerable manhood, and lash out against opponents. Slaves had to calculate their options with the clear knowledge that direct resistance was extremely hazardous to both the bodies and the souls of African Americans themselves. Outright rebellion usually rebounded tenfold, producing genocidal white reprisals that decimated entire slave communities. Further, if enslaved African Americans came to valorize violence, they might corrode their own psyches. Habituation to violence might make some slaves, frustrated and psychologically scarred by their inability to return blow for blow upon their oppressors, likely to turn aggression against their own families and communities.[25]

The latter danger of life in a society where authority exercised its power with erratic violence could have led to an enslaved population split by self-hatred, dissension, and admiration of high-handed masters. Some white observers claimed that blacks, especially men, had caught the disease of frontier hot-bloodedness. The French Comte de Castelnau, who visited Middle Florida during the late 1830s reported that in Tallahassee, "I have seen two hostile planters meet in horseback on the street and immediately start fighting with pistol and bowie knife, a fight in which their slaves took part." Castelnau implied that the love of violence and admiration for whites made all blacks incapable of identifying with each other: "The bodily punishments imposed on the slaves . . . seem to amuse the other negroes greatly, who seem little concerned by the thought that the next day they may experience the same fate; still it is true that at each stroke of the whip they burst out laughing, and by their capers show the pleasures which the charming spectacle they are viewing causes them."[26] Thus the violence of society supposedly transmuted the aggressive impulses of young male African Americans into another bulwark for slavery. And in truth, the slaves' reaction to their circumstances was rarely a simple thing. In the first decades of Middle Florida's settlement, masters and slave traders threw African American migrants together with people they did not know and sometimes did not like. Distinctions among Middle Florida's unfree migrants were sharp: groups and individuals on any single plantation might come from the distinctive cultures of South Carolina, North Carolina, or the Chesapeake. No one could be surprised if the enslaved sought to curry favor with masters to prevent further sale into the slave trade, or if some fought to establish reputations against new neighbors and co-workers to whom they had no ties of family or kinship.[27]

Yet, compared to the bloody record of local white-on-white violence, the almost complete silence of court, newspaper, and plantation records on the subject of black-on-black violent crime is stunning. Masters and overseers clearly carried out many punishments on the plantation itself, but the virtual absence from extant documents of serious slave-on-slave crimes like murder speaks volumes, especially in a region rife with white lawlessness. The facts argue that the level of violence between slaves must have been far lower than that between whites. On the other hand, far more dangerous to them were other frontier forces, outside of slaves' control. If white Middle Florida's descent into internal chaos in the late 1830s opened some opportunities for escape or outright rebellion, those openings created serious risks: for individuals, and for African Americans as a group.[28]

For instance, some African Americans saw the Seminoles' conflict with expansionist plantation society as an opportunity to shield their own behavior. Middle Florida runaways attempted to disguise attacks on whites as Seminole raids. In the summer of 1837, a party of "Indians" surrounded a house northeast of Magnolia. Yelling like Indians were supposed to do, the attackers stole various supplies and then burned the house to the ground. But a newspaper report stated that, while the robbers had put on a good performance as Seminoles, they were in fact "a group of *runaways*, of whom it is reported there are a number out from some of the frontier plantations." Later that same month, a seaman named Curry flashed too much money in a St. Marks dive. Curry accepted a ride to Jefferson County from a slave wagoneer owned by John Gamble. The next morning someone found the seaman lying in the Magnolia road, his throat slashed wide open, near the site of repeated attacks by Seminole raiders. White men questioned and searched Gamble's teamster before he could dispose of a large wad of cash, presumably taken from the late Mr. Curry.[29]

The shape of conflict between whites and Seminoles, however, limited runaway blacks' ability to form alliances, or to use the woods as a place to create a self-sufficient existence. Most of the Africans and African Americans who joined the Seminoles either before or during the Second Seminole War (1835–42) came from East Florida's coastal plantations. Although guerrilla raids brought the war to Middle Florida after 1837, joining the Seminoles was simply not an option for slaves in Jackson and Leon Counties. Black Seminoles and Seminoles had already begun to reach a parting of the ways. When push came to shove, black Seminoles feared—with good reason—that their Indian allies were willing to return them to slavery.[30] And in Middle Florida, African Americans could not expect preferential treatment from Seminole raiders. Some Seminoles allegedly captured slaves from plantations and traded them to Cuban fishermen in the Gulf in return for arms and ammunition. The fishermen then sold the runaways to Cuban plantations. More often, it seems, Seminoles simply killed potential allies. When raiding parties attacked John Gamble's plantation in May 1836, and then Thomas Randall's place a few days later, they left one slave dead. A series of Seminole attacks in late 1839, many along the roads leading north from the St. Marks River ports, culminated with the November murder of four enslaved African Americans at John Johnson's place. In 1841, Seminoles attacked and robbed two wagons rolling north from Port Leon. The culprits tied the drivers, both enslaved blacks, to trees, and beat them to death with clubs. Guerrillas were a long way from their safe territory in the impenetrable South Florida swamps, and escaped or captured slaves might imperil their safe return. We should therefore be wary of romanticizing African Americans' relationships with Native Americans: the two groups based their occasional alliances on instrumental concerns. When mutual usefulness disappeared, so did the alliance.[31]

Where Seminoles roamed the woods, African Americans never knew if they would meet acceptance or murder. And like their encounters with

Seminoles, enslaved rebels' relations with white outlaws simultaneously opened and constricted frontier possibilities for black freedom. In older Southern states, common poverty, cultural similarities, and the rejection of planter society's norms led some of the poorest whites to associate with slaves and free blacks. Resulting social, sexual, and criminal partnerships transgressed racial borders between the two despised groups. On the cotton frontier, some conditions for interracial cooperation grew even more favorable, despite the fact that poor white women and men risked fines, whippings, or imprisonment for stealing, trading, drinking, or sleeping with enslaved African Americans.[32]

Planters' minds inflated any detected assistance to runaways, or friendship between slaves and poor whites, into the specter of a full-scale ring of revolutionaries and/or thieves. When the evidence was not there, planters supplied it from their own myths and fears. Susan Bradford Eppes, born in 1846, grew up hearing this story of the 1834 murder of Leon County farmer James Rountree: brave "Regulators" led by her relative William Lester caught an interracial gang guarding the booty from a robbery. Then "twenty pairs of willing hands did quick work—tree limbs were stout and strong—and five white men and one negro were left hanging high as Haman." Newspaper accounts from 1834 reveal, however, that two slaves named Crittenden and Joe committed the crime by themselves.[33] This account does show the creativity of planters' fears. But their minor myth-making could not hide the fact that some young men, uprooted by forced migration, did find outlawry's possibilities for freedom especially attractive. Runaway slaves joined in the operations of a series of white-led bandit gangs. Two fugitive slaves named Sam and John narrowly escaped lynching with the other members of the "Holloman gang," which robbed mail coaches along the roads from Tallahassee in the 1840s. Their counterpart Jack, an enslaved man "stolen" by John B. Hardin, was not so lucky. Jack joined Hardin in bank-robbing and jail-breaking exploits that stretched from Jacksonville west to Alabama. After Alabamians captured Hardin and Jack in 1851, Floridians brought the audacious pair back, lynched them, and threw their bodies into the same unmarked grave.[34]

Individual poor whites and slaves sometimes ran off together, suggesting that whites who had something to flee were able to overcome at least some racist qualms about associating with African Americans. In 1830, white prisoner Hugh Duncan burned his way out of the Leon County jail cell with the assistance of a slave imprisoned there on an arson charge. Likewise, fear of punishment or need of help could overcome some blacks' reservations about trusting whites. In 1834, Harry ran away from the plantation of Myles Everitt on the southern border of Jackson County. Earlier punishments had left Harry branded with an "O" on both cheeks. Now easily recognized as a fugitive, he allegedly took up with two white thieves named William Stapleton and James Owens. Criminal associations with poor whites could benefit blacks: runaways traveling with whites were much less likely to be questioned than those going alone. Whites could feed or shelter runaways, and, if literate, could write passes for them. Storekeepers or poor farmers purchased stolen goods and cotton from slaves for resale: exchanges which, while fraught with potential for exploitation, also benefited both the thief and his or her partner in crime.[35]

Yet the dangers created by the white criminals who supposedly frequented the woods of Jackson and Leon Counties closed off as many possibilities of freedom for enslaved Middle Floridians as they opened. In the contemporary frontier legend of slave-stealer John Murrell, the great "Land Pirate" and his gang stole slaves. Despite promising to help the slaves escape again and go to freedom, the criminals resold them. Murrell's secret organization of thieves supposedly planned to foment a massive South-wide insurrection. The lurid lines of a fanciful book of Murrell's confessions ignited psychological tinder, and elite whites reacted with panic to the revelations of Murrell's mythical activities. In November 1835, shortly after mass executions of "conspiratorial" slaves and white "Murrellites" in Mississippi, a similar panic broke out in Jackson County. A number of white citizens became convinced that a certain Dr. Borland was a part of Murrell's invisible "Confederacy," a vast criminal network organized for the seemingly incompatible dual purposes of slave stealing and selling and antiplanter insurrection. Claiming that the evidence against Borland was "too dark to render it proper to tolerate him in the community," they threatened to lynch him and a number of other undesirables and gave them three days to leave the territory. And no doubt masters also tried to frighten slaves by telling them what unscrupulous poor white outlaws did to naive would-be runaways. Murrell's legendary "confessions" claimed that when the heat of pursuit got too close, he killed slaves to prevent them from spilling the beans. Gruesome details described Murrell's alleged elimination of evidence, including the disembowelling of carcasses, sunk in creeks, to prevent them from swelling and floating to the surface.[36]

Although few enslaved residents of Jackson and Leon Counties read the accounts of Murrell that appeared in 1835, they all knew where the noose tended to tighten when such rumors filled the air. Murrell's alleged activities also tallied with black fears that poor white criminals were, like planters, unreliable. Slaves who habitually participated in the shared criminal activities of a racist society's margins had long since learned the dangers of trusting poor (or any) white men. Despite common association in a marginal subculture of criminal and rebellious behavior, many poor whites held African Americans in contempt. And such men were often among the most violent individuals in a violent society. Descriptions of poor white criminals, like accused slave stealer Elijah Tucker—5′3″ and stout, "and [had] the end of his nose cut off"—suggested a habituation to violence recorded on their bodies. The experiences of slaves like Dan, "stolen" by George Cushman from Charles Cullock of the Fairfield district of South Carolina in 1830, underlined the signs of appearance. Dan ran away with Cushman, and they traveled toward Middle Florida, but Cushman apparently sold Dan and abandoned him in Florida. Whites turned ruthless were certainly unlikely to offer African Americans any more mercy than the world had showed them.[37]

Consequently, African American parents warned Middle Florida children against too-close association with white criminals. Mothers and fathers used the childhood bogeyman, "Dry [or Raw] Head and Bloody Bones," associated in Middle Florida as elsewhere with the Murrell legend, to teach their children to fear poor white strangers who might tempt young slaves. Parents whispered that the mysterious wagons of poor white migrants contained "'nigger stealer[s]' who kidnapped children and took them to Georgia to sell." The myth of "Raw Head and Bloody Bones" as slave-stealer and runaway-enticer recognized that white outlaws offered certain temptations to young slaves. The semimythical realm of the frontier outlaw was a more attractive—but also more hazardous—world than plantation slavery, especially for young black men. Middle Florida slaves understood that conflicts divided poor and wealthy whites. But the possibilities for freedom or profit were too slim, and the risks too great, for parents—when not separated from offspring—not to warn their children against attempting to exploit white class divisions.[38]

The general rejection of violent resistance, even as some individuals among the enslaved turned to such tactics, suggests a distinct set of beliefs about gender and resistance to power among forced migrants and settlers. Among white planter men, the barest perception of being oppressed or insulted supposedly justified immediate and violent reprisal, or, for yeomen, the refusal to be whipped or "ridden." The enslaved—whether male or female—could indulge in violent resistance only at the peril of their lives, and those of loved ones. In fact, the complex social conditions of the frontier made such acts more dangerous than ever, even though whites' uncertainties appeared to open new paths to escape from slavery. And yet we find very little evidence of the sort of frustrated self-destruction that we would expect if, for instance, individual African American men believed the same things as whites on the subject of what enduring violence and humiliation meant for one's male identity. Women in Middle Florida, of course, had to endure assaults on their identity as women: rape and the theft of children from mothers being two of the most violent.[39] Despite the known fact that these kinds of assaults took place, the scarcity of direct evidence makes it impossible to know what the enslaved really thought about them. But the ways in which slaves reacted to the plantation frontier, even as the crisis of the rag empire generated new waves of disruption, suggest that they adopted an approach of waiting, negotiation, and forbearance. These tactics, necessitated by the harsh limits of their own lives, depended in part upon a moral rejection of planters' claims about slavery's justice—a rejection, in turn, given strength by African Americans' ideas about the history of their southwestward and other passages. The contrast of the tactics of the enslaved with planters' public actions, driven by their masculine obsessions, could hardly have been more stark.

WAITING

Through careful calculation of the forces at war over the plantation frontier, the enslaved determined that the time was still not ripe for direct action against slavery. African Americans in Jackson and Leon Counties turned inward to family and community, trying to repair the damage done by repeated disruptions, forced migrations, and all the other uncertainties of white men. At the same time, the enslaved increasingly generated indirect forms of resistance that may have maintained cultural cohesion, and that certainly ridiculed the self-styled master class. Perhaps by doing so, African Americans were able to release psychological pressures created by dilemmas that, for them, remained insoluble until the configuration of forces in the U.S. South finally changed. Like acts of violent, direct resistance to slavery, the convoluted and clever tactics of indirect resistance have their own history in Middle Florida. In the early years, the disordered conditions of slaves' lives, and the limited interest in paternalism among the planter class, limited the psychological leverage that clever slaves could gain on white slaveowners and overseers. In its own response to crisis, the frontier slaveowning class would redefine itself. In addition to a more stable demography, slaveowners' increased desire to justify themselves as benevolent paternalists helped make possible after the mid-1840s a changed tenor within black-white interactions in Jackson and Leon Counties. The recalibration of resistance by the enslaved to a tuning that re-emphasized indirection and "laying it on thick," was, however, the conscious work and creation of black survivors. Their response to migration and settlement reveals the arc of African American adjustment to—and of—the plantation frontier. This was a historical movement longer in creation and less impulsive than the changes created in white society—but powerful all the same.[40]

In slave societies more long-settled than that of early Middle Florida, rulers often attempted to justify their power by portraying themselves, both in their own eyes and those of the ruled, as benevolent masters who ruled for the common good of all. Public interactions under such conditions often took the form of displays of paternalist care and reciprocating deference. Observers might conclude that the price of such gestures was a limited acceptance, by both sides, of the rules of the paternalist game. If planters treated the enslaved with some kindness, the enslaved would in turn render willing labor and obedience; consenting in what was apparently a "tragic complicity" with paternalist ideology. Of course, one might easily argue that in the antebellum South the enslaved had no better choice. Their participation in such games was necessary for both individuals and communities to avoid punishment and destruction.[41]

Participation in a game does not necessarily mean full mental and emotional commitment to its ostensible rationale, either. But in the 1820s and 1830s, Middle Florida slaves did not even have the opportunity to mime consent. In the slave society that was Middle Florida, would-be masters did not seek even the appearance of willing compliance. Migrant planters paid little attention to extracting performances of deference from African Americans. Instead, they relied upon force and power to squeeze labor and wealth from human property whom they often did not even know by name. They did not even think to claim that their domination of enslaved blacks reflected whites' kindly, paternalistic care for their "inferior" subordinates. Most whites in Jackson and Leon Counties showed near-total disinterest in African Americans as individuals. During these early years of migration, individual slaves were almost completely absent from whites' letters. The conditions of migration limited both the need and the ability of plantation frontier masters to imagine "their" African Americans as individuals. Deaths from disease and the drive to exploit labor created uncertainty and resentment on both sides of the master-slave relationship. The massive influx of slaves brought dozens of new faces to frontier plantations. Hard-driving planters demanded submission from such slaves but were uninterested in anything resembling give-and-take. Migrant masters readily lashed into labor men and women whom they barely recognized. The whip, not deference, ideology, or religion, remained the main instrument of discipline.[42]

For a variety of reasons, some of which Chapters 8 and 9 will explore, Middle Florida's white planters began in the late 1840s and 1850s to desire to act like a historically stable ruling class, shaped by something resembling noblesse oblige. One aspect of this transformed account of the planter self was the increasing concern shown by Middle Florida whites over their relationships with individual slaves. Some began to refer more frequently to African Americans by name in letters. "Tell Maum Amy I think of her all the time," wrote one young man to his sister in 1857.[43] House servants and "mammys" became important figures to members of the master class, admitted to a sort of mascot status within the "family" both on earth and in heaven. Henry Partridge remembered his nurse, "Maum Mollie," who helped raise him in the 1850s, as "a second mother . . . black of skin but pure of heart, she doubtless stands with the faithful upon the right hand of the King." Even record-keeping became better, presenting more African Americans as individuals with families, specific ages, and birthdays. One Leon County family of small planters kept a record book that listed their slave Mary Brown's birth as "about 1831" but provided her children Georgia and Fanny with precise dates of birth: July 20, 1850, and November 29, 1852, respectively. So white masters took more notice of the humanity of some slaves in these last decades, even if they restricted their benevolence mostly to house servants, and implied that individuals' purity of heart and future state were present despite their "black[ness] of skin."[44]

Middle Florida whites increasingly argued that they perpetuated the institution of slavery in order to help an inferior race rather than to develop Florida as an incipient superplantation. In 1860, Thomas Brown's daughter Frances Douglass saw Africans removed from a captured slave-smuggling vessel interned at Key West. She asserted that these men and women, who had barely survived the Middle Passage, would be happier and better off in slavery than freedom: "Does it not seem hard to send these poore [sic] creatures back to barbarism? But what can we do. They do not desire to return to Africa; but want to remain here." She could not, of course, know what they actually desired. But Douglass convinced herself that there could be nothing better for people of African descent than the paternalistic relationship that she imagined as the nature of slavery. Planters now depicted blacks as deferent, willing slaves, rather than as the resistant, potential allies of Seminoles who had crowded white nightmares in previous decades.[45]

Those willing to fool themselves into believing that kidnapped Africans wanted to remain as slaves in a foreign land were, in the 1850s, easy marks for the subtle tricks learned by enslaved survivors of the plantation frontier. African Americans certainly supported the new perceptions of Middle Florida whites by on occasion acting the public role of Sambo, or at least the faithful family servitor. James Page, owned by John and Washington Parkhill, was a Baptist preacher who led worship services in the slave quarters

Maum Mollie (Florida State Archives)

of various plantations in eastern Leon County. The literate Page always de-ferred to white men and women, and never publicly criticized slavery. From time to time he wrote letters to John Parkhill's daughter Harriet, always expressing his gratitude to the members of the extended Parkhill family, and his concern for them and their souls. Always signing himself "Servant James," Page fed paternalist planters' new desire to refer to family slaves as "servants," a distinction of terminology that frosted over the uglier realities of the master–slave relationship with sugary paternalism. In one 1859 letter,

James Page, late 1800s (Florida State Archives)

Page reported going to the capitol building with Washington Parkhill on the Fourth of July. There, at the request of some white men, he danced a deferent step: he "turned about heare amongst the gentlemen and Ladies." The dignified and aged preacher obediently demonstrated that "I still possess the old Virginia spirit," the willingness to enact an increasingly imagined happy image of slavery.[46]

Slaveowners' new attempts to justify their rulership as paternalistic care, and their newly pressing need to see themselves as good masters, opened new windows through which African Americans stealthily imported critique and ridicule directly into the master's presence. Middle Florida slaves already possessed their clandestine narrative of frontier history, which argued that forced migration proved beyond any possible doubt that slavery was "theft" of person. This counseled radical doubt of any argument by which masters claimed that slavery was just, or that it was for the slaves' own good. They were highly skeptical of the planters' new solicitude for (some of) them as individuals. The new concern did not erase the ultimate guarantees of planters' power, which were still whip, gun, and noose. Yet the new paternalism did open a valve for the release of potentially unbearable psychological pressures that could never have been converted into successful revolt against plantation slavery. Such pressures had driven some of the enslaved to take to the woods, with all of its dangers. Others had committed suicide. But beginning in the late 1840s, more and more Middle Florida slaves chose to trespass on indulgence prescribed by the ruling class's paternalist ideology. They criticized the realities identified by their own historiography. Jokes, songs, actions, and so on became occasions of half-concealed ridicule or criticism: old tactics of enslaved people, but now finally feasible in Middle Florida, with the increase in masters' need to experience the illusion of willing submission.

Without repeated submission to indignities, and the writing of carefully worded letters to "Miss Harriet," James Page would have been unable to preach freely to local black men and women. The ties that Page carefully cultivated may have also helped to make divisions of family and community like those that he had witnessed during migration and frontier crisis less likely to occur again. At the same time, behind the deferential facade beloved by the Parkhill family, Page may have organized limited kinds of unrest. D. N. Moxley, overseer of George Noble Jones's El Destino plantation, reported that someone had encouraged slaves angry at his repeated whippings to run to Tallahassee and seek shelter in the town jail. Their actions portrayed Moxley as a violent man who abused his employer's property, and arrayed white benefactors (and perhaps the absentee planter Jones) against the overseer. At first, Moxley suspected the owner of one of the runaways' husband, but eventually he heard whispers that "Jim Page and his crew has been the cause of all the fuss." Moxley stood in a position that made him able to perceive the more puffed-up aspects of planter self-presentation. Perhaps he might in turn have glimpsed the ways in which the enslaved could manipulate the psychological needs of a would-be paternalist like Jones. Page, Moxley believed, had suggested to the slaves that they seek shelter in the jail. The seemingly obsequious slave apparently played whites against each other in order to protect other blacks from corporal punishment.[47]

Another slave whose facade of deference allowed him to import insults and ridicule of whites while acting stereotypically "black" was Bill, the butler on Edward Bradford's Pine Hill plantation during the 1850s. When Bradford ordered a new sausage grinder to replace the old chopping knives, Bill was the first to take charge of the machine on hog-killing day. He cranked it and soon had the ground meat flowing into the casings. "Bill was jubilant," remembered Bradford's daughter Susan, "putting his arms akimbo, after the manner of his race, he called out, 'Jerusa-lem! Ain't dem Yankees smart!'" By exclaiming excitably, and contorting his body in ways that whites found amusing, Bill tricked the master into permitting him to mention some of the failings of the supposedly all-powerful Southern white man. Bill suggested that "Yankees" were smart, while Southern whites came up a little short in the department of industrial ingenuity. Bill's fellow slave Henry Fort created a similar sort of license for himself in 1861. Fort got drunk in town, supposedly celebrating the Confederate victory at Manassas, and headed back to Pine Hill. Upon reaching the grounds, Fort saw a white machinist of Yankee origins. Declaring that he had been waiting all day to kill some Yankees, Fort announced that he would begin with the machinist. Wielding a large stick, he chased the terrified white man around the big house and quarters before passing out—amused, perhaps, at the conjunction of events that had offered him the opportunity to threaten a white man with physical punishment. Masters' increasing need to feel that paternalism created strong bonds between themselves and their slaves—a need so deep that planters desperately desired to hear the enslaved improbably parroting their own sectional prejudices—allowed African Americans to insert into public action subtle attacks on slavery and on white folks. Even Susan Bradford Eppes's retrospective need to remember a paternalist past made her vulnerable, leading her, years later, to insert in her writings events and conversations whose meanings ran in more complex currents than she wished to acknowledge.[48]

Indirect resistance was of course, limited in its effects. What did it do besides maintaining slaves' own self-respect—if it even did that? Of course, given the circumstances of slavery, one wonders what could be both a more important and a more realistic goal. On the other hand, whether one finds such an accomplishment important or not, masked insult was also not an easy weapon to wield. Young slaves needed both instruction and example. Unpleasant reprisals could result if masters found contempt and insult too obvious. During the 1820s and 1830s, the paucity of elders able to teach younger slaves the safest techniques of manipulating the master class endangered audacious young slaves—not that they were likely to succeed in such times anyway. In Tallahassee's early years, according to a story told by Richard Call, his twelve-year-old body servant Logan was a constant truant. When Logan ran away, Call caught him and whipped him with a stick. One day, as Call lay prostrated by a malarial fever, he moaned to the boy, "Logan, your master is not good for much." Logan replied, "Yes you is. You is good fur beaten a fellow." Logan had gone too far, and when Call returned to health, he reenacted the picture that Logan had scrawled on the wall in charcoal: a very big man beating a small boy. Logan was trying to talk back to his master, but he did so without the necessary training in circumlocution.[49]

The smuggling of critique, manipulation, and veiled insult into public dialogue was most successful when and where planters desired to claim that they were paternalists who wanted their slaves to accept bondage as being in their own best interests. When such desires were not present, enslaved African Americans could not exploit whites' need to extract psychological reassurance of their status as good masters. During the 1820s and 1830s, slaveowners who moved to frontiers like Jackson and Leon Counties bought, sold, or lost to debt slaves with dizzying speed, repeatedly breaking up and recombining slave families and communities. Unfree migrants rebuilt, remarried, and created fictive kin, but they could never fully replace those that they lost, or those they were losing every day. The instability of white society on the plantation frontier, culminating in massive crisis by 1839, provoked the desire while limiting the ability to resist or rebel in direct fashion with any real hope of success. Yet the dogged determination of the enslaved to construct new forms of family and community shows that surrender was not their response to the dislocations of the continually unstable frontier. Nor can we find surrender in the searing critique of white society that such migrants generated, and passed down as a version of history. Unlike other groups who migrated to Middle Florida, African Americans did not choose or want to move. They could, however, control the way in which they came to understand the process of migration. That experience had shattered any chance that enslaved African Americans would believe the illusions of masters' later paternalism.

Still, the differences between the earliest frontier of Middle Florida and the stable plantations of a generation later could make a vast difference in the lives of enslaved African Americans. Especially important were the small gains represented by the tenacious building and rebuilding of new families and communities on plantations like El Destino. In concrete terms, such construction projects were as necessary as shelter or food to the long-term survival of African Americans. Family and community instructed young men and women in the way to survive slavery with body and soul intact. Within the quarters, slaves built an alternative to whites' visions of black identity, and indeed, to their whole history of the South and its frontiers. They provided a vocabulary that elaborated a political critique of slavery, one that used the history of forced migration to demolish white racist and paternalist justifications of slavery. And indirect resistance provided, for some, the psychological satisfaction necessary for survival.

Like Daphne Williams's mother, then, enslaved African Americans continued to look toward freedom. The ways in which they did so depended to a large extent on what was possible, and when it was possible. On the Middle Florida frontier, large-scale, violent rebellion was never a real possibility, and probably declined in likelihood as frontier chaos abated. Instead, enslaved blacks turned to manipulating paternalism, and they and their masters increasingly encountered each other as a set of masks. Black played Sambo at times, and white, the good master. Neither was what he pretended to be—one was still held in slavery by force; the other still held him there. Whites came to expect the apparently gratuitous deference that James Page displayed to the Parkhills. Did the wearing of the mask of Sambo become too comfortable? Were the enslaved in some way complicit in their own oppression, or had they found a way to wait for their chance at freedom, surviving domination in a system that neither individual nor group acts of physical resistance could hope, as yet, to change? In Middle Florida, at any rate, the question of slaves' alleged complicity in their own oppression makes no sense in the earlier period, when naked force in all its cruel guises reigned over plantation society. Only in the late 1840s and 1850s did plantation owners in Jackson and Leon Counties stabilize their own society and begin to put paternalistic gestures ahead of earlier self-interest, violence, and unusually high levels of callousness. By that later point enslaved African Americans had seen enough to know that masters would steal their brothers and sisters, spouses or children, as soon as needs—or desires—powerful enough arose. The enslaved knew both how to carry out their subtle resistance and why they should. They taught each other a whole array of "masking" behaviors that allowed them to survive under the eyes of the whites, and at the same time to get away with making fun of them. African Americans became artisans of resistance, crafting small liberties that allowed them to shelter soul and body until the opportunity for something closer to freedom could be seized.[50] In the last decades of slavery, many danced, like James Page, to the new tunes of deference called by whites, but those public performances hardly imply deeper consent. The enslaved played with the mask of deference, fighting off the devastation and anger of loss; showing brief glances of the face of insult to would-be paternalist masters and getting away with it; teaching the young; creating moments of solidarity in the quarters. So most enslaved African Americans in Middle Florida lived in the long run, as they had to—even if that meant, as in the case of Daphne Williams's mother, living beyond Middle Florida and looking past individual lives.

Eight

Creating an Old South

Now such things are surely o'er
We're not the folks we were before

We're captives now, and selfish grown,
As all who look about must own.
Our town too in its outward dress,
Is greatly altered for the worse.
Our streets that once looked smart and gay,
Are marked with ruin and decay,
Business extinct or driven away.
The people crushed with taxes high,
May o'er their failing fortunes sigh —
But who shall all the vagaries tell,
Of Captain Roach and Mister Snell
Who've ranged our streets with David Scutes,
And hung the Mare in Noles' Boots.
— *Tallahassee Star of Florida*, January 1, 1843

In the early 1840s, a succession of disasters had knocked Middle Florida's planter men from their proud perch. Some moved away, some remained defeated, while others struggled to recover. Nowhere was their difficulty more obvious than in the rhetorical contests of politics. These had been transferred, it seemed, from dueling ground to doggery. But over the decade, some things changed. Skip forward, for instance, to the summer of 1848, and one finds an interesting vignette in the *Tallahassee Florida Sentinel*. The state governor's race between William Bailey and Whig Thomas Brown and the presidential race between Democrat Lewis Cass and Zachary Taylor ("Old Rough and Ready," to his Whig backers) were both in full swing. The story carried by the *Sentinel*—once the smug organ of the self-consciously cultured—was probably, strictly speaking, fictional. But it borrowed in certain ways from the views of the yeomen to whom it appealed, just as the *Star*'s tale of "Snell" had done a few years earlier. This time the borrowing was intentional, and far from subtle:

> "As for old Wough and Weady," said an exquisite dandy the other day, drawing on his white silk gloves, and dividing his attention equally between this operation, the frill of his shirt bosom, his whiskers, his glossy patent-leather boots, his gold-headed cane, and the person he was addressing, "As for Old Wough and Weady, I am a dymacwat, and cannot vote for him. And furthermore, I entertain vwery serious doubts, wethaw he is not so ignowant as to disgwace the office, should he be elected. He is nowt a statesman and a scalaw like General Cass, and has spent his life in the bwack woods, among the most savage and ignowant people, whilst General Cass was thought to be the most awistocwatic gentleman ever sent from the country to the Fwench Court. . . . Tom Brown is a man of intaalegence, but he is pwoor, and cannawt entawtain gentlemen in the style that General Bailey can. I think, therefore, that all the higher classes should vwote faw Gen. Cass and Gen. Baalye."[1]

Ridiculous political exaggeration was itself nothing new in Middle Florida. But the projection of foppish and arrogant Democrats as self-conscious opponents of white male equality suggests that Whigs' approach to politics changed drastically from that of their pro-bank predecessors at the beginning of the decade. Manipulation and domination failed. After 1842, the Whigs had, with a few stubborn exceptions like Richard Call, abandoned the banks and all they symbolized.[2] As the decade wore on, yeoman style and yeoman policy had become the lingua franca of politics in Jackson and Leon Counties. On questions of national politics, both Middle Florida Whigs and their Democratic counterparts argued for the rights of slaveholders. But at the state level, they each claimed, above all else, to support white male democracy. As they begged for the votes of the yeoman majority, the two parties became more and more similar in rhetoric, organizational structure, and tactics. The positions held by the mass of yeoman voters were relatively clear. The task for Middle Florida's political parties, from the mid-1840s into the early years of the next decade, became that of apparently aligning themselves with those positions, while dislodging their rival from them. All politicians became anti-bank supporters of white male equality, and the only way for them to distinguish themselves from each other was by painting their party as the defender of yeomen and their opponents as the evil heirs of Federalists and Tories. One's actions, words, and policies must all hang on the principle of equality among white men, and meanwhile, those of the opponents must reek of the love of slavish hierarchy. By making their concerns into the idiom of politics, yeomen had retrained planter-politicians.[3]

Master campaigner E. C. Cabell exemplified the transformation of adaptable former pro-bank men into a new Whig Party. A pro-bank delegate from Jefferson County at the 1838 convention, by the middle of the next decade Cabell had distinguished himself as one of the most malleable members of his class. Unlike his cousin John Gamble, the young Cabell could hold his own on the stump in the country precincts. His popularity in Jackson County helped give that county the nickname "The Gibraltar of the Whiggery." After losing the contest for Congress in 1845, Cabell stumped the state the next year, claiming that Tallahassee wire-pullers had stolen the people's vote. This time he won, and stayed in office for six more years. Using similar tactics, the Whigs won both houses of the state legislature in 1847 and 1848, and claimed most offices in Jackson and Leon Counties. And in 1849, despite his past Union Bank associations, Thomas Brown won the governorship as the Whig version of the common man's candidate.[4]

By the second half of the 1840s, Middle Florida Whigs purveyed a radically different image of the normative citizen from what they had attempted to use earlier in the decade. Now, the *Tallahassee Florida Sentinel* bragged of "Wire-grass Whigs," associating politicians—some of whom had once claimed to be the "gentlemen of sense"—with the poor migrants who had settled the sandy, barren pine- and grasslands between Tallahassee and the gulf coast. Editors made an idol of countryman independence: the "yeomanry of the land" were "honest and hard-handed" but not "*humble*"; while Democrats were "*soft-handed*" and untrustworthy. "Jacob Smith," the yeoman title character of an 1848 series of stories published in the *Sentinel*, fought a mysterious "Sentral Kommittee" (read: Westcott, Levy, and the *Floridian*) that sought to impose a Democratic party line on voters in his "diggins."[5]

Like yeomen, and Democrats, the new Whigs rejected older planter concepts of manhood and argued that white manhood required insubordination in the face of oppression. The Democratic "*party drill*" equaled subservience, and Whigs warned that a single act of submission could lead one down the slippery slope to humiliating enslavement: "Habit reconciles us to every thing, *though restive at first, yet after a while*, [we] *lie still to be skinned*." The one skinned was the prey, not the masculine predator. Democratic leaders were deceitful seducers, seeking to trick voters out of their honor by "skinning" them out of their consent to be ruled. Whigs also alleged that Democratic opponents had supported the whipping of white men. Like many Whig newspapers across the South, in 1848 the *Sentinel* claimed that Democratic presidential candidate Lewis Cass had, as territorial governor of Michigan, backed a law that sold white "common railers" and "stubborn servants" into slavelike servitude for three months. They could also be whipped—a punishment, the editor alleged, that James Westcott had proposed in 1832 for vagrants in Florida. The symbolism of whipping and white slavery attempted to pin Whigs' opponents to caricatures of older, hierarchical ways of understanding white masculinity.[6]

The distance traveled from the open assertion of pro-bank planters' beliefs about which white men were really men, to arguing that only those who suited yeoman ideals of class and gender identity were acceptable political representatives, was a long way indeed. The two parties' pictures of the enemy were now nearly identical. He was a pernicious, effeminate and feminizing, aristocratic, would-be thief of the independence of common white men. Perhaps this characterization of the enemy was merely a different kind of manipulation. Exaggerated deference to the prejudices and views of masculine white identity held by the yeomen became almost parodic. Yet masters who once figuratively and literally whipped their white male opponents now had to wear the mask of equality. Politicians spoke in the vernacular and in the conceptual framework of yeomen. Once, less wealthy white men had chafed under the overt lack of respect accorded to them by many politicians. Now the public reiteration of hierarchy was impossible. One may, of course, wonder if this change merely covered and legitimated some kinds of inequality among whites. But if planter men had their way, politics would have never come to such a pass. Using voices and votes, countrymen had forced planter spokesmen into what were at times uncomfortable and humiliating accommodations to the yeoman desires of the electorate.

The change in the models of white manhood to which planter-politicians proclaimed allegiance was significant, but it was only one of a number of ways in which Middle Florida society transformed itself in the wake of crisis. By the 1850s, local society, culture, and politics would assume an air of stability never seen before. One cause would be the world market's rising demand for cotton, which benefited both yeomen and planters. A change in manners—another retraining of planter men—also took place. Once aggressive, grasping men who posed, postured, and shot each other in the streets in an effort to achieve factional dominance, local planters now trooped, sometimes with once-despised countrymen, into churches on Sundays to hear sermons.[7] Was this apparent coherence an ideal form, a stable "Old South," toward which all Southern creation yearned? Not, it seems, in Middle Florida. Here the creation of harmony among whites was a contingent, late, and haphazard thing. And even when disruptive internal conflict subsided, threats from the outside loomed. Inside, planters—a group of men raised to believe that they could not abide defeat and still be sure that they were men—gnawed at and worked over their past. For the creation of a stable plantation society in Middle Florida did not build upon the victory of elite migrants but rather upon their multiple defeats.

LOSING CREDIT

The Union Bank had been the tool with which Middle Florida's migrant planters had tried to command their own access to credit and the resources of the world economy. But the implosion of the bank's shoddy structure of paper meant that local planters lost control over the financing of plantation operations. Domination of cotton financing passed into the hands of Northern factorage firms, and Northern merchants seized control of consumer goods trades as well. Elite Floridians' newly obvious economic dependence called into question both their future opportunities for economic success and their very identities as men commanded by no others.[8]

During the crisis in the early 1840s, former supporters of the banks rummaged about within their political toolkits for traditional solutions that would block the influence of creditors both in and out of the region. In 1841, "Aristides" suggested to Middle Floridians a time-worn response to their predicament: "I would recommend retrenchment in our ordinary expense, which fashion has rendered extravagant and altogether incompatible with the prosperity of a new country." Imported luxuries, bought on credit, represented more than a negative balance of trade. Many repentant observers saw consumer goods as symbols of a rapacity that had led Jackson and Leon Counties to blunder into economic quicksand. The "people," according to the editor of the *Star*, "have lived too fast. . . . They have imagined they could overtake fortune by the ardour of their pursuit—by their hot haste, and their giant strides." "John Caldwell" struck a familiar note: "Let us call upon the fair Sex . . . and let us tell them we have declined the idea of wearing English cloths." If white women would only put virtuous spinning and weaving over corrupting consumption, they could return planter men to independence: "They will make us a suit of Jeanes, and let us adopt the policy that will dress them in silk of their own manufacturing. "Caldwell" did not pitch his appeal directly at common white men, who had always worn suits of "jeanes" and whose wives did not wear silk of anyone's manufacturing. The rhetoric of retrenchment, a relic of earlier crises and revolutions, could neither solve economic problems nor rally divided frontier communities around traditional political leaders. Other planters recognized that the commercial world had changed for good: "[T]he only hope of a restoration of credit is in a new order of things."[9]

The new order that came, however, brought planter men less, rather than more, economic independence. They increasingly depended on credit and supplies controlled by distant authorities. Most local mercantile firms vanished as independent entities. By the end of the decade, Northern men working directly for Northern companies populated Apalachicola, Tallahassee, Newport, and St. Marks. These large firms rode out the international financial storms that followed the panic of 1837, and had been well-poised to expand afterward—sometimes by swallowing local trading partners. The firm of Brodie and Pettes, for example, which operated in St. Marks and Tallahassee, had by the late 1840s become an extension of New York's Coe, Anderson and Company. Brodie and Pettes consigned cotton from planters to the latter firm, who then took charge of selling it on the New York or Liverpool markets. In turn, Brodie and Pettes took charge of goods shipped on credit to Leon County planters.[10]

Locally owned sources of credit and exchange disappeared, but planters who did not turn to "Tall Walking" still desperately needed financing for each crop year. So each spring, they borrowed money from cotton factors, counting on the growing crop to repay their loans. Indebted planters sank deeper and deeper into the arms of the New York factors who supplied desperately needed capital. In 1844, for example, Robert W. Alston of Leon County, already thousands of dollars in debt to the Union Bank, mortgaged his 1844 crop to J. W. Field of Field and Company in New York. Alston sent Field his crop and allowed Field's house to sell it and charge a commission, but it did not quite pay off his advance. The depression of the world cotton market kept prices low, and so for most of the decade crops would not pay off in December the debt incurred in March. Times were still hard in 1848, when Lawrence O'Bryan Branch wrote: "I have never known the people here so low-spirited, and Tallahassee so dull. Ruin and bankruptcy literally stare many plantations in the face . . . a man will chase you and stand at the rail a week to sue you for a dollar."[11]

Northern merchant houses increasingly served as intermediaries in all dealings between Middle Florida and world markets: acting as sales agents, buyers of necessary plantation supplies and luxury goods alike, bankers, and even litigators for planters. The New York and Baltimore firm of Bryan and Maitland sold John Branch's cotton and loaded his plantation supplies on brigs bound from New York to St. Marks. Bryan and Maitland also allowed Branch considerable advances against future cotton crops. They even held an account for Branch's dissolute son John R. Branch, limiting the young man's spending. Merchant houses also expanded their business to encompass other members of high-status planter families. Bernard and Adams of New York began by employing Joseph and Lawrence Branch to collect debts due to them in Middle Florida. Later they financed the Branches' brother Lewis Henry and his less than successful planting ventures.[12]

The takeover of the financing and selling of the Middle Florida cotton crop was part of a long process of Northern commercial expansion, one that accelerated after 1837. To Florida cotton growers now indebted to factors based in New York, the new situation of the 1840s and 1850s seemed a decidedly unequal relationship, especially when compared to previous experiences of obtaining credit. During the initial stages of migration, debt had bound together webs of kinship and friendship. At the high tide of the Union Bank, members of Middle Florida's ruling class had controlled their own credit supplies, albeit with disastrous results. Now, economic obligations to men unconnected by blood or political alliance put planters in positions of clear dependence. Southerners came to perceive Northern cotton factors' power as part of a wider pattern of economic and political oppression. By the end of the 1840s, planters in Florida and across the South were organizing regional commercial conventions that criticized the South's "colonial" relationship to the North. Yet conventions never made Southern cities into centers of finance, trade, or industry: cash-crop agriculture offered too many rewards.[13]

Meanwhile, Jackson and Leon County planters acted out the resentments of sectional economic honor in microcosm. As John Branch began to sink deeper and deeper into debt during the 1840s, factors Bryan and Maitland pressed him for payment of interest on numerous cash advances. Feeling insulted, Branch switched to another merchant house, but James Bryan continued to seek repayment. Branch took his requests as peremptory demands, accusing Bryan of trying "to coerce the payment of this debt as soon as practicable." Offended by the implication that Bryan could order him around, Branch next resorted to language that typically presaged a duel. He brusquely demanded that Bryan retract his offending statements. Bewildered, Bryan replied, "I have to say that I cannot 'retract' any thing, that I said to you . . . in regard to your failure in almost every instance to meet the payment of interest. I can only state facts which must speak for themselves." Bryan operated upon a new understanding of commercial relationships between men, in which the facts of the ledger balance testified simple truth. But Branch confused demands made in business correspondence with accusations about his honor, perhaps feeling that his debts threatened his status as a planter. In response, Branch could only reply with the bluster of the dueling ground.[14]

"Southern planters are not monied capitalists," John Branch complained to James Bryan, presaging later arguments about the nature of the South. He drew a distinction between the factors and merchants who now controlled planters' credit and the indebted elite of the South, whose economic power now stopped at the edges of their plantations. Branch's reactions to Bryan's demands crystallize the planters' plight. Not all lashed out with such revealing anger, but newly dependent planters had difficulty adjusting to a world seemingly out of control. After being ejected from his position as cashier of the Union Bank amid charges of corruption, a torrent of additional setbacks overwhelmed John Parkhill. The death of his brother Samuel and the collapse of the bank forced him to spend the ensuing decade trying to extricate both Parkhills' estates from mortgages. He lost case after debt case in court to his old ally John G. Gamble and sank into a paralyzing psychological depression. Parkhill's continued "low-spirited" state led his son Washington to abandon his medical studies in New York and return to take over management of what remained of Tuscawilla plantation.[15] Loss of control over ties to the world market, to credit, and to his own economic future left John Parkhill, like other Middle Florida planters, seized by the terror that he had become permanently dependent. And Middle Florida's crisis had undermined not only planters' economic independence vis-à-vis the rest of the commercial world but also the habits and institutions that they had once used to subordinate other white men in their own, local worlds.

LOCAL DEFEATS

The political battles that followed 1838 ended in the metaphorical thrashing of men trained not to bear defeat. While losses in formal politics were hard enough to endure, in some ways the decline in planter authority in everyday contacts was even more devastating. By the mid-1840s, elite white men could use neither intimidation nor local legal forums to deny countrymen the right to use violence to defend their honor. One example of the confusions and reversals engendered by the assertion of yeoman masculinity took place in Jackson County, where Richard Long squabbled with a man named A. M. Bennett. In July 1843, Long seized a group of twenty-five enslaved African Americans—property disputed in a debt case between Bennett and Long's ally, the Georgia speculator Farish Carter. Long and Carter believed they had every right to simply seize the disputed property from Bennett, a merchant of dubious origins. What they had done, Long and Carter assured each other, differed greatly from slave stealing. After all,

Carter owned considerable property in Florida and could thus be held responsible for his actions. Bennett and his friends, new men without prominent allies, evoked little fear of reprisal.[16]

Long took the seized slaves to his plantation near Marianna, where he began to work them with his own bondpeople. A few days later, however, "men of the worst character, picked up from among the vilest of the population of Apalachicola" by Bennett, ran eighteen of the twenty-five slaves off the plantation in the middle of the night. Long asserted in a letter that he could have shot Bennett, but his fear belied his bluster. Panicked, he repeatedly begged Carter to send down a "confidential man" to take the rest of the slaves up to Georgia. Meanwhile, rumors reported that Bennett and his hired common white thugs were hiding the bondpeople in the swamps north of Apalachicola, until he could sell them to the New Orleans slave market. Completely intimidated, Long turned his hopes to the trial of the debt case, which dragged on and on. Long asked Carter to dispense to his overseer Carey Josey, who had guarded the seven remaining slaves day and night, "a present of something — say forty dollars — for his indefatigable exertions to protect your negroes." This gift was meant to manipulate potential jurors: Long named, in his letter to Carter, Josey's extensive friends and family, "and he has many friendly to our cases, when they come up." [17]

Yet when the decision came down in 1848, Long discovered that the courts were not at his command, as they had been fifteen years earlier when he was ejecting squatters from Carter's land. Nor did the ham-handed patronage Long tried to wield in his dealings with Josey buy the results he wanted. Neither Jackson County nor Apalachicola jurors stood "for the defense of planter law and negroes." According to Long, yeoman magistrates, who were appointed as a reward for their Democratic allegiance, were nothing but "scounderels [sic]" who sympathized with the upstart Bennett. Local yeomen also remembered Long's standing as an arrogant old pro-bank man and Carter's history as a land speculator. The Jackson grand jury drew up an indictment against Long, one of the biggest planters in the county, for illegally removing the slaves. Further, an Apalachicola jury found for Bennett, assessing damages by Long and Carter at $23,000, $3,000 above the amount Bennett had requested. Long's son concluded that class resentment caused the decision — "the cry of persecution . . . would operate upon a particular class of jurymen . . . [who have been] long standing in the open air or in the back street polution [sic]." Both Carter and his Middle Florida ally Long represented "planter law." Less wealthy men punished Long and Carter in court for the arrogance of that law. Power once supplied by deference and authority over land, court processes, and government office had drained away in the wake of crisis.[18]

What Long and Carter experienced happened in different ways throughout Middle Florida. Elite violence had once laid down the borders of social and cultural hierarchy among men. Now, when masculine violence appeared, it served only to muddy those same lines. Worried planters perceived a vast expansion in street violence committed by nonplanter whites and in the number and activity of robber gangs in the woods. Although Tallahassee had always merited its reputation for violence, drunkenness, and gambling, the disruption of hierarchy now led many to see its rowdiness as a serious problem. Every store owner seemed to sell liquor from the barrel, and many kept faro or billiard tables in their back rooms. Men went armed, ready to use hidden pistols and sword canes to settle political and personal disagreements. Gambling irritated observers, perhaps because so many had recently lost on the throw of the Union Bank's dice. Many of the antagonists, men of countryman origin, seemed to live in taverns and gambling parlors. Their disorderly realm that spilled out into the streets and crossroads, frightened men and women already convinced that their community was on the brink of economic and political disaster. For instance, North Carolina migrant Rainey C. Ragland strutted around the streets of Tallahassee like a "brute cum dandy." According to multiple court indictments, in 1841, Ragland kept a faro table—probably rigged—fornicated, and fought in taverns. His assertion of the right to display floridly masculine behavior rejected deference, and allegedly corrupted Tallahassee's morals. Violence, alcohol, and chance were confusing the boundaries of class and status.[19]

Perceptions led to a response. By 1841, Tallahassee notables were tired of seeing yeomen, poor white drifters, and even free blacks mingling, playing faro, squabbling, and guzzling whiskey in the taverns and streets of the capital. Political feuding and duels among elite men were bad enough. Now, the kind of disorder that offered "an insult to a gentleman" seemed to be everywhere. Merchants and pro-bank planters with Tallahassee residences managed to get Francis Eppes elected as the intendant, or mayor, of the town and gave him strict instructions to clean up its disorder. With the city council, he produced a string of city ordinances, including one that imposed a $100 fine for "any offense against the rules of public decency . . . any riotous and disorderly conduct." The council and Eppes also established a new patrol system, prohibited the secret wearing of weapons and the firing of guns within the city limits, and cracked down on the sale of liquor without a license.[20]

In 1842, the city council went still further, announcing massive tax increases designed to eliminate gambling and peddling. They levied a $30 annual tax on merchants whose annual stock in trade was less than $30; $12 on carts for hire; $100 on hawkers or peddlers; and $200 on each billiard table. Complaining that "the city [was] overrun with negroes—free blacks, slaves, runaways," the council hoped among other things to drive out the forty-odd free black people in Tallahassee, many of whom survived by peddling. The council also imposed a $200 tax on establishments selling liquor by the drink and levied highly regressive new property and poll taxes. The liquor tax sought to shut down many of the taverns and grog shops where lower-class white men gathered; while the poll taxes levied on them the cost of re-imposing elite control over the uses of violence.[21]

The Leon County Superior Court cooperated with the assault on gambling. Like Eppes, Judge Douglass was eager to "make examples of some of the most hardened offenders." A jury, for instance, ordered the imprisonment of Gustavus West for one hour and fined him $25 for operating an unlicensed billiard table. But Eppes and his allies also ran into opposition. Writers using evocative pseudonyms like "Crockett" or the sarcastic "A Loafer" published letters in newspapers, protesting the new taxes as regressive. On April 4, 1842, a meeting of various Tallahassee citizens signed resolutions opposing the new taxes and appointed a committee "to ask of your honorable body, most respectfully, a 'reconsideration' of 'said ordinance.'" The city council fired back an intemperate response: "One of the City Council" wrote, "there never was, perhaps, a more flagrant insult offered to any body of decent men" than that posed by the apparently indecent men who framed the antitax resolutions. The writer denied that meeting participants had the economic standing that entitled them to claim a voice in town government: "[A] majority of this 'meeting of citizens' consisted of persons of a different character." Finally, he found the language of the petition highly offensive: "If a redress of grievance was the only object of the meeting, why did they not proceed in the usual and more respectful way of petition and remonstrance. Threats," he added, referring to the demand that the council members step aside for a new election, if they did not modify the ordinances, "are not becoming in petitioners!" Francis Eppes's official response was remarkably similar; he "decline[d] the proffered interference in the affairs of the city," coming as it did from those with no right to a voice: "persons who pay but a small portion of the property taxes of said city."[22]

Clearly, opposition to the reordering of Tallahassee's streets had struck a raw nerve. Men like Eppes angrily asserted that wealth should weight the voices of white men differently; as opposed to the new dictum that ostensibly viewed all white male citizens as equals. In fact, to Eppes and others, the petition's claim to equality was an insult. Insults from gentlemen drew one kind of response—the duel—and insults from lesser men drew the assertion that such men should simply remain properly submissive. Implied in the assertion was the promise that force would follow, if necessary. Just as in the debate about the Union Bank, the rejection of popular "interference" did not silence opposition to Eppes and his ordinances. Someone in Tallahassee apparently hung him in effigy one night in September 1842. Two months later, Tallahassee tavern keepers Alfred Hoe and Edward West charged that Eppes did not have the right to assess arbitrary fines against them without any kind of trial. Their case, a direct challenge to the authority of the new regulations, dragged on for months. Eppes finally stepped down in 1843 rather than face re-election. But he continued to be a lightning rod for local hostility to old-fashioned planter arrogance. That same year, while Eppes sat as foreman of the planter-dominated county grand jury, a poor man named William Belden stood up in court and began hurling insults and threats at the former intendant.[23]

Despite the vocal opposition launched by various white men, certain pieces of statistical evidence might suggest that the repression of rowdyism worked exactly as Leon County's better sort intended. Wave after wave of gambling and liquor indictments went to the courts between 1841 and 1844. In one 1840s minute book, covering four years, the grand juries reported as "true bills" ninety-one crimes against public order. By late 1843, the Leon County grand jury could "congratulate their fellow citizens, on the general improvement of the morals in this county." Prosecution had chased many of the most frequent targets of legal action from the county. C. R. Duff and William Hamner, accused of operating a gambling establishment, were nowhere to be found. Joseph G. Williams, supposedly a frequent gambler and rampant fornicator, had skipped town. James Melton stayed around a few days too long. After convicting him of larceny in 1843, a jury sentenced him to receive twenty stripes with the lash.[24]

Perhaps the court system was still planter-dominated, for it defined as disorderly those activities where rich and poor men, or whites and blacks, mixed on relatively equal terms. Or perhaps not: a closer look at the juries of the 1840s suggests that countrymen cooperated with some projects of social control, but not others. In contrast to the 1820s, they defeated planter attempts to curtail yeoman honor. Planters like Thomas Brown, listed in court records as "gentleman—foreman," John Shepard, Edward Bradford, Francis Eppes, and Richard Whitaker were almost always the foremen of the Leon grand jury, and merchants or members of planter families were a majority of the others sitting. However, yeomen comprised most of the petit juries, which sat on cases ranging from debt, to assault and battery, to felony murder. Of the twelve jurors who tried habitual miscreant Josiah Jacobs for larceny on April 29, 1844, only Charles G. English came from a planter

TABLE 8.1. *Leon County Indictments by Category of Crime*

	1825–1833	1843–1847
Crimes of personal violence	129	98
Crimes against property	19	23
Crimes against public peace	46	91
Convictions	48 (24.7%)	63 (28.3%)

Sources: Leon County Superior Court Minute Book 1, 1825–33; Leon County Superior and Circuit Court Minute Book 4, 1843–47, both Leon County Courthouse

family. The rest, like John R. Moore, John Cook, and Joseph Williams, were the very stereotypes of sturdy yeomen. The jury convicted Jacobs and sentenced him to one hour in the pillory, showing that Leon County yeomen were still willing to disfranchise fellow common white men—but only if they stole property.[25]

Yet even as they inflicted harsh punishments on men convicted of dishonorable crimes like petty theft, yeomen on juries staked out claims to once-forbidden territory, insisting on their own right to use manly violence. The four crimes of assault and battery, riot, mayhem, and assault with intent to kill represented male honor in action. Planters who sought to impose order objected to this kind of rowdiness, which suggested a lack of deference, just as much as they wanted to clamp down on drunkenness and gambling. But yeoman juries in the 1840s simply refused to assign disproportionately high fines to countrymen convicted of personal violence. Of 80 individuals tried for crimes of (nonhomicide) personal violence between 1843 and 1847, 23 appear to have been unpropertied poor whites, 16 were yeomen, 2 were planters and 2 merchants, and 37 cannot be identified. Of the 39 indictments of common white men, 15 resulted in convictions. The convicted men paid a median fine of only $1, a punishment that symbolized a jury's tacit approval of their actions. Some, like "piney woods chap" John Anderson, were not even convicted. He bit an ear from S. M. Burritt's head in an 1845 brawl and was later acquitted on charges of assault and battery. Yeoman juries refused to deny men like Anderson, "one of your hardworking, hard-drinking, and hard-fighting sort," the right to defend their honor.[26]

Even when fights and affrays crossed the line into deadly violence, yeomen often escaped serious punishment. In 1846, for example, two nonslaveholding white men, Aaron and William Smith, came to trial for murder. The jury convicted them on a reduced charge of manslaughter and assessed each Smith a symbolic fine of fifty cents plus court costs.[27] Yeoman-dominated juries also refused to scapegoat poor whites for the crime of arson. Planters wanted some one to blame for the rash of burned barns and gin houses that broke out around 1842 and sought a villain in the Tallahassee fire of 1843. But despite strong pressure to convict Thomas Harris as the culprit, yeoman jurors refused to sacrifice him, bringing an acquittal on all charges in December 1843.[28]

Ultimately, Eppes and his peers were unable to maintain deference on the plantation frontier. The records of Leon's courts in the 1840s reveal that lower-class white men assented to some kinds of planter-led order but rejected others. They forced the toleration of crimes of manhood, like street fighting, and class-marked issues like arson that hinted at traditional forms of popular protest (although they rejected "social banditry," the idea that organized groups of outlaws who strike against the rich should be supported by the people in general).[29] Yeoman jurors thus had established the right of their peers to fight for their honor and define themselves as men. The crisis had crippled the "planter law" that had once protected Richard Long, Francis Eppes, and their peers from defeat at the hands of countrymen in everyday conflict.

RITUALS OF ORDER

A way out remained open for those planters who could adjust to a new order of things. Different ideas about order, power, violence, and manhood had divided planters from yeomen, and the repercussions of their conflict continued to cause friction and suspicion. Yet possible grounds of cooperation among white men obviously existed. Planters who put aside or hid their prejudices against countrymen found that white men, acting together, could bring a new kind of order to frontier communities. In part because of their own needs for racial control over the slaves amongst whom they all lived, countrymen and planters realized that together they formed a minority with much in common. During the 1840s, rituals of religious revival and extralegal violence that united white men from multiple classes began to soothe some of the everyday disagreements about class and manhood in Middle Florida.

Violence and its meanings had served as a ground of conflict; now violence brought white men of varying economic status together. Their common cause would be the suppression of outlaw gangs, whose actions threatened not only order but life itself. One hot July night in 1846, Jackson County planter Edward C. Pittman was sitting in his home after dark, reading his newspaper by the light of a candle, while a ten-year-old enslaved boy slept in the next room. As he read, Pittman leaned his chair back against the log wall of his house. Suddenly, an unknown person thrust a shotgun through the unglazed window opposite to Pittman, and fired. The blast of buckshot literally tore off the man's head. Pittman's other slaves rushed to his cabin and found the mangled body, hands still clutching the newspaper. Terrified, they ran to get Shade Merritt, a neighbor. The news spread quickly through the county, but no one blamed the slaves for the murder. Instead, locals feared the bands of outlaws who "infested" the woods of Middle Florida. "The murder," wrote one Jackson resident, "has affected our citizens with a far greater sense of insecurity than any of those with which our county has been disgraced. No one knows where the next blow may fall."[30]

Had Pittman's slaves been guilty of murder, they would have been most atypical. Both in absolute and in relative terms, whites committed far more murders in Middle Florida than did blacks. From December 1841 to May 1847 the Leon County Superior and Circuit Courts indicted whites (all male) for at least seventeen, and perhaps as many as twenty-two killings. At least one additional homicide never produced an indictment. In the same span, the grand jury indicted only three blacks for killings, out of a much larger population. As both an isolated and a relative phenomenon, the number of homicides committed by white men was incredible. Leon County produced an average of three or more homicide indictments per annum.[31] The murder rate among Leon County's approximately 4,500 white inhabitants was thus the equivalent of 55–60 per 100,000, or a rate comparable to that of the most violent urban centers in the late-twentieth-century United States. Even in Jackson County, where the court records from the 1840s are far more spotty, surviving evidence depicts a high rate of murders. Governors' proclamations of fugitive criminals alone reveal that at least one murder per annum was committed by whites during this period in Jackson. Given the county population of approximately 2,500 whites, the annual murder rate in the 1840s remained at least 40 per 100,000 white inhabitants. The actual numbers were surely higher: many additional cases, like the unsolved murder of Pittman, never produced indictments or proclamations.[32]

The violence endemic to both planter and common white codes of masculinity had made deadly assault the preferred response to many kinds of insult. Causes specific to time and place also helped to inspire murderous behavior during the 1840s. Resentment of planter arrogance apparently lay beneath the Burney gang's rampage across northern Leon County in the early 1840s. In earlier decades, local planters had prevented Arthur Burney and his sons from participating in the formation of a new county in northern Leon, thus denying them access to office and status as well. By the early 1840s, when the elder Arthur Burney died, debt upon debt to local creditors piled upon the men of his clan. In purchasing enough slaves to become a cotton planter, Burney had borrowed over $10,000 from the Southern Life and Trust Insurance Company and John Bellamy. Apparently, his sons then began stealing from their neighbors in northeastern Leon County. Soon after, they turned to full-time outlawry: in 1843, William and David Burney murdered Joseph Manning and fled.[33]

The Burneys' conversion from migrant countrymen, to aspirant planters, to lurking outlaws grew out of the same boiling social unrest that also launched the Avant, Flowers, and other Middle Florida gangs. But unlike rough-and-tumbling countrymen, bandit gangs did not receive a blank check from local juries in this decade. The crimes of theft, highway robbery, and premeditated assassination did not square with yeoman ideals of honor. And, indeed, countrymen, like the coach driver killed in 1847 by Alvin Flowers on the road between Leon and Jackson Counties, were often the victims of bandits. And both planters and slaveowning yeomen feared the prospect of a Murrellite alliance that would unite outlaws and slaves against masters (see Chapter 7).[34] Thus, in 1845 and 1846, a round of lynchings in several counties demonstrated the anger of rural white communities against Middle Florida bandits. Designed to prevent a servile insurrection, these rituals also brought both yeomen and planters together on a common ground. Lynchings, of course, meant different things to different groups of participants. Yeomen may have believed that vigilante parties contained equal white men bent on enforcing an order that permitted farmers to produce self-sufficiency on the outskirts of settlement without constantly fearing robbery. The illegal character of lynchings also allowed countrymen to exert their wills in a kind of manly insubordination, even as they enforced a higher law. At the same time, planters calling themselves "Regulators" often took the lead in vigilante posses. If in the process of suppressing disorder they treated some landed yeomen as equals, they could simultaneously act out their contempt for still others. Most important, lynchings trained yeomen and planters to exercise violence together, as communities proving collective manhood.

The first lynching occurred in 1845 in Jackson County, where for some time a gang led by James Avant had "perpetrated murder and robbery" in the swamps between Marianna and Apalachicola. A search party of "Regulators" led by future murder victim Edward Pittman combed the woods and captured Avant. The posse dragged him back to Marianna and hanged him without trial on June 20. Meanwhile, farmers in northern Leon and Jefferson Counties accused a man named Stephen Yeomans of carrying on the slave-stealing legacy of the Burney gang. They eventually captured him in January 1846. Officials brought him to Monticello in Jefferson County to stand trial, but a mob seized the prisoner. The vigilantes, who allegedly included even "men of the gospel," conducted an impromptu "trial" and hanged Yeomans. Two months later, a similar group caught Jackson Jewel, one of Yeomans's associates, and gave him the same treatment. In another case, a Gadsden County mob forced the immediate "trial" of four outlaws who had murdered and killed along the mail stage routes between Tallahassee, Marianna, and points west. Despite Judge Thomas Baltzell's call for a special session to prevent the vigilantes from opening the jail and hanging the accused outlaws, the four captured men, including notorious criminals Samuel Holloman and Alvin Flowers, received speedy and fatal punishment before a cheering crowd — a lynching screened by the presence of a judge.[35]

Most white men stood on common ground when it came to lynchings. In Jackson County, planters either led mobs or remained quiet. In Tallahassee and Leon County, a few men like Francis Eppes and Richard Call remained unreconstructed believers in the deference of the lower sort of white men to their betters. They saw extralegal executions as the death knell of their kind of top-down community control. The *Sentinel* complained that where this sort of community will reigned, "Life, liberty, and property are then only held by *favor* and unpopularity becomes death." But most white men felt differently: Frank Hatheway, a clerk in a Tallahassee shop, reported in a January entry in his diary, "Excitement in Jefferson Co. A man named Roberts, hung by a convention!" William Bailey, the Jefferson County planter who had helped lead the "trial" and "execution" of Stephen Yeomans, became a popular Democratic politician. Supporters proudly advertised his participation in mob justice. Even Governor William Moseley, a planter with holdings in Jefferson and Leon Counties, joined the 1846 posse that hunted Samuel Holloman. Finally, the murder of Edward Pittman, who perhaps was killed out of vengeance for his own vigilante activities, changed the minds of many men who had formerly opposed mob law. Aside from a small, increasingly irrelevant group of conservatives, by the late 1840s, most white men in Jackson and Leon Counties supported lynching.[36]

Lynchings changed white society in Middle Florida. Outlaw gangs essentially disappeared from the area. Vigilante actions enacted the murderous side of the new popular politics. Lynchings were both popular and exclusionary, and in them, mob justice allowed planter and countryman to survive together the contradictions within and between their visions of masculinity. Yeomen could be insubordinate, breaking the law at the same time they enforced the order that made independence possible. Meanwhile, planters leading the mobs felt that they were reinforcing the institution — slavery — that made them strong. In vigilante actions, white men concentrated on what they had in common rather than what divided them. Yet even as planters and yeomen were stringing up some of those who broke rules about the use of violence, others—including some lynch mob members—carried out a different ritual that also brought the classes together, even as it showed wealthy men submitting to yeoman styles.[37]

Religious revivals were, in retrospect, an unsurprising response to Middle Florida's crisis. If confused planters saw their problems as chastisement by God, why would they not turn to evangelical rebirth? Such ceremonies, after all, promised to allow the sinner to pass through trauma into redemption. Yet it was by no means inevitable that evangelical religion would prove an attractive option for a potentially repentant elite. During the first two decades of settlement in Middle Florida, most elite migrants remained unchurched members of a largely nonreligious society. One 1828 correspondent from Jackson County complained that he had lived there for fifteen months "without hearing the sound of the Gospel, and the other counties are not much more favored." Another visitor asserted that planters' lack of religion made them mariners "without a compass." The work of women like Nancy Hagan and the periodic revival meetings of the 1830s rarely gained public notice, much less planter participation. Baptist and Methodist churches in Jackson and Leon Counties remained the province of the common whites who lived in the countryside's new "diggins." Even wealthy Methodist families like the Bradfords of Leon County kept their distance from early frontier revivals and their supposed improprieties.[38]

The magnitude of crisis in the early 1840s sent white Middle Floridians of all classes back to their society's most basic ways of explaining a confusing, treacherous reality. Many of those who wrote to local newspapers called upon the citizens of Jackson and Leon Counties to repent, and to beseech God to return order to a world in chaos. "'Ye cannot serve both God and Mammon,'" preached "John Caldwell" in the *Star.* "[T]he vessel has run aground! She must ultimately sink, without the application of a lever. That lever must be MORAL PRINCIPLE!"[39] Some Jackson and Leon County citizens moved quickly to dislodge the ship. Massive revivals began to sweep the area in 1841. They apparently began in the common white Baptist churches of Jackson County, but soon the planter-dominated lowlands around Marianna also submitted to the gentle yoke. During June of that year, Benjamin Wynns reported to his sister that "there has been a great revolution among the citizens in Marianna and the vicinity and great religious revival. . . . [T]he Methodist quarterly meeting, which continued about ten days . . . resulted in the conversion of about thirty persons, and new ones continue to join on every sabbath."[40]

Both Methodist and Baptist revivals moved on to Leon County the next year, sweeping up whites of all classes, as well as slaves, in their commotion. In 1843, a Methodist meeting held at the Miccosukee campground saw a reported 2,000 attendees. A new Baptist church, Enon, founded near Lake Bradford, seemed to be the favored place of worship for those of the planter set who preferred that denomination. The preacher was a Dr. Lang—once one of Willis Alston's gun-toting bravos, he now heeded a different call. Meanwhile, Trinity Methodist Church, in Tallahassee, which had been dormant during most of the 1830s, saw an explosion in membership. In 1840, thirteen years after its founding, the church listed a pitiful 9 members on its rolls. In 1842, it added 19, and by the end of the decade it claimed 71. By 1860, the names of 160 members were in the church's minute book.[41]

Relieved planters suddenly wanted to praise both evangelical religion and evangelical yeomen as respectable, or at least respectable enough. Newspaper accounts emphasized the good order of these gatherings, suggesting that upper-class men and women could attend meetings without being subjected to the more offensive enthusiasms sometimes displayed by slaves and common whites. At an 1841 revival, reported Joshua Knowles, "we did not witness the slightest disorder on the part of the large audience that attended." Thousands of "the serious and attentive people from the neighboring plantations, and villages" were present at the 1843 meetings in Leon County. They may have been more serious and attentive than in the previous decade. And as revivals became more comfortable for planters, the public eye of the local newspapers began to read yeomen as religiously reputable. Members of the Felkel family, longtime stalwarts of Pisgah Methodist, that touchstone of local "countryman" identity, received long and flattering obituaries upon their deaths in the 1840s. Stories on Jacob and Mary Felkel, and later their son David, recounted conversion experiences and gave full descriptions of their highly Methodist deathbed scenes. This kind of religious incorporation of solid yeoman families into the company of equal, respectable whites was by no means unique to Middle Florida, but in the local context, public and positive recognition of yeoman evangelicalism was a new phenomenon.[42]

Observers credited the revivals with righting the moral compasses of Jackson and Leon Counties. A Marianna resident reported, "By the way, speaking of churches, the morals of this county have undergone a most salutary change within the last few months . . . little or no drinking, gambling, or carousing," before adding, "I am happy to hear that Tallahassee has also improved in that regard. There was certainly much room." Not all of these rosy hopes became reality. Drunkenness and fighting continued to plague both counties through the rest of the decade. But the level of rowdiness declined. Most notably, planters stopped brawling in the streets and abandoned the practice of horsewhipping men with whom they were in conflict. Between 1843 and 1847, the Leon County grand jury indicted only four elite men for physical assaults. Duels disappeared. "Those days," wrote a Middle Florida Methodist minister of the years leading up to the revivals, "with their scenes of horror, had passed away [by the 1850s], and peace and prosperity, religion and morality, had taken their place." And planters and common whites began to see each other in a new light: as fellow members of churches in some cases, or at the least as fellow believers in evangelical dogma and in the ideal of a new kind of social order. Religion was not the only cause of the public shift toward a less assertive, hierarchical planter masculinity, but, along with political needs and the determination of yeomen to resist subordination, revival encouraged planter men to see less wealthy whites as deserving of respect.[43]

Still, many houses of worship remained dominated by yeomen, whereas others were the religious homes of wealthier whites. The Methodist Bradfords still preferred to attend the Bradfordville or Trinity (Tallahassee) churches, rather than Pisgah. In planter churches, evangelical religion became more genteel, less ecstatic and expressive. "I do not like the way things are conducted now," complained Jesse Bernard, a merchant's son married into the Bradford family, to his diary in 1858, "so different from the old-fashioned Methodism—no calling up of mourners, indeed no appeal to sinners." Common participation in evangelical churches may have made planter and yeomen ideas about religious practice, and even masculine behavior, more similar to each other. Some lower-class believers may have preached a more genteel evangelicalism in the effort to win acceptance from wealthier neighbors. Yet one cannot forget that planters had taken up the scorned religion of countrymen (or, rather, the women of that class—and of the slaves). In the rituals of conversion, frontier planter men learned how to hold their peace rather than trying to dominate all encounters with social inferiors.[44]

In both lynchings and revivals, yeomen acted out aspects of their definitions of masculinity. On the one hand, they acted out insubordination with violence, and claimed the recognition of other white men as nominal equals, although this time they acted in concert with planters rather than against them. On the other hand, in churches, they reinforced their rule over subordinates. By the end of the crisis decade, planters had surrendered many forms of hierarchy between white men. Ironically, by the time Middle Florida's economy finally began to recover around 1850, the frontier had become a prosperous region dominated by the plantation economy and a certain kind of plantation order. Perhaps a planter class wiser in dealing with proud yeomen now guided white society with a velvet glove, rather than trying to ride it, horsewhip in hand. Still, change came out of defeat and despair rather than out of a conscious plan of manipulation. Elite whites began to bewail the South's place in the wider national economy only when they lost control over the high ground of their own credit. They hung up the horsewhip before going into town only because they feared the political and physical repercussions of new yeoman assertiveness.

AMBIGUOUS ALLIANCES

Soon after rituals returned a sense of order to Middle Florida, increasing prosperity also began to play a role in defusing any lingering class- and gender-based conflicts among white men. The crucial economic alliances in this development were not those between planters and countrymen but between prosperous yeomen and their less wealthy relatives. But the recovery of the plantation economy in Middle Florida helped most white men in one way or another. International demand for cotton had taken years to recover from the overproduction and financial instability inflicted by, among other things, the excesses of planter banks. Finally, after a decade of depressed prices, the cotton market began a slow recovery by 1849–50. The gradual rise in prices would continue through much of the next decade.[45] The economy of Middle Florida began to heat up again, although this time only to a simmer. The number of plantations that produced large quantities of cotton rose in both Jackson and Leon Counties (see Table A.10). In Jackson, the number of farms producing 50 or more bales of cotton rose from 10 to 50 in the 1850s, while in Leon the number rose from 96 to 108, even as the total number of farms declined. Enslaved African Americans were the workers who made most of the cotton on plantations, and as revenues from cash crops grew, Middle Florida planters began once more to invest money in expanding their labor forces. Between the slave trade, new migrations, and natural increase, the numbers of households owning more than twenty slaves also rose dramatically during the 1850s (see Table A.10).

The cohorts of both planters and successful yeomen broadened by the 1850s. Cotton was crucial to the planters' new prosperity, and in the 1850s it represented a more significant part of the yeoman economy than ever before. In the 1820s and 1830s, cotton was a rare item in surviving inventories of common white estates. Cotton served as a means to the end of obtaining cash, and then self-sufficiency. Yeomen had little reason to grow the crop during the 1840s, when prices were low and the risk of debt high. Increasing prices in the latter part of the decade encouraged small farmers to come back to cotton. By 1850, most Leon County farmers owning more than a small patch of land grew the crop. According to the 1850 U.S. Agricultural Census, for instance, the average farmer who cultivated at least fifty but less than one hundred acres made 9.9 bales of cotton. By 1860, many small farmers were moving out of the county and heading for newer frontiers like Texas. Yet some yeomen continued to add labor and acres and changed production patterns to grow still more cotton. Peter Brown, for instance, farmed forty acres and made no cotton in 1850. By 1860, he had purchased a slave or two and had cleared twenty more acres. He made three bales of cotton, still fewer than most farmers with similar amounts of land. Still, if these developments represented a permanent reorientation rather than a one-year production decision, the turn to cotton production represented a significant change in Brown's approach to farming.[46]

In Jackson County—perhaps less indebted, and thus less desperate for cash—both planters and yeomen increased their production of cotton, although they continued to produce less than Leon farmers working comparable amounts of improved acres. Those who cultivated over fifty but less than one hundred acres in 1850, for instance, made, on average, only 4.8 bales of cotton. While the planters of the Apalachicola and Chipola River valleys ginned scores of bales, smaller farmers often stuck to tobacco and rice. In the piney woods away from the rivers, or scattered through the swamps, hundreds of households scratched out crops on small tracts of a few dozen acres each. An 1850 visitor might have found Irwin and Enoch Miller dividing up their father's old farm. Land that might have provided independence, if not comfort, for one household, barely supported Miller's two sons. Irwin worked twenty-six improved acres, and his brother was listed as working twenty. Each had a single plow horse, neither owned any unimproved acres, and both ran their hogs in woods owned by the government and by their neighbors. They grew barely enough corn and sweet potatoes for subsistence. By 1860, a surge in poor white migrants from South Carolina and Georgia doubled the numbers of Jackson County farmers like the Millers. These new countrymen brought down averages in all types of production for the smaller farms. The overall size of the Jackson County cotton crop increased two and a half times over the decade, while Leon County's remained about the same.[47]

Meanwhile, the more long-occupied "diggins" assumed a settled appearance. Sons and daughters married and settled near their parents, while unrelated neighbors knew each other from long acquaintance. And prosperity overtook those select yeomen who commanded enough land and labor to capitalize on the rise in cotton prices. Countrymen who came to Middle Florida as members of supportive kinship networks, who did not fall victim to drink, disease, Seminoles, outlaws, or the lure of the bank and the faro table, could after a quarter-century of striving, rise. A few moved from working in the fields themselves to a level of slaveownership where we might call them "small planters." These men were unusual, and they were probably the most significant men in their common white neighborhoods. They were the ore that settled to the bottom while the stream of migration, death, and failure carried off most of the other countrymen who had brought their families and slaves to Jackson and Leon Counties during the first two decades of white settlement.

In Leon County, some of the older men in the Pisgah community grew so prosperous that it was sometimes difficult to distinguish their farms—at least on paper—from those of men who had arrived in the county with numerous slaves. Henry Stroman, for example, made fifty-eight bales of cotton on his farm in the Centreville area in 1850. Officially he owned no land, and only four slaves, but he obviously used many of the 373 acres and twenty-five slaves owned by his father, Jacob Stroman, to make the cotton and 1,000 bushels of corn. Brother John Stroman, on his neighboring farm, a 160-acre quarter section, made twenty-five bales with his nine slaves—no doubt borrowing labor from his father and brother. A visiting Methodist preacher who held a "ten days' meeting" at Pisgah in 1855, recalled that he "saw that the church had drifted into worldly-mindedness." "One old South Carolinian, a Dutchman," either Jacob Houck or Jacob Stroman, still retained his old stubbornness, even as his wealth had grown. Angry at the preacher's implication that he had "backslid" in the pursuit of wealth, he stormed out of the Sunday morning service, "saying that God had never made a man that could run over him in that way."[48]

Economic interests increasingly split nonslaveowning whites from planters and prosperous yeomen, but community and kinship limited the development of antagonisms among those who had arrived in the early waves of countryman migration. Virtually without exception, even successful yeoman patriarchs remained firmly ensconced in yeoman neighborhoods. Usually the much smaller farms of sons, sons-in-law, and church brethren surrounded their own larger ones, and through inheritance and mutual assistance they spread some of the boom's benefits out to less successful peers. When they died, they divided a lifetime of accumulated economic independence among the children who had helped make that status. The 1846 will of Gasper Houck, an early settler in the Pisgah neighborhood, provides an example. Houck gave his son John D. F. Houck the 200-acre tract on which Gasper resided at the time, and a 40-acre tract purchased from Adam Gramling to his other son Daniel. The will required John to pay Daniel $200 within four years in order to compensate for this distribution of land. Gasper Houck also willed his slave Tom to John, while Daniel got his father's set of blacksmith tools. The two sons, sisters Ann Felkel, Mary Felkel, Rebecca Barnes, and the children of their deceased sibling Elizabeth Gramling divided the rest of the estate equally. The sisters' marriages to men from neighboring families associated with Pisgah church show the Houcks' entrenchment in the Centreville neighborhood. The small amounts of land and money involved show the small scale of yeoman ambitions, and the close attention paid to trying to make sure each son had the foundations of independence.[49]

By the early 1850s, the foundation willed by Gasper Houck to his sons enabled them both to become self-sufficient and even prosperous. Daniel Houck owned thirteen slaves and worked 125 acres of land. They made twenty-six bales of cotton, and Houck could earn a living as a commercial farmer while his slaves also produced much of the family's subsistence. They raised 600 bushels of corn, while he also owned forty hogs and thirty head of cattle. Self-sufficiency may have allowed him to plan to reinvest a surplus from cotton sales in more enslaved laborers, or in consumer goods, or schooling for his children. Houck's brother, John, was not as successful, claiming only three slaves in 1850, but (no doubt with help from brother Daniel's slaves) he did make twenty-three bales of cotton, 700 bushels of corn, and nearly a ton of rice. Like many other Middle Florida yeoman farmers, the Houck brothers were creeping into the cotton-export commercial economy that sustained planters' wealth. In earlier decades, countrymen used cash crop production as a tool for a specific purpose: the acquisition of land. By the 1850s demand for the staple seemed so great that production appeared to hold less risk than ever before. Cotton and slaveownership became a common ground that united yeomen and planters, once divided by the economic imperatives of frontier settlement.

Yet the daughters of Stromans and Houcks did not marry the sons of the Branches and Bradfords of Leon County, or vice versa. Social and cultural differences continued to divide even prosperous yeomen from those who had come to Middle Florida as planters. Perhaps the Houcks thought that in a generation or two their descendants would mingle on equal terms with the Branches a few miles to the west. Or perhaps they preferred the company of the whites who had treated them as equals all along. We possess no window into the minds of men like Daniel Houck. We cannot know what he thought of continued economic disparities, or the lines of status that evidently still divided yeoman from planter, even though he and his peers could now observe politicians dancing to the rhetorical tune of white male equality.[50]

We can tell, however, that while some yeomen like W. L. Stroman, who owned twenty slaves in 1860, had found economic success on the plantation frontier, most others from similar origins had not. Some remained near family and neighbors, but others, still seeking economic independence, uprooted again, and moved on. Between the 1820s and 1850s, relatively few heads of household remained in Middle Florida from one decade to the next (see Table A.11). Despite cotton prosperity, many white farmers and farm laborers remained landless. Party politics trumpeted their claims to political manhood, but their continued economic dependence might have made the blaring of candidates sound a bit hollow. According to the 1850 Leon County property tax records, 329 white men owned no slaves, and of these, 223 also owned no land (see Table A.12). Some were artisans, clerks, and laborers in Tallahassee, but others lived and worked in the rural neighborhoods of the county. John Evans of Centreville, for example, tried for years to earn money through overseeing but found "as I cannot buy land here without paying two prices for it I have come to the conclusion to hire out" once again. The apparent decline in the number of landless white men in Leon County supports the conclusion that many less deeply rooted countrymen moved on, as the declining number of small farms in Leon might also suggest. Even in Jackson County, where land was cheaper, many men continued to struggle to obtain a freehold. In March 1849, R. L. and R. C. Stephens signed, with their "marks," a contract selling for $55 to local merchant William Harvey "all the crop to be raised by us the present year on the plantation of Hugh Rusk." In order to have any cash for supplies, rent, and taxes, the Stephens brothers had to mortgage their only possession, the crop (probably a bale or two of cotton) that they planned to make with their own labor. Like these two, many of the small farmers in Jackson squatted in the piney woods, clearing a few acres, running cattle and hogs on government land. Some, especially those with local ties, stayed. Others formed an increasingly transient population of poor whites drifting westward across the South.[51]

Yet continuing bonds of community and family between wealthy yeomen and their less successful brethren prevented the fear of economic differentiation from becoming politicized in the 1850s in Middle Florida, and increased the commitment of all common whites to the plantation system. Kinship did not link wealthy planters to yeomen in Jackson and Leon Counties, or at least no real evidence of such ties survives. Instead, blood, marriage, and common membership in yeoman-dominated churches bound successful yeomen to less wealthy peers.[52] These bonds enabled men with fewer resources to benefit from the cotton boom via their relatives, the William Stromans of Middle Florida. They could hope, not to be planters, but to be masters on a smaller scale. That dream was at least a real possibility, although the chance of success may have shrunk steadily with increasing market participation and levels of rural debt during the 1850s cotton boom. The ties between big and little yeoman were perhaps more important to social stability than those that bonded planter and common white. Despite some divergence in basic economic interests between successful slaveowning yeomen and their less wealthy peers, ties of neighborhood and kinship continued to bind countryman households together as a single group.

Perhaps, then, the boom in cotton prices and the return of economic stability did what the crude attempts of pro-bank men to buy off Centreville could not accomplish. Most white men grew more committed to preserving together a vision of Florida as a slaveholders' republic. Planters' acceptance of the fact that they had to behave, in public, as if they believed in white male equality also removed some of the conditions for conflict between them and slaveowning yeomen. Common public commitments to white supremacy and patriarchy as prescriptions for social order linked white men from all classes. Yet one must not overstate areas of agreement between yeomen and planters. Economic distinctions continued, even without the presence of the Union Bank as a constant irritant that politicized issues of class. The rise in yeoman participation in cotton production did not make former countrymen equal masters. Despite changes in political style, and public behavior, overseers and other employees still recognized that differentials in economic power required them to couch their language carefully. Resentment of economic dependence often clouded the statements of men like W. W. Boykin, a Jackson County overseer for absentee planter George Gray. He wrote: "It is my wishes [*sic*] to continue with you Mr. Gray but it is to my interest to get all I can. . . . [E]very man in the settlement says you ought to give me at least $400[. T]here is a grate [*sic*] difference in overseers[,] and when I leave this place you will find it." Employers had to be careful as well. George Jones discharged D. N. Moxley for intemperate language but could not find an effective replacement, so he had to ask his former employee to return.[53]

On the one hand, relations between wealthy white men and their employees had reached a balancing point of ambiguous alliance. On the other hand, yeoman neighbors never stopped insisting that they were planters' equals, and never stopped watching suspiciously for insult. Perhaps no law, and no implicit compromise, could ever quite keep Snell within its grasp. In 1854, John Evans, the overseer for Chemonie plantation, wrote to absentee owner George Jones about the plantation bull named "Doctor." Well known in the neighborhood, Doctor had broken out of his pasture and run loose for several weeks. Residents in "the settlement," a nearby cluster of yeoman households, captured the bull. Angry at his depredations in their fields, and perhaps jealous of Jones's wealth and power, they "altered" him. For good measure they also cropped the new steer's tail. Jones and his neighbors existed in what was at best an uneasy peace, one that existed for the moment of the 1850s.[54]

The frontier conflicts that came to a head in Jackson and Leon Counties during the early 1840s forced a series of accommodations among the white population's social classes. Elite migrant men had not planned to assert their common interests with yeomen as fellow masters, as whites, and as men. But the crisis years "cropped" the power of Middle Florida planters, and they felt at times "altered" indeed. A new relationship to the world market, symbolized by the rise of Northern cotton factors, stripped the Southern elite of control over their credit. Meanwhile, because of the power of yeomen to transform political ideology and practice, Middle Florida communities changed in other ways. White men struck an implicit bargain: planters recognized yeomen as equals in masculinity and white privilege; and the latter accepted their status as citizens and men in lieu of economic equality. And, of course, the steady rise in cotton prices after 1849 helped ease tensions, at least for landowning yeomen. By the 1850s, Jackson and Leon moved beyond the most uncertain years of the frontier, when many aspects of social and cultural order had seemed up for grabs.

The changing relationships did not amount to revolution, except perhaps one in the gendered relationships between different classes of white men. Countrymen did not win control over their world. They won something that they wanted to claim—manhood that both they and their society recognized. Of course, their idea of what manhood meant rendered them incapable of seizing full power over Middle Florida society. They were not going to shoulder aside other white men, other independent householders, if those men could and would deal with yeomen on terms that yeomen recognized as respectful. They were still less likely to turn in allegiance to the enslaved, planters' natural enemy, especially since an increasing number of countrymen were becoming slaveowners themselves.[55]

Still, in part as a consequence of the ambiguity and cloaked hostility that sometimes still permeated day-to-day contacts between elite and common whites, planters were never quite comfortable with the new arrangement. With the advantages of hindsight on our own side, we can argue that non-planter whites supported slavery. Yet planters always feared that their non-planter neighbors were about to desert the bargain—stability and alliance, in return for acknowledgment of yeoman manhood—that countrymen had forced on slaveholders. In 1851, one correspondent, worried about the voting of Georgia yeomen who opposed recent efforts to call a Southern convention to consider secession, wrote to John Branch: "It is startling to slaveholders to contemplate the results of the last elections. . . . I fear it will not be long before we find abolitionists in our midst." Ambiguous hegemony is not a comfortable state for a ruling class raised to desire domination.[56]

As slavery received national criticism, local history made planters uneasy. And so, in order to soothe their fears, they turned to rewriting that history. Many of our histories of the antebellum South show how a stable plantation system slid into the abyss of secession and civil war. In such stories, we look backward, peering at evidence, to see if it signals the war to come. Those who had experienced the Middle Florida frontier also looked backward. From the vantage point of the 1850s, their story rested at an outcome unplanned for all involved, one also difficult to shape into coherent meaning. Enslaved African Americans had not desired this outcome. Nor was it precisely what migrant countrymen, a generation earlier, had in mind, although they got much of the respect for their masculinity that they had wanted. Nor did white women, poor or rich, get what they wanted: reform of manhood in the one case, immediate stability in the other. But the recent past forced male planters, perhaps more than anyone, to reconsider who they were. The course of their frontier experience had gone against their wills. They turned, consciously or unconsciously, to erasing the past that had made their society.

Remaking History

It makes no odds where he [the Virginian] goes, he carries Virginia with him. . . . He may breathe in Alabama, but he lives in Virginia. His treasure is there, and his heart also. If he looks at the Delta of Mississippi, it reminds him of the James River "low grounds;" if he sees the vast prairies of Texas, it is a memorial of the meadows of the Valley.
—Joseph Baldwin, "How the Times Served the Virginians"

Sir Walter Scott had so large a hand in making Southern character, as it existed before the war, that he is great measure responsible for the war. It seems a little harsh towards a dead man to say that we never should have had any war but for Sir Walter, and yet something of a plausible argument might be made in support of that wild proposition.
—Mark Twain, *Life on the Mississippi*

In 1835, in the first bright days of the Union Bank, Rosa Burroughs of Savannah moved with her husband William to Tallahassee. William Burroughs, already prosperous, prospered still more in the flush times of the rag empire. He also survived the bad days of economic crisis and by 1850 could admit to the Leon County tax assessor that he owned thirty-five working slaves. The year before they made seventy-four bales of cotton on his plantation, the Grove.[1] Even as William Burroughs worked at driving his slaves, extracting wealth and status from their bodies, Rosa and her daughters, Mary and Catherine, were far from idle. In one sense, masculinity drowned out the voices of most planter women on Middle Florida's public stage. But in a more private realm, women made their own comments. There, Rosa, Mary, and Catherine worked to re-create their family and house in the new shape of the planter home. The glorification of the imagery of the plantation manor as a place of beauty, inhabited by saintly mother and Southern belle, was a mighty domestic labor under way across the whole South between the 1840s and the Civil War. The Burroughs household, in fact, kept an evocative scrapbook of this process, containing family letters, meticulously inscribed sentimental poems, pressed flowers, scraps of cross-stitch, and cut-out images from magazines. There are page upon page of such icons, carefully pasted into fields of meaning: birds, ladies, cherubic infants, illustrations of New York and Boston, George Washington at prayer, "The Cotton Plant," "The Novel Reader" (a warning for young ladies), Jenny Lind. The whole album is a monument to bourgeois domesticity, sentimental religion, and a gentle nationalism both American and Southern.[2]

The album's effect is a powerful evocation of a planter class's sense of history. Its most elaborate construction combines an up-to-date domesticity available to those who won wealth in commercial markets with a celebration of that most historically minded of romantic novelists, Sir Walter Scott. Facing a page of magazine illustrations with titles like "Young men and the Sabbath" and "The altar of home," there is a carefully constructed collage. At the bottom are three illustrations of women wearing the styles of the day, wrapped in senorita mantillas and, in one case, topped with a Queen Isabella crown. They are grouped carefully across the bottom half of the page: to the left, two young women—sisters, one imagines—in the middle, a regal, more mature lady, and on the right, a mother reading in the shade of a tree while her young daughter plays with a flowered hat. Girlhood, womanhood, and motherhood displayed the idealized life-course, albeit without the presence of older, poorer, or darker women. There are no Nancy Hagans in this world, much less a Daphne Williams. And above this triptych of femininity is an image of the implied male presence under whom they lived: a cut-out engraving of Sir Walter Scott's "Abbotsford," followed by a few valedictory lines about Scott, handwritten and set in lace. Abbotsford was an architectural monstrosity, a quasi-Gothic quasi-castle combining medieval symbols of feudal authority with the latest modern conveniences. The Burroughs women used this concoction of crossbow ports and gas lighting to symbolize their life, pasting the respectability of idealized middle-class families over the harsh realities of coerced labor on frontier plantations. Above everything stood the wished-for social authority idealized by the image of the Middle Ages, when knights were bold and lower-class louts and villeins happily accepted a lower place.[3]

The rejoinder to Middle Florida's recent past is obvious. Wealthy Middle Floridians were attempting to erase a recent past from public discussion and private memory. Although this was not always a conscious project,

Page from scrapbook made by Burroughs family women (Georgia Historical Society)

their attempt to replace the history of crisis with an epic past reveals that they still smarted from multiple defeats. And, just as Abbotsford represented a very contradictory vision, the evidence of change on the frontier persisted in the very efforts of the rewriters to deny what had gone before. The men and women of Middle Florida were not alone. Views of the South as a region without a history of change and conflict were useful and popular throughout the region (and the United States generally) from the late 1830s onward. This period saw the rise of the plantation novel, an altered form of the historical romance made so popular by Scott. Afraid of the accelerating pace of economic and cultural change, writers like John Pendleton Kennedy and William Gilmore Simms likened planters to gracious aristocrats devoted to a less acquisitive life. They compared the supposed courtly manners, concern for family honor, and alleged battlefield valor of the Southern gentry to then-popular romanticism about the Middle Ages.[4]

By implicitly and explicitly comparing themselves to characters enshrined in the new plantation literature, Jackson and Leon County planters distinguished themselves from the North, and connected themselves to the Old Dominion. By making the region more like a mythical Virginia, it seemed less florid, less volatile. During this period, Leon and Jackson County planters chose names borrowed directly from popular historical romances of the antebellum era for their homes, cloaking the relative newness of their frontier money-making operations. John Branch added a second plantation, Waverley, to his older Live Oak. Why a secessionist like Branch would name his plantation after Walter Scott's fictional, half-hearted participant in Britain's failed 1745 rebellion is anyone's guess, but perhaps he missed the irony. Nearby, Edward Bradford's Horseshoe perhaps recalled John Pendleton Kennedy's character, the loyal yeoman Horseshoe Robinson, or even William Carruthers' prototypical Southern imperialist group, the Knights of the Golden Horseshoe. Jackson County planter Jesse Coe drunkenly rode his horse Redgauntlet, named after Scott's border rebel. Middle Florida resident and novelist Caroline Lee Hentz imbued all sorts of local places and people with this aura by setting one of her plantation romances in Jackson County, where she died in 1855.[5]

The past shapes us, and so do the stories that we tell ourselves about events after they have happened, as their aftereffects continue to beat upon our shores. Crucial to the stories, at least in the way in which they shape our perceptions of ourselves, is the structure of their plot. Are they pessimistic or optimistic; comedy, romance, or tragedy? Middle Florida planters began by imposing on the context of local history one particular shape: a template for past, present, and future. The shape of the template then led them to seek out or create evidence, and to do so almost unconsciously as they sought to present their own stories. No single model directed such a process for the entire South. While Tallahassee stores stocked and advertised books by Scott, Simms, and other such authors, such sources did not control Middle Floridians, any more than the Burroughs women were forced to cut images out of magazines by the images themselves. Like those women, Middle Florida's elite assembled available symbols and ideas into a story suiting their own needs. In newspapers and in private memoirs, in novels and in more formal histories, planters wrestled with their own making and remaking on the Florida frontier. In response to the crisis, change, and defeats of their own recent local and regional pasts, Middle Florida's planters produced by the 1850s a new vision of local history—or more accurately, one that forgot local history. Newspaper editors, memoirists, and novelists all helped to create this "popular" interpretation. Even in private letters and conversations, Middle Florida's planter class redrew their particular corner of a very new South as one that was "Old," unchanged from the past and unchanging in present and future.[6]

After the crisis of Middle Florida, planters gradually came to believe that they lived in an old, static region. In this world, they still held authority, albeit now by the gentle reins of lower-class whites' deference and slaves' devoted familial loyalty. Paternalism replaced the whip. The new things that planters told themselves about what social interactions meant enabled them to endure and finesse changing relations with both the enslaved and less wealthy whites. The return of cotton prosperity did not hurt, of course. Meanwhile, yeomen participated only peripherally in collective dreaming, and perhaps they did not care too much about planters' fantasies, as long as in political and everyday life the latter treated them with the manly respect now established as the sine qua non of white class harmony. They had their own historical visions, as did the enslaved. Yet planters were still the most powerful group in Middle Florida, and their ideas about history in the 1850s, like the very different ones they had held in the 1820s, did much to shape this changing plantation frontier.

Like earlier dreams, the new one would lead the local elite into disastrous miscalculations. In the meantime, it did more than salve planter egos more sore than Richard Hayward's head. Local history, as interpreted, also provided a script for Florida's participation in the sectional conflict mounting beyond the young state's borders. The image of a frozen past and an unchanging present said this about the society that Middle Floridians inhabited: here is a unified society, one that does not and cannot change, one more like the old places of the world than the new. They plotted their story as one of unchanging social stability, in past, present, and by implication, future. This story told planters that they were different from the North, and eventually that because of that difference, they could and should prosper on their own. Crucial to such a plot was the absence of anything like a social revolution, and, in fact, the absence of social conflict altogether. The abandonment of revolution did not mean the abandonment of the American Revolution but rather the denial that class-related tensions played any part in the shape of that war, or in the years that followed, including those in which Southerners settled the Old Southwest. The South became in memory a place in which the upper orders could rely on the lower orders of their society. Thus, while many factors would lead to political secession in late 1860, among them was the planters' new view of their own history, shaped by the need to deny the disorder and defeat that haunted the plantation frontier's recent past.

One must pause to note one of the many ironies of this process. Middle Floridians missed one of Scott's major points about the past. He consciously used history and change, situating his plots at points in time, and in the lives of characters, where old ways collided with the new. The new ways usually won, a fact that Scott used to set into strong relief the irrational hold of romantic nostalgia on the psyches of elite men and women. In *Waverley*, for example, the title character's obsession with the knight-errant images of an imagined past leads him into dangerous miscalculations in his present.[7] But perhaps readers saw in such texts only what their own local history disposed them to find. And so we can witness the conception and birth of the idea, at least in its Middle Florida version, that the "South" was "Old." The "popular" historical vision native to this South—a region new in the 1840s and 1850s, reeling from its very newness—depicted it as an old and stable society without internal conflict. Planters, a group sometimes lauded as having a particularly clear historical and political-economic vision, closed their eyes and saw what they what they thought they needed to see. The misreading of Scott implicit in the Burroughs' scrapbook was but one of many ironies.

PIECES OF STORIES: RETELLING LOCAL HISTORY

Middle Floridians had been thinking about their own places and their own antecedents in history from the very beginning of U.S. settlement in the region. Ideas about the past reflected and refracted both experience of the recent past and desires for the future. The first generation of elite white settlers had hoped that the large number of wealthy and cultured migrants would help Middle Florida to escape "that intermediate period of violence and anarchy, that interregnum of law and morals, which had marked the histories of several States less happily constituted." When conflict and lawlessness did appear, many feared that migrants had somehow precipitated themselves back into a barbarous stage of society. The *Pensacola Gazette*'s 1826 serialized "history" of the Florida territory, called "The Chronicles of the Governors of Adirolf," depicted the jockeying of the territory's factions as a parody of the Bible's book of Chronicles. The author implied that the kinship networks that struggled over the frontier's resources resembled the semibarbaric kings of Assyria and Judah. But most elite migrants hoped that energetic exploitation of the frontier's resources and integration with the Anglo-American world would ensure historical progress, rather than regress, for their region.[8]

Twenty years later, elite whites reworked and shifted understandings of their own pasts in the wake of crisis. Some began to tell new stories about the recent past, and about the more distant era of initial settlement. In 1844, the editor of the *Tallahassee Star of Florida* blamed swindlers for the territory's problems: "Florida [has] become the prey of different bands of speculators . . . the theatre of one scheme of fraud and peculation after another." Some observers, he continued, blamed these problems on "things indigenous to the soil, and natural to the climate," but he disagreed: "[N]o portion of our extensive country was ever settled by a better class of people than that which has from time to time immigrated to Florida." Indeed, they were of an historically important root: "[S]cattered over the prairie, the hammocks, or along the rich alluvial bottoms of Florida, may be found the 'best blood of Virginia,' offsets from the best families of the Old Dominion, the Carolinas, and Georgia." And had they changed in Florida's warmer clime? "Have they been corrupted in our atmosphere by the deleterious action of our climate? or our soil? We think not."[9] Neither blue-blooded settlers nor the way they behaved on the plantation frontier were to blame for frauds perpetrated from within or without the territory. A few immigrants might have manipulated the political system, while Northern merchants and investors had fastened on the territory the albatross of the banks. Unchanged and uncorrupted Virginia blood, by contrast, was the answer to the problems of local history. To that "better class of people," and their ultimate ability to shape Middle Florida, the misdeeds of speculators and politicians were irrelevant. So were transformations wrought by soil and climate, metaphors for migration and the frontier. "Corruption" had not occurred.

This point of view—that the Middle Florida ruling class had not changed from its supposed origins in a mystified and idealized Virginia—appeared first in the *Star* but soon came to dominate local thought about local and regional histories. By first placing blame for the crisis of the territory on manipulative outsiders, and then forgetting the crisis altogether, the ruling class would shift the focus. Neither class conflict, nor Indian war, nor the possibility of slave revolt had threatened—or could possibly threaten in the future—their power. In the late 1840s, of course, planters still felt quite threatened. But their assertions were not the less vehement for their doubts. So they moved discussion from the local past to the alleged origins of the planter class in an imagined Old Dominion, or to the cavaliers of a quasi-medieval vision of England. If Florida's planters had not changed in the settlement of Florida but had remained true to their origins, then the history of settlement was irrelevant.[10]

While all sorts of influences drove the shift in visions of past and present, one can find persuasive evidence for the importance of changing ideas of history in the most personal of stories. Individuals, in some cases those who were severely battered by the changing fortunes of local politics and economics, told the past in new ways that emphasized the things that seemed changeless, and not the frontier battles that they had so frequently lost. Thomas Brown's memoir, written for his family in the latter half of the 1850s, included a lyrical paean to social relations in the Old Dominion. John G. Gamble left extensive notes for his son detailing the genealogical heritage of the Grattans and the Gambles, and their role in Virginia history. The memoirs of Leon County's John Parkhill, which his widow began to write up in 1859 from his verbal accounts, shoehorned family and personal histories into classic cavalier plots of feckless heirs and noble quests. Such men helped the Old Dominion blossom as the symbolic origin of Middle Florida's plantation society.[11]

Thomas Brown's memoir paints a loving picture of Virginia and his own family's history there. After claiming that his ancestors were at Jamestown, his recollections return again and again to the crucial symbols of the Old Dominion's timeless stability. Especially important were deferential social relations like those celebrated by plantation novels. Brown's father possessed the devoted loyalty of two sets of stereotyped retainers: one, the prototypical sturdy yeoman, was his father's employee Garland Moore. He was "a strong-minded, straight, athletic man, who was his [Brown's father's] Major Domo." The other was the loyal family slave, Roger Groom, a deeply religious and obedient slave who always "consider[ed] it his mission to save the souls of all his young masters and mistresses."[12]

Each fall, at the "Harvest Home" festivals, Brown's entire community enacted a stable, planter-led order: "At these 'Reapings' there was perfect equality, though the extremes of society met as regarded wealth and condition. No rowdies were admitted, all was conducted in harmony and good order." In Brown's vision of "equality," gentlemen sat under a tree and talked while less privileged whites did the agricultural labor and slaves and white women attended to the gentlemen and cooked. Brown's description of the decline of Virginia set up his migration to Florida as a reconstitution of the supposed customs and the social relations of old Virginia in a fresher soil.[13] In his retrospective account, Brown wanted his and his peers' lives in the new land to repeat the "extravagance of living" and noble ethic of hospitality that he portrayed as the planter class's immemorial characteristics. So his story of his southward trek ignored the division of families and included happy slaves; and his narrative of the settlement of Leon County skipped over events like the violent struggles over his ally Francis Eppes's desire to run Tallahassee like a gentry-dominated Virginia county court. By the time Brown wrote, he had also recovered from the disastrous crash of the Union Bank, in which he had been a central character. He could now more readily claim that he had replicated the lifestyle led by his father than he would have been able to do a few years earlier. Four years as state governor (1849–53) helped Brown to maintain a social status far above that to which his reduced fortune might have sunk him.

In his memoirs, Brown was, in the end, unsure if the "offset" shoot of Virginia could make an Old Dominion of Middle Florida. Perhaps his ambivalence reflected his experience as a Virginian who had suffered repeated defeats on the plantation frontier. But the younger generation could take his memories and stories of Old Virginia and build new castles upon them. Thus, in the 1850s, local planter men and women peered ever deeper into the past for their antecedents, through Virginia and across the Atlantic. As elsewhere in the South, planters in Middle Florida's more exalted circles asserted that their ancestors were English nobility, royalists who had supposedly sought refuge in colonial Virginia after the defeat of Charles I in the English civil war. They traced their lineage even further back, back through alleged cavalier ancestors to feudal England: a society they imagined as ordered by rank, yet without major internal conflicts.[14] While nobles had ruled over yeomen and peasants, the latter groups had accepted their places. The image of the "sturdy yeoman," ever deferent to the local squire, was a central part of this fantasy, and echoed Brown's memories of the Old Dominion. This reevaluation of the past flew in the face of traditional republican interpretations of feudal society as one dominated by nobles and clerics who ruled over honest white men with an unmanning iron rod; a world that placed birth over merit.[15]

Local planter families traced alleged origins not just in memoirs and family histories but also in the rituals they enacted as groups. In 1852, the *Tallahassee Floridian* described a "joust" that matched men of the Leon County planter elite not so much in contest against each other as in harmony with alleged medieval forebears. Here men played at chivalric battle. The "Marshal of the Day," O. H. Burroughs, "rode into the lists." He received his instructions from the "Judge of the Sports, Maj. G. T. Ward" and then marshaled twelve knights on horseback. Among them was "The Knight of the Iron Hand—Dr. G. W. Parkhill." In the jousts that followed, he finished second overall. No doubt some fair Rowena was overjoyed. Arrayed on the field of honor were also chevaliers like the Knight of Jefferson, the Knight of Miccosukee, the Knight of Moss Grove, the Unknown Knight, and the Knight of the Lone Star.[16]

The 1852 joust was only one of dozens of quasi-medieval community rituals performed by Leon County planters during the decade. The jousts lasted until 1859, and many "Queens of Love and Beauty" sat next to their "knights" while presiding over fancy-dress balls in Tallahassee. "The chivalry, as a part of our social organization, is not dead," proclaimed an editor. "Miccosukie," a writer in the *Florida Sentinel*, scorned "our enlightened age" and proclaimed his pleasure at observing the contestants' "chivalry" and luxuriating in the ritual's imagined heritage of unchanging rule.[17] During the early years of Tallahassee, rituals like horse races and the giving of ever more ostentatious balls were explicitly competitive, partaking of the duel's version of manhood. Now, facing a looming outside threat from sectional politics and abolition, planter men closed ranks in the ritual of the joust. The contest involved in the taking of the ring was of little matter compared to cooperative pageantry that dressed planter men and women in the imagined garb of feudal lords and ladies. And they abandoned the custom of making one man pay for each ball, which had in the 1830s led to ever more expensive events as each man tried to exceed his predecessor. Meanwhile, as planters asserted a common identity opposed to that of the North, duels vanished and street fighting among them became a thing of the past. Now, Tallahassee newspapers, once the breeding ground of conflict, romanticized local political debates through quasi-medieval lenses. The 1850 struggle between George Ward and George Walker for control of the Middle Florida Whig Party was "The White and Red Rose . . . [the war] between the houses of York and Lancaster."[18]

The historical vision produced by Middle Florida's planter class after 1844 applied two mental erasers to the local past. First, it brushed away uncomfortable truths. The resistance of enslaved African Americans against slavery, or conflict with lower-status groups of other white settlers, disappeared under sentimentalized depictions of plantation society. Second, in planters' claim that the origins of their class lay in a cavalier tradition channeled via Virginia from feudal England, they denied historical change. And because history establishes present situations and possibilities, the epic vision of an unchanging past denied that the present could change either. The narrative espoused by the *Star* in 1844 became the accepted version of the plantation frontier's past. On the local, almost ephemeral foundations of this narrative in family histories and newspaper stories, other Middle Floridians tried to formalize and institutionalize that understanding of local history.[19]

The events of the rising sectional crisis politicized slaveholders' histories. From 1819, debates over the admission of Missouri as a slave state, slave revolts like those led by Denmark Vesey and Nat Turner, the nullification crisis, the rise in abolitionism, and later debates over the expansion of slavery all made Southern whites anxious about whom they had been, and whom they might be. In plantation novels, and in economic and philosophical tracts, Southern white writers constructed an intellectual historical narrative that defended slavery. For a small percentage of them, proslavery arguments became an outright argument for inequality of rights at all levels of society, but most now recognized their need to pay lip service to the principles of white male republicanism. Still, the disruptive effects of migration south and west, including the drive of yeomen for increased political democracy, had helped make planters unsure of their power and anxious that all seeming verities might change. Authors of the genre of "plantation novels," like William Gilmore Simms and John Pendleton Kennedy, slipped the issue. They depicted a genteel and calm planter class who viewed commercial transactions—like those that had financed their own power on the plantation frontier—with a distaste born of hauteur while conducting easy, paternalist relationships with yeomen.[20]

Although nationwide issues shaped these formal discussions of planters' history and identity, local renditions of the past were not mere derivatives of famous tracts that defended slavery or best-selling plantation novels. This was a dialogue that went both ways, and in more formal productions like novels and histories, elite Middle Floridians dovetailed local and regional issues (even when the latter were repressed) into ruminations about their own group identity. Readers took from such works what they found useful while contributing local interpretations of their particular community's history to wider discussions about the South. Each author came from somewhere. Those who came from Middle Florida channeled the disparate and tributary materials flowing from newspapers, political speech, private conversations, and thoughts together into coherent stories that consciously sought to represent Southern past and Southern present.

One formal expression that put Middle Florida planters on the national literary stage was a novel written by Jackson County's most famous resident, Caroline Lee Hentz. She combined the erasure of local history with the conventions of the standard antebellum plantation novel. Hentz, a New England Yankee by birth, but a Southerner by choice since the 1820s, moved to Jackson County around 1848. She lived in Marianna with her invalid husband, Nicholas, and her son, Charles, practiced medicine in rough neighborhoods along the Apalachicola. In 1852, she published *Marcus Warland*, a local roman à clef fleshed out with elements of regional ideology.[21] The novel contained a paternalist defense of slavery and a critique of Northern individualist feminism, but Hentz also sought to solve the riddle of planter identity on the cotton frontier. Her public response to Middle Florida's recent emergence from the social chaos of which her son privately complained in his diaries was to impose the typical vision of the plantation novel — the planter as representative of unchanging quasi-feudal social and cultural traditions. Her main character, Marcus Warland, begins the novel as a young boy living on a river near the "Long Moss Spring," "near the eastern shores of the rushing Chattahoochee," in what is clearly Jackson County. His father, a ferryman, was a small planter until rowdy political meetings introduced him to the habit of drink. Warland's downfall critiques as destructive and irrational the yeoman style that dominated Middle Florida politics after the fall of the Union Bank. In the first scene, Marcus's chance encounter with planter Edward Bellamy results in a promise to hire Marcus's father as an overseer if the elder Warland will only stop drinking. The elder Warland resolves to do so, and the family moves from the ferry to the Bellamy plantation. There the noble and generous Bellamy recognizes the family's former gentility as an essential characteristic that transcends the accidents of the Warlands' troubled frontier experience. He pays for an education for the young Marcus and introduces him in society. Marcus soon falls in love with Florence, the daughter of a haughty planter named Alston.[22]

Alston's name evoked a memory of arrogance in Middle Florida, but here he represents an overly refined gentry, rather than wild, hyper-masculine violence. Jackson County's "real" Edward Bellamy was a friend of Hentz's who, like his fictional analogue, was the owner of many slaves as well as a plantation called Hickory Hill. Hentz pictured the character as a paternalist lord: "The more prosperous he was, the more grateful he was to God, the more benevolent to his fellow man." The character of the elder Mr. Warland, meanwhile, was based on Edward Bellamy's actual brother. Samuel Bellamy, a doctor who also lived in Jackson County, fell into debt during the crisis years and was forced to sell his Rock Cave plantation to his brother to avoid bankruptcy. Samuel drank heavily but by the end of the 1840s swore to overcome his addiction. He became a public spokesman for local temperance societies. In reality, and unlike Marcus Warland's father, Samuel soon returned to the bottle. Late one night, two years after the novel's publication, he cut his own throat while drinking alone at the Chattahoochee railroad depot.[23]

The novel has a happier ending than did Samuel's life, although Marcus must surmount many more difficulties, such as Alston's opposition to his match with Florence. Meanwhile, Bellamy loses much of his money when he generously "goes security" on notes owed by his false friend Mr. Arnold. Arnold, in classic fashion, tries to run his slaves off to Texas. As Marcus and his allies ride to stop Arnold's escape to the west, he imagines himself as one of the heroic characters admired by romantic literature and shifts out of ordinary time: "Then the forest was converted to a grand and glorious picture gallery, where Shakespeare's wizard pencil drew immortal groups" of characters like Macbeth. He shifts out of his own time again in the fight that takes place after he catches up with Arnold's henchmen. Marcus, along with his father and friends, who had just arrived, subdue these poor white overseers—despite their opponents' "gouging" techniques. Like males of the planter class, Hentz was concerned that lower-class white men had seized the high ground of masculinity during the 1840s. In her novel, she set gender hierarchies among men aright by reversing humiliating economic defeats and showing planters triumphing in physical confrontation over common white men.[24]

After Marcus returns to the plantation and establishes himself as a successful lawyer and planter, Alston consents to his daughter's marriage. When criticized earlier for being the son of a ferryman, Marcus had stated proudly, "My mother was the daughter of a Virginia planter." His essential nobility shone through his earlier disguise of poverty, he "stood beside [Mr. Bellamy] with the air of a young aristocrat, despite his common apparel." Now Warland's innate high rank, initially hidden by his lack of wealth, reappears when he recovers a planter status his father dissipated. The fear that the ups and downs of fortunes on the cotton frontier would let in the unworthy and banish the failed from the cherished status of plantation aristocrat are shown to be groundless. Origins and merit are identical, as with planters and their alleged roots in the mists of "cavalier" feudalism.[25] And while the false pretenses of villains like Arnold disrupt the plantation South, true planters defeat such men and exile pretenders to their rightful status. Everyone returns to their proper place. Yes, some planters ran to Texas to escape debt, but they were only false members of the ruling class, after all. Of course, in Middle Florida the men like Peter Gautier whose "Tall Walking" left behind a host of debts after 1839 had often been important members of the pre-1840 frontier elite. But by viewing class as unchanging inner worth, Hentz was able to sidestep the history of conflict and collapse created by planter migration to the cotton frontier, and the crisis years disappeared with their defeats.[26]

Marcus Warland also claimed to justify the continued subjection of women, poor whites, and, most of all, enslaved African Americans to the paternalistic rule of planter men. White women, of course, should not step out of their sphere. When Florence assumes the disguise of a mulatto woman to nurse the wounded Marcus, all of society assumes that he will reject her later, when he finds out what she, as a white woman, has done. Proximity in status to blacks taints poor whites—a ferryman's wife carries her water bucket on her head "poised in the African style." Yet women can climb a little from their degraded status, if they recognize the superiority of planters and gratefully defer to them. Blacks, on the other hand, are innately childish, although some have good hearts and are willing servants. The elder Warland's faithful Milly, for example, recognizes intrinsic merit and loves the dissolute white planter more than herself. She refuses to be sold away from her bankrupt master's children in order to go with her own. And when the slave Hannibal is offered his freedom after he saves the lives of the Bellamy family in a fire, he rejects the plan to manumit him and send him to Liberia: "Slavery is not an outer garment, that can be taken off at will," for, like class, it, too, is part of a natural hierarchy.[27] In her sentimental *Marcus Warland*, Hentz integrated Middle Florida masters' postcrisis rethinking of local history with the regionwide defense of Southern slavery as a family-based, gently patriarchal institution. The transplantation of old hierarchies replaced the image of disruptive change as the story of their region.

As a part of the defanging of recent local history, the Middle Florida elite suddenly became fascinated with their state's distant origins in Spanish conquest. "A Sketch of the History of Leon County," published by local lawyer John Galbraith in 1853 in the *Tallahassee Floridian and Journal*, focuses almost exclusively on the "strange adventures" of the sixteenth-century Spanish conquistador De Soto and his "knights" among Middle Florida's Apalachee Indians. Galbraith claimed that "this very County of Leon is probably the oldest settled country in North America, with the exception of Mexico."[28] Likewise, the planter-created Florida Historical Society, founded in St. Augustine, focused its research on the sixteenth and seventeenth centuries. The Middle Florida luminaries who traveled east for the first meeting of the society in 1857 listened to a lecture by pioneer Florida historian George R. Fairbanks on the exploration and settlements of Ponce de Leon and Hernando de Soto. The purpose of his study was "to do justice to the men who have figured in the olden time . . . to draw out its [those of the Spanish settlements] secrets, and to bring back to our minds and memories the scenes and actors of the olden times." The "olden times" and its "secrets" were centuries ago. Secrets of the recent past were to be ignored. This new focus corresponded with the shift of the symbolic center of the state's history from Tallahassee, the site of land sales and territorial politics, to St. Augustine. Fairbanks pictured the latter as a place happily divorced from progress or competitive "interest" in frontier wealth: "No corner lots on sale or in demand; with no stocks, save those devoted to disturbers of the public peace, with no excitements or events." Immersed in amber outside of time or change, with rowdy poor whites locked in the pillory for public display, "its life is in the past."[29]

Outsiders also found the Spanish past more fascinating and comfortable than the conflicted process of American migration and settlement. Such impatience comported well with the desires of Middle Florida's planters. However, for the latter, the discussion of the Spanish colony as the real history of Florida, which implied that anything since was not history, served very different purposes from those of contemporary historians of early America. This first generation of nationalist historians, including Francis Parkman and (Samuel) Prescott, deployed a view of American history as an ascension from barbarism, through colonization by the superstitious Catholic Spaniards, to the civilization of Protestant, republican, and Unionist America. The Spanish nobility represented an earlier stage of quasi-barbaric culture and religion, mixed now in Mexico with the not so dissimilar Aztecs. American expansionism was thus the advance of civilization.[30] Such logic could be used against Southern slaveholders as well, and so Florida planters came to identify with the hidalgoes who had supposedly governed the Spanish colony for two long centuries. Certainly for the newborn Florida Historical Society, the secrets of the distant "olden times" were identical to what Fairbanks called "the historical romance of the South." The Spanish nobility, like medieval English knights and their cavalier descendants, became mythical forebears of the ruling class of Middle Florida. By 1859, Southern writer Daniel Hundley could assert as a compliment what Anglo-American Floridians would have rejected scant decades earlier: "In Florida . . . the progenitors of the Southern Gentleman were chiefly Spanish Dons."[31]

PRESERVING THE CHANGELESS PAST
IN THE PRESENT: SECESSION

Barely a year after Hundley's assertion, the "descendants" of Spanish dons prepared to take the extreme step of seceding from the United States. Peculiar understandings of history were not the only reason that Florida seceded in January 1861. Many factors explain the secession of the Southern states, and almost all of these are relevant to understanding the course of events in Florida. The destruction of the two-party system; the pressure on Southern public opinion of abolitionist criticism of the South; and the series of crises from the Wilmot Proviso of 1847 through John Brown's raid on Harpers Ferry, all increased Middle Floridians' sense of interregional confrontation. Like South Carolinians, Middle Florida's whites feared that Northern sectional dominance of the Union's politics would unleash abolitionist emissaries, disguised as federal appointees, into their communities. Slave revolt would be the result. Even Northern politicians who proclaimed that they were for "free soil"—the exclusion of slavery from the new territories, but not the abolition of slavery where it existed—were no better, in the eyes of most whites in Jackson and Leon Counties. The aim of "free soil" was eventual emancipation, they grumbled. And the imputation that Southern institutions were unfit for the land bought by Southern blood in the Mexican War was unfair and insulting.[32]

As the 1840s became the 1850s, and plantation society seemed to solidify and stabilize in Middle Florida, no one knew what was coming. We should not commit the error of making everything lead up to a crashing denouement in the Civil War, as if all 25,000 people in Jackson and Leon Counties were playing instruments to a predefined symphonic score. Instead, past and present issues and anxieties, especially anxiety about recent local and regional pasts, were pushing white Middle Floridians into the awkward position of trying to act upon their claimed beliefs about the past. Given the past experiences that they were trying to erase, they did not completely believe in this script, and as usual in such situations, assertions grew ever stronger. And the new incantation of an "Old" South past, as rewritten by Middle Floridians, stubbornly continued to reveal, in its very emphases and absences, the past that it failed to erase. Dismissal of the commercial North did not conceal the fact that the North dominated Southern trade and finance. Denials by planters that they feared their slaves, or poor white unrest, made one wonder: why the denials? Brooding honor, raw from defeat at the hands of yeomen, sought an outlet in political conflict with the North. Ironically, the defeated now incorporated into their threats of disunion the styles and attitudes of countryman hostility to anything that implied domination. But in another way, planters were still planters; still seeking through assertion to force what they imagined would be a comforting certainty upon their own world. And meanwhile, the loudly enunciated idea of an independent, distinctive, and unchanged South reacted explosively with the North's own charge toward confrontation with the Southern "Slave Power."

From the early 1850s, many Middle Floridians came to argue that secession was not a last resort but an inevitable and desirable outcome of the growing confrontation between North and South. Their justifications for Southern nationalism grew in part from their reinterpretation of history. Their new story about the past, which proclaimed an "Old" South that was essentially different and could go its own way, was an attempt to step out of the frontier's history of dramatic changes, crises, and disruptions of authority. And the ability to imagine one's society as stable in hierarchy, and both disconnected and different from the Anglo-Atlantic world around it, helped enable those who precipitated Florida out of the Union to imagine that secession would work—that it would, in essence, make time stand still. They refused, of course, to face the uncomfortable question that their past might have posed to them: would an independent planter republic be able to quell potential internal opposition from the enslaved and the slaveless? A few planters confided fears on this subject to diaries and intimate letters. But the prevalent historical account of the recent past, whose conventions were shaping public discussion by the 1850s, helps to explain why so few Middle Floridians expressed doubts.

White Middle Floridians shaped their public responses to the developing sectional crisis to the template of the new concept of an "Old" South. As national and sectional politicians debated whether or not the territories acquired from Mexico in the 1846–48 war would be slave or free, leaders from Jackson and Leon Counties scrambled to define why Middle Florida should send delegates to a secession-tinged regional convention at Nashville in June 1850. "Are you the descendants and brothers of Marylanders, Virginians, Carolinians, and Georgians?" asked the proconvention *Tallahassee Floridian and Journal*. Everything that Middle Florida white men and women were reading and hearing said yes, they were such descendants, and descent was the core of their identity. Political speech also depicted the only alternative to submission and destruction as a Southernism based on the consciousness of an identity distinct from the North, and a history derived from older Southern states. The opponents of the convention, and active proponents of the Compromise of 1850, according the editor of the *Tallahassee Floridian and Journal*, would "present the state to the world in [a] slavish attitude—would place her on her knees before her aggressors as a humble suppliant for the boon of being permitted to remain in the Union." Sarcastically, he went on: "Go on . . . Make a Jamaica of Florida, if you please. . . . Yes, a San Domingo, if you are determined on it—but save us, *save us* from separation." The need to protect an unchanging slave society triumphed. Proconvention forces won and elected Charles DuPont and E. C. Cabell to represent Leon and Jackson.[33]

In the same year, Congress constructed a sort of compromise between North and South, admitting (on heavily sectional votes) California as a free state, passing a new fugitive slave law, eliminating the slave trade in the District of Columbia, and leaving open the question of slavery in other territories. The Nashville Convention did little more than issue speeches and resolutions bristling with threats of secession, but the debate in Florida served as a rehearsal for later events. Those who opposed the idea of a separate South sank without a trace. E. C. Cabell, while not proclaiming his willingness to secede at the drop of a hat quite so loudly as some Democrats, stayed afloat and won the election for U.S. representative in the fall in 1850. But Governor Thomas Brown, who had opposed the 1850 convention, ran for Congress as a pro-Union Whig in 1854. He was demolished in Middle Florida, losing badly to Southern nationalist A. E. Maxwell.[34]

Hewing the new line, if not so forcefully as Democrats, local Whigs like Cabell and George T. Ward of Leon, in the wake of their party's collapse, recast themselves as Southern nationalists.[35] The divorce of Northern and Southern Whigs in the early 1850s over the issue of slavery effectively destroyed the two-party system in Middle Florida, a dozen years or so after its violent birth. In 1854–56, politicians in the area agreed with each other on a wide range of formerly divisive issues, such as government-backed economic endeavors like internal improvements. Several railroad lines, paid for in part by a state internal improvement fund, were inching from the west and east ends of the Florida panhandle toward the middle. Democrats even talked about rehabilitating banks and bankers. Without the need to moderate their rhetoric in order to participate in transregional parties, Florida candidates for office sought to distinguish themselves from each other mainly by exaggerating pro-Southern stances.[36]

While process and political structure drove the temperature of sectionalist assertion ever higher, images and ideas also shaped the increasing sense of confrontation with the North. Ever present were the following themes: the wounded honor of Middle Florida's white men; the threat of slave insurrection; and, most of all, a belief in a South that had been and must remain changeless. And after the destruction of the local Whigs and Know-Nothings, writers proclaimed that the fact that only one party still stood on the regional political landscape reflected not just a political but an essential historical unity within the South. Common images, and a unified political system, supposedly reflected basic agreement in the subjective political beliefs of most white Middle Floridians. Nearly all local politicians, and perhaps voters as well, agreed that the North had gone too far. To avoid further humiliation, the South must insist on its rights, returning the nation to an imagined stasis. Southern, and local, unity became essential: division would open the door for additional humiliating defeats of Southern aims at the national level. Normative political unity echoed a historical vision, which stated that in Middle Florida there had been no internal conflict and no change.[37]

In the process, the issue of class—so important in the years since 1839—dropped out of public discussion in the 1850s. The Union Bank no longer entered political debate, although its bonds remained unredeemed by the state. In part, the declining importance of such issues had to do with the stabilization of white society in Middle Florida in the late 1840s and early 1850s. It also had to do with politicians' increasing use of the terms of manhood as descriptors of issues of race and section rather than of local divisions between white men. To oppose secession was supposedly to support the eventual equalization of white and black men, a prospect that touched lower-class whites deeply. "You have so much to fear," wrote "Shanghai" to nonslaveholders in 1856, "if slavery is abolished." Their manly control over and protection of their dependents, was at risk: "How would you like to see yourself, your wife, your sisters and daughters equalized with the negroes and exposed to their insolence and impudence? How would you like to see some great greasy black negro step into your house and pop himself down by the side of your daughter? Then it is as much in your interests as anybody else's to oppose any man whose antecedents are opposed to slavery."[38] In addition to exploiting the fear that the women of poor white households would become the sexual conquests of freed blacks, secessionists used another ploy. They borrowed the language of manly resistance to feminizing oppression that anti-bank forces used to rally yeoman support against "degradation and vassalage" in the late 1830s.[39] Such moves worked, and common whites seemed willing to go with planters to the brink. Given ample opportunity to reject the secessionists' arguments in the 1850s, the yeoman voter did not do so. Meanwhile, planters could now tell themselves the comforting story that white unity in the present indicated an unchanged past of yeoman deference.

With the disappearance of the two-party system in Middle Florida after 1852, local and state politics increasingly focused on national issues. That year's gubernatorial election had brought Leon County planter and die-hard secessionist James Broome to office. Broome's welcoming address to the 1854 session of the General Assembly revealed the new orthodoxy. His discussion of "Federal Relations" argued that, in the sectional controversies of recent years, their region's strength was its stability: "The South is calm and unmoved." For Broome, the Compromise of 1850 was not preserving stability. While the South gave up the possibility of slavery in California, and the slave trade in the nation's capital—"the privilege of converting it [property] into money in the District of Columbia"—what it had received was hardly worth the price. The Fugitive Slave Act was proving unenforceable, while the conflict over the possibilities of expanding slavery into the territories continued.[40]

Broome's concern was not so much the issue of expansion, which one might expect to hit home among planters in a place one generation removed from frontier settlement themselves. Instead, his key issues were the conservative preservation of supposedly old dispensations, and the protection of Southern white male honor. The doctrine of "popular sovereignty" and the Kansas-Nebraska Act, which in 1854 swept away the old Missouri Compromise line dividing free from slave territories, was in Broome's hands; this was no new interpretation of the Constitution "but the acknowledgement of rights already possessed." Pro-secession writers insisted that they preached conservatism from the text of Middle Florida's changeless history. To drive back the Republicans was worth, wrote "Leonidas" in 1856, "any sacrifice short of a revolution." "A thorough revolution and upturning of the foundations of society and government" were what the abolitionists hoped to inflict on the South, wrote one planter, and a society that had not experienced change surely could not allow it to begin.[41]

The alternative was more insult from a North that had already "branded the South with inequality," which of course alluded to the language of earlier resistance to planter authority. Such loaned and loaded words helped candidates to win elections, but perhaps we see again that wearing the mask distorts the face, and even the mind behind it.[42] Elite men now identified their honor—their manliness—with their society's allegedly transplanted and changeless nature, not with their ability to ride roughshod over other white male members of that society. Planters had surrendered their old, dominating, language of honor in order to live with the nonplanter white majority. Their altered descriptions of what was manly and what was unmanning, glorious and humiliating, also meshed with their own quasi-historical views of how Middle Florida plantation society came to be. A static region, whose leaders identified its nature with the absence of change that might threaten the slave system, must reject all forms of transformation. Change was unprecedented, and to say that it was needed meant that what already existed was wrong.

"Can it be glory," asked "Civis" in 1856, "to lay supinely under the galling lashes of an insolent and cowardly majority?" "Civis" feared now not the local, countryman voting majority that Richard Call had once scorned but a Northern majority that would seek to alter the changeless South. Northerners opposed to slavery's continued expansion increasingly implied, or even stated outright, that the South needed and would in fact be forced to change. With the rise of the Republican Party, antislavery forces were apparently amassing the majorities they needed to give the order for a humiliating forced transformation. Instead of accepting such a cup, "Civis" continued, Florida should realize that the dissolution of the Union was little next to the "sacrifice of those rights and privileges which have been bought with the best blood of a noble ancestry." No doubt he meant Virginian blood, and he concluded by calling up the tournaments, cavalier genealogies, and myths of origin that had entertained Middle Floridians for a decade: "The high-born chivalry and courage which characterize our people . . . will not brook insult." The South had made more than enough concessions already: any further and they would be enslaved as a section, destroyed as society. The region, wrote "Alpha" in 1858, was unequal in the current Union. "If this equality is not restored, what assurances have we, as Southerners, that our rights will be respected?" The unequal were still unmanned, the way planters figured things. But now insults derived from the combat between two societies, not from two individuals or different groups of Southern white men. Middle Floridians feared "[t]he arbitrary domination of one section," enforcing like a master over a supine slave, "the abject submission of another." The South must be primed to resist the next attempt by its sectional opponent to make it submit.[43]

Manly honor seemingly shifted from individual-, family-, or even class-owned possession to being a societywide characteristic that must be defended against any incursion that might cut strops from the region's skin. The shift happened in part because outside political forces and events had helped to herd planters into a coherent group that now saw the troops of abolition as would-be thieves of Southerners' manly independence "waiting to strike." But the course of migration and settlement in Middle Florida had also helped to change planters' ideas about who they were. First, countrymen had silenced vaunting planter honor. A sequence of other disasters had also shaken the foundations of their confidence. Then, planters began to look at their manhood and status as collective and conservative — not the need to rule supreme over a frontier world that they were "building up" but the need to prevent any change in a society that had supposedly not changed. All the historical myth-making with which they soothed themselves in the ensuing years had rubbed the idea of being part of a coherent, distinctive, unified society into the very grain of their beings. To attempt to force a transformation of these beloved and compensatory stories would be to demand submission indeed.

Underneath, of course, still lay a current of smothered, ill-defined resentment related to an elite's earlier defeat. But planters' public rhetoric now blended more easily with the beliefs of less wealthy white men, at least in Middle Florida. New planter beliefs that national political issues could touch their honor by forcing change upon the changeless meshed with the yeoman idea that the way to be a man was to, in the words of one humorist recounting a local scuffle, "fight fist and skull like other men, / Our rough-and-tumble, which you know / To be the way most '*comme il faut.*'" In contrast to the duel's version of manhood, the new planter stance toward the world did not require constant conflict with those within Middle Florida who felt that rough-and-tumble white male equality was "*comme il faut.*" Instead, complaining politicians believed that nonplanter men would absorb the news that the North was insulting and oppressing the South, and react as they must.[44]

Of course, to outsiders, the wails of the South's oppression rang false, coming as they did from the already overprivileged. But with the collapse of a national party system that had required alliance-building with Northern wings of political parties, nothing remained to slow the rapid growth of Southern nationalist rhetoric in Middle Florida, or elsewhere in the South. The Northern end of the national party system was coming undone as well. Anger against Democrats who voted for Kansas-Nebraska in 1854 decimated the party's ranks that fall, opening the door for the emergence of the Republican Party in the 1856 presidential election. Although Pennsylvania's James Buchanan emerged victorious, the decline in the strength of the Northern Democrats cast the last nationwide political party into the hands of Southern extremists. Buchanan's mishandling of several 1857 crises, including a brushfire war between proslavery and antislavery settlers in Kansas, the Dred Scott decision, and a stock market panic, only worsened the national situation.[45]

By 1858, many Middle Florida politicians had—at least in rhetoric—already abandoned the idea of reconciliation via compromise. So "Alpha" showed with his claims that the only way to "restore" a lost equality would be for the North to make wide and unilateral concessions. After October 1859, when they heard the news of John Brown's doomed attempt to touch off a massive slave rebellion with his attack on the U.S. arsenal at Harpers Ferry, their mood grew more separatist than ever. "The Union," shrilled one Florida legislator in response to Northern praise of Brown, "at best of doubtful value to the South, would be scarcely an atom in the scale against the perpetual maintenance of the system of African labor." Even old Richard Call, remembered by some as the area's last Unionist, apparently forwarded (through his son-in-law Theodore Brevard) a secessionist manifesto to the General Assembly. Call's proposal agreed with more radical secessionists that the election of a Republican president would signal the need for civil war "to prevent the inauguration of such a President" or outright secession—"any and all steps necessary for the maintenance of their rights." Support was almost unanimous.[46]

The inauguration of a "nigger-worshipping" Republican, as white Middle Floridians called it, would announce a Northern revolution against the stable structure of the South. Not only would a Republican president be able to appoint abolitionists to federal offices in the South, and block slavery from expansion, but these actions would also signal that the majority North could and would dictate still worse to the South. This fear drove leaders to write a script for the Union's end as the only way to preserve the changeless society in which they lived. Brook no more insults. Run as Democrats, but on a strictly Southern-rights basis. If the Northern Democrats leave the party, so be it.[47] When they do, Republican victory and secession become inevitable, and the South will then be left with only two choices: the "dishonor" that accepts the "degrading vassalage of abolition rule," a change imposed from the outside indeed; or the manly "resistance" of secession. Indeed, newspapers reported, egging on their readers, the North "prates about whipping the South into submission." And the South under Republican rule would be subjected to the ultimate social revolution. At best, "the white race will retire, leaving their slaves masters of their happy homes"; at worst, the result would be "a general insurrection." Instead, the (white) people of Florida, along with her "sister" states, would surely prefer secession as a "conservative" alternative to prevent these revolutionary and unmanning changes.[48]

There were now no real Unionists among politicians: all were secessionists, of one stripe or another. Yet as national tension mounted in 1860, and as Southern Democrats, by the script, intentionally split open their national party with the demand of a federal slave code in the territories, there were hints of strains below the apparently unanimous surface of white Middle Florida. Feuding embroiled Calhoun County, which bordered Jackson. Judge J. J. Finley of Jackson County stated that his neighbors were in a state of "insurrectionary war." A company of Jackson militia marched in to preserve peace, and perhaps to quell Unionists. Meanwhile, Thomas Keitt, the Columbia County brother of a notorious South Carolina secessionist politician, was slaughtered in his bed by his own slaves. And an overseer murdered his employer in nearby Madison, where fear of a slave insurrection was also spreading. Such ripples beneath the surface of unity did not prevent John Breckenridge, the candidate of the Southern Democrats who broke up the party convention at Charleston, from winning Jackson and Leon. Still, even unanimous Southern support for Breckenridge would not have prevented Republican Abraham Lincoln—not even on the Florida ballot—from winning the nationwide electoral tally.[49]

To some extent, every people lives on and in its false versions of the past that have become true belief. Now, white Middle Floridians believed, true beliefs about the past and future told them that the present was the time for decision. Governor Madison S. Perry told the legislature not to wait until direct Northern aggression against slavery occurred: "If we wait for such an act our fate will be that of the whites in Santo Domingo." The representatives rushed forward to answer his call. A "black Republican" president was soon to take the oath of office—in effect, the North was calling Southern secessionists' bluff. Middle Floridians had already written their script, and now they urged each other to act on it: "*Resist*. . . . [T]he argument is exhausted." They begged each other to act in unity. Unity would signal the imagined stasis that they hoped to preserve, isolating Southern communities and plantations from outside influences and resting on the continuation of a changeless internal stability to preserve all allegedly old dispensations.[50]

Just as the 1859 resolutions had predicted, then, Florida moved toward "conservative" disunion. The General Assembly immediately voted to hold elections on December 22, 1860, for a state convention to begin in Tallahassee on January 3, 1861. This course of action was, everyone assured each other, not rebellious or revolutionary, but "conservative." It was not frivolous but absolutely necessary in order for white Floridians to remain free and untainted by submission to abolitionist insult. The agenda of the convention would be that of making the dreamed history of the changeless, old South into impervious, independent reality: the only hope, intoned Governor Madison S. Perry, for "domestic peace and safety." The handful of openly Unionist voters in the December 22 election received the derisive term "submissionist." Those who did not take that degrading position were divided between the supporters of "immediate" secession, who did not want to wait for other states, and "cooperationists," who favored waiting a few days to see what neighboring Alabama and Georgia would do.[51]

As Floridians prepared to vote, South Carolina bid farewell to the Union on December 20. That same day, old Unionist Ethelred Phillips, an elitist Jackson County physician from North Carolina, shrewdly noted that those who blindly followed secessionists were the real "submissionists." They feared to oppose what was supposedly universal opinion in white Middle Florida. He suspected, too, that the secessionists' impatience with argument reflected an internalized experience of defeat: "Like all men defeated they lose their temper, and swear the south can whip all creation alone, that cotton is king, and sixty days after the separation we will be happier than ever."[52] As Phillips privately sneered, the secessionists had, out of fear, stacked the historical and rhetorical deck: the choices were submission or the preservation of a changeless South. Yet without a rebuke from the electorate, the wheels of secession rolled forward full speed. The Jackson and Leon County elections selected a mix of immediatists and coopera-tionists. Jackson's delegation included James L. G. Baker, who owned the second-largest number of slaves in the county, Joseph Collier and Adam McNealy, middling plantation owners, and Sidney S. Alderman, a merchant from Marianna. These selections reflected the county's old political habits: a nod to the old conservatives from North Carolina, plus yeomen and small planter representatives. Leon's delegation was more weighted to wealth. Three of the county's top seven slaveholders—James Kirksey, George W. Parkhill, and George T. Ward—were elected, along with lawyer William G. M. Davis and merchant/secession ideologue John Beard.[53]

Right at the outset, the entire convention publicly committed them-selves to secession in order to defend their very reputations as independent men: "All hope of the preservation of the Federal Union upon terms con-sistent with the safety and honor of the slaveholding States has been fully dissipated." A few signs of hesitancy hinted at doubts and suggestive divi-sions. As the convention proceeded rapidly toward the inevitable vote for or against secession on its fifth day, Ward tried to block immediate secession, putting forward repeated amendments to the ordinance. He proposed that Florida wait until the results of Georgia's and Alabama's conventions were known before taking a final vote on the question. Meanwhile, his neighbor Parkhill supported extreme measures.[54]

The convention voted down Ward's amendment 39–30, although he had the support of all the other Jackson and Leon County delegates, save Park-hill. Perhaps they grew anxious. Perhaps they ruminated on past crises. But they were committed to leaving the convention with some form of seces-sion completed, and when Ward proposed an amendment mandating sub-mission of the ordinance of secession to a vote of the people for ratification before taking effect, it received less support and lost 41–26. So, after the defeat of every delaying amendment proposed by the cooperationists, the convention adjourned for the night. When they reconvened the next morn-ing, January 10, delay was no longer possible, and the body proceeded to a vote. The ordinance of secession received sixty-two yeas and seven nays, with only Baker opposing it out of the Jackson and Leon delegates. And so the next day the convention proclaimed and signed the ordinance declar-ing Florida an independent state. Florida was the third state to leave the Union, after South Carolina and Mississippi. Alabama, Texas, Louisiana, and Georgia soon followed.[55]

Even as Elizabeth Eppes, "a lineal descendant of the immortal author of the first Declaration of Independence," prepared a blue ribbon border for the document the delegates would all sign, Jackson County delegates began to go home early. Perhaps they wanted to take the collective temperature

George T. Ward (Florida State Archives)

of their county. Two county delegates, Alderman and Collier, had promised their constituents that they would oppose secession without a ratification by the people. Their public statement after voting for the ordinance suggests the incipient fractures in support for actually going through with secession, as well as why they hurried home. "Knowing that their constituents deemed [popular ratification and cooperation with other states] wise and prudent," wrote the two delegates, "the undersigned have not changed their views . . . but voted for the ordinance to prevent any injurious effect which might arise from a large negative vote being recorded against secession." They hinted at the dilemmas in which planters' history and planters' ideas about how history worked had placed them as an uncertain elite. The acceptance of the yeoman style of politics meant that political representatives had to respond to lower-class white men. Yet the habit of responsiveness internalized its own experience of submissiveness, of planter defeat in time of crisis. Partly in order to deny the memory of that experience, people professed beliefs about the past that denied change and saw the planters' South as an independent and unified society. Any hint otherwise would reopen conflict and division and revive the specters of the past, magnified a hundredfold. Numerous votes against secession could encourage opposition, and so with discomfort Alderman and Collier repressed the well-trained urge to represent their yeoman constituents. More important, they decided, was the belief that the South was distinct and must remain untouched and untainted by Northern political domination.[56]

Still, their skins crawled with uncertainties that they probably could not consciously understand. Had Alderman and Collier, in the pursuit of the new planter honor, overstepped their mandate so far that they trampled on yeoman turf? Were they preparing to ask too much of lower-class whites — preparing to demand obedience in war, taxes from farms, blood and bodies from countryman families — thus imperiling the precious stability and fictive unity that had taken so long to appear? If Alderman and Collier feared such things, they would in time see their fears proved prophetic by the crisis of secession and the necessities of war. In their present, the lure of secession was too great. With a ritual warding-off of the danger of collective dishonor, almost like making the sign of the cross, Alderman and Collier asserted their true belief: "The undersigned wish to announce distinctly to this convention and the county that they have been and are now fully alive to the wrongs perpetrated by the North against the South." Yet the issues thought erased by recent rewritings of history rubbed together again, instead of being rubbed out. While planters half-remembered and wanted to exorcise the shakiness of the frontier past, the carrying out of separation demanded common white support for the planter revolution. Even slaveholding yeomen were not likely to see themselves as equal benefactors from the violence and risk necessary to this kind of preservation of an "Old" South. And so Alderman and Collier rushed back to Jackson to reassure yeomen that the vote for immediate secession was not, after all, a slap in the face to constituents who had wanted secession submitted to a vote of the people.[57]

Meanwhile, the convention whistled in the dark, drawing up a revised state constitution and sending delegates to the Confederate States of America's organizing meeting in Montgomery, Alabama. The committee charged with postal affairs reported with brassy confidence their presumably unnecessary plans for war contingencies: "In case of actual war (which we do not apprehend)." They could not "be brought to believe that either the present or future President of the Northern Confederacy could be so absolutely insane as to imagine that he can, by force, effect a *voluntary* union of states."[58] No one demurred to the committee's statement.

The telling of their own history, whether in novels or in the assumptions of political rhetoric, showed that Middle Floridians were trying to expect something specific of the future. If the past, as they said, was changeless, an inheritance from Old Virginia or even Old England, unstained by internal dissent, then conflict and change should not occur and should not be allowed in their newly "old" society. If white Middle Floridians were all one group without significant divisions—if they in fact were a society and white society was who they were—then Northern criticism of the social system became an insult to every white person in it, one magnified with each ballot cast for Lincoln. In such a world, secession became conservative, a way to run the smooth road of a changeless past forward into a steady future.

Because this book looks at only two communities, it cannot offer an explanation that answers all questions about the secession of the South, or one that explains all areas of the nineteenth century's plantation frontier. Nor has explaining secession been its goal. However, over the years historians have offered literally dozens of explanations for the secession of Southern states, from class conflict, to fear of slave revolt, the breakdown of the national two-party system, the paranoia of republican political ideology, or pure proslavery ideology.[59] In Middle Florida, the history of the plantation frontier helped to shape the process of secession, and those who precipitated secession perceived in it a solution that preserved a supposed past.

In Middle Florida, the push for secession drew strength from the past and from the way in which the past had been obscured. Conflict and crisis driven by migration, economic expansion, and class conflict led to a more popular politics, a more unified white population, but also to a tortured sense of repressed injury and obscured unease among planters. The same dynamics of speculation and economic crisis, political competition, class conflict, and white democratization stirred turmoil in other Southwestern states during their antebellum development.[60] When white male equality became the watchword of politics in the Southwest, and the yeoman style of invective and combativeness was comme il faut, whites across the region were primed to see the election of Lincoln—totally independent of Southern votes—as an insult over which to rough-and-tumble.

So in Middle Florida, and perhaps elsewhere in the South by early 1861, the way in which whites understood the past shaped the political rhetoric and social causes that drove the debate over secession. Middle Florida had been very "new," and self-consciously so, in the 1820s and 1830s. The Southern planters who moved to Jackson and Leon Counties had proclaimed by word and act their faith in progress, in civilization, in change. The crisis of the 1840s brought instead a new dispensation of power. In the last generation before the Civil War, historians, formal and otherwise, from the planter class responded, establishing a new story that explicitly identified local planters with "old" ruling classes, and "old," anticommercial forms of society. This was a vision of the South as "old" indeed, and many white people would return to its myths for sustenance after the Civil War. Perhaps Mark Twain was more than a little hard on Walter Scott when he blamed him for such myths. He clearly exaggerated the power of both the author and the text. In Middle Florida, the planter reader took the images painted by Scott's novels and other symbols where the reader wanted—indeed, needed—them to go, back into an imagined past no longer marked by the disruptions of migration, yeoman defiance, runaway slaves, Seminoles, or economic collapse. Thus they created the myth that stated that their finally stable society had always been so—that it had always been an Old South. Then, they played out the script—although the ending took them by surprise.

Conclusion

Forty years after Andrew Jackson and the United States took possession of the Florida territory, the state left the Union. Soon after secession, many of the white men in Middle Florida marched off to war. A substantial number, like Washington Parkhill and George Ward, never returned. In the reported details of their valiant deaths, some survivors may have seen the confirmation of romanticized stories about the nature of planter self, group, and past. Perhaps the image of a tournament rider poised to charge down a Tallahassee hill flashed before Ward's eyes as he reached the fallen timbers, or Parkhill's as he stalked up and down the rows of his crouching infantry. The imagined cavalier "ancestor" spurred his horse and charged. Perhaps his image resonated in the minds of Southern whites as they considered the way in which Lake Miccosukee planter Joel Blake, in the most futile assault of the war, was shot down charging Union lines with Pickett at Gettysburg. Perhaps these men's deaths confirmed, for some, the changeless past, and the origins of the local ruling class in the supposedly unmodified social structures of the Old Dominion, or Old England. Indeed, that confirmation would be one of several ways in which the bereaved would try to come to grips with the gaping holes that the dead left behind them in the lives of the living.[1]

Florida officer C. Seton Fleming, wounded in the 1862 attempt to recover George T. Ward's body, learned the harsh lesson that other, different versions of history motivated his men moments before his 1864 death in front of Petersburg. He begged his yeoman troops to follow him on a last suicidal charge, but few leapt over the parapet with him. A bullet quickly fulfilled his despair, and the enlisted men who had followed him scattered back to the trenches. They had given up dying for his dreams. By 1864, the war was lost, and with it, any chance of making reality from planters' dreams of a heroic ruling class that triumphed over all opponents and subordinates. They could not escape from a history filled with change. And this was true not only for Middle Florida whites in Fleming's Army of Northern Virginia, pinned around Petersburg, or those in the Army of Tennessee, shattered around Atlanta. The facts that had led Fleming to despair, and most of his troops to stay in their trenches, were by 1864 almost as clear for those at home as well. Many whites had already sacrificed property and family blood to Confederate operations far to the north. Now the battle lines seeped closer and closer to home. Naval raids on the Gulf Coast disrupted Confederate salt-making operations and provided opportunities for some slaves to flee to the Union lines. Poor whites, many of them deserters who refused to die for the slaveholders' republic, stalked the woods between the plantation areas and the coast. "It must be difficult to make soldiers of men by main force," mused one Jackson County planter.[2] And as many of the well-known men who had dominated Jackson and Leon Counties in the 1820s and 1830s died off during these few years, it seemed as if an old world, shrouded in both history and myth, was passing with them. "Old Mr. Betton, Col. Whitner, and Col. Robt. Williams, all died within a few days of each other," Francis Eppes wrote in 1864 to his son in the army, "and another patriarch, old Col. Taylor, is not expected to live." Richard Call had already died in the fall of 1862, soon after the death of his nephew in battle. John Branch took to his bed in January 1863, never to arise, not long after learning that his nephew, Lawrence O'Bryan Branch, had fallen at Antietam.[3]

Most fearful of all to report was that the alleged loyalty of the enslaved to paternalist domination seemed to be crumbling. Bondpeople roamed the woods and roads by night, in greater numbers than ever before. One planter's wife was panicked over the implications of their new restlessness: "I have not a door in the house that can lock and when Mr. Whitner is away the yard is full of negroes at night," including many who were not her own. She feared attack in her sleep if she stayed, and looting if she left the house unoccupied.[4] There were greater shocks to come. Confederates repelled an attack launched toward Middle Florida from Union bases on the east coast of the state in February 1864 at the battle of Olustee. Then, in September 1864, Union cavalry raided Marianna, and war finally brought all its terrors to Middle Florida. Blue-clad riders killed dozens of the old men and boys who lined up to fight. Northern troops burned several buildings and left the town a shambles. They captured many of the men who had resisted and shipped them off to a prison in Elmira, New York, where some died. But "the worst part by far," wrote one resident, "was to see the negroes dressed in Yankee uniforms, and armed in the same way with seven-shooting rifles and revolvers." Much as Confederates did to black Union troops, African American soldiers "killed some [Confederates] after surrender." Perhaps a few settled old scores: "[S]ome were known, who lived here." Others showed more mercy than planters had usually offered: "[O]ne went to his former mistress and gave her protection."[5]

Another Union force landed near St. Marks in early 1865, but Tallahassee-based soldiers stopped them at the "Natural Bridge" in the piney woods of southeastern Leon County. Even as that victory cheered a few, the Confederacy played out its endgame to the north. In Virginia and North Carolina, Robert E. Lee and Joseph Johnston surrendered their battered armies. Among Lee's forces was the 2nd Florida Regiment. In 1861, it had mustered 1,274 men; at Appomattox Courthouse in April 1865, 66 remained to surrender. Perhaps as many as 5,000 Florida white men, out of a white population in 1860 of 77,747, had died in four years of campaigning. As defeat closed in on the Confederacy, Florida governor John Milton retreated from Tallahassee to his Jackson County plantation, Sylvania. On the first day of April, Milton blew out his brains with a shotgun. Confederate president Jefferson Davis fled Richmond and would eventually be captured, allegedly in drag, in southwestern Georgia. By early May, Union general Edwin McCook was advancing on Tallahassee from Macon, Georgia.[6]

On May 20, McCook accepted the formal surrender of the state government and all rebel forces. He then read the Emancipation Proclamation from the steps of a house once owned by Thomas Hagner. That date has become Florida's version of Juneteenth, the celebration of emancipation among many African Americans whose ancestors were in the Southwest in 1865. After McCook arrived, free people left plantations en masse. Some sought work elsewhere, or land of their own. For others, reuniting long-sundered families became the first order of business. Many traveled far and wide, seeking news of spouses and siblings and parents and children sold away years since. African American forced migrants had to wait much longer than had planter or nonplanter whites to impose any significant part of their vision of the plantation frontier on Middle Florida. But now, at last, they could, and they underlined and made real their liberation in rituals that inverted owners' old commands. Ex-slave Neil Coker remembered that some freedmen who had served in the Union Army discarded their blue uniforms and put on former owners' clothes, which they had taken by force. Superannuated Aunt Polly, claimed the ever-resentful Susan Bradford Eppes, hobbled into the Pine Hill manor house and signified at Edward Bradford: "Thank de Lord, I'se free." Eppes later claimed to have been amused, but sixty years later, resentment still smoldered in her words. The remnants of planters' confidence seemed to melt away in that moment of rejection by one's "servants." In 1865, many blacks told whites that they deserved—and might experience—the inversion of the two groups' former positions. Susan Eppes claimed to have heard her maid

Frances telling Bethiah, another former Bradford slave, that within a year, the whites would work while black women sat around and played the piano. Frances added that she would keep Susan for her personal servant. Eppes also remembered a song allegedly popular among local African Americans during this period:

> Hurrah, hurrah for freedom!
> It makes de head spin roun'
> De nigga' in de saddle
> An de white man on de groun'[7]

Now who rode, and who was ridden? Of course, the song did not say that freedpeople actually rode the whites, so we must give them the credit of being more egalitarian or simply more realistic about the nature of power in their brief moment of triumph than the old master class. To white Middle Florida men, and even to women, the destruction of slavery was shocking enough. But by the end of 1865, whites were fighting back, seeking to deny to freedpeople the right to move about, make contracts, vote, raise their own children, assemble, worship, own property, and all that made theoretical freedom practical reality. After 1866–67, a new alliance composed of planter, yeoman, and some (but not all) poor whites chipped away at "Radical Reconstruction" with murderous guerrilla violence and intimidation. Terrible brutality wracked Middle Florida's plantation counties in those years. In Jackson, whites murdered literally scores of blacks in the process of developing a tradition of lynching that would last well into the twentieth century, and make the county nationally infamous with the 1934 killing of Claude Neal.[8]

In 1877, Florida was one of the last three Southern states to be "redeemed": recaptured by white Democrats. Although freedpeople had fought tenaciously for the dream of full political, social, and economic equality, Florida's Reconstruction was deeply disappointing to them. Middle Florida's freedpeople were not able to seize all of their basic human rights during Reconstruction, and it was obvious that white Americans would never simply concede them. But at least African Americans were free, and no longer had to fear shipment from state to state as chattel property. When General McCook stood on the steps of Hagner's old house, Middle Florida's "Old South," created only in the late 1840s, was dead before it reached its third decade.

Or was it? Not only had Reconstruction failed as an effort to make freedpeople full citizens, but now white Southerners, while erecting what they explicitly called a "New South," raised a modified version of the ideology of the late antebellum years to the status of a civic religion. They mourned and mythicized the allegedly static society for which they coined the tag "Old South."[9] They did not have to mold its legend, for antebellum planters had already done that. Thus the Old South found a new, and far more lengthy life after death, which was only fitting. After all, that changeless, contradictory world was invented to cover the wounds produced by frontier instability. In Middle Florida, Ellen Call Long, the daughter of Richard Call, and Susan Bradford Eppes, daughter of Edward Bradford and granddaughter of John Branch, carried on and expanded the tradition of Caroline Lee Hentz.[10] Throughout the defeated region, similar views of a changeless, "moonlight and magnolias" past, disrupted only by tragic war, became accepted as the description of the antebellum South. The imagined past of an Old South served as ex post facto justification for civil war, and the mythos of the timeless and stable plantation realm also helped whites to use nostalgia to validate opposition to black equality for over a century, through both first and second reconstructions.

Historians in the second half of the twentieth century have usually eschewed the sentimentality and racism of Lost Cause apologists. They have not bought cavaliers and belles, moonlight and magnolias at face value, although many people in the United States, North and South, eagerly consume that myth, for various reasons. Yet in one way professional historians have, in telling their stories, followed a path parallel to the writers of plantation memoirs when they projected the image of the last antebellum decade back over the frontier. Instead of looking first for change over time, such as that exemplified in the massive migrations of people to the west- and southward-racing frontiers of the plantation South, most historians have attempted to plumb the depths of the relationships and institutions that supposedly made the antebellum South distinctive: What was the nature of the master-slave relationship? What effect did the institution of the plantation have on Southern politics, white and black culture, and society? Clearly, this generalization cannot describe every historian. However, many have accepted at least one key element of the myth—that of transplantation of the system to the plantation frontier. This is the idea that the Old South was shaped years before 1861, that its essential elements then remained unchanged by migration and massive geographical expansion, and that it foreshadowed the Civil War. That Old South is the "thing" that we analyze, the object on which we focus. Yet it was no thing, no coherent object, no set of ideal characteristics; only a story told by some anxious folks.

The mythmaking lived out (and died in) by men like Washington Parkhill thus came to stand in front of the very real changes that occurred on the plantation frontier. Jackson and Leon Counties did not replicate the cultures formed on the banks of the James, or in the rice swamps of South Carolina. Instead, their Old South was produced as elsewhere in the region: in fits and starts, bold overreaches and strange reversals during the years of alternating crisis and prosperity before the Civil War. Whether these places were Southeast or Southwest, the expansion of the plantation frontier shaped them all. Migration moved blacks and whites to new places. Crop expansion and the capitalization of slave and cotton trades, as well as "feelings" and "interest," drove the ups and downs of the economy. Struggles for land, for political authority and rights, and especially for the status of white manhood, in a society where only that last term meant freedom, reworked the constellations of social, political, and cultural power that structured interactions between whites. The changes set in motion by migration created, out of repeated conflicts and crises, the new social and cultural arrangements that we now interpret as characteristic of the antebellum South. This process was not a foregone conclusion but was instead contingent, unplanned, riddled by conflict—whether between countrymen and planters, factions of hot-blooded fellows, slaves and alleged masters, white men and white women, or creditors and debtors.

Even more than it was a frontier between white society and Native Americans, or between nonmarket economies and the taloned plantation wing stretched out by the capitalist world-system, Middle Florida was a frontier between different groups within the antebellum South. Each group that moved to Middle Florida, whether planter, common white, or enslaved, wanted something different out of the process of migration and settlement. Planters wanted to transplant old hierarchies. Countrymen wanted acceptance as white men equal to planters. They seized the opportunity to force recognition of their masculinity, in many cultural, political, and social senses, during the early 1840s. Economic inequalities remained, and in private, so did many planters' beliefs in hierarchy among white men. Political expediency usually kept such ideas hidden, although we can smell them in the mythos of transplantation that papered over the reality of diminished planter power. Finally, the enslaved sought survival—of body and soul, but also of family, love, friendship, and kinship, the ability to call the theft of human beings by its true name, and if all else failed, the hope that kept them seeking to live until freedom came.

Planter recognition of yeomen had subtle effects. Countrymen increasingly cooperated with planters to keep down those deemed less than manly: women and the poorest of whites, but above all, African Americans. The surrender of planter arrogance created a new stability among wealthy and not-so-wealthy white men. This surrender, plus the evolution of a slave regime staffed by a population now stabilized in age and sex, and bonds of racism between white classes, all added up to a region that seemed stable. Planters, however, resented the imposition of the mask of yeoman manhood while simultaneously beginning to see the world through its peculiar eyeholes. They could not stand the memory of local defeat at the hands of countrymen. Yet at the same time, they began to see the North as an arrogant opponent, seeking to force one's submission. On a seemingly more conscious level, as they tried to explain and justify their own situation to themselves, they told new myths, striving to efface the galling memory of defeat by wiping internal conflicts from their story. This new history was no history, for it claimed a seamless, unchanging past, and helped paint the Old South legend, the colors of which white Southerners would later paint "memories" of the prewar world.

Washington Parkhill died while acting out a role prescribed by the myth of the changeless and old South. But his death tells us little about the way in which—for instance—his father came to Leon County in 1827 and tried to carve out a frontier empire. The earlier event did not foreshadow or prophesy the later one, even if, by torturous and unforeseen paths, human decisions led from one to the other. Only the flies remained with him, not the coherence of meaning that his mourners and descendants summoned up in the image of an Old South cavalier and used to bind his memory to that of his father. Such an image does violence to time, to history, to the experience of those who lived and died in making the plantation frontier of Middle Florida. But indulge a different imagining, one that might harm our understanding less. Imagine that while dying, Washington saw not the flies, or the backs of his men as they rushed past him. Imagine that he saw, grouped around him, the shades of those who had helped in life and death to lead him to where he was. There was his father, John—first, bright in the morning of planters' frontier empire-building, and then fading to gray in the shadow of the ruined Union Bank. There was the unnamed countryman who ridiculed his father's Bel Air resort as "Scratch Ankle" in the story of Snell. Next was Louisa Ross's father, who was taken away from her and her mother and sold by Charles Copland. Here came Isaac Hay, who shadowed John's journey in his old one-horse cart. Washington's uncle Samuel Parkhill, long dead from yellow fever, and Samuel's bride, Lucy Randolph, who had urged her father and family to move south, stood and watched silently. Nancy Hagan passed by, as she had passed Tuscawilla plantation many times in her local journeys. And perhaps the still-living James Page appeared, with his troublesome Bible in hand, to pronounce his ambiguous benediction.

All these people shaped the road of Washington Parkhill's life, and his death, and shaped it in large part by their conflicts with each other. The ways in which they understood their roads south, and their lives once in Middle Florida, helped form the way in which he saw his world as well. And I find here that I cannot apologize for introducing the final speculative image of Washington Parkhill's dying vision. For the shades of these dead are all with us, living on in the still-felt imprint of their actions, the way in which they shaped the choices of those who followed them. They are still with us in the words they spoke, at least those still recorded on paper, and in those acts that others, now shades as well, wrote down while they still lived. My own living vision of them argues that out of the conflicts of migration and settlement of the South's cotton frontier, individuals and groups created a new kind of plantation society. The plantation frontier became, in fact, the model of an antebellum "Old South." Yet this new society, too, was no permanent dispensation—it was a product of contingency. There, planters' ideal of hierarchy drove them to self-delusion even as control slipped through their fingers. There, white males struggled to prove themselves as men, in the dirt or on the dueling ground as individuals and in politics as groups. And there, enslaved African Americans bided their time, husbanding their resources even as they remembered and mourned family members torn away forever by forced migration.

Appendix

TABLE A.1. *Aggregate Population Totals, Jackson and Leon Counties, 1825–1860*

			Whites		
Year	County	Male	Female	Total Whites	Percentage White
1825	Jackson	644	603	1,247	65.4
	Leon	345	228	581	60.2
1830	Jackson	1,186	854	2,040	52.2
	Leon	1,856	1,480	3,336	51.4
1840	Jackson	1,099	903	2,002	42.8
	Leon	2,007	1,454	3,461	32.3
1850	Jackson	1,627	1,448	3,075	46.3
	Leon	1,695	1,488	3,183	27.8
1860	Jackson	2,757	2,506	5,263	51.5
	Leon	1,687	1,507	3,194	25.9

Sources: 1825 Territorial Census, Jackson County; 1830, 1840, 1850, and 1860 U.S. Census of Population, Jackson and Leon Counties

Note: Washington County was created from Jackson County in 1825. Franklin County was created from Jackson County in 1832. Calhoun County was created in 1838 from portions of Jackson, Washington, and Franklin. Wakulla County was created from Leon in 1843.

TABLE A.2. *Slaves Owned by White Households, Jackson and Leon Counties, 1825–1840*

No. Slaves Owned	Jackson		
	1825	1830	1838[a]
0	114 (60.3%)	190 (48.7%)	202 (51.8%)
1–5	42 (22.2)	115 (29.5)	85 (21.8)
6–10	11 (5.8)	34 (8.7)	44 (11.3)
11–20	16 (8.4)	28 (7.2)	29 (7.4)
21+	8 (4.2)	23 (5.9)	30 (7.7)
Total no. of households	189	390	390
Total no. of slaves	660	1,828	2,283
Mean no. slaves per household	3.5	4.7	5.9

Sources: 1825 Territorial Census, Jackson, Leon Counties; 1830 U.S. Census, Jackson, Leon Counties; 1838 Territorial Census, Jackson County; 1840 U.S. Census, Leon County

[a] The 1840 U.S. Census of Population for Jackson County does not record slaveownership by household. The 1838 Territorial Census was substituted instead, although only some 80 percent of the data sheets survive for Jackson County. Therefore totals are more suspect than percentages for that year.

Male	Female	Enslaved Total Slaves	Percentage Slaves	Free People of Color	Total Population
—	—	660	34.6	—	1,907
—	—	383	39.7	—	965
968	886	1,854	47.4	13	3,907
1,623	1,529	3,152	48.5	6	6,494
1,334	1,302	2,636	56.3	21	4,681
3,679	3,552	7,231	67.5	43	10,713
1,794	1,740	3,534	53.2	30	6,639
4,112	4,091	8,203	71.7	56	11,442
2,442	2,461	4,903	48.1	43	10,209
4,599	4,490	9,089	73.4	60	12,343

Leon		
1825	1830	1840
110 (65.7%)	250 (43.9%)	209 (31.4%)
35 (21.0)	152 (26.7)	225 (33.8)
11 (6.6)	78 (13.7)	69 (10.4)
8 (4.8)	48 (8.4)	69 (10.4)
3 (1.8)	41 (7.2)	94 (14.1)
167	569	666
383	3,124	7,237
2.3	5.5	10.9

TABLE A.3. *Landownership, Jackson County, 1830*

No. Slaves Owned	No. of House-holds	No. House-holds Owning Land	% of House-holds Owning Land	Mean Size of Land-holdings (acres)	Median Size of Land-holdings (acres)
0	190	10	5.2	117.0	80
1–10	149	34	22.8	216.8	160
11–20	28	13	46.4	303.6	320
21+	23	11	47.8	660.1	640
Total	390	68	17.4	291.9	160

Sources: 1830 U.S. Census, Jackson County; 1829 Property Tax Books, Jackson County Courthouse

TABLE A.4. *Landownership, Leon County, 1830*

No. Slaves Owned	No. of House-holds	No. House-holds Owning Land	% of House-holds Owning Land	Mean Size of Land-holdings (acres)	Median Size of Land-holdings (acres)
0	250	23	9.2	121.4	80
1–10	230	68	29.6	220.5	160
11–20	48	23	47.9	434.3	400
21+	41	18	43.9	1,528.2	428.5
Total	568	231	23.2	418.8	160

Sources: 1830 U.S. Census, Leon County; 1829 Property Tax Books, Leon County Courthouse

TABLE A.5. *Landownership, Leon County, 1840*

No. Slaves Owned	No. of House-holds	No. House-holds Owning Land	% of House-holds Owning Land	Mean Size of Land-holdings (acres)	Median Size of Land-holdings (acres)
0	209	24	11.5	288.2	120
1–10	294	71	24.2	290.0	205
11–20	69	39	56.5	439.2	360
21+	94	64	68.0	1,250.1	865
Total	568	231	23.2	629.5	322.5

Sources: 1840 U.S. Census, Leon County; 1839 Property Tax Books, Leon County Courthouse

TABLE A.6. *Source States of Enslaved Migrants, 1821–1860*

Decade	Source State Unknown	Ala.	D.C.	Fla.	Ga.	Ky.	La.	Md.	N.C.	S.C.	Tenn.	Va.	Total Enslaved Migrants
1821–1830	1 (2.8%)	0	0	0	5 (13.9%)	2 (5.6%)	0	3 (8.3%)	8 (22.2%)	1 (2.8%)	1 (2.8%)	15 (41.7%)	36 (23.7%)
1831–1840	0	0	1 (2.1)	0	8 (17.0)	0	0	5 (10.6)	15 (31.9)	3 (6.4)	1 (2.1)	14 (29.8)	47 (30.9)
1841–1850	0	1 (2.9)	1 (3.4)	1 (2.9)	5 (17.2)	0	2 (6.9)	1 (3.4)	11 (37.9)	4 (13.8)	0	3 (10.3)	29 (19.1)
1851–1860	0	1 (2.9)	0	1 (2.9)	1 (2.9)	0	0	2 (5.9)	18 (52.9)	4 (11.8)	0	7 (20.6)	34 (22.4)
1861–1865	0	0	0	1 (16.7)	2 (33.3)	0	0	0	1 (16.7)	1 (16.7)	0	1 (16.7)	6 (3.9)
Totals	1 (0.7)	2 (1.3)	2 (1.3)	3 (2.0)	21 (13.8)	2 (1.3)	2 (1.3)	11 (7.2)	53 (34.9)	13 (8.6)	2 (1.3)	40 (26.3)	152

Source: *Register of Signatures of Depositors in Branches of the Freedmen's Savings and Trust Company, 1865–1874. Tallahassee, Fla., Aug. 25, 1866–June 15, 1874*, National Archives Microfilm Series (NAMS) M816, Roll 5

TABLE A.7. *Number of Slaves by Size of Holding, Jackson and Leon Counties, 1830*

Size of Holding	No. of Holdings		Mean No. Slaves		Total Slaves		Percentage of Slaves Held	
	Jackson	Leon	Jackson	Leon	Jackson	Leon	Jackson	Leon
0	190	251	0	0	0	0	0	0
1–5	115	151	2.5	2.4	285	361	16	12
6–10	34	78	7.7	7.7	263	599	14	19
11–20	28	48	14.6	13.7	409	659	22	21
21+	23	41	37.7	36.7	868	1,504	48	48
Totals	390	569	4.7	5.5	1,825	3,123	100.0	10

Sources: 1830 U.S. Census, Jackson County; 1830 U.S. Census, Leon County

TABLE A.8. *Number of Slaves by Size of Holding, Jackson County, 1838, and Leon County, 1840*

Size of Holding	No. of Holdings		Mean No. Slaves		Total Slaves		Percentage of Slaves Held	
	Jackson	Leon	Jackson	Leon	Jackson	Leon	Jackson	Leon
0	202	209	0	0	0	0	0	0
1–5	85	224	2.5	2.6	208	582	9	8
6–10	44	71	7.8	8.0	344	569	15	8
11–20	29	69	15.1	14.7	439	1,016	19	14
21+	30	93	43.1	54.6	1,292	5,075	57	70
Totals	390	666	5.9	10.9	2,283	7,242	100	100

Sources: 1840 U.S. Census, Leon County; surviving sheets from 1838 Territorial Census, Jackson County, Jackson County Courthouse
Note: The 1840 U.S. Census for Jackson County does not enumerate slaves by households, but records 2,636 total slaves, making the surviving sheets of the 1838 Florida census statistically significant.

TABLE A.9. *Number of Runaway Slaves Advertised in Middle Florida, 1826–1860*

Year	Number	Year	Number	Year	Number
1826	7	1838	25	1850	24
1827	0	1839	39	1851	26
1828	2	1840	19	1852	19
1829	4	1841	24	1853	10
1830	10	1842	3	1854	8
1831	5	1843	6	1855	6
1832	8	1844	7	1856	7
1833	9	1845	0	1857	10
1834	7	1846	20	1858	10
1835	7	1847	12	1859	6
1836	11	1848	7	1860	2
1837	18	1849	7	Total	385

Sources: *Tallahassee Florida Advocate, Tallahassee Florida Intelligencer, Tallahassee Floridian, Tallahassee Floridian and Advocate, Tallahassee Floridian and Journal, Tallahassee Southern Journal, Tallahassee Sentinel, Tallahassee Star of Florida, Apalachicola Courier*

TABLE A.10. *Measures of Planter Status, Jackson and Leon Counties, 1840–1860*

Year	Farms Producing More than 50 Bales of Cotton (% of All Farms)	Households Owning More than 20 Slaves (% of All Households)
	Jackson	
1840	a	30 (7.7%)
1850	10 (3.5%)	49 (9.6)
1860	50 (8.7)	70 (8.1)
	Leon	
1840	a	94 (14.1)
1850	96 (26.2)	62 (8.0)
1860	108 (31.2)	97 (14.4)

Sources: 1838 Territorial Census, Jackson County, Jackson County Courthouse; 1840 U.S. Census, Jackson, Leon Counties; 1850–60 U.S. Census of Agriculture, Jackson, Leon Counties; 1850–60 Property Tax Books, Leon County Courthouse; 1860 Property Tax Books, Jackson County Courthouse
[a] There was no agricultural census prior to 1850

TABLE A.11. *Persistence of Heads of Household, Jackson and Leon Counties, 1825–1850*

	1830[a]		1840	
	Jackson	Leon	Jackson	Leon
No. household heads persisting *from* previous census	77	44	70	138
No. not persisting	313	525	280	528
Percentage persisting	24.6	7.8	20.0	20.7
No. household heads persisting *to* next census/tax list	72	137	123	211
No. not persisting	318	432	268	455
Percentage persisting	18.5	24.1	31.5	31.7

Sources: 1825 Territorial Census, 1830 U.S. Census, 1840 U.S. Census; 1850 Property Tax Books, all for Jackson and Leon Counties
[a] Previous census was an 1825 territorial census.

TABLE A.12. *Landownership and Slaveholding, Jackson County, 1860, and Leon County, 1850–1860*

Household Heads	1850 Jackson		1850 Leon		1860 Jackson		1860 Leon	
	Number	Percentage	Number	Percentage	Number	Percentage	Number	Percentage
Owned no slaves[a], owned no land	242	47.4	223	29.0	285	33.1	159	23.7
Owned no slaves, owned land	56	11.0	111	14.4	245	28.5	93	13.8
Owned 1–5 slaves, owned no land	29	5.7	105	13.6	68	7.9	89	13.2
Owned 1–5 slaves, owned land	64	12.5	77	10.0	65	7.6	60	8.9
Owned 6–10 slaves, owned no land	13	2.5	35	4.5	24	2.8	39	5.8
Owned 6–10 slaves, own land	26	5.1	51	6.6	36	4.2	46	6.8
Owned 11–20 slaves, owned no land	8	1.6	24	3.1	16	1.9	27	4.0
Owned 11–20 slaves, owned land	24	4.7	45	5.8	51	5.9	62	9.2
Owned 21+ slaves, owned no land	3	0.6	13	1.7	13	1.5	6	0.8
Owned 21+ slaves, owned land	46	9.0	86	11.2	57	6.6	91	13.5
Total taxpayers	511	100.1[b]	723	99.9[b]	860	100	672	99.7[b]

Sources: 1850 Property Tax Books, Jackson and Leon County Courthouses; 1860 Property Tax Books, Jackson and Leon County Courthouses
[a] Not all slaves were counted in the tax lists, but the tax lists are still probably more accurate than the 1850–60 U.S. Census of Population slave schedules, which contain numerous inaccuracies.
[b] Percentages do not total 100 due to rounding.

Notes

ABBREVIATIONS

Duke   Special Collections, William Perkins Library, Duke University, Durham,
          North Carolina
FHQ   *Florida Historical Quarterly*
FPR   Ulrich B. Phillips and James D. Glunt, *Florida Plantation Records from the
          Papers of George Noble Jones* (St. Louis: Missouri Historical Society, 1927)
FSA   Florida State Archives, Tallahassee, Florida
FSL   Florida State Library, Florida Room, Tallahassee, Florida
FSU   Florida State University, Special Collections, Robert M. Strozier Library,
          Tallahassee, Florida
GHS   Georgia Historical Society, Savannah, Georgia
GLO   Davidson, Alvie, comp. *Florida Land: Records of the Tallahassee and
          Newnansville General Land Office, 1825–1892.* Bowie, Md.: Heritage
          Books, 1989
JCC   Jackson County Courthouse, Marianna, Florida
JLCHD   Jackson and Leon Counties Households Database
JSH   *Journal of Southern History*
LCC   Leon County Courthouse, Tallahassee, Florida
NCDAH   North Carolina Division of Archives and History, Raleigh, North
          Carolina
RSD   *Register of Signatures of Depositors in Branches of the Freedmen's Savings and
          Trust Company, 1865–1874. Tallahassee, Fla., Aug. 25, 1866–June 15, 1874.*
          National Archives Microfilm Series (NAMS) M816, Roll 5
SHC   Southern Historical Collection, Manuscripts Department, Louis R.
          Wilson Library, University of North Carolina, Chapel Hill, North
          Carolina
VHS   Virginia Historical Society, Richmond, Virginia

INTRODUCTION

1. Dick to Mrs. Parkhill, June 28[?], 1862, Folder 8, Parkhill Family Papers, SHC.
2. Quote from Kate P. Cocke to "My Dear Aunt," June 28, 1862; [Mrs. Parkhill] to "My very dear mama," July 8, 1862, both Folder 8, Parkhill Family Papers, SHC.
3. Fleming, *Memoir of Captain Fleming*, 36.
4. Faust, "Civil War Soldier," 3–38, demonstrates that the meanings attached to death

and dying on Civil War battlefields shaped the responses of both the departing and the grieving.

5. Jackson County's location on the west bank of the Apalachicola River led many to consider it part of West Florida, but it was connected to, and similar in settlement patterns and economic base to, the counties of Middle Florida, justifying its inclusion in the latter subregion. Florida-based historians have certainly recognized Middle Florida's role in the antebellum plantation South. See, for example, Doherty, *Richard K. Call* and *Whigs of Florida;* Arthur Thompson, *Jacksonian Democracy;* Denham, *Rogue's Paradise;* Rogers and Clark, *Croom Family;* Shofner, *History of Jefferson County;* and Shofner, *Jackson County.*

6. For the frontier as civilization versus barbarism, see Slotkin, *Regeneration through Violence* and *Fatal Environment.* Compare Dekker, *American Historical Romance,* and Parkman, *Oregon Trail.* For the frontier as the transformative experience that created American democracy, see Turner, "The Significance of the Frontier in American History," in Turner, *Frontier in American History;* and many works influenced by Turner. A few of those used here include Curti, *Making of an American Community;* Elkins and McKitrick, "Meaning for Turner's Frontier," pts. 1 and 2, and Barnhart, "Frontiersmen and Planters." Later historians challenged Turner's conclusions, and a "New Western History" has attacked his valorization of the "frontier," but they still see migration and expansion as a crucial element in shaping region and nation, though for inequality, rather than democracy. See, for example, Limerick, *Legacy of Conquest;* Richard White, *It's Your Misfortune.* For arguments against their semantic decapitation of Turner, see the afterword in Faragher, *Rereading Frederick Jackson Turner;* Nash, *Creating the West;* and Aron, "Lessons in Conquest." For views of the frontier that emphasize the repetition and expression of older cultural and social characteristics, see Adams, *Germanic Origins of New England Towns* (and compare Novick, *That Noble Dream,* 87–89, esp. 88 n), and Fischer, *Albion's Seed.* See also the "Forum" on *Albion's Seed* in the April 1991 issue of the *William and Mary Quarterly,* especially Greene, "Transplanting Moments: Inheritance in the Formation of Early American Culture"; Fischer's rejoinder, "*Albion* and the Critics: Further Evidence and Reflection," 260–308; and Fischer's effort to exorcise Adamsian demons in Fischer and Kelly, *Away, I'm Bound Away,* 9–14.

7. Many historians of the South have claimed that planters were able to transplant patterns of landownership from the old to the new sections of the South. See, for example, Phillips, "Origin and Growth of the Southern Black Belts"; Genovese, *Political Economy of Slavery,* 244–47; and Abernethey, *Three Virginia Frontiers* (quote from 92–93). Others have argued that less wealthy white migrants dominated settlement and made the Old Southwest into a "yeoman democracy" but that they, too, remained unchanged from their cultural origins. See, for example, Owsley, "Pattern of Migration and Settlement"; Owsley, *Plain Folk of the Old South;* Clark, *Tennessee Yeomen;* Weaver, *Mississippi Farmers;* and Lowery, "Great Migration to the Mississippi Territory"; but see also criticisms of the yeoman-democracy thesis in Linden, "Economic Democracy in the Slave South." One might also classify Foust, *Yeoman Farmer and the Westward Expansion,* with the yeoman-democracy historians, although his conclusions are more ambiguous. Other early studies of

the Old Southwest include Craven, "'Turner Theories' and the South"; Lynch, "Westward Flow of Southern Colonists"; Eaton, *Growth of Southern Civilization;* and Coulter, *Old Petersburg.* For some historians, Owsley's herdsmen and plain folk simply express timeless cultural patterns that stretched back into a misty-musty "Celtic" past. See McWhiney, *Cracker Culture;* McDonald and McWhiney, "South from Self-Sufficiency to Peonage"; McDonald and McWhiney, "Antebellum Southern Herdsman; McDonald and McDonald, "Ethnic Origins of the American People"; McWhiney and Jamieson, *Attack and Die;* and Fischer, *Albion's Seed,* 605–782. Other scholars have supplemented this work with a perspective derived from historical-geographical studies of the transmission of cultural patterns. See, for example, Otto, "Migration of the Southern Plain Folk"; Jordan and Kaups, *American Backwoods Frontier;* and Newton, "Cultural Preadaptation and the Upland South."

8. Quote from Long, *Florida Breezes,* 72. See also Eppes, *Negro of the Old South* and *Through Some Eventful Years.*

9. Quote from Eppes, *Through Some Eventful Years,* 11, 30; John David Smith, *Old Creed for the New South;* Foster, *Ghosts of the Confederacy;* Hale, *Making Whiteness.*

10. See Wyatt-Brown, *Southern Honor;* Genovese, *Political Economy of Slavery;* and Fox-Genovese, *Within the Plantation Household.*

11. Like W. J. Cash (*The Mind of the South*), many scholars have argued that the settlement of the South was the eternal repetition of a particular template, differing only on the details. The formation of plantation societies in seaboard states is the key event, whether shaped by an alliance between backcountry and low-country whites, or by compromises within white communities. See Rachel Klein, *Unification of a Slave State;* Ford, *Origins of Southern Radicalism;* McCurry, *Masters of Small Worlds;* Ford, "Frontier Democracy"; Beeman, *Evolution of the Southern Backcountry,* 212–14; Edmund Morgan, *American Slavery, American Freedom;* Kulikoff, *Tobacco and Slaves;* Isaac, *Transformation of Virginia;* Chaplin, *Anxious Pursuit;* and Jeffrey R. Young, *Domesticating Slavery,* 1–14.

12. Eaton, *Freedom-of-Thought Struggle in the Old South;* Sydnor, *Development of Southern Sectionalism;* Freehling, *Road to Disunion;* McNeilly, *Old South Frontier,* esp. 180–81. Walter L. Johnson's pathbreaking work on the slave market (*Soul by Soul*) substitutes the meaning-laden nexus of the slave sale for the Hegelian dialectic of the master-slave relationship as the mode that produced Southern society. Yet one wonders if the slave sale worked in the same way in 1790 as in 1860, and in the same fashion in Mississippi as in Virginia.

13. One of the most widely cited examples of such an argument is Genovese, "Yeoman Farmers in a Slaveholders' Democracy," in their *Fruits of Merchant Capital,* 249–64. Compare Genovese, *Roll, Jordan, Roll.* I have benefited from reading Michael Bernstein's critique of writing on the Shoah in his Bernstein, *Foregone Conclusions,* esp, 1–41, and Ayers, "Narrating the New South." Compare Appleby, Hunt, and Jacob, *Telling the Truth about History,* 241–70.

14. Haywood, *John Branch.* Some historians who do incorporate aspects of the Southern frontier include Oakes, *Ruling Race;* J. Mills Thornton, *Politics and Power;* Tadman, *Speculators and Slaves;* Malone, *Swing Low, Sweet Chariot;* Cashin, *Family Venture;* Censer, "Southwestern Migration"; Terry, "Family Empires"; and Russell,

"Cultural Conflicts." For Brazil, see Metcalf, *Family and Frontier in Colonial Brazil*; and for South Africa, Lamar and Thompson, *Frontier in History*; and Mason, "Hendrik Albertus and His Slave Mey."

15. For the myth of the cavalier and the differentiation between Northern and Southern elites, see William R. Taylor, *Cavalier and Yankee*, and Genovese, *World the Slaveholders Made*.

16. Community studies have revolutionized early American history, but most Southern examples have focused on the seaboard states. See Rutman and Rutman, *Place in Time*; Joyner, *Down by the Riverside*; Harris, *Plain Folk and Gentry*; Kenzer, *Kinship and Neighborhood*; Durrill, *War of Another Kind*; Harry L. Watson, *Jacksonian Politics*; and Burton, *In My Father's House*. Few studies of Southern frontier communities exist; Christopher Morris, *Becoming Southern*; Doyle, *Faulkner's County*; and Dupre, *Transforming the Cotton Frontier*, are the only recently published works conceived and executed as community studies. See also Randolph Campbell, *Southern Community in Crisis*, and Kinard, "Frontier Development."

17. This is my definition of the plantation frontier, reached in the course of this project and in my reading of the existing historiography, including Aron, *How the West Was Lost*; Cashin, *Family Venture*; and Christopher Morris, *Becoming Southern*. For an excellent discussion of the term "frontier," see Lamar and Thompson, *Frontier in History*. For subsistence and exchange economies see Usner, *Indians, Settlers, and Slaves*, 145–275.

18. Some of the works in this historiography include Anne Firor Scott, *Southern Lady*; Deborah Gray White, *Ar'n't I a Woman?*; Catherine Clinton, *Plantation Mistress*; Lebsock, *Free Women of Petersburg*; Cashin, *Family Venture*; Fox-Genovese, *Within the Plantation Household*; Stevenson, *Life in Black and White*; Friedman, *Enclosed Garden*; McCurry, *Masters of Small Worlds*; Weiner, *Mistresses and Slaves*; Bynum, *Unruly Women*; Varon, *We Mean to Be Counted*, but this is far from an exhaustive list.

19. In this task I have been influenced in particular by Mikhail Bakhtin's analyses of language, culture, and literature, Pierre Bourdieu's work on the structures of hierarchy and communication, and James Scott's writings on domination and resistance. See especially Bakhtin, *Dialogic Imagination*; Bakhtin, *Speech Genres and Other Late Essays*; Emerson and Morson, *Bakhtin*; Bourdieu, *Logic of Practice*; and James Scott, *Domination and the Arts of Resistance*.

20. Here the expanding literature on the concept of hegemony has been useful. In particular I have been influenced by Gramsci, *Selections from the Prison Notebooks*; Lears, "Concept of Cultural Hegemony"; and James Scott, *Domination and the Arts of Resistance*; and works that deal with hegemony in more specific contexts: McCurry, *Masters of Small Worlds*; Genovese, *Roll, Jordan, Roll*; Genovese, "Yeoman Farmers in a Slaveholders' Democracy"; Feierman, *Peasant Intellectuals*; and Justice, *Writing and Rebellion*.

21. I say this at the risk of committing what Michael O'Brien ("The Lineaments of Antebellum Southern Romanticism," in O'Brien, *Rethinking the South*, 47) rightly condemns as "the reigning vice of Southern historiography, synecdoche."

22. Saunt, *New Order of Things*; Clifton Paisley, *Red Hills of Florida*, 10–34.

23. Wickman, *Tree That Bends*; Mahon, *Second Seminole War*, 1–17; Bartram, *Travels*.

24. Kinnaird and Kinnaird, "War Comes to San Marcos"; Mahon, *Second Seminole War*,

18–22; Hudson, *Southeastern Indians*, 464–65; Porter, *Black Seminoles*, 3–24; Landers, *Black Society in Spanish Florida*; Lake, "Seminole Slaves Factor"; Saunt, *New Order of Things*, 233–90.

25. Mahon, *Second Seminole War*, 22–28; Remini, *Andrew Jackson*, 341–53.

26. Mahon, *Second Seminole War*, 22–28; Hugh Young, "Topographical Memoir."

27. Governor Jackson to Acting Governor Worthington, July 26, 1821, Carter and Bloom, *Territorial Papers*, 22:133–35; Meinig, *Continental America*.

28. *Pensacola West Florida Gazette and Advertiser*, October 2, 1824. Creation of Jackson County from Shofner, *Jackson County*, 23. Jackson originally stretched from the Gulf to the Alabama border, and west to Escambia County. By the end of the 1830s, the creation of new counties reduced it to its present size.

29. *Pensacola Gazette and West Florida Advertiser*, September 26, 1825, reprinted from *Tallahassee Florida Intelligencer*; Simmons, "Journal."

30. Joseph B. Smith, *Plot to Steal Florida*; Chaplin, *Anxious Pursuit*, 214; Grenelle, "Bellamys of Territorial Florida," [24–26]; Abraham Bellamy to the Secretary of State, June 29, 1822, Carter and Bloom, *Territorial Papers*, 22:476; Benjamin Chaires to Thomas Fitch, July 27, 1820, Folder 11, Thomas Fitch Papers, FSA.

31. Dick, *Lure of the Land*, 19–34.

32. John R. Bell to Thomas Metcalfe, 1822, Carter and Bloom, *Territorial Papers*, 22: 463–65; James Gadsden to the Secretary of War, September 29, 1823, ibid., 752; Governor DuVal to the Secretary of War, July 12, 1824, ibid., 15–17; Mahon, *Second Seminole War*, 29–50. The confrontation between DuVal and Neamathla assumed mythic proportions, at least in DuVal's supposed retelling of the story. See Washington Irving, "The Conspiracy of Neamathla," in *Wolfert's Roost*, 297–304.

33. John Lee Williams, "Sketches of West Florida, No. XII," in *Pensacola Gazette and West Florida Advertiser*, August 27, 1825; Notice of the Land Commissioners of Tallahassee, December 18, 1824, Carter and Bloom, *Territorial Papers*, 23:123–24; *Pensacola Gazette and West Florida Advertiser*, April 23, 1825; "Tallahassee has all the appearance" from Parkhill Diary, 1827, Folder 11, Parkhill Family Papers, SHC. Leon initially included present-day Jefferson and Wakulla Counties. Jefferson separated in 1827, and Wakulla remained part of Leon County until 1843.

CHAPTER ONE

1. Parkhill Diary, Folder 11, Parkhill Family Papers, SHC.

2. Ibid.; John Parkhill land purchases from GLO receipts 1775–77, June 4, 1827; receipt 1859, June 5, 1927; and receipt 1860, June 6, 1827, *GLO*, 210; compare "land prospecting" in Henry Harrington Diary, December 24, 1833, vol. 6, Harrington Papers, SHC. For William Copland, see Charles Copland to John Parkhill, November 16, 1835, Folder 3, Parkhill Family Papers, SHC.

3. Fritot, *Pension Records of Soldiers*, 16–17; Parkhill Diary, Parkhill Family Papers, SHC.

4. P. A. Bolling to Edmund Hubard, February 24, 1837, Folder 72, Hubard Papers, SHC.

5. See Mintz, *Sweetness and Power*, 78–81; Banaji, "Modes of Production"; and Roedi-

ger, "Precapitalism in One Country." Like their Brazilian and Caribbean neighbors to the south, Southern planters were a class originally called into being by the Atlantic market's demand for staple crops like sugar, tobacco, and cotton. For the Atlantic plantation complex see Curtin, *Rise and Fall of the Plantation Complex*; Karras and McNeill, *Atlantic American Societies*; Blackburn, *Overthrow of Colonial Slavery*, 1–32; Blackburn, *Making of New World Slavery*; Solow and Engerman, *British Capitalism*; Eric Williams, *Capitalism and Slavery*, and many, many others. For cotton production and the U.S. economy, see North, *Economic Growth of the United States*. Chaplin, *Anxious Pursuit*, brilliantly describes planters who held modernity, commercial production, and slavery in uncomfortable tension.

6. The transformation of the South through the simultaneous developments of industrialization in the North Atlantic (especially the growth of textile production) and the opening of the Old Southwest as a frontier for plantation development still remains understudied, as noted in my introduction. A few works discuss the topic, whether directly or obliquely; they include Berlin, *Many Thousands Gone*; Deyle, "Irony of Liberty"; Chaplin, *Anxious Pursuit*; Dupre, *Transforming the Cotton Frontier*; Egerton, "Markets without a Market Revolution"; Kulikoff, *Agrarian Origins of American Capitalism*; Christopher Morris, *Becoming Southern*; and Zeitz, "Missouri Compromise Reconsidered."

7. "In time" from Acting Governor Worthington to John Quincy Adams, January 8, 1822, Carter and Bloom, *Territorial Papers*, 22:329; Greene, *Pursuits of Happiness*, 28–54, 195–197.

8. Cashin, *Family Venture*, also emphasizes family as a source of identity but comes to contrasting conclusions about migration's effects upon it. See also Censer, *North Carolina Planters* and "Southwestern Migration."

9. For the best recent account of this shaping, see Walter L. Johnson, *Soul by Soul*; for the argument that (South Carolina, mostly low-country) planters were already obsessed with the defense of slavery, see Sinha, *Counterrevolution of Slavery*, and Jeffrey R. Young, *Domesticating Slavery*.

10. "Florida," 410–20.

11. John Lee Williams, "Journal of an Expedition to the Interior of West Florida, Part V," *Pensacola Gazette*, May 29, 1824; see also Darby, *Memoir on the Geography*; Forbes, *Sketches, Historical and Topographical*; Vignoles, *History of the Floridas*; John Lee Williams, *View of West Florida*; *Pensacola Floridian*, December 17, 1821; and Brinton, *Notes on the Floridian Peninsula*. Brinton mentions another, anonymous, book published between 1821 and 1823, in Charleston, but I have been unable to locate this work, if it in fact survives.

12. Patrick, *Florida Fiasco*; "Florida"; Skinner, "Soil, Climate and Productions of Florida," 244–45; reprint from the *Baltimore Federal Republican*, in *Pensacola Gazette and West Florida Advertiser*, July 10, 1824.

13. "X, Y, and Z," "Notes on the Climate"; Macomb, "Middle Florida"; Chaplin, *Anxious Pursuit*, 220–25; Shofner and Rogers, "Sea Island Cotton"; Lewis C. Gray, *History of Agriculture*, 2:733–34, 737. Very few low-country South Carolina planters seem to have become migrants in the antebellum South, so sea-island cotton in Middle Florida was, like sugar, largely a phenomenon of inexperienced imitation.

14. "Higher game" from McRae, "Of the Agriculture of Florida; "equal" and "We have"

from [*Tallahassee Floridian*] *American Farmer*, December 19, 1828, 211–12. See also *Pensacola Gazette and West Florida Advertiser*, March 10, June 11, 1825, March 18, 1826; and Mintz, *Sweetness and Power*. South Carolina and Georgia planters had tried repeatedly and with little success to grow sugar (Chaplin, *Anxious Pursuit*, 153–55).

15. Mary Eppes to Mrs. Thomas Jefferson Randolph, April 1, 1827, Folder 3, Randolph Family Papers, FSA; compare Francis Eppes to N. P. Trist, June 7, 1828, Folder 43, Trist Papers, SHC; Brown Memoir, Folder 1, Ambler-Brown Papers, Duke; *Tallahassee Floridian and Advocate*, December 15, 1827, December 28, 1830; Plantation Journal, Folder 2, Gamble Family Papers, FSU; Mary Gamble to Emma Breckenridge, December 2, 1833, Thomas Family Papers, VHS; sugar boilers from 200, 219, 286, Armistead Account Book, FSA; H. B. Croom to Bryan Croom, June 5, July 12, 1831, Croom Papers, SHC.

16. Brown Memoir, Ambler-Brown Papers, Duke; McRae, "Of the Agriculture of Florida"; *Pensacola Gazette and West Florida Advertiser*, August 7, 1824.

17. William P. DuVal to John Quincy Adams, February 13, 1824, Carter and Bloom, *Territorial Papers*, 22:848–49.

18. *Tallahassee Floridian*, July 10, 1832; William B. Beverley to Robert Beverley, sect. 3, Beverley Family Papers, VHS.

19. Quotes from Spencer Cotten to William H. Wills, February 6, 1836, Folder 3, Wills Papers, SHC. See also Censer, "Southwestern Migration," and Oakes, *Ruling Race*, 73–91. Joan Cashin argues that a generation of young men who came of age after 1820 rebelled against the restraints imposed by the tight kinship networks of the older plantation states. To show their aggressive, masculine independence from an older generation of men, they dragged unwilling wives and slaves to the plantation frontier in an individualistic exodus (*Family Venture*, 32–52).

20. "Genealogical Sketch," Folder 1, Gamble Family Papers, FSU; "Their property" from Tuckett, *Journey in the United States*, 55; Richard Parish to William Parish, October 4, 1828, Blake Family Papers, SHC. The September 25, 1825, *Pensacola Gazette and West Florida Advertiser* urged Georgia planters to purchase Florida lands to prevent economic failure and thus "save the credit, and the honor, of your state."

21. Mary E. Randolph Eppes to Mrs. Thomas Jefferson Randolph, April 1, 1827, Folder 3, Randolph Family Papers, FSA; see also Thomas Brown from Brown Memoir, Ambler-Brown Papers, Duke.

22. Craven, *Soil Exhaustion in Virginia and Maryland*, 72–121 and 146–47. William Shade (*Democratizing the Old Dominion*, 17–49) argues energetically against both soil exhaustion and the impression that Virginia's economy declined in the early nineteenth century. On agricultural decline as a metaphor revealing a wide spectrum of planters' concerns, see Faust, *Southern Stories*, 29–53, and Allmendinger, *Ruffin*.

23. H. B. Croom to Bryan Croom, January 19, 1830, Croom Papers, SHC; Baptist, "Migration of Planters," 533–34; Cathey, *Agricultural Developments*, 44–47, 106, and 116; Lewis C. Gray, *History of Agriculture*, 2:684, 889–92; Rawle, "Origin and Progress of the Culture of Cotton," 428–29; Guion G. Johnson, *Ante-Bellum North Carolina*, 478, 827–28; James W. Williams, "Emigration from North Carolina." For South Carolina, see Alfred G. Smith, *Economic Readjustment*; for South Carolina and Georgia, see James D. Miller, "South by Southwest."

24. "Aunt Betsey" from Ann to Martha L. H. Bradford, June 5, 1832, Folder 3, Box 367, Pine Hill Plantation Papers, FSU; "spirit of emigration" from John N. Partridge to Eliza Partridge, April 1, 1832, Partridge Papers, Duke; Thomas H. Hagner to Peter Hagner, March 30, 1838, Folder 66, Hagner Papers, SHC. See also Richard Keith Call Journal, Call Papers, FSA; William C. Wirt to Dabney Carr Wirt, December 10, 1835, Folder 5, Wirt Family Papers, SHC; and Robert Davidson to Adam Davidson, December 1, 1835, Folder 1, Davidson Family Papers, SHC.

25. Nuttall from Abbey, "Documents Relating to El Destino and Chemonie Plantations," pt. 1; Whitaker and Branch from R. H. Bradford to John Branch, October 16, 1831, Folder 2, Branch Family Papers, SHC; and *Tallahassee Floridian*, March 28 and August 28, 1832. See also Cashin, "Structure of Antebellum Planter Families," and Baptist, "Migration of Planters," esp. 531–32.

26. "Grace" to Elizabeth G. W. Goldsborough, July 28, 1835, Folder 2, Goldsborough Papers, Duke; A. J. Cabell to W. H. Cabell, March 16, 1828, Section 1, Cabell Papers, VHS; Anna Whitaker Wills to Cary Whitaker, July 14, 1838, Folder 23, and Cary Whitaker to William H. Wills, April 4, 1838, Folder 4, both in Wills Papers, SHC. See also John Branch to "Gentlemen," [n.d.], Folder 3, Joseph Branch Papers, SHC.

27. Thomas H. Hagner to Peter Hagner, September 22, 1837, Folder 64, and April 18, 1841, Folder 85, Hagner Papers, SHC; "Florida," 420.

28. Mary Ann Gregory to W. H. Wills, May 18, 1837, Folder 3, and Anna Whitaker Wills to Cary Whitaker, July 14, 1838, Folder 23, Wills Papers, SHC.

29. Anna C. Gradner to Lydia Turrentine, August 29, 1836, Folder 1, Parish Family Papers, SHC; Anna Whitaker Wills to Cary Whitaker, July 14, 1838, Folder 23, Wills Papers, SHC; Ann to Martha L. H. Bradford, June 5, 1832, Folder 3, Box 367, Pine Hill Plantation Papers, FSU.

30. Francis Eppes to N. P. Trist, March 2, 1828, Folder 42, and June 7, 1828, Folder 43, Trist Papers, SHC; Mary Eppes to Mrs. T. J. Randolph, April 20, 1828, Folder 3, Randolph Family Papers, FSA. Lydia Parish, who reported that numerous Tallahassee "relations" made her Leon County life very sociable, also encouraged emigration ("L.E.P." to Caroline Turnbull, June 3, 1837, Parish Family Papers, SHC).

31. Catherine Wirt to Mrs. Louis Goldsborough, October 6, 1834, September 8, 1834, August 30, 1834, all Folder 4, Wirt Family Papers, SHC; Mary Eppes to Mrs. T. J. Randolph, April 1, 1827, Folder 3, Randolph Family Papers, FSA. See also Laura Randall to Louisa Carrington, May 27, 1829, 269, Randall Letters, VHS, and Terry, "Family Empires."

32. R. H. Bradford to John Branch, September 27, 1831, Folder 2, and July 6, 1833, Folder 3, Branch Family Papers, SHC; "X, Y, and Z," "Notes on the Climate." Planters considering removal to Middle Florida attempted to assure themselves that the region was an exception to the pattern of Southwestern disease. See, for example, Macomb, "Middle Florida"; Robert Davidson to Adam Davidson, October 29, 1837, Folder 1, Davidson Family Papers, SHC; and Francis Eppes to N. P. Trist, June 7, 1828, Folder 43, Trist Papers, SHC. In fact, during the early years of settlement, elite whites escaped the worst ravages of disease. Only after 1830, as Chapter 3 argues, did their alterations of the environment create a deadly "sickly season" each year during the late summer and fall. See K. David Patterson, "Disease Environ-

ments of the Antebellum South," 168–78, and James Cassady, "Medical Men and the Ecology of the Old South," 152–65, both in Numbers and Savitt, *Science and Medicine.*

33. Combining John Locke's environmentalism with a new consciousness of history, Scottish philosophers in the previous century developed a "stadialist" narrative of social development that prevailed among many Anglo-Americans during the late eighteenth and early nineteenth centuries. See Dekker, *American Historical Romance,* 1–98, and Chaplin, *Anxious Pursuit,* 30–37; "*infant* state" from David Macomb in *Pensacola Gazette and West Florida Advertiser,* May 30, 1828; ibid., May 9, October 21, 1828. See also Slotkin, *Fatal Environment,* 33–48.

34. Quotes from the *Pendleton Messenger,* April 12, 1828, reprinted in *Pensacola Gazette and West Florida Advertiser,* May 9, 1828. For complaints about the Seminoles, see *Pensacola Gazette and West Florida Advertiser,* May 4, 1827 (repr. from Natchez *Ariel*). See also "Justicia" in *Pensacola Gazette and West Florida Advertiser,* May 1, 29, 1824.

35. Joseph M. White to James Barbour, July 1827, Carter and Bloom, *Territorial Papers,* 23:899–901.

36. Mary Ann Gregory to W. H. Wills, May 18, 1837, Folder 3, Wills Papers, SHC.

37. Mary E. R. Eppes to Mrs. T. J. Randolph, April 20, 1828, Folder 3, Randolph Family Papers, FSA; Douglass Memoirs, 31, FSU; Brown Memoir, Ambler-Brown Papers, Duke; A. J. Cabell to W. H. Cabell, March 16, 1828, Cabell Papers, VHS; Eli Whitaker to Cary Whitaker, August 31, 1835, Folder 3, Coffield-Bellamy Papers, SHC; Clifton Paisley, *Red Hills of Florida,* 119–24 and 131–39.

38. John Parkhill from GLO receipts 1775–77, June 4, 1827, *GLO,* 210; Francis Eppes from GLO receipts 2717–20, February 12, 1829, and 2712, February 12, 1829, *GLO,* 83; and Thomas E. Randolph from GLO receipts 2967, 2968, 2970, August 1, 1829, *GLO,* 227. For the Wirts, Randalls, Cabells, Gambles, and others, see Wirt Family Papers, SHC; Hagner Papers, SHC; Goldsborough Papers, Duke; Randall Letters, VHS; Jabour, *Marriage in the New Republic;* Clifton Paisley, *Red Hills of Florida,* 82–94; and Shofner, *History of Jefferson County,* 88–95.

39. "I sometimes go and stay" from Cary Whitaker to Anna Wills, March 14, 1837, Folder 3, Wills Papers, SHC; Cary Whitaker to W. H. Wills, n.d., ibid.; see also Mary Taylor to Mary Jane Stokes, May 12, 1837, Hatchett Papers, Duke; "A planter never" from Murat, *United States of North America,* 65; Baptist, "Migration of Planters," 536–41.

40. Nathan Byrd to Richard Parish, November 16, 1827, Folder 3, Byrd Papers, FSU; John Taylor Will, 1842, 64–66, Will Book A, LCC; Abbey, "Documents Relating to El Destino and Chemonie Plantations," pt. 1, 207–9. See also Heirs of Thomas K. White to Joseph White, 1826, Deed Book A, 61–62, LCC.

41. Jefferson's clock from Francis Eppes to N. P. Trist, November 6, 1828, Folder 44, Trist Papers, SHC. Relatives who remained behind could also pay off migrants' debts in the older plantation districts that they had left. See John W. Cotten to W. H. Wills, March 15, 1842, Folder 4, and January 4, 1845, Folder 5, and Cary Whitaker to W. H. Wills, February 3, 1843, Folder 5, all Wills Papers, SHC; Thomas H. Hagner to Alexander Randall, May 18, 1842, Folder 88, Hagner Papers, SHC; Jason Gregory to Daniel and Maryan Thompson, August 29, 1832, Thomp-

son Papers, SHC; Copland and Parkhill from John Parkhill to Charles Copland, March 30, 1830, Deed Book B, 644, LCC; and Claiborne Watkins to Anderson Watkins (of Augusta, Ga.), August 1, 1828, Deed Book A, 419, LCC.

42. William P. Craig to James H. Lorimer, January 3, 1834, Deed Book D, 54; Brown et ux to R. K. Call and E. B. Vass, July 28, 1829, Deed Book B, 471–74; Brown to H. P. Vass, August 8, 1828, Deed Book A, 446; Brown to Philip Alexander and H. P. Vass, December 6, 1828, Deed Book A, 444, all LCC.

43. James F. Trottie vs. Wright and Triplett, 1826, case file 5, Law Case Files, LCC; Daniel Wiggins Diary, vol. 11, November 5, 1838, Wiggins Papers, FSA; Harriet Randolph to Mrs. Thomas E. Randolph, June 19, 1829, Folder 3, Randolph Family Papers, FSA.

44. Robert Gamble Plantation Journal, September 9, 13, 1833, Folder 2, Gamble Family Papers, FSU; Daniel Wiggins Diary, vol. 11, November 5, 1838, Wiggins Papers, FSA; James F. Trottie vs. Wright and Triplett, 1826, case file 5; Cary Bronaugh vs. W. D. Dandridge, 1826, case file 17; and John Addison et al. vs. A. W. Crews, 1826, case file 8, all Law Case Files, LCC; Harriet Randolph to Thomas E. Randolph, September 28, 1829, Folder 3, Randolph Family Papers, FSA; Nathan Byrd to Richard Parish, November 16, 1827, Folder 3, Byrd Papers, FSU. For Tiger Tail, see Douglass Memoirs, 42, FSU.

45. Murat, *United States of North America*, 89 (see also ibid., 64); Brown Memoir, Ambler-Brown Papers, Duke. Eli Whitaker to L. H. B. Whitaker, May 12, 1835, Whitaker-Snipes Papers, SHC; see also Harriet Randolph to Mrs. Thomas E. Randolph, September 8, 1829, Folder 3, Randolph Family Papers, FSA.

46. *Pensacola Gazette and West Florida Advertiser*, February 15, 1828, May 4, 1827; John G. Gamble to Richard K. Call, March 28, 1829, Gamble Letter, FSL; Joe Knetsch, "Canal Fever in North Florida," *Apalachee* 8 (1984–90): 40–53.

47. "Florida," 420.

48. A. J. Cabell to W. H. Cabell, March 18, 1828, Cabell Papers, VHS.

CHAPTER TWO

1. This has been so common an assumption that citation becomes almost unnecessary, but consider one recent formulation: "That most white southerners had little chance of following [someone such as James Henry Hammond of South Carolina, who rose from obscurity to tremendous wealth and plantation ownership] mattered less than their willingness to believe that they too might one day become powerful planters. The white social order held together precisely because poorer whites did not know their place" (Jeffrey R. Young, *Domesticating Slavery*, 199).

2. Pension application of Isaac Hay, April 12, 1832, Circuit Court Minute Book 1, 395–96, LCC; 1790 U.S. Census, Dobbs County; 1800–1820 U.S. Census, Greene County; *State of North Carolina: Entries for Claims for Lands within the County of Dobbs*, 60, 189, 357, 403, 473 (Reubin Hays), NCDAH; Hays, Isaac, soldier, 1333.2, in Secretary of State Revolutionary Military Papers, NCDAH. Dobbs County became Greene County after the Revolution. Changes in the political rights of less wealthy white men occurred in southeastern states as the antebellum years went on, but often not

until long after emigrants had left. See Wooster, *Politicians, Planters, and Plain Folk*; Fletcher M. Green, *Democracy in the Old South*; Durrill, *War of Another Kind*, 13–16; and Lacy K. Ford, "Popular Ideology of the Old South's Plain Folk: The Limits of Egalitarianism in a Slaveholding Society," in Samuel C. Hyde Jr., *Plain Folk*, 228–49.

3. *Tallahassee Floridian*, November 28, 1846; Fritot, *Pension Records of Soldiers*. On lower-class white men and the meaning of service in the American Revolution, see Alfred Young, "George Robert Twelves Hewes."

4. Many scholars have argued that most countrymen who moved to the Old Southwest came from the backcountry. See, for example, Otto, "Migration of the Southern Plain Folk," 184, and Jordan and Kaups, *American Backwoods Frontier*. Yet, too often, evidence from coastal counties creeps into historians' accounts of the eighteenth-century backcountry, and slavery is left out, as in Fischer, *Albion's Seed*, esp. 718 n10. Compare McDonald and McDonald, "Ethnic Origins of the American People," and Purvis, "Why the Accepted Estimates are Unacceptable." For change in the "backcountry" Chesapeake and Carolinas during the eighteenth century, see Fischer and Kelly, *Away, I'm Bound Away*, 43–47; Rachel Klein, *Unification of a Slave State*, 9–46; Coulter, *Old Petersburg*, 20; and Beeman, *Evolution of the Southern Backcountry*, esp. 170–85.

5. For the use of "countryman," see *Pensacola Gazette and West Florida Advertiser*, October 6, 1826; [Myers], "Reminiscences of the Early Days"; and Blake Account Book, March 8, 1828, FSA. The term "common whites," coined by Bill Cecil-Fronsman (*Common Whites*), groups together yeomen (whites who owned land and between zero and ten slaves) and poor whites (nonlandowning whites, excluding professionals, merchants, and members of their respective families). McCurry, *Masters of Small Worlds*, 47–48, defines the slaveowning yeoman as a "self-working farmer," i.e., one who might own slaves but not so many that he and his family did not have to contribute physical field labor. Compare Owsley, *Plain Folk of the Old South*, who uses the term "plain folk." In contrast, Bolton, *Poor Whites*, argues the crucial difference between those who owned and those who did not own slaves. All of these definitions have some validity. However, all of the measures on which they lean were constantly in flux, especially on the frontier.

6. A. J. Cabell to W. H. Cabell, March 28, 1828, Cabell Papers, VHS.

7. From Jackson and Leon Counties Households database, which is a compilation of information on households in these two counties from 1821 to 1860. The information has come from multiple sources: U.S. Census of Population, 1830–60; U.S. Census of Agriculture, 1850–60; Florida Territorial Census, 1825 and 1838; Property tax files (Jackson and Leon) 1829, 1839, 1850, and 1860, plus Jackson and Leon deed, criminal and civil, voting, and probate records. Information on individual householders' origins is from census indexes, censuses, gravestones, newspapers, and the Church of Jesus Christ of Latter-Day Saints International Genealogical Index (IGI). The sample cannot be entirely random, since those individuals with wealth or fairly distinct names are far more easy to track than the Smiths and Joneses who migrated to Middle Florida. This method also must follow migrants almost exclusively through the male line. The only other systematic tracings of large numbers of antebellum Southern migrants of which I am aware are in Cashin, *Family Venture*, and Censer, "Southwestern Migration," both of which trace the migrations

of planter families; Bolton, *Poor Whites*, which traces some individual poor whites from North Carolina to Mississippi; Oberly, "Westward Who?"; and Lathrop, *Migration into East Texas*. The rest of the antebellum South's vast white migration remains terra incognita for historians, occupied mostly by genealogists.

8. On migration from North Carolina and its causes, see James W. Williams, "Emigration from North Carolina," and Calhoon, "Troubled Culture," 76–110. For nonslaveholding whites in Georgia, see Lockley, *Lines in the Sand*.

9. Newsome, "Twelve North Carolina Counties," pt. 3, 178; Bolton, *Poor Whites*, 66–83; Lathrop, *Migration into East Texas*.

10. JLCHD; Magrath, *Yazoo;* James W. Williams, "Emigration from North Carolina"; Huxford, *Pioneers of Wiregrass Georgia*.

11. *Tallahassee Floridian*, November 28, 1846; Joy S. Paisley, *Cemeteries of Leon County*, 164; see also 1790 U.S. Census, North Carolina, Halifax Co.; 1800, 1810, and 1820 U.S. Census, North Carolina, Nash Co.; *Nash County Deed Abstracts*, Books 7, pp. 142, 286, 315; Book 8, pp. 31, 83; Book 9; Books 10–12, 172, all NCDAH.

12. *Tallahassee Star of Florida*, June 9, 1842; see also McCurry, *Masters of Small Worlds*, 37–91, and Sellers, *Market Revolution*, 8–19.

13. Fritot, *Pension Records*, 32; Fields, *Abstracts of the Minutes*, 43.

14. Gilpatrick, *Jeffersonian Democracy*, 14–16; Fletcher M. Green, *Constitutional Development*, 66–90, 176–79, 192–93; Sydnor, *Development of Southern Sectionalism*, 39–49; William E. Dodd, *Life of Nathaniel Macon*.

15. Newsome, "Twelve North Carolina Counties," pt. 2, 81; Durrill, *War of Another Kind*, 10–11; Harry L. Watson, "Squire Oldway and His Friends" and "Common Rights of Mankind"; McCurry, *Masters of Small Worlds*, 92–129; Escott, *Many Excellent People*, 3–31; Guion Griffis Johnson, *Ante-bellum North Carolina*, 61, 71.

16. JLCHD; Klein, *Unification of a Slave State*, 7, 78–108. See also Mann, *History of Telfair County*, 23–25; Newsome, "Twelve North Carolina Counties," pt. 1.

17. For attempts to buy Georgia land and, later, Alabama land see Clifton Paisley, *Red Hills of Florida*, 59; Hay application, Superior Court Minute Book 1, April 12, 1832, 395–96, LCC; Rohrbough, *Land-Office Business*, 110–11, 118–19, although he generally blames squatters for much of the uncertainty surrounding the sale of government lands; and Dupre, *Transforming the Cotton Frontier*, 9–48, which describes the uses of the "speculator" image.

18. Nancy Cone Hagan, "My Farewell to My Friends and Brethren, 1825 in April," Hagan Papers, transcribed by James C. Bryant from private papers of Mrs. Eliza Quarterman of Quincy, Florida, c. 1971; typescript now in FSU.

19. Tuckett, *Journey in the United States*, 33; information on the Boatwrights from JLCHD; quote from Charles Clinton, *Winter from Home*, 36.

20. Clifton Paisley, *Red Hills of Florida*, 57–61; Upchurch, "'Middle Florida,'" 103–8; Tract Book A, JCC; William Chambless to Charles Haire, May 9, 1826, Deed Book A, 26, LCC; "Journal of an Expedition to the Interior of West Florida," *Pensacola Gazette and West Florida Advertiser*, May 29, June 12, 1824; Groene, *Ante-Bellum Tallahassee*, 13–40.

21. Murat, *United States of North America*, 52–53.

22. Upchurch, "Middle Florida," 113–15; Owsley, *Plain Folk of the Old South*, 52–62, 110–11; *Tallahassee Floridian and Advocate*, March 2, 1830; Tuckett, *Journey in the United*

States, 63; Jerah Johnson, "The Vernacular Architecture of the South: Log Building, Dog-Trot Houses, and English Barns," in Samuel C. Hyde Jr., *Plain Folk*, 46–72; Christopher Morris, *Becoming Southern*, 29–30; Murat, *United States of North America*, 52. Farmers intending permanent settlement still had to clear the field completely at some point, especially for plow cultivation of cotton. See Lewis C. Gray, *History of Agriculture*, 1:196–97, and Primock, "Land Clearing."

23. *An Act giving the right of pre-emption, in the purchase of lands, to certain settlers in the states of Alabama, Mississippi, and territory of Florida*, Statutes at Large 4 (1826), sec. 28, 154–55; *An Act to grant pre-emption rights to settlers on the public lands*, Statutes at Large 4 (1830), sec. 208, 420–21.

24. Paul McCormick to Nancy Hagan, January 27, 1826, Deed Book A, 57; Hagan to McCormick, January 4, 1833, Deed Book C, 627; Hagan to McCormick, January 25, 1828, Deed Book A, 419, all LCC.

25. 1830 U.S. Census, Leon County; 1829 Property Tax Book, and Ambrose Cook from Benjamin Singletary and Nathaniel Bryan, July 16, 1827, Deed Book A, 161, both LCC.

26. Long, *Florida Breezes*, 186. McCurry (*Masters of Small Worlds*, 83 n. 89) argues that common white women plowed, which was a "violation" of commonly assumed European gender norms that held that women should not plow; however, the paucity of evidence to prove the point leaves the subject murky. One satirical rendering of a Middle Florida poor white woman, "Dorothy Doolittle," portrays this fictional character as plowing after her husband runs off to Texas. Yet, since it is also an attempt to ridicule poor white women, it is hardly an unproblematic document. See *Tallahassee Star of Florida*, December 6, 1844. For weaving, see Charles Hentz Diary, June 9, 1852, Folder 22, Hentz Family Papers, SHC, and Blake Account Book, 1828, FSA.

27. Groene, *Ante-bellum Tallahassee*, 97. Denham, *Rogue's Paradise*, states that Jane may actually have been hanged in 1835. For yeoman slaveholdings, see 1830 U.S. Census, Jackson and Leon Counties; Territorial Census, JCC; and 1840 U.S. Census, Leon County. For Thomas Coleman, see Will of Thomas Coleman, 1842, 61–63, Will Book A, LCC; see also McCurry, *Masters of Small Worlds*, 49. In contrast, James Oakes (*Slavery and Freedom*, 94) states that "among those who owned only one slave . . . there was a clear preference for adult males."

28. April, August, September, 30, 1829, January 6, 1830, Armistead Account Book, FSA.

29. Singletary land from 1829 Property Tax Book, LCC. Contemporary accounts of family labor include Allen, *Allen's Journal*, 20; McCurry, *Masters of Small Worlds*, 72–85; Owsley, *Plain Folk of the Old South*, 108–11; and Sellers, *Market Revolution*, 13–14.

30. Murat, *America and the Americans*, 53; see also Tuckett, *Journey in the United States*, 53, and *Tallahassee Floridian*, April 27, 1839. For more evidence of a local livestock market, see Willis Bryan to William Allison McRea, January 17, 1828, Deed Book A, 190, LCC. Some scholars have painted yeomen in many areas as existing essentially outside the market until the late nineteenth century. See, for example, Rothstein, "Antebellum South as a Dual Economy"; Hahn, *Roots of Southern Populism*, 16–85; and Genovese, "Yeoman Farmers in a Slaveholders' Democracy," 331–42. Others have argued that yeoman farmers lived along a continuum between self-sufficiency

and market relations. Wright, *Political Economy of the Cotton South*, 22–24, 62–74, for example, argues that small farmers emphasized "safety-first" self-sufficient farming only when it made economic sense. See also Ford, *Origins of Southern Radicalism*, 10–19; McCurry, *Masters of Small Worlds*, 61–72; and Harry L. Watson, "Conflict and Collaboration." Bradley G. Bond, "Herders, Farmers, and Markets on the Inner Frontier: The Mississippi Piney Woods, 1850–1860," in Samuel C. Hyde Jr., *Plain Folk*, 73–99, argues that they did not emphasize it at all.

31. Drury Vickers from *Tallahassee Florida Intelligencer*, March 17, 1826; Richard Long to Farish Carter and Seaton Grantland, January 12, 1835, Folder 11, Carter Papers, SHC; "Journal of an Expedition into the Interior of West Florida," *Pensacola Gazette and West Florida Advertiser*, May 29, 1824; Armistead Account Book, April 29, 1829, FSA; Blake Account Book, February, March 8, FSA. For local rural artisans, see Account of A. B. Wheeler with Edward Bradford, 1861, Folder 2, Bradford Family Papers, FSU; for other labor, see Long to Carter, May 23, 1843, Folder 24, Carter Papers, SHC; Harriet Randolph to Thomas Eston Randolph, September 20, 1829, Folder 3, Randolph Family Papers, FSA; Indenture of Nathan Byrd to Richard Parish, November 16, 1827, Folder 3, Byrd Papers, FSU; Archibald McKay to Hugh Brown, November 11, 1832, Brown Papers, Duke; and John Addison, James Addison, and Harmon Williams vs. A. W. Crews, 1825, case file 8, Law Case Files, LCC.

32. *Tallahassee Floridian and Advocate*, January 6, 1831; Wright, *Political Economy of the Cotton South*, 53–74; Christopher Morris, *Becoming Southern*, 29–30; Lewis C. Gray, *History of Agriculture*, 1:196–97; Primock, "Land Clearing."

33. Geo. Fisher (Sr. and Jr.) to Jacob Horger, January 27, 1829, Deed Book A, 589, LCC; Blake Account Book, November 1830–January 1831, FSA. During the preceding year, Horger also bought on account various goods that his household did not make: needles, sweet oil, spelling books, an atlas, a little bit of silk, coffee, a set of cups and saucers, garden seeds, and bagging and rope for cotton. He had a higher standard of living than many other common whites, but one far less costly to achieved than that of the planters listed in the same account book.

34. Paul McCormick to Nancy Hagan, January 25, 1828, Deed Book A, 419, LCC; Nancy Hagan, "On the Marriage of My Third Daughter Elizabeth . . . ," Hagan Papers, FSU; Benjamin Hagan purchase from November 19, 1827, GLO receipt 2108, 117, GLO; 1830 U.S. Census, Leon County; 1829 Property Tax Book, and Benjamin Hagan to John Taylor, July 10, 1830, Deed Book B, 695, LCC; Lewis C. Gray, *History of Agriculture*, 2:912; Murat, *United States of North America*, 64. Rice, usually grown dry, also found planter buyers. An early commentator claimed that a yeoman farmer could make forty to sixty bushels of rice per acre. See *Pensacola Gazette and West Florida Advertiser*, August 27, 1825.

35. Benjamin Hagan to Mary Elizabeth Hagan, February 20, 1833, Deed Book C, 627, and Benjamin Hagan to John Taylor, July 10, 1830, Deed Book B, 695, LCC.

36. See "Third letter from Mr. Smith," *Tallahassee Florida Sentinel*, July 25, 1848.

37. George Graham to the Marquis de Lafayette, June 22, 1825, Carter and Bloom, *Territorial Papers*, 23:272–73. Figures from Tables A.3–A.5 are probably biased downward for all classes.

38. For the locations and dates of these purchases, see T7N R12W and T6N R12W,

Tract Book A, JCC. For Abraham Phillips, see Clifton Paisley, *Red Hills of Florida*, 58.

39. Thomas Goff from James Webb to Charles Williamson, May 20, 1827, and Thomas Baltzell to Charles Williamson, May 20, 1827, Folder 3; John Smith from J. H. Walker to Farish Carter, May 1, 1830, Folder 5; and quote from Walker to Carter, April 21, 1831, Folder 6, all Carter Papers, SHC.

40. J. H. Walker to Farish Carter, April 21, 1831, Folder 6, and Walker to Carter, November 20, 1830, Folder 5, Carter Papers, SHC; J. T. Bernard Diary, vol. 6, September 30, 1858, Bernard Papers, SHC; Thomas Baltzell to Seaton Grantland, January 3, 1832, Folder 6, Carter Papers, SHC; Bode and Ginter, *Farm Tenancy*.

41. J. H. Walker to Farish Carter, April 21, 1831, Folder 6, Carter Papers, SHC; T6N R12W, Tract Book A, and 1829 Property Tax Book, JCC; 1830 U.S. Census, Jackson County.

42. T7N R12W, T6N R12W, Tract Book A; 1829 Property Tax Book; and Territorial Census, Jackson County, JCC; 1830 and 1840 U.S. Census, Jackson County; Hatheway Diary, January 18, 1846, FSU; Bolton, *Poor Whites*, 66–83.

43. "Habits manners and moral character" from Elijah Hayward to Virgil Maxcy, October 30, 1830, Carter and Bloom, *Territorial Papers*, 24:896–97; T7N R12W, T6N R12W, Tract Book A; 1829 Property Tax Book; and Territorial Census, JCC; 1830 U.S. Census, Jackson County. "Poor & worthless" from Charles Hentz Diary, December 11, 1848, [4], Folder 20, Hentz Family Papers, SHC; Nicholas A. Long to Farish Carter, May 14, 1834, Folder 10, Carter Papers, SHC; Joseph B. Johnston to Dr. Bradford, July 1, 1850, Folder 1, Bradford Papers, FSU.

44. JLCHD; see also Wilbur Gramling Diary, June 16, July 31, August 14, 1864, FSU. The first sale of lands in the Centreville area was proclaimed for May 1825 (Proclamation of Public Land Sales, January 26, 1825, Carter and Bloom, *Territorial Papers*, 23:167).

45. Marriages from JLCHD, and Will Book A, LCC; church memberships from *Register of Members*, vol. 1, 1830–1903, Pisgah United Methodist Church Records, FSA; Boston, *History of "Old Pisgah"*; Alexander Adair to Jacob Horger, January 27, 1829, Deed Book A, 589, LCC.

46. For "Dutch Settlement," see *Tallahassee Floridian*, January 23, 1841; for land purchases of members of the Felkel, Gramling, Horger, Houck, and Stroman families, see Deed Books A–F, LCC; and *GLO*.

47. Ned, Patience, and family from *Tallahassee Star of Florida*, March 9, 1843.

48. Probate Packet 26, Probate Records, LCC. For the concept of "safety-first" farming by common whites, see Wright, *Political Economy of the Cotton South*, 55–74.

49. See Henry Stroman and Thomas John from 1830 and 1840 U.S. Census, Leon County; and 1829 and 1839 Property Tax Books, LCC.

50. *Tallahassee Star of Florida*, July 14, 1841, quoting a "John Slocum" at a Monticello July 4th festival that got far too rowdy and coarse for the editor's tastes.

51. *Pensacola Gazette and West Florida Advertiser*, October 6, 13, 1826.

52. Ibid., October 6, 13, November 2, 1826; for previous murders see ibid., May 15, 1824, and February 11, 1826; for lack of legal structures, see ibid., July 23, 1825.

53. Ibid., October 6, 13, November 2, 1826.

CHAPTER THREE

1. Hulda Alexander, application no. 315, *RSD*; Groves, *Alstons and Allstons*, 110–34; Bank of Florida vs. Willis Alston, October 11, 1833, Superior Court Minute Book 1, 547, and Administrator of Joseph McCants, decd., vs. Willis Alston and Michael Ledwith, January 26, 1842, Superior Court Minute Book 3, 222, LCC; *Tallahassee Floridian*, December 28, 1833, December 5, 1835; Augustus Archer to John Branch, November 25, 1840, Folder 4, Branch Family Papers, SHC.

2. See especially Joseph Miller, *Way of Death*; Eltis, *Rise of African Slavery*; and Curtin, *Atlantic Slave Trade*.

3. Works discussing other "internal" (as opposed to Atlantic) slave migrations include, for the British Caribbean, Dunn, *Sugar and Slaves*, 157; Eltis, "Traffic in Slaves"; and Westbury, "Analysing a Regional Slave Trade"; and for Brazil (among the literature in English), see Conrad, *World of Sorrow*, 171–92 ("The internal traffic, then, was not merely a substitute for the African slave trade [after it was finally banned to Brazil in 1850]; in spirit and purpose, rather, it was its continuation" [189]); Stein, *Vassouras*, 65–73; and Herbert Klein, *Middle Passage*, 95–120.

4. Gutman (*Slavery and the Numbers Game*, 106–7) called attention to the multiple effects of the forced migration on African American families, but perhaps the only work to have explored this issue in depth in the ensuing twenty-five years has been Stevenson, *Life in Black and White*, 218–25.

5. See Bancroft, *Slave Trading in the Old South*; Collins, *Domestic Slave Trade*; Fogel and Engerman, *Time on the Cross*, 42–58; Herbert Gutman and Richard Sutch, "The Slave Family: Protected Agent of Capitalist Masters or Victim of the Slave Trade?" in David et al., *Reckoning with Slavery*; Tadman, *Speculators and Slaves*; Walter L. Johnson, *Soul by Soul* (for the slave trade); Malone, *Swing Low, Sweet Chariot*; and Kulikoff "Uprooted Peoples," 143–71. On slave migration, and movement to the south and west in general, the grand tradition of American slavery studies is oddly quiet. Eugene Genovese, in *Roll, Jordan, Roll*, says little on the subject (the domestic slave trade is mentioned on pages 419, 453, and 625, and slaveowners' migrations are not discussed.) Gutman's *Black Family* (144–84, 318–19) is the only synthetic work on American slavery to discuss sufficiently any aspect of nineteenth-century slave migration. Stampp, *Peculiar Institution*, 239–78, discusses the slave trade but not masters' migrations; Elkins, *Slavery*, mentions the domestic slave trade twice (53, 211); Owens, *This Species of Property*, 173–91, and Blassingame, *Slave Community*, 173–76, discuss the interstate slave trade and family separations. See also Steven Miller, "Plantation Labor Organization," 155–69; Kulikoff, *Agrarian Origins of American Capitalism*, 226–63; Cashin, *Family Venture*, 49–51; Terry, "Sustaining the Bonds of Kinship"; and West, "Surviving Separation."

6. Kulikoff, "Origins of Afro-American Society"; Kulikoff, "Uprooted Peoples"; Sweig, "Reassessing the Human Dimension"; Calderhead, "How Extensive Was the Border States Slave Trade?"; James Smith, application no. 281, and John Green, no. 138, *RSD*. William P. Craig from 1839 Property Tax Book, LCC; Craig to J. H. Lorimer, January 3, 1834, Deed Book D, 560, LCC; for the Union Bank, see Chapter 5.

7. While we cannot know how representative the Freedman's Bank records are, in

a subject starved for "hard" data, they provide a useful sample of one part of the forced migration of African Americans to the Old Southwest. For the Freedman's Bank as an institution, see Osthaus, *Freedmen, Philanthropy, and Fraud,* and Fleming, *Freedman's Savings Bank.*

8. DuVal, *Compilation of the Public Acts,* 216. See also the law described in *Pensacola Floridian,* April 19, 1823. On the need to prohibit criminal slaves, see Acting Governor William McCarty in *Tallahassee Floridian and Advocate,* December 15, 1827.

9. *Tallahassee Floridian and Advocate,* December 22, 1829.

10. For the main flows of the slave trade in this era, see Bancroft, *Slave Trading in the Old South,* and Ingraham, *South-West,* 235–39.

11. Fogel and Engerman, *Time on the Cross,* 42–58, claim that only 13 percent of the slaves in the domestic slave trade were separated from immediate family members; Gutman and Sutch's "Slave Family" acknowledges disruption of extended families, as does Gutman's *Black Family,* but their focus on refuting Fogel and Engerman on the slave trade per se leaves the wider disruptions caused by all the permutations of forced migration underexplored. See also Tadman, *Speculators and Slaves,* 25–28, 228–32, and Fogel, *Without Consent or Contract,* 152, 167.

12. Philip D. Morgan, *Slave Counterpoint,* 498–558; Kulikoff, *Tobacco and Slaves,* 340–80; Gutman, *Black Family,* 135–38.

13. John Walker, application no. 377; William Keno, no. 370; and William Henry Sparks, no. 432, *RSD.* For claims that masters, for various reasons, rarely separated families in migration or in the trade, see Fogel and Engerman, *Time on the Cross,* 142–43; and Genovese, *Roll, Jordan, Roll,* 332. Records from the master class argue that masters did occasionally attempt to purchase slaves upon migration in order to keep abroad marriages together. See Shofner, *History of Jefferson County,* 124, and Eppes, *Negro of the Old South,* 48–51. An authenticated example from early Middle Florida was predictably a house slave (Virginia Trist to N. P. Trist, May 5, 1829, Folder 49, Trist Papers, SHC). Ex-slaves' silence suggests that they viewed such efforts as rare. In addition, the purchase of one partner in an abroad marriage would not prevent forced migration from severing extended family ties. The burdens that fell upon mothers separated from spouses are discussed in Wilma King, "Suffer With Them Till Death: Slave Women and Their Children in Nineteenth-Century America," in Gaspar and Hine, *More Than Chattel,* 156–58.

14. Ellen Paine, application no. 933, *RSD;* 1839 Property Tax Book, LCC.

15. Peter Carter, application no. 359, *RSD.*

16. Quote from Francis Eppes to Eliza Eppes, March 21, 1864, Folder 188, Series 1.10, Hubard Papers, SHC. See Ball, *Fifty Years in Chains,* 19–20, 36, and other memoirs for the recurring image of trickery and subterfuge. One wealthy Virginian wrote of such an occasion, "Tomorrow the negroes are to get off and I expect there will be great crying and mourning; children leaving their mothers, mothers their children, and women their husbands" (quoted in Terry, "Sustaining the Bonds of Kinship," 464, from Unidentified Correspondent to [Polly Cabell Breckinridge], October 12, 1804, Breckinridge Family Papers, Manuscript Division, Library of Congress, Washington, D.C.).

17. Quotes from Douglass Memoirs, 19, FSU; Brown Memoir, Folder 1, Ambler-Brown

Papers, Duke; for a citation of Brown's account, see Cashin, *Family Venture*, 57. See also Abrahams, *Singing the Master*.

18. "Continual *yell*" and "regular loll" from Harriet Randolph to Mrs. Thomas E. Randolph, May 23, 1829; "We have" from Harriet Randolph to Lucy Beverly Randolph, September 8, 1829; all Folder 3, Randolph Family Papers, FSA.

19. For sickness among slaves on the journey, see Harriet Randolph to Mrs. Thomas E. Randolph, June 19, 1829, Folder 3, Randolph Family Papers, FSA; and Eli Whitaker to L. H. B. Whitaker, May 12, 1835, Whitaker-Snipes Papers, SHC; "unfortunate circumstances" from Eli B. Whitaker to Cary Whitaker, August 1, 1835, Whitaker-Bradford-Branch Collection, FSA.

20. Will of John Branch, 383–88, 1863; Will of Absalom B. Whitaker, 96–99, 1845, Will Books A–B, LCC; Lawrence B. Whitaker to Anna Whitaker Wills, Folder 6, Wills Papers, SHC; Brown Memoir, Ambler-Brown Papers, Duke; Francis Eppes to Col. Hubard, March 4, 1864, Folder 188, Hubard Papers, SHC; W. W. Boykin to George Gray, Folder 14, Gray Papers, SHC; *FPR*, 18–27.

21. *Tallahassee Florida Intelligencer*, July 22, 1826; 1830 U.S. Census, Leon County: Samuel Parkhill, 242; John Parkhill, 240; William Copland, 242; "pushing man" from Harriet Randolph to Lucy Beverly Randolph, September 8, 1829, Randolph Family Papers, FSA; 1830 U.S. Census, Jackson County; Steven Miller, "Plantation Labor Organization," 156–57; Malone, *Swing Low, Sweet Chariot*.

22. 1830 U.S. Census, Leon County; Webber, *Deep Like the Rivers*, 67. When he bought slaves directly from the Atlantic trade, Chaires had lived on the east coast of Florida for a few years while it was still under Spanish rule (Benjamin Chaires to Thomas Fitch, July 27, 1820, Folder 11, Fitch Papers, FSA).

23. 1830 U.S. Census, Essex, Halifax, Jackson, and Leon Counties. For North Carolina and Virginia as states, only 47.2 and 46.8 percent, respectively, were between ten and thirty-six. See Steven Miller, "Plantation Labor Organization," 157.

24. William Kenyon, O.A. (Original Application) no. 391, *RSD*; H. B. Croom to B. Croom, June 20, 1833, Croom Papers, SHC; Rogers and Clark, *Croom Family and Goodwood Plantation*, esp. 10, 39.

25. Charley Paine, O.A. no. 263, *RSD*; see also Beverley Fleming, O.A. no. 222, *RSD*; Brown Memoir, Ambler-Brown Papers, Duke.

26. Murat, *United States of North America*, 64 (my emphasis); Achille Murat to John G. Gamble, October 1, 1834, Lipona Letter Book, 1830–35, 459–61, Murat Papers, FSU (film 2657), orig. in Bibliotheque Nationale, Paris; Murat to Thomas Botts, October 4, 1834, Lipona Letter Book, 1830–35, 46, Murat Papers, FSU. He later sent a similar letter to eastern North Carolina: Murat to Wright Stanley, February 21, 1835, Lipona Letter Book, 1830–35, 480–82, ibid. See also *Tallahassee Floridian and Advocate*, September 7, 1830.

27. John Parkhill to Rev. William Atkinson, June 9, 1837, Folder 5, Parkhill Family Papers, SHC. See also Daniel Wiggins Diary, vol. 11, October 16–27, 1838, Wiggins Papers, FSA; *Tallahassee Floridian*, October 3, 1835; and Jabour, "'The Privations and Hardships of a New Country.'"

28. Neither the records of the New Orleans slave market nor the papers of professional slave traders offers an account of the master-borne slave trade, nor do accounts of the master-borne trade lend themselves to quantification. See Tadman, *Speculators*

and Slaves; Kulikoff, *Agrarian Origins of American Capitalism*, 226–63; and Gutman, *Black Family*, 145–49.

29. U.S. Congress, House, *Condition of Banks, 1840*, 325–34; *Tallahassee Floridian*, December 20, 1838, February 9, 1839; Long, *Florida Breezes*, 209.

30. "See if I" from Whipple, *Southern Diary*, 88; Charlotte Moore, application no. 1258; Richard Brewer, no. 749; and Stephen Robison, no. 858, *RSD*; Tadman, *Speculators and Slaves*, 133–78; Walter L. Johnson, *Soul by Soul*.

31. Quote from George A. T. Whitaker to Cary Whitaker, January 17, 1844, Folder 24, Wills Papers, SHC.

32. Eli B. Whitaker to John B. Whitaker, August 16, 1836, Whitaker-Branch-Bradford Collection, FSA; Kiple, *Caribbean Slave*, 15–17, 181; Dusinberre, *Them Dark Days*, 389–90; Hazel, "Geography of Negro Agricultural Slavery," 59–87. For the effects of yellow fever on slaves imported from Piedmont Virginia to Florida, see Lucy B. Randolph to Susan Harrison, January 11, 1834, Folder 3, Randolph Family Papers, FSA.

33. Hazel, "Geography of Negro Agricultural Slavery"; Parkhill Diary, Folder 11, Parkhill Family Papers, SHC; Henry Partridge Diary, FSA; *Tallahassee Florida Sentinel*, August 6, 1841. In addition to mosquito-borne diseases, many slaves from Carolina or Chesapeake plantation districts had not experienced childhood diseases endemic in cities and other areas. In 1837, Cary Whitaker reported, "Some of the negroes are sick with the measles . . . a number are yet to have it" (Cary Whitaker to Anna Whitaker Wills, February 5, 1837, Folder 3, Wills Papers, SHC). See also George A. T. Whitaker to Cary Whitaker, February 12, 1849, Folder 24, Wills Papers, SHC; and John Evans to George Noble Jones, June 15, 1852, *FPR*, 71–72.

34. "Very rich" from James Webb to Dr. Charles Williamson, May 20, 1827, Folder 3, Carter Papers, SHC; "has the reputation" from L. B. Whitaker to Anna Whitaker Wills, 1848, Folder 5, Wills Papers, SHC; W. W. Boykin to George Gray, June 6, 1851, Folder 15, Gray Papers, SHC; Boykin to Gray, August 18, 1851, ibid.; see also J. H. Walker to Farish Carter, June 1, 1832, Folder 8, Carter Papers, and John Evans to George Jones, September 2, 1852, *FPR*, 78–80.

35. *Tallahassee Florida Sentinel*, July 23, 1841; *Tallahassee Floridian*, October 16, September 25, 1841. On October 27, 1848, Lawrence O'Bryan Branch wrote to Nannie Branch: "The Doctors say this has been the healthiest summer since 1832, but many of the citizens look very badly and we have had a great deal of sickness amongst our negroes on the plantations" (Folder 9, Branch Family Papers, Duke).

36. "'Switchel'" from John Parkhill to George W. Parkhill, August 3, 1852, Folder 8, Parkhill Family Papers, SHC; Ann and the mare from L. N. Moxley to George Jones, July 7, 1854, Jones Papers, Duke; "Coatney, Phillis" from D. N. Moxley to George Jones, August 6, 1854, *FPR*, 90–91; Steven Miller, "Plantation Labor Organization," 165–69; for slaves' efforts to feed themselves, see Rivers, *Slavery in Florida*, 128–32.

37. *FPR*, 123–24, 158–60, 169–70, 437–38, 514–15, 545–46; Jones from George N. Jones to W. G. M. Davis, January 22, 1855, *FPR*, 123–24; 1841 numbers and "lack of economic incentive" from Abbey, "Documents Relating to El Destino and Chemonie Plantations," pt. 2," 326–27, 292 n; Ingraham, *South-West*, 235–36.

38. Ball, *Fifty Years in Chains*, 68–69.

39. William Stephens, application no. 634, *RSD*.
40. Douglass Memoirs, 55, FSU; *Tallahassee Floridian*, March 26, 1836; Fanny Henderson, application no. 692, and Melvina Whitehead, no. 783, *RSD*.
41. Martha Ann Hill, O.A. no. 133, *RSD*.
42. Henry from *Tallahassee Floridian*, January 2, 1841; Ball, *Fifty Years in Chains*, 48–49; Hector and Simon from *Tallahassee Floridian and Advocate*, November 11, 1828; Franklin and Schweninger, *Runaway Slaves*.
43. Rebecca from *Tallahassee Floridian*, October 3, 1835; Martha Ann Hill, O.A. no. 133, *RSD*; George and Lettus from *Tallahassee Floridian*, June 1, 1839; see also Grandy, *Narrative*, 33–34.
44. L. E. P. to Caroline Turnbull, June 3, 1837, Parish Family Papers, SHC; see also David Dow, application no. 338, *RSD*.
45. Isaac Wood, application no. 317; see also Henry Gaines, O.A. no. 136; Henry Hall, no. 106; and Henry Johnson, no. 332, *RSD*.
46. Willy Williams, application no. 550, *RSD*; Rawick, *American Slave*, 17:347 (Willis Williams). Information about Duimie Harrison comes from Halifax County genealogist Terence Wyche.
47. Lenn to Memory, c. 1858, Folder 2, Cotten-Elliot Family Papers, FSA.
48. Gutman, *Black Family*, 165, makes the argument that slave culture was the same in both the Southeast and the Southwest.
49. George Jones, application no. 1184, *RSD*.
50. Paul Escott (*Slavery Remembered*, 7–15) and John Blassingame ("Using the Testimony of Ex-Slaves," in Blassingame, *Slave Testimony*, xi–lxv) have demonstrated that those interviewed by African Americans, rather than by whites, were much more open, and undoubtedly more honest, about their own feelings and remembered experiences.
51. The stories of men and women like Frederick Douglass, Harriett Jacobs, and others formed the basis for "a black intertextual or signifying relationship, upon which any meaningful formal literary history of the African-American tradition must be built" (Gates and Davis, *Slave's Narrative*, xiii). See also Charles H. Nichols, "The Slave Narrators and the Picaresque Mode: Archetypes for Modern Black Personae," in ibid., 283–97; Melvin Dixon, "Singing Swords: The Literary Legacy of Slavery," in ibid., 298–318; and Griffin, *"Who Set You Flowin'?."*
52. Ball, *Fifty Years in Chains*, 157.
53. Ibid.; Northup, *Twelve Years a Slave*, 40–49.
54. Henry Gates suggests that African American novels and, before them, fugitive slave narratives, grew from vernacular forms of narrative. Gates's argument draws upon his reading of Mikhail Bakhtin ("From the Prehistory of Novelistic Discourse," in *Dialogic Imagination*, 83), who says that "the familiar strata of folk language . . . played [a] tremendous role in the formation of novelistic discourse." See Gates, *Signifying Monkey*, and Dale Peterson, "Response and Call: The African American Dialogue with Bakhtin and What It Signifies," in Mandelker, *Bakhtin in Contexts*, 89–98.
55. Emerson and Morson, *Mikhail Bakhtin*, 326–27.
56. Rawick, *American Slave*, 17:58 (Patience Campbell), 17:251 (Margaret Nickerson.)

57. Rawick, *American Slave*, 17:101 (Ambrose Douglass), 17:300–301 (Samuel Smalls); see also 17:93 (Douglas Dorsey), and 17:62 (Florida Clayton). Franklin and Schweninger, *Runaway Slaves*, and Carol Wilson, *Freedom at Risk*, 9–39, argue convincingly that kidnapping was a serious danger for free people of color living in both the North and the South.

58. Rawick, *American Slave*, 17:251 (Margaret Nickerson); quote from William Wells Brown, *Narrative*, 13.

59. Ball, *Fifty Years in Chains;* William Wells Brown, *Narrative*, 62, 67; Northup, *Twelve Years a Slave;* Grandy, *Narrative*, 11; Hughes, *Thirty Years a Slave*, 92.

60. Rawick, *American Slave*, 17:251–53 (Margaret Nickerson); Genovese, *World the Slaveholders Made*, 118–244.

61. Quote from Whipple, *Southern Diary*, 17 (my emphasis). Rawick, *American Slave*, 17:335–40.

62. Ball, *Fifty Years in Chains*, 151. Full text reads: "'I have been here,' said she, 'almost two years, and came from the Eastern Shore.'"

CHAPTER FOUR

1. *Pensacola Gazette*, January 8, 1825.

2. "Factions and cabals" from "C. D." to Editor, *Pensacola Floridian*, May 3, 1823; ibid., August 3, 1822; Joseph White to the President, April 15, 1822, Carter and Bloom, *Territorial Papers*, 22:406. Chipola grant from Hill, "Joseph White," 25–31; *Tallahassee Floridian*, March 23, 1833.

3. *Pensacola Floridian*, January 8, 22, 29, 1825; Doherty, *Richard K. Call*, 38; George Graham to Robert Butler, July 9, 1824, Carter and Bloom, *Territorial Papers*, 23:6–9; Graham to Richard Call, February 28, 1825, ibid., 23:197–98; Graham to George W. Ward, May 28, 1825, ibid., 23:253–54; Rohrbough, *Land-Office Business*, 170–71; for Gadsden as Call's sidekick, see *Tallahassee Floridian*, February 9, 1833.

4. "Does he" from "An Escambian" in *Pensacola Floridian*, June 21, 1823; "A Citizen of Jackson County" to Call in *Pensacola Gazette and West Florida Advertiser*, March 12, 1825; "devotée of the pistol" from Richard Call Memoir, Call Papers, FSA. Call here is quoting from his own description in Parton, *Life and Times of General Jackson* (2:653), one of the most widely read biographies of Andrew Jackson published during Call's lifetime; see also *Pensacola Gazette and West Florida Advertiser*, April 9, 1825, and Doherty, *Richard K. Call*, 42.

5. "Citizens" in *Tallahassee Floridian and Advocate*, April 14, 1831.

6. *Pensacola Gazette*, September 24, 1826; *Tallahassee Florida Intelligencer*, October 27, December 3, 1826; Doherty, *Richard K. Call*, 36–44.

7. Quote from *Pensacola Gazette*, October 28, 1827.

8. DuVal to Sec'y of War, August 29, 1826, Carter and Bloom, *Territorial Papers*, 23:636. Although in public the label "speculator" was a political liability, and perhaps something of an insult, in private letters, men like Farish Carter and his allies (who included Joseph White) described themselves by that very word. See, for example, James Webb to Dr. Charles Williamson, May 20, 1827, Folder 3, and

Richard A. Long to Carter and Grantland, January 12, 1835, Folder 11, Carter Papers, SHC; see also Dupre, *Transforming the Cotton Frontier;* Aron, *How the West Was Lost.*

9. Memorial to Congress by the Legislative Council, December 28, 1824, Carter and Bloom, *Territorial Papers,* 23:135–37.

10. Proclamation of Public Land Sales, January 26, 1825, Carter and Bloom, *Territorial Papers,* 23:167–68; George Graham to Robert Butler, July 9, 1824, ibid., 6–9; Graham to Richard Call, February 28, 1825, ibid., 197–98; Graham to George W. Ward, May 28, 1825, ibid., 253–54; Rohrbough, *Land-Office Business,* 170–71; William Wyatt in *Pensacola Gazette,* December 24, 1825.

11. George Graham to Richard Call and George W. Ward, July 13, 1826, Carter and Bloom, *Territorial Papers,* 23:607–8; Graham to Delegate White, January 31, 1827, Proclamation of Public Land Sales, January 26, 1825, ibid., 747; McCoy, *Elusive Republic;* Alan Taylor, *Liberty Men and Great Proprietors* and *William Cooper's Town;* Chaplin, *Anxious Pursuit,* 170–79; Magrath, *Yazoo.*

12. *Tallahassee Florida Intelligencer,* March 24, 1826.

13. *Tallahassee Floridian and Advocate,* November 18, 1828; *Tallahassee Floridian,* April 6, 1833; *Tallahassee Florida Intelligencer,* March 24, 1826; Robert Butler to George Graham, July 1, 1825, Carter and Bloom, *Territorial Papers,* 23:276–77; *Pensacola Gazette and West Florida Advertiser,* January 20, 1827; Rohrbough, *Land-Office Business,* 179. On Adams's policies, see Feller, *Public Lands,* 76–79, 91–93. On Call and Ward's attempts to curtail the general use of preemptions, see Memorial of Inhabitants of Jackson County to Congress, November 6, 1826, Carter and Bloom, *Territorial Papers,* 23:658–59; Richard Call to George Graham, November 10, 1825, ibid., 663; Joseph White to Graham, December 5, 1826, ibid., 680–84; Call and George W. Ward to Graham, January 10, 1827, ibid., 724–26; *Pensacola Gazette and West Florida Advertiser,* January 20, 1827; and *Tallahassee Floridian and Advocate,* February 17, 1831. Reprimand from Graham to Call and Ward, February 17, 1827, Carter and Bloom, *Territorial Papers,* 23:762–63; "we can assign no reason" from Call and Ward to Graham, August 14, 1827, ibid., 904. See also "Q in a corner," *Tallahassee Floridian,* February 9, 1833; Delegate White to George Graham, December 5, 1827, Carter and Bloom, *Territorial Papers,* 23:680–81; and White to Graham, December 1, 1825, ibid., 371.

14. Quotes from "Q in a corner," *Tallahassee Floridian,* February 9, 1833; *Tallahassee Florida Intelligencer,* July 22, 1826; "Middle Florida" in ibid., March 17, 1826; Doherty, *Richard K. Call,* 41–42, 50–51; for charges that Call and Ward misappropriated funds, see George Graham to Richard Call, February 25, 1827, Carter and Bloom, *Territorial Papers,* 23:766, and *Tallahassee Floridian and Advocate,* November 13, 1830.

15. Richard Call to John Shepard, June 17, 1827, Deed Book A, 151, LCC; GLO receipt 593, December 6, 1825, and 718, June 8, 1826, *GLO;* Robert W. Williams and Hector Braden to Richard Call, June 10, 1827, Deed Book A, 150; Littlebury Jones to Call, August 17, 1827, A, 154; David Thomas to Call, August 23, 1827, A, 153, LCC.

16. "Was not" from "Georgian" in *Tallahassee Floridian and Advocate,* February 3, 1831; see also "Georgian" in ibid., December 21, 1830; "Orlando" in ibid., November 30, 1830; "Gentlemen who visit" from *Tallahassee Florida Intelligencer,* July 22, 1826.

17. White from *Tallahassee Floridian,* May 1, 1832; "iron grasp" from "Orlando" in *Tal-*

lahassee Floridian and Advocate, November 30, 1830; for the vision of frontier settlement that simultaneously strengthened the independence of poor white men and the virtue and defensive strength of the nation as a whole, see McCoy, *Elusive Republic*, and Alan Taylor, *Liberty Men and Great Proprietors*.

18. "There may" from *Tallahassee Florida Advocate*, April 4, 1829; "What places" from "Moon Light" in *Tallahassee Floridian*, January 11, 1834.

19. Williamson bought a similar amount in Gadsden County and smaller totals in Leon and Jefferson (*GLO*, May 23–June 6, 1827, 291–96); and received transfers of land from Robert Jamieson (*GLO*, 145–46.)

20. "The Georgians" from Charles Chelfills to Col. Carter, September 11, 1836, Folder 12, Carter Papers, SHC; Richard H. Long to Carter and Grantland, January 12, 1835, Folder 11; Congressmen from S. Grantland to Farish Carter, April 3, 1836, Folder 12; Grantland to Carter, April 10, 1836, Folder 12, all ibid.

21. White also owned a share in what opponents derided as a boondoggle: a live oak plantation of naval timber on the Florida coast, but White asserted that he had lost money on his investment. See *Tallahassee Floridian and Advocate*, February 17, 1831; Hill, "Joseph M. White," 40; Keller, *Nation's Advocate;* and *Tallahassee Floridian*, March 28, 1832.

22. "Intrigues and knavery" from Murat, *Moral and Political Sketch*, 59–60; Hackley, *Titles and Legal Opinions*. For Lafayette, see George Graham to the Marquis de Lafayette, June 22, 1825, Carter and Bloom, *Territorial Papers*, 23:272–73, and Abbey, "Story of the Lafayette Lands."

23. Doherty, *Richard K. Call*, 49–50. "Speculation" by planters who remained in the seaboard states also included, of course, the sale of enslaved people to slave traders and Southwestern planters (Tadman, *Speculators and Slaves*).

24. "Plain Truth" in *Pensacola Gazette*, February 26, 1825; R. K. Call, atty. for Thomas Dunlap to Samuel Parkhill, April 7, 1829, Deed Book A, 150; Call to Dunlap, December 21, 1829, C, 288; Call to Benjamin Dunlap, June 17, 1827, A, 152; Seaton Grantland (exr. of Charles Williamson) to Call, June 10, 1831, C 307; General Lafayette to Robert W. Williams, May 20, 1833, D, 23; Lafayette to William Nuttall, Hector Braden, and John P. Craig, November 18, 1833, D, 20; Nuttall, Braden, and Craig to John Taylor, November 1, 1834, D, 104; Braden and Nuttall to John Dickenson, n.d., C, 408; Braden to various, 1832, C, 411, all LCC.

25. "It appears" from James Exum to William P. DuVal, July 9, 1831, Box 1, Folder 3, Outgoing Correspondence of the Territorial Governors, FSA; William Pope to [?] Pope, November 27, 1825, Box 1, Folder 8, Florida Legislative Council (Unicameral), FSA; Petition to Congress by Inhabitants of Jackson County, December 11, 1827, Carter and Bloom, *Territorial Papers*, 23:947–50; Shofner, *Jackson County*, 31–32; Stanley, *History of Jackson County*, 43–54; Dorothy Dodd, "Locating the County Seat," 44–54; Clifton Paisley, *Red Hills of Florida*, 57–68; county court system from Message of Acting Governor James Westcott, *Tallahassee Floridian*, January 3, 1832.

26. For Robinson and Russ, see 1829 Property Tax Book, JCC; for purchases by Beveridge and the Nucleus, Tract Book A, JCC, and Shofner, *Jackson County*, 32–33. The Nucleus also targeted Webb for defeat in his contest for the Legislative Council but failed ("Jackson" in *Pensacola Gazette*, August 24, 1827).

27. *Tallahassee Florida Advocate*, November 18, 1828; Report of the House Committee on

Public Lands, January 11, 1828, Carter and Bloom, *Territorial Papers*, 23:998 1000; *Tallahassee Florida Advocate*, February 21, 1829.

28. Shofner, *Jackson County*, 34–35; Stanley, *History of Jackson County*, 47; Dorothy Dodd, "Locating the County Seat," 51–52; Joseph White to *Tallahassee Florida Advocate*, February 21, 1829. Stone himself eventually received a federal marshalship for his troubles (Recommendation [by Nucleus men Richard Call, James Gadsden, Robert Butler, and William P. DuVal] of Lackland M. Stone as U.S. Marshal [South Florida District], October 26, 1829, Carter and Bloom, *Territorial Papers*, 24:781; Commission of Lackland M. Stone as U.S. Marshal, March 4, 1830, ibid., 372–73). However, Stone soon turned on his paymasters. They in turn threatened to remove him from his sinecure through the use of their patronage with then-president Andrew Jackson (L. M. Stone in *Tallahassee Floridian and Advocate*, October 19, 1830).

29. Quote from "Serus" to *Tallahassee Florida Advocate*, November 18, December 27, 1828; Shofner, *Jackson County*, 36–37; Stanley, *History of Jackson County*, 52053; Dorothy Dodd, "Locating the County Seat," 54–55. One Jackson County resident told me in 1996 that he had been taught in a local high school that the Marianna inhabitants had gone to Webbville one night and burned the town down. Certainly this was metaphorically, if not literally, true.

30. Even the most cursory examination of Southern political debates shows the influence of republican ideology and rhetoric (even if it was not all-powerful). One cannot disentangle the influence of ideas about slavery, race, and honor, either, making Southern politics of this era a particularly interesting and complex zone of inquiry. See J. Mills Thornton, *Politics and Power*; Harry L. Watson, *Liberty and Power, Jacksonian Politics*, and "Common Rights of Mankind"; Ford, *Origins of Southern Radicalism*; Harris, *Plain Folk and Gentry*; McCurry, "Two Faces of Republicanism" and *Masters of Small Worlds*, and many others. For the historiography of republican ideology in American history as a whole, one might begin with the excellent and skeptical article Rodgers, "Republicanism: The Career of a Concept," and his footnotes of Bernard Bailyn, J. G. A. Pocock, and Caroline Robbins.

31. "Moon Light," *Tallahassee Floridian*, January 11, 1834.

32. Walker-Read duel from Long, *Florida Breezes*, 97–98. See also Denham, "Read-Alston Duel"; Proclamation of Gov. John Eaton, January 8, 1835, Carter and Bloom, *Territorial Papers*, 25:155–56; William Wyatt in *Jacksonville Courier*, April 9, 1835.

33. "Office-Hunters," *Tallahassee Floridian*, June 29, 1839; "all things by turns" from *Marianna Florida Whig*, April 12, 1848; "land office 'tit'" from *Tallahassee Floridian*, February 9, 1833; for DuVal's political meanderings, see Richard Call to George Graham, November 10, 1826, Carter and Bloom, *Territorial Papers*, 23:663; *Tallahassee Floridian and Advocate*, December 15, 1829; "The Querist" in ibid., February 24, 1831; Joseph White, *Tallahassee Floridian*, April 20, 1831; ibid., May 6, 26, 1831; and Doherty, *Whigs of Florida*, 9.

34. "Commission of William P. DuVal as Governor," April 17, 1822, Carter and Bloom, *Territorial Papers*, 22:469–70; "An Act Establishing the Territory of Florida," March 30, 1822, ibid., 389–99; Hall and Rise, *From Local Courts to National Tribunals*, 5–20; "regiment of Colonels" from Joseph White, *Tallahassee Floridian and Advocate*, May 26, 1831. Earlier historians of territorial Florida asserted that factions pre-

figured parties and that lines between factions simply hardened into those shaping parties after 1838. For such views, see Arthur Thompson, *Jacksonian Democracy*, 1–16; Doherty, *Whigs of Florida*, 1–17; Martin, *Florida during Territorial Days*, 50–51; and [Myers], "Reminiscences of the Early Days." However, there was more to territorial politics than a world slouching toward the birth of Democrats and Whigs. For the transition from faction to party elsewhere, see Sellers, "Jackson Men"; Wallace, "Changing Concepts of Party"; and Harry L. Watson, *Jacksonian Politics*, 111–13, 151–97.

35. For the election see Delegate White to the Secretary of State, March 10, 1831, Carter and Bloom, *Territorial Papers*, 24:508–13; and James Westcott in *Tallahassee Floridian and Advocate*, August 11, 1831; "If the majority" from ibid., August 4, 1831; "Gov. DuVal" from ibid., August 17, 1831. The speaker also pointed out the lack of party-based or ideological connections to national politics, which permitted pronullification James Gadsden to draw support via Richard Call from the United States' greatest antebellum Unionist, Andrew Jackson. For DuVal's ability to say one thing in Washington and another in Tallahassee, see Doherty, *Whigs of Florida*, 9, and Joseph White in *Tallahassee Floridian and Advocate*, May 26, 1831.

36. "Another Dreadful Steamboat Disaster" by "Philo Pecum," *Tallahassee Floridian and Advocate*, August 17, 1831.

37. "The oft-told tale" from *Tallahassee Floridian*, May 4, 1839; Randall from *Pensacola Gazette*, May 9, 1828; "political slang" from *Tallahassee Floridian and Advocate*, September 1, 1829.

38. Franklin, *Militant South*, which discusses many of the themes, was later followed by these works: Wyatt-Brown, *Southern Honor*; Ayers, *Vengeance and Justice*; Greenberg, *Honor and Slavery*; Bruce, *Violence and Culture*; and Jack K. Williams, *Dueling in the Old South*. Works incorporating themes of gender, mastery, and honor into broader analyses of Southern social structure include McCurry, *Masters of Small Worlds* and "Two Faces of Republicanism"; Faust, *James Henry Hammond*; Gorn, "'Gouge and Bite,'" 18–43; Stowe, *Intimacy and Power*; Kathleen M. Brown, *Good Wives, Nasty Wenches*; and Heyrman, *Southern Cross*. Wyatt-Brown's work also draws upon anthropological works about violence and honor in Mediterranean society; see Peristiany, *Honor and Shame*, and Pitt-Rivers, *Mediterranean Countrymen*.

39. I use "manhood," "manliness," and "masculinity" interchangeably as analytical vocabulary. The most powerful exemplar of the anthropological view that sees manhood as constant may be Gilmore, *Manhood in the Making*; but see also Badinter, *XY*. Feminist scholars have pioneered the study of gender, including masculinity, as a complex of ideas that change over time. See Kerber, "Separate Spheres," and Bederman, *Manliness and Civilization*. For the burgeoning historiography of masculinity in the United States, see ibid.; Kimmel, *Manhood in America*; Rotundo, *American Manhood*; Carnes and Griffen, *Meanings for Manhood*; Nelson, *National Manhood*; and Castronovo, *Fathering the Nation*.

40. Some scholars see ideas of Southern white masculinity and honor as unchanging sources of stability during the colonial and antebellum periods. See, for example, Wyatt-Brown, *Southern Honor*, and Greenberg, *Honor and Slavery*. Others see sharp changes in the history of white Southern masculinity. See Gorn, "'Gouge

and Bite'"; Kathleen M. Brown, *Good Wives, Nasty Wenches;* Ownby, *Subduing Satan;* and Cashin, *Family Venture.*

41. "Accustomed" from Castelnau, "Essay on Middle Florida," pt. 1, 236; "I am" from *Pensacola Gazette,* February 26, 1825.

42. "There lives" from letter to John Pope, quoted in *Pensacola Gazette and West Florida Advertiser,* April 2, 1825; see also Call, in *Floridian and Advocate,* October 26, 1830; Call to George Graham, September 10, 1825, Carter and Bloom, *Territorial Papers,* 23:316; and "Off-Hand Notes of a Moving Gentleman. No. II. Tallahassee," *The New-Yorker,* vol. 2, January 21, 1837, 286.

43. "Where I rule" quoted by "Junius" in *Tallahassee Floridian,* March 20, 1833; "Some men" from *Tallahassee Floridian,* March 23, 1833, cited in Hill, "Joseph M. White," 30. Jefferson, if he indeed said these words, had in turn borrowed them from a seventeenth-century republican martyr (Adair, "Rumbold's Dying Speech, 1685, and Jefferson's Last Words on Democracy, 1826," in Adair, *Fame and the Founding Fathers,* 192–202).

44. "I am a horse" from Castelnau, "Essay on Middle Florida," pt. 1, 239; "stiffer bit" from "Junius" in *Tallahassee Floridian,* March 20, 1833; Call and Peggy Eaton from Andrew Jackson to William B. Lewis, September 10, 1829, Bassett, *Correspondence of Andrew Jackson,* 4:72–73. See also Isaac Harris to Isaac Jarratt, August 27, 1835, Box 1, Jarrett-Puryear Papers, Duke. For early modern European colonists who used "riding" metaphors to describe both homosexual or heterosexual penetration and gendered class hierarchy among men, see Trexler, *Sex and Conquest,* and Kathleen M. Brown, *Good Wives, Nasty Wenches,* 19. For the horse as submissive male power subordinated to a more manly rider, see Faust, *James Henry Hammond,* 11. For male-male sexuality and power, see ibid., 18 n–19 n.

45. Quote from "A Citizen of Jackson" in *Pensacola Gazette and West Florida Advertiser,* April 2, 1833; Douglass Memoirs, 108–10, FSU; Ormond, *Reminiscences,* 18–20; *Jacksonville Courier,* August 6, 1835. See Chapter 5 for a discussion of the implications of these punishments.

46. On the duel as the ruling metaphor of elite (or, according to some historians, all) Southern white males' masculinities, see Stowe, *Intimacy and Power,* 7, who calls it "the most visible part of the affair of honor, a masculine ritual that went deeply into the realms of authority and manhood in the planter elite," and Greenberg, *Honor and Slavery,* 35. The duel was a metaphor for all planters' ideas about masculinity, but not all fights over honor were duels. Despite Greenberg's contentions, Frederick Douglass and the Maryland slave-breaker Edward Covey did not engage in anything that contemporaries would have recognized as a duel. Covey's planter employers (for whom he subdued or "broke" recalcitrant slaves like Douglass — although Douglass ended up breaking Covey) would not have agreed to fight a formal duel with Covey, a rough and uneducated man of dubious origins.

47. Putnam from *Tallahassee Floridian,* February 22, 1840; repeal (vetoed by Governor DuVal) in *Tallahassee Floridian,* March 3, 1831; differential prosecution from Chapter 5 of this book. See a case in which one planter supposedly prevented his overseer from fighting a duel: [Myers], "Reminiscences of the Early Days."

48. An instructive historiography of honor, dueling, and masculinity has grown up in European history, although historians of the Old South have yet to incorporate

this scholarship into much published work. It offers a consciousness of historical changes in ideals of honor and masculinity absent from much of the scholarship on honor in the Old South. See the text and bibliography of Muir, *Mad Blood Stirring* and "The Double Binds of Manly Revenge," in Trexler, *Gender Rhetorics*; Neuschel, *Word of Honor*; Kelly, *That Damn'd Thing Called Honour*; Nye, *Masculinity and Male Codes of Honor*; Reddy, *Invisible Code*; Spierenburg, *Men and Violence*; and the bibliography in Wyatt-Brown, "Andrew Jackson's Honor."

49. "Citizens" from *Tallahassee Floridian and Advocate*, April 14, 1831; White and Alba from *Pensacola Gazette and West Florida Advertiser*, January 8, 22, 1825; Wyatt and Searcy from *Tallahassee Floridian*, October 23, 1832. See also apocryphal account of George Hamlin's 1835 horsewhipping of Alexander Campbell, which led to a duel fatal to Campbell, in Elizabeth F. Smith, *Life along the Magnolia Road*, xiii, and *Tallahassee Star of Florida*, February 10, 1892. For a series of attempted "postings," see *Tallahassee Floridian and Advocate*, April 20, 1831. For an explicit example of the choice between "flogging" an opponent and submitting to their "domination," see *Tallahassee Florida Sentinel*, July 22, 1842. For dueling as a form of politics (or vice versa?) see *Jacksonville Courier*, August 6, 1835, and Freeman, "Dueling as a Form of Politics."

50. Ward, Parish, and Alston from Denham, "Dueling in Territorial Middle Florida," 46–74; murder of Jordan from Charles Hentz Memoir, 169–74, Hentz Family Papers, SHC; see also *Tallahassee Floridian*, July 29, 1837.

51. *Pensacola Gazette*, from the *Pendleton (S.C.) Messenger*, May 9, 1828; Thomas Randall from *Pensacola Gazette*, May 9, 1828.

52. See [Myers], "Reminiscences of the Early Days."

53. Lewis Taylor to William Haynie Hatchett, September 26, 1836, Hatchett Papers, Duke.

54. [Myers], "Reminiscences of the Early Days"; Stowe, *Intimacy and Power*, 15–23; from Muir, *Mad Blood Stirring*, 68; Black-Michaud, *Cohesive Force*, 80–85; Banfield, *Moral Basis of a Backward Society*.

55. For the Eaton affair (Eaton became Florida's territorial governor in 1834–35), see Marszalek, *Petticoat Affair*; Kirsten F. Wood, "'One Woman So Dangerous'"; and Doherty, *Richard K. Call*, 52–56; "swarms of officers" from *Tallahassee Floridian*, June 20, 1832; see also "land office 'tit'" from ibid., February 9, 1833; "Poll Book River" from *Tallahassee Floridian and Advocate*, August 17, 1831.

56. DuVal's vetoes from *Tallahassee Floridian and Advocate*, December 15, 1829; Mc-Grane, *Foreign Bondholders*, 223–24; and William P. DuVal to Legislative Council, January 31, 1831, Legislative Council Journal, vol. 1 (1831–36), FSA; for requests for banks to improve local currency circulation and provide credit, see Inhabitants of Tallahassee, Leon County, and Gadsden County to the Legislative Council, November 30, 1825, Box 1, Folder 8, Florida Legislative Council (Unicameral), FSA; and William P. DuVal to Nicholas Biddle, February 15, 1831, Box 1, Folder 4, Outgoing Correspondence of the Territorial Governors, FSA.

57. "The time has arrived" from *Tallahassee Floridian*, June 20, 1832; for the Gambles see "Biographical Sketch of the Gamble Family," Folder 1, and "Extracts from the Journal of Major Robert Gamble," Folder 2, Boxes 147–48, Gamble Family Papers, FSU; Tuckett, *Journey in the United States*, 55.

58. *Tallahassee Floridian*, February 9, 1833; "true planters' bank" from ibid., February 23, 1833; Thomas Bradford from Superior Court Minute Book 1, 151, 162, 200, LCC; "congratulate" from *Tallahassee Floridian*, February 2, 1833; McGrane, *Foreign Bondholders*, 225–27; Abbey, "Union Bank of Tallahassee."

59. U.S. Congress, House, *Condition of Banks, 1840;* Abbey, "Union Bank of Tallahassee."

60. Although these banks financed the cotton boom of the 1830s, which in turn drove the wider U.S. economic expansion, they remain to a large extent outside narratives of both Southern and U.S. economic, social, and political changes of the period. Instead, they have been confined to a fairly specialized literature on the history of banking. See Hammond, *Banks and Politics in America;* Engerman, "Note on the Economic Consequences"; McFaul, *Politics of Jacksonian Finance;* George Green, *Finance and Economic Development;* Temin, *Jacksonian Economy;* Schweikart, *Banking in the American South;* Kilbourne, *Debt, Investment, Slaves;* Davis and Cull, *International Capital Markets;* Jenks, *Migration of British Capital*, 65–98; Lewis C. Gray, *History of Agriculture,* 2:898–901 and elsewhere; and Baptist, "Cotton, Credit, and Capital."

61. McGrane, *Foreign Bondholders*, 226–28; William P. DuVal to President of the Legislative Council, January 17, 1834, Carter and Bloom, *Territorial Papers,* 24:943.

62. "New York confederates" from Catherine Wirt to Mrs. Louis Goldsborough, August 30, 1834, Folder 4, Wirt Family Papers, SHC; "hailed with" and "[t]his sudden influx" from *Tallahassee Floridian,* January 17, 1835; "The way" from Thomas Randall to Peter Hagner, March 13, 1838, Folder 66, Hagner Papers, SHC.

63. *Tallahassee Floridian,* July 25, 1835.

64. "I have" from Thomas Randall to Peter Hagner, March 13, 1838, Folder 66, Hagner Papers, SHC; "build[ing] up from *Tallahassee Floridian,* July 25, 1835; Groene, *Ante-Bellum Tallahassee,* 83–85; John Tappan to Benjamin French, December 13, 1841, Tappan Letter, FSL; for the increasing prosperity of Jackson (as well as Leon) County, see R. H. Long to Farish Carter, December 12, 1837, Folder 12, Carter Papers, SHC.

65. John Parkhill to Francis Eppes, August 8, 1838, Folder 6, Parkhill Family Papers, SHC.

66. Report of Florida House Judiciary Committee, in Wilson, "Development of Florida Territory," 95; U.S. Congress, House, *Condition of Banks, 1840,* 325–44; quote on 290. Thomas Brown had the twelfth-largest share.

67. "Masters" and "community" from *Tallahassee Floridian,* January 16, 1841.

68. "Plain Truth" in *Pensacola Gazette and West Florida Advertiser,* February 26, 1825.

CHAPTER FIVE

1. E. E. Blackburn to *Tallahassee Floridian,* August 22, 1840; Lewis Hyde, *Trickster Makes This World.* For Florida Jack Tales, see Reaver, *Florida Folktales;* for Jack as a symbol of manhood, see Sobol, "Jack of a Thousand Faces," 79–80.

2. *Tallahassee Star of Florida,* January 17, 1845.

3. Gramsci, *Selections from the Prison Notebooks;* Lears, "Concept of Cultural Hege-

mony"; Gardiner, *Dialogics of Critique*, 183–87. See also James Scott, *Domination and the Arts of Resistance*, 70–96, on "thick" and "thin" versions of hegemony and false consciousness; by contrast, see the differing interpretation in Genovese, "On Antonio Gramsci," *In Red and Black*, 391–422, esp. 407. For discussions of the differences, and of some of the problems with historians' uses of the theories of Gramsci, see Lears, "Concept of Cultural Hegemony," and Scott, *Domination and the Arts of Resistance*, 70–107. Note also Lears's, "*AHR* Forum," esp. 1423, in which he says, "Legitimation, not manipulation, is the key to cultural hegemony," and the associated footnote, which adds: "I tried to make this point in T. J. Jackson Lears, 'The Concept of Cultural Hegemony,' . . . but scholarly audiences have been misreading it ever since." For the classic exposition of hegemonic incorporation of yeomen in the antebellum South, see Genovese, "Yeoman Farmers in a Slaveholders' Democracy," 249–64. The best use of the concept of hegemony in antebellum Southern historiography is McCurry, *Masters of Small Worlds*. But whether she concludes that hegemony—or manipulation—was the final cause of yeoman support for the slaveholders' regime is open to interpretation.

4. *Tallahassee Florida Advocate*, March 14, 1829; E. J. Bowen to William P. DuVal, September 22, 1831, Box 1, Folder 11, Outgoing Correspondence of the Territorial Governors, FSA; *Jacksonville Courier*, July 2, 1835; Castelnau, "Essay on Middle Florida," pt. 1, 239; Denham, *Rogue's Paradise*, 59–73.

5. See Wyatt-Brown, *Southern Honor*, 353.

6. Chase, *Jack Tales*, 67–75.

7. Statistics from Superior Court Minute Book 1, LCC. Westcott from April 9, 1832, 369, ibid. The eleven different indictments do not include many of the duels or other incidents of political violence discussed in previous chapters. For that reason alone, these eleven indictments can only be the tip of the iceberg when we attempt to measure either the level of elite violence in early Leon County or the degree to which the legal system took no notice.

8. "Citizens" in *Tallahassee Floridian and Advocate*, April 14, 1831. For Richard Hayward, see October 8, 1829, 141, April 9, 1833, 498, April 10, 1833, 500, Superior Court Minute Book 1, LCC. (Jackson County's court records from this period survive only in fragments.) For the system's countenance of elite homicide, see the case of a shootout at Shell Point in Southern Leon County in which three planter men died but no one was prosecuted, reported in *Tallahassee Floridian*, July 29, August 5, 12, 1837, and February 22, 1840.

9. Statistics from Superior Court Minute Book 1, LCC. David C. Wilson, November 10, 1833, 500; Jesse Wiggins, April 9, 1832, 389; John S. Taylor, October 6, 1830, 259; Joel Yancey, October 7, 1830, all ibid. I define poor whites here as those without slaves as recorded in the 1830 U.S. Census or 1829 Property Tax Book, rather than those without land, since so few countrymen had achieved landholding that early. I also excluded cases like that of James Westcott, who owned only one slave in 1830 but who was secretary of the territory.

10. Edward Ballard from October 9, 1828, 88, Superior Court Minute Book 1, LCC. See also Bolton, *Poor Whites*, 58–65, who analyzes differential patterns of punishment and conviction in a North Carolina county. He finds that yeomen were punished less severely than poor whites, especially those without roots in the local commu-

nity. Leon County yeomen convicted of these crimes against person, however, were apparently inflicted with penalties equal to those doled out to the unpropertied. Finally, as I note above, some of those who show up in the nonslaveholding poor white category were in fact members of yeoman families and kinship networks. For fugitives, see John Vickers, April 8, 1828, 54, and Angus Johnson, April 9, 1828, 59, Superior Court Minute Book 1, LCC. Denham, *Rogue's Paradise*, contains dozens of examples of Florida fugitives. See also Bolton and Culclasure, *Confessions of Edward Isham*.

11. Committee on Elections, February 10, 1832, Box 3, Folder 4, Florida Legislative Council (Unicameral), FSA; Gorn, "'Gouge and Bite.'"

12. Murat, *United States of North America*, 66–67, claimed that on juries, "all ranks . . . are here confounded," but actual Leon County jury lists echo Bolton's finding that North Carolina juries included almost no one but slaveholders (Superior Court Minute Book 1, LCC; Bolton, *Poor Whites of the Antebellum South*, 59–60).

13. Statistics from Superior Court Minute Book 1, LCC. Westcott from ibid., April 9, 1932, 369; for George Chew, see Douglass Memoirs, 20, FSU, and April 8, 1828, 53 (nonconviction on a gambling charge), Superior Court Minute Book 1, LCC; "amount to disfranchisement" from Committee on Elections, February 10, 1832, Box 3, Folder 4, Florida Legislative Council (Unicameral), FSA.

14. "Then boast" from George Moses Horton's "The Creditor to his Proud Debtor," in Sherman, *Black Bard of North Carolina*, 96–97; Bob Penn, April 8, 1831, 305; John Pearce, November 17, 1831, 343, and Superior Court Minute Book 1, LCC; Groene, *Ante-bellum Tallahassee*, 97. On the humiliation and dishonoring of whipping and branding, see "Patriotism to be produced by the Cowskin," in *Tallahassee Floridian*, September 12, 1840.

15. For planter arrogance, see "Philo Fair-Fight" in *Tallahassee Floridian*, April 14, 1838. For resentment of the "Tallahassee Gentry," see "Jackson County" in ibid., January 25, 1834.

16. "Freemen of Florida" from Joseph M. White to *Tallahassee Floridian and Advocate*, May 19, 1831, "Patriotism" in *Tallahassee Floridian*, September 12, 1840; Call accused of seeking to restrict ballot in ibid., May 4, 1833; *"nothing less"* from ibid., August 4, 1831.

17. R. B. Kerr quoted in *Tallahassee Floridian*, September 22, 1838; see also ibid., March 28, 1840.

18. Charles Hentz Memoir, 177–78, Hentz Family Papers, SHC; see also Stowe, *Southern Practice*, 1–37.

19. Charles Hentz Memoir, 177–78, Hentz Family Papers, SHC; see also Stowe, *Southern Practice*, 1–37.

20. Wyatt-Brown, *Southern Honor*, 368–69, discusses violence that crossed class lines but denies class differences. See also Gorn, "'Gouge and Bite,'" 36; Bederman, *Manliness and Civilization*, 5–10; Pieter Spierenburg, "Masculinity, Violence, and Honor," in Spierenburg, *Men and Violence*.

21. Quote from Whipple, *Southern Diary*, 24–25; indictments of Dawson and Chesley Boatwright for assault and battery, October 11, 1828, 95–96, Superior Court Minute Book 1, LCC; Shofner, *History of Jefferson County*, 152.

22. Asa W. Chamberlain vs. John and James Dickerson et al., 1828, case file 114, Law

Case Files, LCC. A jury composed almost entirely of yeomen approved the actions of the Dickersons, rejecting Chamberlain's suit against a codefendant, James Willis, and forcing Chamberlain to drop his suit against the brothers (October 12, 1829, 150, Superior Court Minute Book 1, LCC).

23. Quote from Charles Hentz Memoir, 167, Hentz Family Papers, SHC; Gorn, "'Gouge and Bite.'" Edward Muir, "The Double Binds of Manly Revenge," in Trexler, *Gender Rhetorics*, 65–83, discusses the historiography of the rise of dueling, and the perception that only dueling was structured by rules.

24. For quotes on women and men, see toasts by "Mr. Smith" and "G. W. Smith" at Magnolia, in *Tallahassee Floridian and Advertiser*, July 20, 1830.

25. Charles Hentz Memoir, 168–69, 167, Hentz Family Papers, SHC.

26. "Pine Crackers" from Tuckett, *Journey in the United States*, 60; *Tallahassee Floridian*, September 14, 1839; *Marianna Whig*, July 15, 1848; *Tallahassee Star of Florida*, February 16, 1843; *Tallahassee Floridian*, October 3, 1840.

27. Asa W. Chamberlain vs. John and James Dickerson et al., 1828, case file 114, Law Case Files, LCC.

28. Johnson Cook from *Tallahassee Floridian*, February 2, 1839; William Bassett vs. William McGraw and William Wilson, 1829, case file 145; William Wilson vs. George Fisher, 1828, case file 82; and Obadiah Gordon vs. William Rider, 1829, case file 183, all Law Case Files, LCC; February 24, 1849, [35], Charles Hentz Diary, 1848–51, Hentz Family Papers, SHC.

29. John Tappan to Benjamin French, December 13, 1841, Tappan Letter, FSL.

30. "A nondescript" from Whipple, *Southern Journey*, 74–75; "wise acre" from February 24, 1849, Charles Hentz Diary, 1848–51, Hentz Family Papers, SHC; see also *Tallahassee Florida Sentinel*, November 12, 1841.

31. "Big Jack and Little Jack," in Chase, *Jack Tales*.

32. *Tallahassee Star of Florida*, October 6, 1842; Baptist, "Accidental Ethnography." Snell made a brief reappearance (see *Tallahassee Star of Florida*, January 1, 1843).

33. "Some of these fellows" from Whipple, *Southern Diary*, 26–28; Baptist, "Accidental Ethnography"; Long, *Florida Breezes*, 237–39. On the differences between black and white tricksters, see Ellison, "Change the Joke and Slip the Yoke."

34. Longstreet, *Georgia Scenes*, 229–30, and *Longstreet's Georgia Tales Completed;* see also the tactics of Jefferson County planters Abram Bellamy and his father John in Grenelle, "Bellamys of Territorial Florida," 40–41.

35. See the concept of the carnivalesque, as described in Bakhtin, *Rabelais and His World*, and as critiqued in Emerson, "Problems with Baxtin's Poetics," and Stallybrass and White, *Politics and Poetics of Transgression*, 1–30, 38–39. The concept of "authoring" a self through dialogue with others comes in part from Bakhtin's essay "Author and Hero," discussed in Emerson and Morson, *Mikhail Bakhtin*, 184–86.

36. Murat, *United States of North America*, 53; see also McCurry, *Masters of Small Worlds*, 101, and Faragher, *Sugar Creek*, 104, 208–9.

37. M. Hagan to Mrs. Sarah Ann Groover, August 11, 1847, Hagan Papers, FSU; "Dear little" from "On the Death of the Reverend Theophilus Hardie . . . The Widow's Complaint," ibid.; Allen, *Allen's Journal*, 20; see also Charles Hentz Memoir, 251, Hentz Family Papers, SHC, and Faragher, *Sugar Creek*, 87–118.

38. Hagan, "On Staying Alone the First Time in Life All Night," and "My Farewell to

My Friends and Brethren, 1825 in April," Hagan Papers, FSU; Mary C. Johnston to James Dickson, May 2, 1843, Folder 4, Carr Papers, SHC.

39. Petition of Mary Rhymes, January 17, 1832, Box 3, Folder 4; Deposition of David Clements, February 7, 1832, Box 3, Folder 4; Petition of Mahalah T. Waugh, 1831, Box 3, Folder 2; Petition of Lorena Runnell, February 3, 1831, Box 3, Folder 2; Mahala Wadkins Petition, October 14, 1828, Box 2, Folder 6, all Florida Legislative Council (Unicameral), FSA; Hagan, "On the Death of Jesse Butler," Hagan Papers, FSU; "Indictment of John Watkins, yeoman," October 15, 1828, 103–7, Superior Court Minute Book 1, LCC. On intimate violence in yeoman households in other parts of the South, see Edwards, "Sexual Violence"; McCurry, *Masters of Small Worlds*; and Bardaglio, *Reconstructing the Household*, 3–36.

40. "Devlish Mary" from Morris, *Folksongs of Florida*, 151–52.

41. Petition of Alfred Evans, 1832; Petition of Lemuel Turner, January 14, 1832; Petition of Enoch Dudley, January 22, 1832, all Box 3, Folder 4; Petition of H. L. Stone, January 25, 1833, Box 3, Folder 7; Petition of Zachariah Jenkins, December 27, 1830, Box 3, Folder 2, all Florida Legislative Council (Unicameral), FSA.

42. Hagan, "On the Marriage of My Third Daughter Elizabeth to Mr. Ben Hagan in 1827, July 7," Hagan Papers, FSU.

43. Tuckett, *Journey in the United States*, 54 (quote); Long, *Florida Breezes*, 170 (quote), 196. For political consciousness of common white women, see *Tallahassee Floridian*, September 19, 1840, and Brown Memoir, vol. 2, 32, Folder 1, Ambler-Brown Papers, Duke.

44. Petition of Lorena Runnell, Florida Legislative Council (Unicameral), FSA; Castelnau, "Essay on Middle Florida," pt. 2, 237–38.

45. "Render" from Petition of Susan Rhymes, Box 3, Folder 4, Florida Legislative Council (Unicameral), FSA; Petition of Mahalah Waugh; and Petition of Lorena Runnell, ibid.; Petition of Huldah Manning, 1844, Box 4, Folder 3, and Petition of Susan Dozier, 1844, Box 4, Folder 3, Florida Legislative Council (Bicameral), FSA; "bosom friend" from Hagan, "On the Death of the Reverend Theophilus Hardie"; "hold a gentle reign" from Hagan, "On the Marriage of My Third Daughter Elizabeth"; "companion" from Hagan, "My Farewell"; "mate" from "On the Death of Mrs. Mariah Hart, Composed by N. H. for Mr. Hart," all Hagan Papers, FSU. For countrywomen's acceptance of some aspects of manly honor, see "Many of the women" from Eppes, *Through Some Eventful Years*, 224.

46. Hagan, "On the Death of Mrs. Mariah Hart."

47. Historians of Southern women who, among other things, try to explain the absence of Southern women's movements parallel to those in the antebellum North include Friedman, *Enclosed Garden*; Fox-Genovese, *Within the Plantation Household*; and Lebsock, *Free Women of Petersburg*.

48. Sparks, *On Jordan's Stormy Banks*, 41–59; Heyrman, *Southern Cross*, esp. 161–205; Friedman, *Enclosed Garden*; McCurry, *Masters of Small Worlds*, 130–207; Mathews, *Religion in the Old South*, 109–11. The differentials in punishment and attendance like those found by McCurry in low-country South Carolina evangelical churches (*Masters of Small Worlds*, 160) continued after the Civil War. See Ownby, *Subduing Satan*, 134–36.

49. Statistics from *Register of Members*, vol. 1, 1830–1903, Pisgah United Methodist

Church Records, FSA. Of 77 full members by 1841, 33 were male and 44 were female. Of 31 that joined before their families or singly, 13 were male and 18, female. These statistics compare well with those of broader studies: Sparks found that 62 percent of Mississippi evangelicals were female (*On Jordan's Stormy Banks*, 214 n. 6); and Mathews estimated an overall ratio of 65:35 for the antebellum South (*Religion in the Old South*, 47–48, 108).

50. For sex-segregated activities, see Long, *Florida Breezes*, 194, and Faragher, *Sugar Creek*, 110–13. For the closeness and community of some Leon settlements, see, for example, "Deposition of Madison Dancer" in Petition of Enoch Dudley, January 22, 1832, Box 3, Folder 4, Florida Legislative Council (Unicameral), FSA.

51. *Register of Members*, vol. 1, 1830–1903, Pisgah United Methodist Church Records, FSA; Richardson, *Lights and Shadows of Itinerant Life*, 40 (quote), 48, 106, 117–18; Longstreet, *Georgia Scenes*, 216; January 17, 1849, 24, Charles Hentz Diary, 1848–51, Hentz Family Papers, SHC. Shofner, *History of Jefferson County*, 61, identifies Nancy Hagan as a midwife in the Leon-Jefferson County area.

52. James C. Bryant, *Indian Springs*; Hagan, "On the Death of the Reverend Theophilus Hardie."

53. Hagan, "A Letter to a Widow Lady in Virginia by the Name of Osborne on the Death of Her Daughter Mrs. Judah Bach in 1829," Hagan Papers, FSU.

54. Hagan, "On an Evening's Walk with Two Female Friends," Hagan Papers, FSU.

55. Longstreet, *Georgia Scenes*, 215; 1830 U.S. Census, Leon County.

56. Hagan, "On the Death of Mrs. Mariah Hart"; Hagan, "On the Death of Isom Johnson," Hagan Papers, FSU.

57. Hagan, "A Copy of the Letter Laid before Mt. Moriah Church in Jefferson County," Hagan Papers, FSU; circus from Groene, *Ante-Bellum Tallahassee*, 159 (citing *Tallahassee Floridian*, March 13, 1838).

58. Wyatt-Brown, "Anti-Mission Movement"; Hagan, "On the Baptizing of Some Black People in the Miccosukkee Pond in an Extreme Dry Time in 1830"; Hagan, "A Line Written on the Pleasure of Having a New Church Built, Which May Be Called Sweet Liberty, May 20, 1843"; and Copy of Georgia Historical Commission sign at Grooverville, Ga., Hagan Papers, FSU.

59. Ginzburg, *Cheese and the Worms*, esp. xx–xxii, discusses the problems and possibilities of understanding, through the writings of exceptional individuals, the histories of groups who left few documents in their own voices. See also McCurry, *Masters of Small Worlds*, 85, 179–84. For a contrasting perspective, see Ownby, *Subduing Satan*, 122–39.

60. J. W. Hagan to Dear Mother, March 10 and September 17, 1842, Box 4, Folder 3, Florida Legislative Council (Bicameral), FSA; "Mother died" from M. Hagan to Sarah Ann Groover, August 11, 1847, Hagan Papers, FSU; "a very godly woman" from Huxford, *Pioneers of Wiregrass Georgia*, 1:325–26. Genealogist and family historian Huxford, who was so focused on celebrating lines of patriarchal descent that he did not even list women as index entries in his books (they were grouped under the names of husbands and fathers), still noted in his entry for John Hagan: "The church [Liberty]'s centennial a few years ago centered largely on the memory of this old saint," meaning his widow Nancy Hagan, of course.

61. *Tallahassee Floridian*, September 19, 1840.

62. Hagan, "On Staying Alone."

63. Rawick, *American Slave*, 17:347 (Willis Williams); for Hayward as a pro-bank Whig, see *Tallahassee Floridian*, August 22, 1840.

64. [Myers], "Reminiscences of the Early Days."

65. Myers (ibid.) claims that Barnes became Hayward's overseer. Thus, by returning Barnes to the classically subordinate position of overseer (doing the planter's dirty work), he restores a mythical deference shattered by Barnes's act of beating up the elite man. But what Myers does not explain is what it meant to Hayward that his employee had defeated him.

CHAPTER SIX

1. *Tallahassee Floridian*, March 20, 1841.

2. Memorial of the Legislative Council to Congress, January 6, 1827, Carter and Bloom, *Territorial Papers*, 23:712; Mahon, *Second Seminole War*, 68–113.

3. *Tallahassee Floridian*, December 17, 1835; Mahon, *Second Seminole War*, 114–89; Sprague, *Florida War*.

4. Mahon, *Second Seminole War*, 135–89, 245–73; quote from *Tallahassee Floridian*, June 8, 1839.

5. Sec'y of War to Pres. Van Buren, November 29, 1839, Carter and Bloom, *Territorial Papers*, 25:656–65; R. Call to Congress, February 26, 1840, ibid., 26:89–109; Doherty, *Richard K. Call*, 114–17; "The war" from *Tallahassee Floridian*, April 6, 1839.

6. Attack on Chaires plantation from James T. Campbell, "Charles Hutchinson Letters," 19; Douglass Memoirs, 108–10, FSU; attack on Bailey's Mills from *Tallahassee Floridian*, August 4, 1838; Lasley from ibid., July 28, 1838. On other attacks, see ibid., May 7, 1836; January 28, July 1, 1837; March 3, April 14, 21, 1838; March 16, 23, February 16, April 6, May 11, June 8, November 15, 1839; June 6, August 29, 1840; June 6, August 28, October 29, 1841; and August 18, 1842; for the Creeks, see Levin Brown to Gov. Call, May 18, 1836, Folder 1, Box 2, Outgoing Correspondence of Governor Call, FSA; and *Tallahassee Floridian*, November 18, 1837, May 18, 1839, February 15, 1840.

7. Joseph White to James Barbour, July 1827, Carter and Bloom, *Territorial Papers*, 23:898–901.

8. Joseph White to J. Knowles, February 15, 1837, ibid., 25:378–79.

9. Joseph White to Andrew Jackson, May 14, 1836, ibid., 25:283; *Tallahassee Floridian*, August 4, 1838; for more fears see [?] to Elizabeth G. W. Goldsborough, January 25, 1836, Folder 3, Goldsborough Papers, Duke, and William Wilson to Dear Brother and Sister, February 28, 1836, Wilson Papers, FSU.

10. Linton from *Tallahassee Floridian*, June 8, 1839; killing of Perrine and family, ibid., September 12, 1840; and Gov. Reid to Secretary of War, August 22, 1840, Carter and Bloom, *Territorial Papers*, 26:202; "white *devil*" from *Tallahassee Sentinel*, October 29, 1841.

11. Report of Florida House Judiciary Committee, in Wilson, "Development of Florida Territory," 95; "with nothing" from William Wyatt in *Tallahassee Floridian*, May 17, 1838; see also "A Friend of the Prosperity of Florida," ibid., August 11, 1838.

12. *"The brother"* and "the Governor" from John Branch to the President, February 5, 1839, Carter and Bloom, *Territorial Papers*, 25:584–85; "I am opposed" from "Office-Hunters" in *Tallahassee Floridian*, June 29, 1839; U.S. Congress, House, *Condition of Banks, 1840*, 241–438. Local merchants also resented the bank for playing favorites in discounting bills and for destabilizing currency. See, for example, William P. DuVal to John Parkhill, July 23, 1839, Folder 6, Parkhill Family Papers, SHC, and "Calhoun" in *Tallahassee Floridian*, March 14, 1840.

13. "Vassalage" from *Tallahassee Floridian*, January 14, 1837; "galling" from ibid., April 6, 1839; "Journal and Proceedings," December 3, 1838, 133–34 (for members), and "St. Joseph's Convention," 47–66, in Dorothy Dodd, *Florida Becomes a State*.

14. Quoted in Dorothy Dodd, "St. Joseph's Convention," 53. See also Moussalli, "Florida's Frontier Constitution."

15. James D. Westcott Jr. to the President, June 12, 1829, Carter and Bloom, *Territorial Papers*, 24:237; Commission of James Westcott as Secretary, June 15, 1829, ibid., 238–39; Joseph White to Martin Van Buren, January 26, 1830, ibid., 319–37; Thomas Brown to James Westcott, July 3, 1830, ibid., 423–24; toast by James Westcott in *Tallahassee Floridian and Advocate*, July 13, 1830.

16. Dorothy Dodd, "St. Joseph's Convention," 55–60; "Convention Journal," in Dorothy Dodd, *Florida Becomes a State*, December 15, 1938, 184–85; December 27, 1838, 214–18; January 3–4, 1839, 231–51, 316, 322–24; and "Florida Jeffersonian Republican Meeting," January 11, 1839, 334–36.

17. *Tallahassee Floridian*, June 29, 1839; "managers" from Elijah Callaway to William P. DuVal, February 8, 1834, Box 1, Folder 3, Outgoing Correspondence of the Territorial Governors, FSA; R. C. Allen to Richard K. Call, February 15, 1832, Folder 9, Call Correspondence, FSA.

18. Kenneth Bembry in *Tallahassee Floridian*, June 29, 1839.

19. Ibid.; *Register of Members*, Pisgah United Methodist Church Records, FSA; 1840 U.S. Census, Leon County; 1839 Property Tax Book, LCC; *Tallahassee Floridian*, July 13, August 3, 1839; Thomas Baltzell in ibid. See also *Apalachicola Gazette*, December 2, 1839; Shofner, *Jackson County*, 104; *Tallahassee Floridian*, December 28, 1839, November 20, 1841.

20. "We had" from *Tallahassee Floridian*, March 14, 1840; "gentry," "the people," and "capitalists" from "Calhoun" in ibid.; "people" as a contested term from *Tallahassee Star of Florida*, May 21, 1840; "cannot help" from *Tallahassee Floridian*, October 3, 1840.

21. "We began to feel" from *Tallahassee Floridian*, March 7, 1840.

22. Jefferson's warning, etc., from ibid., January 9, 1841; "the Federalists of '98" from ibid., January 25, 1840; "aristocratic idlers" from T. S. Brown to Gov. Reid, May 6, 1840, Carter and Bloom, *Territorial Papers*, 26:171; Revolutionary rhetoric in *Tallahassee Floridian*, September 14, 1839; for Alabama and the "royal party," see J. Mills Thornton, *Politics and Power*, 15–20.

23. "John (x) Smith" from *Tallahassee Floridian*, April 4, 1840; "Spectator" in ibid., July 13, 1840; ibid., December 28, 21, 1839; *Tallahassee Star of Florida*, May 21, 1840; Eppes, *Through Some Eventful Years*, 356–57.

24. "The Banks are" and "shameful vassalage" from *Tallahassee Floridian*, January 16, 1841; "submit" from ibid., February 16, 1841; "defiance" from ibid., March 14, 1840;

"submissive" from ibid., March 28, 1840; "Bank power" from ibid., September 12, 1840.

25. R. R. Reid in ibid., January 18, 1840; class-specific laws from ibid., February 22 and October 3, 1840; whipping white men from ibid., September 12, 1840.

26. For meetings, see (among many possible examples) *Tallahassee Floridian*, August 3, 31, 1839; January 4, August 1, 8, 1840. Quotes are from *Tallahassee Floridian*, January 18, 1840. For Houck's illiteracy, see Leon County Amnesty Oaths, FSA.

27. Quote from Peter Hagner to Peter Hagner, esq., June 21, 1837, Folder 59, Hagner Papers, SHC.

28. Gamble in *Tallahassee Floridian*, August 31, 1839; "High priests of party" from ibid., September 28, 1839; see also "Old Man with Spectacles" in ibid., June 29, 1839.

29. Quote from Denham, "Dueling in Territorial Middle Florida," 66. See also U.S. Congress, House, *Condition of Banks, 1840*, 326, 331, and James Berthelot in *Tallahassee Floridian*, August 3, 1839.

30. "Novi homines" from "Philo Fair-Fight" in *Tallahassee Floridian*, April 14, 1838; "tolerably wild" from *Tallahassee Star of Florida*, July 28, 1841; "Vox Populi" in *Tallahassee Floridian*, March 25, April 22, 1837; "Peter Parley" in ibid., April 15, 1837; John Brickle in ibid. July 13, 1840; [Myers], "Reminiscences of the Early Days"; John Branch to Richard Bradford, May 19, 1840, Folder 62, Branch Papers, SHC; Call, *Florida Breezes*, 209; Baptist, "Migration of Planters to Antebellum Florida," 550.

31. Call's removal from Secretary of War to the President, November 29, 1839, Carter and Bloom, *Territorial Papers*, 25:656–57; McRaeny from "Governor Reid and Others to the President," March 5, 1840, ibid., 120–21; "corrupt" from James D. Westcott Jr. to the President, July 7, 1840, ibid., 26:165–66; Arthur Thompson, *Jacksonian Democracy*, 26–31; U.S. Congress, House, *Condition of Banks, 1840*, 241–438; Governor's [R. R. Reid] Message to the Legislature, *Tallahassee Floridian*, January 18, 4, 1840; excerpt of Pres. Van Buren's address, ibid., January 11, 1840.

32. "A Stockholder" in *Tallahassee Floridian*, March 21, 1840; "Calhoun" in ibid., March 14, February 1, March 7, 1840; John G. Gamble to E. E. Blackburn, February 20, 1840, 343–44; and February 22, 1840, 348–49; and Robert R. Reid to the House, January 24, 1840, all U.S. Congress, House, *Condition of Banks, 1840*, 248; *Tallahassee Floridian*, February 1, 1840. In previous years, the governor had reappointed members from the previous year's board. "defalcations," etc., from *Tallahassee Floridian*, March 7, 1840.

33. "Black cockade" from *Tallahassee Floridian*, March 14, 1840; "claiming to have" from ibid., January 25, 1840; "Hardest Fend Off," ibid., March 28, 1840; Robert R. Reid, ibid., January 18, 1840; see also M. C. Browne to Levi Woodbury, March 9, 1840, Union Bank Letter, FSL. T. S. Brown to Governor Reid, May 6, 1840, Carter and Bloom, *Territorial Papers*, 26:170–80, 171 (quote).

34. "Such is" from Florida House Committee on Banks from *Tallahassee Floridian*, March 7, 1840; see also Committee of the Judiciary Report in ibid., February 29, 1840, and T. S. Brown to Governor Reid, May 6, 1840, Carter and Bloom, *Territorial Papers*, 26:170–80.

35. "Private" and "political" from Petition to the President by Citizens of Tallahassee, August 10, 1840, Carter and Bloom, *Territorial Papers*, 26:186–91.

36. "A Card" (written by Leigh Read), October 26, 1839, Folder 4, Branch Papers, SHC;

Denham, "Read-Alston Duel"; Long, *Florida Breezes*, 209–17; Thompson, *Jacksonian Democracy*, 67–68.

37. "Your Devoted Daughter" to Edward Bradford[?], [n.d.], Folder 1, Box 367, Pine Hill Papers, FSU; Denham, "Read-Alston-Duel"; *St. Augustine Herald-Democrat*, May 7, 1841; Long, *Florida Breezes*, 213–17; Bleser, *Tokens of Affection*, 80, 302.

38. *Tallahassee Floridian*, January 11, 1840; Robert R. Reid to Leigh Read, January 9, 1840, Folder 4, Branch Papers, SHC; *Tallahassee Star of Florida*, July 28, 1841.

39. Ocklocknee Democrats from *Tallahassee Floridian*, August 1, 1840; Elias Blackburn from ibid., August 22, 1840; "Groups" from ibid., September 12, 1840; see also ibid., August 15, 1840; "Petition to the President by Citizens of Tallahassee," August 10, 1840, Carter and Bloom, *Territorial Papers*, 26:186–93; and Thompson, *Jacksonian Democracy*, 68.

40. Quotes from "Petition to the President by Citizens of Tallahassee," August 10, 1840, Carter and Bloom, *Territorial Papers*, 26:186–93, with enclosed "Committee of Tallahassee Citizens," 191–93 (petition to R. R. Reid).

41. "I assure you, sir" from Delegate Downing to the President, August 28, 1840, Carter and Bloom, *Territorial Papers*, 26:206–8; "effrontery" from John Gamble to the President, June 9, 1841, ibid., 26:330–34.

42. "Hardest Fend Off," *Tallahassee Floridian*, March 28, 1840; on confidence and value of bank notes, see Kenneth Bembry in ibid., September 14, May 16, 1840; on hope that the crop would save plantations, see Thomas H. Hagner to Peter Hagner, October 23, 1840, Folder 83, Hagner Papers, SHC; "disappointed" from Judge Balch to the President, April 3, 1840, Carter and Bloom, *Territorial Papers*, 26:128–29; *Tallahassee Floridian*, May 9, 1840. Balch was an old crony of Jackson's and Van Buren's; see Alfred Balch to Andrew Jackson, July 21, 1831, Bassett, ed., *Correspondence of Andrew Jackson*, 4:314–16; for examples of curtailed loans, see September 30 and October 7, 1840, both 7, Union Bank of Florida Minute Book, 1840–52, FSA.

43. *Tallahassee Floridian*, May 9, 1840.

44. Ibid.; "Sucidem," *Tallahassee Floridian*, May 30, 1840; editor, ibid.; Centreville meeting in ibid., May 9, 1840; Arkansas in *Tallahassee Florida Sentinel*, June 25, 1841. Most scholarship on white Southern mobs concerns postbellum lynch mobs, but see Richards, *"Gentlemen of Property and Standing,"* and Waldrep, *Roots of Disorder.*

45. *Tallahassee Floridian*, May 16, 23, 1840.

46. Ibid., October 17, 1840; see also ibid., October 31, September 19, 1840; and "Recommendation of Minor Walker as United States Marshal," February 2, 1841, Carter and Bloom, *Territorial Papers*, 26:252–53, which was signed almost exclusively by pro-bank politicians and planters, including many men from the Chaires, Alston-Parish, and Virginia family networks. For Reid's removal, see *Tallahassee Floridian*, April 3, 1841, and his journal, reproduced in part in Stephen F. Miller, *Bench and Bar of Georgia*, 2:182–236, esp. 225–26; quote from G. W. Call to John J. Crittenden, February 11, 1840, Carter and Bloom, *Territorial Papers*, 26:260–61.

47. Precincts from *Tallahassee Floridian*, October 17, 1840, February 27, March 6, 13, 1841.

48. Augustus Archer to John Branch, November 25, 1840, Folder 4, Branch Papers, SHC; *Tallahassee Star of Florida*, July 28, 1841; *Tallahassee Floridian*, January 23, 1841.

49. *Tallahassee Floridian*, April 3, 1841, May 1, 1840; *St. Augustine Florida Herald and*

Southern Democrat, May 7, 1841; John Gamble to the President, June 9, 1841, Carter and Bloom, *Territorial Papers*, 26:330–34; Denham, "Read-Alston Duel," 442–44.

50. "Reveling" and "insane" from John Branch to Gov. Call, in *Tallahassee Floridian*, April 2, 1842; "The feud," etc., from John G. Gamble to the President, June 9, 1841, Carter and Bloom, *Territorial Papers*, 26:330–34; Charges against Read from *Tallahassee Star of Florida*, July 28, 1841; Thomas H. Hagner to Peter Hagner, esq., May 1, 1841, Folder 86, Hagner Papers, SHC.

51. John G. Camp to the Secretary of State, June 7, 1841, Carter and Bloom, *Territorial Papers*, 26:327–29; Thomas H. Hagner to Peter Hagner, esq., June 14, 1841, Hagner Papers, SHC.

52. For quotes, and for an account of Willis Alston stealing the mail, see John G. Camp to the Secretary of State, June 7, 1841, Carter and Bloom, *Territorial Papers*, 26:327–29; for Call's late proclamation of Willis Alston as an outlaw, see *Tallahassee Floridian*, July 6, 1841, and December 27, 1841, 113, Superior Court Minute Book 3, LCC; for Alston's death, see J. W. Hagan to Nancy Cone Hagan, March 10 and September 17, 1842, Folder 3, Box 4, Florida Legislative Council (Bicameral), FSA. For "man of Blood," see John G. Gamble to the President, June 9, 1841, Carter and Bloom, *Territorial Papers*, 26:334.

53. Indictments of David Brown and John W. Lea, December 31, 1841, 179; their innocence, December 6, 1842, 528–29; indictments of John R. and Joseph Branch, May 5, 1842, 403, all Superior Court Minute Book 3, LCC; trial and pardoning of Ledwith, February 7–March 8, 1842, 264–65, ibid.; *Tallahassee Star of Florida*, March 17, 1842.

54. Call carried such a grudge against the memory of his former ally that he even blocked attempts by the Democrat-controlled territorial legislature to change the name of East Florida's Mosquito County to "Leigh Read" County. For Branch's attack on Call, see *Tallahassee Floridian*, April 2, 1842; pardon of Ledwith and attacks on Branch from *Tallahassee Star of Florida*, March 17, 24, 31, April 7 (quotes), 14, 21, 1842. Branch also attempted to use Washington influence to have Call removed from his gubernatorial post. See David Levy to John Branch, March 19, 1842, Folder 4, Branch Papers, SHC.

55. *Tallahassee Star of Florida*, May 21, 1840.

56. *Tallahassee Floridian*, July 13, 1840.

57. Ibid.

58. "Spectator," *Tallahassee Floridian*, July 13, 1840. For attacks on Bembry as a traitor, see *Tallahassee Floridian*, July 13, 27, September 12, 1840; Bembry's unsuccessful attempts to prevent the seating of Joseph Branch, who defeated him, from ibid., January 2, 9, 16, 23, February 26, 1841.

59. *Tallahassee Floridian*, September 23, 1838. "Subscriptions to the new stock of the Union Bank of Florida," in U.S. Congress, House, *Condition of Banks, 1840*, 307–16; Brown's mortgage from "No. 10—Present list of shareholders in the Union Bank of Florida," ibid., 325–34, esp. 326; Brown's sale of slaves from *Tallahassee Floridian*, January 4, 1840; Call's appointment of Brown from Thomas H. Hagner to Peter Hagner, esq., June 14, 1841, Folder 86, Hagner Papers, SHC; on Brown's conversion to pro-bank principles, see *Tallahassee Floridian*, May 9, 1840; Brown's economic status from 1840 U.S. Census, Leon County.

60. Richard Call to Gentlemen, April 24, 1845, Call Correspondence, FSA; "He has lost

his mind" from Susan Bradford to Sis M., August 23, 1862, Eppes Papers, SHC; "Old G." from S. Towle to John Parkhill, July 10, 1847, Folder 7, Parkhill Papers, SHC; Henry Ince to Thomas Dent, November 17, 1847, Letter Book 1, 128–36, Ince Papers, Duke. Repudiation from *Tallahassee Floridian*, January 8, 1842; ibid., February 19, 1842; *Tallahassee Star of Florida*, March 30, 1843, July 7, 1842, March 30, 1843; *Tallahassee Floridian*, January 8, 1842.

61. *Tallahassee Star of Florida*, May 12, 1842.

62. R. R. Reid in *Tallahassee Floridian*, January 16, 1841.

63. T. S. Brown to Governor Reid, May 6, 1840, Carter and Bloom, *Territorial Papers*, 26:170–80; for blame of the Locofocoes, see *Tallahassee Star of Florida*, January 7, 1842; McGrane, *Foreign Bondholders*, 223–44; for varying perspectives on the wider context of economic crash, see Hammond, *Banks and Politics in America*, 326–68; Mandel, *Marxist Economic Theory*, 1:346–60; and Balleisen, *Navigating Failure*.

64. "The facts" from *Florida Sentinel*, June 4, 1841; Caterpillars in *Tallahassee Star of Florida*, September 17, 1841; J. B. Bull advertisement, *Tallahassee Florida Sentinel*, November 26, 1841.

65. Estate of Samuel Parkhill, Probate Packet 448, Probate Records, LCC; totals from U.S. Congress, House, *Condition of Banks, 1840*; "No. 10—Present list of shareholders in the Union Bank of Florida," ibid., 325–34; and 1840 U.S. Census, Jackson County and Leon County.

66. *Tallahassee Florida Sentinel*, December 3, 1841; *Tallahassee Star of Florida*, December 15, 1841.

67. 1–380, Superior Court Minute Book 3, LCC. For December 29, 1841, suits, see 51–52, ibid.; for William Wyatt, February 16, 19, 1842, 301–7, ibid.; Judge Douglass to Secretary of State, February 12, 1842, Carter and Bloom, *Territorial Papers*, 26:434–35.

68. *Tallahassee Florida Sentinel*, March 25, 1842, February 10, 1843; *Tallahassee Star of Florida*, April 21, 1842; "Fifteen hundred" from "General Presentments of the Grand Jury of Leon County, April Term, 1842," in Governor Call to Delegate Levy, May 10, 1842, Carter and Bloom, *Territorial Papers*, 26:473–76.

69. *Tallahassee Star of Florida*, April 21, 1842; *Tallahassee Florida Sentinel*, March 25, 1842; for bankruptcy petitions, see ibid., April 1, 1842; "It is of great importance" from Joseph Branch to Lawrence O'Bryan Branch, October 2, 1843, Folder 3, Branch Papers, Duke. For a planter who bought up the property of a distressed and deceased relative at an estate (not marshal's) sale, see Estate of John Judge to Edward Bradford, December 6, 1852, Folder 1, Bradford Papers, FSU.

70. R. H. Long to Farish Carter, May 7, 1842, Folder 21, and March 5, 1844, Folder 25, Farish Carter Papers, SHC; "times" and "cultivating" from *Tallahassee Florida Sentinel*, November 19, 1841.

71. Wesley Adams from *Tallahassee Floridian*, March 16, July 10, 1841. For Adams as a debtor to the Union Bank, see U.S. Congress, House, *Condition of Banks, 1840*, and "No. 10—Present list of shareholders in the Union Bank of Florida," 325; see also T. S. Brown to Governor Reid, May 6, 1840, Carter and Bloom, *Territorial Papers*, 26:171; "all of the Neal" from Joseph Branch to My Dear Lairy, April 19, 1844, Folder 4, Branch Papers, Duke; see also L. P. Crain to J. & L. Branch, May 29, 1845, Folder 5, and November 19, 1845, Folder 6, ibid.; on rumors of a planter's plan to

mortgage 150 slaves in Apalachicola and then ship them to Texas, see N. G. Robbins to L. O'B. Branch, November 22, 1844, Folder 4, ibid.

72. "Tall Walking," *Tallahassee Star of Florida*, February 17, 1842; one example of the boot ad in question can be found in the same issue of the same paper. "G.T.T." appears in *Tallahassee Floridian*, January 1, 1842; see also Kelly and Fischer, *Away, I'm Bound Away*, 88. For the pattern of this midnight migration, see Sydnor, *Development of Southern Sectionalism*, 263–64.

73. "Tall Walking," *Tallahassee Star of Florida*, February 17, 1842. Milton later returned to Florida and eventually became the state's governor during most of the Civil War (Shofner, *Jackson County*, 247–48). Thomas Horan case in *Tallahassee Floridian*, February 19, 1842; *Tallahassee Star of Florida*, January 20, February 17, 24, 1842; and Territory of Florida vs. Thomas Horan, December 31, 1841, 179, Superior Court Minute Book 3, LCC; Jesse Willis to John Parkhill, July 7, 1841, Folder 7, Parkhill Papers, SHC; Ambrose Crane from ibid., October 9, 1841; for DuVal, see Snyder, "Nancy Hynes DuVal," and Clifton Paisley, *Red Hills of Florida*, 117–18; "Alas" from *Tallahassee Floridian*, September 25, 1841.

74. "Destruction" from *Tallahassee Star of Florida*, December 15, 1841; "extent" from "General Presentments of the Grand Jury of Leon County, April Term, 1842," in Governor Call to Delegate Levy, May 10, 1842, Carter and Bloom, *Territorial Papers*, 26:473–76; "When the Banks" from *Tallahassee Star of Florida*, June 16, 1842; "hand of Providence" from *Tallahassee Florida Sentinel*, April 29, 1842; "Publicus," ibid., May 6, 1842.

75. Reid from *Tallahassee Floridian*, July 10, 1841; Allen from ibid., August 14, 1841; see also ibid., September 11, 25, October 16, 1841; *Tallahassee Star of Florida*, September 26, 1841; ibid., September 8, 1841. For a list of the dead in Tallahassee, see *Tallahassee Floridian*, October 16, 1841. Some believed that Northerners were more susceptible to yellow fever; see *Tallahassee Florida Sentinel*, February 4, 1842.

76. Bel Air from *Tallahassee Florida Sentinel*, August 6, 1841; ibid., August 13, 1841; Gibson in *Tallahassee Floridian*, August 14, 1841; "the only way" from John Tappan to Benjamin French, December 13, 1841, Tappan Letter, FSL.

77. St. Joseph from Barbara Miller, "Tallahassee and the 1841 Yellow Fever Epidemic"; 400 of 1,600 dead from William P. DuVal to Charles A. Wickliffe, November 13, 1841, Carter and Bloom, *Territorial Papers*, 26:398–99.

78. *Tallahassee Star of Florida*, June 1, 1843; see also ibid., July 6, 1843; *Niles' National Register*, June 10, 1843, 233, and Groene, *Ante-Bellum Tallahassee*, 59–63.

79. Quote from *Niles' National Register*, June 10, 1843, 233.

CHAPTER SEVEN

1. Rawick, *American Slave*, Supplement, series 2, vol. 10 (Texas, part 9), 4076–86.

2. John Walker application no. 136, *RSD*; see also Martha Ann Hill, O.A. (Original Application) no. 133, and Daniel Vaughan, O.A. no. 136, *RSD*; Gutman, *Black Family*, 152–55.

3. Gutman, *Black Family*, and others have assumed as typical the two-parent formation, a position challenged by Stevenson, *Life in Black and White*.

4. "List of Negroes sent to Florida, March 1st, 1828," in Abbey, "Documents Relating to El Destino and Chemonie Plantations," pt. 1, 206–7. The following discussion of El Destino and Chemonie plantations is based on the above article; ibid., pt. 2, 291–329; *FPR* (esp. tables on 329–38, 439–42, 511–71); and a database compiled from all of the above.

5. These individuals appear on neither the mortgages executed by Nuttall between 1834 and 1836, nor on later slave lists. William's brother A. H. Nuttall took several slaves—only four first-rate hands, at going prices—back to Virginia during the 1830s, paying William with a pair of notes totaling $3,430 (A. H. Nuttall to William Nuttall, July 24, 1834, Abbey, "Documents Relating to El Destino and Chemonie Plantations," pt. 1, 208–9).

6. Venus and Aberdeen from D. N. Moxley to George Noble Jones, October 8, 1854, *FPR*, 106–8; compare Billy, Winney, and Rippon from *Tallahassee Floridian*, August 28, 1841. George Jones, application no. 1184; Joe Kilpatrick, no. 1185; Henry Johnson, no. 332; Ned Johnson, no. 333, *RSD*; see also Thomas Davis, O.A. no. 143; George Davis, O.A. no. 144; Samuel Davis, O.A. no. 145, *RSD*.

7. Estate of Thomas Savage, 1820, Probate Packet 24/147, Probate Records of Chatham County, Georgia, Family History Center, Church of Jesus Christ of Latter-Day Saints, Broomall, Pa.; Chaplin, *Anxious Pursuit*, 321; Kulikoff, "Uprooted Peoples." Gullah origins from Joyner, *Down by the Riverside*; Peter Wood, *Black Majority*; and Gomez, *Exchanging Our Country Marks*.

8. D. N. Moxley to G. N. Jones, October 8, 1854, *FPR*, 106–8.

9. Jesse Courtney, application no. 902, Ann Thornton, no. 828, *RSD*; see also Edward Drury, no. 309, *RSD*.

10. Fisher from *Tallahassee Florida Advocate*, June 13, 1829; Brown Memoir, Folder 1, Ambler-Brown Papers, Duke; *Tallahassee Floridian*, November 10, 1833.

11. "Complain[ed]" from Charles Copland to John Parkhill, March 31, 1836, Folder 4, Parkhill Papers, SHC. See also C. Copland to William Copland, March 31, 1836, and C. Copland to John Parkhill, May 4, 1836, Folder 4, Parkhill Papers, SHC. Louisa Ross, application no. 1144, *RSD*. Compare Willis Alston, *Tallahassee Floridian*, December 5, 1835, and "A. B." [Abram Bellamy?], ibid., April 20, 1839.

12. *Tallahassee Star*, April 21, 1842; "31 negroes" from ibid., May 19, 1842; Richard Gads-[d]en, application no. 354; Sancho Thomas, no. 316; Nancy Williams, no. 207; James Givens, O.A. no. 207, *RSD*; purchases of slaves for the New Orleans market from J. & L. O'B. Branch to Wood & Simmons, June 3, 1843, Folder 1, Joseph Branch Papers, SHC; games of creditor vs. debtor in the early 1840s from Folders 3, 5, and 6, Branch Family Papers, Duke; *Tallahassee Floridian*, July 10, 1841; and Folders 23 and 24, Carter Papers, SHC. See also Richard Smith Account Book and Jno. W. P. to E. B. Hicks, November 24, 1842, Box 1, Edward Hicks Papers, both Duke.

13. "A List of the Slaves in the Bequest of Thomas Savage," *FPR*, 529; see also *FPR*, 329–33, 531–33.

14. Carraway Smith to Farish Carter, August 20, 1845, Folder 27, Carter Papers, SHC.

15. Indictments of Ben from October 2, 1827, 37–76, Superior Court Minute Book 1, LCC; *Pensacola Gazette and West Florida Advertiser*, October 26, 1827; Clifton Paisley, *Red Hills of Florida*, 91.

16. For runaways, see Franklin and Schweninger, *Runaway Slaves*; African identities and eighteenth-century rebellions from John Thornton, "African Dimensions of the Stono Rebellion," and Gomez, *Exchanging Our Country Marks*; for resistance and rebellion in a revolutionary age, see Genovese, *From Rebellion to Revolution*; Frey, *Water from the Rock*; and Egerton, *Gabriel's Rebellion*; for masters' fears, see Jeffrey R. Young, *Domesticating Slavery*, 91–122; in contrast to Young, see Jonathan Bryant, *How Strange a Country*.

17. For explicit comparisons of regions of the Americas, see Genovese, *From Rebellion to Revolution*, 1–51. After the publication of Elkins, *Slavery*, arguments over the thorny question of slave resistance reached new heights. For claims that resistance was a central part of African American culture, see Blassingame, *Slave Community*; Rawick, *From Sundown to Sunup*; Levine, *Black Culture*; Aptheker, *American Negro Slave Revolts*; and Owens, *This Species of Property*. For claims that masters' power dampened rebellious spirits and rendered resistance ineffectual as either a cultural or political tool, see Elkins, *Slavery*; Genovese, *Roll, Jordan, Roll*; Kolchin, *Unfree Labor*; Fox-Genovese, *Within the Plantation Household*; Wyatt-Brown, "Mask of Obedience"; Christopher Morris, *Becoming Southern*; Stevenson, *Life in Black and White*; Philip D. Morgan, *Slave Counterpoint*, 385; and Fox-Genovese and Genovese, "Political Crisis of Social History," 219.

18. Studies of colonial slavery do a better job, in general, of taking into account change over time and geographic movement; see Philip D. Morgan, *Slave Counterpoint*, 519–24; Peter Wood, *Black Majority*; Berlin, *Many Thousands Gone*. Caribbean and Brazilian historians have also been less likely to overgeneralize about slave resistance and rebellion from specific contexts; see, for example, James, *Black Jacobins*; Craton, *Testing the Chains*; Gaspar, *Bondmen and Rebels*; Paquette, *Sugar Is Made with Blood*; Beckles, *Natural Rebels*; Price, *First Time* and *Alabi's World*; Da Costa, *Crowns of Glory*; David Geggus, "The Slaves and Free Coloreds of Martinique during the French and Haitian Revolutions," in Paquette and Engerman, *Lesser Antilles*, 280–301; and Fick, *Making of Haiti*.

19. Camp, "Viragoes"; King, *Stolen Childhood*; Blassingame, *Slave Community*, 149, 190–91.

20. Courtwright, *Violent Land*, 1–130; Ayers, *Vengeance and Justice*, 79–80. Florida's young white men, however, were far more violent than any other group of migrants, free or unfree. See Chapter 8 of this work and Denham, *Rogue's Paradise*.

21. Whipping of the marshal from Frank Hatheway Diary, January 25, 1846, FSU. See also Tom and Ned: December 16, 1841, 29, Superior Court Minute Book 3, LCC. C. C. Bryant killing from *Tallahassee Floridian*, April 7, 1849; memories of it from Rawick, *American Slave*, 17:76 (Irene Coates) and 185 ("Prophet" Kemp).

22. Private documents more openly admitted the possibility of resistance by the enslaved; see Eli Whitaker to L. H. B. Whitaker, May 12, 1835, Whitaker-Snipes Papers, SHC; Eppes, *Negro of the Old South*, 78–100; W. W. Boykin to George Gray, October 16, 1850, Folder 14, Gray Papers, SHC; "Hunter" in *Tallahassee Floridian*, March 30, 1839; John Evans to George Noble Jones, August 31, 1854, *FPR*, 94–95.

23. Grand jury presentment of Leon County, April 12, 1828, 66–67, Superior Court Minute Book 1, LCC; "We have lost" from W. W. Boykin to George Gray, July 8, 1851, Folder 15, Gray Papers, SHC; Charlotte from *Tallahassee Floridian*, Novem-

ber 2, 1833; Cain from ibid., April 20, 1839; see also *Tallahassee Floridian and Advocate*, October 5, 1830; ad for Hillary in *Tallahassee Floridian*, January 5, 1833; Hudson (another runaway) in ibid., March 24, 1838; and *Tallahassee Star of Florida*, March 4, 1843.

24. *Pensacola Floridian*, September 22, 1821.

25. Christopher Morris, "Within the Slave Cabin," 268–86. On genocidal reprisals, see Peter Wood, *Black Majority*; Egerton, *Gabriel's Rebellion*; and Winthrop Jordan, *Tumult and Silence at Second Creek*.

26. Castelnau, "Essay on Middle Florida," pt. 1, first quote, 236, second, 215.

27. Daniel Wiggins Diary, vol. 11, October 19, 29, 1838, Wiggins Papers, FSA.

28. Only three black-on-black murders appear in court and other records for the first three decades of settlement: on Ben see *Tallahassee Floridian*, October 8, 1834; on Ned, see *Tallahassee Floridian and Journal*, November 26, 1853; and on Jane, see Chapter 2. Compare this apparently low rate, on the one hand, to the assertions in Genovese, *Roll, Jordan, Roll*, 113–23, and, on the other, to the white violence quantified in Chapter 8 of this work.

29. Christopher Smith house from *Tallahassee Floridian*, July 1, 1837; Curry from ibid., July 22, 1837; see also ibid., August 4, 1838.

30. *Tallahassee Floridian*, June 8, 1839; Joseph White to Andrew Jackson, May 14, 1836, Carter and Bloom, *Territorial Papers*, 25:283; Legislative Council to Governor William P. DuVal, [1823], Folder 6, Box 1, Florida Legislative Council Records (Unicameral), FSA; Marryat, *Diary in America*, 272.

31. Slave trading from Gov. R. K. Call to Alexander Dallas, May 25, 1836, Governors' Letter Books, vol. 1, FSA; attacks from *Tallahassee Floridian*, May 9, 1836; August 4, 1838; November 15, 1839; June 26, 1841. For black-Indian conflict, see Daniel Wiggins Diary, vol. 11, January 5, 1839, Wiggins Papers, FSA; Rawick, *American Slave*, 17:28–29 (Frank Berry); 17:83–84 (Neil Coker). By contrast, see Porter, *Negro and the American Frontier*, 243. Cultural and historical roots of killing captives from Hudson, *Southeastern Indians*, 253–57, and Saunt, *New Order of Things*, 212.

32. DuVal, *Compilation of the Public Acts*, 218–19; November 26, December 12, 1842, 523, 534, Superior Court Minute Book 3, LCC. For patterns of interracial association and criminality in the old states, see Bolton, *Poor Whites*, 44–51, 107–10; Bynum, *Unruly Women*; and Lockley, *Lines in the Sand*, 98–130.

33. Crittenden and Joe from *Tallahassee Floridian*, April 5, November 15, 1834; Eppes's version from *Negro of the Old South*, 95–97.

34. Denham, *Rogue's Paradise*, ch. 13; Frank Hatheway Diary, January 6, 1846, FSU; *Pensacola Gazette*, June 28, 1845; *Tallahassee Florida Sentinel*, August 18, 1846; John T. McCorrie to John Forsyth, April 23, 1851, Folder 4, Box 3, Correspondence of Governor Thomas Brown, FSA; *Jacksonville News*, May 10, June 14, 1851; *Tallahassee Floridian and Journal*, April 26, June 14, 1851; *Pensacola Gazette*, April 19, May 3, 1851; *Jacksonville Republican*, December 14, 1851.

35. Hugh Duncan from *Tallahassee Floridian and Advocate*, September 16, 1830; see also Jesse and Sitzler from ibid., July 13, 1830; Harry from *Tallahassee Floridian*, July 5, 1834; see also Dennis from *Tallahassee Floridian*, January 18, 1840; and the case of Dilsey, from *Tallahassee Star of Florida*, May 21, 1840. For local cases of receiving stolen goods from slaves, see Indictment of Horace Ely, Jackson County Circuit

Court, Fall Term, 1850, Jackson County Historical Documents, 1820–1920 film, FSA; and Indictment of Charles Pindar, April 5, 1826, 9, and Indictment of Reuben Mills, October 15, 1829, 153, Superior Court Minute Book 1, LCC.

36. Howard, *History of Virgil A. Stewart; Tallahassee Floridian*, November 14, 1835; Eli Whitaker to Cary Whitaker, August 31, 1835, Folder 3, Coffield-Bellamy Papers, SHC; Penick, *Great Western Land Pirate*; Denham, *Rogue's Paradise*, ch. 13.

37. *Tallahassee Floridian*, January 3, 1835; *Tallahassee Floridian and Advocate*, May 25, 1830; see also J. B. Lane to Gov. Brown, June 28, 1851, Box 2, Folder 6, Correspondence of Governor Thomas Brown, FSA; Commissioner of Claims to Legislative Council, 1835, Folder 2, Box 5, Florida Legislative Council (Unicameral), FSA; and Bolton and Culclasure, *Confessions of Edward Isham*.

38. Rawick, *American Slave*, 17:63 (Florida Clayton); 17:337 (Shack Thomas); 17:13 (Samuel Simeon Andrews). For a more sanguine view of the frontier's social uncertainty, see Ira Berlin and Philip D. Morgan, "Labor and the Shaping of Slave Life in the Americas," in Berlin and Morgan, *Cultivation and Culture*, 4.

39. Rawick, *American Slave*, 17:62, 95, 167, 185. For the historiography of the topic of assaults on enslaved women, see my own effort at summary in Baptist, "'Cuffy,' 'Fancy Maids,' and 'One-Eyed Men'"; but for the most cogent discussions of the psychosocial experience of black womanhood and the assault on black femininity in slavery, see, for example, Deborah Gray White, *Ar'n't I a Woman;* Stevenson, *Life in Black and White;* Camp, "Viragoes"; King, *Stolen Childhood;* Painter, "Soul Murder and Slavery"; and Jennifer L. Morgan, "'Some Could Suckle.'"

40. James Scott, *Domination and the Arts of Resistance;* Camp, "Viragoes"; Lichtenstein, "'That Disposition to Theft,'"; Kay and Cary, *Slavery in North Carolina*.

41. James Scott, *Domination and the Arts of Resistance*, 18; "tragic complicity" from Philip D. Morgan, *Slave Counterpoint*, 385; Kolchin, *American Slavery.*

42. I have found only a handful of exceptions mentioning slaves by name: one Randolph letter; one Whitaker letter; and L. E. P. to Caroline Turnbull, June 3, 1827, Parish Family Papers, SHC. See also Cashin, *Family Venture*, 112–18. For Florida's reputation for cruelty, see Rawick, *American Slave*, 17:297 (William Sherman), 17:102 (Ambrose Douglass).

43. Bro Max to My Ever Dear Sister, December 3, [1856?], Burroughs Papers, FSL.

44. Henry Partridge Diary, n.p., Partridge Family Papers, FSA; Taylor Family Diary, Taylor Papers, FSA; Francis Eppes to Nicholas Eppes, March 9, 1863, Folder 1, Box 367, Pine Hill Plantation Papers, FSU.

45. Frances Douglass to [unknown cousin], May 8, 1860, Folder 2, Ambler-Brown Papers, Duke; see also *Marianna Florida Whig*, March 22, 1848; James Broome to F. Whitaker, February 16, 1852, Folder 2, Bradford Papers, FSU; and Francis Eppes to Nicholas Eppes, May 13, 1863, Folder 1, Box 367, Pine Hill Plantation Papers, FSU.

46. "Servant James" to Miss Harriet, July 15, August 22, 1859, Folder 8, Parkhill Family Papers, SHC; Rivers, *Slavery in Florida*, 120–22; see also J. M. Galphin to M. E. Galphin, January 31, 1857, Burroughs Papers, FSL. For a different perspective on Page, see Ashford, "Loyal to the End."

47. D. N. Moxley to George Noble Jones, October 8, 1854, *FPR*, 106–8.

48. Eppes, *Negro of the Old South*, 17, and *Through Some Eventful Years*, 161–62. For a

similar incident told from the ex-slave perspective, see Rawick, *American Slave,* 17:178 (Squires Jackson). See also Abrahams, *Singing the Master.*

49. Long, *Florida Breezes,* 229–30.

50. James Scott, *Domination and the Arts of Resistance.*

CHAPTER EIGHT

1. *Tallahassee Florida Sentinel,* August 8, 1848.

2. *Tallahassee Star of Florida,* December 8, 1842, August 23, 1844; *Tallahassee Florida Sentinel,* July 7, October 14, 1842.

3. *Tallahassee Star of Florida,* August 4, 1842; *Tallahassee Florida Sentinel,* September 21, 1847, August 1, 1848. See the extensive historical literature on the second-party system, including Bourke and DeBats, *Washington County,* and Harry L. Watson, *Jacksonian Politics,* 282–313; compare Miccosukee Precinct poll book, October 1, 1849, Byrd Papers, FSL.

4. Doherty, *Whigs of Florida,* 1–46; *Tallahassee Florida Sentinel,* November 4, 1845, August 8, 1848; see also E. C. Cabell to D. M. Barringer, October 13, 1848, Folder 136, Barringer Papers, SHC.

5. *Tallahassee Florida Sentinel,* April 14, 1846, July 4, 11, 18, 1848.

6. Ibid., August 4, 1846; see also ibid., March 7, 1848; Cass from ibid., July 11, November 4, 1848.

7. Robinson, *Pioneer and Agriculturalist,* 462.

8. *Tallahassee Floridian,* January 18, 1834, January 25, 1835, April 2, May 14, 1836.

9. "Aristides" in *Tallahassee Star of Florida,* October 6, 1841; "people" from ibid., June 23, 1842; "John Caldwell" in ibid., May 12, 1842; see also *Tallahassee Florida Sentinel,* June 4, 1841, December 9, 1842; for earlier attempts to enlist women's production to stave off corruption, see Kerber, *Women of the Republic,* 36–41, and Chaplin, *Anxious Pursuit,* 208–20; "the only hope" from "Publicus" in *Tallahassee Florida Sentinel,* May 6, 1842.

10. Groene, *Ante-Bellum Tallahassee,* 31–32; Armistead Account Book, FSA; [Myers], "Reminiscences of the Early Days"; Joseph Gamble to John Branch, March 12, 1840, Folder 62, Branch Papers, SHC; Brodie and Pettes Account Books, vol. 2, September 17–June 18, 1850, FSA; see also Ledger Book, 1850–51, July 11, 1851, 24–25, Williams Papers, FSA; Willoughby, *Fair to Middlin',* 90–115; Woodman, *King Cotton,* 3–72; and Shofner, *Daniel Ladd.*

11. "I have never" from L. O'B. Branch to Nannie Branch, October 27, 1848, Folder 9, Branch Family Papers, Duke; D. S. Walker to J. & L. Branch, January 28, 1845, Folder 6, ibid.; John Parkhill to Smallwood and Anderson, January 20, 1854, Folder 8, Parkhill Papers, SHC; Woodman, *King Cotton,* 132–38.

12. Bryan and Maitland to John Branch, October 31, 1843, Folder 3; John Branch acct. w. Coe, Anderson and Co., July 6, 1849, Folder 10; and Bernard & Adams to J. & L. Branch, March 10, 1846, Folder 7, all Branch Papers, Duke; Taylor and Reitch to E. Bradford, May 19, 1855, Bradford Papers, FSU; George Anderson to John Branch, July 4, 1848, Folder 5, and J. Branch acct. w. E. E., September 20, 1844, Folder 62, Branch Papers, SHC.

13. Woodman, *King Cotton*, 17–18, 151, 154–64. See the role of New York money as early as the late 1830s in "Extracts from the Message of Gov. Reid," House Executive Documents, 26 Cong., 2d sess., no. 111, serial 385. See also U.S. Congress, House, *Condition of Banks, 1840*, 242; William G. Robertson to John Parkhill, November 2, 1839, Folder 6, and Guinn and Dunn to John Parkhill, May 11, 1841, Folder 7, Parkhill Papers, SHC; *Tallahassee Floridian*, August 31, 1839; *Tallahassee Star*, September 1, 1842; *Jacksonville Republican*, August 14, 1851; Vicki Vaughn Johnson, *Men and the Vision*; McCardell, *Idea of a Southern Nation*, 91–140; Bateman and Weiss, *Deplorable Scarcity*; Woodman, *King Cotton*, 139–53, 164–65; and Genovese, *Political Economy of Slavery*.

14. "To coerce the payment" from John Branch to James Bryan, March 26, 1849, Box 2, Folder 11, Hogg Papers, SHC; see also from James Bryan to John Branch, March 15, 1849, ibid.; "I have to say" from Bryan to Branch, April 27, 1849, Folder 5, Branch Papers, SHC. Branch continually shifted from factor to factor; see George Anderson to John Branch, July 4, 1848, and Brown and Rosset to Branch, January 16, 1849, Folder 5, Branch Papers, SHC. A similar incident involved Joseph Gamble; see Tappan and Douglas to Joseph Branch, December 24, 1850, Folder 11, Branch Family Papers, Duke.

15. "Southern planters" from John Branch to James Bryan, March 26, 1849, Box 2, Folder 11, Hogg Papers, SHC; John Parkhill's removal as cashier from *Tallahassee Floridian*, November 8, 1839; Estate of Samuel Parkhill, Probate Packet 48, LCC; S. Towle to John Parkhill, July 10, August 19, 1847, Folder 7; John Parkhill to Robert Parkhill, September 27, 1851, Folder 8; John Parkhill to G. W. Parkhill, August 3, 1852, Folder 8, all Parkhill Papers, SHC; quote from G. W. Parkhill to John Parkhill, January 26, 1845, Folder 7, ibid.

16. John Baird to Farish Carter, July 12, 1842, and Thomas M. Baxter to Carter, August 6, 1842, Folder 22; and J. H. Brockenborough to Carter, January 4, 1843, and George Baltzell to Carter, April 5, 1843, Folder 23, all Carter Papers, SHC.

17. "Men of" from Richard H. Long to Farish Carter, April 29, 1843, Folder 23, Carter Papers, SHC; ibid., April 16, 24, 25, 1843, and Reuben Thornton to Carter, April 22, 1843, Folder 23; and Long to Carter, May 5, 1843, Folder 24, all Carter Papers, SHC.

18. "For the defense" from Richard H. Long to Farish Carter, May 5, 1843, Folder 24, Carter Papers, SHC; "scounderels" from Long to Carter, May 5, 1843, Folder 23, ibid.; Long to Carter, May 23, 1843, ibid.; Long's unpopularity from George S. Hawkins to Carter, November 2, 1843, ibid.; William H. Long to Carter, December 21, 1848, Folder 33, ibid.; William H. Long to Carter, December 22, 1848, ibid.; "cry of persecution" from William H. Long to Carter, December 25, 1848, ibid.

19. Ragland known as "brute cum dandy" from personal communication from James M. Denham to the author, January 1997; for Ragland's alleged gambling and fornicating exploits, see December 20, 1841, 41–42, Superior Court Minute Book 3, LCC, and Leon County grand jury, *Tallahassee Floridian*, November 21, 1840.

20. Eppes from Dorothy Dodd, "Corporation of Tallahassee," 80–95; Groene, *Ante-Bellum Tallahassee*, 102–3; *Tallahassee Florida Sentinel*, May 21, 1841.

21. "One of the City Council" in *Tallahassee Florida Sentinel*, July 30, 1841; fines from ibid., April 1, 1842.

22. Judge Douglass to the Secretary of State, February 12, 1842, Carter and Bloom,

Territorial Papers, 26:434–35; Gustavus West from January 12, 1842, 206–7, Superior Court Minute Book 3, LCC; "Crockett" discussed in *Tallahassee Florida Sentinel*, August 6, 1841; "Loafer" in ibid., June 18, 1841; petition and "One of the City Council" in *Tallahassee Florida Sentinel*, April 8, 1842; Eppes quote from ibid., April 8, 1842. Council members included one unsuccessful merchant (A. J. Fisher), three members of the Virginia faction (T. Brown, R. B. Gamble, and Eppes) and four highly successful merchants (J. B. Bull, R. A. Shine, J. Levinus, and P. Kerr).

23. Hoe and West from December 5, 1843, 112; December 6, 1843, 120; December 7, 1843, 133; and December 18, 1843, 159, all Superior Court Minute Book 4, LCC. Belden from April 27, 1843, 61, ibid. James Berthelot succeeded Eppes as intendant. See also *Tallahassee Florida Sentinel*, March 4, 1843.

24. Grand jury presentment of November 25, 1843, 103, Superior Court Minute Book 4, LCC; Duff, Hamner, and Williams from December 11, 1843, 138, ibid.; Melton from May 5–8, 1843, 64–68, ibid.

25. Thomas Brown from April 28, 1845, 319, ibid.; jury from Jacobs trial from April 29, 1844, 196, ibid. Of the fourteen different indictments for larceny in Leon County Minute Book 4, six cannot be identified by any measure of class, four were yeomen (all members of the Burney family's outlaw gang), and four were local poor whites. Of the fourteen, in two cases the result was unknown, two were found not guilty, three fled, four were dismissed, two spent an hour in the pillory, and one received twenty lashes — a level of punishment considerably less sanguine than the cases discussed in Chapter 2.

26. Numbers from Superior and Circuit Court Minute Book 4, LCC. In an additional case, a woman was charged but ultimately not indicted by the grand jury. Similar developments were afoot in Jackson County; see *Marianna Florida Whig*, May 3, 1848. For Anderson and Burritt, see *Tallahassee Star of Florida*, August 29, 1845; and May 6, 1846, 448–51, Superior and Circuit Court Minute Book 4, LCC.

27. Aaron and William Smith from November 18, 1846, 514, Circuit Court Minute Book 4, LCC. A. P. Smith owned no slaves (1840 U.S. Census, Leon County). For two more cases in which a jury approved a common white man's actions in a fight that turned deadly, see Indictment of Fletcher Hagan, December 27, 1841, 113, Superior Court Minute Book 3, LCC, and trial of James Wells, May 7, 1846, 452–54, Circuit Court Minute Book 4, LCC. See also cases of Matilda, a slave convicted of manslaughter, November 21, 1845, 392, ibid., and John G. Williams, felony charge reduced to manslaughter by the jury, May 6, 1843, 65, Superior and Circuit Court Minute Book 4, LCC.

28. November 20–21, 1843, 163–64, Superior and Circuit Court Minute Book 4, LCC; Charles Sibley to Delegate Levy, December 18, 1843, Carter and Bloom, *Territorial Papers*, 26:813–14. Despite the unusually high number of wealthy whites on this trial jury, which included several merchants who had lost their businesses in the fire, acquittal prevailed after deliberations that lasted through one day and into the next. This lengthy sitting seemingly indicates disagreement among the jurors.

29. For arson and social banditry, see Hobsbawm, *Primitive Rebels*; Hobsbawm and Rudé, *Captain Swing*; and E. P. Thompson, *Whigs and Hunters*.

30. "M." in *Tallahassee Florida Sentinel*, August 4, 1846.

31. Superior and Circuit Court Minute Books 3 and 4, LCC. Almost all "felony" indict-

ments were for homicide, although some could have been for burglary. At least 14 cases were, beyond all doubt, homicides; 3 almost certainly were (thus yielding a total of 17 for a minimum), and 5 may have been killings or burglaries. The additional homicide was the alleged shooting by the sheriff of a drunken man in the street. See John G. Gamble to the President, June 9, 1841, Carter and Bloom, *Territorial Papers*, 26:332, and *Tallahassee Floridian*, January 16, 1841. Slaveowners may have punished some black murderers outside the court system.

32. Jackson County cases include King Gill and Bryant Meredith in 1840, William Bell in 1842, John Shepherd in 1844, and William Watson and James Avant in 184. Avant was wanted for several (an undetermined number) of murders (Proclamations of Robert R. Reid, February 15 and July 14, 1840, Outgoing Correspondence of Robert R. Reid, FSA; Bell from Shofner, *Jackson County*, 170; Shepherd from Proclamation of Thomas H. Duval, Outgoing Correspondence of Richard K. Call, FSA; Watson and Avant from *Pensacola Gazette*, July [?], 1845; and Shofner, *Jackson County*, 170).

33. Indictments from May 18, 1843, 69, and December 22, 1843, 165, and William Burney flees, April 29, 1844, 144, all Superior and Circuit Court Minute Book 4, LCC. Debts from William Bellamy v. A. Burney, April 24, 1843, 50, ibid.; Southern Life and Trust Co. v. William Burney, February 23, 1845, 293, ibid.; Joseph Branch to Lawrence O'Bryan Branch, July 18, 1843, Folder 3, Branch Papers, Duke; *Tallahassee Star of Florida*, August 11, 1843.

34. *Tallahassee Florida Sentinel*, August 16, 1846; Denham, *Rogue's Paradise*, ch. 13.

35. *Pensacola Gazette*, June 28, 1845; *Tallahassee Floridian*, November 22, 1845; *Tallahassee Florida Sentinel*, November 25, 1845; *Niles' National Register*, January 17, June 6, 1846; "men of the gospel" from *Tallahassee Florida Sentinel*, May 5, 1846; Henry Hodson to Eugene Hodson, August 13, 1846, Hodson Letters, FSL; *Tallahassee Florida Sentinel*, August 11, 18, 1846; *Tallahassee Floridian*, August 1, 1846; "Citizens of Gadsden County," ibid., October 10, 1846; "Judge Baltzell's Charge," ibid.; see also Waldrep, *Roots of Disorder.*

36. "Life, liberty" from *Tallahassee Florida Sentinel*, May 5, 1846; Presentment of the Grand Jury, November 21, 1846, 521, Superior Court Minute Book 4, LCC; Frank Hatheway Diary, January 6, 1846, FSU; *Marianna Florida Whig*, April 5, 1848; Henry Hodson to Eugene Hodson, August 13, 1846, Hodson Letters, FSL; Pittman murder from *Tallahassee Florida Sentinel*, August 4, 1846.

37. *Tallahassee Florida Sentinel*, August 18, 1846. In the 1850s, fear of abolitionism and slave revolt sparked new mob violence on the still unstable frontier of East Florida; see Denham, *Rogue's Paradise*, ch. 13.

38. "Without hearing" from J. Evans, "Interesting from Florida" in *Religious Intelligencer*, 13:456, December 13, 1828; Francis Eppes to My Dear Jenny, February 17, 1840, Eppes Family Papers, SHC; Daniel Wiggins Diary, vol. 11, November 12, 26, December 2 ("without a compass"), 15, 1838, Wiggins Papers, FSA.

39. *Tallahassee Star of Florida*, May 12, 1842.

40. Benjamin Wynns to "My dear sister," June 24, 1841, Wynns Family Papers, NCDAH.

41. *Tallahassee Star of Florida*, June 23, 1842, May 25, August 18, 1843; *Tallahassee Florida*

Sentinel, June 10, July 15, 1842, August 4, 1846; Trinity Methodist Church (Tallahassee) Records, FSA.

42. *Tallahassee Star of Florida*, May 25, 1843; *Tallahassee Florida Sentinel*, November 5, 184; obituary of Mary Felkel, ibid., November 11, 1842; obituary of David Felkel, ibid., June 30, 1846; obituary of Jacob Felkel, *Tallahassee Star of Florida*, January 26, 1847.

43. "By the way" from *Tallahassee Florida Sentinel*, November 19, 1842; *Tallahassee Star of Florida*, June 23, 1842; *Tallahassee Southern Journal*, July 7, 1846; numbers from Superior and Circuit Court Minute Book 4, LCC; "Those days" from Richardson, *Lights and Shadows*, 106.

44. Eppes, *Through Some Eventful Years*, 356–57; J. T. Bernard Diaries, vol. 6, October 30, 1858, Bernard Papers, SHC; Richardson, *Lights and Shadows*, 143–46.

45. Lewis C. Gray, *History of Agriculture*, 2:697, 715, 1027.

46. 1850 and 1860 U.S. Census of Agriculture, Leon County.

47. Charles Hentz Memoir, 227, 236, Hentz Family Papers, SHC; Ethelred Philips to James Jones Philips, May 1, 1863, Folder 2, Philips Papers, SHC; 1850 U.S. Census of Agriculture, Jackson County; *Tallahassee Star of Florida*, June 15, 1847.

48. 1850 U.S. Census of Agriculture, Leon County; 1850 Property Tax Book, LCC; Richardson, *Lights and Shadows*, 143–46.

49. Will of Gasper Houck, 1846, 101–3, Will Book A, LCC.

50. 1850 U.S. Census of Agriculture, Leon County.

51. John Evans to George Noble Jones, September 2, 1856, *FPR*, 166; R. C. and R. L. Stephens to William Harvey, March 13, 1849, Deed Book A, 21, JCC; Bolton, *Poor Whites*; Bynum, *Unruly Women*; Bolton and Culclasure, *Confessions of Edward Isham*.

52. This finding contrasts directly with the claims made in Genovese, "Yeoman Farmers in a Slaveholders' Democracy," 331–42, esp. 336–38.

53. W. W. Boykin to George Gray, July 10, 1850, Folder 14, Gray Papers, SHC. For the description of yeomen as "unequal masters," see McCurry, *Masters of Small Worlds*, 92–129.

54. John Evans to George Noble Jones, July 31, 1854, *FPR*, 89; ibid., September 15, 1854, 101.

55. This history both built upon and replicated some of the processes described by Kathleen Brown, *Good Wives, Nasty Wenches*; while occurring in parallel with the process that created a new sense of white manhood in the North, described by Roediger, *Wages of Whiteness*; Nelson, *National Manhood*; and Lott, *Love and Theft*.

56. Charles Colcock[?] to John Branch, October 29, 1851, Folder 7, Branch Papers, SHC.

CHAPTER NINE

1. 1839, 1849 Property Tax Books, LCC; 1850 U.S. Census of Agriculture.

2. The album is found in Box 1, Burroughs Family Papers, Georgia Historical Society, Savannah, Georgia. In contrast to the relative absence of public comment on politics by Middle Florida planter women, see Varon, *We Mean to Be Counted*.

3. Scholars of nineteenth-century American culture have discussed domesticity as an ideology in nineteenth-century literature, especially that by and/or intended for women. See, for example, Tompkins, *Sensational Designs*, and Romero, *Home Fronts*. See also Fox-Genovese, *Within the Plantation Household*. For Scott's own peculiar uses of historical symbols to create an ahistorical vision of himself as a border lord, see Crockett, *Abbotsford*. As usual, A. N. Wilson's vision is idiosyncratic but illuminating; see *Laird of Abbotsford*. For evidence of the popularity of Scott among local planters during the early period of settlement, see Murat, *United States of North America*, 63.

4. William R. Taylor, *Cavalier and Yankee*; Osterweis, *Romanticism and Nationalism*; McCardell, *Idea of a Southern Nation*; Tracy, *In the Master's Eye*; Ritchie D. Watson, *Yeoman versus Cavalier*; Kennedy, *Swallow Barn* and *Horse-Shoe Robinson*; Simms, *Partisan*; and many others by Simms. For additional examples of the plantation novel, consult Taylor and Tracy.

5. Eppes, *Negro of the Old South*; Redgauntlet from Charles Hentz Memoir, 243, Hentz Family Papers, SHC. Odd, too, is the term "Southron," which literary Southerners started to use to refer to their own region's people. In Scott, from whom they probably borrowed the term, the "Southrons" were the rarely heroic English. See *Tallahassee Florida Sentinel*, August 8, 1848, and *Tallahassee Floridian and Journal*, August 12, 19, 1854.

6. See advertisement of P. A. Hayward in *Tallahassee Southern Journal*, January 19, 1847. I borrow the concept of emplotment from Hayden White, *Metahistory*.

7. Scott, *Waverley*; Dekker, *American Historical Romance*, 1–98. See also David Brown, *Walter Scott and the Historical Imagination*; Fleishman, *English Historical Novel*; Lukács, *Historical Novel*, 30–62; and Slotkin, *Fatal Environment*.

8. "That intermediate" from *Pensacola Gazette and West Florida Advertiser*, May 9, 1828; "The Chronicles of the Governors of Adirolf, Book I, Chap. II," ibid., October 6, 1826. See also Chapter 1; Chaplin, *Anxious Pursuit*, 26–37; and Dekker, *American Historical Romance*.

9. *Tallahassee Star of Florida*, July 19, 1844. See also *Tallahassee Sentinel*, September 8, 1846, January 12, 1847; and *Tallahassee Star of Florida*, May 18, September 1, 1843.

10. Compare McCardell, *Idea of Southern Nationalism*, 141–76.

11. Brown Memoir, Ambler-Brown Papers, Duke; "Extracts from the Journal of Major Robert Gamble," Gamble Family Papers, FSU; Parkhill Memoir, Folder 11, Parkhill Family Papers, SHC.

12. Brown Memoir, Ambler-Brown Papers, Duke.

13. Ibid.; Craven, *Soil Exhaustion*; Faust, *Southern Stories*, 29–53; for a rejection of the belief that soil exhaustion was reality rather than rhetoric of "sterility," "exhaustion," etc., see Wright, *Political Economy of the Cotton South*, 17.

14. Osterweis, *Romanticism and Nationalism*; see also O'Brien, *Rethinking the South*, 38–56. O'Brien says: "The origins of Romanticism do not lie chiefly in industrialization, but in a congeries of local social and political crises (42)." He also refers to the movement's European innovators. Might this not apply equally well to the less artistic but still crisis-ridden Florida planters?

15. While Thomas Jefferson and John Adams often disagreed, both believed that in a republican society an aristocracy of birth was unacceptable (William R. Tay-

lor, *Cavalier and Yankee*, 1–10). For an example of the valorization of ties to England, see "R. B. H." in *Tallahassee Floridian and Journal*, March 31, 1849. See also *Tallahassee Florida Sentinel*, June 18, 1850. For Virginia origins and cavalier myths, see Quitt, "Immigrant Origins"; Fischer, *Albion's Seed*, 212–25; Bailyn, "Politics and Social Structure"; and Wertenbaker, *Patrician and Plebian*.

16. *Tallahassee Floridian and Journal*, February 21, 1852.

17. "The chivalry" from *Tallahassee Floridian and Journal*, January 3, 1852; see also ibid. February 14, 1852; *Tallahassee Florida Sentinel*, April 15, May 13, July 8, 1851. For other jousts and rituals, see *Tallahassee Floridian and Journal*, May 5, 19, 1849, February 25, May 20, 1854; *Tallahassee Florida Sentinel*, May 13, December 23, 30, 1851, February 24, 1852, February 25, 1854, January 30, 1858, and January 20, 1859; "Miccosukie" from ibid., May 18, 1852; Groene, *Ante-Bellum Tallahassee*, 146–51; William G. Dodd, "Ring Tournaments in Tallahassee." I agree with Eugene Genovese that planters did not really believe that they were knights of yore, but I must disagree with his argument that the planters' medievalist fetishism derives from an analysis of labor relations (Genovese, "Southern Slaveholders' View of the Middle Ages").

18. The only evidence of street fights or killings by planters found for the late antebellum period is M. E. Whitner to Sallie Galphin, September 5, 1858, Burroughs Papers, FSL; in contrast, see conflicts resolved without duels in *Tallahassee Floridian and Journal*, October 24, 1857, and October 28, 1858; see also *Jacksonville Florida Republican*, November 6, 1851. "White and Red Rose" from *Tallahassee Floridian and Journal*, August 31, 1850. Newspapers now used the language of jousting, rather than that of dueling-producing insults, to describe and contain conflict: defeated parties and candidates were referred to as "unhorsed" (see *Tallahassee Florida Sentinel*, December 3, 1850), while "Southron" offered to "cross swords" or "break a lance" with opponents (see *Tallahassee Floridian and Journal*, September 9, 1854).

19. For nationalism and romance, see Horsman, *Race and Manifest Destiny;* for the "epic" as a time closed off from real historical change and thus more comfortable for a besieged elite, see Bakhtin, *Dialogic Imagination*, 3–40.

20. Proslavery thought from Faust, *Ideology of Slavery*, and Jenkins, *Pro-Slavery Thought*. On tensions between elitism and equality, see Freehling, *Road to Disunion*, and Greenberg, *Masters and Statesmen*. One elitist holdout was George T. Ward (see *Tallahassee Floridian and Journal*, January 21, 1860).

21. Hentz, *Marcus Warland*. See also Stanesa, "Caroline Lee Whiting Hentz"; Tracey, *Plots and Proposals*, 49–75; Moss, *Domestic Novelists*; and Hunt, "Domesticated Slavery."

22. Hentz, *Marcus Warland*.

23. "More prosperous" from Hentz, *Marcus Warland*, 131; for the Bellamy brothers, see *Marianna Whig*, February 2, May 3, 1848; and Bellamy, *Address Delivered before the Chipola Division*; for Samuel's suicide, see *Tallahassee Floridian and Journal*, January 21, 1854.

24. Hentz, *Marcus Warland*, 194; fight from ibid., 167–70, 202–3. In a similar scene in Kennedy, *Swallow Barn* (362–68), a planter's skilled boxing defeats a lower-class bully's brute force.

25. Hentz, *Marcus Warland*, 135, 16; see also Hentz's *Planter's Northern Bride*.

26. *Tallahassee Star of Florida*, February 17, 1842.

27. Hentz, *Marcus Warland*, 188, 16. See also *Tallahassee Floridian and Journal*, April 27, 1850.

28. *Tallahassee Floridian and Journal*, April 9, 16, 1853; *Tallahassee Florida Sentinel*, July 20, 1852.

29. Fairbanks, *Early History of Florida*; Fairbanks, *History and Antiquities*, 9–10. See also "J.B.G.," "A Trip to the Coast" in *Tallahassee Florida Sentinel*, July 20, 1852.

30. See the transition from narratives of frontier settlement like "The Early Experiences of Ralph Ringwood" and "The Conspiracy of Neamathla," collected in Irving, *Wolfert's Roost*, 249–88 and 297–304, to a "Ringwood" character projected back into the sixteenth century in the quasi-pornographic Herbert, *Ringwood the Rover*. Narratives of the Second Seminole War, like Sprague, *Florida War*, were rare and their vogue wore away quickly, except among the abolitionist readers of Giddings, *Exiles of Florida*. For Parkman et al., see Franchot, *Roads to Rome*.

31. Fairbanks, *History and Antiquities*, 51; Hundley, *Social Relations in Our Southern States*, 27.

32. Potter, *Impending Crisis*.

33. *Tallahassee Floridian and Journal*, March 23, 1850; for across-the-board support of most Leon County planters for the convention, see ibid., March 30, 1850.

34. This crisis produced mixed results elsewhere in the South. See, for example, Carey, *Parties, Slavery, and the Union*, 156–83; Ford, *Origins of Southern Radicalism*, 183–214; and J. Mills Thornton, *Politics and Power*. For the theory of secession, see "Revolution vs. Secession" in *Tallahassee Floridian and Journal*, September 6, 1851, April 13, 1850, January 4, 1851. For Brown's stance and his defeat, see ibid., September 16, October 7, 1854.

35. *Tallahassee Florida Sentinel*, October 22, 1850; Dorothy Dodd, "Secession Movement in Florida," 10–12; Wooster, *Secession Conventions of the South*, 67.

36. *Tallahassee Floridian and Journal*, January 1, 1854. The main opposition to partial public funding of railroads, at least in Leon County, came from the old yeoman neighborhood of Centreville; see ibid., May 12, 1855.

37. For paeans to unity, see "Cato" in *Tallahassee Floridian and Journal*, August 29, 1857; ibid., September 19, 1857; Message of the Governor, ibid., November 29, 1856; ibid., July 24, 1857.

38. "Shanghai" in *Tallahassee Floridian and Journal*, November 1, 1856; see also ibid., July 15, 1860, December 20, 1856.

39. *Tallahassee Floridian and Journal*, January 19, 1850; see also ibid., May 10, 1851, September 21, 1850; "An Overseer" in ibid., September 29, 1849; "Madison" in ibid., August 11, 1849.

40. Governor's Message, 1854 House Journal, 28–30. Why were Southern planters so anxious to keep the territories open for slavery? Barney argues in *Secessionist Impulse*, 3–49, that soil depletion was the major impetus for planters' desire to expand westward. Compare Genovese, *Political Economy of Slavery*, 241–75. These authors agree with "The Doom of the South" in *Tallahassee Floridian and Journal*, September 28, 1850, and "Importation of Slaves," ibid., February 10, 1849. But otherwise this issue was mentioned relatively rarely in Middle Florida newspapers, in part because Florida's soil was not particularly depleted.

41. "Leonidas" in *Tallahassee Floridian and Journal*, August 9, 1856; "W.H.B." in ibid., February 14, 1857.

42. Governor's Message, 1854 Legislative Journal, 28–30.

43. "Civis" in *Tallahassee Floridian and Journal*, August 23, 1856; Address of the Governor in ibid., November 29, 1856; "Alpha" in ibid., August 24, 1858; ibid., February 5, 1859; "arbitrary domination" from *Monticello Family Friend*, October 20, 1860.

44. *Tallahassee Floridian and Journal*, October 24, 1857.

45. Stampp, *America in 1857*.

46. Simmons Baker, in Florida, Senate, *Senate Journal*, 1859, 204. The resolution's wording was identical to one offered at the same time in the South Carolina Assembly; see Channing, *Crisis of Fear*, 96. This suggests the issue of secret cooperation, or, as some would call it, conspiracy. Call's alleged proposal from Florida, House of Representatives, *House Journal*, 1859, 188–92; Davis, *Civil War and Reconstruction in Florida*; Meredith, "Secession Movement in Florida"; *Tallahassee Floridian and Journal*, October 29, 1859.

47. "Nigger-worshipping" from *Tallahassee Floridian and Journal*, March 15, 1856; script from "Veritas" in ibid., April 7, 1860; ibid., December 10, 1859, September 19, 1857, February 5, 1859.

48. "Dishonor" and "resistance" from *Tallahassee Floridian and Journal*, December 24, 1859; "degrading vassalage" from ibid., February 18, 1860; see also Richard Call's use of similar terms, in ibid., March 24, 1860; "prates" from ibid., December 24, 1859; "the white race" from Call, in ibid., March 24, 1860; "general insurrection" from Madison Perry, in ibid., December 10, 1859; "sister" states from ibid., February 4, 1860.

49. Calhoun rebellion from Davis, *Civil War and Reconstruction in Florida*, 44, and *Tallahassee Floridian and Journal*, October 13, 1860; Keitt from Laurence Keitt to Susie, February 29, 1860, Keitt Papers, Duke; Madison murder from ibid.; insurrection scare from *Monticello Family Friend*, November 24, 1860.

50. Perry from *Tallahassee Floridian and Journal*, December 1, 1860, cited in Davis, *Civil War and Reconstruction in Florida*, 48; "*Resist*" from ibid., November 10, 1860; see also ibid., August 11, December 22, 1860.

51. *Tallahassee Floridian and Journal*, October 6, November 10, 17, 1860; Perry from ibid., December 1, 1860.

52. Ethelred Philips to J. J. Philips, December 20, 1860, Folder 1, James J. Philips Papers, SHC. See also R. K. Call to Edward Everett, December 31, 1860, Call Correspondence, FSA.

53. *Journal of the Proceedings of the Convention of the People of Florida*, 5; 1860 Property Tax Book, JCC; 1860 Property Tax Book, LCC.

54. *Journal of the Proceedings of the Convention of the People of Florida*, 1–39.

55. Ibid.

56. My analysis here casts the planters' political behavior as the product (in part) of internalized historical experience, i.e., something like the concept of habitus in Bourdieu, *Logic of Practice*.

57. *Journal of the Proceedings of the Convention of the People of Florida*, 34–35.

58. Ibid., 47, 49.

59. Walther, *Fire-Eaters*, 1–7, suggests that the contradictions between historians reflect to some degree the contradictions and wide diversity among secessionists themselves. For explanations focused on class conflict and elite control, see Barney, *Secessionist Impulse*, and Michael P. Johnson, *Towards a Patriarchal Republic*; for fear of insurrection, see Channing, *Crisis of Fear*; for explanations of the acceleration of conflict within electoral politics include, see Potter, *Impending Crisis*, and Nichols, *Disruption of American Democracy*; for republicanism, see Ford, *Origins of Southern Radicalism*, and J. Mills Thornton, *Politics and Power*; for planters' antidemocratic proslavery ideology, see Sinha, *Counterrevolution of Slavery*, which oddly comports well with Hahn, *Roots of Southern Populism*, esp. 105–16; for the yeoman fear of a loss of control over households and society, see McCurry, *Masters of Small Worlds*, 277–304; for the "social ethic," see Bond, *Political Culture*; for the similar argument that slavery was "the main thing," see Carey, *Parties, Slavery, and the Union*, 226–50 (quote on 226); Cooper, *Liberty and Slavery*; or Bryant, *How Curious a Land*. See also Shade, *Democratizing the Old Dominion*, 286, and Olsen, *Political Culture and Secession*. For a multicausal analysis that notes that slaveowners' ideas of their own history also helped to shape their reactions, see Harris, *Plain Folk and Gentry*, 136–39.

60. For Alabama, see Thornton, *Politics and Power*, and Dupre, *Transforming the Cotton Frontier*; for Mississippi, see Christopher Morris's *Becoming Southern*, although Morris sees little evidence of a democratization of Mississippi politics (132–55); for Arkansas, see McNeilly, *Old South Frontier*; for Louisiana, see Shugg, *Origins of Class Struggle*; see also Aron, *How The West Was Lost*.

CONCLUSION

1. On the resignation that they sought to wring from religious consolation as well, see Tribute to Joel Blake, Third Quarterly Conference of the Methodist Church, Leon County, August 1, 1863, Blake Papers, SHC.

2. Ethelred Philips to James J. Philips, January 14, 1864; June 26, November 18, December 25, 1862, December 8, 1863, June 19, 1864, all Folder 2, Philips Papers, SHC; Buker, *Blockaders, Refugees, and Contrabands*.

3. Francis Eppes to N. W. Eppes, October 24, 1864, Box 367, Pine Hill Plantation Papers, FSU; Doherty, *Richard K. Call*, 161.

4. M. E. Whitner to Sallie Galphin, 1865[?], Burroughs Papers, FSL; see also David F. Williams, *Rich Man's War*.

5. Ethelred Philips to James J. Philips, October 14, 1864, Folder 2, Philips Papers, SHC; Nulty, *Confederate Florida*; Johns, *Florida during the Civil War*; Robert W. Taylor, *Rebel Storehouse*; Coles, "'Far from Fields of Glory.'"

6. Davis, *Civil War and Reconstruction in Florida*, 319–30; Shofner, *Nor Is It over Yet*, 19.

7. Eppes, *Negro of the Old South*, 119–42; Rawick, *American Slave*, 17:81–82; see also ibid., 17:215 (Amanda McCray); Berlin and Rowland, eds., *Families and Freedom*, 230–31. The historiography of emancipation and African Americans' attempts to shape freedom and Reconstruction has blossomed in the past two decades. One

might begin with two recent books and their bibliographies: Schwalm, *Hard Fight for We,* and Edwards, *Gendered Strife and Confusion.*

8. Shofner, *Nor Is It over Yet;* Canter E. Brown, *Ossian Bingley Hart;* Shofner, *Jackson County;* Foner, *Reconstruction,* 431. 433; McGovern, *Anatomy of a Lynching.*

9. According to the *Oxford English Dictionary,* the term "Old South" first appeared in *Harper's* in 1871. For the mystification of the antebellum South that followed and its many uses to whites both North and South, one might consult a host of works, beginning with Silber, *Romance of Reunion;* Foster, *Ghosts of the Confederacy;* Burke Davis, *Long Surrender;* John David Smith, *Old Creed for the New South;* Blight, *Race and Reunion;* and Hale, *Making Whiteness,* 43–84.

10. See Eppes, *Negro of the Old South;* Eppes, *Through Some Eventful Years;* and Long, *Florida Breezes.*

Bibliography

MANUSCRIPT PRIMARY SOURCES

Broomall, Pennsylvania
   Family History Center, Church of Jesus Christ of Latter-day Saints
      International Genealogical Index
      Probate Records of Chatham County, Georgia

Chapel Hill, North Carolina
   Southern Historical Collection, Manuscript Department, Louis R. Wilson
   Library, University of North Carolina

D. M. Barringer Papers	Peter Hagner Papers
Jesse T. Bernard Papers	Harrington Papers
Blake Family Papers	Hentz Family Papers
Joseph Branch Papers	Thomas Devereux Hogg Papers
Branch Family Papers	Hubard Family Papers
J. Ozburn Carr Papers	Parish Family Papers
Farish Carter Papers	Parkhill Family Papers
Clingman-Puryear Family Papers	James J. Philips Papers
Coffield-Bellamy Papers	Cyrus Thompson Papers
Hardy B. Croom Papers	Nathaniel P. Trist Papers
Davidson Family Papers	Whitaker-Snipes Papers
Eppes Family Papers	W. H. Wills Papers
George Gray Papers	Wirt Family Papers

Durham, North Carolina
   Special Collections, William Perkins Library, Duke University

Ambler-Brown Papers	Edward Hicks Papers
Elizabeth Blanks Papers	Ince Papers
Branch Family Papers	Jarrett-Puryear Papers
Neill Brown Papers	George Noble Jones Papers
Butler Family Papers	Laurence Keitt Papers
James Gadsden Papers	Benjamin Partridge Papers
Louis Goldsborough Papers	Richard Smith Account Book
William Haynie Hatchett Papers	

Marianna, Florida
   Jackson County Courthouse*

Deed Books A–B	Territorial Census, 1838
List of Taxable Property, 1829	Tract Book A
Property Tax Books, 1842–60	

* I viewed many of the records housed at the Jackson and Leon County Courthouses on microfilm owned by the Family History Library of the Church of Jesus Christ of Latter-day Saints at the Family History Center of the LDS church in Broomall, Pennsylvania.

Raleigh, North Carolina
North Carolina Division of Archives and History
State of North Carolina: Entries for   Secretary of State Revolutionary
  Claims for Lands within the   Military Papers
  County of Dobbs   Wynns Family Papers
Nash County Deed Abstracts

Richmond, Virginia
Virginia Historical Society
  Beverley Family Papers   Harrison Family Papers
  Thomas Brown Letter   John Marr Papers
  Abraham Cabell Papers   Laura Wirt Randall Letters
  Cabell Family Papers   Thomas Family Papers

Savannah, Georgia
Georgia Historical Society
  Burroughs Family Papers   Jones Family Papers

Tallahassee, Florida
Florida State Archives
  L. and M. A. Armistead Account   Florida Legislative Council Journal
    Book   Governors' Letter Books
  Miles Blake Account Book, 1815–30   Jackson County Historical Documents
  Brodie and Pettes Account Books   Outgoing Correspondence of the
  Richard K. Call Correspondence   Territorial Governors, 1821–45
  Richard K. Call Journal and Papers   Partridge Family Papers
  Correspondence of State Governors   Pisgah United Methodist Church
    Moseley, Brown, Broome, Perry,   (Leon County) Records
    and Milton   Randolph Family Papers
  Cotten-Elliot Family Papers   Taylor Papers
  Thomas Fitch Papers   Trinity Methodist Church
  Florida Election Returns, 1824–1926   (Tallahassee) Records
  Florida Legislative Council   Union Bank of Florida Minute Book
    Correspondence (Unicameral)   Whitaker-Bradford-Branch Collection
  Florida Legislative Council   Daniel Wiggins Papers
    Correspondence (Bicameral)   James M. Williams Papers

Florida State Library, Florida Room
  Blake-Parish Family Papers   Thomas J. Hodson Letters
  Sallie Galphin Burroughs Papers   Leon County Amnesty Oaths
  Flavius Byrd Papers   William Moseley Diary
  John Gamble Letter   John S. Tappan Letter
  O. T. Hammond Papers

Florida State University, Special Collections, Robert M. Strozier Library
  Bradford Family Papers   Nancy Cone Hagan Papers
  F. A. Byrd Papers   Frank Hatheway Diary
  Frances Elizabeth Brown   Charles Hutchinson Papers
    Douglass Memoirs   Lipona Letter Book (microfilm copy)
  Robert Gamble Diary (copy)   George W. Parkhill Letters
  Gamble Family Papers   Pine Hill Plantation Papers
  Wilbur Gramling Diary   William Wilson Papers (copy)

Leon County Courthouse
  Deed Books A–K   Superior and Circuit Court
  Law Case Files   Minute Books 1, 3–7
  Probate Packets, 1824–60   Will Books A–B
  Property Tax Books, 1829–60
Washington, D.C.
  National Archives
  Register of Signatures of Depositors in Branches of the Freedmen's Savings and
    Trust Company, 1865–1874. Tallahassee, Fla., Aug. 25, 1866–June 15, 1874.
  National Archives Microfilm Series (NAMS), M816, Roll 5

GOVERNMENT DOCUMENTS

Florida. House of Representatives. *House Journal.* 1845–61.
Florida. Senate. *Senate Journal.* 1845–61.
U.S. Bureau of the Census. *Census,* 1790, 1st, 1800, 2nd, 1810, 3rd, 1840, 4th, 1830, 5th, 1840,
  6th, 1850, 7th, 1860, 8th. Washington: Government Printing Office.
U.S. Congress. House. *Condition of Banks, 1840.* 26th Cong., 2d sess., 1840. H. Doc. 111.
  Serial 385.

NEWSPAPERS

Apalachicola Courier
Apalachicola Gazette
Jacksonville Courier
Jacksonville News
Jacksonville Republican
Marianna Florida Whig
Monticello Family Friend
Niles' National Register
  (Washington, D.C.)
Pensacola Floridian
Pensacola Gazette
Pensacola West Florida Gazette and
Advertiser

St. Augustine Florida Herald and
  Southern Democrat
Tallahassee Florida Advocate
Tallahassee Florida Intelligencer
Tallahassee Florida Sentinel
Tallahassee Floridian
Tallahassee Floridian and Advocate
Tallahassee Floridian and Journal
Tallahassee Southern Journal
Tallahassee Star of Florida

BOOKS AND ARTICLES

Abbey, Kathryn T. "Documents Relating to El Destino and Chemonie Plantations,
  Middle Florida, 1828–1868." Parts 1–5. *Florida Historical Quarterly* 7 (January, April,
  July, October 1929).
———. "The Story of the Lafayette Lands in Florida." *Florida Historical Quarterly* 10
  (January 1932): 118–32.
———. "The Union Bank of Tallahassee: An Experiment in Territorial Finance."
  Florida Historical Quarterly 15 (April 1937): 207–31.

Abernethey, Thomas P. *Three Virginia Frontiers*. Baton Rouge: Louisiana State University Press, 1940.

Abrahams, Roger. *Singing the Master: The Emergence of African-American Culture in the Plantation South*. New York: Pantheon, 1992.

Adair, Douglass. *Fame and the Founding Fathers*. Edited by Robert Shalhope. New York: Norton, 1974.

Adams, Herbert Baxter. *The Germanic Origin of New England Towns*. Baltimore: Johns Hopkins University Press, 1882.

Allen, Alexander. *Allen's Journal: A Trip along the Georgia-Florida Boundary, 1854*. Edited by C. T. Trowell and F. R. Trowell. N.p., 1984.

Allmendinger, David F., Jr. *Ruffin: Family and Reform in the Old South*. New York: Oxford University Press, 1990.

Appleby, Joyce, Lynn Hunt, and Margaret Jacob. *Telling the Truth about History*. New York: Norton, 1994.

Aptheker, Herbert. *American Negro Slave Revolts*. New York: International Publishers, 1969.

Aron, Stephen. *How the West Was Lost: The Transformation of Kentucky From Daniel Boone to Henry Clay*. Baltimore: Johns Hopkins University Press, 1996.

———. "Lessons in Conquest: Towards a Greater Western History." *Pacific Historical Review* 43 (May 1994): 125–47.

Ashford, Leslie L. "Loyal to the End: The Life of James Page, 1808–1883." *Journal of Negro History* 82 (January 1997): 169–79.

Ayers, Edward L. "Narrating the New South." *Journal of Southern History* 61 (August 1995): 555–66.

———. *Vengeance and Justice: Crime and Punishment in the Nineteenth-Century South*. New York: Oxford University Press, 1984.

Badinter, Elisabeth. *XY: On Masculine Identity*. Translated by Lydia Davis. New York: Columbia University Press, 1995.

Bailyn, Bernard. "Politics and Social Structure in Virginia." In *Seventeenth-Century America: Essays on Colonial History*, edited by James M. Smith, 90–115. Chapel Hill: University of North Carolina Press, 1959.

Bakhtin, Mikhail. *The Dialogic Imagination: Four Essays*. Translated by Caryl Emerson and Michael Holquist. Edited by Michael Holquist. Austin: University of Texas Press, 1981.

———. *Rabelais and His World*. Translated by Helene Iswolsky. Cambridge Mass.: MIT Press, 1968.

———. *Speech Genres and Other Late Essays*. Translated by Vern McGee. Edited by Caryl Emerson and Michael Holquist. Austin: University of Texas Press, 1986.

Baldwin, Joseph G. *The Flush Times of Alabama and Mississippi*. New York: D. Appleton and Co., 1853.

Ball, Charles. *Fifty Years in Chains*. 1837. New York: Dover, 1970.

Balleisen, Edward J. *Navigating Failure: Bankruptcy and Commercial Society in Antebellum America*. Chapel Hill: University of North Carolina Press, 2001.

Banaji, J. "Modes of Production in a Materialist Conception of History." *Capital and Class* 3 (Autumn 1977): 1–44.

Bancroft, Frederic. *Slave Trading in the Old South*. 3rd ed. New York: Ungar, 1969.

Banfield, Edward C. *The Moral Basis of a Backward Society*. New York: Free Press, 1967.

Baptist, Edward E. "Accidental Ethnography in an Antebellum Southern Newspaper: Snell's Homecoming Festival." *Journal of American History* 84 (March 1998): 1355–83.

————. "'Cuffy,' 'Fancy Maids,' and 'One-Eyed Men': Rape, Commodification, and the Domestic Slave Trade in the United States." *American Historical Review* 107 (December 2001).

————. "The Migration of Planters to Antebellum Florida: Kinship and Power." *Journal of Southern History* 62 (August 1996): 527–54.

Bardaglio, Peter. *Reconstructing the Household: Families, Sex, and Power in the Nineteenth-Century South.* Chapel Hill: University of North Carolina Press, 1995.

Barney, William. *The Secessionist Impulse: Alabama and Mississippi in 1860.* Princeton: Princeton University Press, 1974.

Barnhart, John D. "Frontiersmen and Planters in the Formation of Kentucky." *Journal of Southern History* 7 (February 1941): 18–36.

Bartram, William. *Travels of William Bartram.* Edited by Mark Van Doren. New York: Dover, 1928.

Bassett, John Spencer, ed. *Correspondence of Andrew Jackson.* 7 vols. Carnegie Institution of Washington Publication. Papers of the Department of Historical Research, no. 371. Washington: Carnegie Institution: 1926–35.

Bateman, Fred, and Robert Weiss. *A Deplorable Scarcity: The Failure of Industrialization in the Slave Economy.* Chapel Hill: University of North Carolina Press, 1981.

Beckles, Hilary McD. *Natural Rebels: A Social History of Enslaved Black Women in Barbados.* New Brunswick, N.J.: Rutgers University Press, 1989.

Bederman, Gail. *Manliness and Civilization: A Cultural History of Gender and Race in the United States, 1880–1917.* Chicago: University of Chicago Press, 1995.

Beeman, Richard R. *The Evolution of the Southern Backcountry: A Case Study of Lunenburg County, Virginia, 1746–1832.* Philadelphia: University of Pennsylvania Press, 1984.

Bellamy, Samuel C., M.D. *An Address Delivered Before the Chipola Division, No. 6, Of the Sons of Temperance, on the 4th July, 1849.* Tallahassee: Office of the Floridian and Journal, 1849.

Benwell, J. *An Englishman's Travels in America: His Observations of Life and Manners in the Free and Slave States.* London: Binns and Goodwin, 1853.

Berlin, Ira. *Many Thousands Gone: The First Two Centuries of Slavery in North America.* Cambridge, Mass.: Belknap Press, 1998.

Berlin, Ira, and Ronald Hoffman, eds. *Slavery and Freedom in the Age of the American Revolution.* Charlottesville: University of Virginia and United States Capitol Historical Society, 1983.

Berlin, Ira, and Philip D. Morgan, eds. *Cultivation and Culture: Labor and the Shaping of Slave Life in the Americas.* Charlottesville: University Press of Virginia, 1993.

Berlin, Ira, and Leslie S. Rowland, eds. *Families and Freedom: A Documentary History of African-American Kinship in the Civil War Era.* New York: New Press, 1997.

Bernstein, Michael André. *Foregone Conclusions: Against Apocalyptic History.* Berkeley: University of California Press, 1994.

Blackburn, Robin. *The Overthrow of Colonial Slavery, 1776–1848.* London: Verso, 1988.

————. *The Making of New World Slavery: From the Baroque to the Modern, 1492–1800.* London: Verso, 1997.

Black-Michaud, Jacob. *Cohesive Force: Feud in the Mediterranean and the Middle East.* New York: St. Martin's, 1975.

Blassingame, John. *The Slave Community.* 2d ed. New York: Oxford University Press, 1979.

————, ed. *Slave Testimony.* Baton Rouge: Louisiana State University Press, 1977.

Bleser, Carol, ed. *Tokens of Affection: The Letters of a Planter's Daughter in the Old South.*
Athens: University of Georgia Press, 1996.

Blight, David. *Race and Reunion: The Civil War in American Memory.* Cambridge: Belknap
Press, 2001.

Bloch, Marc. *The Historian's Craft.* Translated by Peter Putnam. New York: Knopf, 1953.

Bode, Frederick A., and Donald E. Ginter. *Farm Tenancy and the Census in Antebellum
Georgia.* Athens: University of Georgia Press, 1980.

Bolton, Charles S. *Poor Whites of the Antebellum South: Tenants and Laborers in Central
North Carolina and Northeast Mississippi.* Durham: Duke University Press, 1993.

Bolton, Charles S., and Scott P. Culclasure. *The Confessions of Edward Isham: A Poor
White Life of the Old South.* Athens: University of Georgia Press, 1998.

Bond, Bradley. *Political Culture in the Nineteenth-Century South: Mississippi, 1830–1890.*
Baton Rouge: Louisiana State University Press, 1995.

Boston, Norman E. *A History of "Old Pisgah": Highlights and Happenstances, 1830–1976.*
Tallahassee: published by the author, 1976.

Bourdieu, Pierre. *The Logic of Practice.* Translated by Richard Nice. Cambridge: Polity,
1990.

Bourke, Paul, and Donald DeBats. *Washington County: Politics and Community in Antebellum America.* Baltimore: Johns Hopkins University Press, 1995.

Brinton, Daniel G. *Notes on the Floridian Peninsula: Its Literary History, Indian Tribes, and
Antiquities.* Philadelphia: J. Sabin, 1859.

Brown, Canter E., Jr. *Ossian Bingley Hart: Florida's Loyalist Reconstruction Governor.*
Baton Rouge: Louisiana State University Press, 1997.

———. "Race Relations in Territorial Florida, 1821–1845." *Florida Historical Quarterly* 73
(June 1995): 287–307.

Brown, David D. *Walter Scott and the Historical Imagination.* Boston: Routledge and
Kegan Paul, 1979.

Brown, Kathleen M. *Good Wives, Nasty Wenches, and Anxious Patriarchs: Gender, Race, and
Power in Colonial Virginia.* Chapel Hill: University of North Carolina Press, 1996.

Brown, William Wells. *The Narrative of William Wells Brown, A Fugitive Slave, Written by
Himself.* Boston: The Anti-Slavery Office, 1847.

Bruce, Dickson. *Violence and Culture in the Antebellum South.* Austin: University of Texas
Press, 1979.

Bryant, James C. *Indian Springs: The History of a Pioneer Church.* Tallahassee: Florida
State University Press, 1971.

Bryant, Jonathan. *How Curious a Land: Conflict and Change in Green County, Georgia,
1850–1885.* Chapel Hill: University of North Carolina Press, 1996.

Buker, George. *Blockaders, Refugees, and Contrabands: Civil War on Florida's Gulf Coast,
1861–1865.* Tuscaloosa: University of Alabama Press, 1993.

Burton, Orville Vernon. *In My Father's House Are Many Mansions: Family and Community
in Edgefield, South Carolina.* Chapel Hill: University of North Carolina Press, 1985.

Bynum, Victoria. *Unruly Women: The Politics of Social and Sexual Control in the Old South.*
Chapel Hill: University of North Carolina Press, 1992.

Calderhead, William. "How Extensive Was the Border States Slave Trade? A New
Look." *Civil War History* 18 (March 1972): 42–55.

Calhoon, Robert M. "A Troubled Culture: North Carolina in the New Nation, 1790–
1834." In *Writing North Carolina History,* edited by Jeffrey J. Crow and Larry Tise,
76–110. Chapel Hill: University of North Carolina Press, 1979.

Campbell, James T. "The Charles Hutchinson Letters from Territorial Tallahassee, 1839–1843." *Apalachee* 4 (1950–56): 13–28.

Campbell, Randolph. *A Southern Community in Crisis: Harrison County, Texas, 1850–1880.* Austin: University of Texas, 1983.

Carey, Anthony Gene. *Parties, Slavery, and the Union in Antebellum Georgia.* Athens: University of Georgia Press, 1997.

Carnes, Mark C., and Clyde Griffen, eds. *Meanings for Manhood: Constructions of Masculinity in Victorian America.* Chicago: University of Chicago Press, 1990.

Carter, Clarence Edwin, and John Porter Bloom, comps. and eds. *The Territorial Papers of the United States of America.* 28 vols. Washington: U.S. Govt. Printing Office, 1934–75.

Cash, W. J. *The Mind of the South.* New York: A. A. Knopf, 1941.

Cashin, Joan. *A Family Venture: Men and Women on the Southern Frontier.* Baltimore: Johns Hopkins University Press, 1991.

———. "The Structure of Antebellum Planter Families: The Ties That Bound Us Was Strong." *Journal of Southern History* 56 (February 1990): 55–70.

Castelnau, Francis Comte de. "Essay on Middle Florida, 1837–1838." Parts 1 and 2. Translated by Arthur Seymour. *Florida Historical Quarterly* 26 (January 1948): 199–255; (April 1948): 300–324.

———. *Vues et Souvenirs de l'Amérique du Nord.* Paris: A. Bertrand, 1842.

Castronovo, Russ. *Fathering the Nation: American Genealogies of Slavery and Freedom.* Berkeley: University of California Press, 1995.

Cathey, Cornelius O. *Agricultural Developments in North Carolina, 1763–1860.* Chapel Hill: University of North Carolina Press, 1956.

Cecil-Fronsman, Bill. *Common Whites: Class and Culture in Antebellum North Carolina.* Lexington, Ky.: University of Kentucky Press, 1992.

Censer, Jane Turner. *North Carolina Planters and Their Children, 1800–1860.* Baton Rouge: Louisiana State University Press, 1984.

———. "Southwestern Migration among North Carolina Planters: The Disposition to Emigrate." *Journal of Southern History* 57 (April 1991): 407–26.

Channing, Steven A. *Crisis of Fear: Secession in South Carolina.* New York: Simon and Schuster, 1970.

Chaplin, Joyce. *An Anxious Pursuit: Agricultural Innovation and Modernity in the Lower South, 1730–1815.* Chapel Hill: University of North Carolina Press, 1993.

Chase, Richard. *Jack Tales: Folk Tales from the Southern Appalachians Collected and Retold by Richard Chase.* Boston: Houghton Mifflin Company, 1943.

Clark, Blanche Henry. *The Tennessee Yeomen, 1840–1860.* Nashville: Vanderbilt University Press, 1942.

Clinton, Catherine. *The Plantation Mistress: Women's World in the Old South.* New York: Pantheon, 1983.

Clinton, Charles. *A Winter from Home.* New York: J. F. Trow, 1852.

Collins, Winfield. *The Domestic Slave Trade of the Southern States.* 1909. Port Washington. N.Y.: Kennikat Press, 1969.

Conrad, Robert. *World of Sorrow: The African Slave Trade to Brazil.* Baton Rouge: Louisiana State University Press, 1986.

Cooper, William J. *Liberty and Slavery: Southern Politics to 1860.* New York: Knopf, 1983.

Coulter, E. Merton. *Old Petersburg and the Broad River Valley of Georgia: Their Rise and Decline.* Athens: University of Georgia Press, 1965.

Courtwright, David T. *Violent Land: Single Men and Social Disorder from the Frontier to the Inner City.* Cambridge, Mass.: Harvard University Press, 1996.

Covington, James W. *The Seminoles of Florida,* Gainesville: University Press of Florida, 1993.

Craton, Michael. *Testing the Chains: Resistance to Slavery in the British West Indies.* Ithaca: Cornell University Press, 1982.

Craven, Avery O. *Soil Exhaustion as a Factor in the Agricultural History of Virginia and Maryland, 1601–1860.* Urbana: University of Illinois, 1925.

———. "The 'Turner Theories' and the South." *Journal of Southern History* 5 (August 1939): 291–314.

Crockett, W. S. *Abbotsford.* London: Adam and Charles Black, 1905.

Curti, Merle. *The Making of an American Community: A Case Study of Democracy in a Frontier County.* Stanford: Stanford University Press, 1959.

Curtin, Philip. *The Atlantic Slave Trade: A Census.* Madison: University of Wisconsin Press, 1969.

———. *The Rise and Fall of the Atlantic Plantation Complex: Essays in Atlantic History.* Cambridge, Eng.: Cambridge University Press, 1990.

Da Costa, Emilia Viotti. *Crowns of Glory, Tears of Blood: The Demarara Slave Rebellion of 1823.* New York: Oxford University Press, 1994.

Darby, William. *Memoir on the Geography, and Natural and Civil History of Florida: And an Appendix, Containing the Treaty of Cession.* Philadelphia: T. H. Palmer, 1821.

David, Paul, et al., eds. *Reckoning with Slavery: A Critical Study in the Quantitative History of American Negro Slavery.* New York: Oxford University Press, 1976.

Davidson, Alvie, comp. *Florida Land: Records of the Tallahassee and Newnansville General Land Office, 1825–1892.* Bowie, Md.: Heritage Books, 1989.

Davis, Burke. *The Long Surrender.* New York: Random House, 1985.

Davis, Lance E., and Robert J. Cull. *International Capital Markets and American Economic Growth, 1820–1914.* Cambridge: Cambridge University Press, 1994.

Davis, William Watson. *The Civil War and Reconstruction in Florida.* New York: Columbia University, 1913.

Dean, Warren. *Rio Claro: A Brazilian Plantation System, 1820–1920.* Stanford: Stanford University Press, 1976.

DeBow, J. D. B. *Statistical View of the United States . . . Being a Compendium of the Seventh Census.* Washington: A. D. P. Nicholson, 1854.

Dekker, George. *The American Historical Romance.* Cambridge, Eng.: Cambridge University Press, 1987.

Denham, James M. "The Florida Cracker Before the Civil War as Seen Through Travelers Accounts." *Florida Historical Quarterly* 72 (August 1994): 443–55.

———. "The Read-Alston Duel and Politics in Territorial Middle Florida." *Florida Historical Quarterly* 67 (August 1990): 427–46.

———. *A Rogue's Paradise: Crime and Punishment in Antebellum Florida.* Tuscaloosa: University of Alabama Press, 1997.

———. "'Some Prefer the Seminoles': Violence and Disorder among Soldiers and Settlers in the Second Seminole War." *Florida Historical Quarterly* 70 (July 1991): 38–54.

Deyle, Steven. "The Irony of Liberty: Origins of the Domestic Slave Trade." *Journal of the Early Republic* 12 (Spring 1992): 37–62.

Dick, Everett C. *The Dixie Frontier: A Social History of the Southern Frontier from the First Transmontane Beginnings to the Civil War.* 1948. New York: Capricorn Books, 1964.

————. *The Lure of the Land: A Social History of the Public Lands from the Articles of Confederation to the New Deal.* Lincoln: University of Nebraska Press, 1970.

Dodd, Dorothy. "The Corporation of Tallahassee, 1826–1840." *Apalachee* 3 (1948–50): 80–95.

————. "The Florida Census of 1825." *Florida Historical Quarterly* 17 (July 1943): 34–40.

————. "Locating the County Seat of Jackson County." *Florida Historical Quarterly* 26 (July 1947): 44–54.

————. "The Secession Movement in Florida." *Florida Historical Quarterly* 12 (July 1933): 10–12.

————, ed. *Florida Becomes a State.* Tallahassee: Florida Centennial Commission, 1945.

Dodd, William E. *The Life of Nathaniel Macon.* New York: Burt Franklin, 1908.

Dodd, William G. "Ring Tournaments in Tallahassee." *Apalachee* 3 (1948–50): 55–70.

Doherty, Herbert J., Jr. "Andrew Jackson's Cronies in Florida Territorial Politics." *Florida Historical Quarterly* 34 (July 1955): 3–29.

————. "Political Factions in Territorial Florida." *Florida Historical Quarterly* 28 (October 1949): 131–42.

————. *Richard K. Call: Southern Unionist.* Gainesville: University of Florida Press, 1961.

————. *The Whigs of Florida.* Gainesville: University of Florida Press, 1959.

Douglas, Thomas. *Autobiography of Thomas Douglas, Late Judge of the Supreme Court of Florida.* Edited by Henry Stiles. New York: Calkins and Stiles, 1856.

Dovell, Junius. *History of Banking in Florida, 1828–1954.* Orlando: Florida Bankers Association, 1955.

Doyle, Don H. *Faulkner's County: The Historical Roots of Yoknapatawpha.* Chapel Hill: University of North Carolina Press, 2001.

————. *The Social Order of a Frontier Community: Jacksonville, Illinois, 1820–1870.* Urbana, Ill.: University of Illinois Press, 1978.

Dunn, Richard S. *Sugar and Slaves: The Rise of the Planter Class in the British West Indies, 1624–1713.* Chapel Hill: University of North Carolina Press, 1972.

Dupre, Daniel. "Ambivalent Capitalists on the Cotton Frontier: Settlement and Development in the Tennessee Valley of Alabama." *Journal of Southern History* 56 (May 1990): 215–40.

————. *Transforming the Cotton Frontier: Madison County, Alabama, 1800–1840.* Baton Rouge: Louisiana State University Press, 1997.

Durrill, Wayne. *War of Another Kind: A Southern Community in the Great Rebellion.* New York: Oxford University Press, 1990.

Dusinberre, William. *Them Dark Days: Slavery in the American Rice Swamps.* New York: Oxford University Press, 1996.

DuVal, John P. *Compilation of the Public Acts of the Legislative Council of the Territory of Florida Passed Prior to 1840.* Tallahassee: S. S. Sibley, 1839.

Eaton, Clement. *The Freedom-of-Thought Struggle in the Old South.* New York: Harper & Row, 1964.

————. *The Growth of Southern Civilization, 1790–1860.* New York: Harper, 1961.

Edwards, Laura F. *Gendered Strife and Confusion: The Political Culture of Reconstruction,* Urbana: University of Illinois Press, 1997.

————. "Sexual Violence, Gender, Reconstruction, and the Extension of Patriarchy in Granville County, North Carolina." *North Carolina Historical Review* 68 (July 1991): 237–60.

Egerton, Douglas. *Gabriel's Rebellion: The Virginia Slave Conspiracies of 1800 and 1802.* Chapel Hill: University of North Carolina Press, 1993.

―――. "Markets without a Market Revolution: Southern Planters and Capitalism." *Journal of the Early Republic* 16 (Summer 1996): 207–21.

Elkins, Stanley. *Slavery: A Problem in American Institutional and Intellectual Life.* Chicago: University of Chicago Press, 1959.

Elkins, Stanley, and Eric McKitrick. "A Meaning for Turner's Frontier, Part I: Democracy in the Old Northwest." *Political Science Quarterly* 69 (September 1954): 321–53.

―――. "A Meaning for Turner's Frontier, Part II: The Southwest Frontier and New England." *Political Science Quarterly* 69 (December 1954): 565–602.

Ellison, Ralph. "Change the Joke and Slip the Yoke." In *Shadow and Act*, by Ralph Ellison, 45–59. New York: Random House, 1964.

Eltis, David. *The Rise of African Slavery in the Americas.* Cambridge: Cambridge University Press, 2000.

―――. "The Traffic in Slaves between the British West Indian Colonies, 1807–1833." *Economic History Review*, 2d ser., 25 (February 1972): 55–64.

Emerson, Caryl. "Problems with Baxtin's Poetics." *Slavic and East European Journal* 32 (Winter 1988): 503–25.

Emerson, Caryl, and Gary Saul Morson. *Mikhail Bakhtin: Creation of a Prosaics.* Stanford: Stanford University Press, 1990.

Engerman, Stanley. "A Note on the Economic Consequences of the Second Bank of the United States." *Journal of Political Economy* 78 (July/August 1970): 725–28.

Eppes, Susan Bradford. *The Negro of the Old South: A Bit of Period History.* Chicago: Joseph Branch, 1925.

―――. *Through Some Eventful Years.* Macon, Ga.: J. W. Burke, 1926.

Escott, Paul. *Many Excellent People: Power and Privilege in North Carolina, 1850–1900.* Chapel Hill: University of North Carolina Press, 1985.

―――. *Slavery Remembered: A Record of Twentieth-Century Ex-Slave Narratives.* Chapel Hill: University of North Carolina Press, 1977.

Evans, J. "Interesting from Florida." *Religious Intelligencer* 13 (December 13, 1828).

[Extract from the *Tallahassee Floridian*.] *American Farmer* 39 (December 19, 1828).

Fairbanks, George. *The Early History of Florida: An Introductory Lecture, Delivered by George Fairbanks, Esq., before the Florida Historical Society, April 15, 1857, with an Appendix, Containing the Constitution, Organization, and List of Members of the Society.* St. Augustine: 1857.

―――. *History and Antiquities of the City of St. Augustine, Florida . . . .* New York: Charles Norton, 1858.

Faragher, John Mack. *Sugar Creek: Life on the Illinois Prairie.* New Haven: Yale University Press, 1986.

―――, ed. *Rereading Frederick Jackson Turner: The Significance of the Frontier in American History and Other Essays.* New York: H. Holt, 1994.

Faust, Drew Gilpin. "The Civil War Soldier and the Art of Dying." *Journal of Southern History* 67 (February, 2001): 3–38.

―――. "Evangelicalism and the Meaning of the Proslavery Argument: The Reverend Thornton Stringfellow of Virginia." *Virginia Magazine of History and Biography* 85 (January 1977): 3–17.

―――. *James Henry Hammond and the Old South: A Design for Mastery.* Baton Rouge: Louisiana State University Press, 1982.

―――. *Southern Stories: Slaveholders in Peace and War.* Columbia: University of Missouri Press, 1992.

————, ed. *The Ideology of Slavery: Proslavery Thought in the Antebellum South, 1830–1860.* Baton Rouge: Louisiana State University Press, 1981.

Feierman, Steven. *Peasant Intellectuals: Anthropology and History in Tanzania.* Madison: University of Wisconsin Press, 1990.

Feller, Daniel. *The Public Lands in Jacksonian Politics.* Madison: University of Wisconsin Press, 1984.

Fick, Carolyn. *The Making of Haiti: The St. Domingue Revolution from Below.* Knoxville: University of Tennessee Press, 1990.

Fields, William C. *Abstracts of the Minutes of the Court of Pleas and Quarter Sessions of Cumberland County, April 1779–January 1791.* Raleigh: n.p., 1981.

Fischer, David Hackett. "*Albion* and the Critics: Further Evidence and Reflection." *William and Mary Quarterly,* 3d ser., 48 (Spring 1991): 260–308.

————. *Albion's Seed: Four British Folkways in America.* New York: Oxford University Press, 1989.

Fischer, David Hackett, and James Kelly. *Away, I'm Bound Away: Virginia and the Westward Movement.* Richmond: Virginia Historical Society, 1993.

Fleming, Philip. *Memoir of Captain C. Seton Fleming of the Second Florida Infantry.* Jacksonville: Times-Union, 1884.

Fleishman, Avrom. *The English Historical Novel: Walter Scott to Virginia Woolf.* Baltimore: John Hopkins University Press, 1971.

Fleming, Walter L. *The Freedman's Savings Bank: A Chapter in the Economic History of the Negro Race.* Chapel Hill: University of North Carolina Press, 1927.

"Florida." *Southern Review* 6 (November 1830): 410–20.

Florida Bureau of Historical Sites and Properties. *The Delegates to the St. Joseph Constitutional Convention, 1838–1839.* Tallahassee: Florida Department of State, 1980.

Fogel, Robert. *Without Consent or Contract: The Rise and Fall of American Slavery.* New York: Norton, 1989.

Fogel, Robert, and Stanley Engerman. *Time on the Cross: The Economics of American Negro Slavery.* Boston: Little, Brown, 1974.

Foner, Eric, *Reconstruction: America's Unfinished Revolution, 1863–1877.* New York: Harper & Row, 1988.

Forbes, James G. *Sketches, Historical and Topographical, of the Floridas: More Particularly of East Florida.* New York: C. S. Van Winkle, 1821.

Ford, Lacy K. "Frontier Democracy: The Turner Thesis Revisited." *Journal of the Early Republic* 13 (Summer 1993): 144–63.

————. *Origins of Southern Radicalism: The South Carolina Upcountry, 1800–1860.* New York: Oxford University Press, 1988.

Foster, Gaines. *Ghosts of the Confederacy: Defeat, The Lost Cause, and the Emergence of the New South, 1865 to 1913.* Baton Rouge: Louisiana State University Press, 1987.

Foust, James D. *The Yeoman Farmer and the Westward Expansion of Cotton Production.* New York: Arno Press, 1975.

Fox-Genovese, Elizabeth. *Within the Plantation Household: Black and White Women of the Old South.* Chapel Hill: University of North Carolina Press, 1988.

Fox-Genovese, Elizabeth, and Eugene Genovese. *Fruits of Merchant Capital: Slavery and Bourgeois Property in the Rise and Expansion of Capitalism.* New York: Oxford University Press, 1983.

————. "The Political Crisis of Social History: A Marxian Perspective." *Journal of Social History* 10 (Winter 1976): 205–20.

Franchot, Jenny. *Roads to Rome: The Antebellum Protestant Encounter with Catholicism.* Berkeley: University of California Press, 1994.

Franklin, John Hope. *The Militant South, 1800–1861.* Cambridge, Mass.: Harvard University Press, 1956.

Franklin, John Hope, and Loren Schweninger. *Runaway Slaves: Rebels on the Plantation, 1790–1860.* New York: Oxford University Press, 1999.

Freehling, William. *The Road to Disunion.* New York: Oxford University Press, 1990.

Freeman, Joanne B. "Dueling as a Form of Politics: Reinterpreting the Burr-Hamilton Duel." *William and Mary Quarterly,* 3d ser., 53 (Spring 1996): 289–318.

Frey, Sylvia R. *Water from the Rock: Black Resistance in a Revolutionary Age.* Princeton: Princeton University Press, 1991.

Friedman, Jean. *The Enclosed Garden: Women and Community in the Evangelical South, 1830–1900.* Chapel Hill: University of North Carolina Press, 1985.

Fritot, Jessie Robinson. *Pension Records of Soldiers of the Revolution Who Removed to Florida with Record of Service.* Jacksonville, Fla.: D.A.R., 1946.

Gannon, Michael, ed. *The New History of Florida.* Gainesville: University Press of Florida, 1996.

Gardiner, Michael. *The Dialogics of Critique: M. M. Bakhtin and the Theory of Ideology.* London: Routledge, 1992.

Gaspar, David Barry. *Bondmen and Rebels: A Case Study of Master-Slave Relations in Antigua, with Implications for Colonial British America.* Baltimore: Johns Hopkins University Press, 1986.

Gaspar, David Barry, and Darlene Clark Hine, eds. *More Than Chattel: Black Women and Slavery in the Americas.* Bloomington, Ind.: University of Indiana Press, 1996.

Gates, Henry Louis. *The Signifying Monkey: A Theory of Afro-American Literary Criticism.* New York: Oxford University Press, 1988.

Gates, Henry Louis, and Charles T. Davis, eds. *The Slave's Narrative.* New York: Oxford University Press, 1985.

Geertz, Clifford. *The Interpretation of Cultures.* New York: Basic Books, 1973.

Genovese, Eugene. *From Rebellion to Revolution: Afro-American Slave Revolts in the Making of the Modern World.* Baton Rouge: Louisiana State University Press, 1979.

———. *In Red and Black: Marxian Explorations in Southern and Afro-American History.* 2d ed. Knoxville: University of Tennessee Press, 1984.

———. *The Political Economy of Slavery: Studies in the Economy and Society of the Old South.* 1965. New York: Pantheon, 1967.

———. *Roll, Jordan, Roll: The World the Slaves Made.* New York: Pantheon, 1974.

———. "The Southern Slaveholders' View of the Middle Ages." In *Medievalism in American Culture: Papers of the Eighteenth Annual Conference of the Center for Medieval and Renaissance Studies,* edited by Bernard Rosenthal and Paul E. Szarmach, 31–52. Binghampton, N.Y.: Medieval and Renaissance Texts and Studies, 1989.

———. *The World the Slaveholders Made: Two Essays in Interpretation.* New York: Pantheon, 1969.

———. "Yeoman Farmers in a Slaveholders' Democracy." *Agricultural History* 49 (April 1975): 331–42.

Giddings, Joshua R. *The Exiles of Florida: Or; The Crimes Committed by Our Government Against the Maroons, Who Fled from South Carolina and Other Slave States, Seeking Protection under Spanish Law.* Columbus, Ohio: O. Follett, 1858.

Gilmore, David. *Manhood in the Making: Cultural Concepts of Masculinity.* New Haven: Yale University Press, 1990.

Gilpatrick, Delbert H. *Jeffersonian Democracy in North Carolina, 1789–1816.* 2d ed. New York: Octagon, 1967.

Ginzburg, Carlo. *The Cheese and the Worms: The Cosmos of a Sixteenth-Century Miller.* Translated by John and Anne Tedeschi. Baltimore: Johns Hopkins University Press, 1980.

Gomez, Michael. *Exchanging Our Country Marks.* Chapel Hill: University of North Carolina Press, 1998.

Gorn, Elliott. "'Gouge and Bite; Pull Hair and Scratch': The Social Significance of Fighting in the Southern Backcountry." *American Historical Review* 90 (February 1985): 18–43.

Gramsci, Antonio. *Selections from the Prison Notebooks of Antonio Gramsci.* Edited and translated by Quentin Hoare and Geoffrey Nowell Smith. New York: International Publishers, 1971.

Grandy, Moses. *Narrative of the Life of Moses Grandy, Late a Slave in the United States of America.* Boston: O. Johnson, 1844.

Gray, Lewis C. *History of Agriculture in the Southern United States to 1860.* 2 vols. Washington, D.C.: Carnegie Institution, 1933.

Gray, Susan E. *The Yankee West: Community Life on the Michigan Frontier.* Chapel Hill: University of North Carolina Press, 1996.

Green, Fletcher M. *Constitutional Development in the South Atlantic States, 1776–1860.* New York: Norton, 1961.

———. *Democracy in the Old South, and Other Essays.* Edited by Isaac Copeland. Nashville: Vanderbilt University Press, 1969.

Green, George. *Finance and Economic Development in the Old South; Louisiana Banking, 1804–1961.* Stanford: Stanford University Press, 1972.

Greenberg, Kenneth S. *Honor and Slavery: Lies, Duels, Noses, Masks, Dressing as a Woman, Gifts, Strangers, Humanitarianism, Death, Slave Rebellions, The Proslavery Argument, Baseball, Hunting, and Gambling in the Old South.* Princeton: Princeton University Press, 1996.

———. *Masters and Statesmen: The Political Culture of American Slavery.* Baltimore: Johns Hopkins University Press, 1985.

Greene, Jack P. *Pursuits of Happiness: The Social Development of Early Modern British Colonies and the Formation of American Culture.* Chapel Hill: University of North Carolina Press, 1988.

———. "Transplanting Moments: Inheritance in the Formation of Early American Culture." *William and Mary Quarterly,* 3d ser., 48 (Spring 1991): 224–30.

Griffin, Farah Jasmine. *"Who Set You Flowin'?": The African-American Migration Narrative.* New York: Oxford University Press, 1995.

Groene, Bertram H. *Ante-Bellum Tallahassee.* Tallahassee: Florida Heritage Foundation, 1971.

Gutman, Herbert G. *The Black Family in Slavery and Freedom, 1750–1925.* New York: Pantheon, 1976.

———. *Slavery and the Numbers Game: A Critique of Time on the Cross.* Urbana: University of Illinois Press, 1975.

Hackley, Richard. *Titles, and Legal Opinions Thereon, of Lands in East Florida, Belonging to Richard S. Hackley, Esq.* Fayetteville, N.C.: Edmund J. Hale, 1826.

Hahn, Steven. *The Roots of Southern Populism: Yeoman Farmers and the Transformation of the Georgia Upcountry, 1850–1890.* New York: Oxford University Press, 1983.

Hale, Grace Elizabeth. *Making Whiteness: The Culture of Segregation in the South, 1890–1940.* New York: Pantheon, 1999.

Hall, Kermit, and Eric W. Rise. *From Local Courts to National Tribunals: The Federal District Courts of Florida, 1821–1990.* Brooklyn: Carlson, 1991.

Hammond, Bray. *Banks and Politics in America: From the Revolution to the Civil War.* Princeton: Princeton University Press, 1957.

Hanna, A. J. *A Prince in Their Midst: The Adventurous Life of Achille Murat on the American Frontier.* Norman, Okla.: University of Oklahoma Press, 1946.

Harris, J. William. *Plain Folk and Gentry in a Slave Society: White Liberty and Black Slavery in Augusta's Hinterlands.* Middletown, Conn.: Wesleyan University Press, 1985.

Haywood, Marshall. *John Branch, 1782–1863, Governor of North Carolina, United States Senator . . . .* Raleigh: Commercial Printing Co., 1915.

Hentz, Caroline Lee. *Marcus Warland, or, The Long Moss Spring.* Philadelphia: T. B. Peterson, 1852.

———. *The Planter's Northern Bride: A Novel.* Philadelphia: T. B. Peterson, 1854.

Herbert, W. H. [William H.]. *Ringwood the Rover: A Tale of Florida.* Philadelphia: A. J. Rockefeller, 1843.

Heyrman, Christine Leigh. *Southern Cross: The Beginnings of the Bible Belt.* New York: Knopf, 1997.

Hobsbawm, Eric J. *Primitive Rebels: Studies in Archaic Forms of Social Movements in the 19th and 20th Centuries.* New York: W. W. Norton, 1965.

Hobsbawm, Eric J., and George Rudé. *Captain Swing.* New York: Pantheon, 1968.

Hopley, Catherine. *Life in the South from the Commencement of the War.* 2 vols. London: Chapman and Hall, 1863.

Horsman, Reginald. *Race and Manifest Destiny: The Origins of American Racial Anglo-Saxonism.* Cambridge, Mass.: Harvard University Press, 1981.

Howard, H. R. [Virgil Stewart]. *The History of Virgil A. Stewart: And His Adventure in Capturing the Great Western Land Pirate and His Gang . . . .* New York: Harper & Brothers, 1836.

Hudson, Charles. *The Southeastern Indians.* Knoxville: University of Tennessee Press, 1976.

Hughes, Louis. *Thirty Years a Slave: From Bondage to Freedom.* 1897. New York: Negro Universities Press, 1969.

Hundley, D. R. *Social Relations in Our Southern States.* New York: Henry B. Price, 1860.

Hunt, Robert. "A Domesticated Slavery: Political Economy in Caroline Hentz's Fiction." *Southern Quarterly* 34 (Summer 1996): 25–35.

Huxford, Folks, comp. and ed. *Pioneers of Wiregrass Georgia: A Biographical Account of Some of the Early Settlers of the Portion of Wiregrass Georgia Embraced in the Original Counties of Irwin, Appling, Wayne, Camden, and Glynn.* 5 vols. N.p., 1951–c.1988.

Hyde, Lewis. *Trickster Makes This World: Mischief, Myth, and Art.* New York: Farrar, Straus and Giroux, 1998.

Hyde, Samuel C., Jr., ed. *Plain Folk of the South Revisited.* Baton Rouge: Louisiana State University Press, 1997.

Ingraham, Joseph Holt. *The South-West—By a Yankee.* New York: Harper, 1835.

Irving, Washington. *Wolfert's Roost: And Other Papers, Now First Collected.* New York: G. P. Putnam, 1855.

Isaac, Rhys. *The Transformation of Virginia, 1740–1790.* Chapel Hill: University of North Carolina Press, 1982.

Jabour, Anya. *Marriage in the New Republic: Elizabeth and William Wirt and the Companionate Ideal*. Baltimore: Johns Hopkins University Press, 1998.

———. "'The Privations & Hardships of a New Country': Southern Women and Southern Hospitality on the Florida Frontier." *Florida Historical Quarterly* 75 (Winter 1997): 259–75.

James, C. L. R. *The Black Jacobins: Toussaint L'Ouverture and the San Domingo Revolution*. 2d ed. New York: Vintage, 1963.

Jenkins, William Sumner. *Pro-Slavery Thought in the Old South*. Chapel Hill: University of North Carolina Press, 1935.

Jenks, Leland H. *The Migration of British Capital to 1875*. New York: Nelson, 1927.

Johns, John E. *Florida during the Civil War*. Gainesville: University of Florida Press, 1963.

Johnson, Guion Griffis. *Ante-Bellum North Carolina: A Social History*. Chapel Hill: University of North Carolina Press, 1937.

Johnson, Michael P. *Towards a Patriarchal Republic: The Secession of Georgia*. Baton Rouge: Louisiana State University Press, 1977.

Johnson, Vicki Vaughn. *The Men and the Vision of the Southern Commercial Conventions*. Columbia: University of Missouri Press, 1993.

Johnson, Walter L. *Soul by Soul: Life Inside the Antebellum Slave Market*. Cambridge: Harvard University Press, 1999.

Jordan, Terry G., and Mattie Kaups. *The American Backwoods Frontier: An Ethnic and Ecological Interpretation*. Baltimore: Johns Hopkins University Press, 1989.

Jordan, Winthrop. *Tumult and Silence at Second Creek: An Inquiry into a Civil War Slave Conspiracy*. Rev. ed. Baton Rouge: Louisiana State University Press, 1995.

Journal of the Proceedings of the Convention of the People of Florida, Begun and Held at the Capitol in the City of Tallahassee on Thursday, January 3, A.D. 1861. Tallahassee: Office of the Floridian and Journal, 1861.

Joyner, Charles. *Down by the Riverside: A South Carolina Slave Community*. Urbana: University of Illinois Press, 1984.

Justice, Steven. *Writing and Rebellion: England in 1381*. Berkeley: University of California Press, 1996.

Karras, Alan L., and John R. McNeill, eds. *Atlantic American Societies: From Columbus through Abolition, 1492–1888*. New York: Routledge, 1992.

Kay, Marvin L. Michel, and Lorin Lee Cary. *Slavery in North Carolina, 1748–1775*. Chapel Hill: University of North Carolina Press, 1995.

Keller, William F. *The Nation's Advocate: Henry Marie Brackenridge and Young America*. Pittsburgh: University of Pittsburgh Press, 1956.

Kelly, James. *That Damn'd Thing Called Honour: Duelling in Ireland, 1570–1860*. Cork: Cork University Press, 1995.

Kennedy, John Pendleton. *Horse-Shoe Robinson*. London: Pratt, 1845.

———. *Swallow Barn; Or, A Sojourn in the Old Dominion*. Philadelphia: Carey and Lea, 1831.

Kenzer, Robert C. *Kinship and Neighborhood in a Southern Community: Orange County, North Carolina, 1849–1881*. Knoxville, University of Tennessee Press, 1987.

Kerber, Linda. "Separate Spheres, Female Worlds, Woman's Place: The Rhetoric of Women's History." *Journal of American History* 75 (June 1988): 9–39.

———. *Women of the Republic: Intellect and Ideology in Early America*. Chapel Hill: University of North Carolina Press, 1980.

Kilbourne, Richard H., Jr. *Debt, Investment, Slaves: Credit Relations in East Feliciana Parish, 1825–1885*. Tuscaloosa: University of Alabama Press, 1995.

Kimmel, Michael. *Manhood in America: A Cultural History*. New York: Free Press, 1996.

Kinard, Margaret. "Frontier Development of Williamson County." Parts 1 and 2. *Tennessee Historical Quarterly* 8 (March 1949): 3–33; (June 1949): 127–53.

King, Wilma. *Stolen Childhood: Slave Youth in Nineteenth-Century America*. Bloomington: University of Indiana Press, 1995.

Kinnaird, Laurence, and Lucia B. Kinnaird. "War Comes to San Marcos." *Florida Historical Quarterly* 67 (July 1983): 25–43.

Kiple, Kenneth F. *The Caribbean Slave: A Biological History*. Cambridge: Cambridge University Press, 1984.

Klein, Herbert. *The Middle Passage: Comparative Studies in the Atlantic Slave Trade*. Princeton: Princeton University Press, 1978.

Klein, Rachel. *Unification of a Slave State: The Rise of the Planter Class in the South Carolina Backcountry, 1760–1808*. Chapel Hill: University of North Carolina Press, 1990.

Kolchin, Peter. *Unfree Labor: American Slavery and Russian Serfdom*. Cambridge, Mass.: Harvard University Press, 1987.

Kramnick, Isaac. *Republicanism and Bourgeois Radicalism: Political Ideology in Late-Eighteenth-Century England and America*. Ithaca: Cornell University Press, 1990.

Kulikoff, Allan. *The Agrarian Origins of American Capitalism*. Charlottesville: University Press of Virginia, 1993.

———. "The Origins of Afro-American Society in Tidewater Maryland and Virginia, 1700 to 1790." *William and Mary Quarterly*, 3d ser., 35 (April 1978): 226–59.

———. *Tobacco and Slaves: The Development of Southern Cultures in the Chesapeake, 1680–1800*. Chapel Hill: University of North Carolina Press, 1986.

———. "Uprooted Peoples: Black Migrants in the Age of the American Revolution." In *Slavery and Freedom in the Age of the American Revolution*, edited by Ira Berlin and Ronald Hoffman, 143–71. Charlottesville: University of Virginia and United States Capitol Historical Society, 1983.

Lamar, Howard, and Leonard Thompson, eds. *The Frontier in History: North America and Southern Africa Compared*. New Haven: Yale University Press, 1981.

Landers, Jane. *Black Society in Spanish Florida*. Urbana: University of Illinois Press, 1999.

Lathrop, Barnes. *Migration into East Texas, 1835–1860: A Study from the United States Census*. Austin: Texas State Historical Commission, 1949.

Lears, T. J. Jackson. "*AHR* Forum: Making Fun of Popular Culture." *American Historical Review* 97 (December 1992): 1417–26.

———. "The Concept of Cultural Hegemony: Problems and Possibilities." *American Historical Review* 90 (June 1985): 567–93.

Lebsock, Suzanne. *The Free Women of Petersburg: Status and Culture in a Southern Town, 1784–1860*. New York: Norton, 1984.

Levine, Lawrence. *Black Culture and Black Consciousness: Afro-American Folk Thought from Slavery to Freedom*. New York: Oxford University Press, 1977.

Lichtenstein, Alex. "'That Disposition to Theft, with Which They Have Been Branded': Moral Economy, Slave Management, and the Law." *Journal of Social History* 22 (Spring 1988): 413–40.

Limerick, Patricia Nelson. *The Legacy of Conquest: The Unbroken Past of the American West*. New York: Norton, 1987.

Linden, Fabian. "Economic Democracy in the Slave South: An Appraisal of Some Recent Writings." *Journal of Negro History* 31 (April 1946): 140–89.

Lockley, Timothy. *Lines in the Sand: Race and Class in Lowcountry Georgia, 1750–1860.* Athens: University of Georgia Press, 2001.

Long, Ellen Call. *Florida Breezes; Or, Florida, Old and New.* Jacksonville: Ashmead Bros., 1882.

Longstreet, Augustus Baldwin. *Augustus Baldwin Longstreet's Georgia Tales Completed: A Scholarly Text.* Edited by David Rachelis. Athens: University of Georgia Press, 1998.

————. *Georgia Scenes: Characters, Incidents, &c. in the First Half Century of the Republic.* New York: Harper, 1840.

Lowery, Charles D. "The Great Migration to the Mississippi Territory, 1798–1819." *Journal of Mississippi History* 30 (August 1968): 173–92.

Lukács, György. *The Historical Novel.* Translated by Hannah Mitchell and Stanley Mitchell. London: Merlin Press, 1962.

Lynch, William O. "The Westward Flow of Southern Colonists before 1861." *Journal of Southern History* 9 (August 1943): 303–27.

McCardell, John. *The Idea of a Southern Nation: Southern Nationalists and Southern Nationalism, 1830–1860.* New York: Norton, 1979.

McClintock, Anne. *Imperial Leather: Race, Gender, and Sexuality in the Colonial Contest.* New York: Routledge, 1995.

McCoy, Drew. *The Elusive Republic: Political Economy in Jeffersonian America.* Chapel Hill: University of North Carolina Press, 1980.

McCurry, Stephanie. *Masters of Small Worlds: Yeoman Households, Gender Relations, and the Political Culture of the Antebellum South Carolina Low Country.* New York: Oxford University Press, 1995.

————. "The Two Faces of Republicanism: Gender and Proslavery Politics in Antebellum South Carolina." *Journal of American History* 89 (March 1992): 1245–64.

McDonald, Forrest, and Grady McWhiney. "The Antebellum Southern Herdsman: A Reinterpretation." *Journal of Southern History* 51 (May 1973): 147–66.

————. "The South from Self-Sufficiency to Peonage: An Interpretation." *American Historical Review* 75 (December 1980): 1095–118.

McDonald, Forrest, and Ellen Shapiro McDonald. "The Ethnic Origins of the American People." *William and Mary Quarterly,* 3d ser., 37 (April 1980): 179–99.

McFaul, John. *The Politics of Jacksonian Finance.* Ithaca: Cornell University Press, 1972.

McGovern, James R. *Anatomy of a Lynching: The Killing of Claude Neal.* Baton Rouge: Louisiana State University Press, 1982.

McGrane, Reginald C. *Foreign Bondholders and American State Debts.* New York: Macmillian, 1935.

McNeilly, Donald. *The Old South Frontier: Cotton Plantations and the Formation of Arkansas Society, 1819–1860.* Fayetteville: University of Arkansas Press, 2000.

Macomb, David. "Middle Florida." *The American Farmer* 9 (September 28, 1827): 217–19.

McRae, Farquhar. "Of the Agriculture of Florida: The Importance and Value of the Sugar Crop." *The Farmer's Register* 4 (April 12, 1836): [85]–88.

McWhiney, Grady. *Cracker Culture: Celtic Ways in the Old South.* Tuscaloosa: University of Alabama Press, 1988.

McWhiney, Grady, and Perry D. Jamieson. *Attack and Die: Civil War Military Tactics and the Southern Heritage.* University, Ala.: University of Alabama Press, 1982.

Magrath, C. Peter. *Yazoo: Law and Politics in the New Republic, The Case of Fletcher v. Peck.* New York: Norton, 1966.

Mahon, John K. *History of the Second Seminole War, 1835–1842.* 1967. Gainesville: University of Florida Press, 1985.

Malone, Ann Patton. *Swing Low, Sweet Chariot: Slave Family and Household Structure in Nineteenth-Century Louisiana*. Chapel Hill: University of North Carolina Press, 1992.

Mandelker, Amy, ed. *Bakhtin in Contexts: Across the Disciplines*. Evanston: Northwestern University Press, 1995.

Mann, Floris Perkins. *History of Telfair County from 1812 to 1914*. 1949. Spartanburg, S.C.: Reprint Co., 1978.

Marryat, Capt. Frederick, C. B. *A Diary in America, With Remarks on Its Institutions, Part Second*. London: Longman, 1839.

Marszalek, John F. *The Petticoat Affair: Manners, Mutiny, and Sex in Andrew Jackson's White House*. New York: Free Press, 1997.

Martin, Sidney W. *Florida during Territorial Days*. Athens: University of Georgia Press, 1944.

Mason, John Edwin. "Hendrik Albertus and His Slave Mey: A Drama in Three Acts." *Journal of African History* 31, no. 3 (1990): 423–45.

Mathews, Donald. *Religion in the Old South*. Chapel Hill: University of North Carolina Press, 1977.

Meinig, D. W. *Continental America, 1800–1867*. Vol. 2 of *The Shaping of America: A Geographical Perspective on 500 Years of History*. New Haven: Yale University Press, 1996.

Metcalf, Alida. *Family and Frontier in Colonial Brazil: Santana De Parnaíba, 1580–1822*. Berkeley: University of California Press, 1992.

Miller, Barbara. "Tallahassee and the 1841 Yellow Fever Epidemic." *Apalachee* 8 (1971–79): 21–31.

Miller, Joseph. *Way of Death: Merchant Capitalism and the Angola Slave Trade, 1730–1830*. Madison: University of Wisconsin Press, 1988.

Miller, Stephen. "Plantation Labor Organization and Slave Life on the Cotton Frontier: The Alabama-Mississippi Black Belt, 1815–1840." In *Cultivation and Culture*, edited by Ira Berlin and Philip D. Morgan, 155–69. Charlottesville: University Press of Virginia, 1993.

Miller, Stephen F. *The Bench and Bar of Georgia: Memoirs and Sketches*. 2 vols. Philadelphia: J. B. Lippincott, 1858.

Mintz, Sidney. *Sweetness and Power: The Place of Sugar in Modern History*. New York: Viking, 1985.

Morgan, Edmund. *American Slavery, American Freedom: The Ordeal of Colonial Virginia*. New York: Norton, 1975.

Morgan, Jennifer L. "'Some Could Suckle over Their Shoulder': Male Travelers, Female Bodies, and the Gendering of Racial Ideology, 1500–1770." *William and Mary Quarterly*, 3d ser., 54 (January 1997): 167–92.

Morgan, Philip D. *Slave Counterpoint: Black Culture in the Eighteenth-Century Chesapeake and Lowcountry*. Chapel Hill: University of North Carolina Press, 1998.

Morris, Alton C., ed. *Folksongs of Florida*. Gainesville: University of Florida, 1950.

Morris, Christopher. *Becoming Southern: The Evolution of a Way of Life, Warren County and Vicksburg, Mississippi, 1770–1860*. New York: Oxford University Press, 1995.

———. "Within the Slave Cabin: Resistance in Mississippi Slave Families." In *Over the Threshold: Intimate Violence in Early America*, edited by Christine Daniels and Michael Kennedy, 268–86. New York: Routledge, 1999.

Moss, Elizabeth. *Domestic Novelists of the Old South: Defenders of Southern Culture*. Baton Rouge: Louisiana State University, 1992.

Moussalli, Stephanie D. "Florida's Frontier Constitution: The Statehood, Banking, and Slavery Controversies." *Florida Historical Quarterly* 74 (Spring 1996): 423–39.

Muir, Edward. *Mad Blood Stirring: Vendetta and Factions in Friuli during the Renaissance.* Baltimore: Johns Hopkins University Press, 1993.

Murat, Achille. *America and the Americans.* New York, 1849.

———. *The United States of North America.* London: E. Wilson, 1833.

[Myers, Oscar.] "An Old-Timer." "Reminiscences of the Early Days of Tallahassee and Vicinity." Published in *Tallahassee Tallahassean,* 1882 and 1887, repr. 1903, Florida State Library, Tallahassee.

Nash, Gerald. *Creating the West: Historical Interpretations, 1890–1990.* Albuquerque: University of New Mexico Press, 1991.

Nelson, Dana D. *National Manhood: Capitalist Citizenship and the Imagined Fraternity of White Men.* Durham: Duke University Press, 1998.

Neuschel, Kristen Brooke. *Word of Honor: Interpreting Noble Culture in Sixteenth-Century France.* Ithaca: Cornell University Press, 1989.

Newsome, A. R., ed. "Twelve North Carolina Counties in 1810–1811." Parts 1–3. *North Carolina Historical Review* 6 (April 1929): 177–79.

Newton, Milton. "Cultural Preadaptation and the Upland South." In *Man and Cultural Heritage: Papers in Honor of Fred B. Kniffen,* edited by H. J. Walker and W. G. Henry, 143–54. Baton Rouge: Louisiana State University Press, 1974.

Nichols, Roy F. *The Disruption of American Democracy.* New York: Macmillan, 1948.

North, Douglass. *The Economic Growth of the United States, 1790–1860.* New York: Norton, 1966.

Northup, Solomon. *Twelve Years a Slave. Narrative of Solomon Northup, a Citizen of New-York, Kidnapped in Washington City in 1841, and Rescued in 1853, from a Cotton Plantation Near the Red River, in Louisiana.* Buffalo: Derby, Orton, and Mulligan, 1853.

Novick, Peter. *That Noble Dream: The "Objectivity Question" and the American Historical Profession.* New York: Cambridge University Press, 1988.

Nulty, William H. *Confederate Florida: The Road to Olustee.* Tuscaloosa: University of Alabama Press, 1990.

Numbers, Ronald, and Todd L. Savitt, eds. *Science and Medicine in the Old South.* Baton Rouge: Louisiana State University, 1989.

Nye, Robert. *Masculinity and Male Codes of Honor in Modern France.* New York: Oxford University Press, 1993.

Oakes, James. *The Ruling Race: A History of American Slaveholders.* New York: Knopf, 1982.

———. *Slavery and Freedom: An Interpretation of the Old South.* New York: Knopf, 1990.

Oberly, James W. "Westward Who? Estimates of Native White Migration after the War of 1812." *Journal of Economic History* 46 (June 1986): 431–40.

O'Brien, Michael. *Rethinking the South: Essays in Southern Intellectual History.* Baltimore: Johns Hopkins University Press, 1988.

Olsen, Christopher J. *Political Culture and Secession in Mississippi: Masculinity, Honor, and the Antiparty Tradition, 1830–1860.* New York: Oxford University Press, 2000.

Ormond, James. *The Reminiscences of James Ormond . . . .* Edited by Elizabeth F. Smith. Crawfordville, Fla.: Self-published, 1966.

Osterweis, Rollin G. *Romanticism and Nationalism in the Old South.* New Haven: Yale University Press, 1949.

Osthaus, Carl R. *Freedmen, Philanthropy, and Fraud: A History of the Freedman's Savings Bank.* Urbana: University of Illinois Press, 1976.

Otto, John Solomon. "The Migration of the Southern Plain Folk: An Interdisciplinary Synthesis." *Journal of Southern History* 51 (May 1985): 183–200.

Owens, Leslie Howard. *This Species of Property*. New York: Oxford University Press, 1976.

Ownby, Ted. *Subduing Satan: Religion, Recreation, and Manhood in the Rural South, 1865–1920*. Chapel Hill: University of North Carolina Press, 1990.

Owsley, Frank L. "The Pattern of Migration and Settlement on the Southern Frontier." *Journal of Southern History* 11 (May 1945): 147–77.

———. *Plain Folk of the Old South*. Baton Rouge: Louisiana State University Press, 1949.

Painter, Nell Irvin. "Soul Murder and Slavery: Toward a Fully Loaded Cost Accounting." In *U.S. History as Women's History: New Feminist Essays*, edited by Linda K. Kerber, Alica Kessler-Harris, and Kathryn Kish Sklar, 125–46. Chapel Hill: University of North Carolina Press, 1995.

Paisley, Clifton. *The Red Hills of Florida, 1528–1865*. Tuscaloosa: University of Alabama Press, 1989.

Paisley, Joy Smith. *The Cemeteries of Leon County, Florida*. Tallahassee: Colonial Dames XVII Century, 1978.

Paquette, Robert L. *Sugar Is Made with Blood: The Conspiracy of La Escalera and the Conflict between Empires over Slavery in Cuba*. Middletown, Conn.: Wesleyan University Press, 1988.

Paquette, Robert L., and Stanley Engerman, eds. *The Lesser Antilles in the Age of European Expansion*. Gainesville: University Press of Florida, 1996.

Parkman, Francis. *The Oregon Trail*. New York: G. P. Putnam, 1849.

Parton, James. *Life and Times of General Jackson*. 2 vols. New York: Mason Bros., 1860.

Patrick, Rembert W. *Florida Fiasco: Rampant Rebels on the Georgia-Florida Border, 1810–1815*. Athens: University of Georgia Press, 1954.

Penick, James Lal. *The Great Western Land Pirate: John A. Murrell in Legend and History*. Columbia: University of Missouri Press, 1981.

Peristiany, J. G., ed. *Honor and Shame: The Values of Mediterranean Society*. Chicago: University of Chicago Press, 1966.

Phillips, U. B. "The Origin and Growth of the Southern Black Belts." *American Historical Review* 11 (July 1906): 798–816.

Phillips, Ulrich B., and James Glunt, eds. *Florida Plantation Records from the Papers of George Noble Jones*. St. Louis: Missouri Historical Society, 1926.

Pitt-Rivers, Julian, ed. *Mediterranean Countrymen: Essays on the Social Anthropology of the Mediterranean*. Paris: Mouton, 1963.

Porter, Kenneth W. *The Black Seminoles: History of a Freedom-Seeking People*. Revised and edited by Alcione M. Amos and Thomas P. Senter. Gainesville: University Press of Florida, 1996.

———. *The Negro and the American Frontier*. New York: Arno Press, 1971.

Potter, David Morris. *The Impending Crisis, 1848–1861*. New York: Harper & Row, c. 1976.

Price, Richard. *Alabi's World*. Baltimore: Johns Hopkins University Press, 1990.

———. *First Time: The Historical Vision of an Afro-American People*. Baltimore: Johns Hopkins University Press, 1983.

Primock. Martin L. "Land Clearing under Nineteenth-Century Techniques: Some Preliminary Calculations." *Journal of Economic History* 22 (December 1962); 484–97.

The Public Statutes at Large of the United States of America. Boston: Little, Brown, 1799–.

Purvis, Thomas L. "Why the Accepted Estimates of Ethnicity of the American People, 1790, Are Unacceptable: Commentary." *William and Mary Quarterly*, 3d ser., 41, no. 1 (January 1984): 119–35.

Quitt, Martin H. "Immigrant Origins of the Virginia Gentry: A Study of Cultural Transmission and Innovation." *William and Mary Quarterly*, 3d ser., 45 (October 1988): 629–55.

Rawick, George P. *From Sundown to Sunup: The Making of the Black Community.* Westport, Conn.: Greenwood Publishing Co., 1972.

————, ed. *The American Slave: A Composite Autobiography.* 17 vols. Westport, Conn.: Greenwood Publishing Co., 1972–78.

Rawle, J. "Origin and Progress of the Culture of Cotton in America." *DeBow's Review* 17 (October 1854): 428–29.

Reaver, J. Russell, ed. *Florida Folktales.* Gainesville: University Press of Florida, 1987.

Reddy, William. *The Invisible Code: Honor and Sentiment in Postrevolutionary France, 1814–1848.* Berkeley: University of California, 1997.

Reidy, Joseph P. *From Slavery to Agrarian Capitalism in the Cotton Plantation South: Central Georgia, 1800–1880.* Chapel Hill: University of North Carolina Press, 1992.

Remini, Robert V. *Andrew Jackson and the Course of American Empire, 1767–1821.* New York: Harper & Row, 1977.

Richards, Leonard. *"Gentlemen of Property and Standing": Anti-Abolition Mobs in Jacksonian America.* New York: Oxford University Press, 1970.

Richardson, Simon Peter. *The Lights and Shadows of Itinerant Life.* Nashville: Methodist Episcopal Church, 1900.

Rivers, Larry E. *Slavery in Florida: Territorial Days to Emancipation.* Gainesville: University Press of Florida, 2000.

Robinson, Solon. *Pioneer and Agriculturalist: Selected Writings.* Edited by Herbert Anthony Kellar. Indianapolis: Indiana Historical Bureau, 1936.

Rodgers, Daniel T. "Republicanism: The Career of a Concept." *Journal of American History* 79 (June 1992): 11–38.

Roediger, David. "Precapitalism in One Country: A Note on Genovese, Politics, and the Slave South," in *Towards the Abolition of Whiteness: Essays on Race, Politics, and Working-Class History*, by David Roediger, 47–54. New York: Verso, 1994.

————. *Wages of Whiteness: Race and the Making of the American Working Class.* London: Verso, 1991.

Rogers, Tommy W. "The Great Population Exodus from South Carolina, 1850–1860." *South Carolina Historical Magazine* 68 (January 1967): 14–22.

Rogers, William Warren, and Erica R. Clark. *The Croom Family and Goodwood Plantation: Land, Litigation and Southern Lives.* Athens: University of Georgia, 1999.

Rohrbough, Malcolm. *The Land-Office Business: The Settlement and Administration of American Public Lands, 1789–1837.* New York: Oxford University Press, 1968.

Romero, Lara. *Home Fronts: Domesticity and Its Critics in the Antebellum United States.* Durham: Duke University Press, 1997.

Rothstein, Morton. "The Antebellum South as a Dual Economy: A Tentative Hypothesis." *Agricultural History* 41 (October 1967); 373–83.

Rotundo, E. Anthony. *American Manhood: Transformations in Masculinity from the Revolution to the Modern Era.* New York: Basic Books, 1993.

Rutman, Darrett and Anita Rutman. *A Place in Time: Middlesex County, Virginia, 1650–1750.* New York: Norton, 1984.

Saunt, Claudio. *A New Order of Things: Property, Power, and the Transformation of the Creek Indians, 1733–1816.* New York: Cambridge University Press, 1999.

Schene, Michael G. "Robert and John Grattan Gamble: Middle Florida Entrepreneurs." *Florida Historical Quarterly* 54 (July 1975): 61–73.

Schwalm, Leslie. *A Hard Fight for We: Women's Transition from Slavery to Freedom in South Carolina.* Urbana: University of Illinois Press, 1997.

Schweikart, Larry. *Banking in the American South from the Age of Jackson to Reconstruction.* Baton Rouge: Louisiana State University Press, 1987.

Scott, Anne Firor. *The Southern Lady: From Pedestal to Politics, 1830–1930.* Chicago: University of Chicago Press, 1970.

Scott, James. *Domination and the Arts of Resistance: Hidden Transcripts.* New Haven: Yale University Press, 1990.

Scott, Walter. *Waverley.* New York: James Eastbrun et al., 1819.

Sellers, Charles G. "Jackson Men with Feet of Clay." *American Historical Review* 62 (April 1957): 537–51.

——. *The Market Revolution: Jacksonian America, 1815–1846.* New York: Oxford University Press, 1991.

Shade, William G. *Democratizing the Old Dominion: Virginia and the Second Party System, 1824–1861.* Charlottesville: University Press of Virginia, 1996.

Sherman, Joan, ed. *The Black Bard of North Carolina: George Moses Horton and His Poetry.* Chapel Hill: University of North Carolina Press, 1997.

Shofner, Jerrell H. *Daniel Ladd: Merchant Prince of Frontier Florida.* Gainesville: University Press of Florida, 1978.

——. *History of Jefferson County.* Tallahassee: Sentry Press, 1976.

——. *Jackson County, Florida: A History.* Marianna, Fla.: Jackson County Heritage Commission, 1985.

——. *Nor Is It over Yet: Florida in the Era of Reconstruction.* Gainesville: University Press of Florida, 1974.

Shofner, Jerrell H., and William Warren Rogers. "Sea Island Cotton in Antebellum Florida." *Florida Historical Quarterly* 40 (April 1962): 373–80.

Shugg, Roger W. *Origins of Class Struggle in Louisiana: A Social History of White Farmers and Laborers during Slavery and After, 1840–1875.* Baton Rouge: Louisiana State University Press, 1939.

Silber, Nina. *The Romance of Reunion: Northerners and the South, 1865–1900.* Chapel Hill: University of North Carolina Press, 1993.

Simmons, William H. "Journal of William H. Simmons." *Florida Historical Quarterly* 1 (April 1908): 28–36.

Simms, William Gilmore. *The Partisan: A Tale of the Revolution.* New York: Harper, 1835.

Sinha, Manisha. *The Counterrevolution of Slavery: Politics and Ideology in Antebellum South Carolina.* Chapel Hill: University of North Carolina, 2000.

Skinner, J. S. "Soil, Climate, and Productions of Florida." *American Farmer* 8 (October 20, 1826).

Slotkin, Richard. *The Fatal Environment: The Myth of the Frontier in the Age of Industrialization, 1800–1890.* New York: Atheneum, 1985.

——. *Regeneration through Violence: The Mythology of the American Frontier, 1600–1860.* Middletown, Conn.: Wesleyan University Press, 1973.

Smith, Alfred Glaze. *The Economic Readjustment of an Old Cotton State: South Carolina, 1820–1860.* Columbia: University of South Carolina Press, 1958.

Smith, Elizabeth F. *Life along the Magnolia Road.* Crawfordville, Fla.: Self-published, 1972.

Smith, John David. *An Old Creed for the New South: Proslavery Ideology and Historiography, 1865–1918.* Westport, Conn.: Greenwood Press, 1985.

Smith, Joseph Burkholder. *The Plot to Steal Florida: James Madison's Phony War.* New York: Arbor House, 1983.

Smith, Mark M. *Mastered by the Clock: Time, Slavery, and Freedom in the American South.* Chapel Hill: University of North Carolina Press, 1997.

Snyder, Frank L. "Nancy Hynes DuVal: Florida's First Lady, 1822–1834." *Florida Historical Quarterly* 72 (July 1993): 19–34.

Sobol, Joseph Daniel. "Jack of a Thousand Faces: The Jack Tales as Appalachian Hero Cycle." *North Carolina Folklore Journal* 39 (Summer–Fall 1992): 77–108.

Solow, Barbara, and Stanley Engerman, eds. *British Capitalism and Caribbean Slavery: The Legacy of Eric Williams.* Cambridge: Cambridge University Press, 1987.

Sparks, Randy. *On Jordan's Stormy Banks: Evangelicalism in Mississippi, 1773–1876.* Athens: University of Georgia Press, 1994.

Spierenburg, Pieter, ed. *Men and Violence: Gender, Honor, and Rituals in Modern Europe and America.* Columbus: Ohio State University Press, 1998.

Sprague, John T. *The Origin, Progress, and Conclusion of the Florida War.* New York: D. Appleton, 1848.

Stallybrass, Peter, and Allon White. *The Politics and Poetics of Transgression.* Ithaca: Cornell University Press, 1986.

Stampp, Kenneth. *The Peculiar Institution: Slavery in the Antebellum South.* New York: Knopf, 1956.

———. *America in 1857: A Nation on the Brink.* New York: Oxford University Press, 1990.

Stanesa, Jamie. "Caroline Lee Whiting Hentz." *Legacy* 13 (Spring 1996): 130–37.

Stanley, J. Randall. *History of Jackson County.* Marianna, Fla.: The Jackson County Historical Society, 1950.

Stein, Stanley J. *Vassouras: A Brazilian Coffee County, 1850–1900.* Cambridge, Mass.: Harvard University Press, 1957.

Stevenson, Brenda. *Life in Black and White: Family and Community in the Slave South.* New York: Oxford University Press, 1996.

Stowe, Steven M. *Intimacy and Power in the Old South: Ritual in the Lives of the Planters.* Baltimore: Johns Hopkins University Press, 1987.

———, ed. *A Southern Practice: The Diary and Autobiography of Charles Hentz, M.D.* Charlottesville: University Press of Virginia, 2000.

Sweig, Donald M. "Reassessing the Human Dimension of the Interstate Slave Trade." *Prologue* 12 (Spring 1980): 5–21.

Sydnor, Charles. *The Development of Southern Sectionalism, 1819–1848.* Baton Rouge: Louisiana State University Press, 1948.

Tadman, Michael. *Speculators and Slaves: Masters, Traders, and Slaves in the Old South.* Madison: University of Wisconsin Press, 1989.

Taylor, Alan. *Liberty Men and Great Proprietors: The Revolutionary Settlement on the Maine Frontier, 1760–1820.* Chapel Hill: University of North Carolina Press, 1990.

———. *William Cooper's Town: Power and Persuasion on the Frontier of the Early American Republic.* New York: Knopf, 1995.

Taylor, Robert W. *Rebel Storehouse: Florida in the Confederate Economy.* Tuscaloosa: University of Alabama Press, 1995.

Taylor, William R. *Cavalier and Yankee: The Old South and American National Character.* Garden City, N.Y.: Doubleday, 1963.

Temin, Peter. *The Jacksonian Economy.* New York: Norton, 1969.

Terry, Gail S. "Sustaining the Bonds of Kinship in a Trans-Appalachian Migration, 1790–1811: The Cabell-Breckenridge Slaves Move West." *Virginia Magazine of History and Biography* 102 (October 1994): 455–76.

Thompson, Arthur. *Jacksonian Democracy on the Florida Frontier.* Gainesville, Fla.: University of Florida, 1961.

Thompson, E. P. *Whigs and Hunters: The Origins of the Black Act.* New York: Pantheon, 1975.

Thornton, J. Mills, III. *Politics and Power in a Slave Society: Alabama, 1800–1860.* Baton Rouge: Louisiana State University Press, 1978.

Thornton, John. "African Dimensions of the Stono Rebellion." *American Historical Review* 96 (October 1991): 1101–13.

Tompkins, Jane. *Sensational Designs: The Cultural Work of American Fiction, 1790–1860.* New York: Oxford University Press, 1985.

Tracey, Karen. *Plots and Proposals: American Women's Fiction, 1850–1890.* Urbana: University of Illinois Press, 2000.

Tracy, Susan G. *In the Master's Eye: Representations of Women, Blacks, and Poor Whites in Antebellum Southern Literature.* Amherst, Mass.: University of Massachusetts Press, 1995.

Trexler, Richard C. *Sex and Conquest: Gendered Virtue, Political Order, and the European Conquest of the Americas.* Ithaca: Cornell University Press, 1995.

———, ed. *Gender Rhetorics: Postures of Dominance and Submission in History.* Binghampton, N.Y.: Medieval and Renaissance Texts and Studies, 1994.

Tuckett, Francis. *A Journey in the United States in the Years 1829 and 1830.* Edited by Herbert C. Fox. Plymouth, Eng.: St. Nicholas Books, 1976.

Turner, Frederick Jackson. *The Frontier in American History.* New York: H. Holt and Co., 1920.

Twain, Mark [Samuel Clemens]. *Life on the Mississippi.* New York: Harper, 1883.

Usner, Daniel H., Jr. *Indians, Settlers, and Slaves in a Frontier Exchange Economy: The Lower Mississippi Valley before 1783.* Chapel Hill: University of North Carolina Press, 1992.

Varon, Elizabeth R. *We Mean to Be Counted: White Women and Politics in Antebellum Virginia.* Chapel Hill: University of North Carolina Press, 1998.

Vignoles, Charles B. *The History of the Floridas: From the Discovery by Cabot, in 1497, to the Cession of the Same to the United States, in 1821, with Observations on the Climate, Soil, and Productions.* Brooklyn: G. L. Burch, 1824.

Waldrep, Christopher. *Roots of Disorder: Race and Criminal Justice in the American South, 1817–1880.* Urbana: University of Illinois Press, 1998.

Wallace, Michael. "Changing Concepts of Party in the United States: New York, 1815–1828." *American Historical Review* 74 (December 1968): 453–91.

Walther, Eric. *The Fire-Eaters.* Baton Rouge: Louisiana State University Press, 1992.

Walker, Jonathan. *The Trial and Imprisonment of Jonathan Walker at Pensacola, Florida.* Boston: The Anti-Slavery Office, 1845.

Watson, Harry L. "The Common Rights of Mankind: Subsistence, Shad, and Commerce in the Early Republican South." *Journal of American History* 83 (June 1996): 13–43.

———. "Conflict and Collaboration: Yeomen, Slaveholders, and Politics in the Antebellum South." *Social History* 10 (October 1985): 273–98.

————. *Jacksonian Politics and Community Conflict: The Emergence of the Second American Party System in Cumberland County, North Carolina.* Baton Rouge: Louisiana State University Press, 1981.

————. *Liberty and Power: The Politics of Jacksonian America.* New York: Hill and Wang, 1990.

————. "Squire Oldway and His Friends: Opposition to Internal Improvements in Antebellum North Carolina." *North Carolina Historical Review* 54 (April 1977): 105–19.

Watson, Ritchie Devon. *Yeoman versus Cavalier: The Old Southwest's Fictional Road to Rebellion.* Baton Rouge: Louisiana State University Press, 1993.

Wayne, Michael. *Death of an Overseer: Reopening a Murder Investigation from the Plantation South.* New York: Oxford University Press, 2001.

Weaver, Herbert. *Mississippi Farmers, 1850–1860.* Nashville: Vanderbilt University Press, 1946.

Webber, Thomas L. *Deep Like the Rivers: Education in the Slave Quarter Community.* New York: W. W. Norton, 1978.

Weiner, Marli F. *Mistresses and Slaves: Plantation Women in South Carolina, 1830–1880.* Urbana: University of Illinois Press, 1998.

Wertenbaker, Thomas J. *Patrician and Plebian in Virginia; Or, The Origin and Development of the Social Classes of the Old Dominion.* Charlottesville: The Michie Co., 1910.

West, Emily. "Surviving Separation: Cross-Plantation Marriages and the Slave Trade in Antebellum South Carolina." *Journal of Family History* 24 (April 1998): 212–31.

Westbury, Susan. "Analysing a Regional Slave Trade: The West Indies and Virginia, 1698–1775." *Slavery and Abolition* 7 (December 1986): 241–56.

Whipple, Henry B. *Bishop Whipple's Southern Diary, 1843–1844.* Edited by Lester B. Shippee. Minneapolis: University of Minnesota Press, 1937.

White, Deborah Gray. *Ar'n't I a Woman?: Female Slaves in the Plantation South.* New York: Norton, 1985.

White, Hayden. *Metahistory: The Historical Imagination in Nineteenth-Century Europe.* Baltimore: Johns Hopkins University Press, 1973.

White, Richard. *It's Your Misfortune and None of My Own: A History of the American West.* Norman, Okla.: University of Oklahoma Press, 1991.

Wickman, Patricia. *The Tree That Bends: Discourse, Power, and the Survival of the Maskoki People.* Tuscaloosa: University Press of Alabama, 1999.

Williams, David F. *Rich Man's War: Class, Caste, and Confederate Defeat in the Lower Chattahoochee Valley.* Athens: University of Georgia Press, 1998.

Williams, Eric. *Capitalism and Slavery.* Chapel Hill: University of North Carolina Press, 1944.

Williams, Jack K. *Dueling in the Old South: Vignettes of Social History.* College Station: Texas A&M University Press, 1979.

Williams, John Lee. "Journal of John Lee Williams." *Florida Historical Quarterly* 1 (April and July 1908): 18–29; 37–44.

————. *A View of West Florida, Embracing Its Geography, Topography, &c . . . .* Philadelphia: H. S. Tanner, 1827.

Willoughby, Lynn. *Fair to Middlin': The Antebellum Cotton Trade of the Apalachicola-Chattahoochee River Valley.* Tuscaloosa: University of Alabama Press, 1993.

Wilson, A. N. *The Laird of Abbotsford: A View of Sir Walter Scott.* New York: Oxford University Press, 1980.

Wilson, Carol. *Freedom at Risk: The Kidnapping of Free Blacks in America, 1780–1865.* Lexington: University of Kentucky Press, 1994.

Wood, Kirsten F. "'One Woman So Dangerous to Public Morals': Gender and Power in the Eaton Affair." *Journal of the Early Republic* 17 (Spring 1997): 237–75.

Wood, Peter. *Black Majority: Negroes in Colonial South Carolina from 1670 through the Stono Rebellion*. New York: Knopf, 1974.

Woodman, Harold. *King Cotton and His Retainers: Financing and Marketing the Cotton Crop of the South, 1800–1925*. Lexington, Ky.: University Press of Kentucky, 1968.

Wooster, Ralph. *Politicians, Planters, and Plain Folk: Courthouse and Statehouse in the Upper South, 1850–1860*. Knoxville: University of Tennessee Press, 1975.

———. *The Secession Conventions of the South*. Princeton: Princeton University Press, 1962.

Wright, Gavin. *The Political Economy of the Cotton South: Households, Markets, and Wealth in the Nineteenth Century*. New York: Basic Books, 1978.

Wyatt-Brown, Bertram. "Andrew Jackson's Honor." *Journal of the Early Republic* 17 (Spring 1997): 1–35.

———. "The Anti-Mission Movement in the Jacksonian South: A Study in Rural Folk Culture." *Journal of Southern History* 36 (November 1970): 501–29.

———. "The Mask of Obedience: Male Slave Psychology in the Old South." *American Historical Review* 93 (December 1988): 1228–52.

———. *Southern Honor: Ethics and Behavior in the Old South*. New York: Oxford University Press, 1982.

"X, Y, and Z." "Notes on the Climate, Soil, and Productions of Florida." *Southern Agriculturalist* 7 (January 1834): 23–25.

Young, Alfred. "George Robert Twelves Hewes (1742–1840): A Boston Shoemaker and the Memory of the American Revolution." *William and Mary Quarterly*, 3d ser., 38 (October 1981): 561–623.

Young, Hugh. "A Topographical Memoir of East and West Florida with Itineraries of General Jackson's Army." Edited by Mark F. Boyd and Gerald M. Ponton. *Florida Historical Quarterly* 13 (July 1934): 16–50; (October 1934): 82–104; (January 1935): 129–64.

Young, Jeffrey R. *Domesticating Slavery: The Master Class in South Carolina and Georgia*. Chapel Hill: University of North Carolina Press, 1999.

Zeitz, Joshua M. "The Missouri Compromise Reconsidered: Anti-Slavery Rhetoric and the Emergence of the Free-Labor Synthesis." *Journal of the Early Republic* 20 (Fall 2000): 447–85.

THESES, DISSERTATIONS, AND UNPUBLISHED PAPERS

Baptist, Edward E. "Cotton, Credit, and Capital: The Antebellum South and the Panic of 1837." Paper presented to the Society of Historians for the Early American Republic, July 1998.

———. "Creating an Old South: The Plantation Frontier in Jackson and Leon Counties, Florida, 1821–1860." Ph.D. diss., University of Pennsylvania, 1997.

———. "Revisiting the Political History of Territorial Florida: Ideology and Factions." Paper presented to the Florida Historical Association, May 24, 1996.

Camp, Stephanie M. H. "Viragoes: Slave Women's Political Culture in the Antebellum South." Ph.D. diss., University of Pennsylvania, 1998.

Coles, David. "'Far from Fields of Glory': Military Operations in Florida during the Civil War." Ph.D. diss., Florida State University, 1996.

Denham, James M. "Dueling in Territorial Middle Florida." Master's thesis, Florida State University, 1983.

Ershkowitz, Herbert. "The Origin of the Whig and Democratic Parties: New Jersey Politics, 1820–1837." Ph.D. diss., Columbia University, 1982.

Grenelle, Eleanor Hortense. "The Bellamys of Territorial Florida." Master's thesis, University of Florida, 1953.

Hazel, Joseph A. "The Geography of Negro Agricultural Slavery in Alabama, Florida, and Mississippi. Circa 1860." Ph.D. diss., Columbia University, 1963.

Hill, Dorothy E. "Joseph M. White: Florida's Territorial Delegate, 1825–1837." Master's thesis, University of Florida, 1950.

Lake, James. "The Seminole Slaves Factor in the First Seminole War." Paper presented to Florida Conference of Historians, Fort Myers, April 1999.

Meredith, Evelyn T. "The Secession Movement in Florida." A.M. thesis, Duke University, 1940.

Miller, James David. "South by Southwest: Planter Emigration and Elite Ideology in the Deep South, 1815–1861." Ph.D. diss., Emory University, 1996.

Rothman, Adam. "Expansion of Slavery in the Deep South, 1790–1820." Ph.D. diss., Columbia University, 2000.

Russell, Sarah P. "Cultural Conflicts and Common Interests: The Making of the Sugar Planter Class in Louisiana, 1795–1853." Ph.D. diss., University of Maryland, 2000.

Terry, Gail S. "Family Empires: A Frontier Elite in Virginia and Kentucky, 1740–1815." Ph.D. diss., College of William and Mary, 1992.

Troutman, Philip D. "Slave Trade and Sentiment in Antebellum Virginia." Ph.D. diss., University of Virginia, 2000.

Upchurch, John Calhoun. "'Middle Florida': An Historical Geography of the Area between the Apalachicola and Suwannee Rivers," Ph.D. diss., University of Tennessee, 1971.

Williams, James William. "Emigration from North Carolina, 1789–1860." Master's thesis, University of North Carolina, 1939.

Wilson, Osburne Carlyle. "The Development of Florida Territory, 1821–1845." Master's thesis, Vanderbilt University, 1932.

Index

Parish, William, 22
Parkhill, George Washington, 1, 211, 226, 271, 277
Parkhill, Harriet, 212
Parkhill, John, 69, 180, 186, 211; as cashier of Union Bank, 112; on disease-causing conditions on plantations, 75–76; financial ruin of, 226; memoirs of, 254; migration to Florida, 16; raising capital, 31; slave trade and, 73; Union Bank and, 118, 183
Parkhill, Lizzie, 1
Parkhill, Lucy Randolph, 283
Parkhill, Richard, 1
Parkhill, Samuel, 52, 226, 283; as delegate to St. Joseph convention, 160; migration to Florida, 16; number of slaves of, 69; Second Seminole War and, 156; slave trade and, 72–73; Union Bank and, 118, 182
Parkman, Francis, 260
Partridge, Henry, 76, 211
Paternalism: as planters' ideology of master-slave relations, 210–17, 254–55, 260
Pearce, John, 128
Penn, Bob, 128
Pensacola Gazette, 34, 58, 252
Perrine, Henry, 158
Perry, Madison S., 270
Phillips, Abraham, 54
Phillips, Ethelred, 270
Phillips, Nancy, 54
Pine Hill plantation, 215
Pittman, Edward G., 232–33, 235
Plantations: clearing land for, 32–34, 69, 71; disease on, 74–76, 77, 188, 196, 313 (nn. 33, 35); historians on settlement template of, 297 (n. 11); locations of, 29; Middle Florida and early, 14; new literature on, 250–51; provisioning of early, 33; slave demographics on, 69–70, 201–2, 203. *See also* Cotton; *names of specific plantations*
Planter-borne slave trade, 72–73, 312 (n. 28)
Planters: aggressive masculinity of, 90–91, 98–101 (*see also* Manhood/masculinity); anti-bank faction members among, 167; attitude toward countrymen, 43, 165–74, 232, 235, 262; on benefits of migration, 18–19, 22, 87; cotton and, 50; versus countrymen, legal system on theft and, 128–29, 227, 341 (n. 25), 342

(n. 31); and credit, 18, 30–32, 73, 96; debt and stories of worn-out soil, 22–23, 301 (n. 22); decision-making on slave migration, 70–72; and defeat, 222–23, 225–32, 262; differences with countrymen on masculinity, 124–25, 129; disease fears of, 27, 302 (n. 32); dividing line between nonplanters and, 9, 17; and dueling, 99–100, 106–10, 225, 238, 320 (n. 46); economic crisis and, 181–86; and ideas about history, 27–28, 247–61, 263, 269–70, 274–75, 283; in Jack tales, 126, 134–38; juries and, 128, 230; kinship relations of in migration, 19, 24–25, 29–31, 87, 96; lynchings and, 206, 234, 235; masculinity and, 103–4, 110–11, 121, 130, 151–53, 158, 166; memoirs and family histories of, 254–55, 347 (n. 56); migration process of, 29–34; mythology of origins of, 2, 247–56; news about slaves passed by, 80; on North and secession, 264–65; paternalism toward slaves, 210–11, 213–14, 251; pro-bank faction and, 166–67 (*see also* Pro-bank faction); reasons for migration, 17–18, 19, 22–23, 24, 28–29, 301 (n. 19); religious revivals and, 237; rituals and mythologized history of, 255–56; on secession inevitability, 262–63; similarities with countrymen on masculinity, 124; slavery and formation of class of, 18, 210, 257; slaves as sources of capital for, 198–99; sources of capital for, 30–32, 96; Spanish antecedents in mythology of, 260–61; women of, 26, 27, 247–48
Planters' Hotel, 189
Politics: factional, 96–102, 161, 163–65; national, 163, 265–66, 319 (n. 35); parties and, 319 (n. 34); women's involvement in formal, 150. *See also* Anti-bank Democrats; Democratic Party; Elections; Pro-bank faction; Republican Party; Whig Party
Poor whites: definition of, 323 (n. 9). *See also* Countrymen/yeomen
Pope, William, 97
Port Leon, 35, 115
Port Magnolia, 34, 35, 115
Port St. Joseph, 115, 189
Preemptions: land sales and purchases and, 46–47, 92, 93
Prescott, Samuel, 260
Pro-bank faction: anti-bank Democrats' criticism of, 163, 164; on Legislative

indirect forms of resistance to, 209–18; labor force composition under, 69–70, 201–2, 203; legality in Florida, 19–20, 64–65; literature and arguments for, 257–61; Murat on, 33; national criticism of, 245–46; and planter paternalism, 210–17, 254–55, 260; sale patterns of, 297 (n. 12); types of trade in, 65, 72–74, 310 (n. 3); violent resistance to, 199–209, 257

Slaves: birthplaces and states of origin of, 63, 84; capital and minimizing of slave trade, 65–66; changes in migration patterns of, 64–65; communications with separated family members, 80–81; community- and kinship-building among, 68, 74, 81–82, 193, 195, 196–97, 216–17; countrymen and planter's common view of, 124, 138–39; countrymen holdings of, 47, 48–49, 57, 67; differences between early and migrated generations of, 81–82; economic crisis and sale of, 184–85, 198, 335 (n. 5); effects of disease and climate on, 74–77, 188, 196, 313 (nn. 33, 35); escape attempts of, 79; field labor and, 70; freedom and Emancipation Proclamation, 279; house, 83; impact of migration on, 9, 61–62, 77–81, 83–84, 193–94, 311 (n. 11); interviews of ex-, 82, 84–86, 314 (n. 50); kinship networks among, 66–67, 69, 78, 81–87, 196–98; land clearing for plantations and, 33–34, 69, 71; naming practices of, 69–70, 197–98; narratives of as literary tradition, 33, 48, 49, 314 (nn. 51, 54); origins of enslaved migrants from North Carolina, 64, 65; origins of enslaved migrants from Virginia, 64, 65; origins of forced migration of, 62–67; paternalism of whites toward, 210–11, 213–14, 251; population structures of, 69–70; punishment of, 48, 216; renting of, 49; reproduction by female, 49, 78; resistance (direct), 158, 199–209, 269; resistance (indirect), 209–18, 330 (nn. 40–41); responses to migration, 67–72, 191–92, 311 (n. 16); reunions of separated, 80; runaway, 79, 202–3, 205; Second Seminole War and, 158; Seminoles and, 12, 158, 205–7; as source of quick capital, 47, 198–99; sources of narratives by, 82; on "stealing" of freedmen by whites, 83, 84–86; suicides of, 78; survival tactics

of, 195, 211–13; Union Army and former, 278–79; from Upper South, 63–64, 65; variations among, 196; vernacular history of migration among, 81–87, 314 (n. 54). *See also names of individual slaves*

Smalls, Samuel (slave), 85
Smith, Aaron, 231
Smith, Cato (slave), 85
Smith, John, 54
Smith, Powell, 54
Smith, William, 231
Soil exhaustion: myths and fears of, 22–23, 301 (n. 22)
Southern Life and Trust Company, 115, 184–85, 234
Spanish antecedents: in mythology of planter history, 260–61
Sparks, William (slave), 67
Speculators: in land, 43–44, 53, 54, 55, 91, 94–96, 315 (n. 8), 317 (n. 21); in slaves, 317 (n. 23). *See also* Call, Richard; Carter, Farish
Spring Creek/Grant's Pond community, 53, 54
Squatters: land issues and, 47, 55–56, 243, 306 (n. 17)
Stapleton, William, 207
Stay laws, 174–75
Stephens, R. C., 243
Stephens, R. L., 243
Stephens, William (slave), 78
Stevens, Levi (slave), 78
Stevens, Robin (slave), 78
Stevens, Sally (slave), 78
Stevens, Staley (slave), 78
Stevens, Willis (slave), 78
Stone, Lackland, 97–98, 318 (n. 28)
Stroman, Elizabeth Felkel, 56
Stroman, Henry, 241
Stroman, Jacob, 56, 241
Stroman, John, 241
Stroman, W. L., 242
Submissionists, 270
Subsistence farming: among countrymen, 57–58, 307–8 (n. 30)
Sugar cane: in Florida, 20–21
Swain, Isaac, 125
Sylvania plantation, 279

Tallahassa band, 11, 12, 14
Tallahassee: city council of, 228–29, 341 (n. 22); fire in, 189; selected as capital, 13–14

Waters, John, 125
Watson, T., 21
Watson, William, 342 (n. 32)
Waugh, William, 141
Waukeenah plantation, 29
Waverly plantation, 69, 250
Webb, James, 54, 95, 97
Webbville, Fla., 98, 318 (n. 29)
Webster, Daniel, 113, 163
Welaunee plantation, 29
West, Edward, 230
West, Gustavus, 229
West, R. K., 202
West, Zipporah, 146
Westcott, James: as anti-bank outsider, 166; anti–Union Bank rhetoric of, 159; on bank proposals, 112; charges of assault and battery against, 126–27; on creation of Union Bank, 113; political office and, 167, 323 (n. 9); at St. Joseph convention, 160–61
West Indies: as ideal for planters, 21, 336 (n. 18)
Whig Party: changes in, 220; changes in new, 221–22; versus Democrats and countrymen, 163, 172–73, 221; elections of 1840 and, 176; elections of 1841 and 1842 and, 180; North versus South, 264; origins of, 319 (n. 34); symbolism of struggles within, 256
Whipping: of poor whites, 128–29, 230; of slaves, 216; symbolism of, 105, 110, 125, 222
Whitaker, Absalom, 69
Whitaker, Cary: on disease and slaves, 313 (n. 33); location of plantations of, 30, 69; migration and kinship of, 24–25; raising capital, 32
Whitaker, Eli, 24, 68–69, 75, 188
Whitaker, Fletcher, 179
Whitaker, L. B., 75
Whitaker, Mary, 188
Whitaker, Richard, 32, 230
White, Everett, 99
White, Joseph, 28; assaults on, 88–89, 108; Richard Call feud with, 88–89, 104, 111; William DuVal and, 100, 101; on factionalism in politics, 101–2; land business of, 95–96; land speculation and, 94–95, 315 (n. 8), 317 (n. 21); on removal of Seminoles, 156, 157–58; on speculators, 92, 94
White, Oscar, 99

Whitehead, Melvina (slave), 78
White male independence. *See* Manhood/masculinity
Whitfield Place plantation, 69
Whitner, Benjamin, 118, 278
Wiggins, Jesse, 127
Williams, Daphne (slave), 191
Williams, John, 54, 55
Williams, John Lee, 19
Williams, Joseph, 231
Williams, Joseph G., 230
Williams, Nancy (slave), 199
Williams, Owen, 55
Williams, Owen (slave), 199
Williams, Rebecca, 188
Williams, Robert W., 93, 95, 188, 278
Williams, William, 54
Williams, Willy (slave), 80
Williamson, Charles, 54, 94–95, 317 (n. 19)
Willis, James, 325 (n. 22)
Willis, Jesse, 186
Wills, Anna Whitaker, 24, 25
Wills, William H., 25
Wilmot Proviso of 1847, 262
Wilson, David C., 127
"Wire-grass Whigs," 221
Wirt, Catherine, 26, 114
Wirt, Elizabeth Gamble, 29, 118
Wirt, William, 29
Womanhood. *See* Women
Women: adultery of, 141–42; attitudes toward migration, 9, 25–26, 44–45; of countrymen, 39, 42, 139–45; fears of disease, 26; field work and labor of white countrywomen, 47, 143, 307 (n. 26); illiteracy of countrywomen, 149; involvement in formal politics, 150; legal action against, 341 (n. 26); male behavior and church-going, 144, 145–51, 326 (n. 48); male violence against, 140–43; migration fears of, 25–26; migration "fever" of, 23, 26–27, 302 (n. 30); planter, 247–48; rape of slave, 209; reaction to loss of children, 140; rebellious, 141–42; role in migration decision-making process, 26; role of older countrywomen, 146–51; violence by slave, 202; white male masculinity view of, 102, 124–25, 138–39; womanhood ideals and, 8–9
Wood, B. F., 108
Wood, Isaac (slave), 80
Woodward, Alfred, 160
Works Progress Administration (WPA):

ex-slave interviews conducted by, 82,
84–86, 191–92, 314 (n. 50)
Wyatt, William, 100, 160, 173, 183
Wynns, Benjamin, 236

Yancey, Joel, 127
Yellow fever ("yellow jack"), 74–75, 187–89
Yeomans, Stephen, 234, 235
Yeomen. *See* Countrymen/yeomen